A
Philosophical
Commentary
on the
POLITICS
of Aristotle

A
Philosophical
Commentary
on the

POLI

Peter L. Phillips Simpson

THE UNIVERSITY OF NORTH CAROLINA PRESS

CHAPEL HILL AND LONDON

TICS

of Aristotle

© 1998
The University of
North Carolina Press
All rights reserved
Manufactured in the
United States of America
Set in Minion type
by Keystone Typesetting, Inc.
The paper in this book meets
the guidelines for permanence
and durability of the Committee
on Production Guidelines for
Book Longevity of the Council
on Library Resources.

Publication of this book
was aided by a grant from the
Earhart Foundation.

Library of Congress
Cataloging-in-Publication Data
Simpson, Peter, 1951–
A philosophical commentary on the Politics of Aristotle /
by Peter L. Phillips Simpson.
p. cm.
Includes bibliographical references (p.   ) and index.
ISBN 0-8078-2380-5 (cloth : alk. paper)
1. Aristotle. Politics. 2. Aristotle—Contributions in
political science. I. Title.
JC71.A7S56   1998
320.1′01—dc21   97-16515
                         CIP

02   01   00   99   98   5   4   3   2   1

To the students and fellows of

Wadham College, Oxford, England,

where I was first introduced to the

delights of Aristotle

CONTENTS

ACKNOWLEDGMENTS

The debts I have incurred in the course of writing this commentary on Aristotle's *Politics* are pretty much the same as those I incurred in the course of writing the translation. For since the work of translation and the work of understanding are inseparable, and since I was writing the commentary at the same time as I was writing the translation, no one helped me with the one who did not also and by that very fact help me with the other. Accordingly it is my pleasure, no less than my duty, to express my gratitude again to all the many friends and colleagues and students (which categories, I hasten to add, are not all exclusive of each other) who have, sometimes in unknowing ways, played the part of guides and companions for me on the way to understanding Aristotle.

First among them must again come Paul Rahe whose encouragement, advice, and criticism with the commentary were as unstinting and as past calculating as they were with the translation. I have remained as stubborn, doubtless, in what he will consider to be my errors, but he has remained as patient too and his patience has not been without its effect. Certainly the merits of the commentary, as of the translation, are due in no small part to his untiring kindness and friendship.

Among the others who, at various stages and in various ways, have given me of their advice about how to understand Aristotle's *Politics* (advice not always taken, to be sure, but always gratefully appreciated), I should mention the following in particular: Günter Bien, Robert Chiles, Diskin Clay, Ian Crombie, George Forrest, Dieter Harlfinger, Karl-Joachim Hölkeskamp, George Kennedy, Richard Kennington, Carnes Lord, Fred D. Miller Jr., Larry Nachman, Carlo Natali, Martin Ostwald, Pierre Pellegrin, Michael Rohr, Eckart Schütrumpf, Jacob Stern, Zeph Stewart, Robert Talisse. In addition I should thank the readers for the University of North Carolina Press for their careful and helpful comments and criticisms, and also the members (too numerous to name) of the New York Colloquium in Ancient Philosophy during the academic year 1996–97, when we read and studied together the third book of Aristotle's *Politics* and whose lively discussions provided much food for thought. A special word of thanks is also due to Richard Kraut for so kindly letting me see the manuscript of his new translation and commentary on books 7 and 8 of the *Politics* (my books 4 and 5) for the Clarendon Aristotle Series, Oxford 1997. Although, because of time constraints, I was not able to make use of his work in the way I would have liked and in the way the work deserves, I remain most grateful to him for his selfless generosity toward me in this regard.

I have had the privilege of teaching Aristotle's *Politics* several times over the past fifteen years, at University College Dublin, at the Catholic University of America, at the Graduate School of the City University of New York, and at the International Academy for Philosophy in the Principality of Liechtenstein. I would like to thank all my students at each of these places who, in various and sometimes unknowing ways, helped to improve and clarify my thinking. I would also like to thank all my colleagues at the same places, and also at the College of Staten Island of the City University of New York, as well as my many friends scattered in the United States and Europe for support and encouragement of a more general but no less necessary kind.

During the process of working on Aristotle's *Politics* I received much assistance in the form of grants, fellowships, and study leaves. I must first of all thank the College of Staten Island of the City University of New York for awarding me a special summer grant and a year's study leave during my first years there as a junior faculty member, for granting me a further sabbatical leave some years later to finish this work, and also for help with covering the costs of professional proofreading. I must in addition thank the Professional Staff Congress of the same university for generously supporting me with summer travel grants and fellowships over a period of some six years.

I must thank, too, the Center for Hellenic Studies in Washington, D.C., where I spent a delightful year in 1991–92 engrossed in the present work. Special thanks are due in this regard to the director of the Center, Zeph Stewart, and to his engaging wife Diana. Zeph retired as director at the end of the year but that did not prevent him or Diana from being most splendid hosts and making my year there one of great enjoyment and profit. I would also like to offer thanks to the senior fellows for appointing me to a junior fellowship; to all those on the staff of the Center, who each performed their respective jobs with much efficiency and grace; and, last but not least, to the other junior fellows in my year, who, with or without spouses and children, all contributed to the restful atmosphere and collegial scholarship of the place: Mary Whitlock Blundell, Carlo Brillante, Diana Delia, Christopher Faraone, Karl-Joachim Hölkeskamp, Lisa Kallet-Marx, Andrei Rossius.

During my sabbatical leave, the Earhart Foundation in Ann Arbor, Michigan, awarded me a substantial fellowship that enabled me to devote the entire academic year to this project. Without the Foundation's assistance I might not have been sufficiently freed from financial necessities to give myself fully to research and writing. I remain most grateful, therefore, to the Trustees of the Earhart Foundation for their generosity in this regard.

The concluding stages of the study for, and writing of, the commentary (as well as of the translation) were completed in Rome and Athens. I am grateful to the American University of Rome, the American Academy in Rome, the American School of Classical Studies at Athens, and the Australian Archaeological Institute at Athens for their help and support. Those among their staffs and fellows with whom I had most direct contact are remembered with much thankfulness and affection. A special debt of thanks is additionally owed, as it was in the case of the translation, to the staff of the University of North Carolina Press, in particular to Lewis Bateman, Brian MacDonald, and Ron Maner for all the hard work and care they devoted to bringing this work to publication.

I would like to end these acknowledgments, however, rather in the way I ended the acknowledgments to the translation. For as there I closed by expressing my thanks to those who first introduced me to the study of Greek, so here I would like to close by expressing my thanks to those who first introduced me to the study of Aristotle, I mean my tutors at Wadham College, Oxford University, England. The study of Aristotle, I am glad to say, still flourishes amid Oxford's dreaming spires, and to a large extent in Aristotle's own Greek too. This is only fitting. For a university whose first chancellor, Robert Grosseteste, was unusual for his time in knowing his Aristotle in Greek, and a university, moreover, whose student most renowned for subtlety of thought, Blessed John Duns Scotus, was also a remarkably subtle expositor of Aristotle, is bound by strong ties of piety to honor the memory of those medieval giants by continuing to honor the Greek and the Aristotle that they honored. So let me too, as a student of Oxford myself, perform my own duty of piety, and honor my tutors there in Aristotle and Greek by expressing here my heartfelt thanks to them, namely to Michael Ayers, Ian Crombie, George Forrest, and (now sadly deceased) Tom Stinton. I doubt not but they will find some things in this commentary to disagree with (though Tom is by now far beyond such earthly concerns, having received, as I trust and pray, full instruction in all mysteries from Blessed John and other spirits in Glory). I hope, nevertheless, that they will also be able to acknowledge that their patient labor in guiding my awkward steps into the halls of higher learning was not wholly in vain. As this book was going to press, I received the sad news that George Forrest had died. So let my trust and prayer for Tom now also be my trust and prayer for George.

January 1997
New York City

INTRODUCTION

This commentary on Aristotle's *Politics* is a companion to the translation I have made of the same work[1] and, as such, it relies on and uses certain elements of that translation, as notably its division of the text with headings and subheadings. The commentary follows the translation exactly in these respects and accordingly it is patterned after the same analytical outline and has the same divisions and headings. It also repeats the Bekker numbers that begin each new paragraph of the translation. The reader should, therefore, be able to find the part of the translation or of the Greek text that the commentary is referring to without too much difficulty. These references are, moreover, meant to be sufficiently independent of the translation that the commentary can be read and understood without that translation but, say, with the Greek text only, or even with some other translation.

In fact, the commentary as a whole is meant to stand on its own as far as possible (which is in part why the book's design differs in several respects from that of the translation). Consequently I shall repeat here, more or less verbatim, certain of the things I said in the introduction to the translation, but which are also necessary for understanding the commentary, so that those without the translation will not be left at a loss. I have in mind in particular what I said about the unity of the text and the order of the several books, about the last chapter of the *Nicomachean Ethics* as the context of the *Politics*, and about how I translate certain key terms of Aristotle's Greek. I should begin, however, by saying what sort of commentary this commentary is meant to be.

NATURE AND AIM OF THE COMMENTARY

The commentary is called and is meant to be philosophical. It is not meant to be philological or historical. There are already commentaries in existence that deal, and deal well, with these kinds of questions. I have no desire to repeat or rival their work. By calling my commentary philosophical I mean that it is concerned strictly,

1. Simpson (1997).

and even ascetically, with the logical structure of the text and with the analysis of the arguments, both individually and as forming a whole. If the commentary also enters from time to time into properly historical or philological questions, it does so only insofar as these may be necessary for explicating the philosophical sense.

The commentary is also meant to be a commentary. It is not meant to be a tracing of themes from passage to passage, nor a grand overview or summary, nor a speculative elaboration, nor a general contrast or comparison with other thinkers or theories, ancient or modern. This kind of writing on the *Politics* is, of course, necessary and valuable. Many examples have appeared over the years, and some excellent ones only very recently.[2] I have learned much from these writings, but I have not been concerned to imitate them, except incidentally in occasional digressions or in the notes. The commentary, if it is to be related to such writings, should be viewed as focused on what is a sort of preliminary to them. It is meant to give a thorough and accurate analysis of each argument and conclusion in its place and context so that use of such arguments and conclusions for broader speculations, comparisons, tracing of themes, and so forth will be as well grounded as possible. I think, indeed, that a number of writings of this sort have been marred by lack of such preliminary analysis, and conclusions have been drawn or speculations indulged in that Aristotle's text does not warrant or even contradicts.

The style of the commentary is, therefore, perforce analytical. But I think this a positive advantage, for Aristotle's text, being a complex of often subtle arguments, calls for such an analytical treatment. I have, in fact, taken no little inspiration in this regard from the analytical style of the commentaries of St. Thomas Aquinas.[3] There is, however, a view, popular in the scholarly literature, that opposes this

---

2. I would instance Miller (1995) in particular. The character of my own commentary can, in fact, be brought out by contrast with Miller. For Miller is concerned to present and defend the thesis that Aristotle had a doctrine of rights and that his political thought can, in important respects, be cast as a rights theory. I am in no substantial disagreement with Miller on this point, as I indicated in Simpson (1996), yet I hardly talk about rights in my commentary and certainly do not thematize the question. The reason is that Aristotle himself does not thematize the question. Miller readily admits this (1995: 90) and therefore only imputes a theory of rights to Aristotle in the sense that Aristotle recognizes many things as politically just that we naturally call "rights"—and for which "rights" is a natural translation (one I also use, as at 3.12.1282b29)—and that these "rights" have a firm basis in Aristotle's theory of justice. In other words a rights theory does exist in Aristotle but not as explicitly stated (it is surely a truism that any text implies more than it says). Consequently it is not the sort of thing that will naturally get focused on in a commentary that follows the text line by line and thematizes what the text thematizes, but only in a more discursive work that takes disparately treated topics as its theme. The more discursive work, however, will need a literal commentary on the disparate passages it collects to ensure that they are understood correctly and that only genuine implications are drawn out. Much of Miller's book consists of such commentary and it is on that level that my own work comes into comparison, and sometimes conflict, with his, and not on the level of the general thesis.

3. St. Thomas's commentary on the *Politics* is incomplete and finishes at the end of *Politics* 3.8, though there is a continuation of it by Peter of Auvergne.

analytical approach to Aristotle's text.[4] The contention is that the text should be treated, also or instead, with a view to rhetorical subtleties and that it requires reading on several levels. Much is made, for instance, of poetic quotations and of the supposed nonphilosophic character of Aristotle's audience as well as of the practical intention of the writing. The result is not infrequently that the literal argument of the text is rejected in favor of an argument that supposedly lies beneath the surface, or between the lines, and that Aristotle's real views are said to be the opposite of what he expressly says.

Now there can be no objection in principle to the thesis that some texts must be read at more than one level or that a text can appear to say one thing while really saying another. There can certainly be no objection to the thesis that Aristotle's writings, like those of most ancient thinkers, must be read with much care. But I have come across no alleged case of Aristotle saying one thing on the surface and another beneath it that could stand up to scrutiny. Slavery is often said to be such a case, but in fact it is not, and the interpretations of Aristotle's text to establish that it is can be shown to be mistaken (see the text and notes of the commentary at 1.4–6 and 4(7).10.1330a25).[5] The same goes for his views about nature and about women (see in particular 1.8–9, 13, and the commentary thereon). But even if I am wrong and it can be shown that the *Politics* does require, whether in whole or in part, such rhetorical or oblique reading, there would still be need first for a careful analysis of the express arguments. For the rhetorical reading, by the confession of its proponents, is only required because the express arguments are problematic or confused or incomplete or something else of the sort. But the only way to show that the express arguments are thus flawed or lacking is to analyze them properly as they stand. The analytic reading will, therefore, have to precede the rhetorical reading. My own contention is that a correct analytic reading shows that no rhetorical reading is necessary and that all proposed rhetorical readings are mistaken.

Nevertheless, though I disagree with scholars who favor these rhetorical readings, I have learned and benefited much from them, as I have also learned and benefited much from other scholars generally. Indeed I have often benefited most when I have disagreed most. Disagreement is a powerful stimulus to thought, provided the disagreement is honest and one's aim is to get clear about what and why one disagrees. I remain grateful, therefore, to those who have gone before me in the task of interpreting Aristotle's *Politics*, and admire and commend their devotion to so worthy an object. The bibliography and notes to the commentary

---

4. On the general point see Jaffa (1952), and on the *Politics* in particular see, for example, Davis (1996), Lord (1982, 1984), Mansfield (1989: chaps. 2 and 3), and Nichols (1992). A similar approach is taken to Aristotle's *Ethics* by Tessitore (1996).

5. The same thesis is argued by Dobbs (1994: especially 71–73), with whom I am in general agreement; see also Lindsay (1994).

contain only a partial acknowledgment of how much and from whom I have learned. There are many to whom I had no occasion to refer expressly or whom, perhaps, I have forgotten, though they too were my teachers. If in any respect I have seen more than they, or if in any respect I have advanced the study of the *Politics*, it is only because they advanced it and saw more first.

◁ UNITY AND ORDER OF THE TEXT OF THE *POLITICS*

That the *Politics* is the work of Aristotle is not a matter for doubt. What is doubted is whether it forms a single and coherent whole, planned by Aristotle as such, or whether instead it is a composite of disparate parts that were originally written at different times, on different assumptions and for different reasons, and that were put together, in a not very convincing manner, by some editor. The general state of scholarly opinion on this question may be said to be as follows. There are first those scholars who say that the *Politics* is not a coherent whole either in doctrine or form; there are second those who say it is a coherent whole in doctrine but not in form; and there are those who say it is a coherent whole in both doctrine and form.[6]

Those in the first group argue for their view on the ground that the *Politics* contains many contradictions and incoherences, both within and between books, and that these are incompatible with the idea that the *Politics* is a complete whole as opposed to an ill-assorted amalgam. Those in the second group agree that there are incoherences but counter that these are in the form only and do not extend to the doctrine, or only to certain details of the doctrine and not to its substance. Those in the third group also agree that there are incoherences in the form but counter that these are apparent, not real, and that beneath this appearance the whole is coherent in both doctrine and form. Such are those scholars, just mentioned, who prefer rhetorical readings and who accordingly say that Aristotle deliberately gave the appearance of formal disunity since what he wanted to say he did not say openly, in the manner modern readers expect, but hid behind a certain veil of obscurity so as to deter one class of readers and attract another.

My own view is that none of these groups is correct and that the *Politics* is a formal and doctrinal unity without even apparent incoherence.[7] I do not, indeed, maintain that this unity is luminous at a first or cursory reading, but I do maintain that it is really there and that it can eventually become luminous. The divisions and headings of the translation and the analytical table of contents, all of which the commentary repeats, are meant, indeed, to make that unity luminous, and sufficiently so that it can be understood even on a first reading. Any puzzles or diffi-

---

6. Representative of the first group are Jaeger (1923) and Schütrumpf (1991); of the second Barker (1946), Johnson (1990), Mulgan (1977), and Newman (1887–1902); of the third Davis (1996), Lord (1982, 1984), and Nichols (1992).

7. In this regard I am perhaps closest to Miller (1995: 24, 183–90) among modern scholars.

culties that remain will, I hope, be resolved by what I say within the commentary, especially about the passages on which the other views about the unity of the *Politics* especially rest. The reader should, however, keep particularly in view the analytical table of contents, for it provides a visible schema of how I suppose the whole *Politics* breaks down into its parts and how these parts come together to form a steady and logical progression of argument from beginning to end.

There is, nevertheless, one question related to the unity of the *Politics* which does need discussing here, and that is the question of the arrangement or ordering of the books. For I have, in opposition to most commentaries, put these books in an order other than the order they have in the surviving manuscripts, and I need to explain and justify this decision. The view, indeed, that the manuscript ordering of the books of the *Politics* is wrong used to be common among scholars and is reflected in several past translations and editions.[8] It is also the opinion of one contemporary translator (even though he forbore to carry it through into his translation).[9] The view is that books 7 and 8 of the manuscripts have got displaced (whether because of an editor or of some mechanical accident in the process of transmission) and should properly come between books 3 and 4.

The fundamental evidence for this view is that what Aristotle says at the end of book 3 he is going to do next he does not in fact do next but only later in books 7 and 8. This anomaly or oddity is easy to see and cannot have escaped anyone's notice, but caution, perhaps, and a just conservatism induced people to leave the text alone. It was not until 1577 that Scaino da Salo first openly argued for a change of ordering. Scaino was very conscious of the boldness of his proceeding and took great pains to prove that he was not so much changing the order of the books as putting them back into the order originally intended by Aristotle. His arguments were comprehensive and, though not all of equal weight, constituted a convincing case. Unfortunately his work was largely ignored until it was enthusiastically taken up by Barthélemy Saint-Hilaire some 250 years later. Thereafter the view that the ordering of the books should be changed became dominant until the work of Jaeger, first published in 1923, caused it to wane.

Jaeger recognized as much as anyone the oddity in the manuscript ordering of the books, but he gave a different account of it. Aristotle's own thinking, reasoned Jaeger, had undergone development from an early and idealistic stage represented in particular by books 7 and 8 to a later and more realistic stage represented in particular by books 4 to 6. The *Politics* as we now have it was never a coherent whole. It consists instead of disparate and incompatible elements belonging to different stages of intellectual development that were never intended by Aristotle

8. As in the editions of Newman (1887–1902) and Susemihl and Hicks (1894) and the translation of Welldon (1883).

9. Lord (1984: 16).

to constitute a single work. The sort of problems, therefore, that induced Scaino to reorder the books are genuine problems and genuinely there, but they could never be solved or removed by such reordering, for they sprang from incoherences in the content and not in the form only.

Jaeger's work itself, however, is full of problems of its own, from arbitrary assumptions to straight errors,[10] and has itself now fallen out of favor. Besides the thesis on which it rests, that the *Politics* is not a doctrinal and formal unity, can be shown to be false. Scaino's contention, therefore, must be reconsidered and must be accepted or rejected on its own terms. There is, however, a complication that must be considered and set aside first. For among those scholars who agreed that books 7 and 8 should come between books 3 and 4, there were some, including Saint-Hilaire himself, who thought that book 6 should also come before book 5 (thus giving the order 1, 2, 3, 7, 8, 4, 6, 5). Their reasoning was based on a passage where Aristotle is speaking of the questions he is going to examine (4.2.1289b20–26). The second to last of these questions is how to set up the several regimes and the last is how regimes are destroyed and preserved. This last question is manifestly dealt with in book 5 but the other appears to be dealt with in book 6 and so in an order contrary to that which has been allotted to it. The solution seemed to be, therefore, to reorder these books too and put 6 before 5. This solution, however, causes more problems than it solves for it brings one into direct conflict with passages in book 6 that expressly speak of book 5 as having already preceded (6.1.1316b31–36, 1317a37–38, 6.4.1319b4–6, 6.5.1319b37–1320a4). Saint-Hilaire and others therefore had to expunge these passages as later interpolations. But this is a desperate remedy.

Scaino himself, who also agreed that book 6 contained Aristotle's answer to the second to last question in 4.2, had a simpler and neater solution. He left book 6 as and where it was and simply transposed a few words in 4.2 itself so that the question of how regimes are destroyed and preserved was made to come before the question about how to set up regimes.[11] This solution is less drastic than the other and to that extent preferable, but it still requires tampering with the text. A solution that is better still is to note that the whole problem is anyway a false one. For Aristotle makes clear at the beginning of book 6 that that book is an addendum to his discussion of the questions set out in the program at the end of 4.2 and is not the original discussion. The original discussion of the question about how to set up regimes comes earlier in 4.14–16, and so before book 5, as he said (my arguments for this view are given at the relevant points of the commentary).

The question of reordering, then, concerns only whether to put 7 and 8 between

10. Barker (1946: xxxvii–xlvi), Bodéus (1982/1993: 1–2), Grene (1963: chap. 1), Lachterman (1990), Lord (1981: 468–70; 1984: 14–17), Miller (1995: 23–24), Pellegrin (1987), Rowe (1977), Simpson (1993).
11. Scaino (1577: 30–31).

3 and 4. The main arguments for doing so are philological and based simply on Aristotle's own words, and not on any theory about what order he ought, a priori, to have followed.[12] The first is the argument already mentioned, that Aristotle says at the end of book 3 (chapter 18) that he is going next to discuss the best regime and that he also says that books 7 and 8 are that discussion (7.1.1323a14–21, 7.4.1325b33–38, 7.13.1331b24–26). So these words indicate he intended 7 to follow 3. The second argument reinforces the first, for the words that end 3.18 (1288b5–6) are picked up almost literally by the words at the beginning of 7.1 (1323a14–15) and form with them a neat progression of thought (see the commentary ad loc.). The third argument is that Aristotle says in book 4 that the discussion of the best regime has already preceded (4.2.1289a30–35, 4.3.1290a1–3, 4.7.1293b1–7, and by implication at 4.8.1293b22–27; note also the close verbal parallel between 4.7.1293b3–5 and 7.9.1328b37–39). But this discussion is, he says (as just noted), found in books 7 and 8. So these words too indicate that he intended 7 to follow 3.

The above arguments are the more convincing for relying, as they do, on Aristotle's express words. They should be considered decisive.[13] That they are not so considered is largely because of arguments on the other side that seem to bring the matter back into doubt. These arguments, however, all have ready answers. The first and strongest of them is that the outline for the *Politics* laid down at *Ethics* 10.9.1181b15–23 seems to say that the discussion of the best regime, or books 7 and 8, is to come last. But in fact, as I argue in the commentary ad loc., that outline says the opposite and, properly interpreted, requires 7 and 8 to be transposed between 3 and 4 and not left where they are. A second argument is that the best regime of books 7 and 8 is not the best regime spoken of in 3 so that to transpose the books does not solve the problem posed by the end of 3. But this interpretation of books 7 and 8 is not convincing (see the commentary at 4(7).1332b16) and anyway conflicts with the words of Aristotle in 7 noted above. A third argument is that there is a reference in 7 (about "the other regimes" at 4.1325b34) that seems to be to book 4 as if this book had preceded. But this reference is better understood as being to the discussions in book 2. A fourth argument is that book 4 refers back to 3 as if 3, and not 7 and 8, had just preceded. But in fact the references in 4 only show that 3 has preceded and not that it has *just* preceded. A fifth argument is that there seems to be a reference in 7 (about the names for certain kinds of office, at 12.1331b6–15) back to 6.8. But there is no reason to suppose any reference at all here, or no reason to suppose the reference is *back* to 6.8 rather than *forward* to 6.8.

12. They escape, therefore, the problems about arguments based on such a priori theory noted by Pellegrin (1987).

13. It is worth noting that Jaeger considered them decisive (1923/1934: 268). At any rate he agreed that 7 and 8 were originally intended by Aristotle to follow 3. He only claimed that this intention belonged to an earlier stage in Aristotle's thinking and could not be used to help make sense of the books of the *Politics* as we now have them.

The conclusion to draw, then, is that books 7 and 8 were intended by Aristotle to come between books 3 and 4 and so should be put back there. Accordingly that is what I do in both translation and commentary. Still, in deference to the manuscript order (which is the order predominantly followed by scholars and commentators as by most current translations and editions), I number the books after book 3, albeit at the risk of some awkwardness, with two numbers, the first for their correct order and the second (in parentheses) for their manuscript order: 1, 2, 3, 4(7), 5(8), 6(4), 7(5), 8(6).[14]

∿ CONTEXT OF THE *POLITICS*

It is a common assumption that to understand a work one has to understand its context. This assumption is, however, ambiguous for context itself is ambiguous. Generally it is taken to mean historical context or the time and place of the work's composition and the life and times of the author. Such historical placing of a work is often thought to be especially important in the case of the *Politics*, which is not only full of references to historical events but also seems to be about a historical phenomenon, the ancient Greek *polis*. But to make this supposition and to lay it down as a prerequisite for understanding what Aristotle says is to beg the question against him. The *Politics*, according to Aristotle himself, is not about a historical phenomenon, nor is it about a Greek phenomenon. It is about a natural phenomenon which, if prominent in ancient Greece, could in principle exist in any place and at any time and which, moreover, is necessary at every place and at every time if human beings are to attain happiness.

Our modern opinions about history, however, and about its dominance over human life and thought, make us think that there is no such thing as nature in the sense of something prior to history and independent of it. Nature is, on the contrary, something posterior and itself a product of history. So we tend to smile at those, like Aristotle, who believe in an independent nature as we tend to smile at the naïveté of small children. Could we set aside our opinions for a moment, or at least suppose that they need not be as obviously true as we think them to be, we should instead look at Aristotle and his *Politics* with something like shocked astonishment. Really? The *polis* is natural and necessary for happiness? And we, who lack the *polis*, are living unnatural lives and are deprived of happiness? How can this be, and how can our leaders be so careless and indifferent about something so important?

I will not, however, try to settle here this dispute between our modern preference for history and Aristotle's preference for nature. Neither will I assume the modern preference in advance. For that, as I said, would beg the question against Aristotle. I wish at least to give Aristotle the chance to have his say. So I propose to

14. In this I follow the example of Newman (1887–1902).

say nothing about the historical context of the *Politics*.[15] Any notes I have added about the historical events Aristotle refers to in the course of his exposition are rather to satisfy curiosity than to aid understanding.[16] For although Aristotle refers to these events to illustrate his argument, this argument itself, as I have just remarked, is about nature and not about history (save insofar as history reveals and displays nature). One should note, indeed, in this regard that, in order to understand Aristotle's argument, we do not need to know anything more about these events than he himself tells us, even though what he tells us is sometimes only a name. A case in point is the "affair at Andros" used to illustrate the venality of the ephors at Sparta (2.9.1270b11–13). We do not know what event Aristotle is referring to or even a single one of the details, yet our ignorance has not hindered us in the least from understanding what he is saying or arguing. Indeed, scholars are guided in their conjectures about this affair at Andros by their understanding of what Aristotle says, and not guided in their understanding of what Aristotle says by their conjectures about the affair.

But context, as I said, is an ambiguous term and besides historical context there is also philosophical context, knowledge of which, if not of the former, is necessary for understanding the *Politics*. But philosophical context is also ambiguous and can mean the remote and general context or the immediate and particular context. The remote and general context is Aristotle's philosophical writings as a whole and especially, perhaps, his *Physics* and *Metaphysics*, which contain his systematic exposition of certain fundamental terms common to every science, as above all *phusis* or "nature."[17] But knowing this context, while valuable for situating the *Politics* with respect to the other parts of philosophy, does not seem to be as valuable for understanding the *Politics* itself. At any rate one can, as I try to show in the commentary, make sense of Aristotle's arguments without having to refer expressly to any of these other writings; and, significantly enough, Aristotle himself does not so refer.

He does, however, refer, and refer often, to one of his works, namely the *Ethics*. Indeed he considers the *Ethics* already to be politics, or political science (*Ethics* 1.2–3), and does not understand what it studies to be separate from what the *Politics* studies. Repeated reminders of the political character of the *Ethics* are to be found throughout that work. Notable in this regard, in fact, is its very last chapter which is, and is clearly meant to be, an introduction or transition to the study of cities and regimes proper, that is, to the study that is contained in the *Politics*. Contro-

---

15. In this regard I follow the example of St. Thomas Aquinas (1951) whose *prooemium* or introduction to the *Politics* is all about the philosophical placing of the work and is silent about everything historical; see also Mansfield (1989: 27–28).

16. The dates in these notes are therefore B.C. and not A.D.

17. This remote context of the *Politics* is discussed at some length by Kamp (1985).

versy has, however, arisen among scholars on this point and some are of the view that the introduction to the study of regimes at the end of the *Ethics* is not an introduction to the *Politics* as we now have it, and also that the *Ethics* referred to in the *Politics* is not the *Nicomachean Ethics*, in which alone this introduction occurs, but rather the *Eudemian Ethics*.[18] I am myself convinced that this view is mistaken and argue to that effect in the commentary at 4(7).13.1332a19.

But at all events, if the *Politics* does refer to and presuppose the *Nicomachean Ethics*, it is this work alone among Aristotle's writings that will be the immediate and particular context of the *Politics*. A knowledge of it, therefore, and especially of its concluding chapter, will be necessary for an understanding of the *Politics*. Accordingly I have placed, as aid and instruction to the reader, a commentary of that last chapter before the commentary on the *Politics* proper. It will form the proper context, and the only indispensable context, for reading and understanding the *Politics*.

⁓ TRANSLATION OF KEY WORDS IN THE *POLITICS*

The main disputes about the translation of the key words in the *Politics* center on *polis* and the words derived from it, such as *politeia* and *politikos*. These disputes concern, in particular, whether to translate *polis* as "city" or "state" or even "city-state," *politeia* as "polity" or "regime" or "constitution," *politikos* as "politician" or "statesman." It would be desirable to find a set of English words that were similarly related to each other as the original Greek words are. But while it is possible to do this with respect to certain pairs (as "city" and "citizen" for *polis* and *politēs*, "state" and "statesman" for *polis* and *politikos*, "polity" and "politician" for *politeia* and *politikos*), it is not possible to do this for all of them together.

One could, of course, abandon the attempt to find translations and merely transliterate the Greek words instead. But this seems a counsel of despair and, moreover, runs the risk of giving a false impression. For it runs the risk of giving the impression that Aristotle is talking about things or phenomena peculiarly Greek, which can only be referred to using Greek terms, and so about things that are transient and relative to a particular period of human history and not about things that are timeless and relative to universal human nature. But, as I noted earlier, Aristotle supposes himself throughout to be talking of human nature and not of human history (except in relation to human nature), and indeed gives express arguments to this effect (as when he argues that humans are by nature political animals, in 1.2). Perhaps Aristotle is wrong in this regard, but we ought to try to avoid giving this impression in advance or before his arguments have been duly weighed. Likewise, we ought to try to avoid stating these arguments using words that, because they are transliterations and not translations, suggest the

18. Lord (1984: 19–21).

falsity of the arguments they are being used to convey. Transliterations, or even neologisms, might, indeed, be forced on us if our own language and experience proved to be so impoverished or so different that we possessed no word to do the necessary translating. But we ought not to reach that conclusion too quickly or too lightly, and certainly not before we have gone through all the resources available to us and still failed to come up with a defensible translation. And these resources include, one should stress, not only the words and their senses prevalent in current speech but also any words and senses that, even though less used, are still available in our linguistic heritage (provided they have not become so obsolete as to sound outlandish).

The translator and commentator, then, must confront, and not bypass, the problem of translating the words of Aristotle's Greek, and must strive to find acceptable equivalents for these words, or for as many of them as possible, and especially for the key or important words. Now such equivalents can, in my view, be found; indeed most of them already exist somewhere or other in the well-established tradition of translating Aristotle into English. My own choice of which words to use in this regard are, therefore, for the most part not new, but follow one or other of the several already well-trodden paths. The particular path, or rather combination of paths, that I have chosen to follow takes its beginning from the conviction that it is a mistake to translate *polis* as "state."[19] For, first, the word "state" is typically predicated of nations and a nation is not a *polis*. Even if the state is the only modern entity that exercises anything like the control once exercised by the *polis*, it is nevertheless a corruption and not an extension of the *polis*. For it is not at all the sort of community that Aristotle has in mind by the *polis*. The *polis* is that community which responds to the natural desire of human beings to perfect themselves in happy and noble living and which exists by nature in order to realize that goal (1.2, 3.9). It therefore has to be small, or small enough that the citizens can know each others' character and rule with a view to each others' character (4(7).4). It also has to be small enough to be capable of receiving a common political arrangement or a single *politeia*, for a *polis* is identified by its *politeia* (3.3). But the state is far too big to have a single *politeia*, and too big to allow its citizens to know character and to rule with a view to character. The state, indeed, is as big as it is partly to ensure that rule is not exercised with a view to character but that such matters are left to individual choice.

Second, the state does not signify a community or a common way of life. It is understood rather in terms of force, for the state proper is typically defined as that which has a monopoly of legitimate coercion. But the *polis* is first and foremost a community. It does, to be sure, exercise control over other communities and has

19. A view also argued by Berti, in Gigon and Fischer (1988: 90), and by Jaffa, in Strauss and Cropsey (1972: 65–67), and cf. Barker (1946: lxiii–lxiv).

the power to coerce them, but it is still itself a community or a sharing together in a common life. The state, by contrast, stands over against community (for it stands over against society, which is the locus in modern states of community and sharing of life together).[20] A sign is that we can talk of a given community as *our* community, or as something *we* all share together, and so we can also talk of loving and caring for our community and even of dying for it. By contrast, we do not talk, or do not talk happily, of a state as *our* state or of loving and dying for the state.[21]

If *polis*, therefore, does not mean state, neither can it mean city-state (which would imply that the *polis* is a certain kind of state). The option left, then, is to translate *polis* as "city." But this option too is problematic because modern cities are also large (as large, in certain cases, as some modern states) and are just as incapable of ruling with a view to character. But there is this difference: "city," unlike "state," signifies a community, a sign of which is that we can talk of love of our city and even of fighting and dying for our city.[22] Moreover, "city" is a name still in standard use for referring to what Aristotle would call *poleis*, as to the medieval Italian republics, like Venice and Florence. It is also the standard name, outside translations of the *Politics* at any rate, for referring to ancient Athens or Sparta or Thebes or any other ancient Greek *polis*. Indeed the neologism "city-state" helps to confirm this. For that we soften "state" with "city" when speaking of ancient *poleis* shows that "city" is the name for expressing that characteristic of ancient *poleis* that makes them different from states as we now speak of states.

But if *polis* must, therefore, be translated as "city" and not as "state" or "city-state," then this will naturally lead to the translation of *politēs* as "citizen" (even

20. See Miller (1995: 19–20, 358–61) and Mulgan (1977: 16–17). Both Miller and Mulgan accuse Aristotle of equivocation for using *polis* sometimes to mean state and sometimes to mean society. But what this supposed equivocation really shows is not that Aristotle uses *polis* with two different meanings but that he uses it with one meaning that cuts across the division we now draw between state and society. *Polis* does not signify state or society but something that is both and neither at the same time, just as do our terms "country" or "fatherland" when we speak, for instance, of dying for country or fatherland. *Polis* is not an illegitimate fusion of state and society but a third thing altogether, and the real question between Aristotle on the one hand and Miller and Mulgan on the other is whether the single notion of *polis* or the double notion of state and society gives one a truer understanding of political phenomena. To say that *polis* is a fusion of the other two notions begs this question against Aristotle.

21. "Society" will hardly do as a translation of *polis*, for though society carries with it some of the warmth associated with community, it does not carry with it any sense of political organization and rule (for that is said rather to belong to the state). *Polis*, however, does very much carry this sense.

22. Such "fighting" and "dying" typically manifest themselves nowadays at sporting events among fans of teams from rival cities, and then only in the form of high passions and opposing shouts and cheers, when one side is elated at victory and the other dashed by defeat. But these passions can also drive fans into fights and brawls (during which some have died), which shows that even modern cities are still capable of exciting the sort of intense affection and loyalty also excited by what we call fatherland or country, but not by what we call state.

though we use this term for members of nations and states too), but away from the translation of *politikos* as "statesman." True, "statesman" does tend to mean someone with the sort of wisdom, prudence, and care for the common good that Aristotle understands by the true *politikos*, whereas "politician" often means someone who is rather low and devious and concerned to exploit rule for his own private advantage. But even though "politician" can mean this, it does so with the implication that politicians should not be so low and devious and that those who are have somehow failed in their duty and have given their profession, which in itself is something noble, a bad name. In this way, indeed, "politician" is a rather good word to use to translate *politikos*, because the same was true of *politikos* in Aristotle's day. Both words properly mean someone noble and public-spirited but both have derogatory connotations because of the bad example of actual politicians.[23]

Translating *polis* as "city" does not, however, determine anything about how to translate *politeia*. Nevertheless good reasons can be given for not translating it as "constitution." For a constitution is a set of rules (written or unwritten), and though *politeia* includes rules (as the laws that determine the offices), it means above all the people, or the parts of the city—whether the poor, the rich, or the virtuous—who are actually in control. It signifies a body of rulers, in other words, and not a set of rules.[24] Hence Aristotle identifies the *politeia* with the *politeuma* and means by *politeuma* the ruling body, or even, we might say, the ruling class (3.6.1278b8–15). *Politeia* is therefore closer to what we mean by the establishment than to what we mean by the constitution. One could, indeed, not trouble to translate *politeia* at all but transliterate it as "polity," for polity has become a respectable English word that signifies manner of rule. If I prefer to translate it instead as "regime," this is in part because regime is already much in favor as a translation of *politeia*, but mainly because regime conveys, as polity does not, the idea of a way of life (we speak, for instance, of athletes following a regime, or a regimen, and mean thereby a whole pattern of life that they are to follow for a certain period). *Politeia*, by signifying the ruling body, signifies the way of life of the city, since the ruling body necessarily imposes on the whole city, by its ruling, its own vision of happiness and of the best way to live (2.11.1273a37–b1, 4(7).8.1328a35–b2). True, Aristotle also refers to the *politeia* as the kind of composition of the city (3.3.1276b1–11) and also says it is the way cities arrange (*taxis*) their offices (6(4).1.1289a15–18), both of which passages may suggest that he means something of a more institutional character by *politeia*. But a closer look at the contexts shows otherwise. For what Aristotle means in the first passage is how the inhabitants of the city are "composed" with respect to having, or not having, shares in rule. The inhabitants who

23. See Miller (1995: 13 n21).

24. See Mulgan (1977: 56), Susemihl and Hicks (1894: 365–66), and contrast Miller (1995: 79 n21) who prefers "constitution."

do have shares, and so are citizens, are the *politeia*. In the second passage, since the "arrangement," or *taxis*, in question is the arrangement of the offices, it means which of the inhabitants of the city are so arranged as to share in the offices. So in both cases the *politeia* means the arrangement or composition of people with respect to rule; hence it means, first and foremost, the ruling body and the way of living or distinctive character of that ruling body. Such a sense is captured by the word "regime" but not by the word "constitution."[25]

Aristotle also uses *politeia* to mean a particular species or kind of regime, for which "polity" has in fact become a standard translation and the translation I also adopt. But, of course, if one thus translates *politeia* in its general sense as "regime" and in its specific sense as "polity," one is giving to Aristotle's text a greater precision than he himself chose to give it, and there is a case, adopted by some translators, for using the same word to translate *politeia* in both of its senses. Nevertheless, if Aristotle, more in deference to common usage than to philosophical accuracy (*Ethics* 8.10.1160a33–35), uses the same word with two senses, the senses themselves are distinct. For that reason, and with a view to exposition in the commentary, I have preferred to employ a difference of word to keep clear the difference of sense.

So much may be said about the terms of the *Politics* based on the root word *polis*. But there are other important terms that Aristotle uses and about which I ought to say something here. The standard translations for *kurios* include "authority," "sovereign," "supreme," "decisive," and others of the sort. Something can be said for all these suggestions, of course, but I have here decided to depart from the practice of others and to use the word "control" instead. I have found "control" easier to handle than other words in rendering the various ways Aristotle uses *kurios* and its cognates, and "control" does, in addition, include the ideas expressed by these other words. For instance, those who are in control of the city or regime must also be those who are sovereign, supreme, and decisive, for what they say and think must be the final determinant of what the city does and what the regime is like. Further, while "control" can also express the idea of authority, it need merely express the idea of effective power, power that in fact dominates whether or not it has any right or legitimacy so to do. Authority, by contrast, tends to carry with it the idea of right or legitimacy as well as power. But Aristotle uses *kurios* in such a way that it need not mean legitimate power but only effective power. Tyranny, for instance, and tyrannical forms of democracy and oligarchy are never legitimate or just for Aristotle, yet he does not hesitate to speak of them as *kurios* (3.10.1281a11–17, 6(4).4.1292a4–13, 6(4).6.1293a30–34). There is an element,

25. For this reason I would also reject the translation "political system" preferred by Kraut (1997), for that too tends to convey the idea of something institutional rather than a way of life.

if you like, of brute realism in Aristotle's use of *kurios* that the word "authority" can obscure.

The word *kalos* has the fundamental meaning of beautiful, but beautiful in the sense of the full range of beautiful things, not just bodily ones, including in particular beautiful souls, characters, laws, and regimes. Thus it carries a sense that can also, and perhaps better, be expressed in English by the word "noble." Aristotle is very free in his use of *kalos* and employs it in places where we would more naturally employ the tamer and different words "well," or "fine," or "correct." But it is not insignificant, I think, that Aristotle uses *kalos*. For there are other words at his disposal, which he does in fact also use, that literally mean "well" or "fine" or "correct," and yet he prefers so often to use *kalos* instead. The prime reason for this is, no doubt, that one of Aristotle's theses, as fundamental to the *Ethics* as to the *Politics*, is that only the noble is ultimately well and correct and good and that anything that is not noble is not really well or correct or good. The *kaloikagathoi*, however, or those who are (literally) "noble and good" I refer to as gentlemen, since that is what true gentlemen are.

For *dēmos* and its cognates I use "populace," "popular," and so forth. I have refrained from using "people" or "the people" instead mainly because when we say "the people" in a political context in English, we do not typically mean what *dēmos* means in Greek. For by "the people" we typically mean all those who live in or are citizens of a given city or state. But the *dēmos* are only ever part of the people in this sense, for they are only ever the mass of the free poor (and not also the rich or the well-born). So they are rather what we mean by the phrase "the common people." And in fact, while the word "populace" can mean the population in general of a given place, its first meaning is that of the common people. So provided the reader keeps these facts in mind, "the populace" will prove a better and less misleading translation for *dēmos* than "the people."

ANALYTICAL OUTLINE OF THE *POLITICS*

Introduction to the *Politics*: *Nicomachean Ethics* 10.9

Chapter 9

∿ THE INCOMPLETENESS OF THE *ETHICS*

1179a33   The subject of the *Ethics* from its beginning has been the human good or happiness, the final goal of all human activity (1.1–2, 4). So now that Aristotle has discussed all the relevant matters (happiness and the practical and contemplative lives, virtue, friendship, pleasure), one might suppose that he has brought his chosen project to completion. A question arises, however, because the *Ethics* is about matters of practice or action (happiness, or living well, is an activity, the activity of virtue), and the end in such matters is to do, not merely to study. So to know or talk about virtue cannot be enough; there is need rather actually to get it and use it,[1] so that we do actually become good and happy. But that the end in practical matters is doing, and not knowledge only, does not by itself establish that the *Ethics* is incomplete, as Aristotle at once suggests by asking if there is some other way of becoming good. For there is indeed, at least in principle, another possibility here, that knowledge by itself, and the words through which knowledge is communicated, might be enough to make us virtuous and ready to act accordingly. This possibility, that action will immediately follow knowledge, is, in fact, the one adopted by the many who think it enough, in order to become good, to listen to argument (2.4.1105b9–18). For if arguments and words are enough, then the *Ethics* could indeed be complete and there would be no need of anything further.

1179b4   Aristotle had already refuted this view of the many when he first raised it. Here, however, he takes it up and refutes it again, not only because it has become relevant again, but also perhaps because before he was content to refute it using an analogy (that the sick who hear the words of a doctor but do not act on them will not get well). For now he refutes it directly and more thoroughly by also giving the underlying reason.

The basic form of his refutation is: (1) if reasoned words or arguments alone

---

1. To "get" it in the sense of acquiring the habit or virtue of acting best, and to "use" it in the sense of actually doing the actions of which the virtues are the virtues; see St. Thomas Aquinas (1964: 10.14.2138), Gauthier and Jolif (1958–59: 2:900). For happiness is not the result of action but itself action, 1.8.1098b31–1099a7, and note the definitions of happiness at 1.7.1098a16–18 and 1.10.1101a14–21.

were able to make us actually good, it would be enough to provide them; (2) but to provide reasoned words or arguments is not enough; (3) therefore words alone are not able to make us good. Premise (2) is the important one here and is a straightforward appeal to the empirical evidence, that words can be enough but only if something else is first presupposed and that, where that something else is not presupposed, words are useless. For words, as experience shows, are indeed enough to get some of the young possessed by virtue but only those of them who have the right sort of character and training, that is, who are generous, well-bred, and already in love with the noble. Words are not enough, by contrast, for the many who are not of the same sort at all. The many, unlike the young just mentioned, do not love nobility and virtue or hate ugliness and vice. Rather they pursue the first and avoid the second, if they do, only through fear of punishment.

So much is observable fact, but the reason for it is that the many, unlike the nobility-loving young, live by their passions and follow the pleasures of the passions, not the true pleasure and nobility of virtue. So, because they live by their passions, and not by reason, they have no notion of the noble at all (for the nobility in question, virtue, is the object of reason, 1.13.1102b13–b10), and it is manifestly useless to talk about the noble to people who have no notion of the noble; it would be like talking to the deaf. Moreover the difficulty is compounded by the fact that ignorance of the noble and love of the pleasures of the passions have now become a deep and settled habit in the many (who have, presumably, been following their passions ever since childhood). But it is manifest that changing habits and character is not a work of mere argument.

Consequently reasoned words are not enough to make anyone virtuous, whether solely in the case of the nobility-loving young or at all in the case of the many. Hence, further, the chosen project of the *Ethics* cannot be complete.

∼ THE NEED FOR LEGISLATION

1179b18 But if the project of the *Ethics* is incomplete and something else is needed, the next thing to consider is what that something else is. This Aristotle now does. But that he does so by appealing back, in part, to the same facts about words and the passions just mentioned is not indicative that the text as we have it contains a needless repetition of the same material, written, no doubt, by Aristotle though badly put together by a later editor.[2] On the contrary, the repetition is no repetition but serves importantly to advance the discussion. For though the same material is used, it is used for a different purpose. It was first used to show the insufficiency of words; it is now used to show the necessity of law.[3]

The aim of Aristotle's present project is actually to become good, and since this

2. Gauthier and Jolif (1958–59: 2:900).
3. As noted by St. Thomas Aquinas (1964: 10.14.2137, 2139, 2148).

aim is the greatest good of all, the good of living a happy life, one should obviously be glad to use all means available to get hold of it if one can. Now there are generally acknowledged to be three such means: nature, habituation, and teaching. All three are desirable but not all are likewise available. Nature, to begin with, is not in our control, but rather in divine control and so only something we could pray for (as Aristotle himself prays for it later; *Politics* 4(7).4.1325b33–39, 7.1327b20–38). As regards teaching, this, as was just shown, does not have power in every case but only on the presupposition of the other means mentioned, habituation. For if reason and words are to have an effect, the one spoken to and reasoned with must already have been habituated to enjoy and hate nobly, that is, to enjoy the noble and to hate the base. For then, to teach him that such and such is noble or such and such base, which is what teaching virtue is, will move him at the same time toward virtue, since his preexisting love will immediately prompt him to pursue the first and to avoid the second. To teach the same thing to someone living by his passions would be to teach him something he will neither listen to, nor, if he listens, understand (for he does not care about the noble nor does he know what it is). To get such a person to change his behavior what is needed, as experience shows, is force and not persuasion.

1179b31   Of the three ways of getting virtue, then, only two are in our power, and of these two one of them, teaching, is dependent for its effectiveness on the other, habituation. The question, therefore, of how to become virtuous, insofar as this lies within our power, focuses on the question of right habituation. In answer Aristotle argues that such habituation requires law, and not only while young but also through the whole of life, and then that this law must, ultimately, be the law of the political community.

So first, as regards the young, Aristotle argues that to get the right guidance toward virtue will be hard unless one is brought up under the right laws, that is, under laws that will give such guidance. His argument may be stated thus: (1) to live a life of moderation and steadfast endurance is unpleasant and hard for the many, especially when young; (2) to make such living painless and easy, it is necessary to make it habitual, which is done by arranging upbringing and pursuits by law; (3) therefore to live a life of moderation and steadfast endurance is unpleasant and hard unless upbringing and pursuits are arranged by law; (4) to get the right guidance toward virtue is to live a life of moderation and steadfast endurance; (5) therefore to get the right guidance towards virtue will be unpleasant and hard unless upbringing and pursuits are arranged by law.

Premise (1) seems evident to observation and so does premise (2), provided that by "law" is understood a right code of enforced behavior (whether this code be imposed at home, at school, in the political community, or all three). Premise (4), which Aristotle leaves to be assumed from the context, follows from what he has just said about virtue and nobility. For to be well prepared for virtue, since it means not to follow passion but reason, must require being habituated to stand up to noble pains, or pains that reason approves (as the pains of military training), and to flee base pleasures, or pleasures that reason condemns (as the pleasures of indulgence). It requires, in other words, being habituated to steadfast endurance as regards the first and moderation or self-control as regards the second. Such steadfast endurance and moderation are manifestly not going to be pleasant for most of us, least of all when young. We will only acquire them, and only find them painless, if we are forced to get used to them from our youth up. There will be exceptions, of course, for not everyone belongs to the many. The divinely fortunate in particular, whose nature already prompts them to steadfast endurance and moderation, will get the right guidance even without law and coercion. But what is true of them is not true of most, as observation too plainly shows.

Aristotle argues next that the same enforced discipline is necessary throughout life as well: (1) there is need of steadfast endurance and moderation throughout life; (2) the many only continue in steadfast endurance and moderation under the compulsion of law and the threat of punishment; (3) therefore there is need of such law for the many throughout life. Premise (1) is evident, for to lose endurance and moderation is to lose all chance of virtue. Premise (2) is equally evident, for it is clear to empirical observation that enforced discipline in youth does not succeed, as regards most people, in making them self-sufficient or independent with respect to the practice of virtue. They may indeed no longer find steadfast endurance and moderation painful (and so may not resist the law or complain about it as long as it remains in force), but they have not conceived such love of the noble and of virtue that they will go on fleeing base pleasures and enduring noble pains when law and its restraints are removed. Their base desires have been subdued but not overcome.

In confirmation Aristotle refers to the view of those who divide the task of the legislator into three: appeals to nobility for those who are well prepared and will listen to such appeals; punishments for the disobedient and the deficient or ill prepared; banishment for the incurable. To divide legislation like this is to suppose that some citizens will do what is virtuous because it is virtuous but that others will only do what is virtuous if disobedience is punished or, in some cases, not even then. For, certainly, to think punishments are necessary and to attach them to law for all ages, and not for the young alone, is to think that there are many adults who will only do what they should under coercion.

1180a14 Lastly Aristotle argues that the sort of coercive law in question must be the law of the political community or the city. He begins by summarizing the results of his argument so far, that in order to get the right upbringing for virtue and to live out one's life accordingly, a coerced and rational discipline is required (rational so that what one does is right, and coerced so that one actually does it). From this conclusion he then concludes further that only the law of the city has this power of coercion. For, first, the command of a father or a single person generally, even if it is wise, has no such power. It manifestly has none over other adults (who will certainly not listen to a private person telling them what to do), and even over the young it will have none against the opposing pressure or coercion of the community at large. The law by contrast, or the command of a single person who is a king, or ruler of the whole community, and not just a father, does manifestly have such power. Second, not only does the law have this power, but the exercise of its power is anyway less resented. We typically feel hostility toward individuals who stand in our way, thinking they have some personal enmity against us. But law is common and imposed impartially on all and is not perceived as directed at me more than at anyone else.[4]

On both counts, therefore, law is needed for acquiring the right habituation and hence, except in the case of the divinely fortunate, for acquiring virtue and therewith happiness.

～ THE NEED FOR LEGISLATORS

1180a24 The result of the previous reasoning is that the attainment of virtue and happiness requires the city to lay down a regimen of law with a view to virtue, for both young and old. But in fact while Sparta and a few other cities do this (though Sparta does it rather badly; *Politics* 2.9), very few other cities do (they have laws, to be sure, but not laws designed to educate to virtue). In most cities people live as single individuals or families, like the Cyclopes of Homer,[5] and there is no common care for virtue (cf. *Politics* 3.9). The only solution, then, is for those who do care about virtue to do what they can among friends and family instead. For if they are left free by the city to live as they like, they are clearly left free to live with a view to virtue (the Cyclopes and others live as they like but do not care for virtue), and to have their friends and family do the same. This is obviously a second best, but a second best is better than nothing.

The question, then, is how to do this, that is, how to do among friends and family what is not being done in the city. The answer is that it is necessary to learn the art of legislation, or to become a legislator. The reason follows from what has just been said, for: (1) to educate to virtue among friends and family is just to do, if on a smaller scale, the same thing as should be done in the city; but (2) to educate to virtue in the city requires a legislator, or someone skilled in the art of laying down serious laws (laws, that is, which do educate to virtue); so (3) anyone who cares about virtue among his friends and family must become skilled in this art of legislation. Premise (2) is evident, for it merely adds to what has just been argued, that education to virtue requires an upbringing under the right laws, the manifest

---

4. Points made by St. Thomas Aquinas (1964: 10.14.2154) and Gauthier and Jolif (1958–59: 2:903).
5. *Odyssey* 9.114–15.

fact that laying down the right laws requires knowledge and art (for any human activity requires the relevant knowledge or art if it is to be done well). As regards premise (1), this too is evident despite apparent differences between laws in the city and laws in the household or among friends and family. For these differences are not in fact decisive, as Aristotle next proceeds to show.

1180a35   First, laws are still laws whether written and for many persons (as they will be in a city) or unwritten and for a few (as they will be among friends and family), just as this is also true in other arts like gymnastics and music (where the rules for these activities are still rules whether or not they are written and designed for many). For as to the fact, just mentioned, that a father's commands do not have the necessary force, while this does show that a city's commands are ultimately more effective, it does not show that a father's commands can have no effect at all. For at least within the household his commands can prevail in the way laws do in the city and, though they may lack coercive power, they can be strong in attractive power.

1180b7   Second, as regards the superiority of individual education in virtue (such as would exist among friends and family) to common education in virtue (such as will exist in the city), this superiority too does not, in the end, make a decisive difference. It may, to be sure, appear to make such a difference. For the superiority of individual care, which is shown from the analogy with medicine and boxing (where what is beneficial in the general case need not be beneficial in the particular case, and where the individual can get better care if given individual attention), may seem to imply that knowing how to give individual care to one or a few is different from knowing how to give common care to many. Hence it may seem to imply that one does not need to know the general art of legislation to educate to virtue among family and friends.

In fact, however, this is not so. For, first, the case of medicine also shows that individual care is in fact better done by someone with the general or universal art. For the doctor who has the universal art will be the one who knows, in the case of any individual, what suits and what does not (he will know that such and such suits such and such patients and that this individual is such and such a patient). Second, even though someone who had intimate experience of a particular individual could, perhaps, with respect to this individual, equal the doctor in giving good treatment, yet he could not do this for any others but would be limited to this one individual alone. In other words, he would work the same sort of effect as the doctor but not as the doctor works it, for he would work it from a particular experience confined to a given individual and not from a universal art that ranges over all individuals. So if one wants to become skilled in the art, one should proceed to the doctor's universal knowledge. The same, therefore, will hold of educating to virtue too, and anyone who wants to have the art in this (so that he can be of help to anyone and not just to the few individuals he happens to know intimately) will have to press on to the universal knowledge. But this universal knowledge is the art of legislation. Hence whether one's aim is to make many or a few better with respect to virtue, and whether one has command of a city or only of a household, it is the same art of legislation that will apply in every case.

～ HOW TO BECOME A LEGISLATOR: THE NEED FOR THE *POLITICS*

1180b28   The next question, then, is how to become a legislator or where to go to learn the necessary art. The first and most obvious answer would be that one will do this in the same way as in any other area, namely by learning from the experts who, in this case, would seem to be the politicians (for politicians are the only ones who manifestly engage in legislative activity in cities). But the analogy seems to break down here, for whereas in other sciences and arts those who pass on the art are also those who practice it, as doctors and painters for instance, in politics the sophists profess to teach it and yet none of them practices it but only the politicians do. However, since, as Aristotle immediately goes on to show, the sophists do not really teach politics and the politicians do not practice it from knowledge, perhaps the analogy would still hold if those who really teach politics are also those who really practice it, or practice it from knowledge. It may not be, indeed, that any such politicians are actually legislating for any city, but they are likely doing it for their household and among their friends, which, as has just been shown, amounts to the same.

With respect at any rate to existing politicians, that they do not have the universal knowledge but, as sometimes happens in medicine, practice it from a certain power and experience is shown by the fact that they have not written or spoken about politics or taught it to their sons and friends. But they would have done so if they had been able to, since they had all the reason and opportunity for doing it. From this it is evident that they do not have the ability to teach, and that what ability they do have cannot spring from knowledge or thought, for knowledge can be taught; it must spring rather from something like experience, which cannot be taught. Still, the fact that these politicians do have an evident ability in politics, though they cannot teach it, proves that experience has something to contribute. So while experience is not sufficient for the knowledge of politics or, therefore, of legislation, it may well be necessary (as Aristotle does indeed show in what follows).

1181a12   With respect to the sophists, they cannot teach it either, though they claim to, for one cannot teach what one does not know and the sophists manifestly do not know politics, either as regards what sort of thing it is or as regards what it deals with. They do not know what sort of thing it is for otherwise they would not have identified it with rhetoric or something worse, presumably sophistry (for rhetoric is the art of persuasive speech and sophistry the art of deceptive speech, and neither of these is, or includes, the art of laying down good laws). They do not know what politics deals with for otherwise they would not have supposed it consisted in collecting laws that are well reputed and then in selecting the best from them.[6] This is to ignore that selection requires understanding and that the exercise of such understanding in making a right judgment, not the making of a collection, is what really matters.[7]

The point is illustrated by analogy with the other arts, and in two ways. First, it is manifestly the experienced who have the capacity to judge the productions of a given art and, in particular, how these productions are to be brought about. Those who are not experienced must be content if they can judge the quality of the completed work. So, for instance, nonmusicians can judge whether a piece of music is harmonious, and nonpainters can judge whether a painting is a good likeness. But only the painter knows what to do to produce a good likeness and similarly only the musician knows what to do to produce harmonious music. It is the same in politics, where laws are the products (the laws by which this or that regime governs itself). Laws are to politics, therefore, what harmonies and pictures are to music and painting. So while nonexperts may be able to judge how well the legislation has been done in their city (for they can appreciate whether the city is in a good or bad condition), they will not know themselves how to legislate well (just as, for instance, anyone can tell if the economy is in a good condition, but only an expert, if anyone, knows how to bring such a condition about). The sophists are evidently ignorant of this distinction between experts and nonexperts. They suppose that anyone who can judge the results of legislation, and who can collect all the well-made laws, can also legislate. But this must be as foolish as supposing that anyone who can judge and collect fine paintings can thereby himself also produce fine paintings.

Second, matters would not be improved for the sophists even if the collections they talk about included also practical advice, as with medical books that list treatments and also how to use them for particular patients. Experienced doctors will certainly find such books useful but not, as is manifest, those with no medical knowledge or training at all. Amateur physicians are notorious for making mistakes even with the best of textbooks, despite getting lucky now and then; and what is true of amateur physicians is true, for instance, of amateur barbers and amateurs in all fields generally.[8] Collections, in other words, are not the skill or science but

6. These remarks are clearly directed at sophists in general but Aristotle may well have had Isocrates particularly in mind, as Gauthier and Jolif point out (1958–59: 2:906–9) and also Ostwald (1962: 300 n36).

7. The word for "understanding" here in the Greek is *sunesis*, which Aristotle describes in *Ethics* 6.10.

8. One might also compare modern computer books that explain in detail how to use some software program. These are of immense value to people with experience of computers and software programs, but they are, despite their detail and precision, often impenetrable to beginners and amateurs. These latter can, for the most part, only make use of them after having been taught by someone else who is already an expert.

presuppose the skill or science (cf. 5.9.1137a14–17). So only someone already possessed of the knowledge and habit of politics could use well the collections of laws and regimes recommended by sophists and be able to make a judicious selection for the particular city he was legislating for. Someone without this habit could not do this, except by chance.

Aristotle implies here, as the analogy from music and painting indicates, that teaching and practice are required over and above the reading of books. How such teaching and practice will be supplied he does not say. We can suppose, nevertheless, from what he has already said that the training must come, in the first place, from being brought up under good laws. For this is what prepares one to acquire the necessary habits and judgment. Only afterward will books by experts be of much help. There is thus a sort of circle in Aristotle's reasoning. He has said that to acquire and practice virtue one must first be well trained in one's habits. He has then said that those who wish to provide this training, whether for cities or for children and friends, must become legislators. Now he is saying that to become a legislator one must first have been well brought up in one's habits. But the circle is, perhaps, rather a spiral than a circle. For those who received a sufficient education when young might, through acquiring something of legislation, be able to give a better training to their young, who might be able to go further in legislation and so pass on something better to their young, and so on. Of course, there might be many twists and turns in this process, and it might stop and start many times. The first mover, however, at any particular beginning would presumably be that person, or several persons, so endowed by nature that they are good even without training (*Politics* 1.2.1253a27–31, 3.13.1284a10–14). But the gifts of nature come themselves from causes that are divine (1179b21–23), so that, as in the case of the cosmos as a whole, so here in the case of the city and virtue, the god would have to be simply first.

Be that as it may, however, it is at any rate now manifest that, in identifying politics with collections of laws and of regimes, sophists have no idea what politics is about.

1181b12 Consequently neither politicians nor sophists possess the science of politics or, consequently, of legislation. They have all left the subject uninvestigated.[9] But without such investigation the philosophy of human affairs, or the science that studies the human good and how to attain it, which is the intention of

9. In saying that "those who were before us" (1181b12) have left legislation unexamined, Aristotle is referring mainly to the politicians and sophists he has just criticized. But as he seems to be thinking of predecessors in general, he is presumably also referring to Plato and other philosophers, about whom his meaning will therefore be, not that they have altogether failed to examine legislation, but that they have failed to examine it in its entirety (*Politics* 6(4).1), and that the part they did examine they examined imperfectly (*Politics* 2.2–8); see Gauthier and Jolif (1958–59: 2:911–12) and Vander Waerdt (1991: 239–40 n23).

the present work, must remain incomplete. For that part of it which teaches how to get people actually to become virtuous, whether in city or household, is incomplete. The only recourse, then, is for Aristotle himself to supply what is missing and so to undertake, on his own account, this study of legislation and therewith of regimes generally (for the regime, or the arrangement and way of life of the city, is what the legislator sets up by his legislation).[10]

1181b15 In undertaking this study, as in undertaking any art or science, it will obviously be desirable to begin first with a review of previous thinkers to see if they have spoken nobly on any particular. For even though previous thinkers have left the subject as a whole unexamined, they may perhaps have found out something correct about some part of it and, if so, it would be foolish to ignore them and not take advantage of their success (just as this would be foolish in any other art or science). Then, after this review of predecessors, the subject itself can be broached, and since this subject is regimes and how they are to be legislated in order to be legislated well (that is, with a view to virtue), what must be studied is how cities and their regimes are preserved and destroyed, or, in other words, what sort of legislation will make them to be nobly or basely governed. But to do this properly, or to make this study as universal and so as complete as possible, it will obviously be necessary to have a collection of all the kinds of regimes. For then nothing will get left out.

Finally, as a result of all this, one will be able to see from among all these regimes which of them is best and indeed how each of them generally is arranged and legislated (that is, so as to be governed nobly). For though the aim of this study is to find the sort of legislation that will best promote the life of virtue in the citizens (or among family and friends alone where the city is deficient), and so to find the best regime simply, nothing prevents it being the case that some city or household is incapable of the simply best but only of something less. If so, it will be the job of the one who possesses the universal science of legislation to do the best for such a city or household that can be done, even if this is not to do the best simply. Such at any rate is what must be required of the expert in legislation if the analogy just given of the legislator to the medical doctor and the gymnastic trainer

---

10. Because the regime is the ruling body in the city and so has the character and way of life of this ruling body (*Politics* 3.6.1278b8–15, 4(7).8.1328a35–b2), and because the legislator sets up and preserves the ruling body by his laws (the constitutional laws that determine who is to rule and how), to discuss the regime and how to set it up, or at least thus to discuss the best regime, is also to discuss the life of virtue and education in virtue. For the best regime is that arrangement and way of life of the city which is a training in and exercise of complete virtue and which distributes rule only to those so trained and exercised (*Politics* 4(7).1–3, 8–9, 13–15). There is thus no conflict but rather complete harmony between Aristotle's focusing here in *Ethics* 10.9 on virtue and laws and in the *Politics* on regimes, contra Vander Waerdt (1991).

(at 1180b8–28) is to be taken seriously. For the job of the doctor, or at any rate of the doctor who possesses the universal science, is to treat and make as healthy as possible any patient who is put before him, even if this patient is incapable of being made simply healthy (and similarly with the gymnastic trainer; cf. *Politics* 6(4).1).

Such, then, seems to be the rationale for the contents Aristotle lists for the study he is about to undertake. But what is not so clear is whether and how this list of contents is supposed to fit the text of the *Politics* as we now have it (and the *Politics* is the only study of regimes and legislation that has come down to us under Aristotle's name). Some think it does more or less fit our text. So the first part, the review of predecessors, is given, they say, in book 2 of the *Politics*; the next part, the study, from the collected regimes, of what preserves and destroys cities and regimes and why some are well and others badly governed, is given in books 5 and 6 (in the manuscript ordering); the final part, seeing which regime is best and how each is ordered, is given in books 7 and 8 (in the manuscript ordering). But, in carrying out this scheme, they continue, Aristotle saw the necessity of book 1, about the household as the origin of the city, and books 3 and 4 (in the manuscript ordering), the classification and description of regimes.[11] There is, however, one particular problem with this account, which is that the final part of the list cannot, contrary to what is asserted, refer to books 7 and 8 (in the manuscript ordering) because these two books are about the best regime alone and not also, as the list here requires, about the ordering and legislation of each regime generally.[12] Other scholars, therefore, think this list of contents does not refer to the *Politics*.[13]

It is possible, however, to steer a middle way between these two contrasting opinions and make the list fit our text of the *Politics* while still maintaining that the last part of it does not refer to books 7 and 8 (in the manuscript ordering). So, the first part will refer to book 2, as the first opinion supposes, but the next part is more complex. To begin with the collected regimes referred to are generally thought to be the 158 accounts of actual regimes compiled by Aristotle and his school. The sort of information that such a collection would contain was evidently available to Aristotle when he wrote the *Politics* (as his many references to actual cities and their regimes and histories illustrate). But his purpose could never be satisfied by this information alone. What he needs above all is a collection of all the possible kinds of regimes. For his intention, as in the case of medicine, is to teach a science that is universal and covers every possibility, whether actual now or not,

11. The view of Ross, in Düring (1960: 8–9), followed by Guthrie (1981: 334) and Irwin (1988: 603–4 n13); see also Barker (1946: 359 n4) and Rowe (1977: 170–71).

12. As pointed out by Immisch (1935: 61).

13. As Gauthier and Jolif (1958–59: 2:912), Immisch (1935), Lord (1981: 472–74), Vander Waerdt (1991: 240–41), Newman (1887–1902: 1:2–3). (Hereafter references to Newman's four-volume work will be to volume and page only.)

and a collection merely of regimes that happen to have existed, or were known to have existed, in Aristotle's day, need not cover every possibility. It would not, for instance, cover Aristotle's own simply best regime.

An alternative interpretation, then, is to refer the collected regimes to what is contained within the *Politics* itself. For from book 3 onward a collection of all possible kinds of regimes is to be found. At least such a list is to be found if the order of the last two books according to the manuscripts, 7 and 8, is changed and they are made to come between books 3 and 4, because books 3, 7, 8, 4 (in that order) contain a complete collection, along with a detailed treatment, of all the possible regimes. Moreover this collection, as first set out in book 3, and not any empirical collection of actual regimes, is used to do what Aristotle here says the collection is supposed to do, namely furnish the basis for examining how cities and regimes are preserved and destroyed, or why some are nobly governed and others the opposite.

That the manuscript ordering of books 7 and 8 should be changed in this way is the opinion of many scholars and is, in fact, required by the text of the *Politics* itself.[14] But one can also argue that it is required by these final words of the *Ethics*. For what is to be studied from the collected regimes is what preserves and destroys cities and what preserves and destroys regimes. This remark is generally taken to be a reference to book 5 (in the manuscript ordering), but book 5 is only about what preserves and destroys regimes and here a distinction is drawn between cities and regimes. Accordingly, if what preserves and destroys cities is to be something different from what preserves and destroys regimes, the only thing this something different could be is the regimes themselves.[15] For since the city is by nature for the good life of virtue, the city will be so far preserved if its regime is correct and orders it to such life and it will be so far destroyed if its regime is incorrect and does the opposite. Now such a differentiation of regimes into correct and incorrect is introduced in book 3, when the kinds of regimes are first collected, and is continued throughout the detailed treatment of each regime in the succeeding books (7, 8, 4). So if the books are put into this new order, the treatment of what preserves and destroys cities precedes, as the order of the list of contents here requires, the treatment of what preserves and destroys regimes in book 5. But if, by contrast, the order of the books is left as it is, the order required by the list is disrupted because part of the treatment of what preserves cities, the best regime of books 7 and 8, is put after book 5 instead of before it.

I suggest, therefore, that all these five books together and in this order (3, 7, 8, 4, 5) are what Aristotle is referring to in this second part of his list, and that the accompanying remark, about why some of these regimes are nobly governed and

14. As I argued in the introduction, pp. xvii–xx.
15. A point made by St. Thomas Aquinas (1964: 10.14.2180).

others the opposite, is to be read as a clarifying repetition of what this part is about and not as introducing another and third part.[16] For it is evident that Aristotle does much more in these books than collect the several regimes; he also examines them in detail, especially the best regime in books 7 and 8. But provided this second part of Aristotle's list is taken as a whole to mean the study of all the collected regimes and how they are nobly governed or the opposite and how they do and do not preserve cities, then it will fittingly describe what is actually done in these five books and in this order (3, 7, 8, 4, 5). Book 6 in the manuscript ordering will also now fall under the same heading and will not disrupt the order if it is left to follow book 5 because, as Aristotle makes clear at the beginning of it (6.1), it has the nature of an addendum, supplementing what he has said in the preceding books, and so is supposed to come at the end of them and not earlier.

All that remains of the list of contents is the final part, about getting an overall view of which regime is best and how each is arranged. That this cannot refer to books 7 and 8 in the manuscript ordering was remarked earlier, and it will not so refer if books 7 and 8 are, as I have argued, covered in the previous part of the list. Indeed, it cannot refer to any book of the *Politics* if the only books it could refer to have now all been covered. I suggest further, therefore, that it refers, not to anything Aristotle himself does anywhere in the *Politics*, but to what we readers will be able to do after we have finished reading it. For having studied all the things listed, we should indeed be able to look back at the whole and get an overall view of which regime is best (whether simply best or best under these circumstances) and of how each regime is arranged (whether simply so or in such a way as to be the best it can be).

It is in view of these considerations, and of the evidence in general for reordering the books of the *Politics*, that, as already remarked in the introduction, I number them thus: 1, 2, 3, 4(7), 5(8), 6(4), 7(5), 8(6). For as regards book 1, the only book not so far mentioned in Aristotle's list, this is in effect referred to in the very last sentence. For that there is need for such an introductory book before the program of the *Politics* as just outlined is begun is the first thing that Aristotle explains in that book itself.

16. Contra Ross, in Düring (1960: 8). That is why I take the *kai* in the Greek at 1181b19 to mean "that is" and not "and," for *kai* does often have such epexegetic force.

BOOK 1

The Primacy of the City

Chapter 1

1252a1 The topic of investigation for the *Politics* (as the last chapter of the *Ethics* has just shown) is legislation and regimes. But what legislation legislates and what regimes arrange is the city (for the regime is the way the city is arranged with respect to rule and the city is arranged by its laws). Consequently the city must be the focus of the present study since it is the object of both legislation and regimes (see 3.1.1274b32–38). But Aristotle has just argued that anyone who wants to educate to virtue among his friends and family or in his own household, when the city fails to perform this task, must learn the same art of legislation as is needed also for legislating in a city. It might seem, therefore, that the focus of the present study could as well be the household as the city. Partly perhaps to counter this supposition, but partly also to prove, and not merely to assume, that the city is the proper focus of political study, Aristotle begins by showing the primacy of the city.

He argues as follows: since (1) the city is a community, and since (2) every community aims at some good, it is clear that (3), while all communities aim at some good, the community that has most control and embraces all the others is aiming at the most controlling of goods; (4) this community is what is called the city. From (1) and (2) it follows that (5) the city aims at some good, and from (3) and (4) it follows that (6) the city aims at the most controlling of goods.[1] This last conclusion is evidently the one that Aristotle is aiming at, since it proves that the city, and not some lesser community, must be the focus of political study. For if the aim of this study is legislation for the sake of the life of virtue, as the *Ethics* has just proved, and if the life of virtue is the highest human good, which includes and controls all other goods, as the *Ethics* has also proved (in 1.1–2, 7–10), then, if the city is the community that aims at this highest and all embracing good, as has just been proved here, the city must be the focus of political study. Thus even if, because of defective cities, the city's task of legislating for the sake of virtue may

---

1. I follow the analysis of Jowett (1885: 2:1).

have to be carried out in the household, yet this task belongs by its nature to the city and only by default to the household, which is properly a subordinate community with a subordinate good (hence someone who wishes to legislate for his household must learn political, and not household, science, for the science he must learn is proper to the city).

Of the premises used in this argument, (1) is evident to observation and (2) is proved by the parenthetical remark that everyone does everything for the sake of some good (whether real or apparent), for as communities are just people sharing together, communities must be just people who, through their sharing, are pursuing some good together. It also seems clear that these premises, and their accompanying but unexpressed conclusion (5), are introduced to prove (3) and therewith (6). They will indeed prove (3) and (6) but only on the assumptions that communities can include each other and that there is some community which includes all the others. For then, if all communities aim at some good, as (2) asserts, a community that includes other communities must be aiming at a good that includes and controls the goods of these other communities; and if, further, the city is a community and so aims at some good too, as (1) and (5) assert, and if this is the community that controls all other communities whatever, as (4) asserts, the city must have the most controlling good of all as its aim, the good that measures and determines the pursuit of all lesser goods (see *Ethics* 8.9.1160a8–29).

It is true, of course, that cities can also be included in, and feel themselves to be included in, larger groupings and associations, as in leagues or alliances or even broad national linguistic and cultural families. But not every inclusion in a larger group is inclusion in a larger community or under a more controlling good. Cities, for instance, that combine to celebrate some festival or other, as the Greeks did to celebrate the Olympic games (and as we do still in imitation of them), are not combining under a greater or more controlling good. Rather they are combining to share in some lesser good, relaxation or defense, that is subordinate to the higher and more controlling good, happy and noble living. Thus the fact that cities can themselves be members of larger associations does not mean that these associations must therefore be communities that are more controlling than the city.

1252a7 Still, however that may be, the assumption that communities can include and thereby exercise control over other communities is obvious enough, for there are many examples of it (wherever, in fact, there is a chain of command descending from those who control the whole to those who control the parts, as in armies, business companies, schools, and so on). But what seems particularly controversial, for Aristotle's contemporaries as for us, is that there is one community that controls all the others and that this community is the city. We ourselves may, perhaps, be prepared to attribute final control to the state. But the state is huge in comparison with Aristotle's city and we also think its authority should be limited and not all-inclusive (although it usually ends up, nevertheless, exercising the sort of control Aristotle attributes to the city; *Ethics* 1.2.1094a26–b11).[2] As for the state's size, Aristotle would regard that as a serious defect in our political arrangements, since such excessive size must hinder the pursuit of the good life (4(7).4); and as for the state having limited authority, he would perhaps regard that as desirable if the state is to be so large, but he would certainly not regard it as desirable that what is de facto the final authority in our lives should take no care for virtue.[3]

The opponents whom Aristotle himself directly considers also maintain that the city is not the controlling and superordinate community.[4] What they assert is that there is no difference between ruling the city and ruling other or lesser communities, as ruling household and slaves, and that skill in ruling one is the same as skill in ruling another. The difference lies rather in how many people are ruled over and not in the kind of good aimed at. But this view too, like our own today, must be false if the city really is the controlling community and all others are subordinate to it. Accordingly Aristotle turns to prove this assumption, or in other words to prove proposition (4) in his argument above, and therewith to confirm that the city, and not also some other community, is the proper object of political science. The proof, however, turns out to be very extensive, for it requires a detailed examination of each community. It expands, indeed, to occupy the whole of book 1 of the *Politics*.[5]

The method to be followed is that of dividing the whole into its parts. This method applies in the case of any whole (for if the parts are not understood neither will the whole be that is made from these parts), but it applies particularly here. For if the city is the whole of which the other communities are parts, then to divide the city into its parts will be both the way to see how these parts do in fact differ from each other and from the whole (whether in size only or also in kind), and the way to get a proper understanding of their respective kinds of rule or rulers.

---

2. The exception might be the distinction, now often drawn, between church and state, neither of which is supposed to be subordinate to the other. For Aristotle, by contrast, the church, or the priests, are an integral part of the city, though one that has gone beyond the immediate concerns of ruling (4(7).8, 9). This view of his, however, seems further from our theory than from our practice, for church and state interpenetrate and condition each other in a thousand ways in our actual life.

3. See Simpson (1990, 1994).

4. These opponents may be the Stranger in Plato's *Statesman* (258e8–259d1) and Socrates in Xenophon's *Memorabilia* (3.4). But there are nameless others mentioned elsewhere in the *Politics* who would fall under the same criticism, as those who identify political rule with despotic rule (4(7).2.1324b32–34, 8(6).2.1317b11–16), those who identify political rule with that part of household management concerned with making money (1.9.1258a2–14, 11.1259a33–36), those who identify royal rule with despotic rule (3.16), and those who identify household management with despotic rule (1.2.1252b5–7, 8(6).8.1323a5–6).

5. As noted by Natali (1979–80) and Schofield, in Patzig (1990: 16–20).

Chapter 2

~ THE HOUSEHOLD

1252a24   Dividing a whole into its parts may be a necessary step to understanding the whole but getting to the parts cannot be enough. One must also see how the parts come together to form the whole, for otherwise one will have the parts but no whole and, indeed, one will not have the parts either as parts, since parts are parts in view of a whole.[6] Accordingly, Aristotle speaks of understanding the parts of the city, or the other communities, by looking at how they grow or develop naturally from the beginning, that is, at how they come together into the city.[7] For thus the precise nature of their relationship to the city, whether they differ from it in size only or also in good aimed at, should become very clear.

The beginning in the case of the community must be the smallest community possible, the community before which there is no other community. This community is evidently the community of two (one person cannot be a community), and the first such twos that are necessary must be those who cannot be if they are not two. Thus the initial communities are, first, the community of female and male. For these cannot be, at least not as female and male, without each other, since the point of the sexual difference is generation and both are needed for that. Second, no one at all can be without seeing ahead what preservation requires and carrying out what is thus foreseen. So there must also be a coupling of foresight with bodily exertion, that is, of a ruler that commands what is foreseen and a ruled that carries out what is thus commanded, and this is the pairing of natural master and natural slave. Such a master and slave have necessarily, therefore, the same interest, since the preservation of the one is the preservation of the other. These two couplings are thus necessary and the first that are necessary (for, in the case of things that are not individually eternal, their continuing existence includes both preservation of the individual, hence master and slave, and the leaving behind of like offspring, hence male and female).

Aristotle says about both couples that they are natural or by nature. About the

---

6. There is thus, contra Schütrumpf (1991: 1:185), no conflict between the analysis spoken of at the end of the preceding chapter and the synthesis spoken of at the beginning of this, as St. Thomas Aquinas (1951: 1.1.16) and Newman (2:104) correctly note.

7. The development or growth that Aristotle is talking about is perhaps best understood, not as historical, but as "ideational," that is, as tracing the idea of the city from and through the idea of its parts (the household and village). For, as his discussion reveals, the idea or nature of the city comes to light through pushing to its end the idea or nature of the household. Nevertheless elements of history come through too, for actual households and cities exist in time and so it is not surprising that time should reveal the marks of their idea and nature.

first, female and male, this claim would seem obvious and uncontroversial, but not about the second, master and slave. Yet there is for Aristotle a difference between the naturalness of the two couples. The first is said not to be by choice and to be common to plants and animals. The second is said to require what can see ahead with its mind and hence cannot be common to plants and animals and must involve choice. What Aristotle says here about mastery and slavery contains in outline what he says and defends in detail in chapters 4 to 7 (where it also becomes clear that the naturalness of mastery and slavery, unlike that of female and male, seemed as false to some of Aristotle's contemporaries as it does now to us).

1252a34   That female and slave belong to different natural couples devoted to different functions already suggests that they are naturally different. But the two functions could perhaps be served by one and the same thing, in which case female and slave would not differ and the female would by nature be there to serve the male in both respects. Against this supposition Aristotle presents the following argument: (1) nature makes nothing in niggardly fashion but one thing for one thing; (2) if female and slave do not naturally differ, nature would have made something in niggardly fashion; (3) therefore female and slave naturally differ. The crucial premise (1) is proved thus: (4) nature does what is noble; (5) instruments are made nobly when they are made for one thing; (6) therefore nature makes instruments for one thing and not in niggardly fashion.

One might wonder about this argument, if it is indeed true that nature makes nothing in niggardly fashion, why this truth is not applied to male and ruler to show that they must be different too.[8] But male and ruler are evidently to be compared rather to craftsmen who use instruments (for they use women for generation and slaves for preservation), and craftsmen, unlike instruments, are more perfect and more noble the more instruments they can use and use well, for thus they show the excellence of their art. Nevertheless nature has made some instruments to serve more than one function, as the tongue for taste and speech. But these are perhaps the exceptions that prove the rule.[9] Nature makes no tools having more than one function if she is not prevented, or if the two functions do not interfere with each other (which, however, they will do in the case of the functions of female and slave). As for nature doing what is noble, one might say the same here too, that she does what is noble unless prevented. But this claim is evidently an empirical one and to be tested by appeal back to observation (though it may find some theoretical support in the modern idea of evolution, which also stresses that what naturally continues to exist is what is best adapted to its purpose, and such good adaptation is the nobility or beauty Aristotle is talking about).

There is, then, a natural difference between females and slaves because of their

8. Levy (1990: 405) raises this puzzle.
9. See Aristotle's *De Partibus Animalium* 4.6.683a19–26, St. Thomas Aquinas (1951: 1.1.21).

different function (and hence rule over slave cannot be the same thing, or require the same science, as rule over wives). The fact that no such difference exists among barbarians is because female and male are both slaves together and treat each other as such. None of them is naturally able to rule. They are fit, therefore, to be ruled by those who can rule, and these, say the poets, are the Greeks. But while Aristotle quotes the poets to this effect, he can evidently only agree with them to the extent it is true that the Greeks are natural rulers and barbarians natural slaves. For he has just said that the distinction between slave and master is by nature, not by nation, and is based on the presence or absence of foresight by thought. So if some Greeks lack the necessary capacity of thought and some barbarians have it, these barbarians should rule these Greeks instead. At all events it cannot simply be true, as the poets suppose, that to be a barbarian and a slave are by nature the same thing (a point Aristotle returns to more openly later in chapter 6).[10]

1252b9 The two couples of male and female and of master and slave are the first necessary communities. But as human survival is survival of both individual and species, these two couples must unite. The household is their necessary union. The household is the first self-subsisting community, as it were, for the other two only subsist by being fused into it. They are thus, properly speaking, parts of the household, not parts of the city. The names Aristotle quotes from Charondas and Epimenides neatly emphasize the origin of the household in the two couples: its members are fellows, that is, sprung from the same stock, and fellows in food, that is, partners in physical survival.

In quoting Hesiod in this passage (and earlier Euripides) Aristotle is following his practice of using the poets in support of his conclusions. But he often quotes selectively, as he does in this present instance. For Hesiod goes on to say in the next line of his poem that the woman he is talking about is a slave.[11] Hesiod is thus in conflict with Aristotle's argument since Aristotle has just said that female and slave are by nature different. Some commentators are accordingly inclined to think that Aristotle intends his better readers to notice the conflict and to conclude that his real teaching is something other than what is contained in his express arguments.[12] But in reply it may be noted, first, that Aristotle does not think that the poets always speak the truth (see 1.8.1256b31–37). So it is perhaps as or more reasonable to suppose that Aristotle, aware of the unreliability of poets, only quotes from Hesiod the part that is true and omits the part that is false. Second, an appeal to poetic authority could hardly be sufficient to overthrow Aristotle's express argu-

10. See Ambler (1987: 392–93). St. Thomas Aquinas (1951: 1.1.22–23) notes a distinction between the barbarian simply, that is, anyone who is deficient in reason, and the barbarian with respect to a certain person, that is, anyone who does not speak the same language as that person. He comments that Aristotle is speaking here of the barbarian in the first and not the second sense.

11. *Works and Days* 405–6.

12. As Davis (1989).

ments, which have a rigor and conviction of their own. Third, poets would seem to be quoted for the sake of weaker, not stronger or better, readers, that is, for readers who need poetic quotations and are not convinced by reason alone.[13] Fourth, Aristotle would have special reason not to continue this particular quotation. Drawing attention to the fact that Hesiod was a Greek thinking like a barbarian might cause needless offense.

1252b15 The household is a community sufficient for the needs of every day. But it is obviously better, and accords with the foresight characteristic of the master, to try to secure needs that go beyond the every day. So the village arises when several households combine for this purpose. The village is a direct continuation of the household and, as Aristotle's words emphasize, springs from the same natural origins, generation and preservation. Because of its greater size it is able to extend its care beyond the every day, but it is really a large or extended household, a household that, through its children's children, has sent out other households as its colonies.[14]

That households and villages are thus the origins of later human communities, of city and nation, is supported by two facts. First, the form of rule characteristic of the household, rule by the eldest as king, was characteristic of cities previously and is characteristic of nations now. For this implies that cities and nations were formed from those who were ruled as kings, that is, from those who had begun in households and villages, where, as a quotation from Homer confirms,[15] rule was by kings (this same quotation was referred to in the last chapter of the *Ethics*, 1180a27–29, and with similar intent, to show that cities not caring for education are rather collections of independent units, like households or villages, than cities). Second, there is the universal belief that the gods are ruled monarchically, which belief also points to the fact that that is how human beings ruled themselves first and that cities and nations had their origins in households and villages. For stories about the gods go back to the beginning, but since very little is naturally known about the gods, human beings had to fill up their ignorance by attributing to them the same features they found among themselves. So if these stories attribute kingship to the gods, the reason is no doubt that the human beings who first told them were ruled by kings and accordingly had their origin in households and villages.

⁓ THE CITY

1252b27 The next stage beyond the household and village is the city. This arises, as the previous remarks have suggested, from the combination of several villages. But not any combination of villages is a city—only one that is complete or

13. Aristotle *Metaphysics* 994b32–995a17.

14. The word Aristotle uses for colony is *apoikia*, or literally "from the household." The village could accordingly be described as a sort of community of "households from the household."

15. *Odyssey* 9.114–15.

possesses the limit of every self-sufficiency. By every self-sufficiency Aristotle evidently means that it is self-sufficient both for life and for good life.[16] Household and village have their origin in the desire to live, both individually and through offspring, and so does the city since it arises out of them. But the village is sufficient for the needs of life. So if there is an advance in human community beyond the village, this advance must be prompted, not by the desire to live (for the village is already sufficient for that), but by the desire to live well. For even if living well is falsely understood to be sensual indulgence, or the use of the means of survival and generation to satisfy pleasure, not need, still something else is being pursued besides mere life.[17]

1252b30   The city, then, is for an end or a good over and above the good of the household or village and so cannot simply be a larger version of the same thing, or a possible but unnecessary extension. On the contrary, as Aristotle now proceeds to show, it must be the whole that includes these as its subordinate parts and is their natural completion. It must, in other words, be itself a natural whole. It cannot be a mere artifice, as it would effectively be if the household was naturally complete in itself and the city just the name for a large household. So Aristotle first proves this naturalness of the city and then, since the city is a community of human beings, concludes also to the naturally political character of human beings.

The argument for the naturalness of the city is basically this:[18] (1) every city exists by nature if the first communities exist by nature; (2) the first communities exist by nature; (3) therefore every city exists by nature. Premise (2) is obvious from what has just been said, and Aristotle's immediately succeeding remarks ("For the city is the goal of those communities . . ." at 1252b31) seem meant to prove premise (1). They can be formalized thus: (4) the city is the goal or end of the first communities; (5) the goal of things is their nature; (6) therefore the city is the nature of the first communities. For if we add the further premise (too evident to need stating) that (7) the nature of things that exist by nature must itself be by nature, we get the required conclusion that if the first communities exist by nature so also must the city.

16. On the general question of self-sufficiency in the case of the city, see Mayhew (1995).

17. As Saunders notes (1995: 68). One might, however, wonder why the process should stop at the city and not proceed further to the nation or the state. The answer is given later, in 4(7).4, where it is explained that, although anything larger than a city could be self-sufficient in material things, it would not be fit for good life, for it would not be fit for education in virtue. A city might, of course, enter into alliance with other cities for the sake of defense, and the modern state might, indeed, be viewed as such an alliance, as I suggested in Simpson (1990, 1994); but an alliance of cities is not itself a city.

18. Keyt's long and involved analysis of this and the other arguments of Aristotle in this chapter, in Keyt and Miller (1991: 118–41), is flawed by a failure, among other things, to pay sufficient attention to the logical connectives Aristotle uses; Saunders (1995: 68–69) is similarly flawed. The analyses of Miller (1989; 1995: chap. 2) are preferable though still not entirely accurate. My own analysis is closest to that of St. Thomas Aquinas (1951: 1.1.32–33).

The next remarks ("since we say that a thing's nature is the sort of thing it is when its generation has reached its goal," 1252b32–33) seem in turn meant to prove the premises in this further argument. So premise (5) is proved by the claim that each thing's nature is the sort of thing it is when its generation has reached its goal. For a thing only is what it is when it has been brought fully into existence, that is, when its generation is complete and has reached its goal (as is shown by the instances Aristotle gives of human being, horse, and house). So to call complete generation nature is to call the end or goal nature and nature the goal. That the same might be said of artificial things (a shoe's nature is what it is when the shoemaker has finished it) makes no difference to Aristotle's argument. The naturalness of the city does not follow from the fact that the city is the goal, but from the fact that it is the goal of something itself natural, namely the household. Premise (4) is proved by the claim that that for the sake of which something exists—that is, its goal—is best, and self-sufficiency is both a goal and best. For the goal, the best, and the "that for the sake of which" are all terms that naturally go together (they are in some sense interdefinable). So if self-sufficiency is also a goal and best (as it must be, since a thing is complete when it is self-sufficient and needs nothing more; *Ethics* 1.7.1097b6–11), and if the city is the self-sufficient community and the others are not (as has just been shown), then the city must be the end or goal of the other communities.[19]

1253a1 This argument for the naturalness of the city now itself immediately proves that human beings are by nature political. For if human beings by nature belong to the first communities, and if these communities have the city as their goal, then human beings must by nature have the city as their goal too. So they must be by nature political, or must be by nature *polis* animals, animals that are meant to share together in the common life of the city.[20] There are indeed exceptions, but only exceptions that prove the rule. Humans who are cityless by nature (and not by chance, like Philoctetes or Robinson Crusoe) have either not reached, or have gone beyond, the level of humanity; they are either of a base sort or better than a human being. About the first type, the one who is better than human, Aris-

19. This argument and its subarguments obviously rest on teleology, which might seem an objectionable idea to some. But if teleology is not applicable everywhere, it certainly seems applicable to living things and their growth, and communities are nothing but the living human beings who make them up; see Yack (1991: 15–21) and Miller (1989; 1995: 40–45).

20. That other animals can also be said to be political, or that humans can be said to be more political than other animals (as Aristotle does in fact say shortly), does not entail, contra Mulgan (1974b), that "political animal" cannot here mean "*polis* animal," on the supposed grounds that these other animals do not live in *poleis* in any sense at all. Rather it entails that these supposed grounds are false and that the communities the other animals form are *poleis* to the same extent that these animals themselves are political. Both they and their communities are starting to do, though at a primitive level, what only humans and the human *polis* can perfectly do; see Miller (1995: 30–31) and Kullmann, in Keyt and Miller (1991: 94–117).

totle says nothing further here, for the quotation from Homer can only refer to the one who is worse. Someone of surpassing virtue would not be without law but would be law (3.13.1284a3–14). He would, as it were, be a city unto himself.[21] Someone, by contrast, altogether worse than human would neither have law nor be a law and would treat all other humans without any sense of community or right.

1253a7 But there are two further arguments, independent of the argument about the naturalness of the city, that humans are naturally political. The first proves that they are political in a way that no other animal that lives a communal life is. It may be stated thus: (1) nature makes nothing in vain; (2) only humans possess by nature reasoned speech (*logos*), whereas animals merely possess voice; (3) reasoned speech serves to make plain what is advantageous and harmful, just and unjust, good and bad, or it enables human beings to commune with each other about these things (perception of which they alone have among animals), and community in these things makes a household and a city. From (2) and (3) it follows that (4) only humans have by nature something whose point (or part of whose point) is the community of the city, namely the sharing together about good, bad, just, and unjust. From (4) and (1) it follows that (5) humans must be naturally political and more political than any other animal. For if nature does nothing in vain, she must, in giving humans speech, have made them for what speech itself is for, namely life in the city; and since she gave speech to humans alone, she must have made humans more political than all other animals to which she gave merely voice.

The idea that nature does nothing in vain is controversial as a general thesis, but it would be hard to deny in this case, or to say that those who naturally have speech are not naturally made for that for which speech itself is made. It is anyway clear that making plain the just and unjust, the advantageous and harmful, is something that reasoned speech serves to do. A cry might tell us whether an animal was in a state of pain or pleasure, or whether something painful or pleasant was close to hand, but could not tell us whether the pain or pleasure was just or advantageous. Not all pains are unjust and harmful (the pain of punishment and surgery is not), nor all pleasures just and advantageous (the pleasure of vice is not). But the just and advantageous, and sharing them together through speech, are manifestly constitutive of household and city (without them these communities would collapse, or reduce, to interchanges of pleasure and pain and sighs and cries). So humans above all must be political animals.

1253a18 The other argument proves that humans are naturally political by proving that the city is by nature prior to them and defines what they are: (1) the whole is by nature prior to the part; (2) households and individual human beings

---

21. St. Thomas Aquinas (1951: 1.1.35) gives St. John the Baptist and the hermit St. Anthony as examples.

are to the city as part to whole; (3) therefore the city is by nature prior to the household and to individual human beings.[22] Premise (1) is proved from the example of foot and hand and the claim, very evident in this example, that things are defined by their work and their power. For to say what foot and hand are made of, or even to say what shape they have, may tell us something but will not make clear what they are. Saying what they can do, on the contrary, will make everything clear, including the fact that they have this shape and are made of these things. The same result is evident, by induction, from many other cases. Thus if parts no longer have the same definition and are no longer parts when they lack their proper power, and if they lack their proper power when the whole of which they are parts has been destroyed, then the whole is prior to them in the sense of that on which they depend in order to be what they are.

Premise (2) is proved from the fact that individuals are not self-sufficient in separation but need the city to realize themselves. So much is evident to observation, for isolated individuals and households are generally poor and wretched things, capable of daily survival but not much else. They barely rise above the level of beasts that also live solitary lives, unless they are altogether superior and rise above the human to the level of gods (as some philosophers and hermits seem to have done). At any rate, it is clear that anyone who lacks the capacity or power to share in community will be no part of the city (for, lacking the power for community, he must lack the nature for it too); and anyone who does not need community, because self-sufficient on his own, will be no part of the city either (for rather he must amount to a city all by himself). The first of these, as falling below other human beings, must be a beast, and the second, as rising above other human beings, must be a god (cf. the god-man of 3.13.1284a3–11, 17.1288a26–29).

1253a29 There must, then, in everyone be a natural drive toward communal life in the city, if everyone (apart from beasts and gods) is by nature political and finds his completion and, indeed, definition in such community. But it need not follow that this drive operates automatically, or realizes itself spontaneously and by instinct, as it were, without the intervention of thought. On the contrary, if this drive is toward the exercise of speech and reason, the intervention of thought would itself be what we are being driven toward. But further, although this drive inheres in our nature, we need not all be equally aware of it nor equally able to understand what is required to realize it. For if the desire for life in the city is natural to all of us, the knowledge of this fact or the wisdom to set up a city need

22. Such subordination of individual to city need not result in tyranny provided the city is ruled for the common good of the citizens, as Aristotle intends it to be (3.6), and see Miller (1995: 54–56). Nor need such subordination imply the plainly false proposition that humans cannot exist outside a city. Humans can exist in isolation, like Robinson Crusoe, or in households and villages and not yet in cities. But, if Aristotle is right, they could not live well under such conditions nor realize their human nature to the full; Miller (1995: 49–50, 52–53), Zuckert (1983: 188–89).

not be. So if someone else who does have the wisdom sets up a city for us, he will, by fulfilling our nature, be responsible for goods of a very great kind.

There is, therefore, no inconsistency in Aristotle's argument here, as some suppose, who say that if the city is by nature it cannot also be by art, and that to be brought about by human making is to be by art, so that if the city is brought about by some founder it must be by art and not by nature.[23] For Aristotle's combination of nature and human action in the case of the city reflects what he argued about virtue in the *Ethics*.[24] Virtue does not come to be in us by nature nor against nature, but we are naturally born to receive it and later acquire it through habituation (*Ethics* 2.1.1103a18–26). So virtue is by nature insofar as it is the end of nature (we are born, not made by art, to receive virtue), but actually reaching this end is by habituation and not nature. The same holds also of the city. This too is by nature, for it is the end of nature, though particular attempts to realize this end, or the comings to be of particular cities, are by art.

One might still object, however, that this conclusion entails, absurdly, that shoes and other manifest works of art are by nature, since through shoes our natural capacity for walking is perfected.[25] But here the wrong parallel is drawn. The city is to living together well as walking well is to walking well, not as shoes are to walking well. For by the city Aristotle means the living together well of human beings, not the instruments through which they secure such living. The city is the human beings who together compose it (3.1.1274b41); the instruments are rather the regimes, or the particular laws and institutions. For the regime is the way humans arrange themselves so as to live together well (4(7).8.1328a35–b2). Thus it is regimes that are like shoes and are products of design and art (namely of the political art; *Ethics* 10.9.1181a23). But the goal of this art, living together well or the city, is by nature, for it is what nature has all along been aiming at. Every city is by nature, therefore, to the extent that it actually is a city, or to the extent that it actually is an instance of a community for living well. Its being brought into being, however, or the particular way the human beings in it are arranged so as to be a city (and not, say, a disorganized mass), will be by art, for the arranging of a city is its regime and the regime is by art.

Founders, then, are necessary and, as such, clearly causes of things of very great goodness. The argument Aristotle gives may be formalized thus: (1) humans are best with right and justice and worst without it; (2) justice is political or belongs to the city; (3) therefore humans are best with the city and worst without it, and

23. The contention of Keyt in particular, in Keyt and Miller (1991: 118–41). But see Miller's reply (1989: 197–98, 209–11; 1995: 37–45), and also Chan (1992), Dobbs (1994: 75), and Kullmann, in Aubenque (1993: 169–84).

24. A point adverted to by St. Thomas Aquinas (1951: 1.1.40).

25. Keyt, in Keyt and Miller (1991: 131).

hence to found a city is to give humans what they need to be best, which is manifestly something of very great goodness. Premise (1) is shown by the fact that humans have weapons that, though meant to be used with prudence and virtue, can easily be used otherwise, and that injustice so armed with weapons commits the worst deeds (but justice, we understand, the best ones). Aristotle speaks only in general terms about what these crimes may be, but he specifies two of their objects: sex and food. These correspond to the two objects of the first two communities: generation and preservation. Human evil corrupts the human roots; it is radical. The weapons Aristotle is talking about would seem to be intellect and the passions, for prudence perfects the intellect and virtue controls passion (which otherwise would be insatiable) by imposing on it the measure of reason (*Ethics* 1.13.1102b13–1103a10; the other animals seem to have a measure imposed on their passions by nature). The extreme wickedness of humans stems from their following insatiable and untamed passions and putting intellect into this service, that is, from their using intellect and passion without justice. For the justice Aristotle has in mind here must be general or legal justice, the justice that perfects humans in community with others in the exercise of all the virtues (*Ethics* 5.1.1129b11–1130a13).

The proof of premise (2) rests on the further premises: (4) right is the arrangement of a political community, and (5) right is discrimination of what is just (cf. *Ethics* 5.6.1134a31–32). This last premise can, I take it, be converted to: (6) discrimination of what is just is right (or the right). But it is manifest that: (7) justice is discrimination of what is just (justice is the virtue whereby we judge and do what is just). Hence from (6) and (7) it follows that: (8) justice is right, and from (8) and (4) that: justice is the arrangement of a political community, or is something political, which is premise (2). Now Aristotle cannot mean by this that any act of justice is a political act in the sense that it is an act of or about the political community, for then the private acts of private persons could not be considered just. What he must mean is that any act of justice is in principle political because it always somehow concerns humans in their living together, that is, it always somehow concerns the human community. But the perfect human community, of which all others are subordinate parts, is the political community. Hence any act of justice is part of, and ultimately derivative from, the complete justice of the political community.[26]

Of course, political communities can themselves be just or unjust, or can be

26. This political character of justice and right for Aristotle is well stressed by Miller (1995: chap. 4, especially 90–91, 117–23; 1996: 891–92). Aristotle, says Miller, has a theory of rights based on nature, but only in the sense of rights in accordance with what is just by nature and not in the Hobbesian or Lockean sense of rights derived from a prepolitical state of nature. The just by nature for Aristotle is political justice, because what is first by nature (in perfection, though not in time) is the city, the *polis*, and hence all the elements of justice must be understood in terms of political justice, as the parts are to be understood in terms of their whole and as the imperfect is to be understood in terms of the perfect. The Hobbesian and Lockean theories proceed by a sort of inversion of Aristotle's order.

arranged well or badly. But the simply just, by which the justice of any political community is measured, must be the expression of the simply best way of arranging human community and so must necessarily be something political. It will, in fact, be identical with the simply best regime, or that arrangement of the city which accords best with what the city is, namely living together well. Hence it will, as is said in the *Ethics* (5.7.1134b18–1135a5), be the best by nature. For though the best regime, like any regime, is by art, that whereby it is best will not be by art but by nature. For the best regime is best because it realizes the end of nature best.

Chapter 3

~ HOUSEHOLD MANAGEMENT AND ITS PARTS

1253b1 The previous chapter has established what parts the city is made up of, namely households, and also that these parts are genuinely parts, subordinate to and for the sake of the city as their natural whole. One might think, therefore, that sufficient has been done to show that the city is the primary community and that ruling other communities is not the same as ruling the city. But what has been done so far has only been done in general terms, and nothing specific has been said about rule of the household and of its parts, and of how these do concretely differ from rule of the city. Aristotle's case for the primacy of the city will be greatly strengthened if, as he said at the end of the first chapter, he proceeds to get some grasp "proper to art" (*technikon*, 1252a22) of the several kinds of rule.

So since he has established that the parts of the city are households, and since the method here is to understand the whole through the parts, the first thing to do is to understand the household. But the household itself has parts, so to understand the household and rule of the household it is necessary to understand these parts. The parts of the complete household are the free, or male and female, and slaves (incomplete households may have no slaves, as when the ox takes the place of the slave, or no free, as among barbarians). But the two couplings of male and female and of master and slave obviously give rise to three overall, because the coupling for generation naturally creates the coupling of father and children. Aristotle mentions father only, doubtless not because he ignores the role of mothers, but because he is thinking rather of rule than of nurturing and is including mothers under fathers (the father is primary in rule and in educating to virtue everyone in the household, 1.12–13). The supposed fourth part of household management, business (*chrēmatistikē*),[27] which has not so far emerged from Aristotle's

27. I follow Lord (1984) and translate *chrēmatistikē* as "business" because *chrēmatistikē* seems to be just what we now mean by "business." *Chrēmatistikē* is the art concerned with *chrēmata*, and *chrēmata* are "all things whose worth is measured in money" (*Ethics* 4.1.1119b26–27), that is, commodities or

own analysis, is introduced for investigation because of certain opinions about it. Examination, however, proves it to be hardly a part of household management at all, or a very subordinate part.

1253b14 There are thus four things for investigation and Aristotle deals first with master and slave, in chapters 4 to 7, then with business, in chapters 8 to 11, then with husband and wife and father and child, in chapter 12. Finally, in the last chapter, chapter 13, he turns from the parts in separation to consider them in relation to household management as a whole, which consideration, especially of the last two parts (husband and wife and father and child) brings him in turn back to the city.

With respect to slavery, Aristotle's two stated aims neatly pick up on the things he has already said about it. The first aim, to see what relates to the use of slaves, recalls his assertion that the slave is needed for the sake of preservation; the second aim, to get some better understanding than current conceptions, recalls his assertions that slavery is by nature and that knowing how to rule slaves is different from knowing the other kinds of rule, for current conceptions deny both assertions. Accordingly chapter 4 shows what slaves are for, chapters 5 and 6 show that slavery is by nature, and chapter 7 shows that mastery is a distinct science by itself. Of the two chapters devoted to the naturalness of slavery, chapter 5 proves this naturalness directly and chapter 6 refutes the counterarguments Aristotle now immediately summarizes. These counterarguments are, first: (1) slavery is by law; (2) what is by law is not by nature; (3) therefore slavery is not by nature; and second: (4) slavery by law is a matter of force; (5) what is a matter of force is unjust; (6) therefore slavery is unjust.

Chapter 4

∽ SLAVERY

∽ THE DEFINITION OF THE SLAVE

1253b23 The first topic, then, is what the use of slaves is or what slaves are for, and to ask this is the same as to ask for the definition of the slave, since things are defined by their work and their power or capacity (1.2.1253a23). Accordingly this chapter is all about property because that slaves fall into the classification of

---

merchandise but also, by a natural extension, the money that measures commodities. Our name "business" has the same range of reference since we use it to mean precisely this general art or activity concerned with commodities and with making money through the producing or acquiring or exchanging of commodities (or even of money itself). A translation like "moneymaking art" is too narrow, for it loses the connection with commodities, and a translation like "acquisitive art" is too broad, for it loses the connection with money (one can, after all, spend one's time acquiring useless things, like old bottles and newspapers, not for their monetary value—they may have none—but as a hobby or an eccentric passion).

property is manifest and not in dispute (the dispute is about whether anyone should be a slave, not about whether slaves, if they exist, are property).[28] So one will find the definition of the slave by understanding what property is and into which division of property the slave falls.

Aristotle begins by laying down the following propositions:[29] (1) property and the science of it belong to the household and its management; (2) just as any art needs its proper tools to complete its work so does the household manager; (3) tools are either lifeless or living. Proposition (1) follows from the fact that, without necessities, life and good life are impossible (both life and good life fall under the aim of household management since life has to be directed to good life and the household to the city), and also from the fact that property is a supply of such necessities; proposition (2) is obvious from the analogy; proposition (3) is obvious from the instances given. The claim, however, that assistants are living tools is, despite the connotations it may conjure up, relatively innocuous in this context, since all it means is that the job of an assistant is the same as that of a lifeless tool to the extent that both assist the artist to complete his work.

From these propositions Aristotle now draws several conclusions. From (1), together with its reasons, and (2) it follows that a possession or a piece of property is a tool for the purposes of life (for if property belongs to the household manager as what he needs to do his work, which is life, and if these are to him what tools are to any art, then property is tools for life). From this it follows in turn that property, which is the collective name for many possessions, is a multitude of such tools. From (3) it follows that slaves, who are manifestly alive, are a living possession, or must belong to that part of property which is made of living tools. But note that Aristotle does not say tools for the purposes of life are property, nor does he use this proposition to prove that slaves are property. He only says that property is tools for the purposes of life.[30] Not all such tools need in fact be property (as the lookout man need not be). But that slaves are property is given, and the fact that they are alive only shows that within property are included some living tools (just as oxen, the slaves of the poor, are living tools).

That household management has need of such living tools over and above lifeless tools is shown next by an illustration from the statues and tripods of Daedalus and Hephaestus. Living tools make up for the fact that lifeless tools are not like machines, or cannot operate on their own. Lifeless tools need instead to be

28. As Schütrumpf points out (1991: 1:242–43).

29. The Greek begins with a "since" (*epei*) and as this "since" does not seem to be answered until the "thus" or "accordingly" (*houtō*) several lines later, I understand all the intermediate clauses to be dependent on the initial "since." In this I follow the interpretation of Barker (1946: 9), and depart from that of Miller (1995: 315–17), who takes this chapter to be justifying property in general and not to be defining a particular part of property, namely the slave.

30. As Schütrumpf points out (1991: 1:239), contra Barker (1959: 362).

set to work by some other tool that can operate on its own. So living tools are tools for tools, tools that are needed to put other tools to work. But if lifeless tools were like machines, then living tools would no longer be needed.

1254a1　The slave, then, is a possession in the form of a living tool. But he is also a tool for doing, not for making. Two arguments are given for this conclusion. First: (1) property is tools for doing something (as is shown by standard pieces of property like beds and clothing); (2) the slave is property; (3) therefore the slave is for doing something. Second: (4) making and doing are different in kind and the tools proper to making and doing are similarly different in kind;[31] (5) life is doing and slaves are tools for life; (6) therefore slaves are tools for doing, or are assistants in matters that concern doing, and are different in kind from tools for making.

What is curious about this conclusion and about the arguments on which it rests is that they exclude productive tools, or tools for making, from the category of property and deny to slaves any role in making. Yet productive tools are presumably the property of someone and slaves can sometimes be employed in making things (artisans were sometimes slaves, 3.4.1277a37–b1). The explanation must be that Aristotle is taking property in a strict or precise sense to mean just the tools of the household or just tools that are of direct use to life (as beds and clothes are, and as slaves who do the chores about the house and the farm are).[32] So he excludes tools and activities that are not part of this even if they produce what is part of this (as shuttles and weaving, which make the clothes we wear). These things will not strictly be property but will only be for the sake of what is strictly property. Aristotle, therefore, may not so much be excluding these other tools and activities as subordinating them. Productive tools, and slaves involved in production, are at one remove from property and the household. They are not what the household manager needs to do his job; rather they produce what he needs to do his job. They may, therefore, be reduced to property (because they are for the sake of making property), but they are not, strictly speaking, property.[33]

1254a8　From the fact that the slave is property, it has thus been shown that he is a living tool for the sake of life. It is next shown, from the same fact, that the slave wholly belongs to his master: (1) a possession is spoken of in the same way as a part is; (2) a part is not only a part of something else but also wholly belongs to that something else; (3) therefore a possession wholly belongs to the something else of which it is the possession. Hence the slave wholly belongs to the master whose possession he is. The analogy and its point are clear enough. For a part, qua

---

31. The difference is that making has an end beyond itself (as weaving has its end in the finished piece of cloth), but doing is its own end (as living well is its own end), *Ethics* 6.5.1140b6–7.

32. Such slaves will be needed as assistants to make up the bed in the morning, or clean the house, or tend the farm, since none of these things gets done on its own; Barker (1946: 11 nC), against Jowett (1885: 2:14).

33. See Pellegrin (1982: 355–56) and Schütrumpf (1991: 1:241).

part, belongs altogether to the whole and property, qua property, belongs altogether to the owner, and to the extent they cease to be *of* the whole or *of* the owner, they cease to be part or property.

But if the slave is thus wholly of the master, the master is not wholly of the slave. "Master" and "slave" may be correlative terms in the sense that they are predicated with respect to each other, but the being of master and slave is not correlative in the same way. The being of the slave is indeed correlative to his master (for he is his master's property), but the being of the master is not correlative to his slave. This conclusion is not altered by the fact that the master depends on the slave for survival,[34] for the manner of this dependence is not the same. The slave altogether depends on the master since he depends on the master for his whole direction in life (as the body depends on the soul), but the master only depends on the slave for survival (as the soul depends on the body); and indeed, just as the tool in the case of the arts exists for the craftsman who uses it and not vice versa, so the slave also exists for the sake of the master who uses him and not vice versa.[35]

1254a13 The definition of the slave, his nature and power or capacity, is thus clear: someone who belongs to another as a living tool for the doing that is life. Aristotle, however, proceeds at once to what seems the following argument: (1) anyone who, while a human being, does not by nature belong to himself but to another is by nature a slave; (2) he is a human being belonging to another who, while being human, is a possession in the sense of a tool for doing something or for action; (3) therefore he is by nature a slave who is by nature a human possession in the sense of a tool for action. This is certainly to define the slave through his power or capacity (his power or capacity of belonging to another as a tool for life), but it also prepares the way for the next chapter, which is about the slave by nature, since it puts the definition in terms of power or capacity by nature. For now that we know what power or capacity by nature marks the slave by nature, it will be easy enough to see if any humans by nature have this power or capacity.

Chapter 5

~ SLAVE AND MASTER BY NATURE

~ FIRST PROOF

1254a17 Having thus defined the slave and shown what slaves are for, Aristotle turns to consider whether there are any slaves by nature (as he has himself ear-

---

34. Contra Schütrumpf (1991: 1:244).

35. Hence there can be no slave/master dialectic for Aristotle as for Hegel (*Phänomenologie des Geistes* IV A). Aristotle's master only needs the slave for the necessities of life and not for anything else. Besides, Hegel standardly conflates correlativity of terms and correlativity of beings.

lier asserted but as others deny), and therefore whether slavery is good and just for anyone. For if there are any slaves by nature, slavery must be just for them, for thus they will be given their due, and also good, for to be treated justly is good. The answer, says Aristotle, can be seen both "by reason" and "from what actually occurs" (1254a20–21), which implies that two different processes of argument are to follow. Two different processes of argument do indeed follow and, despite lack of definite indications in the text,[36] the second, about what actually occurs, would seem to be given first (it is a frequent practice of Aristotle's to take things in reverse order).

What actually occurs, or is found to be the case generally, is that ruling and being ruled are necessary and beneficial, that some things are separated into ruler and ruled immediately at generation, that there are many kinds of rulers and ruled, and that rule over better subjects is always better. This last claim, which is perhaps less immediately obvious, is supported by the further claims that from better materials a better work is completed and that when one thing rules and another is ruled, there is always some work they have. The claim that the work from better materials is better seems uncontroversial enough, and the claim that ruler and ruled have some work presumably means here that the work of ruler and ruled is the point or essence of ruling (so that rule is better as the work is better), and that this work is completed from the ruled as material by the ruler as agent. If so, this too is plausible enough. The purpose or aim of a ruler is to direct the ruled to achieve something (as victory in the case of a general ruling an army), and in this task the ruler is manifestly agent, as the one directing, and the ruled manifestly material or patient, as the one directed.[37]

But if all these claims or propositions are true then it is already likely that rule over slaves, which is certainly one kind of rule, although evidently not a very high kind (for slaves are not the best subjects), will in some cases be necessary and good, namely in those cases where some are from their beginning marked out as slaves and others as masters.

1254a28 These propositions may be said to be the result of the general thesis, now stated, that in everything that is fashioned into a common unity from the combination of several parts, whether the parts be continuous or discrete, a ruling and ruled part are apparent, and that this is a universal truth of nature, holding of animate and inanimate things alike. For since many natural things are composed of parts, the principle of rule that holds them together will be natural and beneficial, vary in kind and superiority as the things themselves vary, and exist in them from their beginning. In illustration of the thesis Aristotle proceeds to give several examples, the first of which, from harmony (whether in the case of musical modes, where the key note rules and determines the others, or in the case of

---

36. Something remarked on by Newman (2:140), Saunders (1995: 75), and Schütrumpf (1991: 1:250).
37. See 4(7).4.1325b40–1326a8, and *Ethics* 1.13.1102a7–12.

material bodies, where the elements in a mixture are ruled and determined by the predominant element or the form of the mixing),[38] makes the point for inanimate things but is obviously not germane to the present topic. The examples from animals are two of continuous things (soul and body, intellect and appetite) and two of discrete things (humans and animals, male and female).

But first a warning is in order. The ruling and ruled elements in animals are manifestly soul and body, but this is only manifest in specimens that accord with nature and have not become corrupted. In corrupted and depraved ones, the reverse is often the case. Hence only those human beings must be considered who are best disposed in body and soul, that is, who are not corrupted (for merely to count up instances, without distinguishing the best from the corrupted, would not lead to the natural, or even a consistent, result). It may seem prejudicial thus to take the best as the guide to nature. But it is only what scientists regularly do even today. For they do not think it possible to understand a thing's nature from specimens that are spoiled or ruined, nor do doctors or trainers go to the diseased or the weak and lame to understand what health and strength are (except incidentally). Yet if it is thus necessary to know the best to know nature, then those who do not know the best will not be able to know nature nor, consequently, will they be fit students of the present science. But Aristotle already said that long ago (*Ethics* 1.3.1095a2–11).

1254b2   Taking the best as guide, then, we can see that the soul's rule over the body is despotic while that of intellect over appetite is political or royal. The body, for instance, belongs wholly to the soul (the body is what it is because of the soul and it has no principle of action apart from the soul), but appetite does not belong wholly to the intellect (it is something apart from the intellect and has its own principle of action). We can see further that for the body to be subject to the soul (as in the healthy), or for appetite to be subject to intellect (as in the virtuous), is natural and beneficial, while the reverse (as in the paralytic or the vicious) is harmful.

As for animals, the tame are better in nature than the wild ones (it is possible to get better things out of them, as work and companionship and not just food), and they are manifestly better off being ruled by humans since thus they are preserved (they live longer and are more protected from predators and disease). The rule of humans over animals is evidently despotic. Oxen, for instance, belong to farmers as tools for life in the way that slaves belong to masters. Of course we can own some animals, as dogs and cats in particular, for purposes of companionship, but if it can be said that we rule these in some nondespotic way, this only reveals more clearly the despotic way farmers rule the animals used in farming. The latter case is evidently what Aristotle has in mind here.

38. Alternatives noted by St. Thomas Aquinas (1951: 1.3.62).

As for females, that the relation of male to female is by nature that of better to worse and ruler to ruled is asserted as evident to experience (the experience we have of other animals no doubt, as well as of ourselves). Aristotle is, of course, not speaking of all males and females but only of those who are best disposed (some males are doubtless worse than some females). So what he presumably has in mind is, in the case of humans, the superiority in reason of the best males over the best females and in particular the superiority of their capacity for deliberation (the faculty most needed by a ruler, 1.13.1260a12–20). The rule of male over female is, however, not despotic (except among barbarians, 1.2.1252a34–b7); it must rather be political.

1254b14   Accordingly, if the general thesis is true, that things fashioned into a common unity from the combination of several parts divide into natural rulers and ruled, it will be true of all human beings, for human beings are naturally the parts of single communities (household and city). Hence, wherever the like differences are found among human beings as in the examples, there the like kinds of rule will be natural and good. Hence, further, wherever there are human beings as widely separated from others as are soul and body or human and beast (the natural patterns of despotic rule), they will be slaves by nature; and for them to be ruled despotically as slaves by these other human beings, who are their souls as it were, must be beneficial and good. But those whose work is the use of the body, and from whom such work is the best that there is, will be on the same level as animals and the body, which give no better work to humans or the soul. Hence it is these who will be slaves by nature.

This conclusion validly follows from the analogy drawn from nature, but it only establishes that slavery is in principle natural and just. So while it does, as Aristotle requires, refute current conceptions (which deny the justice of slavery everywhere and in principle), it does not establish that there are any people around whose best work is the use of the body and for whom slavery will in fact be just. Or, to put it another way, it only establishes the criterion to use when looking for natural slaves and not whether one will find any natural slaves when one does actually look. Nevertheless one could profitably start, no doubt, by looking at the corrupted specimens Aristotle has just mentioned, those upside-down people, so to speak, in whom the body rules the soul. Such upside-down people will include the mentally deficient, perhaps, but also and more obviously the morally deficient, or those who have no appreciation of the noble, such as the base and vulgar (who must anyway be chastised like beasts of burden; *Ethics* 10.9.1180a11–12).[39]

---

39. Hard labor in prisons, for instance, as punishment for criminals, would thus be a species of Aristotelian natural slavery still very much alive in our modern liberal democratic world. It would also be a species of Aristotelian natural slavery specifically allowed by the Thirteenth Amendment to the United States Constitution. St. Thomas Aquinas (1951: 1.3.68) appositely quotes Solomon's remark (Proverbs 11.29) that "the fool shall serve the wise."

1254b20 The same conclusion, that the slave by nature is one whose best work is the use of the body, is now confirmed by reason, or by a deductive argument based on first principles, namely the definition of the slave from the preceding chapter. Aristotle begins by laying down the propositions that: (1) the slave by nature is someone who has the power or capacity of belonging to another, and (2) who shares reason sufficiently to perceive it but not to have it. Proposition (1) repeats the definition in summary form, for belonging to another was explained in chapter 4 as a human possession in the sense of a tool for doing or for action ("power of belonging to another" must have the force here of "lack of power of belonging to oneself," for someone who could belong to himself would cease to be capable of belonging to another; his power or capacity would be much greater). But if the conclusion, that those whose best work is the use of the body are slaves by nature, is to follow from this definition, the further proposition is needed that those whose best work is the use of the body have the power or capacity of belonging to another in the sense meant. Proposition (2) is intended, I take it, to furnish the proof for this further proposition.

There are two parts to proposition (2): on the one hand that the slave by nature does not have reason, and on the other hand that he can nevertheless perceive it. As regards the first part, it seems evident that those who do not have reason will be such as to belong to another, for to have reason of oneself is the mark of self-possession and enables one to rule oneself by one's own thinking. Conversely, not to have reason must make one subject to those who can do the thinking in one's stead (which is the job of the master with respect to the slave, 1.2.1252a31–34). But if this was all that was meant by the slaves's belonging to another, nothing further about reason need be said. The slave, however, belongs to another as a living tool for the activity of life, and this is, I take it, what the second part of proposition (2) is about. For a living tool is supposed to act by perceiving and obeying the master's command (like the machines of Daedalus and Hephaestus), and as the master's command comes from his reason, to perceive this command is somehow to perceive reason (even if it is not to perceive reason *as* reason). So the slave must share reason enough to be able to do that. How the slave does so is explained in the next sentence about animals, for these also are living tools (1254b23–24).[40] Animals do

---

40. Provided the Greek of this sentence is taken in the way I take it in the translation, namely "for the other animals give of their assistance without perceiving by reason but rather by what they feel." Other translators take the sentence to mean that the other animals do not perceive or follow reason but rather follow their feelings or passions. But such translations treat the text as drawing a distinction between slaves and animals whereas Aristotle has just likened the two to each other and should be continuing the likeness here. The translation I offer overcomes this difficulty. It differs from other translations in taking *hypēretei* absolutely and in its primary sense of "give assistance" (picking up on the word for assistant, *hypēretēs*, in the preceding chapter), and not in its other sense of "follow" or

not have reason yet they too assist their owners by perceiving what these owners command. They do so, not by reason, of course (for they lack reason), but by what they feel, as horses and oxen do by the tug of the reins or sheepdogs by shouts and whistles. Slaves by nature will perceive their master's commands in a similar way, just as the assistance they give to their master is similar to the assistance that animals give, namely bodily help in the supply of necessities.[41]

If proposition (2) is explained in this way it will serve validly to prove that those whose best work is the use of the body belong to another as a living tool for life. For those whose best work is the use of the body cannot have reason of themselves (else they would be capable of some better work), so they must belong to another, but since they can nevertheless provide work with their bodies in the same way animals can (by perceiving a master's commands), they will belong to another in the form of living tools for the necessities of life. Consequently those whose best work is the use of the body will be slaves by nature in the sense defined.

Two clarifications, however, seem necessary. The first concerns what sort of reason is being denied to the slave. For later on Aristotle speaks of slaves as capable of acquiring certain kinds of knowledge and skill (1.7) and as capable of virtue (1.13). It is perhaps necessary, therefore, to distinguish between reason and reasoning.[42] Slaves may have reasoning and be able to learn and work things out (just as some animals can up to a point), but it does not follow that they have reason and can discern the good and the noble. But this kind of discernment must be what Aristotle has in mind. For what the slave lacks and the master has is foresight and delib-

---

"obey" and as governing "feelings" (*pathēmasin*). I have been gratified to discover, since completing the translation, that the same way of taking the Greek was already suggested by Koraes (1821: 236). Susemihl (1886: 343) noted Koraes's suggestion but, unfortunately, rejected it because he failed to see its force in the context.

41. Since the sharing in reason Aristotle attributes to slaves is the same sharing as animals have, it cannot follow that he should have concluded that slaves were related to others as appetite to intellect, not as body to soul or animals to humans, and so should be ruled by political and not despotic rule—contrary to the opinions of Fortenbaugh, in Barnes et al. (1977: 135–39), Smith, in Keyt and Miller (1991: 142–55), Saunders (1995: 78), Schütrumpf (1991: 1:265–66). Appetite shares in intellect in a way that neither animals nor the body do. For appetite belongs to the rational part of the soul and is not separate from it like animals and the body, and something better can also be got out of appetite than from the body and animals, namely the perfection of moral virtue, *Ethics* 1.13.1102b25–1103a10; see also Dobbs (1994: 83–85). The appetite of the slave is not joined to reason *within* the soul of the slave, for the slave lacks reason in the relevant sense. It is only joined, by obedience, to the separate reason of the master (like the appetite of tame animals). Thus the slave can be trained to do well in his work (*Politics* 1.13.1260a33–36), as also can animals, but moral virtue proper requires that appetite be controlled by a reason within the soul of the virtuous (*Ethics* 6.13.1144b25–28).

42. Milani (1972: 117–19), Schofield, in Patzig (1990: 14–16), Swanson (1992: 33–35, 40 n29). Such a distinction is implicit in 1.7.

eration (1.2.1252a31–34, 13.1260a12), and these must be of the good and noble since the master must foresee and deliberate about the end of the household and the city, which is the good and noble life of virtue. Such discernment marks the difference between the few who are fit to learn about virtue and the many who are not, and between prudence and mere cleverness (*Ethics* 1.3.1095a2–b13, 6.12.1144a23–b1). Slaves by nature may have reasoning and be clever, but they cannot have reason or be prudent.[43] That is why, like animals, they only perceive reason by what they feel, for having no understanding themselves of the noble they only perceive and do what they should under command and compulsion applied to their feelings of pleasure and pain (*Ethics* 10.9.1179b10–18, 1180a11–14).

The second clarification ties in with the first. When describing the slave by nature, Aristotle speaks only of a certain *condition* and of those who have it, for he speaks of the condition (*diakeintai*) of those whose best work is the the use of the body (1254b17). He says nothing about how this condition comes about. The phrase "by nature" and his earlier assertion that some things are separated into ruler and ruled immediately at generation suggest that this condition comes about at the beginning or at birth. But if generation refers not to birth only but to any way of coming into being, then perhaps one can come by the relevant condition, and so become a slave by nature, in more ways than birth—as by accident, say, or upbringing, or even by choice. After all, animals acquire their tameness not from birth but from training (by being "broken in" as we say of horses), and yet once they have this condition they are tame by nature.

1254b27 The natural slave's lack of reason has described the condition of his soul. Aristotle next discusses the condition of his body. For it would seem most desirable that slaves, given their function, should have bodies fit for physical labor, and conversely that the free, who are to lead a political way of life, should have bodies fit for the activities of that life (those of war and peace, 4(7).14.1333a30–b5). If therefore nature aims at the best, she must aim at this. Her aim, however, often fails and those who have slavish bodies have free souls and vice versa. Did she not fail so often, there would be far less doubt about the naturalness of slavery. The manifest difference in the bodies of slave and free would convince everyone of the fact. At any rate it is manifest, says Aristotle, that if some people were to develop bodies like the statues of the gods, everyone would say that those left behind deserved to be their slaves. We should not assume that Aristotle's "everyone" here can refer only to ancient pagans. The same thought is far from foreign to us today, as can be discerned from the honor and worship we give to beautiful bodies, as to models, athletes, and film stars. But we also recognize with Aristotle, at least when we reflect, that greater honor and worship are due to beautiful or noble souls (for

43. See the discussion in Dobbs (1994: 80–86).

the soul is better than the body). Nobility of soul, however, is harder to see, being a matter of virtue and not of figure or stature.

But herein may lie the solution to a certain difficulty. That nature sometimes fails is evident; monstrous births are obvious instances. But such failures do not happen often or for the most part. The difficulty is how the failure in the case of slave and free can be so frequent if nature is really at work.[44] The answer seems to be that, whereas beauty or nobility of body lies within nature's control, beauty or nobility of soul does not. We are indeed born by nature for virtue but the achievement of it is by human action, not by nature. The actual achievement of a noble soul requires a legislator and education, and these are no longer an affair of nature. Nature can nevertheless be said to want noble souls in noble bodies for she has made humans for virtue, that is, she has made them to be completed by legislation and training (4(7).13.1332b8–10, 17.1337a1–3). The best thing, of course, would be to have the best body, or the best preconditions, and the best education, for thus would the simply best, the best by nature, be achieved. Hence, when outlining his simply best regime later (in books 4(7) and 5(8)), Aristotle requires the presence of both. But if the preconditions are best and the education deficient, the result will be slavish souls in free bodies; and if the preconditions are poor but the education good, the result will be free souls in slavish bodies (at least provided the souls are capable of education). The failures in nature's wish, therefore, spring rather from us than from nature. For it is we who fail to provide or to get the education that nature has made us for. So it also seems clear from this same fact that slavish souls need not arise from birth alone; they could arise in as many ways as souls could fail to be educated.[45]

1254b39   The chapter has concentrated on slaves by nature as those whose best work is the use of the body and for whom slavery is thus beneficial and just. But, thereby, the free and masters by nature have also become evident as those who have reason of themselves, can discern the good and the noble, and are fit for the life of the city in peace and war. The difference is nevertheless a matter, above all, of souls. The bodies may or may not correspond.

---

44. A problem noted by Cambiano, in Finley (1987: 29–30).

45. See Dobbs (1994: 78–79). Incidentally, St. Thomas Aquinas (1951: 1.3.71) argues that nature does always succeed in matching souls and bodies as far as the interior dispositions are concerned, for no one, he says, can have a well-disposed soul whose imagination and other sensitive powers are not also well disposed. Nature's matching only fails, he continues, when it comes to exterior dispositions, as figure and largeness of body. He also argues (1951: 1.4.86–87) that natural inclinations and natural impediments to virtue can be inherited from parents and come from birth (just as bodily beauty, height, and strength, or their opposites, can be so inherited). But he adds that education and habituation can work counter to this good or bad inheritance. Similar views are expressed by Peter of Auvergne (1951: 7.2.1075, 8.1.1266).

Chapter 6

∽ SLAVE AND MASTER BY LAW

∽ AGAINST THOSE WHO ALTOGETHER CONDEMN SLAVERY

1255a3 Having thus shown that slavery is natural and just, at least under certain conditions, Aristotle turns to refute those who say that slavery is never natural and just. That they are right up to a point is evident from the fact that, besides the slave by nature, there is also the slave by law, namely by the law that says that what is conquered in war belongs to the conquerors. Now the two sorts of slave (by law and by nature) will not necessarily overlap, and so some slaves by law need not be slaves by nature. Slavery in their case will therefore be unnatural and unjust. On the other hand, some slaves by law may very well be slaves by nature and slavery in their case will be natural and just. The opponents of slavery, however, condemn all slavery by law, and make no distinction between those who are also slaves by nature and those who are not. Accordingly these opponents, or those of them versed in the laws, bring against this law the sort of charge or writ of illegality they would bring against an orator in the assembly who proposed a law contrary to the already established laws.[46] In this case, however, they are bringing this charge, not against a proposal for a law, but against a law already in existence. That is perhaps why Aristotle calls it "this principle of justice" (*touto to dikaion*, 1255a7–8), for any law, even a bad one, may be given such an appellation merely because it is a law. In the case of bad laws, of course, the appellation will carry more than a hint of irony, as it clearly must for the opponents of the law in question.

Their argument against the law is: (1) it is a terrible thing if what is forced into submission is to become slave of the stronger; (2) this law says that what is forced into submission is to become slave of the stronger; (3) therefore this law is, or says, a terrible thing. So since, as they further suppose, (4) slavery is by this law of force and force is unjust (1.3.1253b20–23), it follows (5) that slavery is terrible and unjust. Implicit in premises (1) and (4), however, is the further premise that what is by this law of force cannot also be by nature, for if it were also by nature, the force and the law need not be terrible or unjust. For force and law used to support nature can be just (as force against the disobedient, cf. *Ethics* 10.9.1180a5–14). So if there are slaves by nature, to use the law of force against them need not be terrible or unjust. This argument of the opponents of slavery, therefore, only works on the assumption that there are no slaves by nature, and hence it only proves the injustice of

46. In the popular assembly at Athens a writ of illegality (*graphē paranomōn*) could be brought against anyone who proposed a law contrary to established law.

slavery by assuming the injustice of slavery. It is sheer sophistry (though sophistry is, of course, not unusual among those who bring charges in popular assemblies).

1255a11 If the opposition to slavery simply rested on this sophistry, it would not be worth discussing further, but in fact there are some among the wise who also think the law in question is a terrible thing (though others of the wise disagree), and the opinions of the wise at any rate should be taken seriously. Precisely how to interpret Aristotle's next remarks, however, is a matter of much dispute.[47] My own interpretation, which is different from that of others, is based on certain ways of reading the Greek. First of all I take the statement that the conqueror always excels in some form of goodness to depend on the clause about virtue getting hold of equipment (1255a13–15), so that this conqueror excels in virtue and not just in any form of goodness at all, as mere strength for example.[48] A conqueror who excelled in strength or force alone, and not also in virtue, would be a conqueror whose enslavement of the conquered would be terrible because he could not be to them as natural master to natural slave. But one would expect the wise, unlike the opponents of slavery just mentioned, to be expressly mindful that some conquerors can excel in force because they first excel in virtue. That is why, I take it, Aristotle immediately adds that the force in question "seems not to be without virtue" (1255a15–16), because the wise are thinking precisely of such virtuous force and virtuous conquerors. They are not thinking of bare force by itself.

The disagreement among the wise, therefore, is not about the superiority of the conqueror, but about "the principle of justice" (1255a16), that is to say, about the law of conquest mentioned above.[49] So some of the wise think the law kindness (1255a17–18)[50] and not terrible because they think it is meant to apply only to cases where the conqueror excels in virtue, and hence that it only allows the enslavement by natural masters of natural slaves.[51] Others among the wise, by

47. St. Thomas Aquinas (1951: 1.4), Newman (2:150–52), Schütrumpf (1991: 1:272–81), Susemihl and Hicks (1894: 163–66, 205–9); and see also Barker (1959: 368–69), Lord (1984: 248 n19), Saunders (1995: 80) and in Moffat (1984: 25–36), and Schofield, in Patzig (1990: 23–27).

48. My translation reads: "when virtue gets hold of equipment, it has a special capacity to use force, and also the conqueror always excels in some form of goodness."

49. The Greek says literally "the just" (*to dikaion*), which most commentators take to mean the justice of the matter or something of the sort. But "this just" (*touto to dikaion*) was earlier used at 1255a7–8, as all agree, to refer to the law ("this principle of justice" as I translate it), so I take it to mean the same here as well.

50. All the manuscripts have "kindness" (*eunoia*), but the interpretations of some commentators on this passage require "kindness" to be emended to "folly" (*anoia*).

51. To be kind is to want good things for another (*Ethics* 8.2.1155b32), and to want slavery for natural slaves, as the law of conquest effectively does, is to be thus kind, for it is to want for them something good, namely the actual serving as slaves, which, as the previous chapter showed, is beneficial and just for those who are natural slaves.

contrast, think the law of conquest is simply this, "that rule by the stronger is just" (1255a18–19)[52] or, in other words, that this law is saying that it is just for any conqueror to rule, whether excelling in virtue or not. Hence they conclude that the law is terrible as allowing the enslavement of anyone who is conquered, including the enslavement of those who are not natural slaves by those who are not natural masters.

Both groups of the wise are thus relying on a common premise for both agree that (1) the enslavement of natural slaves conquered in war by natural masters or conquerors excelling in virtue is just but the enslavement of the conquered is not just otherwise. What they disagree about is the law of conquest, for some argue that (2) the law of conquest says that conquerors excelling in virtue may enslave the conquered, and so conclude that (3) therefore this law is kind because just. Others, however, argue that (4) the law of conquest says that any conqueror may enslave the conquered, and so conclude that (5) therefore this law is terrible because it allows something that is not just. So their arguments overlap in the common premise (1), and they disagree in their conclusions because they disagree about the law and its correct interpretation. This disagreement presumably arises from the fact that the law gets used in different ways by different people, with some using it in a just and others in an unjust sense. For the law only exists as a convention or an agreement and in what is commonly said, and what is commonly said may not mean the same for all those who say it. Hence there will always be room for disagreement about what the law concretely means.

Aristotle accordingly leaves the dispute among the wise unresolved. Nevertheless once their arguments are set aside, the weakness in the other arguments, namely of those versed in the laws, becomes evident. For these arguments, being stated without any of the qualifications of the wise and condemning all enslavement of the conquered in war, require one to conclude that even the better in virtue ought not to rule and be master, which, in view of the arguments in chapter 5, can carry no strength or conviction.[53]

52. My translation at this point—"others think it [the law of conquest] is this, that rule by the stronger is just"—differs from that of other commentators and translators and rests on punctuating the Greek thus *auto touto, dikaion to* ("it is this, that . . . is just"), and not *auto touto dikaion, to* ("this itself is just, rule . . .") with Dreizehnter and others.

53. It is interesting to note that, in his discussion of slavery, Montesquieu also ignores the qualifications of the wise as well as Aristotle's arguments in chapter 5 (*De l'Esprit des Lois*, 3.15.7 and 2). He just says that Aristotle's arguments hardly work, but he does not try to refute them; indeed he does not even state them—following in this a not uncommon practice among early modern writers noted by Mansfield (1989: 25). In fact, he would seem, in this case, actually to be following the example of those versed in the laws mentioned here, for, like them, all he does is attack the law of conquest and omit any qualifications about conquerors who excel in virtue.

1255a21 The first opponents went too far in condemning slavery and the law of conquest; the next opponents go too far in approving it. They rely entirely on the fact that the law of conquest is a law, and so, since law is something just, conclude that slavery in war is just, that is, just altogether and not merely, as the wise think, on a certain condition (that the conqueror excels in virtue). But then, not surprisingly, they immediately end up contradicting themselves. For not every rule arising from or won by war[54] need be just, as mastery over the conquered who are not slaves by nature is not just, and in these cases one could not call those enslaved really slaves if they do not deserve to be slaves. Otherwise one will have to say that even the most well born are slaves should they be conquered, and in particular the opponents in question here will have to say this about themselves, for they consider themselves well-born. So, to escape this consequence, they deny what they first said, that such slavery is always just, and limit slavery instead to barbarians.

1255a29 In limiting slavery to barbarians, they are really looking for the same thing as Aristotle, namely the slave by nature, the one who is a slave every-where, whether conquered yet or not (though Aristotle himself has not identified slaves with barbarians, since the natural slave was defined in the preceding chapter by condition of soul, and only derivatively by national, or rather geographical, origin; and see 4(7).7.1327b20–36). They are doing the same about themselves and good birth, or they are saying that as the barbarians are slaves everywhere so they themselves are well-born and free everywhere (and so should never be enslaved even if conquered). But thus to appeal, like Theodectes' Helen, to good birth to justify freedom over against barbarian slavery is to think that the goodness of parents is continued in children. So it is to think, as Aristotle says, that what really matters for freedom and slavery is virtue and vice (for otherwise the appeal to the *quality* of birth would be irrelevant).

This view is indeed true, that vice and virtue, or conditions of soul, mark the difference between slave and free, but not the view that virtue is always continued from parents to children. Nature fails here just as she fails to match bodies and souls. Virtue, or nobility of soul, is not just a matter of birth or natural endow-ments, but above all of training under good laws. So one may be the most well born and have the most beautiful or noble body possible, as Helen did, but one

---

54. I translate *archēn . . . tōn polemōn* as "rule arising from war" though most translate it as "the beginning of wars" (*archē* can mean either "beginning" or "rule"). But that the beginning of certain wars might be unjust is not what accounts for the possibility that some of those conquered might not deserve to be enslaved. For even if a war began justly, the conqueror could not justly enslave the conquered unless they were already and independently slaves by nature. Besides, what is relevant to Aristotle's argument is not how wars begin but how they end, namely what one does to the conquered after one has won rule over them.

may still be a slave by nature if one does not also have a noble soul. Helen, we know, did not have a noble soul, for she was an adulteress, and adultery is base, not noble (*Ethics* 2.6.1107a8–17). Helen, we may therefore suppose, is an instance of someone free by birth but by nature, that is, by her condition of soul, a slave.

~ SUMMARY

1255b4　The summary covers chapters 4 to 6 in reverse order. So the dispute about the justice of slavery (chapter 6) has some reason behind it in the fact that, because of the unjust application of the law of conquest, not all those who are slaves deserve to be slaves. But by the same token not all those who are free deserve to be free (as Helen, for instance). Still, where slave and free do deserve to be such, despotic rule by the second over the first is just and beneficial or advantageous (chapter 5). The slave belongs to the master as a part to the whole (chapter 4); hence, to exercise mastery badly cannot be of benefit to either of them, for to harm the part is to harm the whole. The extreme form of such harm must be when master and slave are so only by force and not also by nature, for then they will not really be master and slave and so not really whole and part. In such cases neither master nor slave will have the friendship or advantage involved in mutual benefit: not the slave because he suffers injustice, and not the master because he inflicts it.[55]

Such, then, seems to be, more or less, the burden of Aristotle's reasoning about natural slaves. Once that reasoning is carefully laid out and the necessary clarifications made, his arguments can hardly be said to be as obviously fallacious or as ironical as some commentators have contended.[56] The arguments rest, to be sure, on appeals to experience nowadays considered to be controversial, and also presuppose Aristotle's general theory of virtue, but they proceed validly enough from those bases. There is, in other words, no inconsistency, even if there is controversy, in his thinking. For, as has already been said, what Aristotle means by the natural slave is not only, and not even typically, the mental incompetent most frequently suggested by commentators, but the moral incompetent, those he characterizes in these chapters as the corrupted and vicious (whether this be by birth, upbringing,

55. On the question of friendship between master and slave St. Thomas Aquinas notes (1951: 1.4.88): "the communication of two people in something that benefits each of them is a reason [*ratio*] for friendship." He perhaps has in mind what Aristotle says elsewhere (*Ethics* 8.11.1161b5–8), that there can be friendship between master and slave insofar as the slave is a human being, for the slave, qua human (though not qua slave), can share in justice and law and contract (*nomos* and *sunthēkē*). The slave qua slave, of course, is not much different from a tame animal (both are living tools that belong to another), but the mutual benefit or advantage involved in slavery becomes a reason for friendship in the case of the slave (though not in the case of animals) because the slave is human and qua human has speech and can perceive the mutual benefit for what it is, namely as advantageous and just, not merely as pleasant (1.2.1253a9–18), and hence as a ground of justice and friendship. The condition, of course, is that the slave in question be a natural slave, for otherwise slavery is neither advantageous nor just.

56. See in particular the review by Dobbs (1994), along with the references in the preceding notes.

choice, or whatever). That such people may in some sense have reason is not to the point. Their reason is enslaved to the passions so that it does not operate as reason (that is, it does not discern the good and the noble). For the true commands of reason they do not perceive nor obey by themselves but only insofar as they are subjected to the rule of others, that is to say, only insofar as they perceive these commands through what they experience at the hands of natural masters, the virtuous. With such people it is as if they did not have reason but were no better, in this respect, than tame animals. Doubtless many barbarians will be in this position, but not all of them need be. More to the point, however, is that some Greeks will certainly be in this position, above all the many and those whom the many admire.[57] The problem with natural slaves is, thus, not that they are insufficiently numerous,[58] but that they exist in too great abundance. This point comes out, in fact, in Aristotle's later discussion of regimes, where he indicates that in most cities there are too many wandering around free who are in fact slaves and corrupt (as, above all, in 6(4).11).

But however that may be, Aristotle's views about slavery may be summarized by saying that the natural masters are fundamentally the virtuous, or those who have been perfected in their development, and the natural slaves are fundamentally the vicious, or those who have in some way been damaged or corrupted in their development. This view fits in with, and may in fact be said to fall out of, the teaching of the *Ethics* (where the many are certainly characterized as slavish and bestial, as at 1.5.1095b19–20, 10.9.1179b10–18, 1180a4–14). It is, moreover, not a view peculiar to ancient Greeks or to Aristotle.[59]

Chapter 7

∼ MASTERY AS RULE AND AS SCIENCE

1255b16 Aristotle has thus dealt with the naturalness of slavery and mastery, so now he turns to mastery as a science. Two things were noted in chapter 3 as currently supposed about mastery in this regard, that it is a science and that it is the same science as the other sorts of rule. As regards the second supposition, its falsity is now clear: mastery is not political rule because political rule is over the

57. For this reason Aristotle's arguments for slavery could not safely be used to justify slavery in the antebellum South of the United States, for those arguments would not yield the conclusion that all and only blacks should be enslaved. They would, on the contrary, yield the conclusion that some of the white masters should be enslaved, and to some of their black slaves to boot.

58. As Lear, for instance, thinks (1988: 199).

59. The same idea is found in the quotation from Proverbs 11.29 noted before, that "the fool [the moral fool, that is] will become slave to the wise." Compare also Milton, *Paradise Lost* 12.97–101: "Yet sometimes nations will decline so low / from virtue, which is reason, that no wrong / but justice, and some fatal curse annext / deprives them of their outward libertie, / their inward lost."

free, not slaves, and household management is not political rule because it is monarchical and over unequals (both slave and free), whereas political rule is over equals. Aristotle does not say here that *none* of the kinds are the same; only that *not all* of them are the same, which is only equivalent to saying *some* of them are not the same. So the fact that he allows household rule and monarchical rule to be in some sense the same, or to overlap, involves him in no contradiction. One should nevertheless note that "monarchy" means, as such, simply rule by a single ruler, and that Aristotle does not use it to signify any one *kind* of rule. For he calls both kings and tyrants monarchs, but their rule is by no means of the same kind. Still, there seems to be some special closeness between household rule and kingly rule (1.2.1252b19–21, 3.14.1285b29–33).

1255b20   As regards the first supposition, that mastery is a science, this is partly false and partly true. It is false in that the master is not a master because of science. As chapters 5 and 6 have made clear, the master is a master because he is of a certain character (he is virtuous), and likewise with free and slave. For the free are masters and the masters free, and master and slave are master and slave, because of their condition of soul.

It is true, however, in that there is a science of the master as also of the slave. Slavish science is what is to be taught to slaves so that they can do their chores, and this science comes in several ranks as do the sorts of work and the slaves who do them (and the mastery exercised over them will be ranked similarly). That slaves are capable of being taught and trained does not imply that they must have reason, for animals too can be taught and trained. But it does allow that some slaves could be intelligent, especially if some of them are to be capable of more elaborate and honorable tasks. But intelligence in using the body to do various things is not the same as discernment of the noble (which characterizes the natural master).

The master's science will be the science of using slaves, for the master is a master by using slaves, not just by possessing them (slaves are tools and to rule them means to use them as tools). There can be nothing grand in knowing the master's science, since it consists in knowing the same things as the slave save from the point of view of commanding these things, not doing them. So it is not surprising that masters devote themselves to something grand and dignified if they can, to politics, or ruling the city, and to philosophy. The steward whom such masters leave in charge in their place could perhaps himself be a slave. For in exercising mastery over other slaves, the steward will be exercising only a certain science of mastery, and it is quality of soul, not science, that makes the master. So a master could set slaves in charge of other slaves, and rule slaves through slaves, while yet they all remain his slaves and he their master.[60]

---

60. A point not always noted by commentators, as Newman (2:164) and Schütrumpf (1991: 1:267); see also Smith, in Keyt and Miller (1991: 145).

1255b37   If the sciences of master and slave concern the use of slaves, the science of property, or the getting of slaves by hunting and war, must be different. It will be just, at least when the slaves conquered are natural slaves (as was shown in the preceding chapter), and will fall under the natural kind of property and science of property (as is shown in the next chapter).

Chapter 8

~ PROPERTY

~ THE QUESTIONS ABOUT BUSINESS

1256a1   Business is the topic from chapter 3 that has the closest connection with what has just preceded, as it too has to do with property (namely the getting of property), so it naturally comes next. Two answers were proposed by the supporters of business in chapter 3 about how it relates to household management, namely that it is either household management or a part of it. Aristotle repeats these opinions here but with the further qualification that business could be an assistant, as providing either tools or material (and so, if a part, perhaps only by way of being an assistant in one of these ways). Of these possibilities, that the science of household management is the same as business, or that business exhausts the whole of household management, is quickly dismissed since it belongs to business to provide and to the science of household management to use, and providing and using are not the same thing. But if providing is not the same as using, perhaps providing falls somehow under using as a part of it. So Aristotle poses the question whether providing and business are part of using and the science of household management or a kind different from it. He puts the question in this way, no doubt, because what typically goes under the name of business is indeed a different kind (as he shows in the next chapter).

~ THE SCIENCE OF PROPERTY AND HOUSEHOLD MANAGEMENT

1256a15   Aristotle begins by laying down that if it belongs to the businessman to study where commodities and property will come from, and if property contains many parts, then the first thing to do is to ask about these parts, and whether the provision of any of them is part of business or a class different from it (for the method now being followed is that of dividing a whole into its parts). One should naturally begin, therefore, with the first and most necessary part of property, namely food and the care and property of food (clothing and shelter are also necessary, of course, but in milder climates one can survive without them, whereas without food no one can survive). The reason Aristotle begins his discussion thus is because he is going to propound the following argument: that if (1) the concern with food (or the care and property of food) is part of business, and if (2) this concern is part of the science of household management, then it will follow (3) that business, at least as regards this concern (and anything else of like necessity), is part of the science of household management. At all events Aristotle first argues for premise (2) in this chapter, then for premise (1) in the next, and finally draws the conclusion (3) in chapter 10.

Premise (1) is actually the more controversial of the premises in this argument. For what is standardly meant by business is not concerned with food and other necessities but with money. It is important, therefore, for Aristotle to raise the question whether the concern with food is part of business or is of some other class in order to bring this fact to light, that there are two kinds of business and not, as most people suppose, one only. For the business concerned with food is indeed of a different class from the business concerned with money.[61]

1256a19   It has already been shown before (1.4.1253b23–27) that the concern with property (of which food is a part) does belong to household management. But this was shown only in passing and with a view to the question of slavery. Here it is taken up in detail and on its own account. Aristotle first shows that food is given by nature and then, from this, that the concern with food belongs to the science of household management.

Food itself, however, is of several kinds so again, following the method of dividing a whole into its parts, Aristotle takes these parts and shows that they are all given by nature. The proof is an appeal to two sets of empirical facts, the first about the ways of life that animals and humans naturally pursue, and the second about how they naturally produce food for their young.[62] For food is necessary for life and so, to take the first set of empirical facts, one can readily observe how the different kinds of food have led to a differentiation in the ways of life of the animals and humans who live by eating these kinds. Thus some animals eat crops and plants, others the flesh of animals, and others everything, and nature has divided them into herding animals or into animals that live scattered about as the getting of their respective food requires. She has divided them further among themselves too according to the different tastes and pleasures she has given them (some herbivores naturally enjoy this sort of plant, for instance, and others others).

1256a29   The same is true of humans who also have different ways of life for the same natural reasons. So some live from tame animals, others hunt wild

61. Saunders (1995: 84) and others want to alter the text at this point (1256a17–18) and, instead of "whether the science of farming . . . is a part of *business*," want to read "whether the science of farming . . . is a part of *(the science of) household management*." But not only does this alteration have no warrant in the manuscripts, it also disrupts the neat structure of Aristotle's argument as this is developed through the next three chapters. We should, therefore, leave the text the way it is.

62. I take the argument here to be a relatively straightforward appeal to manifest observable facts; see Miller (1995: 317–18).

ones, others farm. That some also live as pirates may seem strange to mention in this context, but attacking other humans, to take their food and make them slaves, is evidently a sort of hunting and a hunting too for the necessities of life. So if it is done by better humans against worse, it is presumably no more reprehensible, and no less natural, than humans hunting wild animals (which is also the better hunting the worse). At any rate, such are the human ways of life, or those which rely on getting necessities from what is spontaneously grown and do not engage in trade further afield. They are the three hunting kinds (piracy, hunting of animals and birds, fishing), and the two farming kinds (nomadic pasturing of animals and farming of crops). Any deficiencies are made up from mixing one or more such ways according to the pleasures of the humans involved.[63] But in every case these ways, as with animals, are determined by the natural need for food.

1256b7   It already follows from these examples that such property has been given to animals and humans by nature (for it has manifestly been given to satisfy the needs they have by nature). But it also follows that nature has given this property to grown animals in the same way as she gave similar property to animals at generation's very beginning. For one can readily observe, to take the second set of empirical facts, how nature makes animals produce, along with their offspring, other material for food to sustain them (as milk, for instance); and manifestly such material has been given by nature as property for these offspring. The examples from what happens at generation that Aristotle mentions make it very clear, if the earlier examples did not, that what things need for their sustenance exists by nature for that purpose, or that nature has made plants for the sake of animals and animals for the sake of humans.[64]

---

63. Because piracy is here put on a par with hunting animals, Davis (1989: 35–36) suggests that Aristotle is hinting at the fact that some pirates hunt human beings so as to eat them, and not just so as to get them as slaves. Aristotle, of course, was not ignorant that some pirates were cannibals (5(8).4: 1338b19–24), but since this fact plays no role at all in the argument he actually gives about the naturalness of property and business (Davis only manages to make it play a role by a series of misinterpretations), it is highly unlikely that he is hinting at it here. Besides if one wants to look for oblique arguments in Aristotle's writing about property, it is not in cannibalism that one should look but rather in business. Cannibals may indeed live on what is not by nature human food (4(7).2.1324b39–41), but at least they want to live on something that is really edible. They are not so irrational nor so blind to nature as businessmen, who would, if they could, live on something that is not edible at all, namely gold (1.9.1257b14–17). The absurdity of business, not the depravity of cannibalism, is Aristotle's theme.

64. Of course, sometimes animals eat human beings and from this it would follow that humans are, or can be, for the sake of animals as well as the other way round. One could block this inference, however, by noting that the worse is for the sake of the better and that animals are worse than humans; see 4(7).14.1333a21–24 and Miller (1995: 318). On the other hand there is no necessity for Aristotle altogether to reject the inference, for it might well hold in particular cases. If a hungry lion, for instance, comes across a human being whom it can overcome and eat, then there seems no reason to deny that, here at any rate, the human being naturally belongs to the lion. But this case is obviously

The conclusion is, then, that nature has made all these things for the sake of human beings. At least this conclusion must follow if nature makes nothing incomplete and in vain. For if so she could not have made humans and failed to make for them what they needed to live, since that would indeed be to make them incomplete and in vain as it would be to make them only so that they perished at once. This conclusion, however, does not entail that plants and animals only exist for the sake of humans. They could, as far as this argument goes, still exist for their own sake too. But they must exist for the sake of humans to the extent that humans need them to live (though only to this extent, and not also for purposes, say, of greed or vice).[65] The conclusion does, however, entail that the art of war will by nature be an art or science of property, namely the war that is a hunting of wild animals and natural slaves. For if these exist by nature for human beings, then it must be natural and just to do what is necessary to capture them when they resist (that they are unwilling is irrelevant from the point of view of justice; what counts is what they are by nature). Otherwise, by giving these things to us but not the means of getting them, nature would certainly have done something in vain (this argument confirms, therefore, the naturalness of the hunting ways of life mentioned earlier, including piracy against natural slaves).

1256b26   It now follows from the above that one kind of the science of property is naturally part of the science of household management, namely the kind that is concerned with things necessary for life and useful for the community of city or household. For this sort of property has just been shown to belong by nature to human beings to satisfy their needs, and since human beings naturally form the community of the household for this purpose (1.2.1252b12–15), such property must naturally belong to the household. Accordingly the science of such property must, by the same token, naturally belong to the science of household management (how it belongs, or in what way it is a part, is left for precise determination to chapter 10). Aristotle mentions the city again because the household is for the sake of the city, and the supply of necessities must be sufficient for good life and not just for life.

exceptional because nature has given human beings the intelligence to overcome and use for their needs all other creatures put together. So the normal or general case will be that the other animals are by nature for human beings and not vice versa, and that seems enough for Aristotle's purpose.

65. Contra the egregious misinterpretation of Mansfield (1989: 31, 304 n8), who supposes that, because nature has made these things for our sake, Aristotle is insinuating that, as far as this aspect of nature goes, it might be natural for us to acquire property without limit. But if this inference follows according to some understandings of nature (as Locke's perhaps), it certainly does not follow according to Aristotle's. For the truth is, as Aristotle shows in the next lines, that nature made these things for us in the sense of for our self-sufficiency and not our superfluity, that is, for our perfection in living virtuously and not for our perversion in living viciously. On the basis, however, of this misinterpretation (and others), Mansfield argues that Aristotle does not after all have the teleological understanding of nature that he is alleged to have. But this attempt to read between the lines, as it were, is just a failure to read the lines.

From this conclusion it will also now follow that business is part of the science of household management, at least to the extent that business is the same as this kind of science of property. So Aristotle turns next to consider this question. First, however, he draws another conclusion that is necessary for the argument he is about to give, namely the conclusion that true wealth is made up of the property just discussed (crops and animals and natural slaves). The argument is: (1) a self-sufficiency of this sort of property with a view to good life is not unlimited but has a limit; (2) true wealth is property that has a limit; (3) therefore true wealth is made up of this sort of property. Premise (2) is proved shortly. Premise (1) seems obvious, for no one needs to possess an unlimited amount of food and clothes and slaves in order to live well (all that anyone needs is sufficient now and sources from which sufficient can be got later as and when required). But to make the argument formally valid, one has to supply the further premise that there is no other property that has a limit (for otherwise this other property could be true wealth instead). Aristotle is presumably taking this premise for granted for the only other thing that could be property is money and, as is shown shortly (and as is insinuated by the quotation from Solon), property in the form of money has no limit.

Premise (2) is proved thus: (4) no tool of any art is unlimited or without limit in either quantity or size (there always comes a point where anything more or larger is simply useless for the purposes of the art); (5) true wealth consists in a multitude of tools for certain arts, the arts of ruling household and city; (6) therefore true wealth consists in a multitude of tools whose quantity and size is not unlimited. So, since property is by definition such tools (1.4.1253b30–32), true wealth is property that is not unlimited, or is property that has a limit.

Chapter 9

~ THE TWO KINDS OF BUSINESS

~ THE SCIENCE OF PROPERTY AND EXCHANGE

1256b40   The problem with business, and what makes it impossible at once to conclude that business is part of the science of household management, is that there is another class of science of property which is above all called or identified with business and which it is just to call business. This other science cannot be the same as the science just discussed, for the wealth of this other science is indeed unlimited. It is just to call it business, perhaps, because it is above all about money, and the name "business," *chrēmatistikē*, points to *chrēmata*, money and the commodities whose worth is measured in money. It is above all so called because it is the only kind that most people speak about as business and which they also suppose, because of the closeness between the two, to be the same as the kind just discussed (which also helps explain why they identify business with household management, 1.3.1253b12–13). How the two sciences are close Aristotle explains later. Here he notes one particular difference between them (in addition to the difference about the wealth having no limit), namely that the first exists by nature whereas the second does not but rather comes about through a certain sort of experience and art.

This last remark may cause some puzzlement since it seems clear that the first kind of the science of property needs experience and art too (hunting, fishing, and farming certainly do).[66] But the stress must be on the words "comes about" (*ginetai*, 1257a5). The first kind only needs art and experience for aid and improvement, not for coming about in the first place, since the things it deals with exist by nature without art. The second kind, however, is not merely aided by art; it comes about by art. For it consists in what humans invent, namely money. Money does not exist by nature as plants and animals do, so the science of property in money could not come about by nature either, but only after humans, as a result of experience and by means of art, had invented money.[67] To understand business, therefore, requires first an understanding of money, and an understanding of money requires first an understanding of exchange (for money is invented for exchange).

1257a5 Exchange has two features: it is a use of the thing as such but it is not the proper use of the thing. So the proper use of a shoe, for instance, is to wear it, and to exchange is not to wear. Nevertheless when a shoe is exchanged for food, or money, the parties to the exchange are both using the shoe as a shoe. For they are both exchanging it as something for wearing: the buyer wants shoes to wear and the seller sells them as things for the buyer to wear. Thus the shoe enters the exchange because, and insofar as, it is a shoe (whereas to use a shoe, say, to measure things would be to use it, not as a shoe, but as something possessing length).[68] But exchange is not hereby shown to be unnatural,[69] only to be subordinate to, and dependent on, something else. Since exchange uses the shoe as a shoe, it presupposes the proper use of a shoe and makes no sense, and has no point, without it (a shoe that cannot be worn as a shoe cannot be exchanged as a shoe). Exchange is parasitic on use.

---

66. Several of the speculations of Ambler, or shall we say his readings between the lines (1984), turn on this puzzle, as do some of the difficulties raised by Saunders (1995: 91).

67. As is noted by St. Thomas Aquinas (1951: 1.7.111) and by Schütrumpf (1991: 1:326). That analyzing a whole into its parts turns out here to prove the unnaturalness of business, whereas earlier (1.2) it proved the naturalness of the city, is not indicative of any rhetorical indirection or oblique reservations in Aristotle's mind about the method, as Ambler speculates (1984). It rather indicates the method's excellence: to find out the truth about something one does not want a method that will always give the same result no matter what the differences are in the things investigated.

68. As Newman (2:181) notes with reference to *Eudemian Ethics* 3.4.1231b38–1232a4.

69. Contra Davis (1989: 46), Meikle, in Keyt and Miller (1991: 165), and Schütrumpf (1991: 1:327).

What is thus true of shoes is true of all property, for all of it can be used in exchange in the same way. But while this double use of things renders the art of exchange possible, what makes this art actual (and in accord with nature too) is the natural fact that the things needed for life are not evenly distributed. One person, for instance, has too much of one thing and too little of another, while a second has too little of the first and too much of the second. So to make up for their respective lacks and to achieve a balance of self-sufficiency on both sides, they exchange their surpluses with each other. This sort of exchange, therefore, and the art of trading that is concerned with such exchange, cannot belong by nature to business, for by nature it is limited to getting a sufficiency, and a sufficiency moreover in natural wealth (the crops or animals that someone else has and which he exchanges with you for some of the crops and animals that you have). But none of this is true of business.[70]

Such indeed is what Aristotle immediately goes on to explain. For he says that there is no need of exchange in the household, where everyone was sharing everything in common; there would only be need of it, and it would only arise, when people in different households were sharing things from other households as well, and so when they needed to exchange such things with each other, as wine for grain and grain for wine, in the way that the barbarian nations still do. But such exchange evidently only goes as far as required for sufficiency in the goods exchanged, and no further. Hence the art of exchange is neither against nature, since it is for the sake of natural self-sufficiency (a sufficiency in natural wealth), nor, by the same token, is it any kind of business.

THE EMERGENCE FROM EXCHANGE OF ANOTHER KIND OF BUSINESS

1257a30   It is from this art of exchange, however, that business as especially so called arose. The process begins from the fact that the sort of exchange so far

---

70. Such is what the Greek must mean when translated literally as it stands: "Hence it is clear that the art of trading does not by nature belong to business" (1257a17–18). But some think Aristotle is here intending to condemn trade as unnatural (for he appears to do that later), so they either take the term "business" to be meant in the sense of the science of property discussed in the previous chapter, or emend the Greek to read "science of property." They then translate Aristotle as saying that trade does not by nature belong to such science of property, or that the trading part of such science is not by nature. They then understand the next clause ("for people needed to practice exchange only so far as was sufficient for them," 1257a18–19) as meaning that otherwise (that is, if trading did by nature belong to such science of property or if it was by nature) trade would have been for what was sufficient, and not, as it is, for increase without limit: so the interpretations of Barker (1946: 23), Newman (2:181–82), Schütrumpf (1991: 1:328), Sinclair/Saunders (1981: 82), Saunders (1995: 13), Susemihl and Hicks (1894: 180), but not of Lord (1984: 46). There is, however, no need to adopt his interpretation or to emend the Greek. For the exchange Aristotle has just mentioned is surely a kind of trading, indeed the first and natural kind, and what he condemns later is not trade simply but trade for gain and not for sufficiency.

discussed is direct barter. But direct barter may not always be possible and while someone needs your surplus wine, you may have no need of his surplus grain. Instead your need is for fish and the one who has surplus fish has need of the other's grain but not of your wine. To get the fish, therefore, you will first have to carry your wine to the one who has grain, then carry the grain to the one who has fish, and then carry the fish back home (or the series of exchanges may be longer and more complex). It would be more convenient if, instead of grain, you received something more portable but which everyone would find useful for some need of life, as the various metals, and having thus received an amount of such metal for your wine, then took it and exchanged it for fish, and if the one who had the fish then took the metal in turn and exchanged it for grain. Metal of this sort would be all the more necessary if there was a gap in time to overcome, say if you had need of grain now but the other only had need of wine later, and also if you and he were foreign to each other and not bound by any ties of trust. For the metal would serve as a pledge that as he took so much of it for grain earlier, you will take so much of it back for wine later (*Ethics* 5.5.1133b10–13).

Such is the origin of money, which, while made of something useful, nevertheless only exists as money by agreement or convention. So, by convention too, the metal later gets stamped with marks indicating the amount to avoid the need for repeated weighing. But money as so understood evidently exists to facilitate the exchange, which itself exists only to fill up natural self-sufficiency (it is all about people getting, through exchange, the useful things they need). So money cannot, as such, be against nature any more than the exchange which it facilitates can be. But once money was in existence or had been provided, there arose from the necessary exchange just mentioned the other kind of business, the trading kind.[71] This would arise, no doubt, from people noticing that whereas the exchange of wine for grain left both sides with the sufficiency they wanted and no more, the exchange of money for wine, wine for grain, and grain for money, and so forth, would, as often as not, produce an increase in the money itself. So since, in addition, money is exchangeable for all other property, the increase in money would seem to be an increase in one's property. Thus one would think that mere exchange was a way of acquiring property. Thus exchange, or trade generally, would become an art, not of getting a natural sufficiency of useful and necessary things, but of increasing money, or the monetary value of useful

71. Lord (1984: 47) takes the "from necessary exchange" as going with "once money had been provided" to mean that once money had been provided from necessary exchange then the other form of business arose (1257a41–b2). But it is better to take it as I do here and in the translation: "So once money had been provided, there arose from necessary exchange the other kind of business, the trading kind." For, as Schütrumpf (1991: 1:335) correctly remarks, the point of Aristotle's argument is to explain how the other form of business came to be *from* natural exchange; see also Barker (1946: 25), Sinclair/ Saunders (1981: 83), and Saunders (1995: 13).

and necessary things (commodities), simply through the activity of exchanging such things.

1257b5　This art is the other kind of the science of property mentioned at the beginning of the chapter and which is above all called business. It is because this kind seems to be productive of commodities or monetary values, and because it and the trading it engages in are about money, that people come to have the opinions about business and wealth that they do. So they suppose that business is about money, that its work is to study where a multitude of commodities or monetary values will come from, and that wealth is money.

Such at any rate is what appears to be the case from considering this kind of business. On the other hand there is a counter-consideration that shows these appearances cannot be simply correct, namely that at other times money seems to be a nonsense and altogether a thing of law or convention. For money is useful by convention, and if the convention changes, it cannot be used for the necessities of life, and in particular not for that first of necessities, food. But it is absurd to call that wealth which one can have lots of and still, like Midas, starve to death (for even if true wealth also includes clothing and shelter, and even if money, as made of something useful, can have a worth independently of being money,[72] money qua money is useless for exchange if the convention changes and, in any event, cannot of itself sustain life).

1257b17　This counter-consideration, therefore, rightly drives people to seek a different definition of wealth and of business (just as some of the proponents of slavery were earlier driven back to another definition of the slave, 1.6.1255a28–32). For there is such another definition, namely the one given in the preceding chapter. So Aristotle returns now to this definition and shows how the two kinds or definitions of wealth and business differ and how together they explain the conflicting opinions and appearances about business.

Thus, first, the earlier and natural kind of business is proper to household management (it is concerned with providing the property needed for life in household and city), but this other kind is proper to trading and is not productive of commodities in any way except by exchange of commodities (the monetary value of useful things might, of course, increase through mere exchange, but the quantity of useful things available for exchange clearly would not). Second, the other kind of business is or seems to be about money (and not, like the first, about food and other necessities), for money is everything to it, being not only the element but also the limit of the exchange (in the first kind money can be an element, or a medium of exchange, but not the limit, which is natural sufficiency). Third, the wealth of this other kind is without limit, whereas that of the first is not. The proof is: (1) all arts are without limit with respect to their end and only have a limit with

72. These qualifications are noted by Newman (2:188).

respect to what is for the sake of the end; (2) business is an art; (3) therefore business is without limit with respect to its end; (4) the end of business is the sort of wealth just mentioned (that is, money) or property in commodities (that is, monetary values); (5) therefore business is without limit with respect to such wealth (money, as being the end, *is* a limit for business but does not itself *have* a limit). Premise (1) is shown in particular from the medical art, which, as such, aims at making all as healthy as possible for as long as possible. But what it uses for this end, drugs and surgery, it manifestly limits in view of the end. True wealth, by contrast, or the wealth of the first kind of business, does have a limit, as was shown before (1.8.1256b30–37). For it is not an independent art but part of the science of household management. Premise (4) does not therefore hold of this kind, for its end is not wealth but good life, and the wealth it gets is for the sake of this end (its wealth is a multitude of tools sufficient *for* or *with a view to* good life, 1.8.1256b31–32). So it has a limit with respect to its wealth, though none, of course, with respect to the end of good life, which, as part of the science of household management, it has as its proper work.[73]

1257b32   Thus there are two kinds of business which are very different from each other. Nevertheless they are close, as Aristotle remarked earlier, and this closeness explains the fact that, though wealth has a limit, those engaged in business are seen to pursue wealth as if it had no limit. For the two uses of business

73. Locke and Marx, perhaps the two most important influences in contemporary thought on business and wealth, give very different analyses. Locke says that the acquisition of property is naturally limited to that amount which one can consume before it spoils (and where there is enough and as good left for others). Locke therefore differs from Aristotle in not locating the natural limit to property in the end it serves (good life in household and city), but in its material character as corruptible. Any material commodity might be accumulated without limit provided it did not spoil, or at least not very quickly (like nuts, perhaps). Money, which as gold or silver (or even as figures in a bank account) does not spoil, is merely a special case of the same thing (*Second Treatise of Government*, chap. 5, "Of Property"). Marx locates the unlimited accumulation of money in its transformation from a means of exchange into the end of exchange. The cycle c-m-c (commodity exchanged for money exchanged for commodity) is replaced by the cycle m-c-m (money exchanged for commodity exchanged for money). But Marx's objection to this latter cycle is not so much that money is made the end as that the money acquired from exchange is only greater because of the exploitation it involves of the labor of workers (*Capital* 1, parts 1 and 3). Aristotle would hardly object to such "exploitation," since he thinks the use of the labor of natural slaves by natural masters for their own benefit is just. Nor is his objection directed, as such, at the change from the cycle c-m-c to the cycle m-c-m. What he objects to is the making of business into an art that is independent of household management and has wealth, whether in the form of money or commodities, as its end. He would, therefore, object to the cycle c-m-c if this belonged to an independent art, and would not object to the cycle m-c-m if this did not belong to an independent art. What is important is that the end should not be wealth, or that there should be no art or science of property save the one that is proper to the science of household management; see the excellent article by Mansfield (1980–81), and contrast Meikle (1994, 1995) and in Keyt and Miller (1991: 156–81), whose Marxist misreadings of Aristotle are nicely exposed by Natali (1996).

(either for sufficiency or for increase), being of the same thing, overlap or coincide.[74] They are both uses of the same thing, because they are both uses of property, and these uses overlap, because the property has the same use in both cases,[75] that is, both uses are uses of property in exchange. But they are nevertheless different uses, or they are not both uses of property in the same respect, because their ends are different. The exchange is part of the pursuit of natural sufficiency in the one case and is aimed at sheer increase in the other. Hence, because of the sameness of use, those engaged in business confuse the one kind with the other and suppose that the work of the science of household management is increase and that such increase in money is what they should be aiming at. In other, and more modern, words, they think that the work of "economics" (which is what *oikonomikē*, the Greek for the science of household management, is when transliterated) is monetary profit, whereas it is not. Rather its work is to provide a sufficiency of means, and no further, for the sake of a noble life in household and city.

⮜ REASON FOR ITS EMERGENCE

1257b40   But while the closeness between the two forms explains the possibility of confusing them, it does not explain why those engaged in business actually confuse them in the way they do.[76] For it does not explain why they are disposed to pursue the end of increase instead of the end of natural sufficiency. The reason lies instead in themselves, that they are serious about living but not about living well, and so since their desire for living is infinite or unlimited, they also desire an unlimited amount of the things and the wealth that produce it; or, if they apply themselves to living well, they seek this life in bodily enjoyments, and as these seem to exist in property and wealth, the same thing happens. It is their love, therefore, of excess that makes them pursue wealth to excess and hence that concretely gives rise to the second kind of business. This love of excess is, moreover, corrosive in its effects. For if excess cannot be got from business, people try to get it from other things, as courage or generalship or medicine, which are thus all perverted from their natural end and made into businesses or into instruments of making money. For in practical matters everything answers to the end, and so to suppose money-making is the end is to suppose that everything must serve the making of money.

1258a14   The two kinds of business have thus been separated out and distinguished from each other. The first kind, analyzed in the previous chapter, is the

---

74. I read *hekatera* with the manuscripts (not *hekateras* with Dreizehnter) and take it with *chrēsis*: "the two uses of business, being of the same thing, overlap" (1257b35–36). If *hekateras* is read it will have to go with *chrēmatistikēs* and the meaning will be "the use of the two kinds of business."

75. I translate "property has the same use in both cases" (1257b36–37) because I read *chrēseōs ktēsis* (property "has the same use") with the manuscripts and not *ktēseōs chrēsis* ("the use is of the same" property) with Dreizehnter.

76. A point correctly noted by Schütrumpf (1991: 1:330–31).

necessary kind, the kind that is by nature proper to household management, is concerned with food (and suchlike necessities), and is limited. The other kind, analyzed in this chapter, is the unnecessary kind and has the opposite characteristics: it is not proper to household management (but is an independent art), is not concerned with food (but rather with money), and is unlimited. Because it is unnecessary, it is not a kind that we are, strictly speaking, in need of. But a reason could make us in need of it, namely the reason that we care more about life or bodily pleasure than about living well and nobly.

Chapter 10

~ BUSINESS AS PART OF HOUSEHOLD MANAGEMENT

1258a19 Now that the two kinds of business have been distinguished and explained, the answer to the question raised at the beginning (1.8.1256a13–14), and which the present discussion was undertaken to answer, namely whether business belongs to household management as a part of it, can now be made clear. For it has already been implied in the argument just given that the business proper to household management is such a part, whereas the business proper to trading is not. But this conclusion needs to be properly stated, particularly in view of the possibility that even business in the first sense might only be an assistant to household management. At any rate, in what follows Aristotle first poses the question, then gives considerations to show that business is not a part, and finally concludes that it is, nevertheless, in some sense a part. The question then, as posed, is whether business belongs to the household manager and politician (that is, as part of their work), or whether it does not but instead property and food must be to hand as already provided by nature, either land or sea—in the same way that nature, not political science, has to produce human beings, whom political science then takes from nature to use to make virtuous—and whether all that the household manager then has to do is to take what nature has thus given and dispose it properly (for the sustenance of life in household and city).

The considerations that the latter alternative is true, and that business, or the provision of property, is not a part of household management, are two analogies. The first is that it does not belong to the weaving art to make the wool (rather nature does that through providing sheep), but instead to take the wool thus provided and to use it for weaving, discriminating at the same time between which sort of wool is serviceable and fitting for this purpose and which poor and unfitting. So, likewise, it must belong to household management to use property and not also to make or provide it (cf. 1.8.1256a10–13). The second analogy is taken from medicine, and argues that if one says business is a part of household management, then one will have to say that medicine is a part as well, for those in the household must be healthy, which medicine provides, just as they must live or do anything else that is necessary (be clothed, housed, and so forth), which business provides. But medicine is not part of household management, so neither, therefore, can business be.

The answer to these analogies is that in a sense they are right and in a sense wrong. For, with respect to medicine in particular, it is in one way the concern of the household manager and the ruler to see about health, while in another way this concern is not theirs but the doctor's. It cannot, for instance, be the concern of the household manager or the political ruler to study health; that is what doctors do, and the household manager and the ruler are not, as such, doctors. But it must be the concern of the household manager and the ruler to see to it that what doctors say is necessary for health is in fact carried out (as, for instance, to see to it that there is an adequate and pure water supply, that there is protection from winds and heat and so forth, 4(7).11.1330a36–b17).[77] So also, while it cannot be the household manager's concern to study where and how to get property, it must be his concern to ensure that the recommendations of businessmen, whose concern is that study, are carried out so that the needs of the household and city are properly met. The study of business itself, however, will not be his concern, as neither will the study of medicine. These will instead be assistants to his concern (business, of course, being an assistant by way of providing tools, for property is tools).

1258a34   The property that the household manager needs, and which he also needs the assistance of business to help him secure, is provided in the first place, as was said before (in chapter 8), by nature (for that is nature's work). Hence by nature business is the study of how to get such property from the crops and animals provided by nature for the purpose. But there is, as was also said before (in chapter 9), another kind of business different from this one, the kind that gets property from trading alone. It is, of course, the first kind that belongs to household management. For this is the kind that studies how to get the property from nature that household management requires. It is the necessary kind and therewith also the praiseworthy kind. The other kind is, by contrast, blameworthy, since it is not according to nature but is a taking from each other; that is to say, instead of adding to the store of necessities by taking from nature (where such necessities are alone to be found), it simply adds to the pile of money by taking from the other people in the exchange. For since it does not produce anything, it can only get its increase from the exchange itself, that is, from the other exchangers.

---

77. A point noted by St. Thomas Aquinas (1951: 1.8.132). We ourselves nowadays expect politicians to pay much attention to the recommendations of environmentalists about keeping the earth fit for human habitation, and indeed to carry out these recommendations as they judge necessary for the good of the whole. But we do not entrust the job of environmentalists to politicians nor the job of politicians to environmentalists.

Hence, if making profit out of other people through trade is not according to nature and is blameworthy, usury must be even more so, and be most reasonably hated as a result. For trade at least makes its money by exchanging money for commodities or natural goods (which is the point of money). But usury does not even do that; it bypasses commodities altogether and makes its money directly out of money. It is, as it were, twice removed from nature and accordingly a practice that is most contrary to nature.[78]

Chapter 11

~ THE PRACTICE OF BUSINESS

1258b9 This chapter begins rather abruptly with its distinction between knowledge and use, and is peculiar for other reasons too. For it divides business differently (adding a third between the original two), and it seems to counsel some activities just condemned as blameworthy and hateful. Hence some commentators are tempted to regard the chapter as spurious.[79]

But the distinction between knowledge and use has, in a way, been prepared by the preceding chapter. For if business belongs to household management in the sense that the household manager must see to the carrying out of what business recommends (according as the needs of household and city require), then the use or practice of business, and not just the knowledge of the nature and function of business, must belong to household management too. Consequently, since the present question is business and its relation to household management, some discussion of the use or practice of business is appropriate enough. In addition,

78. Aristotle's strictures against usury may read oddly to our modern ears, as they do to Jowett's (1885: 2:34), when charging interest on loans is so much a fact of life and when without it our current manner of living would be well nigh impossible. But that would only show how uncompromising Aristotle's critique is, that if our political community requires usury to survive, it must be unnatural—a thought which is perhaps not so alien as one might think, since it gets reflected in a way in the debate between Jeffersonians and Hamiltonians; see Rahe (1992: 651–725). On the other hand, one should note that Aristotle's argument does not, as such, condemn money, or trade, or even the accumulation of money. What it condemns is the belief that money is wealth (when in fact only goods from nature can be such), that trade is a means of producing wealth (when in fact it produces nothing but only exchanges), and that accumulating money is limitless, or that there is no end to how much money is necessary or useful (when in fact money is only needed as far as exchange for natural sufficiency requires). One should also note that there must be a distinction, even for Aristotle, between lending money at interest and investing money, or at least investing money in a venture acquiring goods from nature. For in the latter case the increase that results is an increase taken from nature and not, like usury, from other people. Provided that such investment was for the sake of natural self-sufficiency, it could itself be natural and praiseworthy.

79. As Barker (1946: 29 n3) and Lord (1984: 17, 246 n45). Newman (2:196–98) and Schütrumpf (1991: 1:354–55) argue the contrary.

making a division now, and not earlier, of business into a further third kind is also appropriate, because this third kind was not needed for understanding the nature of business. It makes a difference, however, to the use of business. Finally, though this discussion of the use of business does include some practices that are unnatural, it is far from clear that Aristotle recommends them, or recommends them for every city. Some cities indeed, namely those with the deviant regimes of tyranny, democracy, and oligarchy, may well have need of such unnatural practices, for they have an unnatural end, and the legislator who is called upon to legislate for a deviant regime cannot afford to be ignorant of what deviant regimes need.[80] The best regime, however, will not have need of, or indulge in, anything unnatural (4(7).6.1327a25–31), though knowledge of what is unnatural will be useful to it nevertheless, for purposes of avoidance.

Having thus drawn a distinction between the knowledge of business and its use, Aristotle draws a similar distinction within use itself, between study of such things, which has something liberal about it, and actual experience in them, which belongs to necessity. What he seems to mean (judging by what he says later at 1258b33–39) is that it becomes rulers of household and city, who are free men, to devote some study to the use and practice of business but it does not become them actually to engage in it.[81] So while they must listen enough to businessmen to know what sources of property may be available for supplying natural needs, they do not have to acquire the detailed experience that comes from actually engaging in business. This belongs rather to those who labor under necessity and do not enjoy the leisured virtue of citizens (4(7).9.1328b33–1329a2). Accordingly Aristotle confines himself in this chapter to saying enough about the several kinds of business, and their relative profitability and worth, so that rulers will be able to judge between them correctly and to command only those that are needed or suitable.

1258b12   His first division, as is fitting, is of business in its most proper sense, that is, of the first and natural kind of business, the kind that studies how to get necessities directly from nature. Not surprisingly, therefore, his division follows the kinds of crops and animals that are the objects of the ways of life listed in chapter 8 (nomads, farmers, hunters, fishermen). The main difference is that now, given his present intention, he notes also the ways in which the profitability of these objects may vary and what needs to be known if one is to get the best out of each.

1258b21   The second division is of the other kind of business, the kind that is exchange. The main part of this kind of business is mercantile activity and involves

---

80. A point rightly made by Newman (2:197).

81. Or, as Jowett puts it (1885: 2:34): "a gentleman may study political economy, but he must not keep a shop." Jowett also suggests that the meaning could instead be that study or speculation is free (in the sense that thinking can go as far and wherever it wants), while practice is bound by the circumstances (in the sense that one can only actually do what the necessities of the case allow).

the three tasks of provisioning a merchant ship, carrying the goods or merchandise (whether by sea or land), and then putting them up for sale at the place of destination. Here too Aristotle notes the relative difference between them with respect to risks and profits. The second part of the business that is exchange is lending at interest, and the third part is wage labor, skilled or unskilled (the second exchanges money for money and the third labor for money). Trade for monetary profit and interest have already been declared unnatural and wage labor is implied to be so later (because it is separated out from the natural slavery where such labor properly belongs, 1.13.1260a39–b2). Such things would not, therefore, exist in the best regime (where trade and money would be for necessities only, and laborers would be slaves, 4(7).6.1327a25–31, 10.1330a25–31); but they might have to exist in others.

1258b27   The third division is of a third kind of business intermediate between the first two. It is, on the one hand, like the kind according to nature in getting useful things from the earth, while, on the other hand, these useful things are, like the money of the second kind, "unfruitful," that is, they are not immediately useful in the way crops and animals are.[82] Timber and metals, for instance, have first to undergo much working (sawing, smelting, and the like) before they are ready for use, and even then have first to be crafted by the artisan (into beds, pots, swords) before something that will count as property, or tools for household management, is produced. This kind of business is presumably not unnatural, since it is a getting of things from nature, even if it is at several removes from immediate utilities.

1258b33   Such is a general division and account of the kinds of business. But since, as was already indicated at the beginning of the chapter, dwelling further on them would be crude and unbecoming a free man, Aristotle contents himself, following his practical intention, with pointing out the relative worth of the several kinds of work involved and with indicating, to anyone who might have the care (as businessmen themselves, and some rulers of household and city), where to get the necessary further information. As regards the worth of these several kinds of work, however, what he notes is their moral, not economic, worth. He is keeping in mind, no doubt, that in deciding what kinds of work to have, and who is to do them, household and political rulers must have an eye on the good life of virtue (5(8).2.1337b4–15). As regards the sources of further information, these are books that already exist and books that could but do not exist, namely the collections of random stories.[83]

1259a6/18   As a contribution to such a collection Aristotle gives two examples, both illustrative of the device of making money from a monopoly. In the famous story of Thales, wisdom may have enabled him to gain his monopoly but it

---

82. As St. Thomas Aquinas notes (1951: 1.9.142).

83. *Oeconomica* 2, attributed to Aristotle but possibly spurious, contains such a collection.

was the reproach, not his wisdom, that moved him to it. The reproach was based on his poverty but it was directed against the value or usefulness of philosophy. Thales was apparently not much disturbed by his poverty, but he was disturbed by the attack on philosophy. He devised his monopoly rather to defend philosophy than to dispel poverty. But at all events, the device is a general one, not peculiar to Thales, as is shown by the fact that some cities and a certain Sicilian have done the same. One may note, however, that in the case of the Sicilian, by contrast with Thales, his name is not given, his device is not attributed to him as a mark of wisdom, and he did not do it for love of philosophy. Indeed, he might seem to have been particularly foolish in doing something that could not but rouse the jealousy of a tyrant like Dionysius.[84]

One might wonder why Aristotle gives two stories, and at some length, about the same business scheme. Perhaps it is to alert the reader to the way of going about collecting such stories, namely that one must extend one's search far and wide since they can be found in diverse places and told for very different reasons. One needs, therefore, to pay attention to general and common business features without being diverted by other facts, and to range disparate stories under the same headings where these features are the same.

1259a33   The cities that need such devices will presumably be those which cannot supply their needs from home, or which, like deviant regimes, put their energy and interest into gain. But it certainly cannot be best that the concern with getting what is needed or with profit (what we now call economics) can come to consume the whole of political activity. Politics is not business (in any sense of business), since the city is for good life, not life alone, and since wealth is the instrument of politics, not its object.

Chapter 12

∼ HUSBAND AND WIFE, FATHER AND CHILD
    1259a37   Of the three parts of household management from chapter 3, Aristotle has dealt only with mastery (the science of property has also been dealt with, of course, but this science is, as science, an assistant rather than a part). What remains is the science of rule over children and over wife. Aristotle first states how these are different, both from each other and from mastery, and then justifies this conclusion. Thus they are different from mastery because they are rule over the free, not over slaves, and they are different from each other because rule over wife is political and over children royal.

In proof Aristotle shows, first, that the man should rule over both and then,

---

84. Whether the younger or older Dionysius is unclear. On the tyrannical practice of getting rid of potential rivals, see 3.14.1284a27–36 and 7(5).11.1313a34–41.

second, that he should rule over both in the different ways stated. So the male should rule the female because he is more fitted for leading than the female, a fact that is again taken as evident to observation, just as it was earlier, but with the same proviso, that the instances observed should be those that accord with nature (1.5.1254a36–39, b13–14). The father should rule the children because the older and complete is more fitted for leading than the younger and incomplete.

1259b4 Second, Aristotle shows that rule by male over female is political and that rule by father over children is royal. He had said earlier that political rule is rule over free and equals (1.7.1255b20), and he is evidently taking for granted here that the female is free and equal (she is certainly no slave, as was shown before, 1.2.1252a34–b5, and, unlike the child, she is an adult equally with the male). At any rate he assumes that rule over female is political in this sense because he passes at once to consider an objection that such an assumption raises, namely why male and female do not alternate in ruling as happens in most cases of political rule. For the political ruler and ruled wish by their nature to stand on equal ground, or to be on an equal footing, and to differ in nothing. The answer is that there is not in fact a total equality and sameness between political rulers and ruled. For the rulers, even though otherwise equal, seek, while ruling, to be different from the ruled, and are in fact so different, in outward form, manner of address, and honors. An illustration is taken from the story of Amasis, who changed the outward form of his golden footpan into that of a god so that the Egyptians then worshiped it; footpan and statue were thus the same stuff but different in outward form. So it is also in the case of the political rule of male over female, save that here these differences are permanent, and the male is always different from the female in outward form, address, and honors (he is bigger and stronger and taller, for instance, and invariably receives the titles and honors of leader).

The evident implication is that alternation in rule, while it may be a particular feature of political rule and a general sign of it, cannot be definitive of it. Indeed this must be the case. For there could in theory, for instance, be alternation in rule between people who exercise mastery over each other. But it would not thereby follow that, just because they alternated in rule, the rule they were exercising was really political instead of despotic. So the fact that the male rules the female permanently need not mean that his rule over her is not political, or not over someone free and equal. But how the female is the male's equal while yet being permanently ruled by him is nicely indicated in the next chapter.

1259b10 That the rule of father over children is royal is shown readily enough by the fact that the begetter is ruler both by virtue of affection and of age, and such rule is a kind of royal rule or kingship (kingship is rule over the willing and by someone surpassingly superior, which a father is to his children, 3.13.1284b25–34). So while all kings need not be the fathers of their subjects, all fathers are kings over their children and all kings may rightly be compared to fathers (as Homer did with Zeus). For they are both different in nature (fathers and kings are vastly superior in virtue) yet the same in family (fathers beget the children they rule and kings come from the people they rule, 3.17.1288a8–9).

The male's rule over the three communities in the household accordingly differs in kind with respect to each. Over the wife it is over someone free and equal; over the child it is over someone free but not equal; over the slave it is over someone neither free nor equal. The kinds of rule, the political, the kingly, and the despotic, are all different, but since one man exercises all of them, not unreasonably did Aristotle say earlier (1.7.1255b19) that the household was ruled monarchically or by a single ruler (which is what *monarchos* literally means).

Chapter 13

~ VIRTUE AS THE OVERALL CONCERN OF
HOUSEHOLD MANAGEMENT

~ VIRTUE IN THE PARTS OF THE HOUSEHOLD
1259b18   Aristotle has thus, in accordance with his intention (1.1.1252a16–23, 3.1253b7–10), expounded all the parts of household management and shown that and how the several sorts of rule differ in kind and not only in numbers of subjects ruled over. His discussion of wives and children is brief in comparison with that of slavery and business, but mainly, as it would seem, because little controversy is raised about them whereas much is raised about the latter two. Certainly the importance of the topics cannot be measured by the space so far given to them. For, having thus discussed each of the parts of the household separately, Aristotle now takes them together and shows how household management sets them into a hierarchically ordered whole, where the concern with property and its virtue or good condition is least, the concern with slaves and their virtue is next least, and the concern with wives and children and their virtue is greatest.

He does not specify the reasons for this conclusion but they are now evident enough: household management is more serious about human beings and their virtue than about property and its virtue, because property is for the sake of human beings; it is more serious about the free and their virtue than about slaves and their virtue, because slaves are for the sake of the free. It is, of course, serious about or concerned with the virtue of all these, that is, with ensuring that they are each in the best condition, because the point of household management is to preserve and perfect the household, which means to preserve and perfect all the parts. The final question about the household, then, in order to complete the analysis of it, is this question about the virtue of the parts and how household management is to secure such virtue.

1259b21   The virtue of property or wealth and how to secure it has in effect already been answered in chapters 8 and 11, namely that such wealth is to be acquired from nature and by using the advice and assistance of businessmen as and where deemed necessary. It has also, in part at least, been answered about slaves in chapter 7, namely that there are sciences they are to be taught. It has not yet been answered about wives and children. So this is what Aristotle turns to next. But there is still something left undecided about slaves, namely whether the only virtues they have are those associated with their bodily forms of assistance (the sciences mentioned in chapter 7), or whether they also have other and more honorable virtues, the moral virtues of moderation, courage, justice, and the like. The puzzles generated by this question lead into similar puzzles about wives and children. So Aristotle first discusses and resolves these puzzles and then turns, in the last part of the chapter, to the question of how the household manager is to secure the relevant virtues in each case.

About the slave and whether he is to have any moral virtues, there are puzzles on both sides. For first, on the one hand, if slaves do have such virtues they would seem not to differ from the free and so not to be slaves after all (for slaves differ from the free as those lacking virtue or nobility of soul from those excelling in it, so to grant them virtue seems to undermine this distinction, 1.5.1254b32–39, 6.1255a39–b2). But second, on the other hand, slaves are also human beings and share in reason (enough to perceive it at any rate, 1.5.1254b22–23), and humans are meant for virtue, and reason is the source of virtue; so to deny slaves virtue seems to deny them humanity.

About wives and children similar puzzles arise and, in fact, about natural ruled and ruler in general (wives and children and slaves are all naturally ruled, though in different ways). For if, on the one hand, the ruled should have the moral virtues too and ruled and rulers together should share the qualities of the complete gentleman (the "nobility and goodness" of the *kalokagathos*), then it would seem that the ruled should not always be ruled, nor the rulers always rule, but that they should alternate with each other (as rulers and ruled alternate in cities governed politically). And one cannot reply to this that they can both have the virtues and still be permanently ruler or permanently ruled because they have the virtues in different degrees, the ruler more so and the ruled less so. For ruling and being ruled differ in kind, not in degree (ruler and ruled have different work—and virtue is relative to the work; *Ethics* 2.6.1106a15–24—for the ruler commands and leads and the ruled obeys and follows; the ruled does not command and lead to a lesser degree). On the other hand, one cannot say either that ruler and ruled do not both need to have virtue but that only one or other of them does. For if the ruler is the one not to have virtue (as the virtues of justice and moderation), he could not do his work, which is to rule nobly, and if the ruled is the one not to have virtue, he could not do his work either, which is to be ruled nobly (cowardice or intemperance would prevent him doing what he should).

1260a2 The preceding dialectical discussion (as is not unusual in Aristotle) itself points toward the answer: ruler and ruled must both have a share in virtue but there must be differences in this virtue, just as there are differences also among those who are by nature ruled (for if the ruled can differ in kind, as free or equal or both or neither, so must their respective habits and characters). Again (as at 1.5.1254a34–b9) the soul furnishes the paradigm, for the soul divides into a naturally ruling and a naturally ruled part and the virtue of each of these is different (as the intellectual virtue of the part that has reason and the moral virtue of the part that does not; *Ethics* 1.13.1103a3–10). What is thus true of the soul by itself will be true of other things too (wherever differences in the soul lead to differences in the things), and so of the natural rulers and ruled now in question. For their natural differences with respect to rule, as Aristotle now proceeds to show, correspond, and follow from, the differences that first exist in their souls.[85]

These differences concern the deliberative part of the soul. For since rule is for the sake of the end and since deliberation determines how to attain the end, it must be by deliberation that the ruler rules and by its lack that the ruled is ruled. Thus while slaves, children, and wives have the parts of the soul (and so are all human), there are differences in how they have them: the slave does not have the element of deliberation at all; the female has it, but it is not in control; the child has it, but it is incomplete. There appears to be a certain oddity in Aristotle's saying that all have the parts of the soul and then denying that the slave has the element of deliberation. But this element must be less a part of the soul than a power within a part of the soul, namely the rational part. The slave has the rational part (he can learn certain kinds of art, for instance, and art belongs to the rational part), but deliberation, in requiring discernment of the end, requires discernment of the noble and good, which the slave does not have.[86] The child, by contrast, does have this power

85. Barker (1946: 35 n1) thinks Aristotle is arguing in a circle here, from the differences between ruled and rulers to differences in the soul back to differences between ruled and rulers. But there are in fact two different arguments proceeding in different directions. The dialectical discussion, which forces the conclusion that the virtues must differ as the rulers and ruled do, proceeds up from the phenomena about rule; the appeal to the soul, which confirms that this conclusion must be correct, proceeds down from the first principle, which is the cause and explanation of the phenomena. Moreover, that slaves, children, and wives differ in soul in the way they do is itself asserted from observation, not deduced from a further first principle.

86. Dobbs (1994: 80–83) argues that this interpretation of how the slave lacks the deliberative element (that the slave lacks it because he lacks discernment of the noble) requires one to translate the Greek as "the slave does not have wholly [*holōs ouk echei*] the element of deliberation [sc. but does have it partially]" and not as "the slave does not have the element of deliberation at all." For if, says Dobbs,

but not in a mature or complete way. He needs proper education to develop it (*Ethics* 10.9).

The female does have a developed or complete power of deliberation and so is, to that extent, the equal of the male. What she lacks is having deliberation along with control. There is some controversy here about what Aristotle means, whether this lack of control is a mere matter of fact (women are not allowed to exercise control in most cities and households), or a matter of nature (the woman does not by nature have this control).[87] But he could hardly mean the former since that would imply that the rule of men over women was conventional and not natural, something he has expressly denied (1.5.1254b13–14). Besides he says this lack of control is a lack in the soul, not a lack merely in concrete political conditions. The sort of lack he means is anyway not hard to conjecture. For women, as constitutionally more subject to bodily functions (the functions associated with generation), and to the passions attendant thereon (what we now speak of as the effect of hormones and the monthly cycle), seem to be less able to impose the results of deliberation on themselves; and, as constitutionally also weaker in body, they often lack the strength, and the will, to impose these results on others.[88] Control must therefore be provided by the male. That is doubtless why the male must rule permanently over her, though he rules her as an equal. For she will only be his equal, having all that he has and in the way that he has it, when her deliberation gets its control from his, that is, only when she is subject to his rule (hence male rule over female is political by way of being aristocratic; *Ethics* 8.10.1160b32–35, 11.1161a22–25).

1260a14   As the souls differ, therefore, so must the virtues of which they are capable. For different souls will not have the same work, and as virtue perfects one with respect to one's work (*Ethics* 2.6.1106a15–24), they must each share virtue according to their work. The ruler then must have complete moral virtue or virtue of character since the work is, simply speaking, his. The ruler possesses deliberation in its fullness and so has the place of reason in the work, directing everything to its proper end like the ruling craftsman. For the ruling craftsman determines the end

---

the slave lacks discernment of the noble but has the capacity for art, then he has one part of deliberation, namely the capacity to work out means to ends, and only lacks the other, namely discernment of the true end. But Aristotle understands deliberation in such a way that not to have discernment of the true end or the noble is not to have deliberation at all; see *Ethics* 6.5.1140a25–31, 8.1141b29–33.

87. See Fortenbaugh, in Barnes (1977: 138), Nichols (1992: 31–32), Saxonhouse (1982: 208–9), Swanson (1992: 53–55).

88. See Fortenbaugh, in Barnes et al. (1977: 138–39). Aristotle may also have in mind that the exclusively female functions of bearing and suckling children belong in the household, not the city, so that the household is the woman's natural place. Consequently rule over the city, and so over the household as the subordinate part of the city, naturally belongs to the man; see Smith (1983: 475–77). For fuller discussion see Bradshaw (1991) and Swanson (1992: chap. 3).

and how best to attain it (which is the work of reason). Those he rules will be his assistants in the work and have the kind of moral virtue or virtue of character appropriate to their manner of assistance. Thus the virtues of the woman, for instance, though having the same names as those of the man, will be specifically different, and his courage will be ruling courage but hers assisting courage, and so on.

1260a24   The truth of this conclusion can be confirmed by considering the virtues one by one, after the manner of Gorgias, and not by speaking, after the manner of Socrates, in general terms only.[89] For while Socrates and others may be right as far as they go in speaking in general terms or aiming for a general definition (for Aristotle himself gives such a general definition too; *Ethics* 2.6.1106b36–1107a8), they deceive themselves in supposing, as a result, that the general definition is sufficient or rules out all differences. For since the soul has different parts and different persons have these parts differently, the general definition cannot in fact mean one and the same thing in every case. What it does mean can only be seen properly when one looks at the particular cases and sees how it differs with respect to each of them. In this regard Gorgias' method, though it omits the general definition, is much better. Evidently, however, both methods should be used if a full account of virtue is to be given (*Ethics* 2.7.1107a28–33).[90]

In imitation of Gorgias' method Aristotle gives an example about virtue in speech, an example that he says applies to everyone (that is, to children and slaves as well), though the quotation he takes from Sophocles ("silence brings adornment to a woman") applies it only to the woman and does not add, as Aristotle immediately does on his own account, that what is thus true of the woman is not true of the man.[91] But that the poet's remark applies to women is evident from what was just said. For while the woman may be as capable as the man of deliberating, she does not have the necessary control. The man, however, does have this control, so he should speak for them both (carrying deliberation into the speech of effective command requires control). Likewise must he also speak for the child and the slave. For the virtues of child and slave are not independent or for their own

---

89. Aristotle is implicitly referring to Plato's *Meno* 71c5–73c5.

90. Note that, contra Jowett (1885: 2:39–40), Aristotle does not simply condemn Socrates, nor does he simply praise Gorgias. He condemns and praises them only in a certain respect.

91. The words from Sophocles are those of a man, Ajax, as quoted by a woman, Tecmessa, which he spoke to her when she tried to dissuade him from a foolish enterprise (*Ajax* 293). Some commentators therefore try to use this fact to argue that Aristotle is really hinting that the opposite of what he expressly says about the inferiority of women might in fact be true; Davis (1989: 44), Nichols (1983: 183–85; 1992: 32–34), Saxonhouse (1982: 208–9). But against this one may note, first, that the saying was a common one (as Tecmessa asserts) and so has no necessary connection with the drama; second, Aristotle deliberately extends its scope and so corrects the poet, not by doubting what he says, but by strengthening it; third, the example is not anyway contrary to Aristotle's argument because he has expressly allowed for exceptions (at 1.12.1259b1–3, when the man is constituted contrary to nature, as Ajax, having gone mad, manifestly is), and exceptions, precisely as exceptions, only prove the rule.

sake, but for the father in the one case and the master in the other. The child's virtue, for instance, is in relation to his father as to his end and leader (the male child will grow up to be like the father and the female child to be married to someone like the father), and the slave's virtue is in relation to his master since he exists to serve his master. So since their virtues are relative to another, that other should speak on their behalf and not they on their own behalf (speech that determines and is decisive, as opposed to chatter or mere talk, is an act of control and leadership).

∾ HOW TO SECURE VIRTUE IN THE HOUSEHOLD

1260a33 Having thus shown how the several parts of the household are capable of virtue, Aristotle shows finally how to secure such virtue. With respect to slaves he first shows what sort of virtue they need, namely just enough to prevent them from being deficient in their slavish work through intemperance or cowardice. Such minor or little virtue is evidently compatible with the kind of lack of virtue that earlier was used to differentiate the slave from the master. For it concerns only a certain reliability in doing physical labor, not any nobility of soul or discernment of the noble and good (or consequently any deliberation).[92]

As for how the slave is to get this virtue, the point is illustrated from a comparison with artisans. For it might seem that if slaves need virtue, so must artisans (for they can be deficient in their work too). But the slave differs from the artisan in two respects: he shares the master's life and he exists by nature. The artisan does not share the master's life and is only his slave temporarily, namely while actually working for him. So the artisan only needs virtue to the extent that he shares in slavery, and not as a regular education. The artisan also does not exist by nature, whereas the slave clearly does (1.5), and so the slave is fitted by nature, unlike the artisan, for the sort of virtue that the master must teach him. Now Aristotle cannot mean by his remark that artisans do not exist by nature that the various arts are unnatural or not needed by the household (for the arts clearly are natural and needed in this sense). Perhaps he simply means that no one is an artisan by nature but only by training or art.[93] But he may also mean that professional artisans, as we might call them, or those who do not belong to anyone as slaves yet make their living from slavish tasks, are unnatural. They divorce themselves from the master and the household to whom they and their work are naturally subordinate, and make a living on their own. They are thus worse and lower than slaves, and only rise to the level of slavery, and of slavish virtue, when actually employed by someone.[94]

92. As Schofield remarks, in Patzig (1990: 15), contra Mulgan (1977: 42) and Susemihl and Hicks (1894: 201).

93. The suggestion of Barker (1946: 37 n2).

94. I follow Dobbs (1994: 90) and Jowett (1885: 2:40), and see also Schütrumpf (1991: 1:379).

The slave, then, will get his virtue from his master, and so the master cannot merely be someone who instructs slaves in their work. He must have the character, not just the science, of a master and must use this character in ruling his slaves. He must reason with slaves, not just command them,[95] for they must not only do what they should (for which commands might be sufficient), but also as they should, with diligence and perseverance (for which reasoning and remonstrance, and even appeals to shame, are necessary). Children, in whom the capacity to understand is still incomplete, are more fit to be ruled by simple commands than slaves are.[96]

1260b8 Further discussion of slaves is evidently unnecessary if household management is more serious about the free and the virtue of the free. The question, then, turns to women and children and their relation to men and fathers and how their virtue is to be secured. But here the answer requires going beyond the household to the city, and so it must be deferred to the discussion of regimes (which discussion begins from the next book onward).[97] The reason is that women and children are parts of the household and the household part of the city. So since the virtue of the part must look to the virtue of the whole, the education in virtue of women and children must be undertaken with an eye to the regime, or to the rule of the city and not to the rule of the household merely. But if this is so, one might wonder why slaves should not be educated to the regime since they are parts of the household too. The difference, as Aristotle immediately indicates, is that the virtue or seriousness of the city depends on that of women and children, but not, evidently, on that of slaves. Women and children are in some sense parts of the city as well as of the household (slaves only belong to the city's preconditions, 4(7).8.1328a33–35, 9.1328b37–1329a2). For women are half the free and from children come those who share in the regime, and a city cannot be serious or virtuous if half the free in it are vicious (women may not share in the offices, but, given their place in the household, they cannot but have a profound effect on rule through their effect on their husbands, 2.9.1269b12–19, 32–34, 1270a11–15).

At all events it follows from this that the household manager's concern with

95. Aristotle may have in mind here Plato *Laws* 777e4–6.

96. See Dobbs (1994: 83).

97. It is generally thought that Aristotle does not return to these questions later; Barker (1946: 38 n1), Jowett (1885: 2:41), Lord (1984: 249 n35), Newman (2:224–25), Schütrumpf (1991: 1:380–82), Vander Waerdt (1991: 242). But this is mainly because these commentators are expecting a discussion of marriage and fatherhood as such and in their totality. Aristotle's argument, however, indicates that the later discussion will be about the education of women and children, or about marriage and fatherhood, only as regards the forming of wife and child in virtue (though this is, anyway, the primary concern of fathers and marriage, if not their whole concern; it is certainly the theme of the present chapter). So since such education must look to the regime, to discuss education to the regime is effectively to discuss marriage and fatherhood in this their essential respect. Hence the later discussion must be what is found, or at least started, in 4(7) and 5(8), which, being about education to the best regime simply, is about education to virtue simply.

virtue in the household must be subordinated to the legislator's concern with virtue in the city. The household manager must be guided by the political ruler or, if a suitable political ruler is lacking, fill up the lack by becoming a legislator himself (*Ethics* 10.9.1180a30–34).

1260b20   It is a noteworthy feature of this chapter that it displays the household growing into the city. The previous chapters have dealt with the analysis of the household into its parts. The present chapter deals, in effect, with the synthesis of the parts into the whole and into the city. It thus returns the book full circle to the beginning, to the city and its primacy. Accordingly Aristotle leaves behind as complete the household and how to arrange it best, and makes a new beginning about the city and how to arrange it best. He turns to his discussion of the best regime.

BOOK 2

Regimes Said by Others to Be Best

Chapter 1

~ REASON AND ORDER OF THE EXAMINATION

1260b27 The opening sentence recalls the choice, or intention, that has been motivating Aristotle since the last chapter of the *Ethics*, namely to investigate how best to arrange the city with a view to virtue, or to investigate the regime in which one could live best. But that chapter of the *Ethics* also indicated that not everyone can live best, but only those who have the right sort of souls and the right sort of upbringing, or only those who, as he says here, can live "as much as possible according to prayer." The reference to prayer seems deliberate and not merely a *façon de parler*. Getting the right sort of souls, or at least the right sort of conditions, is not in our control, but in that of chance (4(7).12.1331b21–22), and only the god could control chance.

This opening sentence also recalls the first part of the outline for the *Politics* at the end of the *Ethics*, but recalls in addition the final words of the previous book, for in both places mention is made of studying what others have said. So since Aristotle is now about to embark on this study he specifies it more precisely, namely that it will cover both regimes actually in use in cities said to be well legislated and regimes spoken of by others. Book 2 divides accordingly, though, as is often Aristotle's practice, in reverse order: chapters 1 to 8 deal with proposed regimes and chapters 9 to 12 with those in actual use.[1]

But having thus indicated the close connection between this book and what has preceded, Aristotle next states, appropriately enough, the reason for it, which consists in two aims. The first aim is the primary and obvious one of seeing what

---

1. It is worth noting that both groups of regimes are the objects of human speech, even those in actual use. For only those in actual use are going to be studied that are said to be well legislated (it would be rather silly, in this context at any rate, to study regimes that had received no praise at all). Hence, contra the reservations of Newman (2:225–26) and Schütrumpf (1991: 1:384, 2:92–93), Aristotle is not departing, even verbally, from the description he gave at the end of the preceding book, or at the end of the *Ethics*, that this study will be about what is said or spoken.

is useful and right in what others have said, for in the case of any study it is wise to begin by learning as much as possible from one's predecessors. But the first aim points to the second, for if the regimes that others praise turn out not to be as they are said to be, then a search for something better must be necessary, and necessary for the best of reasons, not for enhancing one's personal reputation like a sophist. Aristotle would, of course, in the case of a practical treatise, feel a special need to dispel suspicions of bad faith. One can hardly expect others to pay attention to one's advice if they think it is not motivated by a disinterested love of truth.

1260b36   After stating the reason or aims of the book, Aristotle next states its order. One should begin, of course, at the beginning, the natural beginning. But the beginning now is the city (the household was finished in the previous book), and since the city is by definition a community, or a sharing things in common, an examination of views about what is the best way of arranging such a community, or about what is the best regime, must begin with views about what things it is best to share in common (if such views were treated second, one might not be able to judge well views on other matters, since one would not know whether these other views were based on a correct assumption about what must be common). Now it is manifest, to begin with, that the citizens must share something in common, since the city is a community and they must at least share a common place. So the question is whether they should share everything in common that can be shared, or only some and not others. But this question itself points to Plato's *Republic* (461d5–465e3) as the place to begin, for there Socrates is presented as giving a view on this question that directly challenges prevailing views. The view is that everything should be common, including wives, children, and possessions. So the first question has to be whether this view is right or whether instead the contrary and prevailing views are.

An examination, therefore, of the *Republic*'s views about common wives, children, and property in contrast with prevailing views naturally comes first. But from this determination one can readily see how Aristotle might come to order the rest of book 2. For once one has started to discuss the *Republic*, one should naturally finish it and so cover as well all the other views it contains about the arrangement of the best regime (2.2–5). That Plato's other work on the regime, the *Laws*, should be discussed next is naturally enough explained by its closeness to the *Republic* (2.6). Since the *Republic* and *Laws* propose regimes not in use in any city, it would then be natural to continue by discussing any other proposed regimes not in use in any city (2.7–8). The remaining group, that of regimes that are in use, must now, of course, follow on, and here it would be natural to begin with those that are most praised and to group together those that are most akin (2.9–11), leaving any others to be dealt with last (2.12).

Chapter 2

~ THE REGIME OF PLATO'S *REPUBLIC*

~ COMMON WIVES AND CHILDREN

1261a10   Aristotle begins by outlining the problems that Socrates' proposal for common wives (and common children) generates. But there is some dispute about how this outline is supposed to divide up the three chapters that are devoted to common wives and children (chapters 2–4). My own view, that the three criticisms are dealt with in reverse order, is based, first of all, on the fact that the statement of the first criticism (at 1261a11–12) is repeated almost verbatim in chapter 4 (at 1262b3–7) and that what is argued throughout chapter 4 (namely that the result Socrates expects from common wives and children will not in fact be the result but rather the reverse will be) accords with that statement. So if the first criticism is dealt with in chapter 4, the second and third must be dealt with in chapters 2 and 3. But chapter 2 is evidently about a failure of Socrates to qualify his principle of unity, and chapter 3 is manifestly about the impossibility of proving unity from the way Socrates actually speaks about it (namely in terms of all saying mine and not mine together). Hence the second criticism must be dealt with in chapter 3 and the third in the present chapter 2.[2]

Taking a list in reverse order is a common practice of Aristotle's, but it is also worth noting something else about his procedure in these chapters. For Socrates' argument in favor of common wives and children may be summarized in the following way: (1) the city that is to the greatest extent all one is best; (2) the city with common wives and children is to the greatest extent all one; (3) therefore this city is best.[3] Aristotle's criticisms divide accordingly: in chapter 2 he attacks premise (1), in chapter 3 he refutes Socrates' argument in favor of premise (2), and in chapter 4 he shows that both it and the conclusion (3) are false.

~ FAILURE TO QUALIFY THE FUNDAMENTAL
   SUPPOSITION ABOUT UNITY

1261a15   Aristotle states two objections to premise (1), the supposition about unity, of which the first takes up most of the chapter and the second comes at the end. The first is to the effect that the city is a multitude and that to make it more of a unity will destroy this multitude, and so the city, by reducing it first to a household and then to a single human being. The complaint of most commentators, however, is that this criticism misses the point. What Socrates meant by unity

---

2. I have given a more detailed defense of these claims, with full references to the secondary literature, in Simpson (1991).

3. The relevant passage in the *Republic*, 461e5–465e3, does present this argument, though not of course reduced to such a neat form.

was not numerical unity, as the criticism implies, but unity of feeling.[4] But this complaint itself seems to miss the point, since it does nothing to deflect the criticism. For even if the focus of the criticism is unity of feeling, it is still surely the case that such unity would be better secured if the numbers of people involved were reduced. A household, for instance, where there are not only fewer people but people belonging to the same family, would be more united in feeling the same than a city, and a single individual would be more united in this way even than a household.

Aristotle's objection is anyway not to unity as such but to unity pursued *to the greatest extent*. Not unity but progressive unity is the object of his attack (as it is also the supposition that Socrates adopts). For Aristotle agrees that unity is necessary for the city, and what he objects to is unity altogether or in every respect (2.5.1263b31–35). So his point is that the unity of the city must be limited in some way to stop it going too far and his criticism is that Socrates fails to provide any means of stopping, that is, he fails to say how his supposition is to be qualified. To make this point, all Aristotle needs to do is say that the city is a multitude. For if the city is a multitude it cannot be altogether one, so the oneness it has must be qualified in some way to prevent the oneness destroying the multitude.

1261a22 This substantially completes Aristotle's first objection to Socrates' supposition. What he does next is to show how the supposition should be qualified, or rather what more precise supposition it should be replaced with. His argument turns on the fact that a city is a multitude and a multitude of human beings who differ in kind. The point is clarified by reference to alliances and the confederacy of the Arcadians. The Arcadians may have combined together instead of being separated in villages, but they have come together only into the unity of a nation and not into that of a city. A nation only has the unity of an alliance, being an aggregate of more of the same (a sort of collection of villages, 3.9.1280b17–29). Adding or taking away parts does not alter what it is but only how big it is, like increasing or decreasing a weight on a scale. The bigger the alliance, the better it is as an alliance. But a city will be destroyed if it gets too big (just as it will be destroyed if it gets too small, 4(7).4.1326a8–b24). It needs, rather, its proper complement of different kinds of parts (4(7).8, 6(4).4.1290b38–1291b2).

Of course Socrates in the *Republic* was not unaware that the city was a whole consisting of different parts. Aristotle, however, is not accusing him of being ignorant of this fact but of failing to draw out its implications, implications that point to the true account of what saves a city and keeps it united. This true account is the principle of reciprocity from the *Ethics* (5.5.1132b33–1133a5, 9.1.1163b32–35 with 8.1.1155a22–24). The city, being the self-sufficient community that combines within itself all that is necessary for good life, works by having different people

4. See Bornemann in particular (1923–24: 128–30).

doing different jobs and exchanging with each other the benefit of these jobs. A farmer, for instance, provides the doctor with food and the doctor provides the farmer with health care. But this exchange must be equal so that each receives back the equivalent of what he gave (for if one of them gains and the other loses, the one who loses will soon stop exchanging). So cities are held together in unity when each gets back his own, that is when the reciprocation is equal. Hence unity for cities must be understood in terms of this principle of reciprocal equality, not Socrates' principle of undifferentiated and progressive unity.

1261a32 That this principle is indeed what keeps cities together Aristotle confirms by taking the case that might seem to show the opposite, a city of free and equals. For equals might seem to lack the difference necessary for exchange. But a difference arises, and hence reciprocity also, because equals continually alternate between ruling and being ruled. Hence they are after all like farmers and doctors, or shoemakers and carpenters, but shoemakers and carpenters who continually change places instead of always remaining one or the other. Of course, since ruling, like any job, would be done better if done always by the same persons, alternation might, from this point of view, be worse than no alternation. But that does not affect the point at issue, for from another point of view alternation is manifestly necessary and better because manifestly just (that is, when all are on a level and no one excels in virtue like the god-man, 3.13.1284a3–11, 1284b25–34). Nevertheless alternation imitates permanent rule since rulers qua rulers are permanently different from the ruled qua ruled so that even equals, as they pass from one state to the other, are forever becoming different. Hence if it is also the case in a city of equals that reciprocity holds it together, then the unity of the city cannot be understood according to Socrates' principle. On the contrary, that principle, as left unqualified, destroys the differences on which reciprocity and the city rest. But since (to complete Aristotle's objection) the good of each thing preserves it, a principle that destroys the city evidently cannot be the greatest good for the city.

1261b9 Aristotle comes next to his second objection, which may be summarized thus: (1) communities are more self-sufficient the less a unity they are, as the household is more self-sufficient than the individual and the city than the household (the evidence for this is that cities only come into being when the community is self-sufficient); (2) but self-sufficiency is better (it enables the pursuit of the good life, 1.2.1252b27–30); (3) therefore less unity is better than more unity, and better above all for the city. This objection too attacks the lack of qualification in Socrates' principle (for Socrates was again not unaware that the city should be self-sufficient; he just did not draw out the implications). But it more directly attacks the likeness to the individual that Socrates uses to understand the unity of the city.[5]

5. As at *Republic* 462c10–d5.

Chapter 3

∼ UNITY AS APPEALED TO IN THE PROOF OF UNITY IS IMPOSSIBLE

∼ THE WORD "ALL"

1261b16   Aristotle turns next to Socrates' proof for premise (2) in the main argument, the premise that the city with common wives and children is to the greatest extent all one. Socrates' proof for this premise may be formalized thus: (4) the city where all say mine and not mine together is to the greatest extent all one; (5) the city with common wives, children, and property is where all say mine and not mine together; (6) therefore this city is to the greatest extent all one.[6] Aristotle says that Socrates uses the phrase "all say mine and not mine together" as a sign that the city is completely one. Despite the views of some commentators who have supposed that the phrase is used as a means to unity, not a sign of it,[7] Aristotle's comment is correct. What Socrates says binds the city into a unity is the community of pleasure and pain, when all the citizens rejoice and are pained at the same things. That they all *say* mine and not mine of the same things will not cause them to have the same pleasures and pains; it will only be a sign of such common feeling.[8]

Aristotle criticizes this argument first with respect to the word "all," and in two different ways, and then with respect to the word "mine." As regards the word "all," his first criticism is that it is used in different senses in the two premises, the sense of each individually and the sense of all as a group.[9] Hence there is no common middle term and the conclusion is fallaciously inferred. For in premise (4) "all" must be taken in the sense of each man individually saying mine of the same child or woman (only in such a case would it be plausible to say that a city where all spoke in this way was completely united). Premise (5), however, will only be true if

6. *Republic* 462a9–c8, 463e3–5, 464a1–7.

7. As Barker (1946: 43), Jowett (1885: 2:43), Newman (2:236).

8. *Republic* 462b4–6.

9. Some commentators suppose that Aristotle is attacking the word "all," not on the grounds that there is equivocation between the premises, but that when taken in the sense of each individually it makes the phrase in which it occurs simply impossible and so false in both premises. For they say that the same thing cannot belong to more than one person at a time, so that if I say mine of something it cannot be that you could say mine of it as well, Newman (2:236), Saunders (1995: 111), Stalley, in Keyt and Miller (1991: 192). But there are manifestly cases where all could individually say mine of the same thing, as five brothers can all individually say "my father" of the same man. Indeed Aristotle himself refers later to cases of saying "my cousin" and "my clansman" (1262a9–13) which manifestly can be said of the same person by all cousins and all clansmen individually. Premise (4), then, in Socrates' argument could be true taken in this sense. Consequently Aristotle's criticism must be taken as directed at equivocation between the premises and not at impossibility within each premise.

"all" is taken in the sense of all as a group, since those who have common wives, children, and property will only as a group possess them.

For instance, according to the arrangements Socrates lays down,[10] one woman could indeed be individually married to several men so that each of these men could all individually say of her "my wife," but they could not speak thus at the same time since the marriages are not contemporaneous. Moreover, there would be many men who had never been married to her at all and could never, as separate individuals, say of her "my wife." Consequently only one man, taken as this individual, could ever say of her at any one time "my wife." All the others could only do so in the sense that she is, or was, the wife of one of their number. So they could only speak thus of her insofar as they constituted a single group, and not as separate individuals. Exactly the same will hold of the children, for even though Socrates wishes none of the men to know who their real children are, nevertheless one child can only ever be the natural son of one man. All the men therefore cannot individually say of him "my son," but only as a group, in the sense that he is the son of one of their number (whoever that one happens to be). Property too belongs to all in the same collective way so the same criticism will apply here as well.[11]

1261b27   In illustration Aristotle takes a parallel from similar equivocation in numbers. So, for example, all or both of three and five can be both odd and even because they are odd separately and even as a group (they add up to eight). But they are not both odd and even separately. Wives and children also only belong to all the men in the way that "even" belongs to three and five, that is, to all the men as a group but not to each separately. Aristotle's next remark, therefore, that all saying mine is in one sense noble but impossible and in the other sense has nothing of likemindedness in it, must be directed at Socrates' premise (5). The sense is that if "all" in premise (5) is taken as each individually it will be impossible, for Socrates' communism cannot yield such a sense, though it may be noble, for if such a sense were possible Socrates' argument would go through (there would be a common middle term and the argument would not be fallacious). If on the other hand, however, the "all" is taken in the sense of all as a group, premise (5) may now be true but it will not indicate any likemindedness, that is, it will not be the sense that premise (4) has.

One might be tempted to respond to this criticism that, even if technically correct, it rather misses the point. For what Socrates really has in mind is that all the citizens care for each other as for their own, and so, provided they are taught to

10. *Republic* 457c10–461e4.

11. By property must be meant primarily the common provisions received by the guardians from the farmers. That Aristotle mentions property here, even though only wives and children are strictly his topic, is doubtless because to state the same argument over again when he does turn expressly to property (in 2.5) would be needless repetition.

do this, it hardly matters whether they are speaking all individually or only as a group.[12] But such a response itself misses the point both of Aristotle's criticism and of Socrates' argument. For this response concedes that all saying mine and not mine together will not by itself indicate such care. But Socrates' argument proceeds on the opposite supposition, namely that it will, since he maintains that all saying mine together is a sufficient sign that those who have common wives and children are *eo ipso* caring for them as for their own.

1261b32　This point about care is anyway picked up, and refuted, in Aristotle's second criticism about the word "all," which is to the effect that if people only possess wives and children in the collective or group way signified by the "all" in premise (5), the result will be universal neglect, not universal care. The evidence comes from facts of observation, that what everyone shares together in common is least cared for because everyone assumes that someone else is looking after it. The example is many servants doing a worse job than fewer (for the many can always assume that some other servant will do it, whereas the few know that they must do it or no one will). The same will be true of common sons. For of the thousand sons every man has, each of them belongs to everyone else indiscriminately. So everyone will indiscriminately neglect them, on the assumption that someone else will do the caring instead.

～ THE WORD "MINE"

1262a1　About the word "mine" Aristotle also makes two criticisms. The first turns, like the first criticism of "all," on a logical point, this time about disjunctions. For "mine" in Socrates' collective sense is really a sort of shorthand for "mine or his or his or his etc.," a disjunction with a thousand disjuncts or more (depending on the number of those in the city), and of which the "mine" is therefore only a thousandth part. The disjunction will be true, of course, for a disjunction is true if one of its disjuncts is true, and in this case one of the disjuncts must be true since each boy must be the son of someone or other among the thousand who make up the city. But the particular disjunct "mine" is only going to be true on those few occasions when it is said of someone who really is the speaker's son (or brother or father). No one, however, is going to know when it is true, and especially not in this case of "my son," for no one knows if they have had a son or, if so, whether he survived.

The question, then, is whether this disjunctive and uncertain way of saying "mine" is better than the way "mine" is said in cities now. For the phrases "my brother" or "my cousin" or "my tribesman" and so on, as currently used, are not shorthand for a long disjunction nor are they said in ignorance. Instead each signifies a definite and known relationship with a definite and known someone.

12. This is the complaint of Bornemann (1923–24: 135).

Moreover, they signify relationships that enable the same person to be called simply and not disjunctively "mine" by everyone in the city. For one will call him "my brother," another "my cousin," a third "my tribesman," and so on. In other words, paradoxically enough, Socrates could have had what he said he wanted if he had stuck to existing practice and allowed the "mine" to attach to the many forms of relationship that naturally exist instead of confining it to one or two alone. As it is, all he has managed is a verbal trick, and has replaced the real ties of brothers, cousins, and tribesmen with the unreal tie of disjunctive sonship. For it is evident that even if being someone's son is a better or closer relationship than being his cousin, yet really to be someone's cousin is better than unreally to be his son.

1262a14 The second criticism of "mine" is that it will not anyway be true that everyone says mine and not mine together. For it will always be possible (on the basis of the natural likenesses between parents and offspring that Aristotle here refers to) for some people to conjecture who is their real son or father and who is not, and so to say, however secretly, mine and not mine separately. Thus the phrase, on which Socrates' proof relies, will not even be spoken by everyone honestly, let alone mean anything when it is.

Chapter 4

~ THE RESULT IS THE OPPOSITE OF THAT INTENDED

1262a25 Aristotle turns finally to show that, apart from the fallacies in Socrates' proof for his premise (2), neither it nor the conclusion (3) is anyway true, and that the city with common wives and children is in fact neither united nor best. His criticisms here are thus directed at the deeds as opposed to the words. For Socrates had argued that the deeds would agree with the words and that each would not only call others his brothers, sons, fathers, and so on but also treat them accordingly.[13] Aristotle replies, and in six ways, that they will do nothing of the kind.

There is, however, a standard objection to most of these criticisms, namely that Aristotle is supposing that the guardians in Socrates' city will be like people everywhere else, whereas Socrates' point is that they will be educated to be of a superior kind. Hence, even if others would use communism badly, those in Socrates' city will not.[14] But, first, this objection misunderstands Socrates' argument. For while Socrates does intend his guardians to be superior to other men, he means the communism to be part of what will cause this superiority, and not to be something that will follow it. So the objection gets Socrates' argument back to front and there is no

13. *Republic* 463c8–464d6.
14. The objection of Bornemann (1923–24: 135–36, 142).

reason, as far as this goes, to suppose that the guardians will use communism any better than others would.[15] Second, Aristotle's criticisms, as becomes evident, focus on things that this alleged superiority could not anyway change. For ignorance of real family relationships, along with the attendant inability to pay due regard to them, are part and parcel of the communism itself (and not something removable), as is also the system of transferring children from one class in the city to another; and the weakness of friendship when spread out among many people is a function of the limits of space and time (it is physically impossible to spend lots of time in intimate communion with lots of people).[16] Third, one could regard Aristotle's criticisms as directed, not at what communism will supposedly do to people under the altogether extraordinary conditions of Socrates' city, but at what it can be expected to do to people as they in fact are everywhere else.[17] Hence the criticisms will rather be that Socrates is making impossible assumptions (cf. 2.6.1265a10–18), not that he is proposing something incompatible with those assumptions.

At all events, Aristotle's first criticism is that having wives and children in common will lead to more and worse violent crimes. His point evidently is that communism only hides family relationships and does not abolish them (after all, children go on being conceived and born in the same old way). So since the relationships remain, crimes against them can also remain. Since, further, people will be ignorant of these relationships, they will likely offend against them more often (for any offense against anybody is potentially an offense against a close true relative), and will be unable to make the appropriate amends. Yet such crimes are manifestly unholy (and unholiness is ugly, whereas the city exists for a life that is noble), and guardians who have committed them will, through enforced ignorance, be unable to perform the acts of expiation that will rid the city of this unholiness.

1262a32 The same will hold in the case of the second criticism about sexual activity between close relatives, since fathers, sons, and brothers will still be fathers, sons, and brothers even though in ignorance of each other, and sexual activity between them will still be most improper. But the problem in Socrates' case is compounded because Socrates not only wishes to keep these relationships, and not only in deed as well as in word, but also wishes to extend them universally to everyone in the city. But in that case, if he wanted the deeds to match the names, he

15. Something pointed out by Stalley, in Keyt and Miller (1991: 192–93), though this response is criticized by Mayhew (1996: 239 n15) as not altogether sufficient as it stands.

16. A fact stressed by Mayhew (1996: 239–46).

17. William of Ockham seems to have taken this view of Aristotle's criticisms of common property, namely that these criticisms only show, and are only meant to show, that common property would be bad for most people and not that it would be bad for those who are exceptional and perfect; see McGrade (1996: 821).

should have forbidden such kinds of sexual activity precisely because they were between putative fathers, sons, and brothers, and not have simply ignored this fact. The implication of this criticism of Aristotle, then, is that, in order to be consistent, Socrates should have banned homosexual activity altogether (for every male in the city is supposed to regard every other male as father, son, or brother).

1262a40 The third criticism is that common wives and children are given to the wrong part of the city. The reason is that such communism must weaken friendship (it will prevent all those ties of affection that arise within and from particular and recognizable family relations). So it should be imposed on the subject class, the farmers, to foster obedience and discourage subversion (people dare things most when they are united, and friendship unites). One should not suppose, however, that Aristotle is here simply counseling the practice of tyrants (see 7(5).11.1313a40–b18, 1314a17–19). For tyrants would follow this practice as regards everyone, whereas Aristotle is recommending it only for the farmers, or for slaves (4(7).10.1330a25–28). Rather we should regard him as speaking hypothetically, that since common wives and children weaken friendship, if they must be introduced they should be introduced for the subjects, and not, contrary to Socrates' argument, for the rulers.

1262b3 The fourth criticism picks up on and develops the same point about friendship. It also repeats the words from chapter 2 (1261a11–12) and expresses the thrust of all the criticisms given here, that common wives and children will do the opposite of what Socrates intends and will destroy the unity and goodness of the city. But first Aristotle shows the power of friendship in creating unity with an image about lovers taken from Aristophanes in Plato's *Symposium* (1191a5–8, 192d5–e9), an image that has the added benefit of showing how Socrates' arguments actually achieve the opposite of what he intends. For at least Aristophanes' lovers destroy each other through too much unity, in the way that Aristotle earlier argued (2.2) that Socrates' supposition will destroy the city through too much unity. But Socrates has given arguments for this result that will in fact do the opposite and destroy the city by too little unity. Fathers, sons, and brothers will be least united with each other because there will be too many fathers and sons and brothers to care for, and the care will get watered down as wine does when too much water is added to it. For what fosters care and love, and so binds particular people to particular people in intimate relationship, is that the other is one's own and dear, neither of which qualities will hold of anyone in Socrates' city.

1262b24 The fifth criticism concerns the transfer of children born in one class of Socrates' city, but really belonging to another, to that other class (*Republic* 415a1–d2). There is much confusion about how this is to be done, and above all about how it is to be done so as to preserve secrecy. For those who do the transferring must know who has been given to whom and their knowledge will be a standing threat to the regime and its preservation of all saying mine and not mine together.[18] Perhaps there are ways of preventing this knowledge getting out, or even of preventing anyone getting all the knowledge (say, by some system of intermediaries so that those who know from whom someone was taken do not also know to whom he was given). But no such way is going to be fully effective, and working ways out or implementing them will be plagued by many difficulties.

1262b29   The sixth and last criticism returns to the first two, about crimes of violence and sexual passion, but now as applied to those transferred from one class to another. The same problems will obtain here about relations between the classes as there about relations within a class. Those transferred, indeed, will not even call the class where their real parents and siblings are by family names, and so will be even less able to take care against the crimes in question.

Chapter 5

~ COMMON PROPERTY

1262b37   Coming next to property, Aristotle makes it clear at the start that his topic is not simply property as arranged in the *Republic*, but the best arrangement of property as such. That this is a broader question is emphasized by his separating it from the question of common wives and children (for no such separation is made in the *Republic*). In thus broadening the topic, Aristotle is not acting contrary to his aim. Chapter 1 made clear that that aim was not to examine the *Republic*, or any regime, for its own sake but only for what it could reveal about the best regime. So if the *Republic* raises questions that it itself does not explore (as common property without common wives and children), that is no reason why Aristotle should not explore them. At any rate, given this broadness of his intention, one should not expect all the criticisms that follow to be relevant to what is argued in the *Republic*.[19] So much indeed is indicated at once when Aristotle proceeds to set out options with respect to property not considered by Socrates, namely having land private but crops common, or land common and crops private, or both common. The logical fourth possibility, having both private, is not mentioned, perhaps because in a community some of these must in some way be common. But the omission does not affect Aristotle's argument, which proves the preferability of the first possibility, private possession but common use, in such a way as to rule out the other possibilities without the need for a separate refutation of them.[20]

1263a8   Before stating this argument, however, Aristotle mentions an arrangement that comes close to the one actually favored by Socrates: a separate class

18. As Benardete notes (1989: 119).

19. One can thus allay the doubts about the relevance of Aristotle's remarks expressed by Bornemann (1923–24: 142), Newman (2:246), and Schütrumpf (1991: 2:188–89) among others.

20. As noted by Miller (1995: 322).

of farmers doing the work for the citizens. For Socrates seems to have intended the farmers to own and farm the land and to give a proportion of the produce to be shared by the guardians in common.[21] Hence, in saying that a separate class of farmers would be better, Aristotle is not only so far agreeing with Socrates, but also indicating that his next remarks are not to be taken as a direct attack on Socrates. They are rather only what they purport to be: a defense of private possession and common use.

At any rate Aristotle first argues against common possession, and his criticisms are two. First, if the citizens are not equal in work and profits, or in the enjoyments they take and the work they do (a reasonable assumption, as it is hardly likely that everyone's desire and ability for work and enjoyment will be exactly the same), complaints must necessarily arise from those who work more but enjoy or take less against those who work less but enjoy or take more. Second, sharing together is hard enough in any human matter, but especially where those sharing are continually rubbing shoulders (as they would be in the case of common possession). Aristotle's two examples (of quarrels between traveling companions and quarrels with those servants most used for daily chores) make the point well enough and could easily be multiplied.

1263a22   Private possession is thus, as such, better than common possession. So Aristotle next shows that to private possession should be combined common use. For perhaps there might be some who think that common possession has advantages that outweigh the disadvantages. Counter to this idea, and in favor of his own position, Aristotle in effect points out that the advantages arise from common use, not from common possession, and that common use can be combined with private possession provided one has the right laws and character. Property, if held privately, will not cause complaints but will get much better looked after, while virtue, inculcated by correct laws, will ensure that, when it comes to use, the proverb "the things of friends are common" prevails.[22] It is, indeed, this commonness characteristic of friendship that is what motivates the desire for common property and for communism in general, since, as just noted, friendship is a very great good for cities (2.4.1262b7–10). Indeed, Socrates himself actually

21. As at *Republic* 464b8–c3.

22. It is sometimes alleged, as by Miller (1995: 368–69), that Aristotle has no awareness of the possibility, made famous by Adam Smith and much stressed by contemporary economists like Hayek, that common good can arise spontaneously, without conscious direction, from privately centered activity. But it would seem that Aristotle has such an idea in mind here, namely that the overall prosperity of a city will be improved if people are left alone to the private care of their private property and are not forced into some centrally directed communism. What differentiates Aristotle, nevertheless, from Hayek and others is that Aristotle does not think that private property and care, and the resultant spontaneous benefit to the community, are enough. He thinks rather that there is need of moral virtue in addition, or that people have to be moved also to direct and conscious acts of benefit to

quoted the same proverb when he first mentioned common wives and children.[23] By quoting it again here Aristotle implicitly shows that its correct application is to property, not wives and children, and to common use, not common possession. For common use will get the friendship desired, whereas a communism of wives, children, and property will not and brings with it many evils besides.

1263a30 It is a supposition of Aristotle's argument that private possessions can be made common in use (for otherwise indicating the benefits of this arrangement would be pointless). So he now proves that this is indeed possible by citing actual cases, both of cities where such laws exist and of nobly managed cities where the practice already in part exists and could easily be extended, as notably in Sparta. So the combination of private possession and common use is possible and, if it also has all the advantages and none of the disadvantages, it must be the best way to arrange things. Getting the right character, however, which is the key to making the combination work and to ensuring that use is common, depends on the legislator. For it is the legislator's work to make the citizens virtuous, and without virtue private possessors will likely use their goods in immoderate and selfish ways. Socrates' error, and the error of communists generally, is to suppose that common possession can do the work of virtue (a point Aristotle makes explicitly later in this chapter, at 1263b15–23, 37–40).[24]

1263a40 Aristotle next adds two other arguments for private possession (since private possession is what communists most attack). The first appeals to the pleasures of ownership. Now a justification of private property in terms of pleasure might seem rather weak and even offensive, especially to communists. But Aristotle is no puritan about pleasure and defends this pleasure by appeal to nature, the natural love each has for himself and therefore the natural pleasure each gets from wishing and getting good things for himself—as a sufficiency of possessions in particular. Now this love of self is manifestly good and not vain (it is the way nature ensures we do what is necessary to survive). There is, of course, a self-love which is blameworthy, and which may well be what turns some against the pleasures deriving from natural self-love. This is the love of self that goes to excess and which we call selfishness (whereby some love themselves so much they hate others; cf. *Ethics* 9.8). The same difference is found with respect to love of money, which can also go too far but which is natural, and necessary, up to a point (namely, as far as required to get a sufficiency of natural goods).

---

each other by habits of generosity and friendship. He further thinks that moral education, unlike economic prosperity, is not something that can be left to arise spontaneously from private care, but must be made something common (5(8).1). It is in education, therefore, and not in economics (or the family), that Aristotle is a communist (2.5.1263b36–1264a1). One may well wonder if his position is not thereby superior to both sides in the contemporary economic debate.

23. *Republic* 424a1–2.

24. It is also a point stressed by Mayhew (1993a: 829–31).

1263b5 The first argument rested on love of self. This second one rests on love of others, which must be as natural and good as love of self if human beings are naturally political. Hence, the pleasure associated with doing favors for others, and the private property this requires, must be natural and good too.

∿ COMMUNISM IN GENERAL

1263b7 What Aristotle has so far argued is rather a defense in general of private property than an attack on Socrates in the *Republic*. But it leads the way back to such an attack as he now indicates. This attack quickly broadens out from the particular issue of common property to communism as a whole (since these next five criticisms are general enough not to be confined to property).[25] On the matter of property itself, however, Socrates did indeed deprive his guardians of private property since the land belongs to the farmers and the guardians have a possession, and only a common possession, in the produce they receive. Hence, it must also be true that his arrangement deprives the guardians of the two pleasures just mentioned, those arising from love of self and from love of others.

The first of the general criticisms, however, is that common wives and property do away with works of two virtues, namely moderation or self-control as regards women and liberality or generosity as regards property. It might seem false, however, that Socrates takes away moderation as regards women since the strictures on sexual relations in the *Republic* have a certain severity and do require restraint.[26] But Aristotle is objecting less that Socrates takes away virtue than that he takes away *works* of virtue, and Socrates does indeed take away many possibilities of exercising and manifesting virtue. For in his city no woman is exclusively another's and some men (notably the best) may mate with many women one after the other according to the determination of the rulers. Moreover, outside the years set aside for procreation, any man may have sex with any woman in the same age-group. Consequently the kind of moderation Socrates requires of the guardians is going to be fairly limited. It will certainly not include keeping away from a woman because she is another's (for no woman is another's since the women are supposed to belong to all, not to some one man in particular).

The case with possessions is more straightforward, for without private property no one can exercise liberality (which is about possessions), and hence in this case no works at all of the virtue could be displayed.[27]

---

25. The generality of these criticisms shows that Aristotle has now shifted his focus from common property alone and hence that a new section in the logic of his exposition must be marked, as it is by St. Thomas Aquinas (1951: 2.4.204). If this division is noted, and also the division of the next section about the regime as whole, complaints that this chapter is disorganized, as by Barker (1946: 50 n2, 52 n4) and Stalley, in Keyt and Miller (1991: 186, 194 n25), can be satisfactorily answered.

26. *Republic* 459d7–461e4.

27. Against this argument Irwin, in Keyt and Miller (1991: 222–24), has objected that common

1263b15   As regards the second criticism, it is certainly clear that communism has a fair appearance, since it promises a marvelous love of everyone for everyone. Aristotle has already shown (2.4) that this appearance is deceptive. But here he notes two other deceptions that lurk beneath the appearance. The first is that communism pins the blame for human ills on the wrong cause, which is not the absence of common property, or indeed of common wives and children,[28] but depravity. The proof for this is that those who have things in common fall out more often than those who do not (though this fact is apt to be missed unless the "more" is understood proportionately instead of absolutely). The second deception is that communism mentions only the evils it will allegedly remove and is silent about the goods that it will also remove (notably the benefits, pleasures, and virtues mentioned earlier in this chapter).

1263b27   The third criticism is the same as that in chapter 2, namely that while the city must in some sense be a unity, it must not be so absolutely. The criticism is repeated here in order to expose an inconsistency in Socrates' position. For the way to unite the city is through virtue, notably the justice of reciprocal equality, and virtue requires education, which is precisely what Socrates himself says is necessary. So it is inconsistent, counters Aristotle, for Socrates then to have recourse to the device of communism rather than to education through customs, philosophy, and laws. Now one might object to this charge of inconsistency that communism is conceived by Socrates as an education through law and customs, namely the law and customs of communism. But in fact, as Aristotle has pointed out, communism only changes words, not the underlying realities, and its effects on behavior and character will be wholly negative. By contrast the common messes of Sparta and Crete that Aristotle immediately refers to are a genuine training in how to share and live together.

1264a1   The fourth criticism is an appeal to time, namely that if communism really were good it would have been found out long ago. Now Aristotle cannot mean by this that Socrates' proposals have not in any way been carried out anywhere. For in fact some barbarians have common property, as was asserted at the beginning of this chapter, and others have common wives, as was asserted at the end of chapter 3. What he must mean is that such proposals, if they were carried out, were not found to be done well. Nor can he mean that there is nothing

---

possession can still give opportunity for performing works of liberality, since one might be personally in charge of certain common possessions and since the distribution of common possessions is a distribution of what belongs to oneself as a member of the community. But Aristotle's earlier remarks about common wives and children (at 2.3.1261b32–1262a14) sufficiently dispose of this objection. See also Mayhew (1993a: 813–15) and Miller (1995: 324–35).

28. A reference also to common wives and children seems implicit here, for certainly Socrates' argument puts the blame as much on private wives and children as on private property. *Republic* 464c5–465d3.

new to be discovered; rather he must mean that discovery of something new is unlikely so that a search into what already exists should first be made. Most new proposals will turn out to be combinations of what was before tried in separation, or repetitions of previous experiments, or realizations of what others know but have refrained from acting on. Still, even if there are discoveries yet to be made, one can better ensure that one will avoid mistakes and make genuine improvements if one first studies the past.

1264a5 The fifth and last criticism seems to be to the effect that distributing the food and other necessaries provided by the farmers to the guardians en masse, without divisions of them first into messes, clans, and tribes, would prove in practice so unwieldy as to break down. Such divisions would therefore necessarily arise, the guardians would cease to be a single grouping, the institution of common wives and children would be fatally compromised, and all that would be left of Socrates' communist legislation is the Spartan practice of having the guardians not farm. In other words Socrates' proposals, to the extent they are practicable, are already in existence, and, to the extent they are not in existence, are not practicable.[29]

~ THE REGIME AS A WHOLE

~ SUBJECTS

1264a11 Aristotle comes last to examine the manner of Socrates' regime as a whole, that is, the classes it is made up of and how they will in fact form a regime or how they will rule and be ruled.[30] He begins with the subject classes and then turns to the rulers.

As regards the former, the farmers and artisans, the question revolves around whether communism should apply to them also. Commentators standardly object that Socrates has answered this question by confining communism to the guardians.[31] But Aristotle is not asking whether the farmers *have* communism or not but whether they *should* have it or not. He is asking, that is, for some discussion by Socrates of the reasons for his answer. Moreover, he is asking for a discussion that deals with the question in the context of the regime, that is, in the context of ruling and being ruled. There is no such discussion in the *Republic* and Aristotle's inves-

29. As aptly noted by Newman (2:257).

30. That Aristotle returns in this section to a discussion of common wives and children does not betoken any disorder in his exposition, contra Barker (1946: 52 n4). On the contrary, his focus now is not on common wives and children as such but on how the presence or absence of such communism among the farmers will affect the regime, that is, the arrangement of rule.

31. Barker (1946: 52 n4), Bornemann (1923–24: 113–18), Newman (2:258), Susemihl and Hicks (1894: 241); but see also Mayhew (1993b) and Schütrumpf (1991: 2:209). Mayhew argues against these commentators, and with some plausibility, that Socrates has not in fact made clear even whether the communism *will* be confined to the guardians or not, let alone made clear whether it *should* be so confined.

tigation shows that it is hard anyway to determine the matter, as none of the available possibilities will work.

1264a17   Aristotle considers these possibilities in turn and first the possibility that the subjects do have communism. The problem here is that the subjects will not differ from the guardians and could hardly submit willingly to their rule. For, like the guardians, they would be deprived of those private material and family goods that furnish most people with the enduring joys and satisfactions of their life, but, unlike the guardians, they would not have the compensation of sharing in rule, in military training, and in education. The Cretan sophistry might help since it tricks the Cretan slaves into thinking they are equal while in fact they are not (real power must always rest with those who have and know how to use arms). But this sophistry would blur the rather sharp distinction Socrates wants between the guardians and the farmers and, as Aristotle points out later (2.10.1272b15–22), what kept the Cretan slaves in check was less the sophistry than the accident of location.

1264a22   The second possibility is that the subjects do not have communism, and here Aristotle gives four criticisms. First, the subjects and guardians will not constitute a single community but two distinct cities opposed to each other. Socrates had himself said that most cities are really two camps at war, the camps of the rich and the poor.[32] Aristotle here retorts in effect that a city can become two warring camps in other ways as well, and specifically by being divided into non-communist and unarmed farmers and communist and armed guardians.

1264a27   The second criticism is that all the evils Socrates says exist in other cities must exist among the farmers. This criticism is evidently ad hominem. Socrates attributed such evils to the lack of communism and said communism was the cure for them. This view is false (as Aristotle argued earlier in this chapter), but on the supposition that it is true then, if the farmers lack communism, they will suffer all the evils for which communism is supposed to be the cure. Socrates would therefore be required by his own argument to provide some other cure through the laws to prevent disruptive and criminal behavior. But he provides none, relying instead on education, which education (including, ex hypothesi, the education of communism) is denied to the farmers.

1264a32   Such an oversight must by itself make the farmers difficult to control, but, third, they will be made even more so by this other fact, that they are masters of their property and yet have to pay a tribute from it to the guardians. But this combination is fatal to subservience: ownership will give farmers a sense of pride and independence, and tribute a sense of injustice as being forced to hand over to others what is their own.

1264a36   The same point is driven home by the fourth criticism that, independently of how ownership will affect the character of the farmers, so little has

---

32. *Republic* 422e7–423a1.

been said about their character that it is hard to tell how they will be disposed to accept or resist the rule of the guardians. Yet their subservience or lack of it must decisively determine how easily and how long the regime of the guardians will last.

1264a40   The third possibility is that the farmers have common wives but private possessions (the remaining and fourth possibility, that they have private wives but common possessions, is not mentioned, doubtless because it will face almost the same difficulties as the third possibility). Aristotle does not spell out the difficulties here, but the question he asks, about who will manage the household, points to them. For the wives, since they are common, must presumably rotate from one private house to another. But whether they rotate singly or in one large group or many smaller ones, and whether all take all the children with them or some some and others others, nothing but confusion and neglect could follow, to the annoyance and frustration of men and women alike. The same problems would arise also in the case of the first possibility, where possessions and wives are common (and in the case of the fourth, where wives are private). For if there were many households in this case, though everyone shared them all, the same difficulties must arise, and if there was one big household that all the women managed together, the opportunities for confusion and quarreling would be much greater.

A possible reply to the above difficulties might be that Socrates intends there to be no division between men's work and women's work. But apart from the fact that here the possibilities for confusion would be as great (especially if the farmers have private property with common wives), the analogy from animals Socrates uses for this conclusion is false. As Aristotle showed in book 1, household management differs markedly from anything found in the animal kingdom. So if animal pursuits can be shared by male and female alike, it does not follow that the pursuits of the human household can be.

〜 RULERS

1264b6   Having discussed problems relating to subjects, Aristotle ends with a discussion of problems relating to rulers, and raises two criticisms. The first, the danger of faction among the excluded, especially the spirited and warlike, from the same persons always ruling or being in control, is obvious enough and much exercises Aristotle later when he treats of excluded groups in a regime (7(5).8.1309a14– 32, 8(6).5, 7). One cannot, however, say that Socrates has to some extent provided against these problems by ensuring that the warlike and spirited among the citizens will at least be in the silver or guardian class, for in fact if they are not gentle and philosophic as well, they will not be.[33]

33. *Republic* 375c1–376c7, a point apparently overlooked by Barker (1946: 54 n2) and Newman (2:263). Some commentators also raise the puzzle why Aristotle does not anywhere discuss or criticize

1264b15 The second criticism, that Socrates takes happiness away from the guardians, saying it is the whole city the legislator should make happy, while true to what Socrates says,[34] is often itself criticized for being false to his argument. For Socrates does finally conclude that the guardians will live a more blessed life than Olympic victors.[35] However, in reply one may note that the point of Aristotle's criticism is less, perhaps, that Socrates fails to make the guardians happy than that he has gone the wrong way about making the city as a whole happy. For if the legislator is to aim at the happiness of the whole city, the happiness of the parts cannot be incidental to that aim. Happiness is not like evenness in numbers, which can belong to the whole (eight) and not to the parts (three and five). Happiness only exists in the whole if it is made to exist in some part of the whole and cannot otherwise exist in the whole. So not to intend the happiness of the parts is to take it from them and from the whole as far as one's laws are concerned (yet happiness is only achieved through law, *Ethics* 10.9). Hence, if the legislator is to make the whole city happy, as Socrates says he must, then the legislator must after all intend, and intend directly, the happiness of the guardians. For if the guardians are not happy and their happiness is not directly intended by the legislator, then assuredly no other part of the city can be happy (these other parts are unfit for virtue or, as Aristotle earlier suggested about the farmers, are in a state of resentful servitude). Hence the city as a whole cannot be happy either.

Chapter 6

〜 THE REGIME OF PLATO'S *LAWS*

〜 FROM THE REGIME OF THE *REPUBLIC* TO THAT OF THE *LAWS*

1264b26 A discussion of the regime of Plato's *Laws* will naturally follow a discussion of the regime of his *Republic* if the two regimes are similar. So Aristotle first shows the similarity and then turns to criticism.[36] The similarity is not hard to

---

the *Republic*'s proposal for philosopher rulers, as Dobbs (1985: 33). But in fact Aristotle is criticizing that proposal right here. His criticism, however, is not that it is wrong to make philosophers rulers or rulers philosophers, but only that it is unsafe for the same rulers always to rule or, if philosophy is necessary for rule, that it is unsafe only to train some in philosophy. As he argues later, 4(7).15.1334a22–25, 31–36, all the citizens in the best regime need philosophy and should be trained in it.

34. *Republic* 420b3–421c6.

35. *Republic* 465d2–466b2, Bornemann (1923–24: 150).

36. Bornemann (1923–24: 244–51) again takes a negative view of Aristotle's criticism of the *Laws*, as also do Sinclair/Saunders (1981: 120) and Saunders (1995: 126–35). But Morrow, in Düring (1960: 145–62), and Schütrumpf (1991: 2:216–37) do much to show their accuracy.

show since so little has been determined about either regime. So much is evident already about the regime of the *Republic* since Aristotle has just shown, and especially in the previous chapter, how little has been determined about common wives and children, property, and the arrangement of the regime. There are other omissions too, which he immediately notes now.

The omission as regards the farmers and artisans is whether they are to share in any office, that is to say, in any office other than that of the deliberative and controlling body (which Aristotle correctly notes is reserved to another class in the regime). For even if Socrates has made it clear that they are not to share in this office, the question still remains whether they are to share in any of the lesser offices. This question is of no little consequence, partly because the farmers and artisans seem to be treated as part of the citizen body, yet to call those citizens whom one deprives of all share in office is mere deception (3.5.1278a35–40), and also because one way of preserving a regime where, as in this case, some always have control and others never is to give the latter some share in the noncontrolling offices (7(5).8.1309a27–32).

The omission as to whether farmers and artisans should possess arms and go along to war or not is, as before, an omission, not as to the fact, but as to the reason for the fact. One might perhaps think, however, that Socrates does give reasons since he says that one man should have one job so that no one should be both farmer and soldier. Aristotle would doubtless respond that this reason only justifies a general division into classes, and cannot by itself rule out all share by farmers in fighting, say as reserves or as auxiliaries (functions that would seem very useful and not incompatible with farming). A much fuller discussion was required, especially given the problems besetting the relations in general between farmers and guardians raised in the previous chapter. And both these omissions would, anyway, seem omissions even by Socrates' own account, because he did think that the women should share in war, education, and rule. But if it was necessary to decide these things in the case of women, it was hardly less necessary to decide them in the case of farmers and artisans.

The comment about Socrates filling his discourse with extraneous matter cannot mean that Aristotle thinks all concern with education is extraneous, for he himself considers education central to the best regime (in 4(7) and 5(8)). He could, however, think that much of Socrates' discussion was extraneous, as the attack on the poets and poetry, and the theory of knowledge and the Forms. These would be extraneous as belonging to other studies (the study of poetry and metaphysics). For while it may be the task of political science to lay down who should learn what and up to what point, and so to give laws for the sake of the arts and wisdom, it is not its task to raise and answer the questions that properly belong to such other studies (*Ethics* 1.2.1094a27–b7, 6.13.1145a6–11). Politics is not poetry or metaphysics, even if the city needs poetry and metaphysics, just as household management is not business even if the household needs business.[37]

1265a1 Having thus shown what and how little the *Republic* says about the regime, Aristotle next does the same for the regime of the *Laws*. In this work also little has been determined about the regime because, as he wryly remarks, the *Laws* is mainly laws. In one sense, of course, the laws of a regime may be said to be part of it, namely the laws that determine who should rule (as in particular the things Aristotle discusses in 6(4).14–16). But even such laws are not the whole of a regime, and anyway not much of the *Laws* is about laws in this sense, but only parts of books 4, 5, 6, and 12 (and Aristotle's criticisms are in fact concentrated on these books). The suggestion, however, through the use of "he" ("he has said little about the regime," 1265a2), that the main interlocutor of the *Laws*, the Athenian Stranger, is a disguise for Socrates is plausible enough, and that Aristotle makes the suggestion may perhaps be evidence that it was circulating in Plato's Academy (and had even been allowed by Plato). However, Aristotle refrains from expressly naming Socrates in this chapter about the *Laws* (instead he uses "he" or "in the *Laws*" or something similar). The only occasion he does so is in a general reference to all the Platonic dialogues. By contrast he names Socrates many times in his preceding discussion of the *Republic*.

As regards the similarity between the two regimes, Aristotle notes that the main difference is the absence in the second regime of common wives and children and property. Everything else to do with the regime (as notably sharing in rule and possessing arms) is the same. The education is the same (training in moral virtue, mathematics, and dialectic—especially if we take the *Epinomis* to be part of the *Laws*), and the fact that the citizens live free from necessary labor. The separate common messes for women (which will follow from the fact that wives are no longer shared) and the difference in the numbers of the citizen body do not significantly distinguish the two regimes. For though in the *Laws* the citizens have private property, they are forbidden any work save the practice of virtue, and are to leave all necessary labor to a separate class,[38] which class, whether the farmers, who are slaves,[39] or the artisans, who are resident

---

37. One might say in response to these comments of Aristotle that they are misdirected, since in writing the *Republic* Plato was not simply doing politics but something far more complex. There is no reason, however, to suppose that Aristotle would disagree. For it was never his intention to comment on the *Republic* as such but rather to examine those things in it that Plato makes Socrates say about the best regime as such. So if Aristotle, in pursuit of his own intention to study politics, finds things in the *Republic* that are improper to a discussion of the best regime, that does not mean he must find them improper to Plato's intention.

38. *Laws* 739e7–740a2, 807c1–e2, 846d2–847b6.

39. *Laws* 806d7–e2.

aliens,[40] have no share in the regime. So in all respects bearing on the arrangement of the regime, namely who shares in office and who does not and why, the *Laws* and the *Republic* turn out pretty much the same, both as to what they say, and as to how little they say, about this arrangement.

~ PRESUPPOSITIONS OF THE REGIME

1265a10   The words of praise with which Aristotle prefaces his criticisms here are evidently sincere. Aristotle's writings, political and otherwise, are indebted to the Platonic dialogues in all sorts of ways that only a full reading of both can discover. If Aristotle seldom agrees with the results reached (though his debt to the *Laws* in 4(7) and 5(8) is large),[41] it is not because he has any doubt about the importance of the questions or of the treatment they receive. That he spends so much time on the *Republic* and the *Laws*, and that no other work he examines comes close in respect of the same qualities for which these are praised, is proof enough.

Aristotle begins by criticizing the presuppositions of the regime and the things legislated first in the *Laws*.[42] The first criticism, that 5,000 is an impossibly large body of citizens, is often itself criticized because 5,000 cannot, even by Aristotle's own account, be all that impossible if, as he admits later (2.9.1270a29–31), Spartan territory was large enough to sustain 1,500 cavalry and 30,000 hoplites or heavy armed soldiers.[43] But Aristotle is drawing attention to the fact that not just the 5,000 men will be idle (or not involved in farming), but that their wives and families will be too,[44] and hence also their personal attendants (who, though serving the citizens, will not be engaged in any of the tasks of farming and manufacture). It is not clear that the same would hold of Sparta in the same way. Second, Aristotle's criticism of the number 5,000 is not that such a number is impossible simply (Babylon was much larger and did exist after all), but rather that it is impossible "according to prayer" (1265a18). So the meaning perhaps is that a regime according to prayer, one that is devoted to virtue and the whole of virtue (not military virtue alone as in Sparta), could not be so large (4(7).4). Significant in this respect is that Aristotle's own presuppositions later about the best regime include no specific numbers but only general principles (4(7).4–7, and see *Ethics* 9.10, especially 1170b31–33). These principles can be fixed in advance, but not the precise numbers, would seem to be part of his contention.

1265a18   The second criticism, that the legislator is only told to legislate

40. *Laws* 846d1–847b2.

41. See the summary in Barker (1947: 381–82).

42. *Laws* 734e3–745e6.

43. Points raised by Bornemann (1923–24: 246) and Jowett (1885: 2:60); but contrast Barker (1946: 57 n1). The number of citizens is actually said to be 5,040, not a round 5,000, in the *Laws* (737e1–738b1, 753b4–756b6), but nothing in Aristotle's criticisms depends on the imprecision.

44. The requirement to practice only virtue is imposed on both sexes alike (*Laws* 806d7–807e2).

with a view to the territory and human beings but not to neighboring territory, is not directed to anything expressly said in the *Laws*, though it correctly summarizes the only two subjects about which questions are asked when framing the regime begins.[45] Commentators object, nevertheless, that Aristotle has failed to notice that this third subject, the neighboring places or territory, does get dealt with. It is brought in when the size of the population is discussed, where its importance with respect to war is expressly indicated.[46] Aristotle, however, is not complaining that the size of the population should be determined with respect also to the neighboring territory, but that the laws should be.[47] Knowing how to fight on foreign land and to be fearsome to neighbors is not so much a question of how many the citizens are as of how they have been trained and educated, that is, of what laws they have lived under.

1265a28   The third criticism is that the limit for property is unclearly defined, and commentators object to this too because, while accurate to the text cited, it is inaccurate to other passages where what is meant by living moderately is explained (as in the case of sex and drink), and where it is said that the citizens must be neither extremely poor nor extremely rich.[48] But Aristotle is speaking of living moderately with respect to possessions, not sex or drink. Moreover, the lots apportioned to each citizen are measured as the minimum amount below which there would be poverty,[49] but then the only way of determining this amount is given by the formula "live moderately." So the lots could, as far as the formula is concerned, be determined so as to be moderate but mean or wretched, which is Aristotle's complaint. Besides liberality is not given any special praise in the *Laws* where the emphasis is on moderation. But if liberality is one of the two virtues concerned with property, it should be mentioned and emphasized just as much.

1265a38   The fourth criticism, about property in relation to the number of children, needs some careful noting. In the *Laws* several devices are put forward as ways of controlling the population, from adoption, rebukes, and encouragement to colonies and introduction of bastard stock.[50] Nevertheless the device of adoption is the first and primary one and the others are mentioned as supplementary, so Aristotle seems right to suppose that barrenness is implicitly being taken as the normal circumstance that will keep the numbers sufficiently the same. However, his complaint is less that other devices do not exist than that a limit is set for property but none for childbirth, for, whatever the devices, such an arrangement is

45. *Laws* 704a1–708d7.

46. *Laws* 737c1–d8. The objection is made by Morrow, in Düring (1960: 156) and by Susemihl and Hicks (1894: 250).

47. As noted by Newman (2:268) and Schütrumpf (1991: 2:223).

48. *Laws* 635e4–637e7, 741e7–744e5; Bornemann (1923–24: 247–48).

49. *Laws* 744d8–e3.

50. *Laws* 740b1–741a5.

always going to create problems. As he comments shortly, it would be better to have things the other way around, with childbirth limited and not property.

As regards barrenness specifically, no reason is given in the *Laws* as to why this will keep the numbers roughly the same. Aristotle's comment (that such is what happens in cities now) is nevertheless charitably plausible. The trouble is it will not help the regime of the *Laws*, where the numbers of children must be kept very precise (something periodic barrenness could never guarantee), since no division of the original 5,000 lots is allowed. The remark about those left out, or the superfluous offspring (those who are neither natural nor adopted heirs), being few or many in number may be implicitly directed at the device of sending out colonies. Since these need many persons to succeed, what remedy will be available if the superfluous numbers are too few? For certainly the time for regulating births by the other devices of rebukes and encouragements will be well past.

In referring to Pheidon, Aristotle is not necessarily endorsing his solution (which is the opposite of the *Laws* in the sense that Pheidon regulates the numbers of citizens to be born but not the size of the lots, whereas the *Laws* regulates the size of lots but not the numbers of citizens to be born). We should rather read him as seeking to point out the need for legislators to make themselves familiar with the history of their subject so that they do not fail to learn everything possible from past experience, and specifically so that they do not fail to notice problems already detected by others.

1265b18   The fifth criticism, about how the rulers will differ from the ruled, is initially puzzling. Commentators suppose that Aristotle is complaining that the analogy with weaving is left unexplained, which, however, seems true only verbally. For while the analogy is indeed not explicitly referred to again, it seems explained by reference to education. Those are to become rulers who excel and advance furthest in their training.[51] Moreover, there is the problem that this criticism seems to interrupt Aristotle's discussion of the arrangements concerning land and possessions. One would expect it to come a few lines later when the question of rule is expressly taken up.[52] The following solution, however, may be offered. If rulers are to differ from ruled as one wool from another, then something must be said, not just about how the citizens differ in education, but also about how they differ in nature such that some are fit for the education of rulers and others not (for the education will presuppose this difference and not create it). Aristotle is asking, in other words, for some discussion of the sort of natural difference that he himself draws later between ruled and rulers when he says that the first will be the

---

51. *Laws* 734e6–735a4, 951d5–952b5, 961a1–c1, 966a5–d5. Bornemann (1923–24: 248–49), Morrow, in Düring (1960: 158), Newman (2:273), Susemihl and Hicks (1894: 253).

52. As Newman notes (2:272).

younger and the second the older (4(7).9.1329a2–17, 14.1332b32–42). No such explanation of the analogy with weaving is given in the *Laws*. This criticism will come here and not later, even though it is not about land and possessions, because the immediately preceding criticism was about childbirth, which naturally brings to mind the difference between young and old, and also because the nature of the human beings, like that of the land and possessions, belongs among the presuppositions of the regime (4(7).4.1325b38–1326a8, 13.1332a38–b11).

1265b21 The first part of the sixth criticism, that the size of the lot may be increased five times, is itself criticized by some because the passage of the *Laws* referred to speaks of "four times" and not "five times."[53] But this complaint is really about whether the "four times" of Plato's Greek is to be understood as "four times the original lot in addition to the lot" or as "four times the original lot including the lot." Aristotle takes it in the former way and since what is at issue here is the meaning of Plato's Greek, and since Aristotle was a native Greek speaker who knew Plato, we are hardly in a position to say his interpretation cannot be correct.[54]

A more serious difficulty is that this criticism seems to have an obvious reply: all the land has been divided up into inalienable lots of equal value so whatever increase of wealth is allowed cannot be in land. But Aristotle's remark must also be construed as an attack on this reply. Why was the land chosen only sufficient for division into 5,040 lots of moderate, if equal, value in the first place? Since movable property can be increased, why not also choose an amount of land with something left over after the division into lots that the citizens might buy and sell as they please? The argument from moderation cannot be used here because if that was sufficient to rule out greater amounts of wealth in land, it should also be sufficient to rule out greater amounts of wealth in other things too.

1265b23 The last and seventh criticism has been charged by some commentators with inconsistency since Aristotle himself later proposes divided lots for his own best regime (4(7).10.1330a9–25).[55] But there is this difference that he does not adopt the proposal of having two homesteads as well as two lots, and his complaint is only that there are to be two homesteads, not that there are to be two lots. Besides he does not say that having two homesteads is impossible, only that it is difficult, and there can be no inconsistency in adopting oneself another's difficult proposal if it is otherwise desirable and the difficulty can be overcome or mitigated.[56]

53. See Bornemann (1923–24: 249) and Susemihl and Hicks (1894: 254).
54. See Jowett (1885: 2:63), Newman (2:273), Saunders (1995: 131).
55. See Bornemann (1923–24: 249–50), Jowett (1885: 2:63), Susemihl and Hicks (1894: 254–55).
56. As noted by Morrow, in Düring (1960: 154), Newman (2:274), Schütrumpf (1991: 2:230).

1265b26   Following the order of the *Laws* itself,[57] Aristotle now turns from presuppositions to the arrangement of the regime. As regards the first criticism, it may indeed be true that a regime based on those who bear arms, or polity as Aristotle calls it (3.7.1279a37–b4), is what cities have most in common with and also a mean between democracy and oligarchy (since those who bear arms are, as a whole, neither excessively poor nor excessively rich, 6(4).13.1297b1–6). But the most common and the second-best need not necessarily be the same (6(4).7–8, 11, and 2.1289b14–17), since perhaps the Spartan regime is better though it is certainly not most common (6(4).1.1288b39–1289a1). One cannot therefore assume, as the *Laws* does, that the most common and the second-best must be the same.

As proof, in fact, that the regime of the *Laws* is not second-best according to the way it is actually described, Aristotle now shows how the Spartan sort of regime is better according to the way it is actually described. (He does not himself, however, endorse this description of Sparta; his own view is that Sparta is a mixture instead of aristocracy and democracy, 6(4).7.1293b16–18.) For a regime described as a mixture of oligarchy, monarchy, and democracy must be better than one described as a mixture of a kind of democracy and of tyranny that are so extreme (they are described as despotism and license)[58] as to be scarcely even regimes. A regime that has more regimes in its mixture (more, that is, than extreme tyranny and democracy) must be better than this (though perhaps a regime composed of fewer regimes but better ones would be better still).

1266a5   The second criticism is that the regime of the *Laws* does not anyway correspond to its own description, since it lacks any monarchic or despotic element, by which Aristotle must mean that it contains no office with controlling powers filled by one man. That there are offices in the *Laws* with controlling powers occupied by several men (as the guardians of the laws) is not to the point[59] since regimes differ from each other in who exercises office, not in what offices they exercise (3.7). Hence a regime that has no great office in it filled by one man lacks a monarchical element.

That the regime is instead a mixture of democracy and oligarchy though leaning toward oligarchy is proved by reference to the details of election to office. Aristotle discusses these sorts of details more at length later (6(4).14–16), but as regards the *Laws*, its regime contains enough instances of the sort of devices Aristotle mentions to justify his general charge. For even if having most offices in the hands of the well-off, and the greatest offices in the hands of those with the

---

57. *Laws* 737c1 with 751a1–3.
58. *Laws* 693d2–701e8, 709e6–710a2.
59. Contra Morrow, in Düring (1960: 159), and Susemihl and Hicks (1894: 257).

greatest assessments, are not expressly legislated, the regime nevertheless does "try" (*peirasthai*, 1266a12) to bring this result about. Service in the highest offices requires leisure and there is no payment for such service, both of which facts will tend to ensure that de facto, if not de iure, the well-off will alone or most occupy these offices.[60] The same will hold of the election of the council (itself a very high office), which is also oligarchic as Aristotle explains. For although there are some puzzles about precisely what the arrangements for election to the council amount to,[61] there is no doubt that the better off classes will have a disproportionate say in who gets elected.

Hence it is clear that the sort of mixed regime, or polity, that the *Laws* is after should not be or be described as a mixture of democracy and monarchy but rather of democracy and oligarchy, a point Aristotle argues further in his later discussion of polity (6(4).8–9, 13).

1266a26 The third and last criticism is directed in particular at the appointment of the council just described. What Aristotle has in mind seems to be something like the following. In the first round of election the number of votes required for election will be small since many must be elected, so a smallish group could manage on its own to get its candidate among the winners. In the second round the same overall number of electors will be voting for a smaller number of candidates, but since other electors have not, ex hypothesi, banded together, their votes will tend to be spread out and not markedly in favor of one candidate more than another. Consequently, those who have banded together and are voting as a block could easily constitute the critical mass to get the candidates they want elected yet again. Sectarian interests might thus come to dominate in the regime.[62]

1266a28 These criticisms of the *Laws* are not as severe and damaging as those of the *Republic* (for the severest were directed at the communism, which the *Laws* lacks). Some of them do not seem very weighty and others are directed at faults that could be put right without too much difficulty. Little is exposed that seems radically irreformable. Aristotle is thus, in a way, anticipating his use of the *Laws* in constructing his own best regime later (4(7) and 5(8)): some things he borrows as they stand and others he borrows along with the changes here recommended. His admiration for the "Socratic speeches" of the *Laws* is genuine, if discriminating.

---

60. As noted by Morrow, in Düring (1960: 149), Newman (2:279), and Saunders (1995: 134–35, 171), against Susemihl and Hicks (1894: 258–59).

61. See Susemihl and Hicks (1894: 259).

62. The point finds some parallel in the system of primary elections in the United States, which effectively puts the choice of the candidate who eventually wins the main election into the hands of the few party faithful who are permitted, and bother, to vote in the primaries. Consider also the practice, in some countries, of having runoff elections between the top candidates in the previous round of voting.

Chapter 7

~ THE REGIME OF PHALEAS OF CHALCEDON

~ PHALEAS' MATERIALISM

1266a31 In accordance with his program (2.1.1260b29–32), Aristotle turns next to consider other proposed regimes. These lack the imaginative novelties of the *Republic* and *Laws* and start rather from necessities, that is, things that cities must share in common (rather than could share in common), notably land and its distribution. In Plato's dialogues, of course, there is no lack of concern with necessities, but the emphasis is on more spiritual matters, above all the education of the soul (common wives and children as well as messes are introduced to improve character). The most important thing is certainly not material possessions, as Phaleas and others think.[63]

1266a39 Aristotle first summarizes Phaleas' proposals, but evidently just to illustrate that Phaleas thought property should be equalized. For he refrains from commenting on Phaleas' suggestions of how to go about doing it, though these suggestions rest on several false assumptions. There is no guarantee, for instance, that equalization will be easy at the founding of a city, for in any joint project there are likely to be some, notably the leaders or those who have gone to some special risk or expense, who think they deserve more.[64] As for cities already in existence, Phaleas is falsely supposing that the rich and poor will intermarry instead of marrying their own kind, that dowries will go with sons as well as daughters (if a rich son marries a poor wife), and that the rich will put up with seeing their wealth equalized. One cannot, however, expect these things to happen voluntarily and to impose them by force would require the power of a tyrant or provoke a revolution. Aristotle's silence about such problems is probably because they do not concern the substance of Phaleas' proposal but rather the manner chosen to implement it. For the comparison with Plato in the *Laws* seems meant to suggest that Phaleas' objections to inequality of property might be as well or better answered by limitations on the size of the inequality rather than by its total abolition. If so, there would be no need for so unreal a law about dowries.

~ CRITICISM OF PHALEAS

1266b8 The first criticism recalls the one already made in the previous chapter about the *Laws*. Admittedly there is the difference in Phaleas' case that he only limits the relative amount of property (everyone is to have the same), not the absolute amount (no limit seems to have been set on how large this same amount

---

63. *Laws* 731d6–e1.

64. Phaleas evidently did not pay the sort of attention to the problems of founding a city as is paid in the *Laws* 704a1–712a7.

could be). Hence one might say that, in theory at least, Phaleas need put no limit on the number of children, provided the amount of possessions could be increased without limit as well. But since everyone is supposed always to have the same, no one could be allowed to increase his property to accommodate more children if the property of everyone else was not increased by the same amount at the same time. This requirement could, of course, hardly ever be met, and certainly not at the whim of parents who want more children. So Phaleas' proposal, without legislation about children, will have the effects noted: a breaking of the law and revolution on the part of the rich who become poor because they have large families but no means to increase property.

1266b14 The second criticism is about whether leveling of property will anyway have the effect Phaleas attributes to it. Aristotle first notes from examples that it does have some effect on the regime, though his examples cut both ways: in the case of Solon property was kept leveled in order to prevent revolution, whereas in that of Leucas the leveling of property was the cause of revolution. Still the examples do confirm, what Phaleas and others maintain, that revolutions or factions can be controlled by arrangements about property. The question is rather about the sufficiency of Phaleas' arrangements, and it is evident that equality is not enough. For equality, being relative, can be too great or too small, and both these (extravagance in the one case, penury in the other) are political ills and cause of others, including revolution (cf. 6(4).11). There is need, then, that the amount of property also be a mean between these extremes.

1266b28/31/38 The third criticism naturally follows on from the second but, along with the fourth, fifth, and sixth, turns the focus on the problem of controlling human desires, a matter to which Phaleas remained strangely blind. So it is manifest, to take the third criticism, that controlling or leveling property will not be of much help if desires are left uncontrolled or unleveled, and controlling desires requires education, not property equalization. Further, and fourth, it is not enough to say in answer that there must be equal education along with equal property, since education, like property, can be deficient even when equal. Fifth, there can be inordinate desires for the good of honors or office as well as for property, and these desires too are cause of faction, for whose cure, however, Phaleas has proposed nothing.

1267a2 The sixth criticism in a way sharpens the fifth. For Aristotle distinguishes three kinds of wrongdoer: those lacking necessities; those who desire something more than necessities; those who desire to enjoy painless pleasures. As cures he proposes few possessions with hard work for the first, moderation for the second, and philosophy for the third. For if the poor, or the first group, have enough, but no more, and with hard work, they will be adequately clothed and fed but kept too busy to fall into mischief, and if the greedy, or the second group, are taught moderation, they will no longer have excessive desires for more. Those in the third group present a harder problem. They are presumably those who wish to be so abundantly endowed with property and power that they never have to feel the pain of waiting for what they want but can get it as and when they please. They have the passion that will drive them into tyranny, though in fact philosophy, not tyranny, is their only cure, since only philosophy, or learning in general, will give them the independence they crave (tyrants, for all their wealth and power, cannot escape the pains associated with waiting for and depending on other people). At all events, the problem with those in the third group is not that they desire material things too much (for which moderation would be a cure), but that they desire, however unknowingly, something of a different order.

The inadequacy of Phaleas' proposals is well illustrated by the third and second groups. For the greatest crime, tyranny, is committed by them if by anyone, not by the first group. His proposals, therefore, would be of no help against tyranny, but only against the lesser crimes caused by need.

1267a17 The seventh criticism is that, as Phaleas has forgotten tyranny (or attacks on the city from within), so he has forgotten foreign affairs (or attacks on it from without). His proposals say nothing about how to organize the city for defense. He has not even said anything about property in this regard, though property is all his concern. The trick is to find an amount of property that will not be so great as to inspire attacks from more powerful neighbors, whom it would yet not be great enough to enable the possessors to repel, nor so little that it would not enable them to resist equal neighbors. In other words, the amount of property should be such that those who could win will not want to attack (at least not for the sake of gain) and that those who might want to attack could not win. Phaleas was silent on this matter, as he was on tyranny, so Aristotle supplies the deficiency here as he has just done there by offering a proposal that will certainly ensure that any wars with superiors are not about property but about something else, as the example of Eubulus and Autophradates helps to illustrate.

1267a37 Phaleas' proposal of equalizing possessions thus has no value as regards war and defense. What value it has can only be confined to the internal matter of preventing faction. Here, in his eighth criticism, Aristotle returns to issues he raised in the fifth and sixth. But now the criticism is less that Phaleas has ignored certain facts about desire than that these facts make his proposal to be of little use, since equality will not in fact satisfy anybody: not the refined sort because they always think they deserve more, and not the many because they always want more. The proper solution is instead to limit the desires of the naturally respectable and to limit the power of the base. The respectable will have their desires limited if they are educated (in moderation and, if necessary, philosophy), and the base will have their power limited if they are kept inferior through hard work and few possessions and are not provoked by injustice at the hands of intemperate superiors. Education for the few and hard work for the many, not welfare and high taxes (like Athens' dole and Phaleas' dowries), are thus Aristotle's solution to what we now call social injustice.[65]

1267b9   The ninth criticism shows that, quite apart from Phaleas' failure to notice the facts of desire and foreign war, he has even failed to notice all the facts about possessions, and specifically that possessions include more than landed property. The effect of this oversight, however, which is extraordinary in a man who professed to pay so much attention to property, is altogether to overturn his regime, since the inequality he removes in one form of wealth will be nullified by the inequality he fails to remove in the rest. Consequently he will not even reap from the policy the minor benefits to be had from it.

1267b13   The tenth and last criticism concerns the size of the city. This must be small under Phaleas' scheme because, we may suppose, if the citizen body were large the number of public slaves to supply all their needs would also have to be large, which would be both expensive and dangerous. So if these slave-artisans must instead be few, so also must the number of citizens whose needs they serve. This requirement would still hold even if the land was rich and extensive and could sustain many more. Aristotle's objection, then, will not to be that citizenship is denied to artisans or that the city is small[66] (his own best city has both features), but that the smallness will be imposed for a wrong and unnecessary reason, namely that the artisans will be public slaves (as opposed to aliens or even, in some instances, private slaves). For though smallness might not itself be a disadvantage to a city, smallness imposed for a reason that has no regard to prosperity or defense would certainly be. The difficulty would be overcome if only those engaged on communal works were public slaves, for then the numbers of citizens could be expanded without much regard to how few the publicly owned artisans were.

1267b19   Looked at as a whole, what Aristotle's criticisms of Phaleas most reveal is a failure to deal with anything except material property and above all a failure to take account of the human soul and its desires. The other omissions, as about foreign affairs and movable property, might also be traced to the same cause (ignorance of the other things people desire besides landed property). The criticism of Phaleas may thus serve, and be regarded, as a criticism of political materialism in general.

---

65. One may note that Aristotle says nothing about changing the desires of the many and the base, a pessimism about educating them in virtue which recalls the last chapter of the *Ethics*. Note also that all the preceding criticisms directed by Aristotle against Phaleas could be directed with equal justice against contemporary socialists and liberals, who seem no less obsessed with leveling property (but not desires or political power), and no less indifferent to the complexities of the human soul—though contemporary conservatives are often not much better in this regard.

66. Contra Schütrumpf (1991: 2:256).

Chapter 8

~ THE REGIME OF HIPPODAMUS OF MILETUS

~ HIPPODAMUS AS MAN AND AS LEGISLATOR

1267b22 If Phaleas is an example of a political materialist, Hippodamus is an example of a political technocrat. Judging by Aristotle's criticisms, one may find it hard to say whose proposals are worse. But Phaleas at least had a genuine concern with political justice, the removal of faction, whereas Hippodamus seems to have had no such concern at all. His specialty was dividing the street plan of cities, not legislating for them. It is perhaps for this reason that Aristotle draws attention to Hippodamus' peculiar personal habits, something he does not do as regards anyone else he criticizes. For these habits show that if Hippodamus cared about anything, it was hardly the political good or the just. His failings as a political thinker seem elementary.

The word "extraordinary" (*perittos*, 1267b24) that Aristotle uses to describe Hippodamus is the same word used earlier to describe the speeches of Socrates (2.6.1265a11). But Hippodamus is extraordinary through ambition, not out of a concern for truth, and for appearance and dress, not for his discourses or speeches. Aristotle's particular comments here look merely anecdotal but they curiously anticipate what follows. For Hippodamus' chief error would seem to be his failure to grasp the peculiar character of political study and his attempt to reduce it to mathematics or technique. He applies to one study principles and methods that properly belong to another (doing so, no doubt, about the "whole of nature" and not just politics). In other words, despite his reputation as a divider, he fails to divide what he should divide. The same might be said of his hair and clothing, for in the first he does not divide himself from women[67] and in the second he does not divide summer from winter. If ambition could make Hippodamus collapse the divisions between the sexes and the seasons, one should not be too surprised if it also made him collapse the other, and less obvious, divisions between the kinds of knowledge or science.

By thus drawing our attention to the eccentricity and ambition of Hippodamus the man, Aristotle in effect warns us not to expect anything better from Hippodamus the political thinker. Such a warning would seem all the more necessary in this context because Hippodamus was also the first not engaged in politics to speak about the best regime. There is doubtless nothing wrong in principle with non-politicians doing this, but there is something wrong if they do it without knowing

---

67. Long hair among men was, however, also a practice of the Spartans and the admirers of Spartans, Newman (2:296), though the Spartans seem hardly to be commended for their knowledge of women, or indeed of men (2.9, 5(8).4).

what they are talking about, especially if their priority in the matter, and their fame in other things, has given them a name to attract and impress an audience.

1267b30/37/1268a11 Having thus described Hippodamus the man, Aristotle gives next a summary of the proposals of Hippodamus the legislator. They concern population and land, law, and rulers. First, Hippodamus composed his city of ten thousand men divided into the three parts of artisans, farmers, and warriors; second, he divided the land into the three parts of sacred, public, and private; third, he thought there were three kinds of law, concerning cases of insolence, of injury, and of death; fourth, he legislated for a single supreme court; fifth, he wanted changes in the way courts reached decisions (instead of balloting, the jurors do one of three things: write the verdict, write nothing, or write distinctions); sixth, he laid down a law awarding honor to anyone who discovered something useful for the city; seventh, he laid down a law providing public sustenance for the children of those who died in battle (thinking, falsely, he was the first to discover it); eighth, the rulers were all to be elected by the people, that is, by the three parts of the city; ninth, the elected rulers were to take care of three things: common matters, foreign matters, and matters affecting orphans.[68]

There are three striking features to these proposals: they display a passion for neat divisions (reflecting Hippodamus' training as a divider of cities); they are extraordinary in making division always into threes; they display a keen desire for honor (the law about discoveries is presumably meant to have honor for Hippodamus as its primary effect). A wish to be distinguished for technical ingenuity seems to be the main motive behind them. Certainly, as Aristotle proceeds to show, they are not motivated by much care for, or understanding of, political realities. He focuses his criticisms, however, on Hippodamus' division of citizens and land, on the jurors, and on the law about discoveries. He omits to criticize the other proposals, doubtless not because they are altogether sound, but because it is unnecessary to say everything. Much can fairly be left to the reader to think out for himself, especially when he has before him the model of Aristotle's criticisms of the other proposals (but see 6(4).16 on jury courts).

~ CRITICISM OF HIPPODAMUS

~ CITIZENS AND LAND

1268a16 The first criticism is that those who do not have arms must effectively be slaves of those who do. For, as is manifest, the armed will always be able to

---

68. It is perhaps only incidental that one can number Aristotle's list of Hippodamus' proposals as a multiple of three, but the fact is amusing nevertheless. Schütrumpf, however, counts the proposals as ten, not nine (1991: 2:30–31, 262), apparently taking that about the composition of the single supreme court (that it will be constituted from certain elected senators) as a separate proposal.

force their will on the unarmed as and when they want to.[69] It is also manifest that only warriors can furnish generals[70] and only those with arms can guard the regime from external and internal threats. The warriors must therefore have ultimate control over deliberation, legislation, the courts, and in short the whole life of the city. Consequently the farmers and artisans, being excluded from any real say in the regime, could not be friendly to it. Hippodamus, in other words, has produced a citizen body of soldiers and slaves in conflict with itself.

1268a25 Supposing such a conflict, therefore, Aristotle points out, second, that if the armed are to keep the farmers and artisans in check, they will need to be stronger, and strength requires numbers as well as arms. So if Hippodamus allows the armed to be large enough to keep imposing their will, there will be no need in the first place for him to give a share to the farmers and artisans in the regime, and certainly no need to give them a share in deciding who the rulers will be, for the warriors will be sufficient for everything by themselves.

1268a29 The third criticism is that the farmers serve no use since they do not provide food for the warriors (which is the usual point of having a separate, and subservient, farming class). To this it has been objected that, on the contrary, they serve the use of providing food for the artisans. For how else could the artisans get their food?[71] A first answer is that they could get their food from the warriors, for the warriors are supposed to have provisions from land set aside for them and could give their surplus to the artisans in exchange for manufactures (how the warriors get these provisions from their land is of course a problem but it gets discussed next). Alternatively, the artisans could get food by trading with farmers in some other city. Hence there is no need, as far as provisioning the artisans is concerned, that the city have in it a separate class of farmers.

The farmers will serve a use, of course, if they are there to provide food for the warriors. For the job of the warriors is to protect and defend the city, which is a service they could only exchange in return for food with farmers who belonged to the same city. As it is, however, Hippodamus has arranged for the warriors to be

---

69. This truth applies, one would think, as much to modern nation-states as to ancient cities, even if it is a truth that remains hidden and (hitherto) unacted on in liberal democracies because of the conventions of representative rule. But military coups elsewhere prove what the possibilities are, and the Soviet empire, among others, proved that huge nation-states can come entirely under the sway of professional armies. The hostility with which the National Rifle Association in the United States views any limitation by federal and state governments on the right to bear arms owes something, perhaps, to the lingering awareness of such facts.

70. The convention that untrained civilians can be commanders in chief, as in the case of the president of the United States, is only a convention and would easily be nullified by any general who was powerful and daring enough to ignore it.

71. A point raised by Newman (2:302–3) and Schütrumpf (1991: 2:273).

provisioned from their own land and the farmers are a third class farming separate land separately. They are a fifth wheel in the regime, as it were, spinning uselessly.

1268a35   The mention of nourishing the warriors leads naturally to the fourth criticism about the land set aside for them. None of the possibilities of how this land is to be farmed makes much sense in the context, as Aristotle has little trouble pointing out. For whether the warriors farm it or the farmers or someone else, conflicts will arise with Hippodamus' other proposals and intentions. And even if one might perhaps be able to think up some solutions to these conflicts (though Hippodamus did not do so), there was nevertheless no need in the first place to propose the arrangement that generates them, an arrangement that, moreover, serves no obvious point beyond mathematical neatness.

It is evident from these four criticisms how little thought of a political nature Hippodamus devoted to his proposals. It would seem that his thinking about citizens and land simply stopped when he had got a pleasing division of them into threes and the possibility that this division might give rise to problems and questions of a nontechnical sort did not occur to him.

~ JURORS
1268b4   The first criticism here, that Hippodamus' proposals about jurors could only be carried out properly if jurors were arbitrators (after the fashion of our own system of juries), is clear enough. What is not so clear is what the criticism is a criticism of. Some commentators think that, because of Aristotle's reference to what is possible in existing jury courts and to the practice of most legislators in forbidding jurors to confer, he is criticizing the idea of making jurors into arbitrators.[72] But Aristotle makes no comment about the correctness of existing practice nor about whether most legislators are right. Perhaps he thinks that either system would do (whether making or not making jurors arbitrators), provided it were done properly.[73] His objection may therefore be rather that Hippodamus' proposal is inconsistent with current practice and that therefore he ought to have proposed a change in that practice as well. In other words, since Hippo-

72. The view of Saunders (1995: 144–45), and also of Susemihl and Hicks (1894: 271, 275) who accuse Aristotle in addition of failing to notice the superiority and originality of Hippodamus' proposal.

73. Jury courts containing hundreds of jurors are, after all, a democratic feature (8(6).2.1317b25–28). In other regimes, notably oligarchies and aristocracies, cases are decided not by jurors but by certain officeholders, who doubtless could and did confer (3.1.1275b5–12). Aristotle cannot, therefore, be understood as being simply in favor of jury courts as opposed to trial by official (for he was not simply in favor of democracy, or even polity). Our modern jury system is a combination of trial by official (for the presiding judge is such an official) and by jurors. Moreover, our jurors are very few in number (twelve usually); are obliged to confer in order to reach, if possible, a unanimous verdict; and only decide guilt, not also the penalty (which is decided instead by the judge according to law).

damus is in effect requiring his jurors to be arbitrators, he ought also to have made it possible for them to behave as such, that is, to confer and reach collective decisions. But Hippodamus has done no such thing. On the contrary he clearly supposes that the jurors are to continue deciding their verdict separately, since he speaks of them as still casting separate ballots, and that the decision is reached by counting the ballots so cast.

1268b11   The second criticism naturally follows on and reinforces the first by showing what confusion will result from the fact that the jurors are being required to behave and not behave like arbitrators at the same time. Inevitably all these hundreds of jurors (for Hippodamus says nothing about changing current practice in this respect) are going to have different opinions about what is just, with some thinking acquittal is just, others a fine of this much, others of that much. But since they are not to confer and try to reconcile their opinions in a collective decision beforehand, what they write on their ballots will be these differing opinions. And then, of course, it will be impossible or hard to count them so as to get a single, overall verdict.[74]

1268b17   The third criticism concerns the reason Hippodamus gave for his proposal, namely to prevent the jurors from committing perjury if they are forced simply to acquit or condemn when they really think the verdict should lie somewhere in between. Aristotle's response is simple and decisive. The matter is a mere question of logic: to deny that the defendant deserves a fine of twenty minas, say, is not to deny that he deserves some lesser fine. It is simply to say he does not deserve to pay a fine of twenty minas. The two denials are different and the first is not the same as, nor does it entail, the second, so there is no perjury.

One might complain, of course, that in this way the accused gets off scot-free and pays nothing when the juror thought he owed at least something. This and the like worries seem to be what lie behind Hippodamus' proposal[75] and we might well wonder why Aristotle does not address them. But, in a way, he has addressed them. For if there is a problem here, it is not that the jurors forswear, but that there is no room given for them to confer and arbitrate. The issue then is arbitration, not perjury. Hippodamus has failed to see this fact and so has mistaken what sorts of solution are appropriate. Moreover, since any solution would require some major change in existing practice, Hippodamus has also failed to consider if the problem,

74. Saunders (1995: 144) suggests that one could add up all the figures of the fines proposed and then divide by the number of jurors. But while this may solve the problem mathematically, it will not solve it politically. For, first, there are other sorts of punishment where averaging could hardly work (as whether to inflict the death penalty, or hard labor, or a long prison term), and, second, averaging will be a standing temptation to jurors to play the game of exaggerating, or of reducing, their assessment of the fine in order to force the average as close as possible to what they really think is just (that is, it will tempt jurors to forswear themselves in exactly the way Hippodamus wants to avoid).

75. As is noted by Newman (2:306) and Saunders (1995: 144–45).

to the extent there is one, could not be solved in some less drastic way within the existing system.

1268b22   That Aristotle turns next to Hippodamus' proposal about giving honor to those who discover something of advantage to the city is perhaps not accidental. The proposal about jurors is something that Hippodamus doubtless considered useful and wished to be honored for. That it would also require a major change in existing practice makes it an instance of one of the dangers in the present proposal, namely the danger involved in changing established law.

So, first, there is the criticism that this proposal will encourage informers and changes of regime. For one of the things useful to a city is to discover threats or conspiracies against it. But the prospect of winning honor will be a temptation to the greedy and ambitious to bring charges of conspiracy against prominent figures, quite regardless of truth and public safety. Such mischief, however, not untypically provokes changes of regime, as from democracy to oligarchy or from democracy to tyranny (7(5).5).

1268b25   Second is the criticism that whether Hippodamus' proposal is a good one or not depends on the answer to another and prior question, namely whether it is harmful or beneficial to change the ancestral laws if a better one comes along. For if this question is answered in the negative, then Hippodamus' proposal can hardly be accepted, and evidence for a negative answer is provided by the fact that the proposal could serve as an occasion for some to introduce novelties that would overthrow the regime. Of course, if the question were answered in the affirmative, then Hippodamus' proposal might be allowed to stand. But Aristotle's complaint still holds. Hippodamus' proposal is logically posterior to this other question, but he has not even realized that there is another question, let alone made any attempt to answer it.

1268b31   Not unreasonably, therefore, does Aristotle decide, third, to complete his study of Hippodamus with a discussion of this other question. Arguing, as is his wont, on either side, Aristotle comes to an answer that mediates both extremes, an answer that avoids the defects while retaining the merits of each. First he argues on the side of changing ancestral law if some better one is available, and gives several reasons.

The first is an appeal to the other arts and sciences where changing the ancestral precepts for better ones has proved advantageous. So if political science is like these, then the same change in it should also be advantageous. Evidence that the likeness does hold is then taken from instances of ancient laws. These are overly simple and barbaric and so, being like the ancestral precepts in medicine and gymnastics, would seem to need changing in the same way. The practice of buying wives is barbaric since it treats wives like slaves (1.2.1252b5–7), but so also is the practice of carrying arms about, since it would seem to indicate that those who do so are not yet acting as fellows of one city sharing a common life but remain wary of each other as of potential enemies.[76] The law from Cyme seems simple in not paying regard to the probability that family members will tell lies for each other against strangers.[77]

1269a3 The previous reference to ancient laws might, however, be taken as a separate argument if one takes it with the remark here about everyone seeking for what is good, not for what is ancestral. For one could read it thus: (1) what is good is preferable to the ancestral if the ancestral is not also good; (2) ancestral laws are often not good (they are in fact simple and barbaric); (3) therefore new and better laws are preferable to existing and ancestral ones. Alternatively the remark might be taken as by itself a separate argument: (1) what is good is preferable to the ancestral; (2) existing laws are ancestral; (3) therefore good and new laws are preferable to existing and worse ones. The point, however, remains the same whichever way one takes it.

1269a4/8 The third argument appeals to the likely foolishness and simplicity of the first humans and their laws, and hence to the folly of abiding by their folly instead of changing the laws whenever something better is found. The fourth argument, unlike the other three, is independent of any supposed simpleness or folly in ancient law and refers to a defect that must attach to any law, even the best. For particular cases may always arise that do not fit a given universal rule, and so the rule may need either to be qualified in some way, or at least to be suspended for this or that particular. If the latter, the action of a judge might be sufficient; if the former, a change in the law might be required (*Ethics* 5.10).

1269a12 These four arguments show that sometimes laws should be changed, for since they show that existing laws can be bad or defective and that better laws can be found to replace them, they show that one cannot reasonably hold that no law should ever be changed. They do not, however, show that laws should always be changed in favor of better ones, for other factors are relevant to change in the law over and above the quality of their particular content. So Aristotle now argues on the other side of the question.

His first counterargument refers to the fact that frequent change by itself involves a certain damage, the damage of accustoming people to disobeying the law.

76. One is reminded, perhaps, of the Wild West in the United States, which is supposed to have been wild for this sort of reason, though one may note that such wildness can be found in many a large modern city. The Spartans also carried arms about, but because of their slaves rather than because of each other (2.9.1269a38–39).

77. As noted by Newman (2:309) and Susemihl and Hicks (1894: 277). Aristotle need not be understood as speaking in his own voice at this point. Since he is arguing dialectically he need only repeat what could plausibly be said, whether or not he would himself fully agree.

For as people see laws often being changed, and as they find themselves required now to follow and now not to follow the same law, they will come to regard no law seriously and will follow or not follow law as they please, expecting that if a law has not yet been changed it soon will be.[78] Consequently, to avoid such damage, change, if change there must be, should be rare and confined to those that promise major improvements.

1269a19 The second counterargument picks up on the same fact of custom and habit but uses it to attack the supposition behind the first of the arguments in favor of change, namely the analogy with the other arts and sciences. The analogy is false because rules in the case of the arts and sciences do not get their force from habit, whereas laws in the case of politics do. Here indeed is a major difference between technique and law or between art and morals. The first is acquired by learning, the second by habituation (*Ethics* 2.1.1103a14–18), and while one can always be learning new and better things without destroying the existing art (for rather the changes perfect the art), one cannot always be getting used to new and better habits without destroying those one has already acquired, and indeed without introducing other ones (specifically disobedience to rulers) which are bad.

1269a24 The third counterargument is also, in a way, directed at the falsity of the analogy with the arts. It draws attention to the fact that it matters much in politics, if not in art, which laws are changed and by whom. For if those laws on which the regime depends are changed (as laws about elections and who may serve in what offices), the regime will be changed, and if anyone at all may change the laws, including someone who holds no office or authority, the same result may follow (thus indeed have tyrants arisen). In an art or science, by contrast, it matters little who introduces an improvement (young or old, layman or expert) or whether the improvement concerns something peripheral to the art or something central (indeed the latter are the better and more significant improvements). The reason is doubtless that the well-being of an art does not depend on an authority vested in persons whereas the well-being of the political order does.[79]

---

78. Such change of existing laws is also a cause of revolution, as Aristotle notes later, 7(5).7.1307a40–b19, 8.1307b30–40.

79. Aristotle's argument in these sections needs noting with some care. For he is not arguing against improvement in the arts, nor he is saying, or implying, that technical innovations are a threat to the political stability of the city such that, for instance, a technically innovative city would be forever undermining itself, contra Rahe (1992: 82–83). All he is doing is noting the difference between the arts and politics and between improvements in the one and improvements in the other. A politically stable but technically innovative city, as far as these arguments are concerned at any rate, need not be an impossibility, provided it carefully distinguished between politics and technology (in the way that Hippodamus and his law evidently did not). For Aristotle's distinction works as much against the validity of reasoning from the premise that the arts change frequently to the conclusion that the laws must be changed frequently, as against the validity of reasoning from the premise that the laws must

When he proposed his law about honor, Hippodamus ignored such considerations. Once again his knowledge of and interest in political realities seem nonexistent, and while he doubtless possessed much technique, he possessed little or no prudence. But politics is, above all, a work of prudence (for this is the peculiar virtue of the ruler, 3.4.1277b25–30). Prudence and its role in human affairs may be said to be a distinctively Aristotelian discovery, or Aristotelian emphasis,[80] whose usefulness for the city could hardly be overestimated. It is also, interestingly enough, a useful discovery that the city could honor without fear.

Chapter 9

~ THE REGIME OF THE SPARTANS

~ SLAVERY

1269a29 Aristotle turns next to regimes actually in use in certain cities. He names only two such regimes here, the Spartan and Cretan, omitting the Carthaginian (to which, however, he shortly devotes a whole chapter). The reason is, perhaps, that the quality of the Carthaginian regime, and its likeness to the Spartan and Cretan, are not generally acknowledged and Aristotle has to draw attention to the fact at the beginning of his chapter on Carthage. The reason for this lack of acknowledgment may, in turn, be that Carthage was not Greek, but Phoenician, and most Greeks would find it hard to admit that any barbarians could be equal or even superior to the Greeks, at least until all Greek candidates had been canvassed and found wanting first.

The two questions Aristotle poses for his investigation of regimes in use have appeared also in the previous discussions,[81] but there is perhaps some point raising them explicitly here because admirers of regimes in use seem not to have distinguished the two but to have supposed (especially in the case of Sparta, 4(7).14.1333b5–1334a10) that because the legislation fit the regime, the legislation also fit the best arrangement; or that because the regime had the best order, all its legislation fit that arrangement too.

---

not be allowed to change frequently to the conclusion that the arts must not be allowed to change frequently. If one wants to show that innovation in the arts always brings with it innovation in the laws, one will need some other or additional argument.

80. As Bien argues at some length (1968–69).

81. So the regime of the *Laws*, for instance, apart from being criticized for legislation that is not noble with a view to the best, is also criticized for legislation about elections that conflicts with the supposition of the regime, namely polity; and the regime of Phaleas is criticized for legislation that will not in fact achieve its supposition of equality. The two topics of the end and what leads to the end are mentioned explicitly again later, 4(7).13.1331b26–38, where it is also stressed that both need to be correct.

1269a34/b7   Aristotle first discusses, as he did with the *Laws*, certain presuppositions of the regime, notably the parts of the household (slaves, women, and property), and then the regime itself or the offices. He also begins with a matter relating to the first of his two questions, legislation with a view to the best arrangement, or, as he says here, noble government (1269a34–35). For since the best is virtue and since virtue requires leisure, or freedom from necessity (4(7).9.1329a1–2), legislation to secure leisure is manifestly necessary. But about the only way to secure leisure is through the use of slaves.[82] The slaves chosen by Sparta and Crete, however, were an indigenous and conquered population who, as Aristotle shows, caused, at least in the case of Sparta, more trouble and burdens than they were worth by rising up in armed revolt or by being impossible to control, whether through leniency or harshness. Hence this cannot be the best way to secure the needed leisure.[83]

∿ WOMEN

1269b12   As regards women, Aristotle quickly makes it clear that worse harm can come to a city from unruly women than from unruly slaves. He criticizes the Spartans in this regard on the basis of both of his two questions, that of the best arrangement and that of the supposition of the regime. For the first question is, I take it, what he intends by referring to the happiness of the city, since the city is arranged best when it is arranged for the good and happy life. At any rate the first criticism (which is, in fact, a general one, applying to all cities) is of the following sort. The household (as shown in book 1) has man and woman as its principal parts (the other parts, slaves and children, are either not free or not adult), and households are parts of the city. But the household is part of the city concretely through its head, the man, who is a citizen of the city. For the man is a citizen, not as a mere individual, but as heading a household and so as joined intimately to a woman. Consequently the woman, in a way, enters the city through the man and the city becomes divided, in effect, into men and women (for even if the women do not personally share in office, they effectively do so through the men whose other

---

82. Machines and robots are also another answer (1.4.1253b33–1254a1), but while labor-saving machines are now available in abundance, robots sufficiently sophisticated to do everything necessary on their own do not yet exist. Hired laborers and servants who work for pay might also do the job (as they do now for those who can afford them), but Aristotle would presumably regard these as slaves in fact if not in name, since the best that is being got from them is the use of the body (1.5.1254b16–20).

83. The solution Aristotle himself proposes later is to import slaves from abroad who are lacking in spirit (4(7).10.1330a25–28). Their coming from abroad would make them less ready to revolt, as they would not have the belief that the land was really theirs; and their lacking spirit would make them natural slaves, for spirit would seem to be a necessary, if not a sufficient, condition for the virtue of a master, especially the virtue of courage; see Dobbs (1994: 83).

half they are). To leave women without legislation, therefore, is to leave half the city without legislation, which is clearly contrary to the best arrangement.

1269b19 From this general criticism it follows that the happiness of the Spartans has been harmed by their failure to legislate for the women. So Aristotle shows, second, that this failure has also harmed the supposition of the regime. For that supposition is steadfast endurance and the women, being left without legislation, live completely dissolute lives, which is patently in conflict with such endurance.

1269b23 But the problem is not only that the women are dissolute, for from them the vice has infected the whole regime, and with respect to wealth, rule, and usefulness. That wealth must become an object of honor is obvious enough. License sets free the passions and to satisfy passions requires much wealth, not least when the passions are for expensive things like fine clothes, perfumes, and jewelry. To please their womenfolk, therefore, the men will have to pursue wealth, and all the more so the more unable they are to resist female charms. So if, as Aristotle contends quoting the story of Ares and Aphrodite, martial pursuits stimulate in men love of women, Spartans will be even more overcome by their women than men in other cities and so even more in pursuit of the money their women crave.[84]

1269b31 When the men are conquered by their women, rule must effectively be in the hands of the women, however much it remains nominally in those of the men.[85] But women can scarcely be made as steadfast in endurance as men can, so rule by women must take away from steadfast endurance in the city, and all the more so given that the women in question were sunk in luxury. We may note, too, that Aristotle indicates that the rule of women was at its height during the Spartan empire (which would be reasonable enough, since that is when the men would have been in the best position to satisfy the women's passions, and so when the women would have been most keen to exploit their power). But if so, then it follows that the power of women was greatest when it could also do the most damage, which makes the effect of their license even worse. Nevertheless, it is nicely ironic that when the Spartans held their greatest empire over others, the women held their greatest power over the Spartans. Aristotle doubtless notes this fact with a wry smile. Spartans prided themselves on manliness and were famed throughout Greece because of it. But in truth their rule was womanly.

1269b34 This womanliness or lack of steadfast endurance in the city comes

---

84. Although Aristotle mentions homosexuality among the Celts here, he is silent about it among the Spartans. Spartan homosexuality, however, was ritual homosexuality, as noted by Rahe (1992: 152–56), which does not, as such, mean that the Spartans honored or preferred sex with men as opposed to sex with women. It is the honoring or preferring of homosexuality, however, that Aristotle notes among the Celts.

85. For some of the historical evidence about Sparta, see Bradford (1986).

out also in the women's brazenness or boldness (an inevitable result of their license and of their dominance over the men), something that did not fit them for peace and made them a positive nuisance in war. Hence, the city, instead of holding up manfully in the face of invasion (by the Thebans in 369 B.C.), fell into more uproar because of its womanliness than because of the enemy.

1269b39 The Theban invasion happened late in Sparta's history, and it might appear that the unruliness of the women was a fault that was also late, indeed a degeneration in the regime, and not something essential or integral to its construction.[86] So Aristotle forestalls this conclusion by pointing out that it goes back to the very beginning and is coeval with the regime (for Lycurgus, who is here mentioned by name, was supposed to be the first founder). That Aristotle is nevertheless prepared to allow Lycurgus some excuse does not alter the force of his criticism: the error was a capital one and, as he makes progressively clear, lies at the bottom of almost everything that was wrong with the regime.

~ PROPERTY

1270a11 Aristotle turns next to property, and naturally enough, for the women are as much behind the evils here as elsewhere. So their license has contributed to the greed that marks the excessively unequal distribution of the property. Such inequality could not, of course, have arisen had the citizens not been greedy, and greed is a vice and manifestly contrary to the best arrangement. But the unequal division of property is also contrary to the supposition of the regime, as is noted shortly. First, however, mention is made of other faults that compound it. These faults are certain laws (free bequests of land, large dowries, marrying off of heiresses to anyone) whose effect can only be the further concentration of land into few hands. That they may not go back to the beginning of the regime[87] does not matter much since the sources of them must, or at least the source they have in the greed and the license of the women. Indeed, these laws seem tailor-made for the women. For, being bold or brazen as well as dissolute, these women will browbeat the already submissive men into giving extra land to their husbands (and

86. Some modern commentators have taken this line, explaining that when Aristotle praises the Spartan regime he is thinking of its early years, and that when he blames it he is thinking of its later decline, as David (1982–83). There is, however, no conflict between the praise and blame, since what Aristotle praises is Sparta's principle of educating the citizens throughout life, and what he blames is the miserable education that was actually given, 4(7).14 and 5(8).4, with *Ethics* 10.9.1180a24–29, and see also Braun (1956) and Schütrumpf (1991: 2:294). Moreover, while it may be true that some of what Aristotle singles out for criticism was of later origin (as perhaps the law about the disposition of heiresses), there is no doubt that he finds the root cause in the original dissoluteness of the women. That the effects of this evil became more pervasive over time is only to be expected, but the evil itself was there from the beginning.

87. The question, however, is a controversial one and much debated by scholars; see Newman (2:325–26), Rahe (1992: 169–72), Schütrumpf (1991: 2:308–9).

not to needier families), into bestowing large dowries on them when they marry, and, especially if heiresses (of whom there will be not a few if their brothers are often risking their lives in war), into giving them in marriage only to already rich men, so that their wealth and the man's might be enough to sate their passions.

All these practices and passions must inevitably narrow the distribution of wealth so that poorer sons, instead of being helped back up by marriage to wealthier wives, will become poorer still. Hence the number of families producing male children rich enough to take part in the regime must fall. The drastic decline in the numbers of citizen-soldiers was therefore perfectly predictable, as was also the military defeat (at the hands of the Thebans in 371 B.C.), which, in these circumstances, was simply waiting to happen. Greed could cause no greater harm.

1270a34   This problem of numbers, of course, could not go unnoticed, but the two remedies proposed failed to do anything to solve it. About the first, Aristotle expressly notes that it was said to belong to the time of the earlier kings and was therefore near to the founding, and perhaps he means us to suppose the same about the second.[88] This problem of numbers, then, also goes back to the beginning, like the greed from which it sprang.

The first remedy, however, of introducing outsiders into the regime, is at best a stopgap measure and would solve nothing unless continually repeated (which it was not, doubtless because greed got in the way). Aristotle's own solution, a permanent leveling of possessions, while much superior, would be opposed by greed and hence especially by the women, which is perhaps why it was never proposed or adopted. Neither legislator nor kings seem to have been man enough to face the women down.

The second remedy, a law about releasing fathers of sons from military duties, is clearly not even a temporary solution to the problem but only makes matters worse by increasing the numbers of the poor, that is, of those excluded from the regime and unable to become soldiers. Yet it only makes matters worse, as Aristotle expressly notes, because of the way the land is divided. But the land is so divided, and kept that way, largely because of greed and the women.

〜 OFFICES

〜 THE EPHORATE

1270b6   Aristotle turns finally to the regime proper or the offices, and first to the ephorate. The opening criticism here is that the ephorate has great power and yet is filled from the populace and so from the needy, who are easy to corrupt

---

88. It would therefore seem necessary to suppose, with Newman (2:325–36), that Aristotle thought the laws he has just mentioned, which are a main contributory cause of the dearth of citizens, also went back close to the same time and were not of more recent origin, though he does admittedly express his doubts about the truth of the story he relates in this present passage.

with bribes (it is better, as Aristotle notes later, to give control to the populace only as a mass and not through offices they hold individually, 3.11.1281b21–38). In Sparta's case, of course, the poverty of the populace is made worse by the unequal division of property and their venality by the greed of the city as a whole (for the same impulsions toward greed must operate on them as on anyone else), or, in other words, by the women again. Such poverty and venality would not matter so much if the ephors had little power. As it is, though, they are in a position to sell out the whole city and have almost done so.

1270b13   The second criticism is that, being poor yet powerful, the ephors function like the poor in an extreme democracy and force the kings, or those who must lead, to play the demagogue (see 6(4).4.1292a4–37). Hence the kings become subservient to the democratic element in the regime and cease to function as an independent element marked by, and caring for, virtue. The regime has thus ceased to be a mixture of democracy and aristocracy and become simply democratic.

1270b17   These first two criticisms are serious enough to make one think the ephorate is altogether a bad institution that would be better away. But Aristotle, looking for the good as well as the bad (2.1.1260b32–35), next notes that the ephorate performs the very necessary function of reconciling the populace to the regime and so of completing its balance (something of no little importance, 6(4).9). He would therefore not be in favor of abolishing it. His final three criticisms, in fact, while further showing up how bad the institution is, also point to the sorts of corrections that, if made, would remove pretty well all the faults, including the first two just mentioned.

So the first correction would be to change the manner of election, presumably to a form of popular and written vote. Aristotle does not explain how election was actually done in Sparta, but indeed he really has no need to. Election should manifestly be done in a mature way if it is to be done at all, and such ways are not hard to think out (including some way to do it that might reduce the chances of the very needy and venal getting elected; see 6(4).14–16). Still, that those famed for their manhood, but really dominated by women, should elect their rulers like children has a certain wry humor to it.

1270b28/31   The second correction would be to have the ephors use their great judicial power according to law and not at their own discretion. In this way too their venality would do less harm since they would be less able to sell their decisions. The third correction would complement this reduction in the ephors' ability to sell decisions by reducing also their desire to do so. For given the tyrannical power they have in office, ephors are clearly in a position to do just about whatever they want, but only *as* ephors. As citizens they are subject to all the harsh rigors that every other Spartan is subject to. The resulting tension between the two conditions would evidently be a severe trial even for good men, let alone for the rather base sorts who become ephors. It is not surprising, then, that poor men, subjected to excessive hardship on the one hand and grasping women on the other, should, when in possession of great power, use it to seek relief in base gratifications. Far better, therefore, to remove or mitigate the tension by putting some restrictions on the ephorate's power and bringing it more in line with the steadfast endurance desired by the regime.

∾ THE SENATE

1270b35/71a1/a5 The senate was earlier said to be the reward of virtue (1270b24–25), which would make it a beneficial office if those who filled it were in fact virtuous. Aristotle's reasonable comment here is, first, that even so, because of possible senility, they should not be allowed to go on exercising control over the greatest matters throughout life, and, second, that anyway the condition is not met. The senators are venal like the ephors, and no doubt for similar reasons: not poverty perhaps, but certainly the excessive harshness of their military life (the common education of all Spartans) combined with subjection to greedy and licentious women. Consequently they should, third, not go unaudited. Auditing would impose, if only through fear, some of the missing restraint (see 8(6).4.1318b27–1319a4).[89] The ephors might seem to be those who should do the auditing (since they are the popular part of the regime), but it is clear that the ephors already have too much power and that they would only use any extra to sell themselves and the city all over again. Although he makes no further comment here, Aristotle would presumably want auditing instead to be in the hands of the whole assembly (as in Solon's Athens, 2.12.1274a15–18, 3.11.1281b32–38, and cf. 8(6).4.1318b29–30).

1271a9 Of the three criticisms about election to the senate, the first, the childish manner, repeats the same point made about election to the ephorate. The second and third raise a more serious point about the evils of having to campaign for office: the second that only those who want office will get it (and to the exclusion of those who deserve it but do not want it), and the third that having to campaign for office promotes love of honor, the cause, along with love of money, of most voluntary wrongs or deliberate acts of injustice.[90]

Love of honor in Sparta, as opposed to love of money, is mentioned here for the first time by Aristotle. The love of money, as we already know, was not desired by the legislator but came about mainly because he failed to tame the women. The love of honor, however, is said to be his express work. How it is so in the case of the senate is clear. As regards the rest of the regime, Aristotle seems to have in mind what he mentions later, that the regime is wholly directed to war. Sparta is not de-

---

89. "Auditing" here (*euthunō*) refers to the practice of examining the accounts and conduct of outgoing officeholders to ensure they have not abused office. See MacDowell (1978: 170–72) for a description of the procedure at Athens.

90. The truth of these charges has surely not been much lessened by our own modern experience of campaigning for election.

signed to be at peace, and if defense at home is already secure, fighting can only be for domination of others abroad. The Spartans have been trained to want lordship over everyone else and so to want honor, the honor that is inseparable from empire. Thus imbued with the two chief causes of injustice, love of honor and love of money, the Spartans would seem fitted only for a life of tyranny and crime (as indeed Aristotle more or less says later, at 4(7).14.1333b24–1334a2, 5(8).4.1338b29–36).

∾ KINGS, COMMON MESSES, AND ADMIRALS

1271a18 The first criticism of the kings, that they should not be hereditary and for life but chosen according to character or way of life, appeals to the requirements of a king, that he must excel in virtue in his own right (3.17.1288a15–29, 7(5).10.1310b9–12). It also anticipates Aristotle's approval of the way kings are chosen in Carthage (2.11.1272b38–41). The second proves, from the practice of the regime itself, that the kings actually chosen are neither virtuous nor deemed capable of virtue (for they are not deemed capable of exercising their powers unsupervised and unopposed). The kings, in other words, are no better than the ephors and senators: none is fit to exercise office.

1271a26 It may seem strange that Aristotle deals with the common messes in the context of a discussion of offices. But the messes are in effect a sort of office, for not to belong to a mess is to be excluded from sharing in the regime. The fault Aristotle notes here is clear enough and it opposes the intention of the regime not unlike the way the ephorate does. For as the ephorate shifts the balance of the regime from aristocracy to democracy, so the messes shift the balance of the regime from democracy to oligarchy. Once again, however, we can trace here the perverse influence of the women and of greed. For land and provisions set aside as a common store for the messes, as in Crete, would be land and provisions not available for concentration in private hands to satisfy private greed. It is hardly surprising, therefore, that the Spartans have not arranged for any such way of provisioning the messes.

1271a37 The office of admiral (even though not hereditary nor held in perpetuity) was as powerful on sea as that of the kings was on land, and, since the Spartans love honor, any admiral would be bound to wield his power factionally, in opposition to the kings. For those who love honor always feel it is diminished if shared. Such resentment would be compounded in the case of Sparta, for the kings had their honor by birth. So those excluded by birth from the kingship would not only leap at the chance to seize the equivalent but also jealously assert it when acquired (as in the case of Lysander, 7(5).1.1301b19–20, 7.1306b31–33).

∾ SUPPOSITION OF THE REGIME AND FINANCES

1271a41 Having just criticized offices to do with war, Aristotle turns not unnaturally to criticize finally the orientation of the whole regime toward war. His two criticisms recall the two questions from the beginning of the chapter, about the best arrangement and about conflicts with the supposition of the regime. For he first shows that arranging everything toward war is not best and then that the handling of common finances is anyway in conflict with this arrangement.

That it is an error to suppose military virtue or courage is the only virtue is manifest of itself (and also from the *Ethics*), but Aristotle shows further how bad an error it is from the damage it inflicted on the Spartans. For, first, while it enabled them to win empire, it destroyed them when empire was won (their means were, in other words, opposed to their end, for they evidently wanted to keep empire, not merely to win it); second, it induced in them a false belief about which goods are for the sake of which (4(7).1.1323a34–b29). The mention of leisure in this context recalls the criticism with which Aristotle began, that slavery in Sparta was not arranged so as to secure leisure but required them to be forever on their guard against revolt. This error about slavery might well have been instrumental in causing their other error about the supposition of the regime, since it would necessarily force them to prize military dominance as the only key to survival.

1271b10   The last fault, about the deficiency of the common finances, clearly compounds those just noted, and puts the regime in even greater conflict with itself as well as perverting it from the best arrangement (no arrangement that starves the city of needed money and makes the individual citizens lovers of it can be best). The cause, however, of the failure of the Spartans to ensure they each pay their taxes returns to the greed that, as Aristotle's analysis has shown, infects the whole Spartan regime. It was greed, perhaps, as much as or more than the love of honor and empire, that was the undoing of the Spartans, and behind the greed we know lie the women. The women, in fact, seem like a cancer rotting the whole city. But if such harm can be done by vicious women left undisciplined by the legislator, what good, we may wonder, might not be done by virtuous ones whom the legislator has expressly taken in hand along with the men?

Chapter 10

～ THE REGIME OF THE CRETANS

～ HOW IT IS LIKE THE REGIME OF THE SPARTANS
1271b20/b32   About the Cretan regime Aristotle has less to say, and about the women he says nothing (Sparta seems something of an exception in this regard). That the Cretan regime is the older and the more primitive model from which the Spartan was derived is given support by the story of Lycurgus here related. This story must indeed be given some credence, for were it not ancient and

possessed of some truth, one would expect the Spartans to have invented a story giving themselves the original authorship of their own arrangements. What Aristotle next relates about Crete's suitability for empire and its actual possession of empire, even as far as Sicily, under Minos, gives some further credence to the idea of Cretan priority.[91] For if the Cretans could have attempted in the remote past what was only attempted again and recently by the Athenians at their most daring,[92] then that Crete was once sufficiently organized and powerful to have developed traditions that could be taken by the Spartans as a model is not implausible.

1271b40   Having stated the similarity of the two regimes as a general fact, Aristotle next confirms it from details about slaves, common messes (including the priority of the Cretan name for them), and the several offices (save that the Cretans abolished the kingship and the cosmoi have its powers as well, which makes them in principle, therefore, more powerful than the ephors at Sparta). There was no express mention earlier of the assembly at Sparta but it was implicit in the reference to elections and to the messes. What is said about the power possessed by the assembly is new but Aristotle apparently wishes it to be understood that in this respect too Sparta was like Crete, for later he treats the two as one when he contrasts the greater power given to the assembly in Carthage (2.11.1273a6–13).

HOW IT IS BETTER AND WORSE
THAN THE REGIME OF THE SPARTANS

1272a12   Aristotle's criticisms of the Cretan regime follow the ordering of topics he has just given, save that he does not say anything about the slaves (having already explained this point at the beginning of the last chapter, 2.9.1269a39–14). He begins instead with the messes, for although he mentioned these too in the same chapter, and as being superior to the Spartan because more common, only here does he give the details, including the rather striking one that the provisions from the common store are sufficient to sustain not only the common functions of divine worship and public service in the city, but also the whole of a man's family. A similar arrangement at Sparta would have done much to prevent depletion of the citizen body.

1272a22   The remarkable success of the Cretans in doing so much with the common store is attributed to the philosophy of the legislator in forcing on the people a certain abstinence in both food and sex, or at least in sex between men and women. For too many children would obviously make provisioning the messes from common stock difficult or impossible. That the Cretan legislator was aware of this fact, and aimed accordingly to limit both wealth and children, shows

91. As Newman (2:349) and Schütrumpf (1991: 2:335) rightly note, against Susemihl and Hicks (1894: 300).

92. The Athenian expedition to conquer Sicily set out in 415 B.C.

why one might describe his thinking as philosophical, since he had noticed what Plato and Phaleas did not (2.6.1265a38–b12, 7.1266b8–14).[93]

Aristotle is, however, more reserved about the device of homosexuality that the legislator chose as the means to limit children.[94] At least he puts off saying whether he approves of it or not. We can nevertheless conjecture on our own account that if the legislator's aim was to discourage luxury, the policy was bad since it did not limit sex but only changed the partners (homosexuality among the women perhaps developed also). If his aim was merely to discourage childbirth, he would succeed but at the expense of the virtue of moderation. Although Aristotle does not return to this question expressly later, he says enough to indicate that he would prevent luxury in food and sex by education in virtue (4(7).15.1334a11–36).[95] The Cretan legislator philosophized indeed, but surely not well enough.

1272a26   Apart from the messes, everything else in Crete appears much worse than in Sparta, especially the arrangement of the offices. For while the office of cosmoi has the Spartan fault that the cosmoi can be any chance persons who lack the virtue required of so great an office, it does not have the Spartan benefit of reconciling the populace to the regime, for it is not drawn from the whole populace but only from certain families. The fault is compounded by the fact that all the senators are drawn from the cosmoi. Hence all the offices (for there are no longer kings in Crete) are confined to the same families and it is not the case, as it is in Sparta, that the senators are representing a different part of the city from the cosmoi. These senators, moreover, have all the faults of the senators at Sparta.

1272a39   One would therefore expect the populace in Crete to be always on the verge of revolt, and since they are not, one might be tempted to conclude that the arrangements in Crete cannot be as bad as Aristotle alleges. To counter this, Aristotle points out that the acquiescence of the populace has other causes, one accidental and one deliberate.

The accidental cause is the isolation of the island, which means, not indeed that the rulers are more virtuous than in Sparta, but that they have no opportunity to behave as badly by accepting bribes and perverting justice. So profiting from office and injustice on the part of rulers, which are things that especially alienate the populace and drive them to faction (6(4).13.1297b6–8, 7(5).8.1308b34–38), are not prevalent in Crete.

1272b1   The deliberate one is the peculiar, and dynastic, practice of periodically suspending the office of cosmoi, by forced expulsion or resignation. Dynasty

---

93. Reason to doubt whether Aristotle can be right about the legislator's intention to limit childbirth has been sought in the fact that Crete seems always to have been so abundant in men that Cretans can be found serving as mercenaries throughout the Greek world; see Spyridakis (1979). But perhaps this fact is not decisive, or concerns rather the legislator's success, or lack thereof, than his intention.

94. Homosexuality in Crete seems to have been of the same ritualistic sort as it was in Sparta.

95. As Newman correctly notes (2:356).

is the technical name for an extreme oligarchy in the hands of a few very rich and powerful families (6(4).5.1292b5–10), and these expulsions and resignations in Crete are evidently at the behest of such families. Aristotle, of course, does not object in principle to the expulsion or resignation of officials (there might always be cases when someone was behaving so badly he should be removed or forced to resign), but he does rightly object to either happening at human whim and not according to law, for that is to invite abuse. But worse than expulsion and resignation is the abolition of the office of cosmoi altogether by the powerful who do not wish to submit to punishment. The dynastic character of this is evident, as it is further evident from the practice of the powerful in splitting up populace and friends and forming them into rival followings, in setting up monarchies (or centers of one-man rule), and in then fighting against each other. For this simply reduces rule to the arbitrary despotism of the powerful families.

But one can see, nevertheless, how these practices would tend to pacify the populace. For the populace will seldom come to resent rulers who are bad or unjust, since they will see all rulers so often expelled or resigning, and, perhaps more importantly, they will see themselves continually courted by the rich and powerful.[96]

1272b13   The problem with such a cure, however (which makes it in fact worse than the disease), is itself twofold: first, it amounts to periodic dissolutions of city and regime (the city is dissolved into rival gangs and the regime, or the offices, into control by powerful families); second, it makes the city an inviting prey to attackers (it is easy to defeat people who are already fighting themselves, 7(5).6.1305b18). That Crete has escaped paying the penalty for these faults, as for its fault with the slaves, is again because of the accident of isolation, and also because, since Minos' time, Crete has not been interested in empire. But the faults remain faults, nevertheless, as recent successful invasions have finally shown.

Chapter 11

~ THE REGIME OF THE CARTHAGINIANS

~ HOW IT IS BETTER THAN THE REGIME
OF THE SPARTANS AND CRETANS

1272b24   As regards the Carthaginian regime, Aristotle begins by pointing out why it too should be treated in a discussion of regimes reputed to be nobly

---

96. One might say something similar about the periodic elections in modern states, when all candidates are obliged to court the populace to create followings for themselves, by outdoing each other in making promises or in distributing public largesse (we forbear to call such promises and largesse bribes). These candidates and their followings, or followers, also fight each other, with slander and accusations if not with weapons.

governed and along with the Spartan and Cretan regimes. Indeed, it might seem more deserving of such treatment since it receives more praise. At any rate, the three regimes stand out from all others (perhaps because they alone make some effort at having a common education; *Ethics* 10.9.1180a24–29), and the Carthaginian most of all, as it turns out. For Carthage now receives from Aristotle both more praise and less blame than either of the others.

1272b29   The praise comes first and the fact that it is deserved is shown in general by a sign and then specifically by reference to details. The sign is threefold: that the populace acquiesce in the regime,[97] that there has been no faction, and also no tyranny worth speaking of.[98] The fact that acquiescence is accompanied here by the other two features helps explain why it can be taken as a sign of a tight arrangement in Carthage but not in Crete (where acquiescence was in large part secured precisely by faction and tyranny). As regards details, Carthage has what is good in Sparta (messes and a mixture of different offices) but escapes what is bad by choosing its offices according to merit instead of by birth or from anyone at all.[99] Nothing is said about the women.

~ DEVIATIONS IN THE REGIME OF THE CARTHAGINIANS

~ DEVIATIONS IN GENERAL

1273a2   The blame or the criticisms of Carthage get involved in constitutional details that are passed over in Aristotle's discussion of Sparta and Crete.[100] Perhaps the reason is that so many other things are at fault in the latter two regimes that only in the case of Carthage does Aristotle feel himself free to expand the scope of his review. His opening reference to deviations common to all three regimes seems to refer to the first question of chapter 9, that is, to deviations from what is best,[101] and he presumably means making the goal of the regime military

97. I accept the emendation of *echousan* to *hekousion* here (1272b32) and translate: "the populace willingly abide by the way the regime is arranged." If *echousan* is retained the meaning will be something like: "though possessing its popular element, or populace, Carthage abides by the way the regime is arranged"; see Newman (2:361). Perhaps not much hangs on the difference since the same meaning, that the populace accept the regime, follows on the second reading as on the first (for the second reading indicates that the populace do not do anything, or anything effective, to stop Carthage abiding by its regime). The first reading has the advantage of making the point clearer.

98. Apparent exceptions, as Hanno, mentioned later 7(5).2.1307a2–5, and certain others, rather confirm than refute Aristotle's point here, as Susemihl and Hicks remark (1894: 307).

99. In the text as we have it, nothing is said about whether the senators are also chosen by merit, so some suppose there is a lacuna that would have said that they were, as Lord (1984: 81).

100. See the detailed discussion in Schütrumpf (1991: 2:348, 352–53), who himself, however, is not convinced on this point.

101. Schütrumpf (1991: 2:351–52) again discusses the point in detail and is again not convinced; he

virtue and success in war (and also, perhaps, using indigenous subjects as slaves). It is clear at any rate that his other criticisms refer to the second question from chapter 9, conflicts with the supposition of the regime.

1273a6/13/17 The democratic features are deviations from aristocracy, not just because they are absent in the regimes of Sparta and Crete (which also aim at aristocracy), but mainly because they clearly derogate from the power of the rulers (who are chosen by merit) to determine the direction of the city. That the oligarchic features are also oligarchic and deviations seems clear, since they put great and uncontrolled power in the hands of a self-selecting few (an aristocracy or polity would combine control by the few with control by all, 6(4).15.1300a34–b5) and, moreover, of a few who are not singled out for their virtue (or at least Aristotle is silent about their virtue). The absences of payment for office and of the lot are, by contrast, aristocratic (and not oligarchic, as they might initially appear) because, being nondemocratic, they are compatible with both aristocracy and oligarchy and will promote one or the other depending on circumstances. At any rate they are not oligarchic here because they are not, as such, deviations *toward* oligarchy.[102] The way cases are tried is also not oligarchic, at least to the extent that, by spreading jurisdiction broadly, it ensures that no one office, occupied by a self-selecting few, has exclusive jurisdiction in any area. On the other hand, by limiting jurisdiction to certain offices and denying it to the populace gathered in assembly, it is also nondemocratic.[103]

~ PARTICULAR OLIGARCHIC DEVIATIONS

1273a21 This next oligarchic deviation is of a rather serious sort and accordingly receives extended treatment. It might indeed be said to lie at the root of all the oligarchic deviations, for it is an error in reasoning about the qualifications for office. The Carthaginian regime is in fact a third kind of regime between aristocracy and oligarchy since it elects to office both on the basis of wealth and desert or merit—a point Aristotle draws express attention to, perhaps, because it shows something he insists on later (6(4).7), that there are kinds of aristocracy after the best kind (as there are also kinds of the other regimes too). Aristotle agrees, of course, that leisure, and so some degree of wealth, are necessary for rule. What he objects to is the Carthaginian inference that one should therefore choose rulers on the basis of wealth and not just merit. This inference, if allowed, would

---

thinks that some remark that the deviations are from the best should have been given in the text, whereas all we have is a reference to deviations simply.

102. As noted by Newman (2:366).

103. As is implied in 3.1.1275b6–12; see Barker (1946: 85 n2) and Newman (2:366), against Lord (1984: 253 n94).

imply that a pure aristocracy was impossible. Accordingly Aristotle points out that it is erroneous, and that in three ways.

1273a31   First, and most importantly, he rejects the validity of the inference: if office requires leisure, then the conclusion to draw is not that the virtuous but poor should be disqualified (as the Carthaginians suppose), but that arrangements should be made to ensure that the virtuous have means or are not needy. Thus in his own best regime later Aristotle requires that his citizens both have education in virtue and own all the property (4(7).9.1329a1–2, 17–26).

1273b35   Second, he rejects the additional inference that offices, in particular the greatest ones like king and general, should be put up for sale. Two reasons seem to be given.[104] First, such a law undermines aristocracy: it sets up for the whole city wealth and not virtue as the object of honor and of love. For what the rulers honor (that is, in this case, those wealthy enough to buy office) everyone else will come to honor also (what one looks up to one wishes to imitate, and in any regime the controlling part is looked up to). Second, such a law fosters injustice since it will necessarily encourage the rulers to use office as a means of making money. The point is obvious enough but it is reinforced by the consideration that poverty makes even the virtuous seek wealth (all need wealth to survive), so that one can hardly expect someone of no or less virtue, who moreover has to use his money to get office, not to seek wealth also, and specifically one can hardly expect him not to seek it through the office he has just bought. But to rule with an eye on profit is a sure recipe for injustice. The proper qualification for rule, therefore, must be ability or fitness for doing it well, or virtue, not wealth; and wealth, as the first argument said, should be something that is given to the virtuous so that they can rule.

1273b6   Third, if despite these arguments, the legislator still does not try to make the virtuous wealthy, he ought at least to make sure they are at leisure while ruling so that they are not forced to make money from office. He certainly ought not to do nothing at all, as seems to be the case in Carthage.

1273b8   The last deviation toward oligarchy is connected with the one just criticized (for if wealth is made a requirement for office, and someone has the wealth to occupy several offices at once, what reason could there be to prevent him?). It is a deviation, however, that is not strictly required by the other, and indeed could exist without it. Aristotle therefore gives express reasons against it. First, things are best done when one man does one work and not when he does two or more. Second, if several share in office, it is more political and more popular, for things get shared out more (which is more popular as being more communal and involving more people in rule) and get done more nobly and quicker (which is

104. I follow Newman (2:368).

more political as helping the city to do its work better as a city, a *polis*). A neat illustration is taken from armies and navies (where almost everyone has some share in rule, however minimal). But as for the last point, having many involved in doing the same work, this is not, of course, in conflict with the earlier point about having one man do one work, for the latter is meant to rule out the case where one man does many works, whereas what the former commends is many men together doing one work. Further, that Aristotle speaks well here of a measure that is more popular does not betoken any preference for democracy over aristocracy. Rather it expresses a preference for polity over oligarchy, especially in Carthage where oligarchic features are destroying the aristocratic ones by making the regime too unmixed.

1273b18   These last two deviations toward oligarchy are sufficiently serious, and introduce sufficient imbalance, to make one wonder why there has not been more faction and tyranny in Carthage. The answer is given here next, that the Carthaginians make sure that parts of the populace always have a chance to get rich and so to share in the regime. Still the fact that there are subject cities to which some of the populace can be sent (whether as rulers, colonists, or something else is not clear)[105] is a work of chance, whereas it ought to be the work of design. What should be done instead, therefore, is what Aristotle has just suggested: make the regime internally more balanced and stable by making it less oligarchic.

1273b24   The closing remark (that the Spartan, Cretan, and Carthaginian regimes are "justly esteemed") is a bit surprising given how bad Sparta and Crete in particular have been shown to be. But, in fact, Aristotle adopts several of their practices for his own best regime later (as common messes and a public training for all the citizens). For these regimes do indeed have excellent institutions that most other regimes altogether lack. Their fault is not to have used or arranged them well.[106]

Chapter 12

~ OTHER LEGISLATORS

~ FRAMERS OF REGIMES

1273b27   This last chapter is somewhat peculiar and its relevance is not immediately obvious. Apart from some instructive remarks about Solon, it appears to be little more than a catalog of legislators that does not much aid the under-

---

105. See the discussions in Newman (2:371), Saunders (1995: 166), Schütrumpf (1991: 2:361), Susemihl and Hicks (1894: 313–14).

106. As Schütrumpf rightly notes (1991: 2:294–95).

standing of the best regime. Hence some commentators doubt its authenticity.[107] But the doubt is unnecessary for the chapter does fit Aristotle's intention. All the legislators mentioned in it are held in honor by some as having legislated well, and since this book is about well-reputed regimes, an examination of these legislators and what they did for particular regimes is certainly appropriate and, from the point of view of completeness, desirable. Further, we should recall that Aristotle is under some pressure to prove the honesty of his intentions (2.1.1260b33–36). He would fail to do so were he to begin his own opinions without at least acknowledging all or most of those legislators whom his audience might favor, and without recording anything they might have discovered or proposed of relevance to the study of the best regime. His brief comments on these legislators, however, serve to show both why they might be worth a mention and yet why they do not deserve more than a mention.

To reduce the catalog to some sort of order, Aristotle begins with a series of divisions,[108] the first between those who did not take part in politics (that is, who did not do any legislating for some actual regime) and those who did. By the former he doubtless means Plato, Phaleas, and Hippodamus, who have already been dealt with.[109] The latter he divides further into those who legislated for their own cities or for foreign ones, and into those who framed laws and those who framed regimes as well. There are thus four different groups. Those who (a) framed laws and regimes for their own city or (b) for some foreign city, and those who (c) framed laws for their own city or (d) for some foreign city. Each of these groups is now dealt with in turn.

1273b35 Lycurgus and Solon are representatives of group (a), and as Lycurgus has been dealt with (in 2.9, for he legislated the Spartan regime), Solon alone remains for treatment here. Solon is praised by some and blamed by others: praised for what he did and blamed for what came of what he did. Aristotle, as is his wont, mediates and moderates the excesses of each side. Solon is praised on the one hand for abolishing an extreme oligarchy, freeing the populace, and setting up the ancestral democracy with a fine balance between oligarchic, aristocratic, and democratic elements. Aristotle responds that Solon seems to be responsible only for the last, having retained the first two from what already existed. The praise, therefore, is too strong in attributing all the institutions to Solon instead of the addition of one of them to balance the others.

1274a3 Solon is blamed on the other hand, however, precisely for this fact.

107. As Barker (1946: 91), Newman (2:372–73), Saunders (1995: 166–67), Schütrumpf (1991: 2:362–69), Susemihl and Hicks (1894: 314). The authenticity of the chapter is, however, defended by Martin Ferrero (1984) and Keaney (1981).

108. I follow Martin Ferrero (1984).

109. Plato did, it is true, try to influence Dionysius of Syracuse, but he effected nothing there in the laws or regime and thus might be said not to have shared in political deeds.

He is accused of destroying the other two elements and giving control to the democratic jury court. As this grew strong, the present democracy developed under the influence of demagogues. Aristotle responds that this result was against Solon's choice and happened by accident because of the naval empire secured by the populace during the Persian Wars. Solon himself only gave the populace the minimum power necessary to prevent them being slaves, while distributing the offices only among the notables and well-off.

Thus Solon changed an oligarchy into a polity[110] and even, to some extent, toward aristocracy (since the notables are, as it were, the aristocrats in regimes that make no common care for virtue, 6(4).7.1293b12–14), thereby securing the freedom, and acquiescence, of the populace. His regime seems not dissimilar in this respect to that of Carthage, which also distributed office to wealth and virtue. Perhaps it is for this reason that Aristotle devotes no more space to Solon.[111] The good in his regime has already been sufficiently noted in the examination of Carthage. But the striking difference between Solon and Carthage is their luck. Carthage, like Crete, was saved by chance but Solon's regime was destroyed by chance. Regimes, however, should be judged by their legislation or their design, not their luck.

1274a22/31 Aristotle comes now to group (b), those who framed laws and regimes for a foreign city. He first relates who they were and then describes what is noteworthy in their legislation. That they deserve to be discussed at all, however, at least in this context, is shown by the fame attaching to them: Zaleucus and Charondas have had chronology twisted in their favor so as to make them companions of other famous men, including another legislator, Onomacritus, and Philolaus has become a tourist attraction at Thebes (though for his life and love rather than for his legislation). Fame is generally a sign of worth, so Aristotle would at least have this reason to give these legislators a mention.

1274b1 Philolaus' legislation, the regulation of childbirth with a view to preserving the number of allotments, concerns no mean matter, as Aristotle has remarked several times (2.6.1265a38–b17, 7.1266b8–14). But precisely because the matter has already been discussed there is no need to say more here. As for Zaleucus and Charondas, nothing of note is recorded about the first but two things are recorded about the second: trials for perjury and the accuracy of his laws. Accuracy of expression is doubtless an excellent thing in laws but it is subordinate to the quality of the laws themselves. In this regard Charondas appears deficient.

---

110. Solon's regime should be called a polity rather than a moderate democracy, even though it is referred to as an ancestral democracy, for it did not give control to the populace (which is the essential condition for any democracy). It divided control between notables and populace, and this is the mark of polity, 3.11.1281b32–34 with 6(4).8.1293b32–34 and 13.1297b22–25.

111. Something which has appeared a problem to commentators, as to Barker (1946: 91) and Newman (2:376–77).

Trials for perjury are mentioned by Aristotle earlier as an evil arising from human depravity (2.5.1263b16–23). Charondas seems to have indulged this depravity instead of trying to remove it.

∾ FRAMERS OF LAWS

1274b9 Aristotle seems now to turn to groups (c) and (d), though the opening remarks about Phaleas and Plato look rather out of place.[112] One might nevertheless rescue them in the following way, that as Aristotle had earlier introduced his discussion about framers of regimes by briefly recalling those who spoke about the regime without themselves taking part in politics or political deeds, so here he recalls these same persons again at the beginning of his discussion of framers of laws, but this time only with respect to what is peculiar in the laws they proposed.[113] That he only mentions Phaleas and Plato and not Hippodamus may be because Hippodamus could be said to have taken part in political deeds when it came to laws since he did lay out the Peiraeus, and how a city should be geographically divided is a matter of law and no mean matter either (4(7).11.1330b21–31). The list of laws, especially of Plato, is manifestly not meant to be exhaustive, but it is presumably meant to cover the most peculiar or distinctive proposals that Plato's two dialogues contain.[114] Aristotle's concern here is, after all, not to report everything that reputed legislators did, which would doubtless involve much repetition, but only what is peculiar to each. For only here, if at all, might one find something of interest to the best regime that is not to be found elsewhere.[115]

1274b15 With this brief introduction, Aristotle turns to group (c), those who framed laws for their own city, of whom are Draco and Pittacus. As regards Pittacus, Aristotle clearly regards his law about drunkards as unusual but it is not clear he regards it as altogether bad (whereas the severity of Draco's punishments does seem to be bad). Perhaps utility should sometimes be preferred to forgiveness, and not just in the case of the drunk either. At any rate Pittacus' law, whether good or bad, has the merit of drawing attention to the problem (which is the point of noting peculiarities in others' legislation, so that nothing important is missed).

112. As remarked by Newman (2:377) and Susemihl and Hicks (1894: 320).

113. This way of rescuing these remarks requires one to divide the text as I have done and not, for instance, as do St. Thomas Aquinas (1951: 2.17.345, 347) and Schütrumpf (1991: 2:362), who take all the proposals of particular legislators (including the proposals of Philolaus and Charondas) as forming one section. One could, however, rescue them in that way too, if one regarded them as a continuation of the discussion of what is peculiar in the laws of noted legislators, as does Keaney (1981).

114. There is no problem, as Newman supposes (2:377, 382–83), in the fact that common property is also listed here as a peculiarity of Plato's when earlier it was not (2.7.1266a34–36) and when common property was also said earlier to exist among some barbarians (2.5.1263a5–8). For common property along with common wives and children is peculiar to Plato.

115. Schütrumpf (1991: 2:366) fails to consider this fact in censuring this chapter's concern with the peculiarities of particular legislators.

1274b23   Aristotle comes finally to group (d), those who gave laws to a foreign city. The sole representative is Androdamas of Rhegium about whom, however, there is nothing peculiar to note. His laws about homicides and heiresses are presumably of the sort one might find anywhere, or they do not raise any questions not already obvious or not already discussed (as heiresses were in the chapter on Sparta, 2.9.1270a23–34). So there is evidently no need, from the point of view of an investigation into the best regime at any rate, to discuss details.

1274b26   Aristotle's review of legislators has been comprehensive in covering all the four groups into which any legislator must fall, though it may perhaps not be comprehensive in covering all legislators by name. But any omissions in this regard are doubtless of no great consequence, for given the little that Aristotle has been able to say about those he does name, we may reasonably assume that any he has passed over are even less worthy of note. So he may now not unreasonably regard his intention from chapter 1 as completed.

BOOK 3

Definition and Division of Regime

Chapter 1

~ DEFINITION OF CITY AND CITIZEN

~ PRIORITY OF THE CITIZEN

1274b32 Having discussed the views of others on the best regime, Aristotle comes now to state his own view. But obviously he cannot say which regime is best without also saying what the several kinds of regime are or what as such is meant by regime. Hence a book about the regime and its kinds is the next logical step in the analysis.[1] It is also the next logical step required by the program outlined at the end of the *Ethics*. For that program next requires a study, from the collected regimes, of what saves and destroys cities. But as what saves cities most of all is the best regime, since thus the city becomes most completely devoted to living well, the best regime must be the next topic (followed by the other regimes that preserve cities less well or destroy them). Such a study of regimes obviously requires a comprehensive collection of them (lest some get overlooked). But no mere empirical catalog of existing regimes (which might not include all the possibilities) could be sufficient for this purpose. Rather a rational catalog is required, one that can be guaranteed to omit nothing because it begins from what is first, namely from the very idea of regime and its primary logical articulations. Such then is the subject matter of this book and from it, and from the several remarks Aristotle makes along the way, can be drawn out a coherent division of the chapters. Scholarly doubts about whether such a coherent division can be found turn, to be sure, on real matters of controversy, but closer examination can put these doubts pretty largely to rest.[2] Such at any rate is my contention.

An examination of the regime as such, then, is what Aristotle must undertake

---

1. Contra Newman (3:129), Schütrumpf (1991: 1:39–40), Susemihl and Hicks (1894: 37), who suggest a book directly about the best regime, as books 4(7) and 5(8), should logically have come next. But anyway this third book is about the best regime since it identifies which regime is best; books 4(7) and 5(8), by contrast, consider its details and how to set it up.

2. Doubts are expressed by Schütrumpf (1991: 2:109), Susemihl and Hicks (1894: 37–44). Newman discusses the issue (1:570–72) and suggests that the doubts may not be decisive.

first. But this, he now says, requires a preliminary examination of the city. Three reasons, it appears, are given and all seem to point to the same conclusion, made explicit by the third, that the regime is some way of arranging the city. So, as regards the first reason, there could be no dispute about whether the city or the regime (the tyranny or the oligarchy) did the deed if the city were not what regimes arise in or get imposed on. As regards the second reason, politicians and legislators preserve and legislate regimes, so if this concern of theirs wholly revolves about the city (as is evident and as the previous book showed), the city must again be what regimes, as patterns of rule and legislation, are about. As regards the third reason, it is evident to inspection (especially after the discussions of the last book) that regimes differ in the way they arrange cities and their inhabitants, and hence that regimes are some structuring of cities. Add next to this conclusion the further and fairly obvious claim (left unexpressed by Aristotle) that a thing which structures another thing cannot be understood without understanding that other thing, and the required result follows (that the city, or whatever one calls the political community, must be studied first).

1274b38 The conclusion that Aristotle next draws, that to understand the city it is necessary first to understand the parts of the city, namely the citizen, follows clearly enough from the principle of analysis and synthesis laid down before (1.1 and 1.2.1252a18–26). But what excites puzzlement is why this should be the conclusion next to be drawn. For why does not a study of the city return us to book 1 where an understanding of the city was, it would appear, already given? And why, secondly, are the parts of the city now said to be citizens when before they were said to be households? It is tempting to claim that there are signs here of confusion and contradiction in Aristotle's text.[3]

But in reply one may note first, as regards the second question, that the citizens are in a way the households and the households in a way the citizens. For the households enter the city and its rule through the man who is their head, and the citizen is part of the city as a man who heads a household (the man, in other words, is not a citizen as a mere individual but as representing a household). Second one may note, as regards both this question and the other about why an examination of the city does not return us to book 1, that there are differences of context and intention.[4] For in book 1 the intention was to explain the origin of the city and how it differed from other communities. So the parts of the city were the subordinate communities within it and from which it emerged. But here the intention is to define what this distinct community of the city is, so its parts are those who immediately share in it and constitute it, and these are, by common consent and parlance, the citizens. The city, in other words, *comes to be* out of households, but

---

3. Schütrumpf (1991: 2:383) and Susemihl and Hicks (1894: 355) make this claim.
4. Quinn (1986: 577) and Mulgan (1977: 52) draw attention to such differences.

it *is* a multitude of citizens. That is presumably also why earlier the city was said to be prior to households and individuals (1.2.1253a18–26), but why here the citizen is implied to be prior to the city. For the city, one may say, is prior as the whole to the parts that it perfects, but the citizens are prior as the parts to the whole that they define. Individuals as individuals thus exist for the city (since it perfects them), but the city subsists in the individuals as citizens (since it *is* them).

That who is to count as a citizen is, like regime and city, a matter of dispute and varies from regime to regime shows, of course, that this question needs careful consideration. But it also confirms that the city, or the assemblage of citizens, is what the regime structures. For it shows that citizen is in some way a function of the regime.

⌁ PRELIMINARY DEFINITION OF CITIZEN

1275a5   So Aristotle's task is to get an understanding of citizen and thence of city, and this he now does in the rest of this chapter. He proceeds by a process of elimination.[5] He first dismisses those who are called citizens but in some sense other than that required, as honorary or "made" citizens (who have the name but little of the reality of citizens).[6] He next dismisses criteria for citizenship that may be necessary but clearly not sufficient (as residence and liability to legal proceedings), and finally he dismisses those who may indeed be accounted citizens but only with a disabling condition, as children and the aged (who are perhaps to be called "incomplete" and "overage" citizens), the exiled and the disenfranchised (who are perhaps to be called "former" or "suspended" citizens).

1275a22   This process of elimination and the reasons given for it already point to what Aristotle now concludes to be the understanding of citizen, namely someone who shares in judgment and rule. For, especially in the case of those last listed, all that seems left to make them fully citizens, or to remove from them the disabling condition, is precisely to share in the full life of the city, that is, above all, to share in deciding how the city is to be run or governed.

Such deciding is done by those who possess office of some sort, but office cannot be confined to definite office alone (perhaps the most obvious kind of office) since, as Aristotle immediately notes, that would have the absurd result of excluding from rule those who, in democracies at any rate, are in most control, namely the populace through the assembly and jury courts. The understanding of office and thence of citizenship must be made broad enough to cover all or most citizens. An

---

5. As Miller rightly notes (1995: 143–48).

6. On the meaning of "made" citizens, Quinn (1986) and Winthrop (1975) indulge in some rather fanciful speculations. For saner views see the references in Newman (3:132) and Schütrumpf (1991: 2:386).

understanding that confined citizenship to those who shared in definite office would thus be too narrow; indefinite office (or whatever else one may care to call membership of assembly and of jury courts) must be the criterion instead.

∼ PRECISE DEFINITION OF CITIZEN AND CITY

1275a34/b5 The above result fundamentally decides the definition of citizen, namely that citizenship is a question of sharing in rule or office. The further qualification Aristotle now adds does not alter this result but only serves to make more precise, and more universal, what such sharing must concretely mean. The qualification falls out of an argument that is straightforward enough: (1) what is common to things that include in their understanding a reference to something else that is articulated into prior and posterior is minimal; (2) citizen involves in its understanding such a reference (a citizen is a citizen in some regime or other, and regimes differ as prior and posterior); (3) therefore what is common to citizens across the several regimes is minimal. Hence, further (to complete the process of reasoning), an account of citizen that is going to cover all cases or all regimes must be minimal too.

But the account just given is not minimal; it includes in it reference to kinds of office that are found only in some regimes and not in all. What is required, then, is to remove this reference and find something more universal, as Aristotle immediately does. One may note, however, about the metaphysical principle he uses in premise (1) of his argument that, though seemingly rather abstruse, it is reasonable enough and has other applications, as in the case, say, of the uniform of a military officer. Such uniforms can differ widely from the highest to the lowest rank of officers and one would, in many cases, be hard put to find very much that was common between them (other than the vague and general "dress distinctive of one who shares in military rule"). And so it is also in the case of citizen and regime.

1275b13/b17 To find something more universal, or less specific, Aristotle speaks now, not of assembly and jury courts, but of what assembly and jury courts do, namely deliberate and pass judgment. These powers or functions exist in all regimes even if the offices in which they are concretely realized are different. Hence a citizen of a given city can now more precisely be defined as anyone entitled in that city to share in these functions (whether indefinitely, as in a democracy, or at definite times, as in an oligarchy).[7] The corresponding definition of city ("a multi-

---

7. Some scholars, as Irwin, in Patzig (1990: 82), and Schofield (1996: 840–42), doubt that this is Aristotle's precise and final definition of the citizen and suppose that the precise definition is the one given earlier (1275a22–23), namely that the citizen is someone who (actually) shares in judgment and rule or office and not someone who is entitled so to share without actually now sharing. But this view is contrary to what Aristotle actually says here at the end of this chapter, as well as to what he says later at

tude of such persons adequate for self-sufficiency of life") now falls out more or less straightforwardly (with a suitable reference back to the self-sufficiency that was found to be the mark of the city in 1.2).

Such then is Aristotle's definition of citizen and city. But the value of his detour, if you like, through democratic citizenship (which otherwise might appear rather tortuous) is that it enables him to isolate those aspects of rule which properly make the citizen.[8] For the populace are citizens, if anywhere, in a democracy, so the share in rule that is finally extended to them in a democracy (though denied to them elsewhere) must be enough to make the citizen. But this sharing is sharing in the assembly and law courts, for these, in a democracy, control the city. Hence sharing in the equivalent control, namely in deliberation and judgment, must be what is sufficient to make the citizen simply.

Chapter 2

~ CONFIRMATION OF THE DEFINITIONS

1275b22 Aristotle has now answered his two questions from chapter 1, so the way is in principle open to examine the regime. Aristotle's wont, however, is not to be satisfied with formal definitions until he has confirmed their truth by reference to the phenomena, in particular the prevailing opinions, and has resolved any difficulties they contain.[9] And this is what he does now. In this chapter he shows how his account fits, by ultimately explaining the common definition of citizen, and in chapters 3 to 5 he solves certain disputes, notably those he raised at the beginning of chapter 1.

The common definition of citizen in terms of citizen descent[10] may be fair enough in practice, for it serves the purpose of enabling cities to expedite the determination of whom to admit into shares in rule (hence Aristotle's characterization of it as "political and swift," 1275b25). The problem, of course, is that it

---

3.5.1277b34–35. It also entails that someone eligible for office but not now in office is not actually or fully a citizen. This means that citizens who alternate in ruling and being ruled are not really citizens when they are being ruled, and this means in turn that the virtue of citizens cannot include the virtue they have when being ruled (for, on this view, they are not citizens when being ruled), which conflicts with Aristotle's teaching in chapter 4 (especially 1277b7–16; and see also 3.6.1279a8–13). This view is rightly rejected by Miller (1995: 147; 1996: 902–3).

8. I follow the discussion in Johnson (1984).

9. As Johnson rightly notes (1984: 81).

10. Such descent obviously requires that women too can be regarded as citizens, and this raises a problem since women were typically denied access to office, including indefinite office. Hence they could not be citizens in Aristotle's precise sense. But they could be called citizens derivatively, because from them and a citizen in the precise sense, their husbands, will come citizens in the precise sense, their sons.

cannot serve for more than this purpose, and specifically it cannot serve as a formal definition. The first citizens could certainly not be defined in this way since, precisely as first, they could not have had citizen forbears. This is the point of Gorgias' witticism, namely that citizenship must ultimately be a matter of political decision and not of descent. Gorgias' witticism is, however, little more than that and does not push the matter to its proper conclusion (Gorgias was after all reputed for skill in words, not in philosophy). For the question is what sort of political decision makes for citizenship, and the answer can only be what Aristotle has just determined, namely that it is decision about who is to share in rule: those who have such shares are citizens and those who do not are not.

1275b34   The next case Aristotle raises is more serious and is perhaps what is really lying behind the previous one, since at a revolution many might be enrolled as citizens whose parents were not enrolled. Such indeed happened at Athens under Cleisthenes,[11] and Athens after Cleisthenes would, in fact, seem to be just the place where disputes about deciding citizens by means of parentage would arise. For later opponents of what Cleisthenes did might, in their desire to get rid of the descendants of those whom he had enfranchised, try to push the requirement that citizens have citizen parents back to the third or fourth generation.[12] Moreover a debating point against Pericles, who introduced the requirement of citizen parents,[13] might well have been that if Pericles was going to require citizen parentage for citizens now, he should in consistency also require it for citizens in the past. This jibe might then have given Gorgias, who after all taught people how to be good at speaking, the opportunity later to display his skill by inventing a clever pun.

But however that may be, the real issue here, as Aristotle quickly points out, is not the definition of citizen but the justice of this or that grant of citizenship. Cleisthenes' opponents would certainly have to admit as much, for their complaint precisely is that he gave a share in rule—that is, he gave real citizenship—to those who had no just claim to it. Conflating the unjust and the false by saying that those not justly citizens are not truly citizens will not alter this point. For this conflation is itself false and those who possess rule unjustly (as Cleisthenes' opponents allege about the citizens he made) are nevertheless still really in possession of rule, and so are citizens in fact whatever one may think of the justice of the matter.

So we are brought back, as before in the case of parentage, to Aristotle's definition of citizen, and hence of city, in terms of shares in rule.

---

11. In the power struggles among the notables that followed the expulsion of the tyrants from Athens in 510 B.C., Cleisthenes successfully used the device of enfranchising new citizens to increase the number of his opponents and so to win out against rivals (*Athēnaiōn Politeia* 20–21).

12. Newman notes some of the evidence for this idea (3:145–46).

13. *Athēnaiōn Politeia* 26.

Chapter 3

~ RESOLUTION OF DISPUTES

~ AS REGARDS THE CITY

1276a6 Aristotle comes now to resolve the disputes raised in chapter 1, and first about the city and then, in the next chapter, about the citizen. The dispute about whether the city did the deed is like that just mentioned in raising a question of justice and also in confusing this question with a question of identity. For it is used to decide a matter of justice, the keeping of previous agreements, but turns on a question of identity: is the city to be identified by reference to the regime or not? Aristotle's definition of city (a multitude of those who share in deliberation and judgment) effectively identifies the city with those who are in control of the city and hence with the regime. The dispute about the city clearly brings his definition into question (since it denies that the city is to identified by reference to its regime), and so it needs to be sorted out. So Aristotle first proceeds against the standard argument used in the dispute and then directly takes up the question itself.

As regards the argument Aristotle is able quickly to show that it is inconsistently, not to say hypocritically, applied. The argument is that regimes that exist by force and not for the common benefit, as democrats allege is the case with tyranny and oligarchy, are not the city and that the actions of these regimes are not the actions of the city. But this argument works as much against a democracy that opposes the common benefit as against a tyranny or an oligarchy, even though the democrats who propound it clearly want to exempt democracy from its scope. But while this response of Aristotle's may be sufficient to silence or embarrass certain democrats, it does nothing to show that the argument's conclusion, that at least in some cases the city is not the regime, is false. So he turns directly to the question of when the city is the same or not.

1276a17/a24 The two most obvious criteria for identity of city would seem to be identity of place and persons. So Aristotle takes each in turn, beginning with identity of place. He considers two opposed cases. The first is where the persons are geographically split but politically united (as, say, with Athens and its port of the Peiraeus). Such a city is in a sense the same city and in another sense different cities. For if by city is meant a geographical unit then such a city may be called two (as with the two of Athens proper and the Peiraeus), but if by city is meant a political community then it is clearly one. The second case is where the persons are geographically united but politically split, as with the Peloponnese and Babylon. One can, in a way, regard these as one place but the Peloponnese is certainly not one political community, and a city as big as Babylon, where a part could carry on without noticing what had happened to the rest, is not one political community either. Some limit to size and diversity of place, then, is required for sameness of

[*138*] 1276a6 · POLITICS 3.3

city, but this limit admits of a certain latitude (how much latitude is left for later consideration, 4(7).4–6, 12). Athens and the Peiraeus may be within this limit but Babylon and the Peloponnese are certainly not.

1276a34 Assuming now that the limit on place, whatever it is, is met, Aristotle considers whether the city will be the same in such a case provided the human beings are also the same. Human beings of course are born and die and, over time, they will only be the same in family or descent and not individually (like the sameness of a river). Is such sameness, while sufficient for sameness of the human family, sufficient for sameness of city? Aristotle says no, because a city is not just a family of human beings but a community of human beings in a regime (that is, human beings sharing a common and ordered pattern of life). Like other communities and composites (dramatic choruses and musical modes), it gets its unity from its organization, not from the elements so organized. Hence it is sameness of regime that primarily makes for sameness of city. The sameness of the persons, unlike unity of place, does not even seem to be a prerequisite. For the city could have the same name or not (that is, I presume, it could remain an oligarchy, say, or change to a democracy)[14] regardless of what happens to the persons. Or, in other words, the persons could remain the same (whether individually or in family) and yet the city could be different (if it became a democracy from an oligarchy); or the persons could change (individually or in family, as when at Athens under Cleisthenes some are expelled and others introduced) and the city could remain the same (if its regime remained the same); or again both could change together (as did in fact happen under Cleisthenes). But in every case it is sameness or difference of regime, and not of persons, that determines sameness or difference of city.

1276b13 From this result it now follows, of course, that when the tyrant or the oligarchy acts, so does the city. But this conclusion does not settle what lay beneath the democratic argument quoted at the beginning. For that argument was really about whether a democracy was bound by the contracts of a previous regime and that, as Aristotle now expressly notes, is a different question. How he would answer it he does not say, but one can conjecture that it would depend on the circumstances, that is, on whether keeping this or that agreement would really serve the common good (which is what is meant by political justice, 3.12.1282b16–18).[15] At all events, the first dispute from chapter 1, about the identity of the city, has now been resolved and in such a way as to confirm the definition of city in terms of the citizens or the regime.

14. Newman (3:154) thinks "name" here means the city's proper name, as Athens or Thebes, and not its regime, as oligarchy or democracy. But a reference to proper names seems irrelevant in this context, which is about real sameness, not nominal sameness, as Lord notes (1984: 254 n12).

15. Barker (1946: 100 nQ), contra Susemihl and Hicks (1894: 366).

Chapter 4

∾ AS REGARDS THE CITIZEN

∾ VIRTUE OF MAN AND CITIZEN

1276b16 The next thing for Aristotle to do, after resolving the disputes about the city, would be to resolve the disputes about the citizen. That he does in fact now do that becomes clear from what follows (especially in chapter 5), but an initial puzzle is why this should require him to turn to a discussion of the virtue of man and citizen.[16] One may, however, suggest the following. The dispute about the citizen mentioned in chapter 1, and raised again specifically with reference to Athens in chapter 2, turns on a question of desert. Those, for instance, who, like oligarchs, wish to deny citizenship to the populace, or, like the opponents of Cleisthenes, to slaves and aliens, are saying in effect that such should not be citizens, or are unjustly citizens, because they do not deserve to be citizens, and that they do not deserve to be citizens because they are not good men (they are vulgar and slaves). But as it is virtue that makes one good, the implicit claim here is that it is necessary to have the virtue of a good man to be fit to be a citizen, or, in other words, that the virtue of good man and of good and deserving citizen are the same. So while Aristotle's response so far, that anyone who shares in rule is a citizen whether he is justly so or not, may have answered the earlier disputants as to the fact they allege (for it shows that a slave or alien must be a citizen if he shares in rule), it has not answered them as to the reason they give (for it has not confronted the contention that a slave or alien does not deserve to share in rule). Hence, in order properly to resolve the disputes about the citizen, Aristotle must confront the problem of virtue, and whether and to what extent the virtue of the citizen is the same as that of a man. Accordingly he deals with this question of virtue in the present chapter and then applies the results to his resolution of the disputes in the next.

1276b20 An examination of this question obviously requires that one have some idea of what is meant by virtue in the case of both man and citizen. What is meant by the virtue of a man has presumably been sufficiently dealt with in the *Ethics* (though certain relevant points are recalled shortly), so Aristotle first considers what is meant by the virtue of a citizen. He takes an analogy from virtue in members of another sort of community, sailors, whose virtue is both relative to their individual capacity and work and to their common work of a safe voyage. So, similarly, virtue in the members of other communities, as notably the political

---

16. Schütrumpf sees here another indication of incoherence in Aristotle's text (1991: 2:413–17), but Johnson argues the contrary (1990: 122).

community, must be relative to their capacity and work and, in particular, to the common work of the community, which, in this case, is preserving the regime.

∼ THAT THE VIRTUE OF BOTH CANNOT IN EVERY CASE BE THE SAME

1276b31   Aristotle comes now to the main question and uses this understanding of citizen virtue, first to argue that such virtue cannot always be the same as the virtue of the man, and then to argue that in some cases it can be. On the former point he develops three arguments. The first rests on the idea that citizen virtue is relative to the regime. For if so and the regimes are of several kinds, then it follows that (1) citizen virtue must also be of several kinds; but (2) the virtue of a man is of a single kind; therefore (3) not every citizen virtue can be the same as the virtue of a man, or it is possible to be a virtuous citizen without having the virtue of the good man.

The virtue being talked of here in both cases must, as Aristotle indicates, be virtue understood in its complete sense. For the virtue of the citizen and of the man are going to be made up of several particular virtues (courage, self-control, justice), so there is a sense in which neither is a single virtue. But both are nevertheless single taken as a whole, that is, in their completion, and in this sense there are as many completions of citizen virtue as there are regimes, whereas there is only one completion of the virtue of a man (the completion dealt with in the *Ethics*).[17]

1276b35   The second argument rests on the idea that citizen virtue is also relative to the citizen. Although somewhat complex in expression, it can be analyzed thus:[18] if (1) it is impossible for everyone in a city to be serious (or a good man), but (2) it is necessary for each of them to do his work well, that is, with virtue, then, since (3) all citizens cannot be alike, it follows that (4) there cannot just be one virtue for both citizen and man. This is because (5) the city cannot be best unless all have the virtue of the citizen, but (6) they cannot all have the virtue of the man unless everyone in the serious city must be good men. The conclusion (4) follows if (1) and (2) are true; but (3) is meant, I take it, to prove (1) and (5) is meant to prove (2). The last proposition (6) serves to make explicit how it is that (3) is meant to prove (1), namely because unlike citizens will have unlike virtues and so will not all be good in the same way and, specifically, they will not all be good in the way that the good man is good.

---

17. To bring out this fact I translate the Greek at this point as follows: "the complete virtue of the serious citizen clearly cannot be a single one. But the good man we do say is good by reference to a single complete virtue." Other translators give a sense more along these lines: "the virtue of the serious citizen cannot be a single and complete virtue, but the virtue of the good man is a single virtue, the complete virtue."

18. I follow the outline of Newman (3:157–58).

This second argument applies, as Aristotle says, only to the case of the best city since only in this case must proposition (5) be true (in other cases it need not be true). The argument also appeals to the idea that citizen virtue is relative to the citizen, or to their respective work, because this is presumably the point of propositions (3) and (6). The idea, however, that not all the citizens in the best city must be good might seem to be in conflict with Aristotle's later claim that a city can only be serious if all the citizens are serious men (4(7).13.1332a32–36).[19] But Aristotle is not so much saying there that all the citizens in the serious city must be good as that they must all either be good or becoming good. For the young who are serving in the army are citizens (they are being ruled as citizens and indeed are engaged already in some deliberation and judgment and will be fully so when older, 4(7).9.1329a2–17 and 12), and must have the virtue appropriate to their age and work, but, precisely as young, they cannot yet have the virtue of the good man.[20] That Aristotle already has this difference in mind here is shown by the fact that it is the theme of the last section of this chapter.

Alternatively, one might regard this argument as ad hominem, that is, as directed at what others (though not Aristotle himself) would regard as the best city. For mixed regimes, like the Spartan and Carthaginian, which some regard as best, give the poor a share in rule along with the respectable, and expect the poor to perform their work well, yet presumably the poor are not held to be good men as the respectable are. Similar things might be said of Solon's regime at Athens where laborers were given a share in rule. Yet laborers would presumably not be called good men even by those who praised Solon's regime as best. One might even take the more extreme cases of oligarchy and democracy which oligarchs and democrats think to be best. Democrats, for instance, allow the rich also to be citizens and even impose on them important office, which they expect to be exercised well. But they could hardly say that a rich man who preferred oligarchy but exercised office well in a democracy was a good man. For according to them only democrats could be good men. Likewise, oligarchs would have to admit the same if any citizen in their regime exercised office well though preferring a tyranny or a democracy. Taken in this way Aristotle's argument has the merit of neatly complementing his first argument. For there he argued to the nonidentity of the virtues of serious citizen and good man from what would generally be accepted as an account of the serious citizen (the one who does well the job of preserving the regime). Here he does the same by arguing from what would generally be accepted as an account of the good man (the best citizen in the best city or regime).

1277a5   The third argument also rests on the idea of the relativity of citizen virtue to the citizen, or that different citizens have different virtues. For (1) if this is

19. A conflict noted by Newman (1:236 n2, 3:158) and by Susemihl and Hicks (1894: 368–69).
20. As Schütrumpf rightly notes (1991: 2:420–21).

true, and (2) if, as Aristotle now expressly asserts, the city is composed of dissimilars, it follows (3) that the virtues of citizens, who compose the city, are also dissimilar from each other or are not all one and the same virtue. So, evidently, (4) they cannot all be the same as the virtue of the good man either.[21]

To illustrate the fact that the city is composed of dissimilars Aristotle takes examples from animals, the soul, the household, and property. These examples all recall 1.5 where they were used to illustrate the different kinds of ruler and ruled. Aristotle, however, cannot mean that the city is composed of body, soul, reason, desire, man, woman, master, slave as if each was independently a citizen (how could reason or desire be citizens?).[22] Besides, he does not say that the city is composed "immediately" of these parts (1277a6, 9). So what perhaps he means is that the city is composed mediately of these parts (because they are the parts of the parts of the city, namely men and households) but immediately of other parts, namely citizens, and that it is composed of these other parts "in the same way" (1277a8), that is, these parts too divide into ruler and ruled. Then the sense is that citizens divide into many kinds of ruler and ruled (there are many sorts of office in cities and many ways in which citizens share in rule, as in the case of Sparta for instance), and so citizens cannot all have the same virtue as each other but must have different ones for different kinds of rule. That is presumably why Aristotle adds the example from the dramatic chorus, for such differentiation of ruling and being ruled in one and the same community is what we find in a chorus with its several members and their several functions.

~ THAT THE VIRTUE OF BOTH CAN IN SOME CASES BE THE SAME

1277a13 The above three arguments only prove that the virtue of citizen and man cannot in every case be the same. They leave open the possibility that in some cases they are the same. Aristotle now considers these cases. He first proposes an answer on the basis of accepted opinion, then clarifies it in response to a difficulty that other accepted opinions generate. The answer is that the serious ruler or politician must be a good man and have the prudence that is the mark of the simply good man. This is asserted on the basis of what "we say" (1277a14) and may be a reference back to the *Ethics* (in particular to 6.12 and 13), or also to generally accepted views.[23] It is also asserted on the basis of a difference in education that some say marks out the ruler. For the belief that rulers need special training (though Aristotle would not agree that war and riding constituted this training) lends support to the view that the goodness of rulers must be superior to that of others and that rulers above all must be simply good men. So in this case of

21. I follow Newman (3:158–59).

22. Schütrumpf (1991: 2:422–23) does think that Aristotle must be meaning this; see also Susemihl and Hicks (1894: 369–70).

23. As Newman (3:160) and Schütrumpf (1991: 2:424) rightly note.

the good ruler, the virtue of man and citizen would be the same since the same virtue that makes the ruler a good man also makes him a good citizen, that is good at doing his work in the city, namely ruling it.

1277a20 The difficulty that arises is this. The virtue of the good man and the good citizen qua ruler may be the same, but the citizen is also ruled (as for instance when he is still young or when rule is exercised by turns) and his virtue qua ruled cannot be the same. Now the accepted opinions just appealed to separate the ruler from the ruled and suggest that the ruler, and so the good man, will neither be ruled nor trained to be ruled. Like the tyrant Jason, he will only be fit to rule. There are, however, accepted opinions on the other side that praise the virtue of being ruled as well as of ruling and say that the citizen's virtue consists in both. But if ruling virtue is the good man's virtue, ruled virtue is not going to be as praiseworthy as these other opinions suggest. There are these two views then: the view that says rulers should learn one thing and the ruled another and praises the virtue of ruling, and the view that praises the virtues of both and says that both virtues should be learned and practiced.

1277a33/b7 Aristotle resolves this conflict of opinions by drawing a distinction between despotic and political rule. Despotic rule was discussed earlier (1.4–7) and Aristotle briefly recapitulates the relevant point that in this sense of rule the ruler, or the master, does not need to know what the ruled, or the slave, knows.[24] The remarks about laborers and artisans are added, no doubt, to show that slavish knowledge is not to be narrowly construed[25] but includes things that some citizens in some regimes, namely ultimate democracy, do in fact learn and practice. But these things are not to be learned by the good man or the good citizen in the sense under consideration. Or at least not learned and practiced in the slavish way the vulgar do, which is as work in the hire of others. So here the opinion that rulers should not learn the same as the ruled or have their virtue is true. The second sense of rule is political rule, and again Aristotle recalls the relevant point from earlier (1.7.1255b16–18 and 12.1259b4–6), that such rule is over free and similars. This rule must be learned through being ruled, as the examples drawn from military rule sufficiently attest.[26] So here the opinion that the good citizen should learn how to rule and be ruled, and that his virtue consists in both, is true.

1277b16 From this result it now follows that the good man too will have both virtues, since ruling virtue is acquired through ruled virtue. But it does not

24. That there is a reference back to book 1 here is not made explicit but it is clear enough by itself, contra Schütrumpf (1991: 2:415).

25. As Newman rightly says (3:165).

26. Newman mentions examples, as Alcibiades and Lord Stratford de Redcliffe, whose too rapid rise to high office seem to have been factors in making them overly masterful and unfitted for political rule (3:169).

follow that both virtues are equally praiseworthy, or that the good man is a good man through both virtues (and not through his ruling virtue alone) in the way that the good citizen is a good citizen through both virtues.[27] That the two virtues are not equally praiseworthy Aristotle illustrates from another case of ruler and ruled, namely man and woman. Courage and moderation are superior in a man for they require him to act and speak where they require her to hold back and be silent (virtue is relative to the work, and the work of man and woman is different). So likewise ruling virtue in general is superior to ruled virtue (the works here too are different). That the good man is nevertheless a good man only through his ruling virtue (and not also through his ruled virtue) Aristotle indicates by saying of the virtue of prudence, which is the mark of the good man (as was said at the beginning of this section), that it alone is proper to the ruler whereas the ruled (qua ruled) only has right opinion. So the pipe maker does not need to know, for instance, what the best pipes for playing are; he only needs to follow instructions. He has opinion only, but right opinion because derived from the knowledge of the pipe player. Thus it is also with the citizen when ruled.

1277b30 The virtue of good man and serious citizen is thus both the same and different. It is the same because the virtue of both consists in ruling virtue; it is different because the virtue of the good man consists simply in ruling virtue while that of the serious citizen consists also in ruled virtue. The good man does indeed have ruled virtue but incidentally, not essentially. He has it because that was the way he acquired ruling virtue.

Note, however, three things. First, it does not follow from this that the good man is only a good man when ruling, as if, absurdly, he were to lose prudence when he left office. Rather what follows is that the virtue by which he is a good man will only be the same as the virtue by which he is a good citizen when he is actually ruling. When he is ruled his virtue as a good citizen will be different, and his virtue of prudence will not be exercised (at least not in ruling the city). Nor, second, does it follow that the good man can never be a good citizen in a defective regime.[28] For ruling and preserving a defective regime is above all a question of moderating and controlling its defects, which is the job of the politician, that is, of someone with the virtue of prudence (6(4).1).[29] Nor, third, does it follow that to be a good man it is necessary to be, or to have been, a citizen or a ruler anywhere. It is sufficient to

27. Newman (3:171) and Barker (1946: 107) think it does follow that the good man must be good through both virtues. But that leads to a conflict with what Aristotle said at the beginning of the section, that what makes the good man is ruling virtue and prudence alone. This conflict is readily avoided if one understands the text in the way that, with help from St. Thomas Aquinas (1951: 3.3.375–76), I argue here.

28. Contra Newman (3:155); and see also Mulgan (1977: 57).

29. Consider the praise of Theramenes in *Athēnaiōn Politeia* 28.

have the virtue that fits one to be a ruler, namely prudence, and though this will ordinarily be achieved through being a citizen, it could be achieved in the family or even perhaps be a natural or divine gift (*Ethics* 10.9.1179b20–23, 1180a30–32).

Chapter 5

~ CITIZENSHIP AND VIRTUE OF THE VULGAR

~ PRELIMINARY DISCUSSION

1277b33 Having thus dealt with the question of virtue, Aristotle comes now to respond directly to the disputes about the citizen. These disputes focus round the question of whether or how the vulgar populace, and slaves and aliens, are to count as citizens. So Aristotle now recalls that question, but he poses it dialectically, that is, in a way that reflects, not his own views, but the views of those who are party to the dispute. Indeed the question, in the way it is posed, proceeds on the oligarchic or antidemocratic view that those who do not share in the determinate offices are not citizens (something he himself has expressly rejected).[30] But perhaps Aristotle decides now to begin speaking in the name of oligarchs and others because what he has just decided (that only those are good citizens, or are capable of ruling and being ruled well, who are also good men) seems to support their view that the vulgar populace and slaves and aliens should not be allowed to count as citizens. It might therefore also seem to give some support to their companion view that those who only share in the indeterminate office of assemblyman and juror, and who include the vulgar, should not count as citizens either.

At all events, Aristotle states the dispute thus: is citizenship to be defined in terms of sharing office (as opponents of democracy may wish), or are the vulgar also to be regarded as citizens (as democrats would wish) even though they do not share in office, that is, determinate office? If the latter, then not all citizens, and specifically not the vulgar, can be good citizens or can have the virtue of citizen just discussed (the vulgar, as Aristotle noted at 1277a33–b7, learn how to be ruled slavishly; they also live lives incompatible with the acquisition of more than slavish virtue—see 1.13.1260a33–b7, 4(7).9.1328b39–41). If the former, then how are the vulgar, who are not aliens or foreigners, to be classified in the city?

1277b39 But however puzzling at first sight, neither of these alternatives raises any serious problems—not even about the notion of citizenship on which it rests, let alone about Aristotle's own. The second alternative is easily dismissed

---

30. If the question is thus interpreted as dialectical, there will be no need to follow Barker (1946: 107 n1), Newman (3:173–74), and Schütrumpf (1991: 2:438) in supposing that in this chapter Aristotle is espousing a different view of citizenship. See also Susemihl and Hicks (1894: 375).

because not everyone in a city needs to be a citizen or a foreigner. Slaves and freedmen are not and, of course, mechanics used to be slaves (and so perhaps could now be classed as freedmen). But anyway the supposition that is lurking behind this argument, that all those whom a city needs must be citizens of it, is false. For people can belong to the city without being citizens. Aristotle discusses this point more fully later (4(7).8), but here he contents himself with showing the fact from an evident example, namely children, who are clearly parts of the city though not citizens of it (they do not yet share in rule). Mechanics, of course, unlike children, are not in the process of growing up, but that does not affect the point of the example, which rests on the present, not the future, status of children.

The first alternative, that the vulgar cannot have citizen virtue, only requires one to say that the vulgar will not be allowed to be citizens in the simply best city (since they could never be good citizens in the simply best city), and that if they are allowed to be citizens anywhere, then not all the citizens in that case can be allowed to be good citizens (specifically not those bound, as the vulgar are, to slavish tasks).

～ DETERMINATIVE ANSWER

1278a13/21   Aristotle has so far been speaking only dialectically, and though no difficulties have been uncovered that need any further answer, the matter still needs to be resolved in the light of Aristotle's own account of citizen and not just in the light of a dialectical one. The solution was, in fact, already given in the first chapter. For there are several kinds of regime and so several kinds of citizen relative to these regimes. The way of life of the vulgar would prevent them being citizens in any regime that cares about virtue, such as aristocracy, but wealthy artisans among them could be citizens in an oligarchy (unless the oligarchy prevents it), while laborers could be so in a democracy, as could also slaves and aliens (until the democracy thinks it has enough people). Hence the view that the vulgar cannot be citizens is right in one way, because they cannot be citizens in an aristocracy, but wrong in another, because they can be citizens in some other regime.

As regards Aristotle's remark that there must be several kinds of citizen, *especially* of the citizen when he is being ruled (1278a16–17), I take this to reflect the fact that in some regimes there may, besides the sharing in office that makes the citizen, also be kinds of sharing in office that go beyond this and for which not all citizens are eligible (for instance, all may be members of the assembly but not all may be eligible for this or that determinate office). Hence in this case sharing the rule that makes the citizen will be one thing (membership of the assembly) whereas being ruled as a citizen will be many things.

1278a34/40   At all events, having thus resolved the difficulties, Aristotle can now end with a summary, and he briefly states his views both on what a citizen is and on citizen virtue. So, as about what a citizen is: there are several kinds of citizen (depending in particular on the kinds of regimes); a citizen is properly someone who shares in the honors of office (determinate or indeterminate); those who do not so share are not really citizens, even if, for reasons of deception, they are, say, allowed the name. As about citizen virtue: the virtue that makes the good man may also make the good citizen because in some cities, such as aristocracies, the same man is good as both; in others, however, this need not be so (some, for instance, may be good as citizens when being ruled but not good as men, nor hence as citizens when ruling); the man who is good as both citizen and man is the politician (he has the ruling virtue of prudence, either individually or collectively, 3.11).

Chapter 6

~ DEFINITION AND DIVISION OF REGIME

~ DEFINITION OF REGIME
1278b6/8 Now that city and citizen, and the disputes relative to them, have been dealt with, Aristotle can return to discuss the regime and its kinds. So he first gives a definition of regime and then, in the light of it, divides the kinds. The regime is defined as an arrangement of a city's offices and especially of its controlling office. This definition is in fact a consequence of the preceding discussion. For if a regime is a name for the arrangement of a city, and if a city is a multitude of citizens and citizens are those who share or are entitled to share in deliberative and judicial rule, which is the controlling office, then the way a city is arranged is the way its controlling office is arranged, or the way this office is distributed among those in the city. Aristotle, however, chooses to confirm the definition by an argument that appeals rather to direct experience: (1) the ruling body has control in the city; (2) the ruling body is the regime (and conversely); (3) therefore the regime is those who have control in the city. Premise (1) is proved from the examples of democracies and oligarchies where the manifestly ruling body of the populace has control in the first and the manifestly ruling body of the few has control in the second. Premise (2) is proved from the fact that we call democracies and oligarchies different regimes, or that we determine difference of regime by difference of ruling body.

It is worth noting about this definition that it identifies regime with a body of persons, not with a body of laws or a certain document (which is what we typically mean, for instance, by constitution).[31] This identification helps to explain why Aristotle's preoccupation throughout his discussion of regimes is with kinds of persons and not, or not first, with kinds of laws.

31. Mulgan (1977: 56), Robinson (1962: xv–xvi), Susemihl and Hicks (1894: 365).

1278b15 To find the kinds of regime Aristotle says two things must first be set down, the end of the city and the kinds of rule. The need to determine these follows, in fact, from the preceding definition. For if the regime is essentially an arrangement of rule in the city, and if the city exists for a certain end, then the kinds of regime will in some way be determined by differences in ways of arranging rule for the sake of this end (just as the several kinds of other things, as of animals, are determined by differences in their essential elements, 6(4).4.1290b25–1291b15). Aristotle turns, therefore, to consider the end of the city and the kinds of rule that human community admits of, and then, in the light of these, to divide the kinds of regime.

1278b17 The end of the city was already stated, in a way, in 1.2. But it was not fully set out there, and anyway the context there was the household whereas here it is the regime. So although Aristotle refers back to that discussion, he only recalls from it what is of most use for a fuller determination of the city's end, namely that human beings are naturally political or naturally belong in political community. From this two things follow: (1) that human beings desire to live together for its own sake; (2) that the common good also draws them together, at least to the extent they can partake of such good or noble living. These two, says Aristotle, are "above all" (1278b23) the end of human life, singly and in common. For he allows next (3) that mere life may also play a role, but only because mere life has something noble and sweet in it. That is why people will endure much to stay alive (it is perhaps only overwhelming misfortune or wickedness that can make life seem hateful; *Ethics* 1.9.1100a5–9, 1166b2–13).

Point (3) is asserted on the basis of empirical evidence, but points (1) and (2) also, though founded on the political character of human beings, seem to be asserted as empirically observable claims. At all events, by (1) Aristotle denies that only need or advantage could work to bring people together; by (2) he denies that, to the extent advantage does work, this advantage is private as opposed to common advantage, and mere life as opposed to good life or the noble; by (3) he denies that, to the extent mere life also works, this advantage is itself not to be understood in terms of the noble. These propositions state, in simple and direct terms, Aristotle's rejection of all theories, ancient and modern, that understand the point of political community to be the securing of private and material goods (as property and bodily survival). Such theories, he implies, are contrary both to the observable facts and to the political or communal nature of humanity.

1278b30/1279a8 The kinds of rule were also spoken of earlier in book 1, and though Aristotle seems to refer back to that discussion, at least in passing (the force, I take it, of the word "too" at 1278b31),[32] he chooses to make express mention of external discourses instead.[33] Possibly he wishes to show how obvious and common the distinction is, and hence that those who rule in cities as if rule was of only one kind (and the worse kind at that) are without serious excuse.

The distinction is straightforward: one kind of rule is over slaves and is exercised for the sake of the ruler (the slave is, of course, property, and, though he is preserved by his master's rule, that rule is manifestly not for the sake of property but for the sake of that for which property itself is for the sake of); another kind of rule is rule over those who are not slaves, as wife and child, and is clearly for the sake of the ruled (provided of course that the examples of such rule are taken from the practice of civilized peoples and not from that of barbarians who treat their wives like slaves, 1.2.1252b5–9). If the ruler also benefits from this rule, it is incidental, as it is in the case of doctors, sailors, and gymnasts who become objects of their own art. The same distinction of rule is also admitted in the case of cities where all are equal and similar (and so where none could be so different as to be by nature slaves of another). What is thought right here is ruling by turns, and ruling for the sake of the ruled. If some nowadays wish to overturn this opinion and rule permanently and for their own benefit, it is not because they have come to think the opinion false, but because they have been seduced by the wealth rulers have access to (they have caught the disease of the tyrant Jason, as it were, and are incapable of stepping down, 3.4.1277a24–25).

1279a17 Given these determinations about the city's end and about the kinds of rule, and given too that the city is a community of the free, Aristotle now concludes that the first and main division of regimes is into correct ones, those that look to the common advantage,[34] and mistaken or deviant ones, those that look to the advantage of the rulers. This division is obviously an evaluative one, but so it must be if the city is essentially for the end of noble living. For the end of a

32. Schütrumpf proceeds rather hastily in denying that any such back reference is intended here (1991: 2:445).

33. What these external discourses were is a matter of some dispute, though a common opinion is that they are Aristotle's dialogues (now lost). Another opinion (which I borrow from conversation with John Cooper) is that, at least in the passage here, they could be Plato's own dialogues, and perhaps the *Republic*. For Aristotle would doubtless regard these as external discourses and as "ours" (because belonging to us students of Plato), and the difference between ruling for the sake of the ruled and for the sake of the ruler is an important theme in *Republic* book 1.

34. Scholarly controversies have arisen about whether Aristotle means by "common advantage" the advantage of each and every citizen in the city or only the advantage of some or most of them. But since by "common advantage" Aristotle means noble or virtuous living, this is actually a false dichotomy. No one can harm either their own or another's advantage by acting virtuously, for everyone's advantage is to act virtuously, so that the common advantage, if this is understood as virtuous living, is at one and the same time the advantage of each individually and of all together (cf. 4(7).13.1332a32–38). But see Miller (1995: chap. 6) for an extensive discussion of the issues and the scholarly debates.

thing is its good and judgments of good and bad are made by reference to the end, and the regime, since it is the arrangement of a city, must naturally have the same end as the city.[35]

A problem, however, arises about what is meant by "advantage of the rulers" in the case of deviant regimes. For since, by Aristotle's definition of citizen, only those are citizens who share in rule, it might seem that for the rulers to rule for their own advantage was for them to rule for the advantage of all the citizens, that is to say, for the common advantage. Hence their rule would turn out, paradoxically, to be correct and not deviant.[36] But here one must recall that the division of regimes into correct and deviant is based on two criteria—not only on the difference between rule over slaves and rule over free but also on what the end of the city is. Hence, when Aristotle speaks of the "simply just" (1279a18–19) in the context of the correct regimes, he must mean by this (as he does in 3.9) the city's true end, which is living together well or nobly. So even if one were to assume that a given regime was ruling for the advantage of all (including all the free noncitizens, like wives and children), and yet that it was not ruling for noble life, then it would not be ruling for the common advantage.[37]

But this solution leads to another problem. For if a regime is ruling for the advantage of all (ruled as well as rulers) but does not understand this advantage as noble living, then, while it might be deviant according to the end of the city, it will not be deviant for the reason Aristotle gives, namely that it rules for the advantage of the rulers alone.[38] The answer must be that it is in fact false to suppose that a regime can really be said to be ruling for the advantage of all if it is not ruling for the common advantage of noble life. For if noble life is the end of the city, then only such life will, properly speaking, be the advantage of all, for only such life will be the advantage that the city naturally exists to provide and that people naturally enter the city to gain. Anything else that might be said to be the advantage of all will, despite appearances and despite what people say, not be the advantage of all. Accordingly what one should say about a regime that, while professedly for the advantage of all, is not for the advantage of noble living is that its rule, since it is not for such advantage, can only be for what the rulers themselves say or suppose

35. Hobbes's rather hostile rejection of Aristotle's division of regimes into good and bad or tyranni-cal is motivated by his rejection of Aristotle's understanding of the end of political life. For Hobbes this end is peace, not noble living, and any effective organization of rule (including one that Aristotle would call despotic) can achieve this end; see *Leviathan*, chap. 19.

36. A puzzle noted by Mulgan (1977: 61), Miller (1995: 212), Newman (1:216 n2), Schütrumpf (1991: 2:458).

37. Modern liberal democracies, as they are called, might be a case in point. For they rule, or claim to rule, for the advantage of all (both rulers and ruled), but do not understand this advantage as noble living, nor make that their aim.

38. As Newman remarks (3:xxviii).

advantage is. But then if the rulers are judging according to their own opinion, and not according to the truth (or not according to the "simply just"), they are after all ruling for their own advantage, because they are ruling for the prevalence of their own opinion in the city and for the continuance in rule of themselves and of those who have the same opinion as themselves.

Consequently one must read the phrase "the advantage of the rulers" in the account of deviant regimes as meaning the advantage of the rulers in their continuance in rule and in their permanent exclusion from rule of others who have different opinions (and specifically of those who have the true opinion). That this is how the phrase is to be read is suggested by what Aristotle has just mentioned (people who want to remain always in power) and by what he argues in 3.9. For he shows there that the democratic and oligarchic opinions about justice are precisely to the advantage of the poor or rich in their desire to stay in power. In other words, it does not matter how much the rulers suppose that their regime is for the advantage of all (and probably most rulers, including some tyrants, think this). Nor does it matter how well they actually treat the ruled (Aristotle allows that some oligarchical regimes do treat the ruled well, and even counsels them to do so, but he still holds that they are deviations, 2.11.1273b18–24, 7(5).8.1309a20–32). For if they are not ruling for the sake of noble living, their rule cannot be for the common advantage of all. Conversely, a regime that is ruling for the sake of noble living is ruling for the common advantage of all even if it excludes some in the city from rule and even if these some hate it.[39]

Take, for instance, the case of two groups of rulers both of whom are ruling with a view to wealth or material prosperity. Suppose that one of these groups is ruling to keep or concentrate wealth in its own hands, and that the other is ruling to distribute wealth broadly among everyone. According to many opinions (ancient and modern), the former group of rulers would be ruling unjustly while the latter would, at least to this extent, be ruling justly. But according to Aristotle both would be ruling unjustly, because both would be ruling for a deviant end, namely wealth and not noble living. The difference in the way these two groups of rulers treated the ruled, whether distributing or not distributing wealth to them, would not make one group to be correct and the other deviant. Rather it would only make them to

39. Schütrumpf (1991: 1:50, 2:580) says that Aristotle is here distinguishing correct and incorrect regimes by the criterion of how they treat the mass of the free who are not part of the ruling body (and hence that 3 is incompatible with 4(7) and 5(8) because the best regime in these latter books has no mass of the free outside the ruling body). But what Aristotle is really saying here is that a regime is correct if it rules for noble living and incorrect if it rules for something other than noble living, whether or not there are any free outside the ruling body. Of course, any regime will try to exclude from rule those who disagree with its principle of rule (its conception of advantage); but correct regimes will do this correctly (they only exclude those who have a false view of the end of the city), and incorrect regimes will do it incorrectly (they also exclude those who do have a correct view of the end of the city).

be different classes of deviant regime (one an oligarchy, say, and the other a democracy), or different varieties within the same class of deviant regime (one an extreme oligarchy, say, and the other a more measured one, 6(4).2.1289b9–11, 4–6).

Again, take another example. A modern liberal democracy does not rule for noble living (it does not use rule to make people virtuous), but rather for allowing everyone the freedom to pursue, as far as possible, their own idea of advantage (or of happiness). Thus such a modern liberal democracy is not ruling for the common advantage. It is really ruling for the advantage, or for the continuance in rule, of those who believe that the regime should not use rule to make people virtuous. It is accordingly a deviant regime and is ruling for the advantage of the rulers only.[40] By contrast, a modern regime that did rule to make people virtuous, and used the laws to prohibit vicious and promote virtuous behavior, would, according to Aristotle, be ruling for the common advantage. Hence it would be a correct regime. The fact that it was preventing people from living as they liked, and was forcing them instead to live in ways the rulers liked, would not, contrary to prevailing modern opinions, make it deviant or unjust.

Of course, all this only holds on the supposition that the end of political community is noble living. If it is not, then whatever is posited as the end instead (freedom, perhaps, or wealth) will be the measure of correctness and deviation. But disagreement on the end of political community is precisely what separates Aristotle, not only from ancient oligarchs and democrats (3.9), but from their modern counterparts too.[41]

Chapter 7

~ SECOND PART OF THE DIVISION

1279a22   Having divided regimes into correct and deviant, Aristotle now divides these further into their several kinds. The correct are taken first because a deviation is a deviation from something and so presupposes knowledge of that from which it deviates (just as crookedness is understood from straightness).[42] Aristotle presents the following argument: (1) a regime is the same as the ruling body (so that what varies the ruling body must vary the regime); (2) the ruling body is what has control in cities; (3) this control must either be exercised by one

40. One way out of this conclusion would be to deny that the modern liberal democratic state is supposed to be like a city or a regime and to say instead that it is, or should be viewed as, a sort of defensive alliance of cities, as I in fact suggested in Simpson (1990, 1994). But then, in order to keep to its role as a defensive alliance, it would have to be far more limited in power, and far more tolerant of communities that do use rule to make people virtuous, than in fact it is.

41. Above all Hobbes and his inspirers and followers. See Rahe (1992: book 2).

42. Fortenbaugh (1976: 136–37).

or few or many; (4) therefore regimes must be divided into correct or deviant rule by the one, the few, or the many.

Propositions (1) and (2) follow from the definition of regime given earlier so the only new question this argument raises concerns proposition (3). Now while it may be proper enough to divide a quantity of persons according to the possible kinds of quantity, one may ask why "all" is not included among these kinds and also whether the few and the many could not be more or less few or many. But presumably Aristotle here intends "many" to include "all" ("all" is, as it were, the extreme case of "many"), and also intends "many" and "few" to be taken broadly and to admit of variations (indeed these variations become later the basis for further divisions within the kinds of regimes, 6(4).4–6). So his division of possible quantities can be seen as appropriately exhaustive.

As regards the parenthetical remark ("either participants should not be called citizens or they should share together in the advantage," 1279a31–32),[43] it seems added just to confirm that ruling for private advantage must be deviant. It constitutes, as it were, an acid test of correctness: either use words properly and admit that those ruled for someone else's advantage are being treated like slaves and so should not be called citizens, or exercise rule for their advantage also. To do the first is to admit despotism openly; to fail to do the second is to admit it in fact.

1279a32   The division according to numbers just given is evidently schematic and only a first step. So Aristotle says now what it actually means in fact. For the one, few, and many are meant here as concrete and not abstract numbers, as numbers qualified, as it were, by the particular features attendant on what they are applied to, namely human beings in cities. Accordingly Aristotle first names the three correct regimes of kingship, aristocracy, and polity, and then explains that these names arise because the one, few, and many that they specify are a virtuous one, few, and many. That correct regimes must be in the hands of the virtuous is required, of course, by the fact that they rule the city for the common advantage, and the common advantage is noble living, which only the virtuous pursue and realize. These regimes concretely differ, then, according to the ways that one, few, or many can be virtuous. Hence regimes run by one or a few virtuous are simply best because, as Aristotle says and as is obvious to observation, perfect virtue can only be found in one or a few. A regime run by many virtuous will therefore not be best (and so will not deserve a name signifying perfection), but it will be virtuous

---

43. On the question of whom "participants" refers to in this phrase (probably fellow citizens who, while entitled to share in rule, are effectively excluded from it), see Schütrumpf (1991: 2:464–65). There is, however, a scholarly emendation that would give the sense "either those who are *not* participants should not be called citizens. . . ." This, perhaps, makes the sentence easier to comprehend, but it is not required for the sentence can be given an acceptable sense as it stands.

with the virtue that a mass can have, namely military virtue (and so will deserve a name signifying correctness but nothing more). For soldiers are manifestly trained to act for the advantage of the whole, and the military life contains many parts of virtue (2.9.1270a4–8). Such a regime, because it is not best, will not deserve a name signifying perfection as the names kingship and aristocracy do, but, because it is a case of rule by the virtuous, it will nevertheless deserve a name signifying correctness. Polity is such a name. For it means regime, and as regime properly refers to a certain end (for city refers to a certain end), and as deviant regimes are thus, to this extent, not regimes (they have fallen away from what the regime is for), polity, in signifying regime, properly signifies something correct.[44]

This division, therefore, of correct regimes according to one, few, and many is concretely a division of regimes according to perfect and imperfect virtue. It is still a division according to quantities but qualified quantities. But once this quality is noted, an interesting fact emerges. For whereas polity clearly differs in point of virtue from kingship and aristocracy, kingship and aristocracy do not seem to differ in point of virtue from each other. They are, in respect of the virtue that characterizes them, one and not two regimes (kingship is just a sort of concentration or intensification of aristocracy). This oneness of kingship and aristocracy is confirmed in what follows where Aristotle treats them as more or less the same (3.18.1288a32–b2, 6(4).2.1289a30–33).

1279b4   The incorrect regimes must follow the same pattern and what distinguishes them will also be quantities that are qualified or concretized. So tyranny deviates from kingship, oligarchy from aristocracy, and democracy from polity when the one, few, and many are not marked by virtue and so do not pursue the common advantage (which is virtue) but their own. These regimes will be marked instead by what constitutes the one, few, or many in cities as distinct interest groups, opposed to the rule of any other or rival interest group. For the tyrant this is himself alone; but for the few, says Aristotle, it is wealth, and for the many poverty. For, as he indicates in the succeeding chapters and as is evident, not just any few or many are going to coalesce sufficiently to form a regime; only a few or many that are united by a common and abiding interest will manage that. But in cities wealth is what makes for such an interest among a few (provided wealth is

44. In the *Ethics* timocracy is preferred as a name for polity, because polity is a regime based on property assessments or *timēmata* (*Ethics* 8.10.1160a33–35; the assessments are designed to ensure that control is in the hands of those able to afford heavy arms, *Politics* 6(4).13.1297b1–6). Polity is nevertheless admitted, even in the *Ethics*, to be the more customary name, which is presumably why it is the name used in the *Politics*, because it keeps closer to common usage. One should also, perhaps, note the possibility that polity could be the common name for this kind of regime because *politeia* also carries the general sense of "citizenship," so that polity might be popularly called polity because in it all the citizens get their due while in deviant regimes some get oppressed by others.

understood broadly to include advantages that tend to accompany wealth, as abundance of friends, education, family tradition), and poverty is what makes for it among many (provided poverty too is understood broadly to include all those who have no time for leisure but have to work for a living, 6(4).4.1291b16–30).

The deviant regimes are thus, in a sense, the dominance in the city of one or other interest group, or part of the city. The correct regimes are also, in a sense, the dominance in the city of a certain interest group, whether the simply virtuous or those who are virtuous in the mass. The difference is that the deviant have a deviant interest (something other than the common advantage of noble living), while the virtuous have a correct interest (precisely this common advantage). These regimes are nevertheless also in fact distinguished by numbers (perfect virtue goes with a few, as does wealth, and mass virtue with many, as does poverty), save that it is not the numbers as numbers that are significant, but the interests, or the quality of the different groups in the city, that these numbers pick out (a point that gets reinforced in the next chapter). This focus on qualified numbers, as opposed to numbers merely, follows the focus on the end of the city as noble life. It is because the city has such an end, and has it by nature, that correctness in politics or justice is not a matter of giving every individual an equal say (as we tend to suppose nowadays and as democrats supposed in Aristotle's day), but a matter, rather, of giving the best individuals, or the best mass of individuals, the whole say (as emerges particularly in 3.13).

This idea, that qualified numbers, not mere numbers, count when it comes to the kinds of regimes and their correctness or deviance, persists throughout the *Politics*. It is picked up significantly in 6(4).3–10, where it is again stressed that the decisive factor for understanding the differences among regimes is not how many rule but which part of the city rules, whether the virtuous or the well-off or the needy, and which sort of virtuous or well-off or needy. For since individuals differ in kind or in their quality and character, and do so according to the part of the city they belong to, the regimes composed of these individuals or founded on these parts differ in kind too. Individuals are thus, because of the varying worth of their character, fundamentally unequal when it comes to political rule. For their respective characters make them unequal with respect to what political rule is all about, namely noble living. Hence correctness or justice in politics is not a matter of equality for each individual; nor is it even a matter of equality for each of the parts of the city. Rather it is a matter of superiority for some part or parts over the others. At least these conclusions must follow if noble living is the true end of the city.[45]

45. That is why theories, whether ancient or modern, that assert the political equality of all individuals deny this supposition and assert that something else, as property or physical survival, is the true end of the political community.

Chapter 8

~ CONFIRMATION OF THE DIVISION
AGAINST CERTAIN DIFFICULTIES

~ FIRST DIFFICULTY: WHETHER THE
DEVIANT REGIMES ARE RIGHTLY DEFINED

1279b11   Aristotle's division of regimes seems now essentially complete, but
he does not pass at once to investigate the best regime, which is his next object. Instead, he pauses to consider the matter further in the light of certain problems, for
this, he says, is what philosophy, as opposed to practice, requires. That the *Politics* is
a contribution to philosophy was asserted already in the *Ethics* (10.9.1181b14–15),
and one need not suppose that there is any conflict here with Aristotle's overall
practical intention, because that intention is the art of the legislator as such, not
some particular case of legislation, and art requires a universal treatment.[46] In fact,
Aristotle only does now in his treatment of regimes what he did earlier in chapters
2–5 in his treatment of citizen and city: he goes through and resolves the several
difficulties.

An important question nevertheless arises over the point and coherence of the
remaining chapters of this book. The question concerns not only the appropriateness of having four chapters at the end about kingship, but also whether chapters
8–13 are internally harmonious since they treat the same problems several times
and with seemingly conflicting results.[47] To reach an answer that saves the overall
coherence of these remaining chapters, one must note, first, that the turn to the
next stage in Aristotle's intention, the discussion of the best regime by itself, is not
made until the last chapter (chapter 18). For if this is so, then this book can hardly
count as a coherent whole unless all the remaining chapters, including especially
the chapters on kingship, can be read as belonging to the discussion of the regime
in general and of its kinds (the subject matter announced at the beginning of chapter 1). But the only way to do this is to suppose that the difficulties Aristotle says he
is now going to examine cover the whole of the rest of the book and not just the
next one or two chapters. Such a supposition is in fact easier to sustain than the
scholarly disputes make it appear and can be given strong support if one notes Aristotle's several programmatic remarks as well as the actual content of each chapter.
So the discussion of kingship, for instance, is not a discussion of kingship as such

---

46. As Schütrumpf rightly recalls (1991: 2:472).

47. For details of the scholarly disputes see in particular Schütrumpf (1991: 2:109–18, with references) and his introductions to the several chapters; also Leandri, in Aubenque (1993: 316–29), Newman (1:570–72, 3:xxvii–xxxiii), Robinson (1962: viii–xii), Susemihl and Hicks (1894: 37–44), Wolff
(1988: 273–78) and also in Aubenque (1993: 289–313).

but of whether it is a good thing for cities, or, in short, whether it really is a correct regime as Aristotle has contended. If kingship as such is discussed anywhere, it is along with aristocracy in books 4(7) and 5(8), since both are names for the best regime (6(4).2.1289a30–33). All the intervening chapters 8–13 are also about difficulties confronting the division of regimes that Aristotle has just given, but about different difficulties. That is why the same points get taken up more than once, because they are relevant to more than one difficulty. But no conflict arises between their several treatments provided the differences of context are duly considered.

1279b15   The first difficulty noted by Aristotle concerns the definitions of the deviant regimes. These definitions, as he here recalls, contain two parts: that these regimes are deviant, or despotic, and that the one, the rich, or the poor have control in them. Now no serious difficulty is going to arise about whether tyranny is rule by one man or whether it is despotic (indeed even many tyrants admit they are despots). But serious difficulties do arise about whether oligarchy and democracy are despotic (oligarchs and democrats certainly claim that their regimes are not despotic), and about whether they are rule of the few rich and the many poor. That difficulties thus arise about oligarchy and democracy but not about tyranny will explain why Aristotle does not speak of tyranny further.[48] He focuses instead on the two difficulties about oligarchy and democracy. He deals with the difficulty about numbers in this chapter and with that about despotism in the next.

1279b20   The difficulty about numbers is that situations can be conceived where the poor are few and rule and where the rich are many and rule. So, in these cases, if oligarchy means rule of the few, it cannot also mean rule of the rich, and if democracy means rule of the many, it cannot also mean rule of the poor (and vice versa). The situation is obviously not improved by combining the criteria, since that creates the difficulty of what to call regimes where the poor few and the rich many rule (as opposed to the poor many and rich few).

~   FIRST PART OF THE SOLUTION:
QUANTITY AND QUALITY IN THE DEFINITION

1279b34   The difficulty in question here arises because of the customary definitions of democracy and oligarchy as rule of the many and rule of the few. But while Aristotle had, in the preceding chapter, called democracy and oligarchy deviations from rule of the virtuous many and from the virtuous few, he had not defined them in terms of many and few but in terms of who the many and few are in deviant regimes, namely the poor and rich. The discussion of the present difficulty confirms what he did there. It points to the fact that the numbers are incidental to the definition of these regimes, being a result of the fact that rich and

48. As Newman remarks (3:196).

poor are everywhere few and many. As proof Aristotle refers to the rival claims to rule made by democrats and oligarchs. Oligarchs appeal, not to their fewness, but to their wealth; democrats appeal, not to their manyness, but to their freedom and so effectively to their poverty. Democrats dispute over the regime on the basis of freedom rather than poverty, because poverty does not furnish a proper claim to rule, whereas freedom does. For freedom, unlike poverty, is necessary to the existence of a city (3.12.1283a16–19), and the poor have no place in the city qua poor but only qua fulfilling necessary occupations (6(4).4.1290b39–1291a6). So freedom is the way in practice to claim control for the poor, since freedom puts everyone on a level and so excludes the rich qua rich and gives rule to the majority who are poor.[49]

Thus what distinguishes oligarchy and democracy, and makes them different regimes, is the wealth and poverty that mark those who compose the ruling body. As noted earlier, Aristotle's concern with numbers in the case of regimes is with concrete and not abstract numbers, and so it is the qualities which these concrete numbers take on that really make the different regimes to be the sorts of regime they are. Oligarchy is, nevertheless, rightly called a deviation from rule by the virtuous few and democracy rightly called a deviation from rule by the virtuous many, because the only few and many in the city who constitute a regular and deviant interest are the rich and the poor (that many are rich and few poor is altogether exceptional). So the names naturally get imposed because of this incidental fact of fewness and manyness, yet, once imposed, they of necessity signify the essential fact of deviant interest, namely wealth or poverty.

Chapter 9

~ SECOND PART OF THE SOLUTION:
DESPOTISM IN THE DEFINITION

~ THAT OLIGARCHIC AND DEMOCRATIC JUSTICE ARE PARTIAL

1280a7 This chapter is directed to a discussion of democratic and oligarchic justice and of how neither is justice simply. It is directed, in other words, to showing that both regimes are despotic in the sense stated at the end of chapter 6. Aristotle first states that both kinds of justice are partial, and then gives proof of the fact.

49. The point is confirmed by the exceptional case of rule by the few free over the many poor and unfree, 6(4).4.1290b9–14, where the regime is in fact an oligarchy, and not a democracy, because it is rule by the rich and not by the poor. Freedom may be the basis on which democrats dispute, but it is not the defining mark of their regime, contra Mulgan (1977: 65).

Democrats and oligarchs err, says Aristotle, in speaking of only part of justice and not of the whole of it. His explanation is a little involved and may even appear misleading,[50] but it can be expanded as follows. In their dispute over who should rule, democrats argue that justice is equality and so requires all to have equal shares, while oligarchs argue that justice is inequality and so requires the few rich to have unequal shares. But these arguments are incompletely expressed, for justice is only equality when it is between equals and only inequality when it is between unequals. So the respective arguments are really of the form: (1) justice is equality for equals, and (2) we are all equal, (3) therefore justice requires all of us to have equal shares; or (4) justice is inequality for unequals, and (5) we oligarchs are unequal, (6) therefore justice requires us to have unequal shares. But in their statement of their positions, democrats and oligarchs simply say that justice is equality or inequality, and omit to add for whom it is equality or inequality. So they each state their first premise incompletely, dispensing with the "for whom," and proceed at once to their conclusion without even bothering to state their second premise. They do this because they are judging in their own cause and take for granted their own equality or inequality (their arguments may anyway be more rhetorically convincing if the complication of the "for whom" is left out and no attention is brought to it).

1280a16 But if the "for whom" is not made explicit in what they say, it is still implicit in the way they argue. For their arguments are resting on the (correct) idea that justice is a matter of equalizing the things to the persons between whom these things are to be shared (equal to equals and unequal to unequals). This truth about the just distribution of the things they both implicitly admit. What they are really disagreeing about is whether they themselves are equal or unequal. Or, to put it another way, they both implicitly concede each other's first premise (that justice is equality for equals and inequality for unequals), but dispute each other's second premise ("we are all equal" or "we oligarchs are unequal"). They assume their own equality or inequality, of course, and deny the inequality or equality of their opponents, because they are each judging in their own cause. But a sort of reasoning does lie behind their thinking, namely that since they are equal in one thing, they are equal in everything; or that since they are unequal in one thing, they are unequal in everything. Now they are not, or need not be, wrong about the respect in which they are equal or unequal, so to this extent they are both speaking about justice correctly. But they are wrong to suppose that this respect is all that matters for a just distribution of shares, or that it constitutes justice simply. On the contrary, they fail to speak of what carries most weight or authority in the case of justice.

50. Newman (3:199) remarks that while Aristotle says oligarchs and democrats dispense with the "for whom" in their arguments, in fact these arguments, as Aristotle reports them, say a great deal about the "for whom." I address this puzzle immediately in what follows.

1280a25 What does carry most weight or authority Aristotle now proceeds to explain. He does so by taking his cue from the preceding arguments. The oligarchic argument, for instance, would work if people formed cities for the sake of possessions. For then how much wealth each contributed would be the measure for determining just shares, as it already does determine shares in the case of certain business transactions (and likewise, one might add, the democratic argument would work if people formed cities for the sake of defending freedom). But at all events, to settle the question of just distributions in the city, what really matters is the true end of the city, or what people form cities for, since that will determine what the relevant equality or inequality is.

1280a31 The city's true end Aristotle has already determined before to be noble life (1.2, 3.6). Here he proves the same conclusion again, but since he is now arguing against oligarchs and democrats he does so by directly challenging their conceptions of the end.[51] He presents three arguments.[52] The first is directed at the supposition, implicit in the oligarchic appeal to property (which is essentially for satisfying bodily needs, 1.8), that people form cities for the sake of life and not good life. For (1) if so, then there would be a city of slaves and the other animals; but (2) there is no such city; therefore (3) people do not form cities for life instead of for good life. Premise (2) is presumably meant to be evident to observation (animals live in herds and slaves, such as barbarians, in despotic empires or wild tribes), but is supported by (4) that neither slaves nor animals share in happiness and deliberate choice (which are distinctive of human communities). Aristotle is evidently speaking here of a properly human, and not vulgar, notion of happiness. For unless happiness is taken in this way then, as premise (1) says, human life will never rise above anything better than the life that even slaves and animals can attain (who do not deliberate or make considered choices and yet can have their fill, just as much as others, of the pleasures associated with physical life). But this is an absurd supposition, and even oligarchs and democrats, who claim that they are much better than slaves, would be ashamed to assert it.

1280a34 The second argument is directed at the suppositions that people form cities for defense, as democrats might say (for those who cannot repay evils seem not to be free; *Ethics* 5.5.1132b33–1133a1), or for exchange and mutual utility, as oligarchs might say (for such things are aimed at producing wealth). For (1) if so Etruscans and Carthaginians and others who have defensive and commercial

---

51. The fact that this chapter is directed against oligarchs and democrats helps explain, contra Schütrumpf (1991: 2:477), why Aristotle argues the question without referring back to his earlier discussions.

52. Keyt, in Keyt and Miller (1991: 251–52), thinks these arguments are parts of a single elimination argument. But this view does not, I think, make full sense of the logic of the text.

treaties with each other would be citizens of one city; but (2) they are manifestly not citizens of one city (Etruscans and Carthaginians live hundreds of miles apart across an open sea); therefore (3) the city is not for defense and commerce. That the city is for virtue instead (the city truly and not verbally so called) is shown by the fact that virtue is precisely what cities care about whereas alliances, such as that between Etruscans and Carthaginians, do not. So alliances neither have a common office for their treaties (they monitor observance by their own separate offices), nor do they have concern for each others' character as opposed to each others' behavior (they only care that the treaty be observed, not whether those observing it are just). The city, by contrast, has both common offices (sharing in office makes the citizen), and also those who care that the legislation in cities be in a good condition (including especially the legislation about shared offices) care about character. Common offices would, of course, be needed if there is to be common concern for the virtue of all those subject to the treaties; and as for the claim that those who care about good legislation in cities care about character, this is doubtless to be assumed from the previous book, where regimes reputed to be well legislated[53] (whether merely proposed or also in use) all cared about character, even if their proposals or their practice were not entirely successful in this regard.

1280b8   Aristotle, however, added something when stating his conclusion that the city must make virtue its care, for he said that the city "truly and not verbally so called" must make this its care (1280b7–8). What he does next is to explain and to prove this remark. He first explains it by saying that otherwise, that is, if one does not say the city is for virtue, one will effectively be saying that "city" is just a word, for one will be saying that it does not serve to mean anything other than what the word "alliance" already means, or that it does so only to the extent of meaning an alliance differing from other alliances (such as the alliance between Etruscans and Carthaginians) by not being between allies who live far apart. What it will not do, however, is mean any distinct kind of community. Nor will good legislation mean anything other than what "treaty" means or what, to use Lycophron's words, "guarantor of rights" means, or again, to use a modern phrase, what "social contract" means.[54] It will not mean anything that is designed to make people virtuous.

That "city" and "law" will come to mean this, and not anything else, Aristotle next proves by a sort of thought experiment. Take, first, two cities, Megara and

53. The Greek word that is used is of the same root in both cases. Here it is the noun *eunomia*, 1280b6, and in the previous book it was the verb *eunomeisthai*, 2.1.1260b30.

54. The likeness between this view of the city and law, especially Lycophron's phrase "guarantor of rights," and the modern social contract theory of the state and law, as found say in Hobbes's *Leviathan* and recently in Rawls (1971) and Gauthier (1986), is very marked.

Corinth, and remove the distance between them and assume intermarriage; they are still only an alliance and not a city. Or, second, take a number of scattered households united by a commercial and defensive alliance but sharing nothing else; these too are still only an alliance and not yet a city. But it is not because of distance that they are not yet a city. For, third, take distance away and keep the manner of community the same, and still they are an alliance and not a city. Or at least they are not a city in any sense of "city" that would make it signify something other than what "alliance" signifies (for the sort of sharing, or the things shared, are still the same and all that is altered is distance).

1280b29   The third argument, like the second, again picks up on this idea that the city, if it is to be more than another word for an alliance, must signify a community for virtue. It is to the effect that while the sorts of sharing already possible in an alliance, as sharing a common place and commerce and defense and even intermarriage, may be necessary for a city, the city does not emerge as a distinct community until the households come together in such a way as to form a community in living well. The proof is found in the change that is undergone in cities, as opposed to alliances, by the sharing of a common place and intermarriage (both of which things could, as such, be features of an alliance). The city needs these as conditions but they occasion, precisely when in the city, the marriage connections, clans, sacrifices, and cultured pursuits involved in living together. Such things, however, do not arise from these conditions alone (for they do not arise in alliances). They can only be the result of friendship, for they are, as activities of living together, expressions of the choice so to live, and such choice is friendship. The city, therefore, is a community in friendship (whereas an alliance is not), and friendship belongs not to life alone but to living well,[55] and living well is living happily and nobly, that is, with virtue.

1281a2   These three arguments all issue in the same conclusion: the city's end is noble deeds and not mere living together, that is, its end is living together nobly and not merely the living together that might be found among animals, slaves, and alliances. From this it in turn follows, according to the principles of distributive justice admitted by both oligarchs and democrats alike (equal shares for equals, unequal shares for unequals), that greater shares should go to those

55. Barker (1946: 120), Newman (3:208–9), and Schütrumpf (1991: 2:487–88) all suppose that Aristotle is making these remarks at this point to distinguish living together from living well and to show that the living together here under discussion is not the end of the city. But such an interpretation runs into conflict, as Schütrumpf himself notes, with the *Ethics* (8.1.1155a23–31, 3, 11–12), where friendship, in particular virtuous friendship, is regarded as integral to the city and to living well; note also Jaffa, in Strauss and Cropsey (1972: 104). It also runs into conflict, because of the reference to cultured pursuits (*diagōgē*), with Aristotle's claim (*Politics* 4(7).13–15, 5(8).3) that living well in the city consists principally in such pursuits.

who contribute most to this end of noble life than to those, as oligarchs and democrats, who contribute only to its conditions.[56] Oligarchs and democrats therefore have a partial conception of justice, since they have a partial grasp of the end of the city (which is what determines justice). Accordingly their regimes were correctly defined earlier as deviant (although deviant not so much because they pursue something bad as because they pursue the good partially or incompletely).

Chapter 10

~ SECOND DIFFICULTY: WHETHER ANY OF THE
REGIMES IS CORRECT

~ STATEMENT OF THE DIFFICULTY

1281a11 The previous two chapters have been about the deviant regimes. This one raises a difficulty about all regimes. It is therefore a new difficulty, but as it is a difficulty about which regimes, if any, are correct, it must be construed as another of the difficulties in need of examination mentioned at the beginning of chapter 8. Hence it may rightly be called the second of such difficulties. But further, since it is about all regimes, it necessarily covers, to some extent, the same ground as has just been covered in the case of the deviant regimes. We should therefore expect a certain repetition, though a repetition that is not useless or inappropriate in the context since it is given from a different angle and to answer a different and broader question. Moreover, it fits the intention announced at the beginning of chapter 8, for to treat every particular thoroughly and leave nothing out may well require treating the same points more than once.[57] This chapter, however, must be regarded as dialectical (as the first sentence of the next chapter implies) and as only stating the difficulty without giving a determinative answer. Otherwise it might appear that in raising objections to the correct regimes as well as to the deviant ones Aristotle is contradicting earlier results.[58]

Aristotle begins by listing the candidates for control in the city. They correspond to the six types of regime already listed save that the multitude is not distinguished into a kind proper to polity and a kind proper to democracy (which perhaps reflects the fact that most people fail to distinguish democracy from polity, 6(4).7.1293a39–b1). As against putting control in the hands of the multitude Aristotle raises three objections. The first is specifically about rule by the poor: if the poor are in control, they could despoil the rich (an act whose manifest injustice is not removed by appeal to oaths), but rule is for justice and not injustice, so

---

56. See also Miller, in Keyt and Miller (1991: 238–78).

57. Schütrumpf's remarks here are exact (1991: 2:490).

58. Schütrumpf incorrectly takes this view (1991: 2:491–92).

putting the poor in control cannot be correct. The second is about any majority that despoiled the few (whatever the composition, presumably, of the many and few): such a majority would destroy the city (it would destroy the community or sharing that marks the city), but no virtue destroys what has it and, specifically, justice, the virtue of the city, does not destroy the city (virtue is rather what perfects each thing), so again control by the multitude cannot be correct. The third is a *reductio*: if acts of violence by the multitude against the rich are just, so must the violent acts of a tyrant (who is as much in control in a tyranny as the multitude in a democracy) be just; but this is absurd, as well as denied by democrats themselves; so such acts cannot be correct nor, therefore, can control by the multitude that commits such acts be correct.

It is worth noting about all these three arguments that they proceed on the supposition that the multitude in control is corrupt; consequently they will not work, as Aristotle shows in the next chapter, against a multitude that is not corrupt.

1281a24 As against rule by the rich, Aristotle repeats the same *reductio*: if the rich use control to commit the same crimes and despoil the multitude and this is just, then the crimes of the multitude and the tyrant will be just, but this is absurd, as well as denied by oligarchs themselves; therefore, control by the rich cannot be correct either.

1281a28/32 As against rule by the decent few and the one best man, Aristotle no longer speaks of the possibility of their committing crimes (for then they would not be the decent nor he the best), but simply points out that in these cases few have the honors and the multitude are excluded. The problem with this is presumably that there is an appearance of injustice in excluding all from office save one or a few (the multitude who suppose themselves equal would think so), and a resentful multitude in a city is a source of instability (2.5.1264b6–10, 2.12.1274a15–18, 3.11.1281b29–30). This argument is manifestly dialectical since if the multitude are neither equal nor resentful, rule by the one or few best would certainly not be unjust (and, as Aristotle shows later in chapter 13, fewness need not be a problem if the few are not too few for the work of ruling the city and if their vast superiority over everyone else is manifest).

1281a34 Aristotle presents no argument against rule by the tyrant since the injustice of tyranny is manifest and was in fact used in the earlier *reductio* against the multitude. Instead he rejects a possible answer to the problem of who should rule, namely that this should not be human beings but the law.[59] Aristotle needs to confront this possibility for, if it is allowed, the question *who* should rule would be falsely posed and regimes would be distinguished, not, as Aristotle has said, by who rules in them, but by whether law rules. This view can, however, easily be

59. This opinion may be taken from Plato's *Laws* (713c2–715d6), but it need not be since it was doubtless a common enough opinion in Aristotle's day, as it still is even now.

rejected because law too can be democratic or oligarchic (law is made by human beings and need be no better than they are), and if so it will be no less unjust.

Chapter 11

〜 PARTIAL SOLUTION SPECIFIC TO POLITY

〜 STATEMENT AND ILLUSTRATION OF THE SOLUTION

1281a39 Having thus stated the difficulties against all regimes, Aristotle now turns to show, according to his earlier conclusion, that three of these regimes are nevertheless correct. The order of his treatment, however, can appear obscure and some suppose that in this and the next chapters much confusion and repetition are to be found.[60] But the opening sentence of this chapter indicates that only part of the difficulty is going to be dealt with here and the whole of it later. Further the content of this chapter indicates that its subject is the correctness of rule in the hands of a virtuous multitude, that is to say, of polity (for polity was defined earlier, 3.7, as control by a virtuous multitude). The conclusions of the chapter therefore concern the case of polity alone, and are not general to all regimes. In chapters 12 and 13, however, it is clear that Aristotle is dealing with all the regimes together. These chapters, in fact, give his complete answer to the difficulties raised in chapter 10. They must, therefore, be the later discussion he here refers forward to, and while they do contain repetition, they only contain as much as is necessary to make the truth in each case clear.

That there should be need first, however, for a separate treatment of polity seems to be partly because the results are needed for the complete solution stated later, and partly because, as Aristotle here says, the case for polity, especially when rule can be given to the few best instead, might seem to be manifestly refuted.[61] It might seem to be manifestly refuted because it might seem impossible that the multitude could be virtuous, or more virtuous than the few. So there is some pressure on Aristotle first to confront this belief and state separately the case for such a multitude.

1281a42 Aristotle first states and illustrates this case and then responds to certain objections. The case itself is straightforward enough: the many, while not virtuous singly, could nevertheless be virtuous as a whole. This thesis of combined

---

60. Newman (1:570–73, 3:225), Schütrumpf (1991: 2:508–10), Susemihl and Hicks (1894: 42–43).

61. Certainly this is what the text must mean if it is taken literally. My translation runs: "the view would seem to be refuted and involved in some difficulty that says the multitude should be in control rather than the few best. Perhaps, however, it might also seem to have truth to it." Since this way of taking the text makes sense of what follows, there is no need for emendations—on which, however, see the discussions by Newman (3:212–13), Narcy, in Aubenque (1993: 276–77), and Schütrumpf (1991: 2:497).

qualities has occasioned some surprise among scholars,[62] but that it must be a possibility is evident from the four examples Aristotle gives: collective meals, collective physical ability, collective judgment of poetry and music, and nobility or beauty in persons and paintings. These examples prove the possibility of combining good qualities because they present actual cases of such combining, and, manifestly, if something is actual then it is also possible.

That collective meals can be superior to those provisioned by one person is perhaps something everyone has experienced in one way or another, and that a crowd of relatively weak people could complete a task (say a massive clean-up operation) faster and better than a few abler men can scarcely be doubted. The case of musical and dramatic competitions (which is presumably what Aristotle is thinking of in his third example) is perhaps less obvious, but if one imagines that each person in the crowd can appreciate well some aspect of music or drama and gives a vote or his applause to each of the pieces that excel in the aspect he individually appreciates, then the piece that excelled in all or more aspects would get more votes or applause than a piece that excelled in fewer. Such a collective decision by the crowd might thus easily be better than that by a panel of experts. This example perhaps also best illustrates how collective virtue could be possible, especially if, as Aristotle suggests shortly, the multitude is only meant to judge, as at a music competition, which candidates are better or worse fitted for a determinate office and which officials have performed well or badly.

1281b10 The fourth example illustrates the same point but rather from the perspective of how the few best can be superior individually though still inferior to the multitude as a whole. A noble or beautiful person or painting excels in nobility by combining many noble parts into one. Elsewhere, by contrast, these parts are scattered among many different individuals, each of whom is not noble, save with respect to the one isolated part he happens to have. But it is, of course, possible that these scattered parts are more noble than the corresponding parts in the single painting or person, in which case the nobility to be found in the multitude as a whole, none of whom could be called noble individually, would exceed that of the one noble person or painting.

1281b15 These examples, of course, do not prove that the many can or must always be better than the few. For if the many are especially deficient, or the few especially excellent, or both, the few will be manifestly better (just as a meal provided by one very rich man will be better than a meal provided by many beggars). Some individuals, for instance, as Aristotle notes later in chapter 13, could be

62. Lindsay (1992: 104–6), Mulgan (1977: 105), Newman (3:215), Schütrumpf (1991: 2:497–500), Susemihl and Hicks (1894: 398). It is necessary to keep in mind, however, that Aristotle is not saying that a multitude must always combine its good qualities instead of its bad, but only that nothing prevents this happening sometimes. Such collective virtue was hinted at earlier, 3.5.1278b4.

so superior that they exceed all collective virtue too. Conversely, as he expressly notes here, some multitudes could be positively bestial and combine bad qualities, not good ones (notably the democratic multitudes mentioned in the preceding chapter who despoil the rich). Still, the possibility that some multitudes could sometimes be superior to the few best remains. The typical case would doubtless be the one Aristotle expressly associates with polity, namely a multitude with military virtue. For soldiers are trained to act as a whole and to do their proper work in and for the whole, and indeed a well-disciplined army of mediocre men could easily be superior to a few outstanding champions. Moreover, they could very well be better than the experts at judging good generals and rulers from bad.

1281b21/31   So much then for the thesis, which, as stated, does solve the difficulty about how the many could be better than the few best.[63] It also points to the solution of another difficulty, not before mentioned but clearly implied in the previous one, about how such a multitude should exercise control. The difficulty is that the multitude cannot exercise control in offices that require virtue in individuals (for as individuals they are not virtuous), nor can they be deprived of office altogether, since they will be hostile to the regime if they get nothing from it, and justly so, since they are, taken as a whole, superior to the few who do exercise office. The solution is of course that they should exercise control, or judge and deliberate, through the sort of office for which their virtue fits them, namely office that they can hold and exercise as a multitude, like the choosing and auditing of officials. The example of the food—that raw mixed with wholesome food is more useful than a small amount of wholesome food on its own—illustrates how this way of mixing the multitude with the few best can help the city. But it is an example that implies at the same time, as chapter 13 says more expressly, that such a mixture is only necessary and just when the few best are not good enough to have control all by themselves (for if they were good enough, there could be no need to mix in something impure as well). Further, the example also shows that the sort of regime Aristotle has in mind in this chapter is not democracy proper but the mixed regime of polity.

〜 ANSWER TO OBJECTIONS
1281b38/1282a7   So much solves the original difficulty about whether and how the multitude should rule and have control. But the solution itself is subject to objections or difficulties of its own, and two in particular. The first takes the

---

63. Some think that the difficulty Aristotle here (1281b21–22) refers back to is the general one raised at the beginning of chapter 10 about who should be in control in cities, as Barker (1946: 124), Leandri, in Aubenque (1993: 320–21), Newman (3:218), Schütrumpf (1991: 2:502), Susemihl and Hicks (1894: 399). But if we accept this interpretation we have to conclude that Aristotle is now deciding the general question in favor of the multitude alone and so is saying that only polity is a correct regime, and that makes havoc of his whole teaching in book 3.

following form: (1) those who should judge whether the job has been done well or badly, or who should choose which candidate is to do the job, are the experts; (2) the multitude are not experts; (3) therefore the multitude should not, contrary to the solution just proposed, have control over judging and choosing officials. Premise (1) is defended by an analogy with the arts, specifically with medicine, where experts in the art judge whether a cure has been correctly administered, and with geometry and navigation, where again experts in the art choose who should do the job. For although, as in the case of medicine, the experts may include some who are not practicing the art, yet they include none who do not have the art; and although, as in the case of geometry and navigation, some laymen may be involved in the choosing, yet the laymen have no greater voice than the experts.

1282a14 Aristotle responds to this argument by attacking each premise in turn. Against premise (2) he appeals back to his earlier claims that the multitude, not singly but as a whole, may well be expert in the relevant sense (provided they are a virtuous multitude, as in a polity, and not a slavish one, as in a democracy). Against premise (1) he points out that the analogy is not true of all arts, and specifically not of those where the user, who may not have the art, is a better judge of the results than the maker or doer (as in the case of houses, rudders, and a feast). So since it is manifestly the multitude who use or experience the works of office-holders, it can sometimes be they, and not the few best, who are superior at auditing and electing officials.

1282a23/33 The second objection is: (1) it is absurd for inferior types to have control over greater things than the decent sort do; (2) but the multitude is composed of inferior types and, on the solution just proposed, has control over the very great things of auditing and choosing the offices; (3) therefore this solution is absurd. Aristotle responds by attacking the second premise (the first premise he would doubtless accept): the multitude may consist of inferior individuals but it is as a whole that they rule, not as individuals, and as a whole, gathered together in assembly, council, and law courts, they can very well be superior and not inferior (in wealth as much as in virtue).

1282a41 Aristotle has thus answered the objections and shown that polity, or rule by a virtuous multitude, is possible and, in principle, correct. But his argument has only shown this in a certain way. For his answer to the first of the objections in particular[64] makes it clear that the multitude are only fit to rule as a whole and not as individuals, and then only when it is the case both that they are

---

64. The "first mentioned difficulty" (1282b1) must be a reference to the first of the two objections, as Barker (1946: 127) notes (or possibly also to the difficulty with which the whole chapter began). To suppose the reference is to difficulties raised in chapter 10, as Newman (3:224), Schütrumpf (1991: 2:506), Susemihl and Hicks (1894: 403) do, not only makes less sense but renders it hard, or even impossible, to save the overall coherence of Aristotle's argument.

virtuous as a whole and that the few best are not superior enough to rule all alone. Consequently polity requires control to rest finally in laws that lay down the relative spheres of competence in each case and that, in particular, deny to the few best, or to those who are fit to hold office individually, the power to act as they choose, but only to make corrections in particular and exceptional cases (for they are, ex hypothesi, not good enough, unlike the god-man of chapter 13.1284a3–15, to be themselves law).[65]

1282b6 Of course, this conclusion only raises the question which these laws should be and hence recalls the difficulty from the end of chapter 10 that laws can also be bad. Or perhaps there is a reference here also back to the *Ethics* (10.9.1181a15–19) about how to pick out and judge the best laws (which was the question that launched Aristotle into his study of regimes). For if laws must be laid down with a view to the regimes (since otherwise they would be self-defeating), then laws in accordance with the correct regimes alone can be just—hence, the need to have a full account of the several regimes (which is Aristotle's object through the rest of the *Politics*).

The problem with this final comment, however, is that the relation between polity and law now seems to be circular. For we have just been told that polity needs to be ruled by rightly legislated laws, and now we are told that its laws will be rightly legislated if they accord with the correct regimes, of which polity of course is one. What Aristotle says later (in 6(4).8–9, 11–13) would seem to provide a solution, and it is a solution that accords with what he has argued in this chapter. For polity is composed by mixing elements from democracy and oligarchy and by giving control, as far as possible, to the middle element in the city. In this way the multitude that has control will in fact possess the necessary collective virtue. But

65. Note, contra Newman (3:224–25) in particular, that Aristotle only concludes to the superiority of law in the case of polity, and not to its superiority universally. There is thus no conflict between the conclusion of this chapter and what Aristotle argues in chapter 13. There is a conflict, however, between what Aristotle argues, both here and there, and what Mansfield would have him argue (1989: 38). For when Aristotle says that the laws cannot speak with precision (1282b4–6), Mansfield wants to translate the reason Aristotle gives as "because of the difficulty of making clear the whole for all things," and not as "because of the difficulty of giving clear declarations in universal terms about everything." But this is to treat *katholou* ("the whole") as a noun and object of the verb, when it is really an adverb ("in universal terms"), and to translate *peri* as "for" when it really means "about" or "concerning." This misinterpretation is part of Mansfield's extended argument (1989: 38–46), marked by other misinterpretations, to show that politics, according to Aristotle, requires a sort of reconciliation between humanity and nature as a whole that would be provided by the god-man, or total king, if such a god-man were a possibility. But, Mansfield argues, the god-man is not a possibility. Hence politics has to be understood as inherently incapable of completion, or as striving for something which cannot be realized (compare Davis [1996] for similarly gloomy views). There is, however, no evidence to suggest that Aristotle shares Mansfield's pessimism. On the contrary, it is clear from chapters 13 and 17 in particular that, unlike Mansfield, he does very much believe in the god-man.

the dominance of the middle is achieved only because the laws are arranged to achieve it and because these laws rule. Hence the rule of law is what makes and keeps the regime a polity, but these laws are correct because they accord with the principle of polity, namely control by the virtuous middle.

Chapter 12

~ COMPLETE SOLUTION GENERAL TO ALL REGIMES

~ WHO MAY JUSTLY MAKE CLAIMS TO RULE

1282b14   The abruptness with which this chapter begins and the repetitions that it and the next chapter contain have led many scholars to doubt whether they are in the right place and whether they cohere with the previous chapters.[66] But if we recall that at the beginning of the previous chapter Aristotle expressly put off a general discussion of all the difficulties noted in chapter 10 in order to concentrate on the case of the virtuous multitude alone, and if we note further that he now proceeds to give that postponed general discussion, neither the abruptness with which this chapter begins nor the repetitions need occasion any surprise. For he has already told us of a coming general discussion so he can now launch into it without telling us again, and the repetitions are only what one would expect in a general treatment of something that has already been treated in part. But anyway, as was said at the beginning of chapter 8, Aristotle's intention now is not to avoid repeating something as rather to avoid omitting anything.

Aristotle's solution to the general problem of who should have control in cities is given in two stages. In this chapter he determines who may justly make a claim to share in rule and in the next he determines who may justly make a claim to have control of rule. He begins, as is fitting, by a return to first principles and presents an argument of the following sort:[67] (1) since the end in every science and art is some good, the end of the science or art that has the most control will be the greatest good; (2) the science or art that has the most control is politics (cf. 1.1, and *Ethics* 1.2.1094a26–b11); (3) therefore the political good is the greatest good; (4) justice or the common advantage is the political good (cf. 3.6); (5) therefore justice is the greatest good. This argument deduces the supremacy of justice from the nature itself of political science, and though the supremacy of justice might seem obvious and not in need of proof (even to those who disagree about what justice

66. For some discussion of these doubts, see Newman (1:570–72, 3:xxx–xxxi), Schütrumpf (1991: 2:508–10, 517–19), Susemihl and Hicks (1894: 42–43), Wolff (1988: 273–75).

67. The opening argument is difficult to interpret because though it begins with a "since" there is no clear indication of where the answering apodosis is supposed to come, as Newman notes (3:226). The interpretation I offer is not the only one possible, but it does give sense to the whole.

is), Aristotle's intention here is to establish things philosophically and not merely to assume them as given.

The point of this argument would seem to be that in establishing justice as the greatest good it establishes justice as that good which will determine all other goods, including specifically the good of distributing office. Hence to determine how offices should be distributed, or who should be in control in cities (the topic of these chapters), it is necessary to determine what justice or the common advantage is, and that is precisely what Aristotle next proceeds to do. Of course, he has in a way done it already (in chapters 6 and 9 in particular), but he comes back to it now in a different context and in answer to different questions. Moreover in his treatment of these questions he makes certain things clear that have not yet been made clear.

1282b18 The nature of justice is, at one level, obvious and not in dispute, for everyone agrees, including philosophy itself, that justice is equality for equals (and conversely inequality for unequals). But problems arise when the question turns to what the relevant equality or inequality is (which question, as noted earlier in chapter 9, most people ignore or beg to their own advantage). This is a matter for political philosophy, the philosophy whose concern it is to penetrate the human things (and justice in particular; *Ethics* 10.9.1181b14–15).

1282b23 The question is about which equalities and inequalities are relevant for determining justice in the case of shares in rule. Aristotle confronts it by beginning with the possibility that all of them are. This possibility may seem obviously implausible, and indeed it is, but this very implausibility makes it a good place to begin. For since everyone will agree *that* it should be rejected, an explanation of *why* it should be that also shows what should replace it can perhaps ease the way to agreement on this replacement.

Those who say that any inequality at all is ground for having unequal shares in rule argue something as follows: (1) justice requires unequal shares for unequals; (2) those who are superior in any good at all, though equal in other respects, are unequal; (3) therefore justice requires these to have unequal shares. Aristotle first shows that this argument is false and then why it is so. That it is false is manifest from the fact that it would lead to such absurdities as that those superior in color or height should have greater shares in rule (which not even a hardened oligarch is likely to say).[68] Why it is false is shown by an analogy with the arts, and that in three

68. In the translation I use here the term "rights" to render Aristotle's meaning: "if this be true, then those who excel in color . . . would have the advantage in claims to political rights [*tōn politikōn dikaiōn*]" (1282b27–30), and a controversy has arisen as to whether this is legitimate, or whether there is really any notion of rights in Aristotle, or a notion that plays any significant role; see Miller (1995: chap. 4, 1996, with references). But that there are certain things in Aristotle's discussions of justice for which the English word "rights" is a natural enough equivalent seems clear enough; see Miller (1995: 87–91, 93–111). The controversy focuses on whether the term "rights" has not accumulated, over the

ways. The first way appeals to pipe playing and to the fact that those superior in other respects, but equal in the art of pipe playing, do not thereby deserve the better pipes, for the obvious reason that only superiority in a good relevant to the work to be done gives just grounds for a superior claim to pipes. So likewise, to apply the analogy, only superiority in a good relevant to the work of ruling, and not just any good at all, could give just grounds for a claim to unequal shares in rule.

1282b34 The second way takes this analogy a step further, and supposes, first, someone superior (instead of equal) in the art of pipe playing but surpassed in other goods (as birth and beauty), and supposes, second, that these other goods are superior as goods and outweigh any superiority he has in pipe playing. Still even in this more extreme case, where the one superior in the art is worse placed in comparison with others, it remains true that he justly deserves the better pipes. The reason is again the same and no less obvious, that these other goods, whatever their superiority, contribute nothing to the work of playing the pipes. So the same will also hold of rule, and only those superior in goods relevant to ruling, not superior in any good at all (regardless of how much better those goods may as goods be thought to be), will have the juster claim to rule.

1283a3 The third way is a little more complex, but is essentially of the following sort: (1) if superiority in any good at all can count as a greater claim (whether to pipes or rule), all goods will be commensurable; (2) but all goods are manifestly not commensurable; (3) therefore superiority in any good at all cannot count as a greater claim. The main difficulty here concerns how Aristotle establishes premise (1).[69] I take his argument to be rather elliptical but to be essentially as follows. If, as the argument being criticized here supposes, any good, however irrelevant, can ground a superior claim to pipes (or to rule), then the good of size, say, will not only be competing for pipes against skill or virtue in the art, but also against any other good, like wealth or freedom. So assume that a certain size is more of a claim to pipes than a certain amount of skill or virtue in the art, then some lesser size must equal, in claims to pipes, that amount of virtue. Thus the goods of size and virtue will be commensurable. But the same supposition can be made about any other good, like wealth or freedom, if all goods can ground a superior claim to pipes. For here too, if some amount of wealth or freedom is assumed to be more of a claim to pipes than that original amount of virtue, some other amount must be equal to it. Hence the goods of wealth and freedom will be com-

---

years, too much excess baggage from modern and non-Aristotelian political theories (as the Hobbesian in particular) to be anything but misleading, or even false, when used of Aristotle's thinking. The correct response seems to be that, provided one explains, in the way Miller does, that one is using the term in an innocent sense without all the excess baggage, there is no reason at all not to employ it to translate or expound Aristotle's ideas; see Simpson (1996), and the introduction to the commentary, p. xiv n2.

69. The explanations of Barker (1946: 130–31), Newman (3:230–31), Schütrumpf (1991: 2:514) are not entirely clear or convincing.

mensurable with the good of virtue. But then the goods of wealth and freedom must also be commensurable with the good of size (for they were all assumed to be commensurable with the good of virtue), and indeed any good at all will be commensurable with any good at all since all are allowed to ground claims to pipes.

1283a9 The falsity of this supposition, however, that all goods are commensurable, is manifest. For it is manifest that no amount of size or wealth or freedom or beauty or anything else, however great, is going to make up for deficiency in pipe playing such that, for instance, a person is going to play the pipes as well or better than someone else superior in the art just because he is taller or wealthier or prettier. But what is false here is not that differences in quality are reduced to differences in quantity;[70] it is rather that qualities relevant to doing one work or task are also taken to be relevant to doing some other, completely different, work or task (which is manifestly absurd).

Accordingly, in the case of rule too, not just any claim based on any good is going to count. Superior speed in running, for instance, is only relevant to gymnastic contests, not to distributions of office. So manifest is this truth, in fact, that no one disputes it, but all those who make claims to rule base their claims on goods that are relevant to rule, namely on things that constitute the city or are integral to living together in political community, for such living together is the work of ruling. So wealth and freedom contribute to the life of the city and virtue to its good life, and it is on the basis of these and the like qualities that people should and do dispute about rule (as in fact do all those mentioned at the beginning of chapter 10). What is left, then, is to mediate between these several disputants and decide which of them may justly claim to have control of rule in the city.

Chapter 13

∾ WHO MAY JUSTLY MAKE CLAIMS TO HAVE CONTROL OF RULE

∾ PRELIMINARY DISCUSSION

1283a23 To decide who should have control in the city, Aristotle first discusses the question in a preliminary way and then proposes a determinate answer. He recalls and lays down certain points already established in chapter 9. First, the claim of virtue is the most just of all the claims mentioned because it is based on what concerns good life and not on what concerns life alone (the point of the city is good life and what concerns life is for the sake of what concerns good life). Second, if those equal or unequal in one only of the things relevant to the life and rule of the city claim equality or inequality in everything, it is unjust and the regime in question deviant. Third, all the claims are in a way just (they all rest their

---

70. Contrary to what Barker (1946: 131) and Schütrumpf (1991: 2:514) suppose.

case on something relevant to the life of the city and the work of ruling) but are not simply so (they do not base their claim on everything that is relevant nor even on what is most relevant).

As regards the second and third of these points one might wonder if they are also supposed to be true of the claims of virtue or whether, that is, a regime in the hands of the virtuous that excluded, say, all the rich would be a deviant regime, and if so what sort of deviant regime it would be.[71] But it is evident, first, that Aristotle is thinking here of oligarchy and democracy (as he was in chapter 9), and, second, that the supposed case of the virtuous excluding all the wealthy could not in fact arise. For if the virtuous did not also have wealth they could not be at leisure to rule, and so either their rule would rest on despoiling the rich (in which case they would not be virtuous but the corrupt poor), or they would, of themselves, have to be in possession of sufficient wealth (in which case the wealthy would not after all be excluded).[72] It is also evident that in the regimes of polity, aristocracy, and kingship the virtuous rulers are understood to possess wealth (in polity they are the moderately wealthy and in aristocracy and kingship they possess the property). In like manner, no case could arise where the virtuous ruled to the exclusion of all the free, for the virtuous are certainly free by nature and must also be free by law since they could certainly not be ruling if they were enslaved to someone.

1283a31   Having stated the three points Aristotle explains the third one, not, however, as to how the claims in question are unjust (that was done before in chapters 9 and 10) but as to how they can be just.[73] So all the claimants are brought forward as capable of justifying their claim with respect to some aspect of the life and rule of the city: the rich because they possess the land and know how to keep treaties (a city needs a common territory and must stay on friendly terms with other cities whose help or trade it might need); the free and well-born because of their descent (which preserves the city's connection with its founding and with at least one of the sources of virtue, nature); the virtuous because of their justice (which is the virtue of common life and includes the other virtues too); the multitude because they might, taken as a whole if not individually, possess all or some of these qualities to greater degree.

1283a42   Having thus reviewed the rival claims to rule, Aristotle turns to consider how the dispute between them is to be resolved. Of course, in each of the several regimes the dispute has already been resolved, for better or worse, in favor of one or other claimant.[74] But the question now is not how the dispute has in fact

71. This is a puzzle raised by Newell, in Lord and O'Connor (1991: 203 n16), by Newman (3:xxxii–xxxiii), and by Schütrumpf (1991: 2:519–20); cf. also Wolff (1988).

72. Cf. the criticisms brought against the regime of the Carthaginians in 2.11.1273a21–b7.

73. Cf. Wolff (1988: 274).

74. Though, interestingly enough, in Aristotle's own best regime the dispute has been resolved in

been resolved in this or that city, but how it should be resolved or which way of resolving it is just. A situation must accordingly be taken where all the rivals are imagined to be present and separately pressing their claim. So when Aristotle asks whether there will be a dispute in this case, the force of his question cannot be whether there will be any disputing going on (manifestly there will be), but whether this dispute will or will not admit of a resolution, that is, whether one or more claims will eventually prove superior to the others, and superior by right, not by force (for manifestly in some regimes, as tyranny in particular, the case has been settled by force and not by right).

1283b9 Aristotle had begun the chapter by recalling three points from chapter 9, and these points together indicate that, of all the claims, that of the few virtuous is the most just. For their claim is based on contribution to good life, not mere life; it is thus the claim that is most of all simply just; and those superior or unequal in virtue would seem, as a result, most to deserve inequality in everything.[75] Not unnaturally, therefore, Aristotle starts with this case of the few virtuous, since their claim seems strongest.

Now the main problem with this case (as stated in chapter 10) was precisely the fewness of the few. But a possible way out of this difficulty has been suggested by chapter 12, which showed that a just distribution of rule must have reference to the work to be done. So the fewness of the few need not be a problem from the point of view of justice provided they are not too few to do the work. This possible solution, however, only leads at once to another difficulty. For if sufficiency for the work is what counts, then why could not one man alone, instead of a few, be sufficient? Moreover this problem is going to arise for all the claimants to rule. For if the wealthy claim that they should be in control because wealth is what counts for the work of ruling, then it will follow, by parity of reasoning, that if one man is wealthier than all of them he should be in control. The same thing will happen with all the candidates, the well-born, the virtuous, and the multitude, since if one man excels in the quality on which they each rest their case, the argument will prove that he and not they should be in control.

∽ THE CASE FOR POLITY

1283b27 The result of the above discussion seems to be that none of the candidates for control in the city can be arguing correctly. For none of them succeed in proving what they want to prove, that they alone should be in control,

---

favor of all the claimants at once, for his best regime is so arranged that the citizens constitute all the wealthy, all the free, all the well-born, and all the virtuous together; see 4(7).8–9.

75. One might also note that of all the candidates mentioned in chapter 10, where the dispute in question here was first introduced, the few best would seem to have presented the case that was most just. For the others either deprived more people of office, as the one best man, or were manifestly involved in injustice, as the many, the rich, or the tyrant.

since in each case their argument also justifies rule by one man, and by one man, moreover, who, as far as the argument itself is concerned, could well turn out to be a tyrant. At any rate this result is going to hold of democrats and oligarchs, who argue on the basis of freedom or wealth, for one who exceeds in these qualities could well be a tyrant, and democrats and oligarchs are certainly not intending to yield control to such a one, or indeed to anyone. It need not, however, hold of those who argue on the basis of virtue, for one who exceeds in virtue could never be a tyrant (otherwise he would not be virtuous), and those who argue on this basis might well be prepared to follow the logic of their position and yield control to the one best man, should he emerge.

In effect, this is what Aristotle now proceeds to show, that the argument from virtue is alone correct because it alone can justly be followed wherever it leads. This argument, however, is going to lead in both directions, not just to rule by the one best but also to rule by the many best. This latter case is of course that of polity discussed in chapter 11 where the many, though individually worse and poorer, are collectively better and richer. Hence the argument from virtue, to be correct, must be allowed to justify also rule by the multitude when this multitude is indeed more virtuous as a whole.

1283b35 In illustration of this result, Aristotle shows how to answer a difficulty that some use to exclude the multitude from rule. The difficulty is put in the form of a question: is a legislator who, in the case just mentioned, wishes to lay down the most correct laws to legislate for the advantage of the multitude or of the best? This question is so phrased as to insinuate the answer that of course he should legislate for the advantage of the best (for how could it be just to legislate for the advantage of the worst?). But quite apart from the fact that in this case the many, and not the few, are best (so that the question proceeds on a false assumption), what is correct in laws has to be understood, as chapter 6 indicated, by reference to the common advantage of the whole city and its citizens. This common advantage is, of course, the good life of virtue, and in polity the multitude, because collectively virtuous, partake of this life and are properly citizens. The most correct laws must here, therefore, favor the rule of the multitude. But a citizen, while having a common definition, varies from regime to regime (as noted in chapter 1), and in some other regime, notably aristocracy, the citizens would indeed be confined to the few best. Only in this case, where the few are simply superior, will the most correct laws regard the common good of perfect virtue and favor rule by these few alone.

~ THE CASE FOR ARISTOCRACY AND KINGSHIP

1284a3/11 But then this brings us precisely to the case of aristocracy and rule by the surpassingly best. Here if there is one or several so outstanding in the excess of virtue that there is no commensurability between them and others, then they can no longer be regarded as part of a city (rather they are themselves a city, in power and virtue if not in numbers). So to treat them as being part of the city and to give them equal shares, as in the case of polity, would clearly be unjust. Such persons cannot be subjected to laws (as to laws limiting their power or tenure of office or requiring them to share rule with others). Legal restraints of this sort are only in place, and only needed, in a regime like polity where (as noted in chapter 11) there is an equality among the citizens such that, for instance, those fit to hold high office are nevertheless not fit to choose or audit themselves but must be subject in these respects to the better judgment of the multitude. For in polity the superiority of the few as individuals is outweighed by the superiority of the many as a collectivity. In the case now under consideration, however, the few or one best are, ex hypothesi, so surpassing in power and virtue that no common measure exists by which they could be weighed against others.[76] They are, instead, themselves law and like gods among men or, to use Aristotle's other example, like lions among hares, and manifestly no number of men or hares could make up for a god or a lion.

1284a17/33   The question then is what to do with people like this. The example of the lions and hares might suggest that the two should simply be separated, or, in other words, that the lions should be expelled (for they will altogether destroy the hares).[77] So Aristotle turns to this possibility. He first states the several ways and regimes in which it is realized and how it can be just up to a point, even in correct regimes. Then he shows that it is not just in the case of those who excel in virtue.

The practice of expelling the preeminent is perhaps especially and immediately obvious in the ostracism practiced by democracies, for democracies have a particular love of equality and hate inequality, and the parallel case of the Argonauts and Heracles that Aristotle immediately adds shows that this practice can sometimes be correct. Hence the fact that tyrants also do the same thing, as in the notorious

---

76. The virtue of the one or few best is perfect virtue, whereas that of the many best, or of the few who are not better than the many best taken as a whole, is partial or imperfect virtue; see 3.7.1279a39–b4. That is why the first sort of virtue is surpassing and incommensurable with respect to the second (for the perfect is surpassing with respect to the partial or imperfect as the whole is surpassing with respect to the part). One should not suppose, therefore, with Nichols (1992: 170), that such surpassing virtue is a contradiction in terms on the grounds that virtue is a mean and what is surpassing is at an extreme. For virtue is a mean only with respect to its matter (actions and passions); it is an extreme with respect to its goodness (*Ethics* 2.6.1107a6–27). There is no reason, therefore, why some might not have achieved this goodness in a way that surpasses everyone else; cf. Newell, in Lord and O'Connor (1991: 193n), Mulgan (1974a).

77. This is the suggestion of Peter of Auvergne (1951: 3.12.465). But teeth and claws could be used to protect and guard as well as to kill, and Aristotle may rather wish us to think of this possibility.

piece of advice given by Periander to Thrasybulus, cannot be blamed as simply incorrect (not everything that tyrants do need be unjust). Ostracism is like such tyrannical cutting down of the preeminent, and it is also like the cutting down of the preeminent practiced by imperial cities and nations against their subjects, as with Greek (and democratic) Athens and barbarian (and tyrannical) Persia.

1284b3/17 Most of these instances are clearly unjust and done for private advantage (those, for instance, who argue that control should be distributed according to wealth or freedom cannot consistently deny that one man who surpasses all others in these respects should rule instead; if they do deny this they are following rather their own private desire to rule than the logic of their argument). But the preeminent can pose problems in correct regimes too and it can sometimes be of benefit to the common good to expel such people. The examples from the arts, as painting, shipbuilding, and singing, clearly prove the point. So provided such expulsions are indeed for the common good, they are so far just (even when done by monarchs or single rulers like tyrants).[78] Of course, it would be preferable if the city was so ordered that no such preeminent men could emerge who, because they threatened the balance of the city, would need to be expelled (it would be better to limit, for instance, the acquisition of wealth; cf. 2.7 and 9). Prevention is clearly better than cure, though if there is no prevention cure is necessary and just. At all events it is now manifest first, from the examples of history, that expelling the preeminent has worked to private advantage in deviant regimes (as democracies and tyrannies) and, second, from the examples of the arts, that such expulsions can, even in deviant regimes, be just (they can benefit the common good) even if these expulsions (because done for private advantage) are not simply just.

1284b25 The question then is whether the same is true of the expulsion of the preeminent in virtue. This poses a particular problem for the best regime. For, on the one hand, it has just been shown that expelling the preeminent can be correct, but, on the other hand, the best regime makes its claim to rule on the basis of virtue and, as was shown earlier, if this argument is to be sound, it will have to be allowed to justify putting control in the hands of the one or few preeminently virtuous men. The solution is clear: expulsion (or prevention) of those who are preeminent in respects other than virtue will be just, but expulsion (or prevention) of those who are preeminent in virtue will not be. To think that this would be just is like thinking it would be just for mere humans to rule over Zeus and take turns with him in ruling. Consequently the preeminent in virtue (whether the one

78. There is a solitary *men* at this point in the Greek, 1284b13, as Newman (3:251) notes (a *men*, "on the one hand," is ordinarily followed by an answering *de*, "on the other hand"). It may perhaps be a silent caution that while tyrants might, to this extent, be acting justly, nothing is implied about whether what they do in other respects is just.

of kingship or the several of aristocracy) should willingly be submitted to as to permanent kings.[79]

With this conclusion Aristotle completes his answer to the difficulty raised in chapter 10 about who should be in control in cities. In summary form his answer is as follows. Each claimant for control argues justly up to a point (for all appeal to something relevant to the life and rule of the city), but not all do so simply. For, first, not all claims are equal but that of virtue outweighs the others (for this concerns the well-being of the city and not its being merely), and, second, not all these claims are or can be consistently pursued. The claims, for instance, of oligarchs and democrats will sometimes justify rule by one man, if this one man turns out to be richer or stronger or better-born, but oligarchs and democrats do not want to follow the logic of their argument and yield control to this one man (rather they do what they can to expel him), and, anyway, no argument can be just or followed to its conclusion that justifies rule by a man who, though superior in other respects, could well be vicious and a tyrant. Only the claims of virtue can consistently and justly be followed and these are the claims either of the multitude of polity, when the multitude is more virtuous as a whole, or of the few of aristocracy or the one of kingship, when the few or one are surpassing in virtue. Consequently these and these alone, as stated in chapter 7, are correct or simply just regimes.

Chapter 14

〜 THIRD DIFFICULTY: WHETHER KINGSHIP IS A CORRECT REGIME

〜 THE KINDS OF KINGSHIP

1284b35 Aristotle next turns to examine kingship and to ask whether such a regime is of advantage to a city or country that is going to be nobly managed. His turning now to this subject and this question has caused some difficulties for scholars and has led to doubts about the coherence and completeness of the book.[80] Not much help, however, is provided by referring back to Aristotle's remark in chapter 7 (1279a23–25) that the correct regimes are to be treated first.[81] For that remark properly refers to what he does immediately there, namely state how many and which the regimes are, and does not read like an outline of a program for the rest of the book. Besides, the programmatic remark that has been governing the chapters so far is the one from the beginning of chapter 8 (1279b11–15)

---

79. In their case, their lionlike teeth and claws, or their virtue, are clearly to be considered as of benefit, not harm, to the ruled.

80. Robinson (1962: 51–52), Schütrumpf (1991: 1:46–47, 2:538–39).

81. As Newman (3:255) and Schütrumpf (1991: 2:535) do.

about the need to examine the difficulties that concern the division of regimes into three correct and three deviant. This remark is more likely to be the one that is still relevant. In fact to ask, as Aristotle now does, whether kingship is of advantage for a city that is going to be nobly ruled is to ask whether kingship is a correct regime (for correct regimes are those where the city is ruled nobly or for its proper end). Therefore, it seems better, and makes more coherent sense of this book as a whole, to read these chapters on kingship as dealing with another difficulty about the division of regimes, namely whether kingship is after all a correct regime.

So it is also worth noting in this regard that this difficulty is the one that the preceding chapter is most of all likely to generate. For the solution there given to the question which candidates should have control in cities basically rested on the idea that only the argument of virtue could consistently and justly be followed through to the end. But the end was total control in the hands of the one most virtuous man, and it has seemed to many people (in Aristotle's day and since) manifestly foolish and unjust to give one man, however good, total control.[82] For this would be in effect to set up a tyranny, and tyranny is never of advantage to any city. Consequently, on this ground too, it is a "noble thing" (to quote the opening words of the chapter) for Aristotle now to raise the present difficulty since thus, in addition to confirming generally that kingship is, as he said at the beginning, a correct regime, he can also confirm what he concluded at the end of the previous chapter.

1284b40   But, manifestly, to answer the question whether kingship is of advantage or not, it is necessary to know how many kinds of it there are, so that it will be clear which kind (or kinds) is the one that is now in need of being discussed. Aristotle lists five kinds, the initial four of which he describes from historical examples. The first kind is the perpetual generalship found particularly in Sparta and which is according to law because, evidently, it is governed by laws that limit its extent and application (it does not have control over everything and its greatest power is confined to war outside the territory). It also need not be hereditary but can be elected.

1285a16   The second is the sort found particularly among barbarians. It is, in the largeness of its powers and the despotic character of its rule (the barbarian king rules for his own advantage),[83] really the same as tyranny. What makes it

---

82. Robinson expresses this view (1962: 66).

83. Newman (3:266) and Schütrumpf (1991: 2:542) deny that despotic can mean here, as it does in 3.6, ruling for the ruler's own advantage. But in fact it can mean nothing else, for the explanation Aristotle gives for the barbarians' putting up with such rule, that they are (natural) slaves, could only be an explanation if the rule they are putting up with is the sort of rule slaves are subject to, which is rule for the advantage of the ruler. Recall, however, that to rule for one's own advantage is to rule for one's own continuance in rule and to exclude from rule others who are equally or more worthy, and this was certainly true of the barbarian kings Aristotle here has in mind (who were anything but worthy of having total control).

different from tyranny proper is that it is according to law (as opposed, presumably, to being arbitrarily imposed) and the subjects put up with it willingly and even willingly defend it (a feature of kingships). So these subjects are in effect natural slaves (willingly to put up with a slavish condition is a sure mark of a slavish character; it betokens in particular a lack of spirit and spirit is necessary for virtue, which is the mark of the naturally free man, 1.5–7).

1285a30 The third kind is the ancient dictatorship (*aisymnētēs*), which is in effect another sort of tyranny (the dictator must thus be understood as someone who rules for his own advantage), but one that is also willingly accepted, though through election instead of inheritance. That it is a phenomenon found among Greeks is an indication that Greeks too can be naturally slavish.

1285b3 The fourth kind is genuinely kingship and no tyranny. It is rule by outstanding men of the heroic ages who were benefactors, that is, who used their superiority for the benefit of the ruled and not of themselves. Their powers were clearly extensive though not unlimited, and the fact that many of these powers were given up or removed over time, that is, as the later successors ceased to be able, or needed, to perform similar benefactions, is an indication of the original kingly character of the rule. For rule that is for the benefit of the ruled should naturally be given up or taken away if such rule ceases to be for their benefit (that is, in particular, if the king ceases to possess the necessary superiority). It seems to be the kingship of which the perpetual generalship of Spartan-style kingship is the last vestige.

1285b20 The summary description of these four kinds of kingship makes it clear that only the last listed is anything like a kingship (control by one man over many great matters for the common benefit). The second and third are quasi tyrannies (6(4).10.1295a7–17) and the first is just a general for life. They are drawn, more or less, from actual cases of monarchical rule,[84] but the last kind, the fifth, is not referred to any historical case but is constructed by analogy with the household: as household management is kingship over the household, so this kingship is household management over cities and nations. It is a form of kingship that combines what the other forms divide up, for it has control over everything, like forms two and three, but is household management, not tyranny, and so, like the fourth form, is for the common advantage of the ruled. It is also a combination of the political and domestic since, though the king rules a city or a nation, he rules it as a household. It seems to be the one exception to the thesis of 1.1 that political and household rule are different in kind (cf. *Ethics* 10.9.1180a18–21). But, in fact, already in book 1 kingship was seen to unite the domestic and the political, since

84. For some discussion of the historical aspects, see Newman (3:258–77), Schütrumpf (1991: 2:540–44), and Romer (1982).

the ruler of a household was there described as king and monarch (1.2.1252b20–21, 7.1255b19).

The further peculiarity, that in this last form of kingship only the king himself counts as a citizen (for only he has the control), implies, interestingly enough, that being a citizen, or sharing control, need not be simply best for everyone, but that belonging to the household of a god-man (as the total king must be) would be better, should such a god-man arise. But this too only continues something that Aristotle has said earlier, namely about everyone gladly obeying such a king (3.13.1284b32–33). It also anticipates something he says later. For if the virtues most characteristic of a life of leisure, which will be the life of the best regime, are justice, moderation, and philosophy (4(7).15.1334a23–25), then those who do not rule but are ruled by a god-man will not be deprived of this life, for the ruled must still have justice and moderation (3.4.1277b26–29), and one does not need to rule in order to philosophize.

Chapter 15

 DIFFICULTIES WITH TOTAL KINGSHIP

 ARGUMENTS FOR RULE OF LAW
RATHER THAN RULE BY ONE MAN

1285b33 Aristotle's aim is to examine whether kingship can be of advantage to cities. So if most kingships fall within a range bounded by two of them (Aristotle says "most" and not "all" presumably because some of them, as the barbarian, may in power and duration sometimes equal, and not be less than, total kingship), then to ask the question about these will in effect be to ask it about all. For if it is not of advantage to have one man in control of few things, then, a minori, it will not be of advantage to have him in control of all things; and, conversely, if it is of advantage to have one man in control of all things, then, a fortiori, it will be of advantage to have him in control of fewer things too.

1286a2 But these questions can in fact be reduced further. For the least kingship is not a kind of regime. It is rather a kind of office that could be legislated in any regime. Accordingly it poses more a question about the advantage of a certain kind of law than about a certain kind of regime. But Aristotle's concern now is with regimes and specifically with the advantage or correctness of kingship insofar as kingship constitutes a kind of regime. So the question turns to the advantage of having one man in control of everything.

1286a7/20 Aristotle takes as his beginning whether it is better to be ruled by the best man or the best laws. There is a certain appropriateness to this beginning because if the best man is the best simply, then only rule by the best laws could conceivably pose a challenge to him. For the other candidates of the many and the few will ex hypothesi be inferior, provided he really is the best simply, whereas if the best laws could have the same surpassing excellence as the one best man, then being ruled by them could perhaps be better than being ruled by him. Further, one particular philosophical argument in favor of kingship rests on a contrast between rule by law and rule by man, and so for this reason too beginning here would be appropriate.

The philosophical argument in question is drawn from Plato's *Statesman* (294a10–b6, 295b10–e2, 300c9–d2), and Aristotle significantly does not assert it in his own name. In fact the present chapter is a sustained critique of the argument showing that it fails to prove what it purports to prove.[85] The argument is as follows: (1) laws speak of the universal and do not command or rule relative to actual circumstances; (2) men can correct universal law and rule relative to the circumstances (as in the case of doctors changing a patient's treatment); (3) therefore men are better at ruling than laws.

Aristotle responds that this argument does not prove that men are in fact simply better. For premise (2) in effect concedes that men still need the universal account provided by law (for men have to rely on this account to judge particular exceptions, as doctors do for instance). In addition, law, unlike men, lacks the passion that can corrupt judgment. So men are not in fact simply better at ruling, and accordingly the conclusion (3) cannot be read as if it meant that they were simply better. Indeed, all that the conclusion can really be understood to mean is that men are better at ruling in the case of particulars. But then in that case this conclusion is conceding that the laws are superior as regards the universal, and so it is conceding that the ruler will have to lay down such laws and rule by reference to them. It will be these laws, therefore, which must, save in the case of particular exceptions, have the control, and not any one man.

1286a24 The argument thus fails to prove that men are simply superior to law as opposed to superior in certain respects. But Aristotle next shows that it fails to prove the superiority of one man even in these respects, since several men might be better. Here he gives a series of arguments, the first of which is the one already stated in 3.11, that the multitude might, as a whole, be better at judging than one man. The second is that a multitude is harder to corrupt all at once whereas it is relatively easy for one man alone to be swayed by passion. The proviso must of course be added in this case that the multitude in question is a virtuous one, and not the corrupt one of democracy (which is, in fact, worse when it is united

---

85. The chapter is therefore entirely dialectical, like the next one; see Newell, in Lord and O'Connor (1991: 208). Aristotle's own view is not given until chapter 17.

together, 6(4).4.1292a10–18). The third is that, even if this proviso is not met, it could still be the case that a few good men, as opposed to a multitude, are better at judging than one alone. And if, fourth, it be retorted that these few might fall to faction and be at odds with each other whereas one man will not be, the response is that the few could be as virtuous as the one man and so need be no more at odds with each other than he with himself (for virtue unites the virtuous).

1286b3 Hence, in these cases, aristocracy must be better for cities than kingship, regardless, fifth, of the question of the king's bodyguard. For someone might think that a kingship is only worse because it involves giving the king his own private troops (which could be a threat to liberty). Aristotle therefore points out that the case for aristocracy just given will not diminish, nor the case for kingship increase, if the king is thought of as not having a bodyguard. For the other difficulties with one-man rule will stay the same just as before. Or at any rate this will be so provided that a few men of like high quality can be found. Otherwise a single man might stand out as superior.

At this point Aristotle's discussion takes a turn into a series of remarks about the historical rise and fall of different regimes that seem directed at this proviso. For these remarks, whose point can seem obscure, are perhaps best understood as supporting the case against kingship by showing that, whatever may have been true of the past, kingship now is no longer good or correct because now the numbers of the virtuous, or of those capable of exercising rule, are much greater, and there is no one man who stands out above the rest. Thus understood, these remarks will form a continuation of the dialectical discussion and will not be spoken in Aristotle's own name but rather in that of the opponents of kingship (who would doubtless be keen to insinuate that kingship is a feature of primitive and bygone ages).[86] At any rate it is clear that this historical excursus does not agree with what Aristotle says elsewhere about changes in regimes (notably in 6(4).13.1297b16–28 and 7(5).12.1316a1–b27). Nor does it agree with others of his opinions. For he himself supports kingship (though not, of course, for the reason he is criticizing in this chapter), and a kingship that is not confined to the past but could in principle arise at any time, if there is someone who is surpassingly virtuous (cf. 4(7).14.1332b16–27). Moreover he would not agree that the historical progress of regimes must have followed the spread of virtue. For though he would say that kingship or aristocracy is just where there is one or a few surpassingly virtuous men, he would not allow that polity becomes just in their place merely because virtue spreads among the multitude, since if the virtue of the one or few remains incommensurably superior,

---

86. As Newman suggests (3:286). There is no justification, therefore, for using this passage, with Schütrumpf (1991: 2:546) and others, as a basis for speculations about the genesis of different books of the *Politics*.

polity will not be just. Nor would he agree that only democracy is possible when cities have become larger. On the contrary the greater size of cities makes polity, or the middle regime, more of a possibility (cf. 6(4).11.1296a8–13).

1286b22   Having shown that rule by many or few where particulars are concerned may well be better than rule by one man, Aristotle now argues that, even if the one man is allowed to be better in this respect, still there are difficulties. The first concerns the succession. For (1) either the kingship must descend to his children or it must not; but (2) if it does and they are bad, then this will be worse and not better for cities, and the contrary supposition, that it does not, is too much to expect from any man, including a very virtuous one; therefore (3) on this ground, too, rule by one man, even a very good man, is not better.

1286b27   A second difficulty arises with respect to the armed force about the person of the king. Such a force he must have in order to defend the laws and coerce the disobedient, but he might also abuse this force to satisfy his will against the laws. The general principle Aristotle lays down about how large this force should be—large enough to be stronger than several but not large enough to be stronger than the multitude—may work well in the case of a king obedient to law. But there can be no guarantee that even this limited force could not be abused, or secretly enlarged, and employed for tyrannical purposes. The closing reference to the tyrant Dionysius is perhaps meant to suggest this possibility to the reader. At all events where many rule, as opposed to one, this problem will not arise, since the many will be their own bodyguard or armed force.

Chapter 16

◞⁓ ARGUMENTS AGAINST TOTAL KINGSHIP

1287a1   The previous chapter has shown that to argue for kingship in preference to law on the grounds that law is general and does not speak of particular eventualities is, first, really to argue for law and not for the king (since it is only to argue for the superiority of the king with respect to particulars and not for his superiority simply) and, second, to leave open the possibility that even in the case of particulars rule by several is better than rule by one. The argument has, in other words, not even reached the idea of the total king who rules everything by his own will without subjection to law. It has in fact only introduced another instance of Spartan-style kingship and has not been about a kind of regime but about a kind of office that could exist in any regime. For this king is really an officeholder who has been given certain duties to interpret and correct law where law, because of its universality, gives out. He is therefore subject to law, both because the law is what he is supposed to be following generally and to be correcting only in particular cases, and because the appointment and competence of his office are evidently also limited by law (the law that determines which offices shall exist in cities and how chosen and with what authority). Such, at any rate, is the case with the "kings" or kingly offices in Sparta, Epidamnus, and Opus.

This failure of the main philosophic argument for kingship (the argument from Plato's *Statesman*) means that the question about kingship proper, the kingship that is a regime and not an office within a regime, has not yet even been started. The discussion has not, however, been useless, for it has at least made evident what the question is. It has brought us, as it were, to a "stand" (1287a2) at the right place, namely at the realization that the king to be discussed must be understood as a king who is not subject to law at all, not even to its general prescriptions and not even to any limitation on the scope or duration of his power. Without the discussion in the previous chapter, this realization might never have been reached (as it is not in fact reached in Plato's *Statesman*).[87]

1287a8 Once, however, it has been made clear what sort of king is being talked about, a king who is wholly lawless, it may seem simply obvious that such a king cannot possibly be good nor such a regime correct.[88] Indeed even to suggest the possibility may seem shocking. At all events to discuss the arguments about such a king is now Aristotle's express object. In this chapter he rehearses the arguments against, and then in the next chapter gives his answers to them as well as the argument for.

The first argument against may be summarized as follows: (1) justice is by nature the same for those who are by nature similar; (2) the total king in a city of similars does not have the same but vastly more; (3) therefore the total king is unnatural. To premise (2) is then added the further premise (4) that it is harmful (as the examples of clothing and food show) for the equal to have what is unequal or the unequal what is equal, whence it follows (5) that total kingship is harmful. What is unnatural and harmful is evidently to be rejected, hence that anyone should be total king and have more, as stated in premise (2), must be rejected. The alternative, then, is that (6) rule should be exercised by turns, and since (7) a system of ruling by turns is law (there is a universal rule, to which all are subject, about who should rule, for how long, over what things, how chosen, and so forth), it follows that (8) law and not a total king should rule. This last conclusion (8) also then entails the further conclusion that (9) officeholders, if there is need of them, should rule subject to law and not be lawless like the total king.

87. In this way one can largely lay to rest the many doubts of scholars about whether chapters 15 and 16 are not doublets of each other or whether there is not a great deal of confusion in their argumentation; see the discussion in Schütrumpf (1991: 2:559–61) and Susemihl and Hicks (1894: 83–86, 428–42). That they are not doublets, even though some of the same arguments are repeated, is clear from the fact that these arguments are deployed for different purposes: once against the Platonic king of the previous chapter, and once against the Aristotelian total king of this.

88. It so seems obvious to Robinson (1962: 66).

Such is how I take the argument to proceed, but of course as so taken it rests on the assumption, made explicit in premise (2), that the total king is a king among similars (a fact that Aristotle perhaps intends to stress by repeating it at the end, 1287a23). So if this does not hold in the case of some particular king, then none of the conclusions will follow. Such a case is, in fact, precisely what Aristotle has in mind and which he sets out in the next chapter.

1287a23 The second argument is to the effect that human beings are anyway not sufficient by themselves to decide even those particular cases which the law (because of its generality) has to pass over. Rather the law must first educate them and only then can they properly judge how to add to it or correct it. In other words, even where humans do the deciding, the law is still operative, but as educating them how to decide not as telling them what to decide (they are, after all, to decide what the law itself would decide if it could speak to the particular case at hand; cf. *Ethics* 5.10). This claim is supported by appeal to the actual practice of cities and to the fact that, while human beings do have intellect, they also have passions and these passions can turn them into beasts, whereas the law is intellect alone without appetite. So it is law, and not any man, who is really like god and fit to have control in cities.

1287a32 The third argument attacks the analogy from the arts, specifically medicine, used in the previous chapter to give the initial defense for kingship. The analogy is faulty or falsely applied because (a) doctors are paid according to how well they cure the sick (so their own interest coincides with that of their patients), whereas rulers often act out of favoritism or hostility toward particular persons (so their own interest is often contrary to the advantage of the ruled); (b) if doctors were as bad as politicians in this respect, patients would seek a cure from medical books instead (as now people seek a cure from written laws instead of from corrupt politicians); (c) doctors do not treat themselves when sick but call in some other doctor instead because they fear their own pain will corrupt their judgment, and it is to find the same freedom from passion in politics or the same impartiality that people have recourse to laws; (d) laws are either written or unwritten and the latter have more control, so even if a ruler can sometimes be more reliable or safer than the former, it does not follow that he must or can be more reliable than the latter. The sort of unwritten laws Aristotle has in mind in this last argument are presumably long-established traditions, customs, precedents, and the like. For it is indeed true, and remains true even today, that such preexisting customs can be too strong for written laws and can make those laws, even when backed up by force, a dead letter.

Consequently the analogy from the arts, when properly considered, either does not prove that persons are better than laws or even proves the opposite.

1287b8 The fourth argument is that a king is going to need subordinate officials to help him so that his rule is in fact not going to be single but divided among many. So there is no real difference between rule by one man and rule by several and hence no reason to have a single ruler in the first place.

1287b11   The fifth argument, recalling one from the previous chapter, is that if one good man should rule because he is better, then two good men will be better still and hence aristocracy or even polity, but not kingship, will be what is of advantage for cities.

1287b15   The sixth argument rests on a claim about what is really at issue in the debate about kingship. Note is taken to begin with of the fact that cities already observe in their political practice the distinction between things that law can decide and things that officials must decide. It is this distinction between what thus falls under the competence of law and what does not that is the cause of the debate about whether the best man or the best laws should rule (as was in fact the case with the way the debate in the preceding chapter started). But this debate is not really about what it appears to be about. For neither do those who support kingship deny that law should rule where it can rule, nor do those who oppose kingship deny that human beings should rule where law cannot rule. The debate therefore cannot really be about the king and the law; it can only be about whether, where law is admitted by both sides to be incapable of ruling, one man or several should rule. Consequently the counterclaim of the opponents of kingship is that in fact several are better at ruling in these cases than one.

These opponents give two arguments: (a) anyone properly educated by the laws can rule in cases where law is too general, so since many are or can be educated by the laws many should rule in this way instead of one; (b) it is contrary to reason, and to the actual practice of monarchs, to suppose that one man can rule better than many can, so therefore again many should rule. For reason says that if two of a thing are better than one, then many must be better still; but one man sees and acts better with two eyes, hands, and feet; therefore many seeing and acting with many eyes, hands, and feet must see and act better still; consequently many will be better at ruling than one. The actual practice of monarchs is that in fact they do make many eyes, hands, and feet for themselves, since they make joint rulers of their friends. But lest it be thought that these joint rulers are subordinates and not equals, to be counted as means whereby the king rules instead of as sharers in ruling (so that the king would remain the sole ruler and they would only be his instruments), the following argument is added: (1) these joint rulers are either friends of the king and his rule or not; (2) but they cannot not be friends, for then they would not do what he wants and so he would not make them joint rulers; (3) therefore they must be friends; (4) friends are equals and similars; (5) therefore the king's joint rulers are his equals and similars (and hence not mere subordinates or instruments).

1287b35   Such then are the collected arguments against kingship, and it is easy to see already that, apart from any other difficulties they may labor under, they all proceed on the assumption that the king in question is not surpassingly superior to everyone else. This is made an express premise in the first argument but it is implicit in all the rest since a surpassingly virtuous man would not need the laws to guide him (being himself a law and a god), would not be corrupted by anything from within or without, would be the exemplar of good habits and customs, would have the capacity to manage many things all at once, would have no equal with whom he could rule better, would be superior even to universal laws, and would only have subordinates in rule (who could be friendly to him without being equals, for children too are friendly to their father without being equals). This is effectively what Aristotle argues in the next chapter.

Chapter 17

≈ ANSWER TO THE DIFFICULTIES

1287b36   Aristotle first shows, in answer to the preceding arguments, that they only hold of some cases and need not hold of all. Then he shows what cases they will not hold of and why. So, first, the above arguments, he says, only hold of some persons and need not hold of others because what is by nature just and advantageous is different in the different kinds of correct rule[89] (there can, of course, be no natural right or advantage in deviant or unnatural kinds of rule, though there is in them a deviant right and advantage). Hence what is just or advantageous in the case of polity, say, need not be just or advantageous in kingship. The above arguments are really only about polity, or aristocracy, which are regimes where there are many or several who are equal and similar. In these cases it is indeed not just or advantageous for one man to have total control, whatever his control and whoever he be: whether his control is also over the laws or subject to them (with respect to universal principles), whether he is bad or good (swayed by his passions or not), whether the laws are bad or good (relative to the incorrect or correct regimes), whether he is superior (to the many individually, if not to them as a whole). But nothing follows from this about whether total control in the hands of one man would be unjust and harmful if the superiority of this one man is of an exceptional kind.

1288a6   Having thus shown that none of the arguments against kingship is decisive simply or universally, Aristotle now shows when and why kingship will be just. To do so he needs only to return to things discussed before (in chapter 13), things that he now repeats and enlarges with a view to the present question. He has just said that what is by nature just and advantageous differs in the case of each of the correct kinds of rule. So, picking up on that point, he states when kingship is

89. A point argued in book 1.

appropriate by contrasting its conditions with those for aristocracy and polity.[90] The description of these conditions is involved but nevertheless rather precise. In each case there is a first multitude containing a second and smaller multitude, and evidently the first multitude are the inhabitants of the city as a whole (including wives, children, aliens, and slaves) and the second those from among them who exercise rule. For since the rule being talked of is rule over the city, to say what conditions favor what kind of rule is to say what sort of city, and hence what sort of multitude, favors what kinds of rule.

Accordingly kingship, given the sort of rule it is, will be appropriate where the multitude of the city naturally carries with it a family surpassing in virtue for political leadership. The king, of course, is only one man but, since he is human, he must belong to and grow up in some family or other, and as by nature the good tend to be born to the good (1.6.1255b1–3, 3.13.1283a36–37), such a king is most likely to come from a surpassing family. Moreover, the virtue he must have (and virtue is, in the end, the only just title to rule) is virtue precisely for leading the political community, and hence prudence in particular (3.4.1277b25–30). Aristocracy, by contrast, is appropriate in a multitude that naturally carries with it a multitude capable of being ruled as free men by several others who have this same virtue for being leaders in political rule. Here Aristotle makes express reference to the multitude that is ruled as well as to the several who rule. The reason is presumably that in an aristocracy the aristocrats are understood to be training the young whom they rule to become rulers after them, and hence some reference to those fit to be so trained for rule (rule over the free who will themselves one day rule) is necessary. In a kingship, by contrast, those who are ruled will not later become rulers themselves but will always remain the political household of the king (provided there is always someone fit to be king, which is of course the assumption behind kingship). Finally polity is appropriate where from the multitude of the city a multitude of soldiers emerges who will be able to share ruling and being ruled according to a law that distributes rule to people fit to be soldiers, that is, to those who have military virtue and are well enough off to afford arms. Here it is significant, first, that law has the place previously occupied by the king or the aristocrats and, second, that ruling and being ruled are shared by turns (some ruling in the offices, some ruling through membership of the assembly, and so forth, as explained in 3.11), whereas the king and aristocrats always rule (they are ruled only when too young or too old).

90. Scholars have raised a number of doubts about whether this paragraph is genuine or placed where it should be; see the discussions and references in Newman (1:573, 3:303–4), Schütrumpf (1991: 2:573–75), Susemihl and Hicks (1894: 443–44). But these doubts are not decisive (as Newman already noted). The passage can in fact be given an acceptable sense where it stands as, following Lord (1984: 256 n57), I proceed to show.

1288a15   Having thus shown when kingship is naturally appropriate, Aristotle now states why it should be so or why kingship in these conditions is just. The argument is the same as the one given earlier (in chapter 13). First, all the claims to justice (virtue, wealth, strength, freedom, birth) eventually end up supporting rule by one man alone. Of course, it is not excess in wealth or birth or strength that fits a man to be king, but Aristotle is doubtless not saying that it does. Rather we must suppose he is saying that those who argue on these bases have no grounds for denying that total rule by one man is just, for their own argument logically compels them to admit that sometimes it must be. Second, as regards the true ground for total rule, namely surpassing virtue, expelling or killing such a man is manifestly not just, for if virtue gives the true title to rule, surpassing virtue must give a surpassing title to rule. Hence neither is it just to force such a man to share rule with others, since his surpassing virtue makes him a whole by himself. His virtue is, ex hypothesi, incommensurable and so such as not to be capable of being increased or improved by the addition to it of the virtue of others who are not on the same scale as he (just as the virtue of lions or gods cannot be increased or improved by the addition to them of the virtue of hares or human beings, 3.13.1284a3–17).[91] The conclusion is, therefore, inescapable that such a one should in justice rule all by himself and that everyone else should obey him.

1288a30   Aristotle has thus shown that kingship is sometimes just and therewith answered the objection that kingship cannot be a correct regime. Whether such a regime is actually possible will depend on whether any man could ever be so good as to be, in contrast with others, a god. There is nothing in Aristotle's writing, here or elsewhere, to suggest that he thought the emergence of a man of divine goodness impossible. The evidence certainly shows that he thought such a man worth praying for (since he thought kingship, along with aristocracy, worth praying for). If we are inclined to disagree, that can only be because we, unlike Aristotle, do not believe in the god-man or in the power and usefulness of prayer.

At any rate, having answered the difficulties about the regime of kingship, which is the last difficulty Aristotle notes for his division of regimes, he can now pass on to the next subject, which is the best regime itself.

Chapter 18

〜 TRANSITION TO INVESTIGATION OF THE BEST REGIME

1288a32   The general division of regimes, their number, and kinds has thus been completed. But Aristotle's intention was not merely to state the kinds but to say what each is like (3.1.1274b32–33) and this second task has yet to be done.

---

91. A comparison rightly recalled by Mulgan (1974a).

Further, what first motivated Aristotle at the beginning to investigate regimes was a concern with the best regime, the regime that would enable people actually to achieve the virtue that makes the happy life (*Ethics* 10.9; cf. 2.1.1260b27–29). Consequently, an investigation of what the best regime is like (an investigation that descends to details) should properly come next. Such an investigation is exactly what Aristotle now proceeds to give. First he argues, from conclusions just established, which of all the possible regimes is best and, second, how investigating this regime will answer the question of how to make people virtuous.

Aristotle's argument may be summarized as follows:[92] (1) the best regime must be one of the correct regimes (a deviant regime could not possibly be best, 3.6), and it must, further, be that correct regime which is managed by the best men (for these are those who rule for the sake of the best, namely the noble life of virtue, 3.7, 9); but (2) the best men are manifestly those who are most virtuous and such men rule either in kingship, where one man or a family is surpassing in virtue, or in aristocracy, where a number of men are surpassing in virtue (3.13, 17) and are, further, composed of those able to rule (the mature) and those able to be ruled (the young) with a view to the best life (3.4); hence (3) the best regime is kingship or aristocracy indifferently (polity may be a correct regime but it is not marked by perfect virtue, 3.7). Further, (4) the virtue of the good man and the good citizen is the same in the best regime (that is, when the citizen is fully mature and knows how to rule and not just how to be ruled, 3.4).[93] Hence (5) to know how to make a man virtuous is the same as to know how to make a city a kingship or an aristocracy (for a city will only be a kingship or an aristocracy if some in it have the virtue of kings or aristocrats). Hence also the education that makes a man virtuous will be the same as the education that makes him aristocratic or kingly.

It is worth noting that Aristotle does not mean here that to make a man good or serious it is necessary to establish an aristocracy or a kingship, but only that to know how to make him good is to know also how to set up an aristocracy or a kingship. This neatly fits in with the *Ethics* (10.9.1180a30–34) where Aristotle said that one could make a man good in one's own home if the city provided no help, but that to do this was the same as to be a legislator, that is, as one who knows how to set up regimes and in particular the best regime.

1288b2   The question then is how to set up the best regime, which Aristotle glosses as how the best regime naturally comes to be and gets somehow or other established. This double question is perhaps meant to refer to the fact that the life

---

92. I follow Newman (1:293, 3:306).

93. Commentators have professed to find conflicts between what Aristotle says here about the virtue of man and citizen and what he said earlier in 3.4, especially at 1276b35–1277a5; see the discussion in Newman (3:158) and Schütrumpf (1991: 2:582). But there is no conflict if one recalls the teaching of that whole earlier chapter, that the virtue of man and citizen is the same when the citizen is fully mature and is already exercising rule, not when he is still young and is being trained for rule by being ruled.

of virtue needs both education and equipment.[94] Equipment, however, is the work of fortune or chance so that, in this respect, the best regime only naturally comes to be according to prayer. Education, by contrast, is the proper work of the legislator and so, in this respect, the best regime naturally gets established by art. At all events this double question divides the discussion of the best regime in the next two books that follow (equipment is dealt with in 4(7).4–12 and education in 4(7).13–17 and 5(8).1–7).

The last sentence is problematic. Taken just by itself it is grammatically incomplete. Hence many commentators translate it as so incomplete: "Anyone, then, who is going to conduct the examination that is proper to the subject must . . ." However, as I argue in the notes to the translation, there is no need to do this. Taken in context the sentence need not be read as incomplete, for the missing sense can be provided by the immediately previous sentence. That sentence says that it is necessary to speak about the best regime and how it naturally comes to be, and the last sentence then just continues the same thought by saying, as I do in the translation: "Anyone, then, who is going to do this [namely, speak about the best regime] must conduct the examination that is proper to the subject."[95]

Anyway, as so construed, this last sentence neatly introduces the next book, and in particular the first three chapters of it (provided, of course, that the next book is 4(7) and not 6(4)). For what is last said here is that the examination that must be made is one that is proper to the subject (a manifest truth about any examination into anything), and what is first said there is what this proper examination is.

94. *Ethics* 1.8 (especially 1099a31–b8) and *Politics* 4(7).12.1331b18–23, 13.1332b8–11. Also note that at 4(7).4.1325b35–38 Aristotle expressly speaks of equipment being necessary if the city is to "come to be" and that such equipment is part of what must be presupposed if a city is going to be "set up" according to prayer. Mansfield (1989: 46) and in Silver and Schramm (1984: 170) suggests that how the best regime naturally comes to be means how the best regime will come to be through a reform of existing regimes, and that the phrase refers to books 6(4)–8(6), which books should therefore come next and not books 4(7) and 5(8). But this is not persuasive. For while it is probably true that deviant regimes transformed into polity could in a certain respect prepare the way for aristocracy and kingship, such reform could never guarantee the advantages of fortune as well. Prayer must remain an important, if not the most important, element in how the best regime naturally comes to be.

95. Davis (1996: 65–66) suggests another translation. He joins the last sentence to the last part of the previous sentence (taking *pōs* interrogatively to mean "how" and not adverbally to mean "somehow or other") and translates: ". . . and how it is in fact necessary for the one intending to make an appropriate inquiry about it [= the best regime] to establish it." This suggestion is similar to a suggestion contained in a marginal gloss to some of the manuscripts, as noted in the apparatus criticus of Dreizehnter: ". . . and how it is in fact necessary for those going to examine these things to establish themselves, that is, what sort of beginning to their discussion they should use." If we are to follow this way of construing the Greek, the second suggestion is preferable since it relates conducting an appropriate examination to how to begin that examination. The first relates conducting an appropriate examination to how to set up the best regime, which does not seem very appropriate (Davis tries to make it seem appropriate by appeal to his strained rhetorical readings of the *Politics*).

BOOK 4

The Best Regime

Chapter 1

~ PREFACE TO THE DISCUSSION: THE BEST WAY OF LIFE

~ THAT THE LIFE OF VIRTUE IS THE BEST LIFE FOR EVERYONE

1323a14 The final sentence of the preceding book and the first sentence of this produce, when put together, a rather neat progression of thought. For the preceding book ends by saying: "Anyone who is going to [speak about the best regime] must conduct the examination that is proper to the subject"; and this book opens by saying: "Anyone who is going to conduct the investigation into the best regime that is proper to the subject must first determine what the most choiceworthy way of life is." This progression of thought follows the schema: anyone who is going to do x must do y; anyone who is going to do y must do z. There is thus a tight logical connection between the two books that can do nothing but strengthen the view that they are meant to follow each other immediately (the variation in the words, from "examination" *skepsis* there to "investigation" *zētēsis* here, is hardly significant since there is no variation in the sense). Furthermore, the final remark at the end of the last book, that the examination of the best regime must be made in the proper way, has, apart from expressing an obvious truth, neatly prepared us for what Aristotle does now, which is not to embark at once on that investigation but rather to preface it with a determination of the most choice-worthy way of life. The reason, he says, is that the best regime cannot be clear if the most choiceworthy way of life is itself not clear. So if that is true, then, since making the best regime clear is now the purpose of investigation, the only proper way to conduct that investigation must be first to make clear the most choice-worthy way of life.[1]

The conditional premise here, that the best regime cannot be clear if the most choiceworthy way of life is not clear, is supported by an argument that may be

---

1. In view of this very neat and tight connection, in both form and thought, between the end of the last book and the beginning of this, the complaints of certain scholars, as Newman (1:294) and Schütrumpf (1991: 2:580), that there is no such connection can readily be set aside.

formalized thus: (1) the end proper to those who govern themselves in the best way (that is, who have the best regime) is to do the best (that is, to live the most choiceworthy life); (2) to be unclear about the end proper to a thing is to be unclear about the thing; (3) therefore to be unclear about the most choiceworthy life is to be unclear about the best regime. Premise (2) would seem obvious and is left unexpressed. Premise (1) is a rephrasing of the fundamental claim from the preceding book (3.6, 9, 13) that living best is the point or end of the city (Aristotle does not use the word "end" in his rephrasing but it is manifestly what the premise is about), and hence that the best ordering of the city, or the best regime, must be the one where the citizens live best. This rephrasing seems simply designed to make manifest, even in the words themselves, the essential connection between best life and best regime.[2]

As for the words Aristotle adds ("from what is available to them," 1323a18–19), these are usually taken with "those who govern themselves in the best way" to give the sense "those who govern themselves in the best way from what is available to them" or, alternatively, "those who govern themselves in the best way that their circumstances permit." But, so taken, these words read as if they were in conflict with Aristotle's claim elsewhere that the best regime is the regime that is absolutely best, and not the regime that is only best under the circumstances (6(4).1.1288b21–33).[3] One could, however, keep this order of words and yet avoid the conflict by taking "from what is available to them" as referring to the best conditions simply, not as a limiting qualification, for what is available to those with the best regime must precisely be the simply best conditions. The sense will then be "those who govern themselves in the best way in the best circumstances," which is not in conflict with the idea that the best regime is the best absolutely. On the other hand, to make the point a little clearer, one can take these words, as I do in the translation, with what follows and read "to do the best from what is available to them," and again understand what is available to them as being the best conditions simply. At all events these words, when taken in either of these ways, reinforce, instead of weakening, Aristotle's argument, because they now say that those with the best regime must do or live the best without any impediments from imperfect conditions, and hence must live the best or most choiceworthy life absolutely. The other phrase "unless something unreasonable happens" (1323a19) now also serves to stress the same point, namely that to suppose those who have the best regime and the best conditions do not live the best life is to suppose something unreasonable.

2. Newman therefore seems wrong in his complaint (1:293–94) that since the preceding book has just repeated the premise about the point of the best regime being the most desirable life (3.18.1288a36–37) we should expect Aristotle now directly to appeal to it instead of introducing this "fresh reason" about governing best and doing the best things. For this fresh reason is not fresh at all but the same premise restated in a verbally manifest way.

3. This puzzle is raised by Barker (1946: 279 n2) and Newman (3:307–8).

The question of the most choiceworthy life is next divided by Aristotle into two, into what is the most choiceworthy life for everyone and into whether this life is the same for all in common as well as for each separately. One might think the second question is unnecessary once the first is answered since humans, being by nature political, must be living best when living politically, that is when living together in a city, so that the best life must be the same for communities as for individuals. In fact Aristotle does answer the second question using his answer to the first but he presumably takes the trouble to ask and answer the second because, as will be seen, there is a common, and respectable, opinion that the two questions do not have the same answer and this opinion, on a matter of such importance, ought not to be passed over in silence.[4]

1323a21 Aristotle starts with the first question and, since there are some things agreed and true about it and other things not, he notes the former before turning to discuss the latter. He appeals to certain external discourses (instead of, say, the *Ethics*) perhaps because these would, as being more popular in character, display truths popularly agreed in a more readily accessible way.[5] So here, for instance, the division of goods into external, those of the body, and those of the soul, is rather obvious, once made explicit, and would naturally meet with general agreement, as would also, of course, the idea that the first two (wealth and health in particular) are necessary for blessedness (blessedness being what is most choice-worthy). That the goods of the soul, the virtues, are also necessary would be likewise agreed, at any rate as soon as the extreme cases Aristotle here describes are presented.[6] For it is manifest that blessedness needs at least as much virtue as is necessary to avoid such sorts of barbarity and stupidity. But while everyone would agree that all three kinds of goods are necessary, they would not agree that they are all needed in equal amount. For while a modicum of virtue (enough, at least, to avoid the extremes just mentioned) is thought sufficient, the other goods, external ones in particular, are pursued without limit. Here, however, is where the popular view becomes erroneous, so Aristotle turns next to show that it is so and which view is true instead.

1323a38 His first argument appeals to the facts (1) that the other goods are preserved by the virtues and not vice versa (so that, if all three sorts of goods are

4. The opinion that the best life in common is not the same as the best life separately, or that the best life separately is something individual and not something common, is of course a key point in modern liberal political theory.

5. As Newman suggests (3:309). On the question of external discourses see Newman (1:299 n1, 3:308–9), Susemihl and Hicks (1894: 561–65). Vahlen (1911: 1:177–226), however, suggests the reference might in fact be to the *Ethics*, especially to 1.8. But see also p. 150 n33 above.

6. Here, as elsewhere (3.4.1277b16–30, 1.13.1260a17–24), Aristotle speaks of virtue according to its traditional division into four cardinal virtues (courage, moderation, justice, prudence). Presumably this is for reasons of brevity and not because he is ignoring the fuller list of virtues given in the *Ethics* (2.7); cf. Susemihl and Hicks (1894: 471).

necessary, the virtues are more necessary since they bring the others with them but not conversely); and (2) that those who put no limit to virtue but do put a limit to getting the other goods enjoy more happiness or blessedness than those who do the opposite. Aristotle does not bother to say what facts he has in mind, nor indeed need he. These facts were doubtless as obvious in his day as they still are in ours. So we have traditional sayings like "a fool and his money are soon parted" and "pride comes before a fall," and we can point to numerous examples of the rich, famous, and powerful who have awful characters and are miserable, and to the moderate or poor, the obscure and powerless who have beautiful characters and are happy.

1323b6 The second argument appeals, as do the rest, rather to certain principles of reason. It may be formalized as follows: (1) external and useful goods are limited with respect to amount and are harmful or useless in excess, whereas the goods of the soul are more useful the more they exist to excess; (2) what is more useful the more it exists to excess is more choiceworthy than what is less useful or limited in usefulness; (3) therefore the goods of the soul are more choiceworthy. Premise (2) here is evident and left unexpressed, and premise (1) is also evident (the useful is by definition only useful for something else, beyond which it can no longer be useful; cf. 1.8.1256b31–37), but it also appeals back to the fact that by the virtues the other goods are acquired and preserved and not vice versa.

There nevertheless seems a certain oddity, or at least verbal awkwardness, in Aristotle's speaking, in premise (1), of the usefulness of the goods of the soul. For if they were simply useful then, according to the very idea of the useful, an excess of them, going beyond what they were useful for, would be harmful and useless. Aristotle indeed expresses some reluctance about calling them useful as opposed to noble. But they are of course useful with respect to acquiring and preserving the other goods, which is doubtless why he does speak of their usefulness alongside their nobility. For because their usefulness in this respect has no limit, usefulness cannot be the nature or essence of their goodness (as it is, say, in the case of instruments) but must be more like an overflow from what is the essence of their goodness. So the fact that the virtues are more useful even than properly useful things (like wealth) and also break the pattern of properly useful things (becoming more useful the more there is of them) makes manifest, especially to those capti-vated by useful things, that useful things are not the best things simply but are surpassed, even in terms of usefulness, by other things whose goodness is not usefulness but nobility.

1323b13 The third argument may be formalized as follows: (1) the best condition of one thing stands to the best condition of another thing as those things themselves stand to each other; (2) the soul is more honorable than property and the body; (3) therefore the best condition of the soul (virtue) must be more honorable than the best condition of property and the body (wealth and health).

Premise (2) is, perhaps, meant to be proved by the next remark that (4) the other things are by nature to be chosen for the sake of the soul and not vice versa, since that for the sake of which something else is must be more honorable, and certainly more desirable, than that something else. Alternatively one could regard premise (2) as something manifest by itself (for the soul rules and uses both the body and property and what rules and uses is more honorable than what is ruled and used, both simply, or by nature, and for us whose nature this soul and body are). Then premise (4) could be regarded as forming a separate argument, as is perhaps intended by the word "further" at 1323b18: (4) that for which something else is to be chosen is more desirable; (5) the soul is that for which goods of the body and property are to be chosen (property is for health and health is for activity, which is the work of soul); (6) therefore the soul and its good, the virtues, are more desirable.

1323b21   The fourth (or fifth) argument takes a testimony, as it were, from the god: (1) the god is happy through himself and his nature not by external goods (of which he could have no need); (2) divine happiness is the model or archetype of happiness (cf. *Ethics* 10.8.1178b25–27); (3) therefore human happiness must be similar and consist likewise in internal qualities of soul and in acting accordingly. The addition of "acting accordingly" (1323b22–23) is necessary since to have virtue but not to act on it, or not to be able to act on it, is not yet actually to be happy (cf. *Ethics* 1.8.1098b31–1099a7). But the god must be actually happy and active, and human happiness can be no different. Of course the god, unlike humans, is of a certain sort "in his nature" (1323b26), for manifestly he must have the character and activity he has by nature and not by habituation and training (the god could hardly be god if he had to learn how to be noble and wise).

The last sentence may be a sort of corollary: (1) happiness, as has just been proved, lies in virtue and not goods external to the soul (goods of the body or property); (2) fortune or chance can cause external goods but not virtues; (3) therefore good fortune is different from happiness. Alternatively one could, by taking this difference not as a corollary but as a premise, read here another (and sixth) argument:[7] (1) good fortune is different from happiness; (2) only the thesis that happiness is virtue could explain this difference (if happiness were any of the goods outside the soul, which are all subject to fortune, happiness and fortune would not be different); (3) therefore happiness is virtue.

∼ THAT THE LIFE OF VIRTUE IS THE BEST LIFE FOR THE CITY

1323b29   Aristotle has just concluded that each of us individually has as much of happiness as we have of virtue and virtuous activity. So he turns next to his other question (the one he posed second at the beginning), whether the same is true of the city, that is, of all in common. The opening sentence here is, however,

7. As Newman does (3:317).

controversial and is often translated along these lines: "Next, and requiring the same arguments, is that the best city is happy and acts nobly."[8] It is also often remarked that the phrase "acts nobly" can also mean, more neutrally, "fares well" and that Aristotle trades on this ambiguity or verbal association in his next argument, which is generally understood as follows: (1) the city can only be happy or "fare well" if it "acts nobly"; (2) a city cannot "act nobly" if it does not do "noble things"; (3) no act is "noble" without virtue; (4) therefore a city cannot be happy or "fare well" if it is not the best city, that is, the city that acts with virtue.[9]

There are problems, however, with this interpretation, the first and not the least of which is that this argument is a sophistical play on words and would surely have appeared so to many in Aristotle's audience (it simply begs the question by assuming, instead of proving, that faring well is faring nobly in the sense of doing the deeds of virtue). Second, Aristotle has said that the same arguments are to be used for the city as were just used for each separately but this argument was precisely not used for each separately.[10]

The translation I offer, "next, and requiring the same arguments, is that a city is happy when it is best or acting nobly," avoids these problems. To begin with it helps avoid the sophistry since "acting nobly" can now be read literally and not also in the looser sense of "faring well." The sophistry can altogether be avoided if one accepts Aristotle's statement that the same arguments prove of the city what has just been proved of each separately. For what this statement must mean, if taken seriously, is that all these same arguments (the ones just given) are simply to be repeated with "city" taken as the subject instead of "each individually," though Aristotle does not himself bother to repeat them, for that would be unnecessary (he leaves us to do it for ourselves). But if so, then the immediately following remarks cannot be meant as another argument for the same conclusion (the *same* arguments are needed, not additional ones), and indeed, without the sophistry of "act nobly" and "fare well," they cannot even constitute such an argument (for to show that acting nobly is acting virtuously does nothing by itself to show that acting nobly is to be happy).

I suggest then that they be read instead as proving that the same arguments can indeed be applied to the city. For it might well be thought that there is a problem here because an individual is not a city and so to take the same arguments and make city the subject instead of individuals might generate equivocation in the terms and, above all, in the key terms of "virtue" and "happiness." For if these terms do not mean the same when predicated of the city, then there can be no

8. So Barker (1946: 281), Lord (1984: 198), Newman (3:317), Susemihl and Hicks (1894: 476); but cf. the several readings suggested by Jowett (1885: 2:255).

9. So in particular Sinclair/Saunders (1981: 389–90), Susemihl and Hicks (1894: 476–77), but see also Barker (1946: 282 nAAA), Lord (1984: 266 n4), Newman (3:317–18).

10. As Newman correctly notes (3:318) and also Susemihl and Hicks (1894: 476).

guarantee that the same arguments can be applied to the city to prove the same conclusion. Aristotle accordingly proceeds to show that there will be no equivocation, first of the term "virtue" and second of the term "happiness."[11]

The argument about virtue may be formalized as follows: (1) to act nobly is to do noble deeds; (2) noble deeds are impossible for anyone, whether a man or a city of men, without the virtues; (3) therefore the city that acts nobly acts with the virtues; (4) the virtues of the city have the same power and form as those by which a man is said to be virtuous; (5) therefore the city that acts nobly acts with virtues that have the same power and form as those that are said of a virtuous man. Premise (1) here simply says what acting nobly concretely is, namely doing noble deeds (a city can be said to do things just as much as a man can). Premise (2) may be regarded as a sort of definition, for virtue precisely is that whereby noble deeds are done, whoever it is who does them. Premise (4) may be regarded as implied by or contained in premise (2), for if the virtues of the city make the city do noble deeds just as the virtues of a man make a man do noble deeds then the virtues that are said of a city must have the same power and form (they cause the same deeds) as those by which a man is said to be virtuous. Consequently virtue is predicated of a city in the same way as it is of a man.[12]

1323b36 This argument need not, perhaps, fully exhaust the question of the likeness or identity of the virtue of a city and a man (the fact, for instance, that both virtues cause the same deeds still leaves open the possibility that they are not in other respects the same). Still, something had to be said on this question for the purposes of the present discussion (the arguments about the virtue of a man had to be shown to be applicable to the virtue of a city), and enough has now been said for those purposes (for if both virtues cause the same deeds, then arguments that a life of such deeds is best for an individual man must prove the same too of the community of men in a city). So Aristotle is now able to lay down the thesis that the best life for each separately and for cities in common is the life of virtue sufficiently equipped for taking part in the deeds of virtue (cf. *Ethics* 1.8.1099a31–b2). Further discussion, while still perhaps possible, is not necessary, and the curious or dissatisfied can, for the time being, be dismissed. The further discussion about virtue in man and city is perhaps to be found in the treatment of which virtues specifically the city needs (4(7).13–15). On the other hand it may not be found anywhere in the *Politics* at all. For Aristotle does say here that it is "work for

11. This possibility of equivocation in the terms, at least as regards "virtue," is noted by Peter of Auvergne (1951: 7.1.1057).

12. Peter of Auvergne's comment is perhaps worth quoting here: "The virtue of the whole city and the virtue of each individually are of the same nature, in themselves and in relation to action, and do not differ save as the whole differs from the part and the more from the less. For the moral virtue of a city is an aggregate of the individual virtues of the citizens. That is why, just as the capacity to laugh is of the same nature in one man as in a hundred, so virtue is the same in one man and in a whole city" (1951: 7.1.1057).

leisure of another sort" (1323b39–40), which other sort of leisure could well be metaphysics or psychology. For certainly to go much deeper into the general question of when and how the same qualities can be predicated of different subjects would take one into metaphysics, and to go much deeper into the particular question of when and how the same dispositions or habits can be said to belong to each soul individually and to several souls in common would take one into psychology, or the science of the soul.

Chapter 2: 1324a5   This next paragraph has posed problems for commentators since it looks, first, like needless repetition and, second, like inappropriate arguing. It is needless repetition because this question about the city's happiness has surely just been decided, for it has just been shown that the best life for city and individual is a life of virtuous deeds. It is inappropriate arguing because if Aristotle had thought it now necessary to draw in express words this conclusion that the happiness of the city must therefore be the same as the individual, he should simply have appealed back to what he has just proved and not have appealed instead to what people say, including what those people say who deny that the happy life is a life of virtue.[13]

All these problems can, however, be removed by reading the paragraph instead as a direct continuation of the previous chapter.[14] For though the sameness of virtue in individual and city has just been argued, there remains the question of whether the other key term in the arguments to be applied to the city, namely happiness, is the same. So this is what Aristotle does now. Accordingly his argument is neither repetition nor inappropriate. It establishes a different point and does so by appeal to what it should appeal to, namely how the term "happiness" is actually and universally used. For if everyone predicates happiness of the city in the same way and for the same reason as they predicate it of the individual (regardless of what that reason is), then no one can object that arguments used to prove of an individual that happiness is a life of virtue must be false or improper if used to prove the same of the city.

~ WHAT THE LIFE OF VIRTUE IS

~ THE KINDS OF VIRTUOUS LIFE

1324a13   Aristotle has just established that the most choiceworthy way of life for each individually and for all in common is the life of virtue, and so has, to

---

13. See Barker (1946: 282 n1, 283 n1), Jowett (1885: 2:255–56), Lord (1978b: 341), Susemihl and Hicks (1894: 86–87, 478–79). Kraut (1997: ad loc.) notes several additional problems with the paragraph as standardly interpreted.

14. In the way that Newman does (3:319–20), whom I follow here. This is one of the few places in the *Politics* where I think one of the chapter divisions (which do not go back to Aristotle himself) does not help to reveal the articulations of the argument.

this extent, answered his opening question from the preceding chapter. But he has not yet determined what the virtuous life consists in. So he turns to this subject now and raises two questions. The first, whether the most choiceworthy life is sharing a city together or is an alien one, picks up, in a way, on that from the preceding chapter. For this first question, which is not simply about the priority or superiority of the theoretical as opposed to the political or moral virtues[15] (for both virtues can exist within the city), raises the possibility that, despite the general identity of the best life for individual and city, some people might be so self-sufficient as to be able to live this life like gods, without need of others (cf. 1.2.1253a27–29). This question, however, though a real one, departs from the question of the best regime, for regardless of how it gets answered the question of which regime is best will still arise for those (whether all or only most) for whom life in the city is most worth choosing. Not surprisingly, therefore, Aristotle declares the first question to be outside the work of the present study.

1324a23 The second question is what regime and disposition of the city are to be set down as best. It has, of course, already been shown in the preceding book that the best regime is a kingship or an aristocracy. But the question now is not about this general point but about what such a regime should concretely be like, and in particular about what virtues it should be aiming at. So Aristotle begins by recalling the first principle, as it were, of the best regime, namely that it must be that arrangement in which anyone might act best and live blessedly (for such life is the end of the city and so must also be the end that the simply best regime should order the city toward, 3.6). This life has just been shown to be the life of virtue but there is dispute about whether the virtues in question are the political or the philosophic virtues. This dispute is consequently what must be dealt with next, both because there is no other candidate for the life of virtue (these are the only two that those ambitious for virtue have championed), and because the best goal is what the regime, like the individual, should clearly aim at.

Now it might appear that Aristotle is here sliding back into the question that he has just set aside as not proper to the present study, namely whether the political life or the life outside the city is better.[16] But there is a difference in the words he uses. Before he spoke of "the alien way of life" and a life "released from the political community" (1324a16–17); here he speaks of a life that is "released from all externals" as "the contemplative life, for instance" (1324a27–28). The first two quotations could not describe a way of life possible for the city or for those whose best life is in the city (who could certainly not be aliens or released from the political community), but the second two quotations could. For a city could live "released from all externals" and could pursue a "contemplative" life alone (as is indeed noted at 4(7).3.1325b16–30). So perhaps Aristotle is thinking of a dispute about

15. Contra Lord (1978b: 341; 1982: 183–84).
16. So Newman (1:303), Kraut (1997: ad loc.), Lord (1978b: 342–43; 1982: 184–85).

how the city, and not about how individuals, should live. But even if he is thinking of a dispute about individuals, and about whether they should live apart from the city or not, still he is not referring to this dispute insofar as it is about individuals but insofar as it is about a life of detached philosophy.[17] For if those who commend such a life are right and this life is best, then, as he says, it must be the goal, not just for individuals, but for the best regime too, and the best regime must also live as much as possible alone philosophizing by itself. At all events, Aristotle is not going back to the question he earlier dismissed but is continuing with the question about the best regime.

～ THAT THE LIFE OF VIRTUE IS NOT DESPOTIC RULE OVER NEIGHBORS

1324a35 There are three parties to the dispute about the virtuous life, one on the side of philosophy and two on that of politics. Those who favor the philosophic life say that the political life is either a matter of despotic rule or political rule and that, since despotic rule is unjust and political rule an impediment to happiness, the nonpolitical life must be better. Those who favor political life divide into those on the side of political rule and those on the side of despotic rule. Both, as it seems, would assert that a political way of life is the only one fit for a man, but the former at any rate also allege as reason that the deeds of each virtue no more belong to private persons than to those engaged in politics. This reason does not so much prove the manliness of political life (its manliness seems rather to be assumed as obvious) as attack the conclusion that the private life must be better. The argument would seem to be that since the political can be at least as equally virtuous, and since this life is manifestly manly while the private life is not, the political life must instead be the better one.

Those who favor despotic rule, however, simply assert that political life, even if manly, is nevertheless only happy when it is tyrannical (the objection, leveled by those who favor the philosophic life, that despotic rule is unjust they would seem implicitly to concede by passing over in silence). This third party Aristotle considers first and rejects. The other two he considers in the next chapter and, by moderating each, accepts both.

1324b3 That the opinion of the third party needs dealing with first is hardly surprising. Not only is it widely held but it is the only one that has actually been used anywhere to give unity to the laws of a city. For those cities which, as we learned in book 2, are most praised for the way their regime is organized all aim at

---

17. So Barker (1946: 284 n2). As regards those who say such a detached life is "the only philosophic way to live," these are, if the subject is individuals, probably the pre-Socratic philosophers suggested by Lord (1978b: 345; 1982: 188 n10) and Newman (1:306–8, 3:321–23), but if the subject is cities, probably Plato (*Laws* 704a1–705b6, and cf. 2.6.1265a21–26). Aristotle would doubtless reject the opinions of both as extreme.

war, and war for the sake of conquest and rule over neighbors. Moreover this same opinion is found in nations as well as cities, among barbarians as well as Greeks, in customs as well as laws. It is truly universal and, indeed, the only universal opinion that seems to have given much unity to human life anywhere.

1324b22 This opinion is, nevertheless, false, as Aristotle now proves by several arguments. The first is as follows: (1) what is not lawful is not the work of politician or legislator; (2) studying how to rule despotically over neighbors regardless of whether it is just to rule despotically over these neighbors is not lawful; (3) therefore this is not the work of politician or legislator, or consequently of political rule in general. Premise (1) is obvious (both city and legislator aim at what is lawful and just), and premise (2) is also obvious (despotic rule is only lawful and just over natural slaves, so not to care about whether those one rules or wants to rule are natural slaves is not to care about law or justice). And lest it be thought that any conqueror must have superior right just because he conquered, Aristotle adds the obvious point that conquerors can conquer unjustly (a successful tyrant is manifestly such; cf. 1.6.1255a24–26).

1324b29 The second argument is: (1) it is not the work of the other arts, as medicine and sailing, to impose their rule on their subjects willy nilly; (2) politics is an art, or indeed the architectonic art; (3) therefore it is not the work of politics either to impose its rule willy nilly. One should note about this argument that it does not say that the arts should never use compulsion when persuasion fails; it only says that they should not always use it. Sometimes perhaps the arts should compel.

1324b32 The third argument is: (1) the many think that political rule is despotic rule and want justice for themselves but not for others, the implication of which is that the distinction between those fit and those not fit for despotic rule is the distinction between "us" and "them"; (2) but the distinction between what is fit and what is not fit for despotic rule is by nature (just as the distinction between what is fit and what is not fit for being hunted for food is by nature); (3) therefore the many are drawing the distinction wrongly and not everyone should be ruled despotically but only those naturally fit for it. Premise (1) is manifest since to say that despotic rule is unjust for "us" but not to bother about justice when it comes to "them" is to distinguish justice by what distinguishes "us" from "them." Premise (2) was proved earlier (in 1.5), is anyway implicit in the opinion of the many (who really want to say that "we" are not naturally fit for despotic rule but that "they" are; cf. 1.6.1255a21–32), and is nicely illustrated by the case of hunting for food (where the distinction between what is so fit and what is not so fit is manifestly by nature). Hence it must be wrong to want to rule everyone else despotically just because they are not "us" instead of because, or if, they are natural slaves.

1324b41 The fourth argument is: (1) a city could be nobly governed and happy while yet existing apart by itself somewhere; (2) such a city would not have a

regime arranged for war and dominating enemies (ex hypothesi there are no enemies to hand for it to fight and rule over); (3) therefore a city can be nobly
governed and happy without having a regime arranged for war and domination,
and so such domination or despotic rule cannot be the work or end of the city.
Premise (2) is manifest ex hypothesi and to reject premise (1) would in effect be to
say that a city could only be nobly governed and happy if there were hostile neighbors around for it to conquer, or that without enemies it is impossible to be happy.
But this is an absurd, not to say, murderous supposition (cf. *Ethics* 10.7.1177b9–12).

1325a5/14   The conclusion is now manifest: war may indeed be noble, and
necessary, but only for the sake of the end and not as the end. The end or the happy
life of city and household, which is the object of the legislator, must be something
else, though this object must include relations with neighbors, and hence even
training for war and rule, insofar as circumstances may require it. Consequently
there is still need for further discussion of what this end is, and specifically of what
virtues and virtuous acts it consists in, but enough has obviously been said for now
to refute the view that the end is despotic rule. This further discussion of the end,
however, does not come until chapters 13–15. What has to come next is the completion of the present discussion by examining the two other disputants mentioned at
the beginning.

Chapter 3

~ THAT THE LIFE OF VIRTUE IS BOTH
PRACTICAL AND PHILOSOPHICAL

1325a16   The remaining disputants agree that happiness is virtue, and not
the criminal activity of tyranny, but disagree about its exercise (about how the
virtuous life is actually to be lived). Aristotle first states what their differing opinions are and then shows how both are partly right and partly wrong. The partisans
of contemplation and philosophy, on one side, say a free life is not one of political
activity (such activity, they say, impedes well-being, as was noted at the beginning
of the last section, 2.1324a38). The partisans of politics, on the other side, praise the
active life of politics. Their argument is that happiness is good activity, that those
who are not doing anything or are not acting at all cannot be doing or acting well,
and that therefore they are not happy or living best.

Both these sets of reasoning are, one may note, of a negative character; each side
is only arguing against the opposing position and not also for its own. So the
partisans of philosophy argue that the political life is not free but take for granted
that the life of philosophic withdrawal is the only free one; the partisans of politics
argue that the life of philosophic withdrawal is not active and take for granted that
the life of political activity is the only active one. It is partly because of this one-
sided arguing that Aristotle is able to steer a middle course between them.

1325a23 He first argues against the partisans of philosophy. These are right in one respect but wrong in two others. They are right to suppose that the life of a free man is better than that of the despotic ruler, because there is nothing grand or noble about ruling over slaves. They are wrong to suppose that all rule is despotic or that there is no such thing as rule over the free. They are also wrong to suppose that inactivity is better than activity, both because happiness is activity and because in virtuous actions many noble things reach their goal. The partisans of philosophy, in short, not only fail to show that the free life is not the practical life; they even fail to show that this life is not the political life of ruling over the free.

1325a34 To this extent, then, the partisans of the political life have been vindicated. But Aristotle next proceeds against them too because of a certain false inference that this refutation of the partisans of philosophy might generate. Someone might now suppose that the best life is the activity of ruling over the free, and hence that the best thing is to secure for oneself the position of ruler over everyone. For since, as has just been said, happiness is activity and many noble things reach their goal in virtuous activity, then if one was in control of all the free, one would be in control of the greatest number of the noblest actions. Hence it might further seem that one should prevent everyone else from ruling or sharing in rule, including one's closest relatives and friends, in order to possess for oneself what is most worth choosing, namely the best activity of ruling.

1325a41 Aristotle responds to this reasoning, first, by showing that it is wrong and, second, by showing why it is wrong. That it is wrong is manifest because it entails that one should commit violent crimes in order to secure rule for oneself, and a life of crime cannot possibly be most worth choosing. Why it is wrong is that it falsely assumes that ruling over everyone is always and in all circumstances noble. But, on the contrary, if the ruler is not superior in kind to those he rules, his ruling will not be noble. Among those who are equal what is noble and just is sharing rule by turns, for in that way everyone is treated equally. But to rule over equals permanently is to treat them unequally and that is unnatural and so not noble. Someone, therefore, who secured permanent rule for himself over equals would, in his very ruling, be committing such wrongs against virtue that no actions he did as ruler could ever make up for them. Consequently, if one is not superior in the way required for permanent rule, the only way to do noble deeds is either to share rule with one's equals or not to rule at all but to yield rule and obedience to someone who is superior (and superior in virtue and the power so to act since virtue without action is vain and incomplete).

1325b14 This refutation of the false inference from the superiority of the active life, while necessary, does not overthrow that superiority (a proposition from which something is falsely inferred is not refuted just because that inference is refuted). The discussion has indeed shown that the partisans of the practical life are right in saying, against the partisans of philosophy, that happiness is activity and hence that the practical life is the best and happiest life for both individual and city. But the refutation of the false inference does nevertheless generate a problem. For if it is sometimes noble not to rule and act but instead to rule and be ruled by turns, or even to follow and obey permanently the one superior man, how can the active life always be the best and most noble life?

The solution is to be found, as before with the partisans of philosophy, by distinguishing between the several things that the partisans of the political life assert, and by accepting some and rejecting others. So, activity must indeed be admitted to be best but this activity need not, as they suppose, always be like rule in being directed toward others; nor need all thoughts except those for the sake of something else be inactive. On the contrary those thoughts are active, and indeed more active, that are ends in themselves and exist for their own sake. Having stated these points, Aristotle proceeds next to prove them, first of the individual and then of the city.

As regards the individual, Aristotle first removes the false opinion that thoughts that are ends and for their own sake cannot be active. His argument is: (1) acting well is an end; (2) acting well is an activity; (3) therefore some activity is an end and, conversely, some end is an activity. Consequently the mere fact that thoughts that are ends in themselves and for their own sake are not directed to others, nor are for the sake of anything else, does not show (contrary to the opinion of the partisans both of philosophy and of politics) that such thoughts cannot be, or be called, active. Second, Aristotle proves that thoughts are active and, indeed, more active than external actions. He appeals to the fact that ruling craftsmen whose thinking concerns some external action are more properly said to be acting than those who carry out this thinking (one might take as examples architects, who are more properly said to have built buildings than the bricklayers, or generals, who are more properly said to have won battles than the soldiers). So if thoughts for the sake of external actions are, as thoughts, active and more active than external actions, then thoughts that are for their own sake can, as thoughts, also be active and more active than external actions.

1325b23   As regards the city, Aristotle proves that cities living and choosing to live apart (and not ruling over, or involved with, other cities) can still be active. The first reason picks up on what he has just said, for cities too can be active by themselves alone, namely by the way the parts commune with each other (as men with women, fathers with children, rulers with soldiers, rulers and soldiers with priests, and so on; cf. 4(7).8, 9). The same is true of a single human being where the parts also act in relation to each other, as notably in acts of thinking (which involve sensation, memory, and thought together). The second reason appeals to the example of the god and the cosmos, which are manifestly in a noble condition but only act within themselves. Consequently it is possible, both for the city and the individual, to be active and happy even though not ruling over anyone, because they can be happy in other activities.

1325b30   The conclusion Aristotle now gives, that the same way of life is best both for each human being and for cities and humans in common, indicates that the previous discussion has all been about the question posed at the beginning of chapter 1. And indeed so it has, for while in that first chapter he proved that the best life for both was the life of virtue, in chapters 2 and 3 he has so resolved the debate about whether this life is one of political or philosophical virtue that the same answer is to be given for both individual and city. Chapter 2 refuted the idea that despotic rule could be best, or even a life of virtue, and, with despotism thus removed, chapter 3 proved that the debate between the partisans of the political and philosophical lives was a false one, generated only by partial understandings of action, rule, and freedom. Consequently there is no case for saying that there is one life for the city and another for the individual, or that what is best for one is not best for the other. The political and philosophical lives form a unity, both for the individual and the city.[18] Indeed the form of Aristotle's concluding words (the same life is best for "each human being" as well as "for cities and humans in common") suggests that this conclusion is meant to hold for everyone, not just for most people, and therefore also for those few, mentioned at the beginning of chapter 2, for whom an alien way of life might be better.[19] For even if these few live, or can live, in some sense apart from any city, yet they could lead no better life than the active and philosophical life, a life that perhaps they could lead in seclusion or, like Aristotle himself, for the benefit, not of one city only, but of many cities.

One should note, nevertheless, that Aristotle has not decided any questions about the relative superiorities of the different virtues (that is, of the moral and intellectual virtues). He has only spoken of virtue in general terms and the specific questions he has left, as he said at the end of chapter 2, for later investigation. But he has shown here that any debate about the virtues is not properly posed in terms of the political or philosophical lives as if these were exclusive of each other. So, when he comes to that later investigation, he poses the question instead in terms of the virtues of war and peace, of occupation and leisure. It then emerges again, as has been shown here, that the political and philosophical lives combine into one, since the active life in the city turns out to be, above all, a matter of the virtues of peace and leisure, and the primary virtue of leisure is philosophy.[20] One should

18. As Newman rightly notes (1:308–9), and as Peter of Auvergne also argues (1951: 7.1.1082).

19. Lord's understanding of these words (1978b: 346 n27; 1982: 189 n13), that they are meant to indicate that the best life for "so to speak everyone" is not necessarily the best life for "every single human being," seems therefore to be mistaken.

20. On the meaning of philosophy in this context there has been much debate among scholars, and some maintain that the term is not to be taken in its full or literal sense of all the branches of philosophical or theoretical study but only in a lesser sense of "culture" and a culture that is primarily poetry and music, so Lord (1978b; 1982: chap. 5), Solmsen (1962), and Vander Waerdt (1985). This opinion is, however, rightly criticized and rejected by Depew, in Keyt and Miller (1991), and also in

nevertheless note in this connection that nothing has been said here, or is said later, to show that the city must not live with others and must not be involved in empire. All that has been said is that it *need* not be.[21] In fact, occasions may arise where it should be so involved, or where, in effect, the city should be both philosophical and imperial (cf. 4(7).6.1327a40–b6, 14.1333b38–1334a2).

Chapter 4

~ PRESUPPOSITIONS OF THE BEST REGIME

~ THE AMOUNT AND SORT OF MATERIAL

1325b33   Since the best way of life, for both individual and city, has been shown to be the life of virtue, and since other accounts of what the best regime is like were studied earlier and the good and bad in them distinguished,[22] the way is now open for Aristotle himself directly to examine the best regime. Now the best regime is according to prayer, so the first thing to do is say what equipment should be prayed for, since the best regime, as was just shown, will live the life of virtue and the life of virtue requires the full complement of all necessary equipment (though these prayers for equipment, or these presuppositions of the best regime, must not be impossible, a fault in Plato's *Laws* noted earlier, 2.6.1265a17–18).

1325b39   What equipment is needed, or should be prayed for, is shown by Aristotle from analogy with the other arts, which produce something better the better the materials they have to work with. So the political art too, if it is to produce the best regime, must have the best materials to work with. These materials are, first, human beings, for to make the best regime is the same as to make human beings virtuous (3.18.1288a39–b2), and, second, territory, for human beings must have somewhere to live and something to live off. Both these materials must exist in the right amount and be of the right sort.

~ THE NUMBER OF HUMAN BEINGS

1326a8   As regards the number of human beings, Aristotle begins with the popular view, which he accepts, but only with the necessary reservations and

---

effect by Peter of Auvergne (1951: 7.2.1083–84, 7.11.1216) when he argues, with respect to the present passage, that the contemplative life, or the activity of the theoretical intellect, is best for both individual and city.

21. So Depew, in Keyt and Miller (1991: 349–51).

22. The reference to the "other regimes" (1325b34) must be to the other best regimes studied in book 2, since only a prior examination of opinions about the best regime could be relevant to an examination of the best regime (as 2.1.1260b27–36 in fact argues).

qualifications. The view is that the happy or best city must be great. But greatness is popularly understood in terms of numbers or largeness of population and this is false, as Aristotle proceeds to show. His first argument is that greatness is to be measured by power or capacity, not numbers: (1) the city has a certain work to do; (2) things that have a work to do are great according to their capacity to do the work, as in the case of Hippocrates who is great as a doctor because of his capacity in medicine, not because of his bodily size; (3) therefore the city is great according to the capacity of its human beings to do the work and not according to their numbers merely.

1326a17 The second argument is that, even if greatness is to be judged by reference to numbers of persons, it is not just any persons that are relevant but only certain sorts: (1) greatness in a city is measured by the superiority in numbers of its proper parts; (2) the proper parts of a city are not just any multitude, and specifically not slaves, resident aliens, and foreigners; (3) therefore greatness in a city is not measured by numbers of just any multitude. What is meant by proper parts is explained later (4(7).8). Here Aristotle contents himself with a manifest example: a city that marches out with few heavy armed troops but many vulgar mechanics cannot be great (it would easily be defeated by a city with a smaller population and army but more heavy armed troops). Such a city may indeed be populous but not with parts that are proper to it, namely soldiers for its defense.

1326a25/29 The third argument is that a city's numbers, even indeed its numbers of proper parts, can become too large: (1) a city with too many people in it cannot be well legislated; (2) a city needs to be well legislated (the city is for good life and good life requires good laws); (3) therefore a city needs to avoid having too many people in it. Premise (1) is proved first by appeal to facts and then by argument. The facts, then, are that no city confessedly well legislated is seen to be lax about its numbers or to allow its population to grow unchecked. The argument is: (1) law is an arrangement and a good state of law is good arrangement; (2) a number that exceeds too much is incapable of receiving arrangement; (3) therefore a city with a number that exceeds too much, or that has too many people in it, cannot have good laws, or be well legislated. Premise (2) here is proved by the fact that only the god who holds the whole cosmos together could arrange such an excessive population, and human legislators are not gods, or at any rate not the cosmic god. It is also proved by appeal to the fact that the noble or beautiful exists in number and size, for (1) if so and (2) good arrangement is noble, then (3) good arrangement can only exist in number and size, and hence not in a population that exceeds number and size (exceeds, that is, with respect to being managed or arranged by human power). From this last argument it also follows, as a corollary, that the city which limits itself to a size that can be well legislated will not only be greatest but also most noble.

1326a35 The arguments so far have proved that the city is not great by reference to numbers and that its numbers must be limited. The fourth argument not only proves this last point again but also moves to what must logically come next, namely what the limit is: (1) whatever is destroyed or damaged in its power and nature by being too small or too big has a limit to its size as determined by that power and nature; (2) the city is destroyed or damaged in its power and nature by being too small or too big; (3) therefore the city has a limit as determined by its power and nature. Premise (1) here is obvious once stated but it is drawn by Aristotle from induction or example from other things. For other things all have a limit and they are limited precisely because they are destroyed if they go beyond their limit either by excess or defect. So the same will be true of anything else that is destroyed in the same way. The example Aristotle gives of a ship proves the point even if nowadays ships—in particular, oil tankers—can be much bigger than he supposed. For even an oil tanker can be too big (an oil tanker that stretched halfway round the globe would not be a ship but rather a pipe line).

Premise (2) is proved from the fact that a city too small will not be self-sufficient (but a city is self-sufficient); and a city too big will not sustain a regime, or be capable of receiving arrangement (but a city must have an arrangement, for that is necessary for living well). That a city too big could not receive arrangement or a regime is proved by appeal to the impossibility of marshaling and addressing an excessive crowd of people (though a city must be marshaled for purposes of defense and be addressed for purposes of judgment and decision). These problems of size can be, and have been, overcome to some extent by modern technology (as they have been also in the case of ships), but clearly only at the expense of the intimate human contact that a city, which is a community of people sharing together in one and the same life, properly requires.

1326b7 What the limit of the city's size should be, both lower and upper, now follows straightforwardly from the power or work of the city. As regards the lower limit, this will be determined by the work of self-sufficiency, so anything too small for this cannot be a city and a city will only be possible after this limit is reached. As for the upper limit, this will be determined by the work of a regime, that is, by ruling and being ruled and specifically by decisions about justice and distribution of office. Anything bigger than this will not be a city (but a nation or something similar). Here the limit must be determined by the capacity of the citizens to know each other, since justice requires knowledge of people's merits and hence of their character or their virtue. Too large a number will result in decisions about justice being made without this knowledge, and hence badly. In addition too large a number will make it easy for resident aliens and foreigners to get a share in the regime who, being likely unfit or even hostile, will damage or overthrow it. Hence the city should not, in its upper limit, be larger than is easy to survey, that is, than is easy for the character of the citizens to be discerned and for detecting aliens.[23]

1326b24 This limit, one should note, is not given as a fixed number but only as a fixed function (self-sufficiency and good rule). It allows the numbers, therefore, to vary according to circumstances and eventualities, especially of births and deaths. Consequently it avoids the problems noted earlier about Plato's *Laws* (2.6.1265a38–b17, and cf. *Ethics* 9.10.1170b31–33).

Chapter 5

⁓ THE AMOUNT AND SORT OF TERRITORY

⁓ AMOUNT AND QUALITY

1326b26 The determination of the territory also now follows from the preceding discussion. It too must be self-sufficient both in quality, that is, it must be capable of producing everything, and in amount, that is, there must be enough of it to satisfy the whole population. The limit here is defined by a life of leisure lived in moderation and liberality. The citizens of the best city must have leisure (as noted in the case of Sparta, 2.9.1269a34–36, and as noted again later, 4(7).9.1329a1–2), and must have both of the virtues associated with property (as noted in the case of Plato's *Laws*, 2.6.1265a28–38). Aristotle, however, defers further discussion of this point to later. No such discussion is to be found in the *Politics* as we have it, and one might wonder indeed why a "general discussion of property" could not come now instead of needing to be postponed. An answer is provided by Aristotle's comment that the question is involved in many disputes because of people who argue for one or other of the extremes of meanness and luxury. For such disputes must evidently focus on the question of what sort of life is best and only on property insofar as amount of property affects how one lives. In other words, the disputes are more about the virtue and way of life of the regime than about its material presuppositions. Consequently an examination of them properly belongs later in the discussion of virtue, that is, in the discussion of education and how to make the citizens good. Such examination would, therefore, naturally follow somewhere after the end of the unfinished book 5(8).

23. Newman (3:348–49) collects some interesting materials to support Aristotle's claims here, including this quotation from Bryce's *American Commonwealth* (3.62): "In moderately-sized communities men's characters are known, and the presence of a bad man in office brings on his fellow-citizens evils which they are not too numerous to feel individually. . . . In large cities the results are different because the circumstances are different." Our own experience will surely confirm this judgment.

1326b39 In the previous section Aristotle has dealt with the amount of territory and also of its quality in terms of sustenance. Here he deals with its quality in terms of defense. What he says is brief and general: the territory must be hard for enemies to enter (so that invasion is difficult) but easy for citizens to leave and to survey (so that counterattacks and defense are not difficult). That he leaves the rest to be learned from military experts is less perhaps because he has himself little interest in such questions[24] than because they belong in treatises on subordinate topics.[25] So he only says enough now to indicate the sorts of things that need to be considered and where to go for the necessary further discussions.[26] By contrast his more extended discussion in the next chapter on nearness to the sea seems to reflect the fact that disputes about good legislation are raised in this connection that are not raised about the territory (no one says that an easily defended territory is harmful to good legislation),[27] and because questions of good legislation do properly belong to politics itself.

1327a3 The comments about positioning the city well from the point of view of defending the territory and of getting in provisions are also brief and general, and doubtless for the same reasons.

Chapter 6

◠ AS REGARDS THE SEA

1327a11 As regards closeness to the sea, Aristotle first states the disadvantages that are alleged against it; then he says what the contrasting advantages are and that having these advantages would be better if the disadvantages can be avoided; and finally he argues that such avoidance will not be hard. The disadvantages, which are undoubtedly real and serious, are two: first, that closeness to the sea means there will be many foreigners around brought up under different laws who will be a threat to good legislation (law gets its force from custom, 2.8.1269a20–21, and so the city's laws, however good, will not be regarded by those with different customs); second, that there will be many traders around who will be a similar threat (too large a

---

24. As is supposed by Newman (1:340) and Sinclair/Saunders (1981: 426).

25. Strategy is subordinate to politics, *Ethics* 1.1.1094a27–b7, and Aristotle later leaves many things about music to be learned from experts, though his own interest in music seems very marked, 5(8).7.1341b27–32.

26. Compare the similar treatment of the practice of business in 1.11.

27. As Newman notes (3:359).

number cannot be reduced to the arrangement of a regime, 4(7).4.1326a31–32, and a trader's life is incompatible with virtue, 4(7).9.1328b39–41).

1327a18 The contrary advantages are also two: first, that a city with access to the sea will be better able both to defend itself against enemies and to inflict damage on them in return; second, that such a city will be better provisioned by being able to import what it lacks and to export what it has in abundance. These advantages are clearly such that, if the contrary disadvantages can be avoided, it is better to have access to the sea than not to have it. But, as Aristotle now proceeds to argue, it is possible to have the advantages in such a way as to avoid the disadvantages; therefore access to the sea must be better.

1327a27 With respect, first of all, to the advantages associated with trade, two things can be done. One, the port should only be for the city's own needs and not for that of others as well. The latter sort of port is only needed for accumulating revenue, but the best city, according to earlier teaching (1.8, 9), will not be involved in such greedy accumulation. The former sort of port, however, will be relatively small in size and so keep the influx of foreigners and traders to a minimum. Two, the port should be close to the city but separate from it and under its control, and hence contact with foreigners will be subject to the city and any danger to the laws can be prevented by the laws themselves (a topic Aristotle expressly comes to in 4(7).12).

1327a40 With respect, second, to the advantages of defense, the problem here is that such defense requires a navy, which will be larger or smaller depending on whether there is need to help defend neighbors and on whether the city is going to be involved in leadership. But a navy requires sailors and many sailors would seem certainly to bring to the city the problems of an excessive population. Aristotle's response is that this need not be so because there is no need to have a separate mass of sailors. For, first, the marines, or the fighting men who control the ships, will already belong to the city as part of its citizen soldiery (they do on ships what they are already trained to do on land), and, second, the oarsmen, the subject laborers on the ship, as it were, can be taken from those who already belong to the city as its subject laborers on the land, namely the farmers and serfs. And lest this last suggestion appear implausible, Aristotle proves its feasibility from an actual example. This example is, moreover, of a small city that has a large navy. Consequently, even if the city were living a life of leadership, it could still have an adequate navy and avoid problems of excessive population.

Chapter 7

~ THE SORT OF HUMAN BEINGS

1327b18/33 Having just dealt with the sort, as well as the amount, of territory, and having dealt with the amount of human beings earlier, Aristotle turns now to consider the sort of human beings.[28] The quality or character in question here is not the character that the legislator has to introduce by education, but the character that must be presupposed prior to education. For education presupposes nature, and the better the nature the better the education can be. So since the best regime requires the best education, it requires also the best natures. Which peoples have the best natures Aristotle determines by looking at the empirical evidence and at the materials for virtue, namely intelligence and spirit. That virtue presupposes intelligence needs no arguing (for the chief or ruling virtue, prudence, is a virtue of intelligence), but that it also presupposes spirit is argued expressly at the end.

The empirical evidence comes first from the world as a whole and then from Greece itself. In the world as a whole, people from colder climes are full of spirit, so are seldom ruled, but deficient in thought and art, so cannot rule themselves or others. People from the hotter climes of Asia[29] have thought and art, so could rule, but lack spirit, so are ruled and enslaved. The Greeks, by contrast, have both characteristics and so could rule the others: their spirit would enable them to conquer both and their thought and art would enable them to rule both—provided, however, that they had a single regime. By this last remark, Aristotle perhaps means "provided they cease their factional squabbles and, resting content with a similar and moderate regime everywhere, combine under some sort of federation" (they would be too big to form a single city together). So he may be thinking of what happened during the Persian Wars or under the rule of Philip of Macedon and his son Alexander.[30]

The evidence from Greece is similar, continues Aristotle, since some here are rather one-sided while others are well mixed.[31] Consequently, if those with a well-mixed character are best for exercising rule, and since the aim of the best regime is to produce good rulers (for such are also good men), it is this sort of character that will be most able to be educated to virtue by the legislator and which therefore the best regime will want in its citizens.

Since Aristotle's argument here is empirical, its truth depends on the accuracy

28. There is thus a chiastic form to Aristotle's arrangement of topics, and the material conditions of property and land are embraced on either side by the human conditions of population.

29. Aristotle does not actually say that Asia is hotter but he would seem to have this in mind, as Susemihl and Hicks note (1894: 499), especially if Greece is supposed to be in the middle, for the contrary extreme to cold is hot. Kraut, however (1997: ad loc.), conjectures that Aristotle may also be thinking of other factors, as dryness and moisture.

30. Barker (1946: 296 n2), Newman (1:321 n1, 3:366). Whether a reference to the conquests of Alexander is to be understood here is supposed by some but denied by others, Lord (1978b: 350–52). A peace similar to what Aristotle seems to have in mind was accepted by the Greek cities at the Congress of Corinth convened by Philip after his victory at Chaeronea in 338, the text of which can be found in Defourny (1932: 536–37 n1). The peace was continued by Alexander.

31. Newman suggests (3:366) that Aristotle is thinking of the Ionians as more intelligent than spirited and the Arcadians and Aetolians as more spirited than intelligent.

of his observations (it cannot, for instance, be dismissed simply because it seems racist). One should perhaps note, though, that the characteristics he finds in the different regions need not be geographically fixed in the sense that they cannot be changed.[32] For perhaps rule by the Greeks would do the changing, at least over time and with the young. One may suggest indeed that to the extent northern Europeans seem no longer to be as Aristotle describes, this may be due to the fact that the Greeks did come to rule over all, not by political power but by education, and mediated through a nation situated in the middle just like the Greeks, namely the Romans. For one should also note that Aristotle's preference for Greeks is not Hellenic chauvinism, because it is not a preference for Greeks as such but for Greeks as instances of a people lying in the mean between extremes. Any other people, therefore, that was similarly in the mean would be similarly praiseworthy and similarly suited to education in virtue.

1327b38 To illustrate the role and need of spirit for virtue (the role and need of thought being obvious), Aristotle picks up on some remarks of Socrates in Plato's *Republic*, which he partly accepts and partly rejects. Socrates is right, on the one hand, in requiring friendliness of rulers, or guardians (as he calls them). For spirit is the seat of friendship as well as of freedom and rule, and the citizens and rulers in the best regime must certainly be friendly to each other (cf. 2.5.1262b7–10), as well as free and capable of ruling. The quotation from Archilochus is apposite since both Aristotle and Archilochus are thinking of fast and firm friendships, not weak ones. In such friendships there is a certain fierceness involved, which is particularly manifest when something threatens or destroys them (as in Archilochus' case). Love must be fierce if it is to endure, and endure even unto death (as will especially be required of soldiers defending the city).

1328a8 Socrates is, however, wrong, on the other hand, in requiring rulers or guardians also to be harsh to strangers. For to be harsh to someone without cause is not a mark of virtue, and magnanimity, which is a virtue and a very great virtue (even if it is not one of the standard four cardinal virtues; *Ethics* 4.3, especially 1124a1–3), is moreover not savage save to wrongdoers who deserve it. Hence the magnanimous will be fiercely disposed particularly toward relatives and friends who do them wrong, for thus they suffer a double harm. Such fierceness toward injustice mirrors the fierceness in loving just mentioned and on both counts shows why spirit, if it is such a powerful aid to justice and friendship, is needed in the citizens of the best regime. It will have to be directed by prudence, of course (*Ethics* 6.13.1144b8–17), and that is why to spirit thought must be added for thus the citizens will be educable in all necessary respects.[33]

---

32. Newman thinks that Aristotle does suppose they are fixed (1:320–22).

33. There is therefore no reason to suppose with Lord (1978b: 348–50) that Aristotle thinks, or is trying to insinuate, that spirit is as much a threat to political life as a support. In its unformed and

1328a17   The summary indicates that Aristotle has reached the end of this part of his discussion, but he adds, to forestall, no doubt, objections about the brevity and generality of his remarks, that more cannot be expected in matters that are properly to be understood through observation on the spot (something that will presumably also be the case with doctors using medical text books; cf. *Ethics* 10.9.1181b2–12).

Chapter 8

~ THE DISPOSITION OF THE MATERIAL

~ THE CLASSES OF HUMAN BEINGS NECESSARY TO A CITY

1328a21   The preceding chapter has ended with a summary and this one begins with the laying down of a fresh principle, so it is evident a further topic is being introduced. The topic, however, is still one concerned with the presuppositions of the best regime, since the discussion of the best regime itself and of its education clearly does not begin until chapter 13. The content of these intervening chapters reveals that they are not about further materials the city needs (they are as much about human beings and territory as the previous four), but rather about how these materials must be disposed within the city if the city is to be best. The disposition of human beings is examined first and then the disposition of the territory and the site of city.

As regards disposing the human beings, it is obviously necessary first to know what human beings there are to be disposed and what differences exist among them. Hence it is necessary to know all the human beings that must be present if there is to be a city and how they must be present. To accomplish this Aristotle first considers how the things a city needs in order to exist differ among each other. The principle he lays down is a general one about the difference between proper parts and necessary conditions. The principle itself is regarded as obvious and to be found in any natural whole (one may think of plants where the earth is not part of them but something they certainly need in order to be, and of animals or fish where air and water have the same character). As regards communities, such as a city is, what distinguishes proper parts from necessary conditions is the sharing together that constitutes the community as the community it is (just as in the case of plants and animals the proper parts are things that constitute the body that the animal or plant is).

The point that Aristotle is making here is evidently a definitional one, for only

---

uneducated state, spirit may well be double-edged, just like any other natural quality. But without it the citizens will not be properly educable and it is as educable that Aristotle is now speaking of both it and them; cf. Saxonhouse (1983).

those who share something in common can be said to form a community, and only as regards what they thus share. So those, for instance, are parts of a community in food or land who share together in the food or land, whether equally or not. By contrast things that are related to the community as for its sake, but not also as sharing in what is common, are only related to each other by way of making and receiving and not by way of sharing; hence they can only be necessary conditions. The examples of tool and maker illustrate the point: the parts of a house are the bricks and mortar that constitute it (as the parts of the body are what constitute the animal), but the builder and his tools are external agents that are necessary for the existence of the house but are manifestly not part of it.[34]

1328a33 The immediate consequence of this principle as applied to the city is that property, which is merely an instrument for the city, is not a proper part of the city, and hence no living things that belong to property are part of the city either (notably animals and slaves, which are, however, parts of the household, 1.3). The parts of the city can only be those in it who are similar and commune together in the best possible life (and slaves are not similar nor indeed capable of the best life). A corollary that Aristotle next expressly draws is that since happiness understood as the complete exercise of virtue, which is the point of the city, cannot be shared in by everyone to the same degree, and by some not at all, then that is why actual cities and regimes come in different kinds. For because of the different ways people's capacity makes them conceive and pursue happiness (whether truly or falsely), the regimes they make when they are in control of the city are necessarily different too (as was in effect stated earlier, 3.7 and 8, but also 6.1278b11–15, for regimes differ according to the character of the ruling body, and the ruling body gets its character from what it pursues and thinks is most worth pursuing). This corollary anticipates what Aristotle argues in the next chapter, that in the best regime, by contrast with others that are not best, not everyone in the city will share in the regime.

1328b2 Having distinguished between parts and necessary conditions, Aristotle comes now to list what are all the things a city needs, since under this head must be included parts as well as conditions. What a city needs can in turn be discovered from all the things that a city needs to have done if it is to exist. They are six in total: food, the arts (the instruments of life), arms (the instruments of defense both within and without), wealth (to supply these instruments), care of

---

34. Barker's complaint (1946: 298 n2) that the builder is not the "means" but rather the house is, since the builder is a man and an "end in himself," misses the point. The builder qua builder is a means to the building of the house and not part of the house, however much it may also be true that the house, once built, is a means or instrument for those who live in it. Still it is true that Aristotle regards some human beings as instruments because they are natural slaves. That slaves are nevertheless said to form a community with masters (1.2.1252b9–10) is doubtless because slaves, though instruments for masters, do also share something in common with them, namely preservation and life in the household (1.2.1252a30–34, 13.1260a39–40; and cf. *Ethics* 8.11.1161a32–b8).

the gods (which is primary or first in importance, since all things depend on the gods, especially in a city according to prayer), judgment concerning the just and advantageous (which is most necessary since by this the disposition of the other things are determined).

1328b15 The reason for all these things is straightforward: the city is a community self-sufficient for life and all these are needed together if the city is to be self-sufficient. Consequently the human beings needed must follow accordingly and there must be human beings to do each of these works.

Later, in 6(4).4.1290b39–1291a40, Aristotle lists eight parts of a city, adding merchants, laborers, and officials to the list he gives here, and omitting priests. This difference between the two lists, which has naturally exercised scholars,[35] may perhaps best be explained by the fact that here Aristotle's aim is to decide things in the best regime, while there his aim is to decide how and why there are several kinds of regimes. So merchants, for instance, while they exist in most cities, need not exist in the best city, which is supposed to be self-sufficient from its own resources, and moreover any merchants there are will not inhabit the city but be separated off in the port. Again, laborers need not exist in the best city, or not a class of laborers distinct from artisans and farmers. Officials, by contrast, will be needed, but since all the citizens in the best city are part of the ruling body, there need be no officials over and above those who are deciding questions of justice and advantage generally. As for priests, they must clearly be present in the best city, for, apart from the fact that the best city depends on prayer, piety to the gods must be part of the best life just as theology is part of philosophy (*Metaphysics* 5.1.1026a15–25)—and philosophy is the main virtue of leisure in the best city (4(7).15.1334a23, 31–34). Further, priesthood is to be the work of the retired citizens. Priests will, of course, exist in other cities as well, even in those that do not care about philosophy and virtue. But cities will not have different regimes because of priests qua priests (for priests will doubtless tend to be drawn from the ruling body, whoever that ruling body is). So priests do not need to be mentioned in the later list. Cities will, however, have different regimes because of the presence or absence in the ruling body of merchants and laborers, so these do need to be mentioned in the later list.

Chapter 9

～ THE SEPARATION OF THE CLASSES FROM EACH OTHER

～ STATEMENT AND PROOF OF THE SEPARATION

1328b24 Having stated the classes necessary to a city, Aristotle turns now to ask whether everyone is to share in every work or class or not. One might have

---

35. Barker (1946: 299 n2), Newman (1:567–69), Schütrumpf (1991: 1:51–53).

expected him to ask instead which of these classes are parts as opposed to necessary conditions. But that is in fact what he is doing, for to ask whether everyone should do every work is to ask whether every work is compatible with sharing the happiness of the city, and sharing the happiness of the city is, as he showed in the previous chapter, the criterion for distinguishing parts from necessary conditions.

In stating his opening question, Aristotle lists three possibilities: whether everyone is to do every work, whether different persons are to do each work, whether some works must be private and some common. We might gloss this as whether every work is shared, or none is, or only some. But as regards the third Aristotle asks if some must *of necessity* (1328b28) be private and others common, by which he must mean (as he goes on to argue) whether a differentiation of works, some shared and others not, is necessary with respect to living the best life. For that every work could in principle be shared by everyone is proved by the existence of democracy (where everyone shares in rule and where, in principle, anyone might have any office). But Aristotle's concern now is the best regime, and what he proceeds to argue is that in the best regime some tasks must be shared by some and others not. Thereby he is able to exclude, without having to treat separately, all the other possibilities, for these, even if actual in other regimes, are not fit for the best regime.[36]

1328b33   The question, then, concerns the separation of the classes and their respective work in the best regime, and Aristotle proceeds to answer it from the first principle of what a regime is. He lays down the following argument: (1) the best regime is that under which the city, that is, the multitude of citizens, can live the best and happiest life; (2) this life is the life of virtue (as was shown in 4(7).1–3); (3) therefore the best regime is that under which the citizens live virtuously. From this and from the further premise that (4) the mechanical and commercial and farming lives are incompatible with a life of virtue, it follows that (5) the citizens cannot share in these works or be members of these classes and, conversely, that members of these classes cannot be citizens.[37] For artisans, or mechanics,

---

36. Of the other possibilities some are impractical (if some or all works are done by no one, the city could not survive, and if some or all people do nothing, they cannot belong to the city), and as regards the others (everyone does every work; no one does every work but each a separate one; everyone does some works but others are done only by some; some do every work, but others only some or one work; some do some works and others others), the first four automatically fall away when Aristotle proves that the last, with the "some" differentiated according to virtue, is what fits the best regime. That he nevertheless remarks here that the first of them is actual in democracy and the last, with the "some" differentiated according to wealth, actual in oligarchy (and, we might perhaps add, the third and fourth actual in certain mixed regimes—the second only being actual, if at all, in Plato's *Republic*), serves to show how the principles he uses to determine the best regime also determine the other regimes, and hence serves to keep in view the practical reality of those principles (a point that is also proved by his remark in the previous chapter that different ways of understanding and pursuing happiness determine different regimes). But he turns to these points and makes them explicit later, 6(4).4–6.

37. This conclusion would, of course, be rejected by most modern political theorists and practi-

and businessmen live lives that damage the body and give no place to virtue (1.11.1258b37–39, 8(6).4.1319a26–28), and farmers have no leisure, and leisure is evidently needed for the life of virtue.

1329a2 Aristotle has thus excluded the first two works or classes from the parts of the city and from the citizens. He now shows how all the remaining classes are parts and must be citizens. This is manifest, to begin with, about the warriors and those who judge and deliberate (since the whole regime and its life are in their control). The only problem is whether the same people should be in both classes, for reason requires that they both should and should not be. They should not be because the works are different and require different qualities; they should be because warriors, who have the power to preserve or destroy the regime, will not put up with being ruled all the time. The answer is neatly provided by nature herself. People become different as they grow, and so they should be, and be educated to be, warriors when younger and judges and deliberators when older. This is certainly possible because ruling is learned by being ruled (3.4), and because such learning occurs especially in armies where the young progressively rise up the ranks to higher levels of rule as they get older, becoming generals, and thereby sharers in the highest counsels of the city, by maturity. In this simple and rather obvious way Aristotle himself neatly avoids a problem in Carthage (2.11.1273b8–18), since he does not concentrate rule in few hands but has it spread progressively through the whole mass of citizens,[38] and also a problem in Plato's *Republic* (2.5.1264b6–15), since he preserves the difference between the functions and qualities of soldiers and rulers but is not saddled with a class of soldiers most of whom are prevented from ruling.

1329a17 As regards the next class, that of the wealthy, this too should be the same as the class of soldiers and of judges and deliberators. The reason is simple: (1) the citizens need prosperity (otherwise they would not have the leisure or the equipment required to practice virtue); (2) these classes, and not the others, are the citizens; (3) therefore these should have the property which is the basis of

---

tioners, socialists and liberal democrats in particular. But the reason is that they would reject Aristotle's premise, that the city, or the state, exists for virtue and that virtue is aristocratic; cf. Sinclair/Saunders (1981: 412). Note also that those in the best regime who live mechanical or commercial or farming lives will necessarily have the condition of natural slaves (for they are manifestly incapable of the happiness that is the object of the best regime, 4(7).8.1328a35–b2, and so will be such that their best work from the point of view of the best regime is the use of the body, 1.5.1254b17–20). There will be no injustice therefore in their being treated as slaves (that is, in their being regarded as necessary to, but not part of, the city), and so no reason to doubt, on this account, the justice of Aristotle's best regime; contra Annas (1996), and see also Miller (1996: 898–900), both of whom, however, suppose, falsely, that slave by nature means, for Aristotle, slave by birth (see the commentary on 1.5).

38. Newman's reservations here about the wisdom of excluding the young from deliberation (3:371) rather miss Aristotle's point, which allows for *progressive* introduction to deliberation, and would doubtless allow for quicker introduction for the young who advanced quicker.

prosperity. That the others are not citizens has just been shown and is evident from the very supposition of the best regime: the mechanics lack virtue and so are incapable of the happiness that, by definition, all the citizens in the best regime should have, and the farmers, as is shown at the end of the next chapter, are to be slaves. By thus giving the wealth to the citizens Aristotle avoids another fault criticized earlier, the Carthaginian fault of not ensuring that the virtuous have the wealth to be at leisure for rule (2.11.1273a21–b7).

1329a27 The only class now left is the priests and these too must be citizens (priesthood is first in importance, as noted earlier, at 4(7).8.1328b11–13, and so should presumably be exercised by those having importance in the city, namely citizens). But as the citizens have been distributed among the armed and deliberative class, and as it befits the old to give service to the gods and to rest in their company (for death is near and earthly concerns are fading away), the solution is again to follow a natural discrimination and give the priesthood to citizens who have passed through the other two stages and are now worn out with age.

Aristotle thus arranges for the old to retire from rule while still giving them something important to do for the city, whereby he neatly avoids another fault noted earlier, that of Sparta, where senators served for life despite the fact that thought too gets old (2.9.1270b38–1271a1). Feebleness of thought would, doubtless, only be a hindrance in the priesthood if it was especially severe, since the performance of rituals is regular and fixed and unhurried; and the aged could hardly rest better than in devotion to the highest things, which are the gods, or in theology, which is first in philosophy (*Metaphysics* 6.1.1026a10–32), as the care of the gods is first in the city (4(7).8.1328b11–13).

Chapter 10

~ CONFIRMATION FROM ANCIENT PRECEDENTS

1329a40 Doubts have been expressed by scholars about the authenticity of this next passage.[39] But it actually fits very well where it is since to confirm the conclusions of reason by appeal to common and long-established opinion and practice is not only Aristotelian in style[40] but makes much philosophical sense. The correctness of a deduction can be confirmed if we see that others, and others with a reputation for wisdom, have long reached the same conclusion (cf. 2.5.1264a1–5, *Ethics* 1.8.1098b9–12). So Aristotle accordingly confirms the correctness of dividing the city's inhabitants into classes, and in particular of separating the fighting from the farming class, by appeal to ancient practice in Egypt and Crete.

39. Barker (1946: 306 nDDD), Newman (1:573–75, 3:382–83), Susemihl and Hicks (1894: 511).
40. As Newman notes (1:574).

1329b5 The following remarks about Italy and common messes, with their seemingly irrelevant and merely antiquarian detail, are what mainly cause the scholarly doubts about this passage. But we can defend it on the ground, first, that common messes naturally tie in with the separation of fighters from farmers (and messes are anyway about to be discussed by Aristotle). For a class of fighters devoted to training and the practice of virtue, and who are not just away from home on occasions of particular need but as a matter of course, will necessarily be eating much together. They will therefore need someone to provide them with food, and these others must be a class distinct from them. For even if, as a matter of fact, both ideas, distinct classes on the one hand and common messes on the other, can be separately developed, they naturally belong together. Second, as regards the anecdotal details, it can be argued that they are designed to confirm the basic coherence of the story being told and so to confirm its reliability and therewith the philosophical point at issue, namely the antiquity of such practices.

So, as regards the story of Italus and common messes, the size of the area of land named after him is noted and so shown to be large enough to have been home to nomads and small enough for Italus to have been able to settle them into farmers and give them all laws. That they lacked laws as nomads and received them, and common messes, only when settled, and that this was due to one man and that, in honor of him, they changed their name, all add to the coherence and plausibility of the story. But even were the story not wholly true, it is manifestly old. This is shown by the specially noted facts that, first, the practice of common messes is widely scattered over the whole area as well as beyond, and that, second, the preservation of this practice and of other laws of Italus is not universal among those who trace themselves back to him. For traditions take time both to spread widely and to suffer here and there some decay. Hence, if the story is old, the idea and practice of common messes must be old too.

1329b22 Having told the tale, Aristotle now points the philosophical moral. Since the separation of classes and common messes are both ancient and were, indeed, discovered more than once, it is reasonable to suppose the same of other discoveries too. Confirmation of this can be taken from the fact that there is an abiding and universal cause of discovery among men, namely need first and afterward desire for what goes beyond need. Consequently the same must be supposed about the regime, a supposition that the case of Egypt helps confirm (for if Egyptians are the most ancient people and have a tradition of political arrangement, political arrangement must have been discovered in the past and not just have been discovered for the first time now). The proper procedure, then, for philosophers of the regime is not to make proposals as if they were first and were starting from scratch (like Socrates and Hippodamus, 2.5, 8), but instead to follow what has already been discovered and only to look for something new where they find a lack.

1329b36 Next Aristotle turns to the disposition of the territory and first from the point of view of getting provisions and then from the point of view of the site of the city. That he is beginning a new section he indicates by summarizing the relevant conclusions from earlier parts of the discussion. But since now he intends to speak of the division of the territory and who is to farm it, he also recalls and lays down the conditions or ends that the answers to these questions must satisfy, for it is clearly from these conditions that the answers will be discovered.

The conditions he lays down are four: (1) property should be privately possessed, though be made common in use and be such that no one lacks for food (from 2.5.1263a22–40); (2) there should be common messes (from the practice of all the regimes praised in book 2); (3) all citizens should share in these messes and not be excluded by poverty (from 2.9.1271a26–37); (4) expenses relating to the gods are a common concern. Aristotle promises a later discussion of point (2) but takes its necessity now from common agreement. No such later discussion is to be found but, since, like the postponed discussion of the measure for determining the amount of property (4(7).5.1326b30–39), it would seem to belong to the question of education in virtue (for messes are a means of such education, 2.5.1263b37–1264a1), it was probably meant to come somewhere after the present end of book 5(8).

1330a9 The solution Aristotle offers, wherein, as in other matters of the best regime, he partially follows and partially corrects Plato's *Laws*,[41] is to divide the land into two divisions of two: common land with one part for the gods and another for the common messes; and private land with one part near the city and another near the border, something that is both equal, he says (property near the city being intrinsically more desirable), and, for the obvious reason given, better with respect to war against neighbors.[42] There will doubtless be some inconveniences involved in managing two plots of land, but the advantages are greater and the inconveniences are not such as would be involved in managing a household on each plot as well (a problem in the *Laws*, 2.6.1265b24–26).

1330a25 As for the class of farmers, they will be slaves of different races and lacking in spirit, or alternatively barbarian subjects similarly lacking in spirit. They will accordingly, unlike the helots in Sparta for instance (2.9.1269a36–b12), be natural slaves (no spirit means no or little capacity for virtue), and easy to control. The unspoken implication, judging by earlier remarks (4(7).7.1327b27–29), is that

---

41. Newman (3:391–92). On the overall question of Aristotle's indebtedness to the *Laws*, see Barker (1959: 380–82), as well as Newman's notes generally.

42. Cf. the evidence collected by Newman (3:392–93).

these slaves should ideally be taken from the different nations of Asia (those whom Alexander famously conquered).

These slaves will, further, be common on common land and private on private (as recommended earlier in the case of a problem in the regime of Phaleas, 2.7.1267b16–19). The later discussion of how slaves should be treated and why freedom should be held out as a reward is lacking but would again properly belong in the discussion of education in virtue (for how to treat inferiors is part of virtue).[43] The offer of freedom, however, does not mean that these slaves cannot be natural slaves, as several commentators suppose (some of whom also go on to conclude that therefore Aristotle is implicitly conceding that his best regime must be to some extent unjust because it will have to enslave those who do not deserve to be enslaved).[44] For what he argued about slaves earlier (1.6) was that it was unjust to enslave those who are not natural slaves, but this is not the same as saying, nor does it imply, that it is unjust to free (or even not to enslave) some natural slaves.[45]

Further, nothing in that earlier discussion excluded the possibility that natural slaves might be educated out of being natural slaves and thus might earn the right to be free. Worth noting in this regard, indeed, is that some slavish works differ in what they are done for rather than in what is done (4(7).14.1333a6–11), so such works might become a means of educating some slaves to do things for a noble end, and thus of educating them toward freedom.[46]

Chapter 11

~ WITH RESPECT TO THE SITE OF THE CITY

~ HEALTH

1330a34 Aristotle turns next, as he did in chapter 6, to the site of the city and how it should be disposed. Four things are needed, he says, which four are health, military action, political action, and nobility.[47] Health is, of course, a simple necessity, but since health is for action and the actions of the citizens are defense and rule, and since, further, these actions must be virtuous, that is, noble,

---

43. There is in fact a discussion of this question in the possibly spurious *Oeconomica* at 1.5.

44. Annas (1996: 740), Davis (1991–92: 162), Lord (1978b: 343 n17), Nichols (1992: 145, 164), Shulsky, in Lord and O'Connor (1991: 98), Susemihl and Hicks (1894: 518). See also Dobbs (1994: 71–72, 79–80) and Lindsay (1994: 130–34).

45. Cf. Miller (1995: 242 n127).

46. Dobbs (1994: 87–92) suggests that farming might be particularly appropriate for slaves in this regard.

47. Nobility would seem to be the fourth thing, if one goes by the prominence it has in the ensuing discussion, so Newman (3:396), but some suggest that air or water might be, as Sinclair/Saunders (1981: 421) and Jowett (1885: 2:273), though these are perhaps better understood as falling under health.

these three other factors are not only necessary but of greater dignity. Hence they are the focus of most of the discussion. As regards health, Aristotle contents himself with some brief remarks about position with respect to the compass and winds. Doubtless more could be said but doubtless more does not need to be said here; much can be got instead from experts and much else will have to be determined by direct perception (cf. 4(7).5.1326b39–40, 7.1328a19–21).[48]

~ MILITARY ACTION AND NOBILITY

1330a41 Aristotle's remarks on the disposition of the city with respect to military action are all concerned with defense (that the city is near the sea and its territory easy to exit will be enough to secure its capacity for offense and, if necessary, imperial leadership). His initial remarks concern getting in and out of the city and health. They focus on obvious and straightforward but nevertheless vital things that cities have sometimes ignored to their cost.[49] The remarks on health are, despite appearances, not really a return to the previous topic, for they concern disposing the city so that it can survive under siege (and preserving the health of the citizens is vital to that).

1330b17 The fortifications within the city are said to reflect the character of the regime and seem to relate to defense against attack from within as much as from without. So a citadel or acropolis is oligarchic or monarchic presumably because it provides a single defense for the single man or the single group that rule; a plain fits a democracy presumably so that everyone is on a level and no one can achieve a dominance over the mass; several fortified places fit an aristocracy presumably because aristocrats are several, unlike monarchs, and are virtuous, unlike oligarchs, and so can have several centers of defense and control without running the risk of splitting up into opposing factions.[50]

What is curious, however, is that Aristotle makes no recommendation here on his own account, though if the best regime is a kingship or an aristocracy it will need an acropolis in the first case and several fortified places in the second. Perhaps, too, since the best regime might be at times kingly and at times aristocratic, a combination could be achieved: one central and higher acropolis with

48. Jowett (1885: 2:273) cites Vitruvius 1.6 about Mytilene in Lesbos: "The town is magnificently and elegantly built, but it is not wisely positioned. When the south wind blows in the city, people fall ill; when the east wind, they cough; when the north wind, they are restored to health, but they cannot stand in the lanes and streets because of the vehemence of the cold."

49. Newman (3:400) suggests that Aristotle's remarks about securing abundant supplies of water may be directed at Athens. For Athens was not well supplied with drinkable spring water, a lack that must have been keenly felt during the Peloponnesian War when the city was cut off from its territory by enemy action.

50. Jowett makes several of these points (1885: 2:274), as do Kraut (1997: ad loc.) and Peter of Auvergne (1951: 7.9.1160).

several lesser ones round about. At any rate Aristotle is silent, leaving the matter, no doubt, here as elsewhere, for particular decision in particular cases.

1330b21   Aristotle turns finally to two matters more directly under human control: arranging the houses and streets and having or not having walls. For the first he adopts a characteristic mean between the neatness of Hippodamus' pleasing geometry (2.8.1267b22–23) and the safety of traditional randomness (presumably randomness on the outskirts and in residential areas and neatness toward the center).[51] This mean is provided by another geometrical figure, but taken (with Aristotle's characteristic dry humor) from farmers and not mathematicians or town planners.

1330b32   As regards walls, Aristotle mounts a strong defense of them against attack.[52] The attack is that walls are contrary to virtue (the citizens are to be brave enough to defend the city by themselves and not run for protection behind walls). The defense is fourfold: (1) this view is refuted by the facts—presumably the fall of Sparta, where even the reputedly bravest soldiers were defeated in open battle and the city was left wide open; (2) retreating behind walls may be ignoble if the enemy is not greatly superior, but enemies can be too numerous, and too technically advanced, even for human virtue (divine virtue being another matter), and so walls are a more warlike defense, and hence more in accord with military virtue, than hopeless pitched battles (courage too is a mean, and the rash are no more virtuous than the cowardly); (3) no one thinks it necessary to remove the mountains from the territory or walls from around houses in order to preserve courage, but not having walls around the city is just like doing that; (4) with walls one can use the city in both ways and so have resources against any enemy, but without them one cannot.

1331a10   Walls therefore are necessary and so must be arranged in such a way as to be beautiful as well as militarily adequate, which means in turn keeping up with, and even anticipating, technical advances in offensive warfare. Aristotle is evidently not opposed to technical progress, provided it is governed by the noble, or the concern with virtue, as well as effectiveness.

Chapter 12

∾ POLITICAL ACTION AND NOBILITY

1331a19   Aristotle turns next to dispositions with a view to other activities of the city, and in particular the location of messes for the different classes of

51. The suggestion of Kraut (1997: ad loc.) and Lord (1984: 267 n44). Washington, D.C., illustrates the idea, at least in part, with its broad avenues on the one hand and more irregular residential areas on the other.

52. The attackers are, probably, Plato's *Laws* 778d3–779b7 and admirers of Sparta, Newman (3:406) and Susemihl and Hicks (1894: 522); and see also Dherbey, in Aubenque (1993: 119–32), for a more general discussion of the present passage.

citizens, which messes are of course both necessary and instruments of education. So first, and picking up from the previous chapter, the messes for the young in the army who are serving on garrison duty along the walls should be in their guard-houses, which will obviously assist defense and stimulate to courage and justice (since even meals will be occasions for watchfulness on the city's behalf).

1331a24 Temples and the messes for the offices with most control in the city should obviously go together (for those who judge and deliberate about the useful and the just should be ever mindful of the gods, who are the guardians of justice). But exceptions are to be made in the case of temples specially set aside by law (sacred things set apart and reserved stimulate to reverence and awe) or by the oracle (revelations from the gods themselves obviously take precedence over human wisdom and tradition). These most eminent buildings, and these messes for the most eminent officials, should have an appropriately eminent position over the rest of the city, to celebrate the eminence of virtue and for defense, that is, for both nobility and utility.

1331a30/b1 Below this eminence comes the free square, the square uncontaminated by anything mercenary and vulgar, where the citizens are obviously meant to associate for the sake of virtuous leisure. Consequently putting the gymnasium of the old there is also fitting. The old, of course, are now busy about the temples as priests, and it will be fitting for them to have their place of recreation close at hand. But the reason Aristotle mentions is that thus the teaching of noble fear will not cease even among the old, since their recreation too will be taken under the eyes of the most eminent magistrates and the gods. The fear in question is evidently the fear of offending, by doing something base or ugly in their sight, those whom one is taught to admire and respect (the fear is not the base one of those who are afraid lest they be found out and punished). Hence the same teaching must be secured for the young by having other rulers (those perhaps more directly involved in military matters) spend time among them in their gymnasium.

It is significant that Aristotle wants to continue this teaching of noble fear also for the old. One can perhaps detect a special kindness here. He does not wish to deprive even the old of the helps to the practice of virtue, and so he contrives to have the rulers always in their presence, not, as with the young, by special imposition (which might appear offensive), but rather as a matter of course. It would certainly be tragic (not to say scandalous, especially to the young) if an older man, reaching the end of a life full of virtue, should fall away at its close and through the want of a help that could thus so inoffensively and easily be provided.

1331b1 The commercial square should certainly be separate from the first one (in order not to mix inferior and necessary tasks with higher and free ones), and should naturally also, because of its function, be easy of access for goods from land and sea. It will thus necessarily occupy a lower place away from the free square and the temples, so its position in the physical order of the city will, like theirs, suitably mirror its position in the political order.[53]

1331b4   The messes of the old men will also, like their gymnasia, be near the temples in which they now serve as priests, and the messes of other officials near their place of rule, including the commercial square (where, of course, the regular presence of these magistrates, even when "off duty" as it were, will aid in the preservation of decency and order).

1331b13   The same principles will govern the disposition of buildings about the countryside, where the young again will be on guard duty and must therefore also have their messes. But holy fear and the sanctification of the whole must be continued here by distributing about it temples to gods and heroes.[54]

1331b18   Once these ideas have been put forward, it is easy to see that many other such questions will arise as one descends more to details and particular cases. But it is also easy to see that the answers will be similar and not hard to work out on the basis of the examples already provided. So Aristotle leaves such thinking to our own acts of prayer, and the realization of these prayers to chance (or to the divine providence that controls chance and hears prayer).

Chapter 13

〰 THE BEST REGIME ITSELF

〰 THE GOAL THAT THE REGIME
MUST BE CAPABLE OF ACHIEVING

1331b24   Having dealt with the presuppositions of the regime, Aristotle now turns to the regime itself and how it is made up. The Greek, however, is vague and leaves ambiguous whether this question is about "from which and what sort of persons" or "from which and what sort of things (or elements)" the city is made up (1331b24–25).[55] What, however, Aristotle now proceeds to concentrate on is persons or human beings and to show that those in the best regime must be simply and altogether good, and that, in order to be such, they must be properly educated.

53. Davis (1991–92: 163–68) is right to stress the poetic or symbolic character of Aristotle's town planning here, but he is unduly pessimistic about how far such symbolism in the city can be successful. For what Aristotle points to here, and elsewhere, would seem to have been realized, more or less, whenever and wherever religion has played a dominant role in human life, which is to say always and everywhere—with the possible exception of certain parts of our modern world.

54. A practice not only of the pagan world but of Christendom too, with its ubiquitous shrines and churches to saints, those "heroes of virtue."

55. For instance, Barker (1946: 312) and Jowett (1885: 1:229) say "elements," Lord (1984: 217) says "things," Sinclair/Saunders (1981: 427) says "people."

Besides, the city and the regime are by definition the persons who make them up, for the city is a multitude of citizens (3.1.1274b41, 1275b20–21), and the regime is the ruling body (3.6.1278b11–15). Also, the parts of the city were said earlier to be the citizens (4(7).9). So it is perhaps better to read "persons" or "human beings" and not "things" in this first sentence (compare the opening words of the next chapter: "But since every political community is made up of rulers and ruled . . . ," 1332b12–13). Aristotle has already discussed the quality of the persons who must make up the best regime (4(7).7), but only with respect to what nature they are to have. Here by contrast he intends, as the next section makes clear, to determine how, given this nature, they are to be educated so that they will actually come to possess blessedness and be nobly governed (and not merely have the natural capacity for this).

Aristotle begins, as is his wont, by a return to first principles. The first principle in the case of living blessedly is that such living, or such well-being, must necessarily consist in two things, namely getting the goal of blessedness right and getting the way to it right. Or, to use Aristotle's words, it consists in the right laying down of the end of actions and in the finding of the actions that bear on that end (which actions will not simply be those that are means to the end, but also and much more those that constitute it, for the end is itself activity, 4(7).3.1325b14–30). Error can occur in either or both respects, as the illustration from medicine shows, and it is clear from the concrete instances in book 2 (especially Sparta) that such errors have often enough been committed. But clearly politics, like medicine or any other art, must have both end and the way to it correct. So Aristotle proceeds now to determine these. First he determines the end, and then, from the next section onward, the way to it.

1331b39　The end, as is universally agreed, is happiness, but happiness does not come automatically and it presupposes conditions. Not everyone is fit for happiness, or fit in the same way: some lack the necessary fortune (happiness requires the goods of fortune); some need more fortune than others (the sickly and weak, for instance, than the healthy and strong); some lack the requisite nature (happiness requires people with the natural capacity for happiness, which natural slaves, for instance, do not have); some lack the necessary knowledge or choice (they are capable of happiness but pursue it wrongly).[56] The best regime, however, must be that under which the city would be best governed, and the best governed city must be that under a regime where it can most of all be happy. Hence

---

56. The belief that happiness, or its pursuit, is everyone's right, and something everyone can attain, rests on the belief that happiness is peculiar to each and is the satisfaction of one's desires, whatever those desires may happen to be. But, for Aristotle, happiness is something one and the same for all and consists in acts of virtue, not any acts and not any pleasures.

it can lack nothing of what belongs to happiness. Accordingly happiness and its conditions need to be set down first.

Now Aristotle has discussed this question several times before, so one might wonder why he needs to discuss it again. But it is typical of him to go over the same point several times when it arises in several different contexts, especially if, as here, the point concerns a matter of the highest importance which people nevertheless persist in getting wrong.[57] Moreover, it is typical of him to repeat such points in ways that differ significantly according to the context. So here, for instance, he refers to the *Ethics* and not, as he did in 4(7).1, to external discourses, and he does so, perhaps, in order to stress, what is also stressed in the *Ethics*, that happiness needs not only an abundance of external goods but also the right use of them, and that therefore happiness needs good education, not just good fortune (contrary to the opinion of many), and education in using external goods, not just in acquiring them (contrary to the opinion of the Spartans).

1332a7 Continuing his return to first principles, Aristotle recalls the first principle in the case of happiness, namely its definition. He refers to the *Ethics*, but somewhat casually, perhaps because the definition is not given there in exactly the same words as it is here. The thought is, nevertheless, the same, and Aristotle is doubtless more interested in accurate repetition of thought than accurate repetition of words. The definition stresses two things: first, that happiness is not virtue merely but the exercising or using of virtue and, second, that this exercise must not be compromised or limited in any way but must instead be unconditional and absolute. The first point is clear (happiness is acting well, not merely being able to act well), and the second Aristotle at once explains. An act of virtue is conditional if it is necessitated, and it is not absolute if it is noble only because of that necessity. So punishment is an act of virtue and noble, but only on the supposition that someone has done something that is not noble. For it is crime that makes punishment necessary (one only chooses to punish because one is compelled to do so by crime), and only this necessity makes it noble (inflicting pain is not in itself or absolutely noble). By contrast, bestowing rewards and honors is an act of virtue that is unconditional and absolute, for bestowing goods is in itself absolutely or simply good, and one would naturally choose to have acts that deserve to be rewarded whereas one would not choose to have acts that deserve to be punished.[58]

57. Some remarks of Cicero, *Disputationes Tusculanae* 5.7.18–19, quoted by Newman (2:xxix–xxx), about the style of philosophic writings are also very much to the point: "But such is the manner of geometricians; it is not the manner of philosophers. For when geometricians want to teach something, they assume as agreed and proved anything relevant to the matter that has been taught already. They only expound what they have written nothing about previously. Philosophers collect all that bears on the matter in hand, whatever it is, even though it has been discussed elsewhere."

58. As Newman rightly remarks (3:424).

1332a19   This explanation is now applied to happiness. A serious man confronted by misfortune would act nobly by bearing his misfortune well, but such acting is, like punishment, noble only by necessity. For misfortune is not choiceworthy for its own sake (just as crime is not either), and bearing misfortune well is noble only because misfortune makes it necessary (as punishment is only noble because crime makes it necessary). Blessedness, however, consists in the opposite, that is, in good fortune and using good fortune well, for the serious man is such that, because of his virtue, good fortune is good for him. That is why people suppose that happiness exists in good fortune simply, and not first and foremost in virtue (an opinion that is, however, as absurd as supposing good lyre playing is caused by having a good lyre). In fact, however, hardship and punishment are better for the nonvirtuous, both to deprive them of opportunities for vice and also to move them, if possible, toward virtue.

There is some dispute here among scholars as to whether Aristotle's references are to the *Nicomachean Ethics* (which I refer to normally as the *Ethics* simply) or to the *Eudemian Ethics*.[59] The opinion that they are to the latter is based on certain verbal resemblances. But similar verbal resemblances can be found in the former.[60] More relevantly, however, there is more doctrinal, as opposed to verbal, resemblance to the *Nicomachean* than to the *Eudemian*, for the latter has no equivalent of the long discussion in the former about the virtuous man needing the goods of fortune to be fully happy but being able to use misfortune well if it befalls him.[61] That the doctrinal or substantial resemblances should be given greater weight is not only reasonable in itself but is perhaps confirmed by Aristotle's opening casual or even dismissive reference to his ethical discussions, for that suggests, as already noted, that his concern is less to give exact quotations than to repeat certain teachings.

∾ THAT ACHIEVING THIS GOAL REQUIRES EDUCATION

1332a28   Having thus stated the goal, Aristotle comes now to determine the way to reach it, and as this way is chiefly education, the discussion of this second question continues in effect to the end of the next book when the treatment of the best regime itself ends. The goal, as just stated, is both the exercise of virtue and the enjoyment of an abundance of external goods; hence the way to this goal must

59. That they are to the *Eudemian* was argued by Jaeger (1923/1934: 283–85); see also Kraut (1997: ad loc.), Keyt and Miller (1991: 6), Newman (1:575–76, 3:428), Vander Waerdt (1991: 235).

60. On the definition of happiness as perfect exercise and use of virtue, see *Nicomachean Ethics* 1.8.1098b31–33, 11.1101a14–21, 13.11025a5–6, and *Eudemian Ethics* 2.1.1219a38–b3. On the serious man being such that what is simply good is good for him, see *Nicomachean Ethics* 1.8.1099a11–15, 3.4, 5.1.1129b1–6, 5.9.1137a26–30, 9.9.1170a14–16, and *Eudemian Ethics* 7.2.1236b36–1237a3, 8.15.1248b26–37. Cf. also *Magna Moralia* 2.9.

61. As Jowett rightly notes (1885: 2:280).

require getting both virtue and such goods. The latter, however, can only be assumed as being the work of chance and prayer. The former is not the work of chance but of knowledge and choice, namely the knowledge and choice of the legislator in making the citizens, and thereby the city, virtuous. The question then returns to the work of the legislator in making all the citizens serious or virtuous (which was the question posed at the end of the *Ethics* and at the end of the preceding book, 3.18).

In saying that in the best city all the citizens share in the regime, Aristotle is following his determination from 3.1, that a citizen is one who shares in deliberation and judgment. He is also following his determination (from 4(7).9) that the young will be in the army but not in the body that deliberates and judges. For the young are not citizens in the strict sense but are becoming citizens in the strict sense through the education to rule that, in part, they are getting through service in the army (as argued in 3.4).[62] That each citizen individually is to be serious or virtuous is not only better in itself, as Aristotle here says, but it follows from the fact that the best regime is to be a kingship or an aristocracy as opposed to a polity, for in the former all are virtuous individually whereas in the latter all are virtuous only as a body and not individually.

1332a38　The three things through which people become serious or virtuous—nature, habits, and reason—are the same, of course, as those listed in the *Ethics* (10.9.1179b20–31), and Aristotle repeats here more or less what he said there. For it is here, in fact, that he most directly answers the questions posed at the end of the *Ethics*. One must indeed be born first, and born human and of a certain sort in body and soul[63] (which are not trivial remarks, because some human beings are born not much different from animals—as for instance some natural slaves and barbarians; cf. *Ethics* 7.1.1145a27–32—and because some human beings do not have the nature for education in the best regime; see 4(7).7.1327b20–38 and 7(5).12.1316a8–11). But since habits can make us worse, nature is not enough; and even if our habits are good, reason can be persuaded to make us go against habits as well as nature. All three, therefore, need to be harmonized. The sort of nature, however, that the legislator needs in the citizens was explained before, so since habits and reason are developed through the two sorts of education, habituation and listening, the legislator's work is education. Education, therefore, becomes necessarily the whole content of Aristotle's discussion of the best regime.

---

62. There is thus, properly considered, no disharmony between what Aristotle says here and what he said in those previous chapters. Newman thinks there is some disharmony (1:324), though he seems to be in two minds on the issue since he speaks otherwise later (1:570).

63. My rendering in the translation at this point (1332a40–42) is rather inaccurate. I wrote: "For nature must first produce us with the quality of body and soul of a human being and not of some other animal." A more accurate rendering would be: "For one must be born first such as a human being is and not some other animal, so also born of a certain sort in body and soul."

Chapter 14

∽ THE EDUCATION REQUIRED

∽ EDUCATION IS TO FORM BOTH RULED AND RULERS

1332b12 Since education is now the object of concern, the obvious thing to do next is to determine what the education will be. Aristotle proceeds now to do this step by step. The first step is to consider if there is to be one education or several, or whether everyone is to have the same education or different persons are to have different ones. A political community is a combination of rulers and ruled, and so different persons will have different educations if some are to be educated for ruling and others for being ruled, while they will all have the same education if everyone is to be educated for both. The question, then, is whether different persons are to be the rulers and ruled (that is, some always ruling and some always being ruled) or the same persons must be both (that is, the same persons sometimes being ruled and sometimes ruling).

1332b16 The condition for some always ruling and others always being ruled is, as argued before (3.13), such a superiority of the rulers over the ruled that there is no commensurability between them.[64] This will be the case if the rulers are as superior in body and soul as gods and heroes are (for then they will be incommensurable), and if this is manifest and indisputable to the ruled (for then their rule will be voluntarily embraced and be a source of unity and friendship and not of faction and enmity). This superiority will also have to be manifest in body as well as in soul, and in body first, for superiority in soul only emerges over time, but the superiority of permanent rulers must be manifest already at birth if they are to be educated for rule from the beginning. Still, provided these conditions are met, then clearly the permanent rule of such persons will be best.

Getting these conditions is, however, the problem; not indeed that it is impossible, but it is certainly not easy. It is not impossible because the conditions are, according to Scylax' report, met in India, but it is not easy because the conditions are not obviously met elsewhere (and perhaps even Scylax' report should be regarded with skepticism).[65] So, in the absence of such superiority on the part of

---

64. That the citizens of the best regime have this sort of incommensurable superiority over the noncitizens goes without saying, because the noncitizens are to be natural slaves and the citizens natural masters. But what is now in question is whether any among the free in the best regime will have this sort of superiority over the rest of the free. If so, they will rule as kings; if not, the body of the free will together rule as aristocrats.

65. One may nevertheless note the following that Newman quotes from a more recent report about Polynesia (3:435): "Throughout Polynesia the chiefs and upper classes are taller than the lower orders, and with a finer physical they combine a greater mental development. They are in every respect superior to the people whom they rule. They are as genuine an aristocracy as ever existed in any

some, everyone must share in ruling and being ruled by turns. This is both just, since justice for equals or similars is sharing equally, and safe, since there will be no disaffected body of unjustly excluded similars who could easily make themselves strong enough to overthrow the regime.

Now, in thus leaving aside Indian-style kings, Aristotle would seem to be excluding kingship from further consideration and concentrating only on aristocracy. But this seems to create a problem. For he had earlier spoken of the best city as either a kingship or an aristocracy and that, under the heading of the best regime, both were included. He had also said that the education and habits that make a man good would also make him political (that is, aristocratic) and kingly (3.18.1288a39–b2). But now it appears that he is only going to discuss aristocracy and the education of aristocrats. This problem is less serious than has been supposed.[66] For if both regimes are the best regime and if the education that makes aristocrats also makes kings, then to speak about aristocracy and aristocratic education is also to speak about kingship and royal education. The difference would presumably be, first, that in an aristocracy there would be no one or no family so surpassing the others in excellence of soul and body as to deserve to rule alone while the rest were always ruled, and, second, that aristocratic education would include education to be ruled as well as to rule while royal education would only include the latter. But an aristocracy could, one supposes, easily become a kingship if some man or some family emerged that was manifestly superior, and aristocratic education could easily become kingly education if the king received one part of it and not the other and received it at a more intense and elevated level. Conversely a kingship could easily become an aristocracy if the king perished without leaving anyone his like to succeed him. For the ruled, because educated to be ruled by a king, and because actually having been ruled by a king, would have been educated also to rule (though as aristocrats and not as kings).

1332b32   Still, even in the case of aristocracy where the same persons both rule and are ruled, rulers and ruled must differ qua rulers and ruled (cf. 1.12.1259b6–10, 2.2.1261a37–b6). Their difference in this respect, however, was stated earlier, namely that, following the natural distinction of ages, they are ruled as younger and rule as older (and this arrangement does not run the risk of provoking the young to revolt, especially the young educated to virtue and to the exercise of rule later in the place of their retired fathers). So the same persons rule and are ruled but at different

country." A natural king, then, among the Polynesians would be one of the aristocrats who possessed and manifested these aristocratic qualities in a supreme or surpassing way.

66. Newman (1:294–95, 4:144) thinks the problem poses a genuine puzzle. Schütrumpf (1991: 2:580–81) goes so far as to reject altogether the idea that the best regime of 4(7) and 5(8) is the best regime spoken of in 3. But even if the apparent absence of kingship is a problem here, such a rejection is too extreme for, as Mulgan correctly argues (1977: 101), the aristocracy of 4(7) and 5(8) is an aristocracy in the sense of 3; cf. also Vander Waerdt (1985: 252–53, 268).

ages. Consequently their education too will be the same and different. It will be the same because all will be taught the same things but it will be different because they will be taught different things at different times (taught to be ruled first, and then, through being ruled, taught to rule).

1333a3/11 As regards being taught to be ruled, this will concern teaching the young how to be ruled as free men (and not how to be ruled despotically as slaves), and also how to do whatever they do for the right end. Hence the young should even be commanded to do some menial and seemingly slavish things, for these things are not slavish in themselves but in why they are done (whether nobly, on one's own account and for virtue, or slavishly, on account of others, 5(8).2.1337b17–21). As regards being taught to rule, which is achieved through being ruled, this is the same as being taught to be a good man. So the question becomes how to rule citizens so as to make them good men, or what pursuits to give them and what the end of the best life is toward which they are to be directed. Aristotle mentions the end of the best life again because, though it was decided earlier that the best life was a life of virtue, what has to be decided now (as becomes clear) is which virtues and which actions a life of virtue has its end in.

~ EDUCATION MUST FOLLOW THE DIVISION OF THE SOUL

~ WHAT THE DIVISION IS

1333a16 Aristotle comes now to answer this question of what the end of the best life is (the other question of what pursuits the citizens are to follow, both as younger and older, is taken up from chapter 16 onward). The answer is to be found from the nature or parts of the soul, since it is by the virtues of these parts, the part that has reason and the part that follows reason, that men are good (*Ethics* 1.13). What decides which of these the end is more to be found in is the principle, universal to nature and art, that (1) the worse is for the sake of the better. So since (2) the part that has reason is clearly better than the part that only listens to reason (the goodness of the second is derivative from the goodness of the first), it necessarily follows that (3) the end is in the part of the soul that has reason. This part is itself divided into parts, practical and theoretical. The acts of all these parts are divided similarly, namely the acts of the part that does not have reason and the acts of the two parts within the part that does have reason. The latter two acts must again be better. Consequently for those who can attain "all or the two" (1333a29), the acts of the part that is by nature better must be better, since the highest attainable is always most worth choosing.

What Aristotle means here by "all or the two" is a little unclear. The standard view takes "all" and "two" as alternatives and interprets "all" as being all three acts (those of the part without reason, those of practical reason, and those of contemplative or theoretical reason), and "two" as being the acts of the part without reason and the acts of practical reason, but not the acts of contemplative or theoretical reason.[67] Aristotle is then understood to be saying that those in the best city who can attain only the two acts should prefer the acts of practical reason, but that those who can attain all three should prefer the acts of contemplative or theoretical reason, for these belong to the superior part of the soul. Aristotle is then sometimes further understood as implying that many or most in the best city will not be capable of contemplative or theoretical reason. But one could perhaps regard "the two" as referring to the two parts of the soul (the part without and the part with reason),[68] and then understand Aristotle to be speaking of those capable of attaining all three acts or both parts of the soul and so not to be proposing alternatives but just saying the same thing in a different way. Or again one could regard "the two" as referring to the acts of practical reason and the acts of contemplative or theoretical reason, and understand Aristotle to be speaking of those capable of attaining all three acts or of attaining these two in particular.

One or other of these latter interpretations is perhaps better because, despite the standard view, Aristotle does not say anything here about the superiority of contemplative or theoretical to practical reason (though he does so speak elsewhere; Ethics 10.7.1177a12–18, 1177b30–1178a8). Indeed, since he argued earlier for a combination of the political and contemplative, or philosophical, in the "practical life" of the best city (4(7).2–3), it would seem contrary to his intention now to be separating them and to be implying that some in the best city will be capable of a practical life but not of a philosophical or contemplative life. The hierarchy he draws in this section is not between the practical and contemplative or theoretical lives, but between war and peace, occupation and leisure (where the practical and theoretical are together constitutive of peace and leisure), and indeed, as the next chapter indicates, all the citizens in the best regime will need, and so must be capable of, the virtue of philosophy.[69]

1333a30   As regards the division of life as a whole into occupation and leisure, war and peace, and of actions into the useful and the noble, choice must be

67. Barker (1946: 320 nEEE), Kraut (1997: ad loc.), Lord (1978b: 355; 1982: 49–50), Miller (1995: 226 n86), Newman (3:441), Solmsen (1964: 218), Vander Waerdt (1985: 258). But see the criticisms of Depew, in Keyt and Miller (1991: 371–72).

68. The interpretation of Demont, in Aubenque (1993: 219 n30).

69. See the exact remarks of Demont, in Aubenque (1993: 218–21). There is no reason to suppose that by philosophy is meant philosophy in some lesser sense, and not in the full sense which includes theoretical contemplation. For even if the present passage (about "all or the two") is read and interpreted according to the standard view, it still does not mean that the education of the citizens of the best city will not include, or will downplay, theoretical philosophy (as Kraut, Lord, Solmsen, and Vander Waerdt wish). On the contrary, it means that as many citizens as possible will be given such philosophical education, since acts of the contemplative or theoretical part will, even according to the standard view, be best. But what is best is most choiceworthy for those capable of it, and all in the best city are supposed to be capable of the best; cf. Susemihl and Hicks (1894: 50–51, 619–20).

made in the same way, that is the worse are to be chosen for the sake of the better. So war, occupation, and the useful (which are worse) are for the sake of peace, leisure, and the noble (which are better). That the former are worse and the latter better is here assumed (it was argued earlier in the *Ethics* 10.7.1177b4–15), but the fact is fairly obvious and is anyway proved shortly by refutation of the contrary view.

1333a37   The conclusion now clearly follows that the politician and legislator must legislate for all these activities (for they all belong to the soul and to life generally) but for the better more so and for the worse only in view of the better. Hence education (the proper work of the legislator) must be organized in the same way, during childhood and beyond. This last remark is perhaps a reference back to the previous chapter where it was shown that education must be for being ruled and for ruling—for education for ruling comes through being ruled, and being ruled is something all experience until they are old enough to take part in deliberation and judgment (which point will certainly come later than twenty-one, at least for those who are not by nature kings).[70] Perhaps, however, one might better understand the remark as a reference to what has just been said about the activity of contemplation, and read it to mean that the citizens will go on being educated in philosophy throughout life, even into old age (when they are priests and should be meditating on the theological part of philosophy?).

~   REFUTATION OF THE OPPOSING VIEW

1333b5   The opposing view, that the end is to be found in the useful virtues and in war and conquest, while clearly vulgar (for it is vulgar to value useful things over noble ones), is nevertheless promoted by the example of Sparta and the admirers of Sparta—hence the need to refute the example and opinion of Sparta, in this respect as in many others (Aristotle admires the Spartan concern with education but not the education they chose). Aristotle first argues against this view by reason and lastly by the facts. The burden of what he says is—interestingly enough in view of the beginning of chapter 13—that the Spartans have entirely failed, not only of the right end, but also of the way to the (wrong) end that they did choose.

1333b16   The first reason is that the praise of Sparta is self-refuting: (1) the ground for praising the Spartans as happy and their legislator as good is their domination over others; (2) but the Spartans do not now dominate over others; (3) therefore they and their legislator are not now to be praised as happy or good. By the same token, of course, Sparta is not to be praised in the past either, because its regime and education have not changed despite the loss of empire, so if this regime

---

70. Some commentators, as Depew, in Keyt and Miller (1991: 373–74), doubt if Aristotle intended education to continue through life, that is, for grown men too. But the evidence to the contrary (above all about the need for education for ruling) seems decisive; see Newman (3:443, 497).

and education are not to be praised now (because not cause of empire, or thereby of happiness, now), neither are they to be praised in the past (because they could not have been cause of empire, or thereby of happiness, then either, but rather something else must have been instead, 5(8).4.1338b24–38).

1333b23 The second reason is to similar effect: (1) if the Spartan regime and laws are the cause of noble living (as the partisans of the Spartans say, who praise empire as noble living), then it cannot be that by keeping to this regime and laws they should have lost noble living; (2) but the Spartans have kept to their regime and laws and have lost noble living (they have lost empire); (3) therefore the Spartan regime and laws are not the cause of noble living, and to suppose that they are is clearly ridiculous.

1333b26 These first two arguments only show that praising Sparta on the basis of domination and empire is absurd. They do not as such show that praising domination as the goal of life is itself wrong or absurd. Aristotle's next arguments do prove this. So the third argument, which is straightforward enough, is that domination over others is not best because rule over the free is better than despotic rule and involves more virtue (to dominate others as the Spartans did is to treat them like slaves, and slaves are much inferior to the free and ruling them has nothing grand about it).

1333b29 Fourth, to praise domination as happiness is, first, harmful because this is in effect to teach those who can to aim at domination at home too (as happened in the case of Pausanias), and, second, not political, beneficial, or true because it is to suppose that what is best for the individual is not best for all in common, and vice versa, and that rule is for enslaving everybody (instead of for enslaving natural slaves, escaping slavery for oneself, and ruling for others' benefit). But these views are clearly false (it was shown earlier, at 4(7).1–3, that the best life for individual and city is the same), not political (they promote tyrannical instead of political rule), and not beneficial (they set individual in conflict with city).

It is worth noting Aristotle's admission here that empire for the benefit of the ruled, that is, empire in the sense of leadership and not despotism, may be an object of pursuit for the city, and that empire in the sense of despotism over natural slaves may be also. Aristotle clearly does not think leadership over other cities is necessary for happiness (4(7).3.1325b23–25), but it is also clear that he does not think it need be an impediment either.[71]

71. The relationship of Aristotle to Philip and Alexander, and his approval, or disapproval, of the empires and conquests of both, has been a source of much speculation and controversy. See, for instance, Kelsen, in Barnes et al. (1977), Lord (1978b: 350–53; 1982: 195 n19), Simpson (1990: 161–62), Stern (1968), Vander Waerdt (1985). These controversies and speculations are as fascinating to pursue as they are perhaps impossible to resolve.

1334a2   The concluding argument is an appeal to facts, namely that cities ordered toward war and empire are destroyed when they get empire because they have not been trained for peace and leisure, which is what the exercise of empire, not the getting of it, requires (examples would be Sparta, doubtless, and Thebes).[72] Hence these facts too show that war should be for peace and occupation for leisure and that the legislator should educate the city accordingly.

Chapter 15

~ WHAT VIRTUES EDUCATION MUST INCULCATE

1334a11   Having established that the end of the best life is found in the life of peace and leisure, Aristotle comes now to consider what virtues are required for this life. The arguments he has just given, however, have partly concerned the city and partly the individual, so he begins by recalling that, in respect of the end and the best life, city and individual do not differ; hence, in either case, there is need of the same virtues. But the virtues of leisure include those of occupation, since leisure needs many things that can only be secured by occupation. Hence the city needs also the virtues associated with occupation and war: moderation, courage, and steadfast endurance (the virtues particularly favored by the Spartans). For without these it will be slave to any attacker, and slaves have no leisure (their time is consumed in occupation to benefit another).

1334a22   But these are only some of the virtues and there are others more proper to leisure itself, notably philosophy and justice. Courage and endurance are only necessary for occupation and war (they concern facing pain and death, which are present in abundance in occupation and war but not in leisure and peace). Justice and moderation are also needed for occupation but evidently much more so for leisure. Aristotle appears to give two arguments for this conclusion. The first is: (1) in war people are compelled to be moderate and just (survival itself is at stake), while in leisure amid the goods of fortune there is no such pressure and people tend to become insolent; (2) but the best regime will have an abundance of the goods of fortune and be at leisure; (3) therefore, in order to use leisure and abundant good fortune well and not become insolent, the best regime must have an equal or greater abundance of justice and moderation and philosophy. Philosophy will be needed, and more so, as it alone of the virtues is confined to leisure. For leisure must be filled with some activity or other, and if, because of moderation and justice, it is not filled with acts of lust and greed and the like, there is nothing else to fill it with but the exercise of the intellect, and that for its own sake (and there is no reason to suppose that Aristotle does not mean such exercise to cover

72. As Newman suggests (2:342, 3:448–49).

the whole range of intellectual endeavor, or the whole scope of philosophy, as far as each citizen can go).[73]

The second argument is something as follows: (1) it is shameful not to be able to use good things, and more shameful to appear able to do so when compelled but to be shown up, when left free, as in fact incapable and slavish; (2) there is nothing shameful or slavish in the best regime and its citizens (otherwise neither it nor they could be best); (3) therefore the best city must really be able to use good things (and not only under compulsion of war); (4) but to be really able to do this one needs moderation and justice and philosophy; (5) therefore the best city needs moderation and justice and philosophy. Premises (2) and (4) here are evident and left unexpressed. As regards (1), not to be able to use what is good is certainly shameful, since it indicates that one is oneself not good; and it is more shameful, and slavish to boot, to do good things only because one is forced and to do base things when one is left free. For in the former case the inability could be a result of weakness; but in the latter case it is evidently a result of depraved choice and corrupt character (cf. 1.5.1254a36–b2).

1334a40 The above argument is presumably directed in no small part against Sparta, which manifestly proved itself slavish in the way stated. So Aristotle remarks specifically that the Spartan example is not to be followed. The Spartans are as vulgar or as slavish as others in supposing that the external goods of fortune and despotic empire are best, and differ only in supposing that these goods are to be secured by some sort of virtue. So they pursue the virtue that appears to get these things, namely warlike virtue. But in this they are doubly wrong: they pursue only part of virtue, not the whole of it, and they do not pursue virtue for its own sake but for lesser and baser things[74] (in which respect, indeed, they would seem

73. As Depew rightly insists, in Keyt and Miller (1991: 362–74), and Peter of Auvergne (1951: 7.1.1081–84, 7.11.1216). Note also that Aristotle's combining here of moral and intellectual virtues in the activity of leisure shows how he would unite the practical and theoretical lives that he sets in contrast with each other at the end of the *Ethics* (10.7–8)—or at least how he would unite them in the best regime. The exercise of the virtues of the practical life would be necessary for the winning of leisure and also for the right enjoyment of leisure once won, but that enjoyment itself would consist properly in the exercise of the virtues of the theoretical life, namely philosophy. Hence the theoretical life is truly better, as the end of the *Ethics* argues, for it forms the substance of leisure, but the practical life and its virtues are still indispensable, for they form the defense and preservation of leisure. But on this whole question about how to unite the theoretical and practical lives in Aristotle and the scholarly disputes thereby generated, see in particular Miller (1995: 351–53, with references), Natali (1989: chap. 5), Tessitore (1996: chap. 5).

74. Aristotle's text seems to have a lacuna at this point (1334b3–5). For the reconstruction of the text and argument I follow the suggestions of Newman (3:453): "But since [they think] these goods to be greater, and the enjoyment of them to be better than the enjoyment of the virtues, [they practice only the virtue useful for war. That the whole of virtue, however, must be practiced,] and for its own sake, is manifest from what has been said."

worse than others, since they not only pursue base goods but pervert virtue to a base end as well; cf. 1.9.1258a8–14).

But now that it has been shown that all the virtues are needed, and those of leisure and peace more than those of occupation and war, the next question is obviously to ask how, or by what education, these virtues will be secured.

~ THE ORDER OF EDUCATION

1334b6   Of the three things through which education in goodness is achieved, nature was considered earlier, which leaves habit and reason as the object of the legislator's concern. The question then is where to begin, with education in reason or in habits, and this question arises because both of these, or education in both of these, must harmonize "in the best of harmonies" (1334b9–10). The harmony must be best because one can mistake the best supposition (about the end of life) both through reason and through habits, that is, by both intellectual and moral error (bad habits can corrupt knowledge of the true end as much as bad reasoning). Hence, merely to have reason and habits, and the education of each, in harmony with each other is not enough, for both might be in error and so their harmony would be a harmony in error. Rather their harmony must not merely be with each other but must also be a harmony with the true end; that is why it must be the "best" harmony (two singers, for instance, are not in the best harmony if they are in tune with each other but out of tune with the music).

Consequently two things need to be understood: how to harmonize education in habits with education in reason, and how to harmonize both to the best supposition. The second point is dealt with first.[75]

1334b12   The argument is as follows: (1) generation comes from a beginning (the union of parents), and the end of this beginning (birth) is for a further end (education), and so on to the (final) end; (2) the (final) end is reason and intellect; (3) therefore all the other beginnings and ends are for reason and intellect. This establishes what the best supposition is, namely that the end to which education is to be harmonized is reason and intellect. But from this it necessarily follows, first, that training in habits must be for the end of reason and intellect, and, second, that training in reason and intellect is to be for the end of reason and intellect, or that such training is to be for its own sake. This, however, was already implied by, and now neatly picks up on, the earlier claim that the end of the best life is leisure and that the virtue and activity of leisure are philosophy, or intellectual activity simply.

1334b17   In answer to the first point, how to harmonize education in habits with education in reason, Aristotle argues that education in habits, while second in nature (for it is not the end but for the sake of the end), is to come first in time. The

75. I follow, more or less, the interpretation of Newman (3:454).

argument is: (1) of the two of body and soul, and of the two parts of the soul, namely the part without reason (appetite) and the part with reason (intellect), body is prior in time to soul and appetite is prior in time to intellect (as is evident from the case of children); (2) what is prior in time to another must be educated before that other; (3) therefore education or care of the body must come before care of the soul, and then care of the appetite, or education in habits, must come before care of the intellect. Also, of course, the first care must be for the sake of the second, which must be for the sake of the third (for, as just argued, the first beginning is for the first end and this end is for the next and final end).

The mention of the body might seem a bit out of place here, for Aristotle's concern is now, as he has said, with education in habits and reason, not also education in body. But the state of the body must manifestly affect the state of the appetite and indeed of the intellect (for poor or damaged bodies tend to bring with them damage in appetite and spirit and intellectual capacity too). So the care of the body must manifestly be a concern for anyone concerned with the care of appetite and intellect. This care must also begin right at the start with conception and pregnancy, since the state of offspring in both body and soul is manifestly affected by how they begin and grow in the womb. Hence, not surprisingly, Aristotle devotes the next chapter to marriage and childbirth.

Chapter 16

~ PRELIMINARY STAGES

~ CHILDBIRTH

1334b29/b38/1335a4   Ensuring children have the best bodies obviously means regulating the condition of those who get married and when (for what the children being born are like must necessarily be affected by what their parents are like). Here Aristotle lays down three conditions that the legislator is to observe. First, the spouses must reach simultaneously the time of no longer being able to generate, so as to avoid factions in the marriage. Second, the generation of offspring must be such that they are neither too close to nor too far from fathers in age (otherwise the succession of sons to fathers, which is the point of having an heir, will not go well). Third, the bodies of the offspring must be such as are most fit for what the legislator wants. Of these three conditions, the first concerns the good of the parents, the second the good of parents and children together, and the third the good of children.

1335a6   Aristotle secures all three by regulating the time of marriage with respect to the age of parents. He begins from when the capacity to generate ends, seventy in general for men and fifty for women, for this determines that husband

and wife should, to reach these times simultaneously (the first condition), be about twenty years apart. But this only determines the relative, and not absolute, ages for marriage. The absolute ages are understood from the other two conditions. So, to avoid offspring with poor bodies (the third condition), men and women should not couple when too young. The defects mentioned (deformed and small bodies and liability to produce females) are manifestly defects (liability to produce females must be a defect, for it must be better for the city to have roughly equal numbers of each sex and not a great deal more of one than another), as are also the damages in health of body and virtue of soul suffered by parents who couple at too young an age. Aristotle therefore suggests eighteen as the age for coupling for women, and thirty-seven or a little before for men, which is both close to twenty years older than eighteen and such that the father will be about seventy and ready to retire when his eldest son is about thirty-seven and ready to get married himself and take over (the third condition).

The truth of Aristotle's claims here, which are about other animals as well as humans, will depend, since they are empirical, on empirical observation. We are doubtless in as good a position to make the necessary observations as Aristotle, so any disputes his claims raise can be left to such observations for settlement.[76] Of course many other questions might arise about his determinations, as whether eighteen and thirty-seven are the physical primes for women and men, whether a twenty-year gap is suitable between spouses, whether the problem of their generative capacities not ending at the same time is the only or the worst one they can face, and so forth. But one particular objection that might well arise is that these arrangements seem designed more with a view to the happiness of the city (that it have the right sort of children) than to that of the spouses (will an eighteen-year-old woman be happy with a thirty-seven-year-old man, or will she be or remain in love with him?). So perhaps it is worth noting that the friendship between man and woman Aristotle has in mind is an aristocratic one, where both have their proper sphere and duties, and not one of equality and romantic passion (*Ethics* 8.7.1158b11–28, 10.1160b32–35, 12.1162a16–33). There seems no compelling reason, especially in an aristocracy, to suppose that such aristocratic friendships will not work as well or be as happy for the couple as those based on equality and the passion for romance; they might in fact work better.[77]

1335a35 So much concerns the age for getting offspring, and Aristotle next adds some remarks about season of year (he suggests winter), whose accuracy is

---

76. For Aristotle's own observations on this point, and some more recent confirmations of them, Newman's rich notes are worth consulting, but they are rather too long to quote here (3:462–64).

77. Aristotle's own marriage seems to have conformed to his own recommendations and to have been a happy one; see Newman (3:461). As for the follies and tragedies of romance, one may well consult the dramas of Shakespeare.

again a matter of empirical observation.[78] There is no doubt, though, that such factors must affect the quality of offspring, just as do environmental factors generally, hence there is need for the legislator and parents themselves to pay attention to them.

1335b2 Having determined time and season of generation, Aristotle now comes to the other matter for consideration he mentioned at the beginning of the chapter, the condition of the parents, or rather their quality of body. He first speaks of both sexes generally and then more specifically of women. The condition of body must be a mean between the excess of athletes and the defect of the pampered, as becomes free persons (who should clearly make their bodies serve them and not make themselves serve their bodies, by devotion either to physical exercise or to physical indulgence). But as these matters more properly concern education in virtue (for how one treats the body is a function of one's virtue or lack of it), they are deferred for later consideration.

1335b11 That women must have the same well-rounded bodies is evident. They are as much involved in child-getting, indeed they are more so, which is doubtless why Aristotle adds some specific remarks about what they should be doing when pregnant. The combination of physical exercise and religious worship may not be original[79] but it is a striking way of ensuring that the biological necessities of childbirth are not divorced from the higher goals of the best life (of which the gods are the model), and that women do not forget these goals, especially at a time when their thought is to be more relaxed as they nourish the child within. The worth of these pieces of advice with respect to the biological point is again a matter for empirical observation, but their worth with respect to the higher goals of the city would seem not in doubt.[80]

1335b19 So much concerns regulating marriage and childbirth to ensure sufficient children of the right sort. But there remains the question what to do if, despite the best intentions, something goes wrong. Aristotle's recommendations are against nourishing defective children but also against failing to nourish, or against exposing, sound and healthy children just on the ground that there are too many.[81] Instead, the control of numbers should be done by regulating intercourse

78. Newman quotes a paper, published in 1876 by a Dr. Kulischer, to the effect that the two especial pairing-times among human beings, as judged by a statistical analysis of the timings of matrimonial ceremonies and of births, were about New Year and late spring (3:468).

79. Newman suggests that Aristotle is following a hint of Plato (3:472).

80. Barker (1946: 327 n2) thinks these remarks indicate a certain contempt for women on Aristotle's part, but in fact they indicate the opposite. Aristotle is very clear on the need to educate women, as well as men, in virtue and the good life (1.13.1260b15–20, 2.9.1269b12–19).

81. I translate the text at this point (1335b20–23) as follows: "let the law be to nourish nothing that is defective but not to expose anything born, where the arrangement of custom forbids [more than a

and by aborting conceptions contrary to this number, but only before quickening occurs and not afterward. Abortion after quickening is said not to be holy and this word "holy" appears in only two other places in the *Politics*, when Aristotle says outrages, murders, and so on are not holy between close relatives (2.4.1262a25–32), and when he says that humans are the most unholy without virtue (1.2.1253a35–36). A child is of course a close relative, so Aristotle is evidently of the view that to kill the child in the womb (when it is a child and alive, which Aristotle evidently, though mistakenly, thought was true only after quickening) is unholy, and an offense against virtue and the gods.[82] He would therefore rather the city have too many children than that it do something unholy and vicious.

Indeed even his recommendations about exposure have something of the pious about them. For, first, all sound children are to be nourished, and, second, the defective are not to be killed but to be abandoned to fate, as it were, or to the gods (it was not unknown for exposed children, even deformed ones, to be found and cared for by others). The legislator is to do what he can, by regulating the timing of marriage and the quality of parents, to ensure that offspring are sound and healthy, so if, despite his best efforts, fate still produces something defective, then it is perhaps not unholy to return it to fate. Certainly defective children could not be citizens in the best city, since they would not have the physical or mental abilities required (Aristotle must be talking about real deficiencies of body and intellect, not harmless blemishes).[83]

1335b26 Aristotle now completes his recommendations by regulating when getting children is to end, namely before the age when parents are likely to have offspring who are defective and unsuitable, which he places at about fifty-five (for the man, presumably, and hence about thirty-five or thirty-seven for the woman). This conclusion is not necessarily in conflict with Aristotle's earlier concern to ensure that the capacity for generation of both husband and wife cease at the same time and at about seventy for a man and fifty for a woman. For he did not say there that generation should continue to those ages, but only appealed to these ages to establish the beginning of union. Perhaps also he understands by the end of the age for generation also the end of the age for having intercourse, so that

---

certain number of children], merely because of numbers. For there should be a limit to the amount of child getting." See Lord (1984: 226).

82. Cf. Dobbs (1994: 70–71 n2), who rightly remarks that if Aristotle had known what we now know about embryology he would have been opposed to abortion altogether.

83. Peter of Auvergne (1951: 7.12.1241) thinks that in these remarks about exposure and abortion Aristotle is not speaking in accordance with his own intention but with the law of nations (the Latin translation Peter used has "nations" in place of "custom" at 1335b21), and that even then he is not recommending either of them as positively good but only as less bad. Kraut (1997: ad loc.) adopts the more standard interpretation and judges Aristotle to be personally in favor of both.

his intention is to ensure that husband and wife cease at the same time to want to have intercourse (a discrepancy here would certainly lead to quarrels in the marriage). Perhaps, finally, he is thinking of exceptional cases, where older parents, whose already existing children have met untimely deaths, could, if their ages were not too discrepant, still have heirs by starting a family again. At any rate he goes on to allow, though not to require, intercourse after the age for getting offspring, but for health or some other purpose (which other purpose could, perhaps, be harmonious relations between the spouses).

That other purpose is certainly not going to be mere pleasure, for intercourse with someone other than one's spouse (which could doubtless be very pleasant) is declared not noble and, if done while one is of an age to have children for the city, punishable with dishonor. Adultery is base and destructive of marital friendship (which friendship Aristotle evidently intends to endure through life),[84] and as for the punishment of dishonor Aristotle may perhaps mean loss of citizenship. If so, this would be appropriate. Those who, despising marriage and legitimate offspring, show open contempt for the good of the city should also be openly shown to deserve no part in that good.

Chapter 17

~ INFANCY TO AGE SEVEN

1336a3 Aristotle turns next to what must be done after the child is born,[85] which concerns both bodily growth and now also the direct training of habits. His remarks on the body concern food and movement, and on body and habits together inurement to cold. Clearly habituation should begin as soon as children are capable of it, which, in the case in question, means immediately after birth. As before, the soundness of the advice is matter for empirical investigation.[86]

1336a23 For the age from this point, namely shortly after birth, to five, Aristotle's remarks focus more on matters to do with habits, though with necessary references also to movement and the developing of bodily strength. The oblique reference to Plato's *Laws*, if it is indeed such a reference ("those who, in their laws, prevent children from stretching their lungs and crying are not correct in their prohibition," 1336a34–36), need not be understood as petty carping, but a

---

84. The importance of fidelity and the baseness of adultery form the theme of *Oeconomica* 3.2 which, if spurious, seems nevertheless to express Aristotelian ideas.

85. Aristotle's indebtedness to Plato's *Laws* is particularly marked here, and is so noted by Newman (3:478–79).

86. Newman quotes some more recent medical advice on this point that directly opposes Aristotle's. He does not, however, quote the evidence on which this advice is based (3:482).

sort of silent debt of acknowledgment: if so little of what the *Laws* says about education deserves to be criticized and so much else to be accepted, this is an indication of how valuable Aristotle took that book to be.

But since children are going to start learning and developing habits already in their play, it is evident that, for children who are to be educated for virtue and the best life, this play should not be slavish and should already be anticipating what is to come later. For children are going to play with what they are given and to imitate what they see and hear no matter what, so it makes sense to ensure that this is not detrimental to, but rather prepares, serious education later.

1336a39/b12   Aristotle is rightly concerned, therefore, to prevent children picking up illiberal habits from slaves and vulgar habits from shameful stories and representations—hence the rather severe punishments he recommends for those older persons who infringe this rule in the presence of the young. Slaves, of course, will only be a problem for the impressionable young; the mature, by contrast, should suffer no ill effects from the presence of slaves. Rather the influence will be the reverse: slaves will be refined by hearing and seeing well-educated citizens instead of citizens being coarsened by hearing and seeing slaves.

What is interesting, nevertheless, is the exceptions Aristotle makes to the ban on hearing and seeing crude representations, lampoons, and comedies, namely that those may hear and watch them who are already educated, but only in the context of worshiping certain gods. Education will, as he says, grant immunity to the harm that those without education will suffer, and the connection with worship will also fix the whole in a context of religious awe as well as limit it to certain times and places. But that exceptions are allowed at all is striking. Perhaps it is because some things are worthy of being lampooned and mocked and indeed guffawed over, especially when drink, which gladdens the heart, has relaxed the tongue. So not wishing, in any puritanical way, to deny even these things their place in a full human life, Aristotle allows them but is careful at the same time to keep them controlled.[87] The exclusion, therefore, of women and children fits the same context, if such crudity would harm the latter and unbecome the former.

1336b24   In giving such recommendations, Aristotle is, of course, straying into the broad realm of censorship in general, a full discussion of which, as he says, should come later (in the treatment of education in virtue that presumably followed somewhere after the end of 5(8)). Still there was need to mention censorship now, since it must certainly cover all ages of education, especially that of the most impressionable. The argument in support of censorship of comedy and suchlike is

87. Barker (1946: 330 n2) interestingly compares mock ceremonies in churches during the Middle Ages.

taken, with suitable dry wit, from a tragic, and not a comic, actor. Its truth, however, seems evident enough.[88]

1336b35 For the years from five to seven, Aristotle presumably means the same conclusions to hold save that now children must be more directly readied for serious education, by watching what older children are doing. Since children learn much by imitation, and admire older children especially, such watching will get them already to start in play what they are soon to do in earnest.

Aristotle has passed quickly over these first seven years and one might legitimately wonder if he has not passed too quickly and whether some other kinds of learning should not already have begun, as in letters and numbers particularly. But given his readiness to defer to experts, and to follow later discoveries, in other matters, perhaps he would do the same here, and expect any legislator to do likewise. His overall ideas and intentions, however, are plain enough.

✑ EDUCATION PROPER

✑ THE DIVISION OF EDUCATION AND QUESTIONS TO EXAMINE

1336b37 Aristotle passes now to education in earnest and divides it with respect to the age after seven to puberty and the age after puberty to twenty-one. The wording here is peculiar but evidently meant to be taken seriously, and must mean that the education from seven to puberty is to regard the age puberty to twenty-one and the education from puberty to twenty-one to regard the age after twenty-one. His point, however, is the same as he laid down before (4(7).15.1334b12–28), that what comes earlier must be educated in view of what comes later. But his remarks do not strictly entail that there will be education after twenty-one (only that education from puberty to twenty-one will have that age in view),[89] though there is perhaps no strong reason to doubt this (especially if the citizens are to learn philosophy). As for the division at puberty, this need not be strictly at the age of fourteen. For since education is aimed at completing nature (that is, at bringing to completion what nature has first set going), nature, rather than neat schemas, must be taken as the guide with respect to what needs completing and when.[90]

Of the three questions Aristotle now lays down for investigation—whether

88. That education to virtue requires considerable censorship should occasion no surprise; cf. Barker (1946: 330 n1). If virtue and vice are habits, then not to encourage the first and not to prohibit the second, especially for the young (which is what censorship does), is to ensure that virtue will rarely, if ever, be acquired; see *Ethics* 2.3.1104b8–13, 10.9.

89. Contra Newman (3:497) and Lord (1982: 45).

90. I translate as follows at this point (1336b40–1337a1): "For those who divide ages into sevens are not, for the most part, speaking nobly; nature's division should be followed." Many commentators wish to emend "nobly" (*kalōs*) to "badly" (*kakōs*). But the text makes sense as it stands.

children should be educated, whether in common or privately, and what the education should be—the first two have in a way been answered already (in 4(7).13, 15, and also *Ethics* 10.9). But it is, as noted earlier, Aristotle's wont to reargue the same points several times, and, especially because of difference of context, in different ways and with different arguments.[91] *Bis repetita docent.*

91. As Kraut (1997: ad loc.) notes specifically in this case.

BOOK 5

Education in the Best Regime

Chapter 1

⁓ THAT EDUCATION IS NECESSARY AND MUST BE COMMON

1337a11 Aristotle turns first to the first question set out at the end of the preceding book, whether education of the young is necessary. As regards his opening remark, that no one would dispute that the legislator should especially busy himself about the education of the young, one might think that many would dispute this, namely all those cities where no care is taken of the young (the majority, as it would appear; *Ethics* 10.9.1180a24–29). However, what happens in the majority of cities is not that no care is taken over education but that no *common* care is taken over it; education is rather a private matter left to each family (as Aristotle notes shortly). Many cities may, indeed, dispute or disregard the need for common education, but none disputes the need for education, and education to the regime, for none disputes that an uneducated citizenry damages or destroys the regime.[1] So since Aristotle is now arguing for education only, and not yet for common education, his appeal to universal opinion is not unfair.

In support of this opinion, however, that the young need to be educated to the regime, he gives two arguments. The first is: (1) the character proper to a regime is what preserves and establishes that regime; (2) to educate the young to the regime is to educate them in the character proper to the regime; (3) therefore to educate the young to the regime is to preserve and establish that regime. Hence, also, not to educate the young to the regime is to allow them to develop some other character opposed to the regime, which would certainly damage, if not destroy, the

---

1. As in the case of democratic Athens in particular, since one of the charges against Socrates was precisely that he had corrupted the young, that is, not educated them to love and want to preserve the democracy (see Plato's *Apology*). Modern states, liberal democratic and otherwise, seem no less concerned about "civic education" or "civics," as it is called, and for the same reason: fear of a youth and a citizenry that do not care for, or even oppose, the existing system of government. On the other hand, while democrats, ancient and modern, care that the youth be not corrupted, they understand freedom, on the basis of which democrats claim the right to rule, in a self-destructive way, namely as doing whatever one wants. For sometimes what the democratic multitude wants is actually destructive of democracy; see 7(5).9.1310.25–36. Curren (1993–94) has an extended and generally helpful discussion of the context and contemporary significance of Aristotle's arguments in this chapter.

regime. Premise (2) here is manifest, and premise (1) follows from the idea of a regime as the way rule is distributed to a given ruling body according to that ruling body's idea of justice. So democracy is rule by the poor on the supposition that justice is equal shares for all, and oligarchy is rule by the rich on the supposition that justice is unequal shares for the wealthy (3.6.1278b8–15, 9.1280a7–25). It is those, therefore, who are formed by this or that idea of justice who will establish and preserve the regime that is formed by the same idea of justice. So, as Aristotle continues, the best character is cause of a better regime, that is, the character formed by the correct view of justice will produce a regime formed by a similarly correct view of justice. The regime will therefore be better, because ruled by those with the correct view of justice. But Aristotle significantly does not say that the regime will therefore be best, or rather he does not say that the best character is cause of the *best* regime. For a city also needs the best equipment if it is to have the best regime, and the best equipment is not a matter of character but of prayer (4(7).4.1325b37–39).

1337a18 The second argument is: (1) in order to put any art or ability into practice, there are things that one has to learn and get accustomed to first; (2) virtue is an ability; (3) therefore to put virtue into practice there are things that one has to learn and get accustomed to first (or there is need of education). This argument applies, of course, most obviously to the best regime that makes virtue its end. But it will actually work of any regime since any regime, even a deviant one, needs the habits proper to its own conception of justice to be put into practice if it is to survive (7(5).9.1309a36–39, 1310a12–19). Hence, again, failure to educate the young for the practice of these habits must be damaging to the regime.

1337a21 Aristotle turns next to the second question from the preceding book, whether education must be common. He gives two arguments that it should be. The first is stated with a double conclusion—that everyone must have one and the same education, and that taking care of this education must be a common matter. As it turns out, the first conclusion is needed as a premise for the second. The first conclusion would seem to follow thus: (1) the whole city has one end; (2) the young must be educated to the city; (3) therefore the young must be educated to this one end, or their education must be one and the same (what the education should be is manifestly a matter of what its end should be; cf. 4(7).15). Premise (1) again applies most obviously to the best city, but it will also apply to others more or less. Premise (2) repeats in effect the result of the first two arguments of this chapter.

The second conclusion would seem to follow thus: (1) of common things the care should be common; (2) education is a common thing; (3) therefore the care of education should be common. Premise (2) is in effect the conclusion of the argument just given, that education must be one and the same. For if all the young are to be educated (as the two opening arguments effectively showed), and if they are to be educated to the one end of the city, which is manifestly common to all, then education must be a common thing. Premise (1) would seem to be evident, though it should perhaps be read as stating what it is better to do rather than what it is strictly necessary to do.[2] For a common education could in principle be given to all the young separately within individual families (as it certainly will be up to the age of seven, 4(7).17.1336a41–b2). Still, the city as a whole would have to ensure that this educating did go on and that it was the same education in each case. Moreover some parts of the education would have to be done in common, as physical training for military purposes in particular. Consequently making education a care of the city or of the citizens as a whole, and not of families separately, must be better.

1337a27 But in case some might want to make education a private matter nevertheless, Aristotle responds that no one should think he belongs to himself alone but rather to the city, for each is part of the city and the part belongs to the whole. One should note here, however, if only by the way, that the citizen is not part of the whole as subordinate to the whole but as constitutive of the whole. The city *is* the multitude of the citizens, and the citizens *are* the city (3.1.1274b41, 1275b17–21). City and citizen are, as it were, on the same level.[3]

At any rate, on the basis of this claim Aristotle presents a second argument: (1) the care of a part naturally looks to the care of the whole; (2) each citizen is part of the whole city; (3) therefore the care of each citizen, or his education, should look to the care of the whole city, or, in other words, education should be part of the common care of the whole city. This argument is, again like the previous one (and for the same reasons), best understood as indicating what is better rather than as what is strictly necessary.[4]

A problem nevertheless arises. For if the citizen is to consider himself as part of the city and as needing to be educated with a view to the regime of his city, then this would seem to entail, if the regime is a deviant one, that everyone, including good men, should be, and should consent to be, educated in deviance or in the virtue of preserving a deviant regime.[5] But in response it is necessary to bear in mind that, as Aristotle indicates later (4(6).1), the ability to preserve a deviant regime is part of the same ability that preserves the best regime, or that the good man's prudence is such that it embraces all regimes and the setting up and ruling of

2. Newman (3:501) takes it in the latter way and therefore finds the argument faulty.

3. Contra Barnes, in Patzig (1990: 262), and cf. Mayhew (1993a: 830 n87). Individuals may perhaps, according to 1.2.1253a18–29, be said to be subordinate to the city, but only in the sense that a city is a multitude of citizens, and so only in the sense that an individual may be said to be subordinate to himself. For the individual qua imperfect is by nature directed to becoming, and so is by nature subordinate to, the individual qua perfect, and the perfect individual is the full citizen in the best city, or at least fit to be such.

4. Contra Newman (3:501).

5. Newman raises this problem (3:502).

all regimes (just as a doctor's skill includes caring for those who are or can be made completely healthy as well as for those who cannot). Consequently the good man, or the good citizen in the best regime, would be capable of being a good citizen in any regime, and, conversely, anyone educated in the virtue proper to a deviant regime would have been educated in a part of the ability proper to the good man and to the best regime. He would have taken a step, if a partial and incomplete step, in the right direction (just as a sick patient who can only be cured a little, or who can only be stabilized where he is, has taken a step in the direction of health). The problem as initially posed is falsely assuming, in other words, that deviance is a total negation of simple justice so that education in deviant justice is education in simple injustice. Properly considered, however, deviant justice is a partial approach to justice and education in deviant justice a partial education in justice.[6]

Chapter 2

~ THE CONTENT AND MANNER OF EDUCATION

~ REVIEW OF DIFFICULTIES

1337a33 Aristotle comes now to the third question from the preceding book, what the education should be like. Since the matter is in dispute, he begins, as is his wont, with a review of difficulties. These difficulties cover, to some extent, questions he has already discussed elsewhere, but as it is only now in this context that they arise, some repetition of earlier points is not inappropriate—if, at any rate, no significant dispute is to go unnoticed.[7]

The two questions he poses about what the education should be like concern what its content is and the manner of carrying it out, and the disputes he mentions concern the same two questions: people disagree about what should be taught, either with respect to virtue or the best life (content), and also about whether thought or habits should more be kept in view (manner). Virtue and the best life are separately mentioned here, perhaps because some do not think the life of virtue is the best life and not all those who pursue virtue pursue it as if it, instead of its results, constituted the best life. The first question, about content, is discussed at length and answered in the rest of this chapter and in the next, and an answer to the second question, about manner, is implicitly given at the same time (for the conclusion reached in chapter 3, that subjects need to be taught with a view to leisure spent in cultured pursuits, is also in effect a conclusion that thought is more to be aimed at than habits—though not, of course, to the exclusion of habits).

6. Which is doubtless in part why those educated to deviant regimes will in fact be closer to justice simply than others in those same regimes who have not been so educated; see 7(5).9.1310a19–36.

7. Cf. Newman (1:354 n2).

1337a39   The disputes about content and manner are next more specifically noted. As regards content, the dispute concerns whether this should be in things useful, things virtuous, or things extraordinary. The latter phrase is unclear and could refer to several things, including the extraordinary kinds of musical skill Aristotle mentions later (5(8).6.1341a9–17). Perhaps, however, it is better to take it as referring to the things required for a noble leisure, since Aristotle solves the problem of content in the next chapter in favor of these things, and philosophy, which is the virtue of leisure, certainly had the reputation of being extraordinary.[8]

As regards manner, or whether habits or thought is more to be aimed at, the dispute concerns which virtues are held in honor. For those who, like the Spartans, prefer the virtues of occupation, notably courage, will presumably aim at habits, while those who prefer the virtues of leisure, notably philosophy, will presumably aim more at thought.

✑ SOLUTION TO THE DIFFICULTIES

✑ EDUCATION MUST BE LIBERAL

1337b4   Aristotle proceeds now to solve these disputes, and particularly about content. First he corrects the division into three (things useful, things virtuous, things extraordinary) by making a different division that cuts across the first one. Second, with the help of this different division he resolves, in the next chapter, the disputes themselves. So, first, that the division just given requires some correction is evident from the fact that the three categories are not exclusive of each other: for some virtues can fall into the class of the useful (as the courage of virtue, which can be regarded as useful for empire), and others into that of the extraordinary (as the virtue of philosophy, which some regard as extraordinary). Aristotle replaces all three by another division, that of the liberal and illiberal, or of the free and the unfree. This division, combined with his contentions about leisure (from 4(7).14–15 but reargued, from the point of view of the present context, in the next chapter), resolves the disputes about the useful, the virtuous, and the extraordinary, and also about habits and thought. In brief the resolution is that those useful, virtuous, and extraordinary things should be learned that are free and promote the cultured activities of leisure, and that education should aim, through the training of habits, at the training of thought.

Aristotle approaches his division between the free and the unfree by taking that member of the original division that would seem least subject to controversy, namely the class of the useful. Everyone would presumably agree that useful things should be taught, or at any rate the necessary ones among them, though there

---

8. See Newman (1:354 n3) and Susemihl and Hicks (1894: 571). Lord (1982: 53), in accordance with his view that Aristotle does not mean to teach the citizens of the best regime philosophy in the full sense, takes "extraordinary" to refer only to extraordinary musical and gymnastic skills.

might well be dispute about which ones were necessary. Aristotle's response is to distinguish between works that are free and those that are unfree. On this basis he denies that the young should learn anything, whether useful or necessary, that is vulgarly mechanical.[9] Those things are vulgarly mechanical, he says recalling earlier determinations (1.11.1258b35–39, 4(7).9.1328b39–41), that render the body of the free, or their soul or thought, useless for the deeds of virtue. For if free works are those that are proper to the free, and if it is proper to the free to be and act virtuously (cf. 1.5–6), then no mechanical work is a free work. Among mechanical works must be included those which put the body into a worse condition (for then the body will be unfit for the performance of virtuous acts, in particular warlike ones), and those which, like wage-earning labor, may not damage the body but do, by making one subject to others' needs for one's livelihood, deprive thought of leisure and make it abject (for then thought will be unfit for discerning virtue).

1337b15 The distinction, however, between the free and unfree, or the liberal and illiberal, is not simply a matter of the things done or learned; it is also a matter of how these things are done or learned. Things that are liberal in themselves can be done illiberally if done to excess or with too much attention to detail (an example would be playing a musical instrument, which is fit learning for the free provided they do not do it with the technical pyrotechnics and attention to detail of professionals; see 5(8).6.1341a9–13, 1341b8–18). Conversely things otherwise illiberal could be done in a liberal way if done for their own sake, or for friends, or for virtue, and not done for others like a laborer or a slave, that is, not done for pay or for a master (points already made earlier, at 3.4.1277b1–7, 4(7).14.1333a6–11).

Chapter 3

~ EDUCATION MUST BE FOR NOBLE LEISURE

1337b21 Aristotle turns next to consider directly the question of the subjects to be taught. The problem here, that existing educational practice points in two directions, is presumably a reference back to the dispute about whether things useful or things virtuous are to be taught.[10] Aristotle has just qualified this distinction by introducing the further distinction between the free and the unfree. He

9. Newman (3:506) thinks that the question at this point concerns only the useful works that are not admitted to be necessary, and not also those of them that are admitted to be necessary. But it is clear that Aristotle would say that even the necessary among useful works should be avoided if they are slavish. So perhaps one should understand him to be thinking here of the necessary as well as the useful.

10. As Newman suggests (3:510). A reference to the category of the extraordinary is omitted presumably because Aristotle is about to speak of the accepted or standard subjects of education, not of novelties that some may have introduced, and also because it is his intention now to argue from these standard subjects to the conclusion that leisure must be introduced into the analysis of education.

now qualifies it by introducing the idea of noble leisure, but again he draws the point out of matters of general agreement, namely, in this case, the subjects of education. The four subjects he lists are the accepted or prevailing ones; they are not to be taken as being all those Aristotle would himself accept, for doubtless he would include others and did so do in the missing chapters.

As for these accepted subjects, they fall into the categories of the useful or the virtuous, or specifically the virtue of courage. But all these are things proper to occupation, not leisure. The exception is music whose role in education is puzzling, for it certainly does not seem to be useful nor part of occupation. Most people, when faced with this puzzle, opt for pleasure as its purpose, but Aristotle counters that music was introduced at the beginning with a view to noble leisure. The argument he gives suggests, rather than proves, that that is why those at the beginning introduced music into education. It more immediately proves that some education for leisure is needed: (1) our nature seeks not only to be capable of a right occupation but also of a noble leisure; (2) education is for completing nature (cf. 4(7).17.1337a1–3); (3) therefore there is need of education for noble leisure; and this need will be all the greater if (4) leisure is more choiceworthy than occupation and is its end (a point made forcibly in 4(7).14–15). Consequently (we may add) it is highly likely that some part of the traditional education was introduced for the sake of leisure, and, if so, it could only be music.

But if music is for leisure, that does not prove it cannot be for pleasure as well. Indeed leisure would seem to need to be spent in activity that is pleasurable. Pleasure, however, is an ambiguous term, for there is more than one sort of pleasure or pleasurable activity and not all sorts need be fit for noble leisure. So Aristotle turns to consider what activity leisure must be spent in. He proceeds to argue, first, that it cannot be the activity and pleasure of play, second, that it must be some activity and pleasure proper to leisure itself, and then, third, that it must be the noble activity and pleasure of the best man. From this he then draws his intended conclusion, that some subjects must be taught with a view to leisure spent in cultured pursuits (the noble pursuits of the best man).

1337b35   As regards play, Aristotle gives two arguments that it cannot be the activity of leisure. The first is: (1) if leisure is to be spent in play, play would be the end of life (for leisure is the end of life); (2) but play is not the end of life; (3) therefore leisure is not to be spent in play. Premise (2) is assumed and not argued for, but would seem to be obvious from the fact that play, taken in its strict sense (for perhaps leisure could be called play in some looser sense insofar as it is not occupation), is by definition not serious, but the end of life is manifestly something serious.[11]

The second argument proves the same point by proving that play, far from

---

11. This point is argued explicitly in *Ethics* 10.6.1177b27–35.

being the activity of leisure, is not even for the sake of leisure but rather for the sake of occupation. It may be formalized thus: (1) those engaged in toil need rest; (2) those who are occupied are engaged in toil; (3) therefore those who are occupied need rest; (4) play is for the sake of rest (it is a movement of soul that relaxes and gives rest through its pleasure); (5) therefore play is for the sake of something that is needed by those who are occupied and should, accordingly, be introduced by way of remedy for the occupied (and not, understand, for those at leisure who, though active, are not toiling and so do not need rest, or not for this reason).

1337b39   Having shown that play cannot be the activity of leisure, Aristotle next shows that this activity must be something proper to leisure itself. He gives an argument of the following sort: (1) leisure activity contains pleasure and happiness and blest living; (2) such happiness and blest living are not the possession of those who are occupied; (3) therefore leisure activity is not something that is the possession of those who are occupied, or it is something that is proper to leisure itself. Premise (2) is proved as follows: (4) those who are occupied are occupied for the sake of an end that they regard as not yet present to them, and they also suffer the pain of toil; (5) happiness is an end and is accompanied by pleasure and not by pain; (6) therefore those who are occupied do not possess happiness.

It thus also becomes clear, incidentally, that the three things, play, occupation, and leisure, are related in a direct line of subordination. Play is a remedy for toil and pain and so must be for occupation. It relaxes those who are occupied so that, after periods of rest, they can return refreshed to occupation. Occupation in turn is a striving for a future and not a present end, and so must be for leisure that is precisely the present and pleasurable possessing of the end or, in particular, of happiness.

1338a7   To find the activity of leisure, then, it is presumably necessary to look to the pleasurable activities that people set down as belonging to the end, that is, to leisure and not to occupation. So next we have something like the following argument: (1) people set down different pleasures as the pleasures proper to the end according to their own disposition or habits, and it is the best person who sets down the best pleasure, that is, the pleasure that comes from the most noble sources; (2) leisure (insofar as it is here under discussion) is something noble; (3) therefore the pleasurable activities of leisure are those set down by the best man. Premise (2) was asserted just above (1337a30–32), when Aristotle recalled that our nature itself seeks to be capable of a noble leisure.

So if we now add to this conclusion (3) the further premise (a premise basic to the whole present discussion) that (4) education is for making the citizens into best men, it follows that (5) there is need for some subjects to be learned and taught with a view to the pleasurable activities pursued by the best man or, in other words, with a view to a leisure spent in cultured (not base or vulgar) pursuits (what Aristotle calls *diagōgē*). Education in these subjects must, moreover, be for its own sake (for leisure, containing the end, is for its own sake), and not, like education for occupation and necessities, for the sake of something beyond.

1338a13   That there is thus a need for an education in subjects proper to leisure itself, over and above education in subjects for other purposes, is the main conclusion Aristotle has been driving at. But he now confirms it by appeal to the ancients, confirming also at the same time that this is what they had in mind when they introduced music into education. First he argues by way of elimination and then by appeal to certain quotations from the most authoritative of all the ancients, Homer. His first argument seems to be as follows: (1) the ancients introduced music as something either necessary or useful or for the cultured pursuits of leisure; (2) but they could not have introduced it as necessary or useful, for music is manifestly neither; (3) therefore they introduced it for the cultured pursuits of leisure.

A problem with this argument is that premise (1) seems not to be exhaustive since Aristotle himself argues later (in chapter 5) that music is useful also for generating virtue. Hence the conclusion need not follow, for perhaps the ancients introduced music only for this reason and not for leisure.[12] But we should recall that Aristotle is arguing here, as the opening of the chapter indicates, from what people currently say about music education, and the only reason people currently give for such education is that music is pleasant. Now Aristotle's preceding discussion has just shown that pleasure is ambiguous and covers the pleasures of play, of the vulgar, and of the cultured pursuits of the best man. The ancients, however, can hardly be supposed to have meant by education for pleasure education for the first two kinds of pleasure (for the ancients are universally regarded as being serious and noble), therefore they must have meant education for the pleasures of cultured pursuits. Accordingly if, as people currently concede, the ancients did not introduce music into education for its necessity or its utility (whether its utility for life or for courage), then they must have introduced it for the cultured pursuits proper to noble leisure. So taken in this ad hominem way, premise (1) does exhaust all the relevant possibilities and the argument goes through.

In addition, one should note that current conceptions do not allow for any education in virtue save the virtue of courage, which is a virtue belonging to occupation, not leisure, and is freely conceded not to be a result of music. So even if one were to add to premise (1) the further possibility that the ancients introduced music as something useful for generating virtue, these virtues would have to be understood as those of leisure, and so they would not, after all, be a further possibility but the same as that of the cultured pursuits of leisure already included in that premise. Hence in this way too premise (1) turns out to be suitably exhaustive.

1338a22   But to confirm that the ancients did introduce music for this reason, Aristotle shows next, from quotations, that they regarded music as belonging to the cultured pursuits of the free (and so, if that is what they saw in music, it

12. A problem noted by Newman (3:515) and Susemihl and Hicks (1894: 577).

must also have been what they saw in education in music). The quotations do indicate that the kind of feasting and singing in question was understood as something other than relaxation from toil and as good and delightful for its own sake, and hence do show that music had, among the ancients, a place in the leisured activities of the free (and not, or not only, in the activities of play and of the vulgar).[13] And even if the Homeric poems do not now enjoy the same authority as they did among the Greeks, yet they still preserve important evidence about ancient practices and opinions.

1338a30 From all these considerations, Aristotle is now able to conclude, with respect to the subjects education should teach, that, over and above useful and necessary subjects, there is need also for the subjects of noble leisure. He has not yet, however, concluded what specifically these subjects are to be (and whether, in particular, they are to cover more than music or not), or how they are to be taught. These questions are still outstanding and, unfortunately, Aristotle does not return to them in the *Politics* as we have it. Still we were told earlier that the virtue proper to leisure was philosophy (4(7).15.1334a23), so we can conclude that these other subjects must have included philosophy and all that prepares for philosophy.[14]

Nevertheless, Aristotle does note further now that, besides the evidence for education in leisure just acquired from the ancients and the traditional training in music, it is possible also to conclude two other things. First, some useful subjects, like letters (or speaking, reading, writing), must be taught, not only because they are useful, but also because they prepare the way for other subjects, and specifically, that is, for these subjects of leisure. Second, drawing in particular should be taught, not for the utilitarian purpose of making good purchases, but for the contemplation of physical beauty, that is, again for noble leisure (contemplating beautiful things for their own sake, including physically beautiful things, must be an activity of leisure too).

In further proof, it would appear, of these two conclusions, Aristotle adds a final comment that may be expanded into the following argument: (1) the magnanimous and the free should not be looking everywhere for what is useful; (2) the

13. Davis (1991–92: 165) indulges in speculations about Aristotle's intention at this point based on the Homeric context of the quotations. For since, in the second case, the bard is about to sing of the deeds of war and since, in the first, Odysseus is plotting to kill the suitors, the leisure spent in listening to this music is leisure spent in meditating the deeds of war and of occupation. Hence these quotations seem to undermine, rather than to support, Aristotle's contentions about the priority of leisure and the place of music in leisure. But even if these speculations about the context of the quotations have some relevance to the meaning of Homer's poems (though that is not clear), nothing thereby follows about the intention of Aristotle's argument. It is as likely—indeed given this argument's own context, it is far more likely—that the Homeric context is of no relevance to Aristotle's argument at all. That is doubtless why he is entirely silent about that context. Cf. also Lord (1982: 81–82), Nichols (1992: 159).

14. Hence we can get some idea of what this would involve from Aristotle's own writings on philosophy.

citizens of the best city are to be magnanimous and free (they are to be good men); (3) therefore the citizens of the best city should not be looking everywhere for what is useful. Hence, if possible, they must be taught even useful subjects for other than useful reasons, and specifically for reasons of beauty and noble leisure.

～ TREATMENT OF PARTICULAR SUBJECTS

～ GYMNASTICS

1338b4 Aristotle has thus answered the questions, and solved the disputes, from chapter 2 about the content and manner of education. The first he has done explicitly and the second implicitly, since education for leisure is education for thought more than for habits. It remains now, therefore, for him to proceed to particulars. So this is what he now does, and he first concludes to the necessity of gymnastics and physical training. He recalls, for this purpose, what he had established about education earlier (4(7).15.1334b8–28), that it should be in habits before reason and concern the body before the soul. From this it necessarily follows that there is need for education of body, that is, need for gymnastics and physical training. By the first of these, says Aristotle, the body itself is put into a certain condition and by the second its actions are. What he means by this remark is presumably that gymnastics will develop general bodily well-being (as health, strength, suppleness, muscular tone, and so forth), and that physical training will develop particular physical skills (as running, throwing, riding, and other such activities of a martial sort). Certainly without the right disposition of the body the right activities could not be well performed, and without the right activities the right virtues, and particularly courage in war, could not be well developed. Hence Aristotle first turns to this education of body.

Chapter 4: 1338b9[15] With respect to such education, Aristotle comes to his conclusions about what should be taught and when by again starting from prevailing opinions and practice—this time, of cities reputed to take most care of their children. This prevailing practice is twofold and in both ways it errs, in the first by ruining the body and in the second by ruining the soul. Aristotle accordingly opts for a middle course that properly trains the body while not ruining the soul.

One prevailing practice, then, is to give children the condition of professional athletes. But this destroys both shape and growth. The fact of the fault here is presumably manifest enough not to require further discussion (one needs merely to look at professional athletes), so Aristotle passes at once to the other prevailing practice, that of the Spartans. The fault of the Spartans is perhaps more serious and, since they enjoy high repute, less likely to be recognized as a fault. Accordingly Aristotle dwells on it at some length. The fault is that, while they do not ruin

15. Here also, as with 4(7).2, I ignore the chapter divisions for the purpose of the analysis of the argument.

the body in the way just mentioned, they do impose such toil on the young as to make them into wild beasts. The Spartans' aim is to produce courage, but they commit a double error with respect to this aim. The first Aristotle has mentioned before (as 2.9.1271b2–10 and 4(7).15.1334a11–b5), that the care of education should not be carried out with a view to one virtue and especially not to this one in particular (the virtues of leisure and peace are more important than those of occupation and war). So leaving aside this error as already sufficiently exposed, he turns to the second (which he has not before mentioned), that the Spartans have failed even to find the way to produce courage.

1338b17   Here Aristotle gives two arguments. The first is taken from a comparison with other animals and other nations and the second from Spartan history. The first is that the milder and more lionlike animals (as lions themselves in fact) are more courageous than the wilder ones (as perhaps wolves),[16] and that the same is true of nations. So the Achaeans, the Heniochi, and others may be savage and cannibals and robbers, but are not courageous. To be courageous is to be able to face death in war because this is noble and according to the judgment of right reason (*Ethics* 3.6–7), but such savages have a reputation for running away when they see the fight going against them, and face death, if at all, rather out of savagery than because they have exercised right reason or have any sense of dying in a noble cause.[17]

The second argument is taken from the evidence of Spartan history, that the Spartans' superiority in the past was due to the fact that in the past they alone exercised or trained but now when others train too the Spartans are regularly surpassed. So Spartan training cannot be the best if it only produces superiority when others do not train but produces inferiority when others do train.

1338b29   Having stated his criticisms and arguments, Aristotle now summarizes his general conclusion about Spartan education. So, from the first argument, it follows that courage is to be found in the good man only (who alone would face a noble danger because it was noble), not in the wild beast or savages. From the second, together with the fact, mentioned initially, that the Spartans only trained for courage, it follows that they made their children, like vulgar mechanics, useful for one thing only and made them worse for this than others do. The reference to vulgar mechanics is appropriate because, as stated earlier (5(8).2.1337b8–15), whatever work, art, or learning renders body, soul, or thought useless for the deeds of virtue is vulgar, and the Spartan training made the young wild and useless for any virtue, including courage (not to mention moderation, justice, and philosophy). And lest any admirer of Sparta object that this conclusion ignores Sparta's

---

16. See Newman (3:522) and Susemihl and Hicks (1894: 580) both of whom refer, among other things, to Aristotle's discussion of the lion in *Historia Animalium* 9.44.

17. As Peter of Auvergne (1951: 8.1.1283) notes.

success in the past, Aristotle repeats that it is present and not past evidence that must be decisive here, for only in the present is there any competition to put Spartan training to the test.

1338b38 Aristotle now comes, on the basis of this discussion, to his own conclusion about gymnastics. It can be now agreed that gymnastics is to be employed in education (for the body certainly needs to be trained), and also how it is to be employed (namely with a view to the soul and habits, and to allow for all habits, not some, and for true courage, not false). But what this means specifically is, first, with respect to the age up to puberty, that the young should only be put to lighter gymnastic exercises and not be subjected to an athletic sort of training with its toil and constrained diets. For, as he said initially about athletic training, it impedes growth (that is, in both shape and bulk). Now, in further proof, he cites evidence from the Olympic games, that few were successful both as boys and as grown men.[18] Second, about the age from puberty onward, he concludes that, for the first three years (that is, up to seventeen in most cases), time should be spent on other subjects of learning and heavy physical exercises should only be begun after that. For while it is evident that soldiers, especially courageous soldiers, must be trained to undergo many toils (to this extent, no doubt, the Spartans were right), yet these toils must not begin too soon, and they will not do so if they begin three years after puberty (for at about seventeen most bodily growth will have been completed). Nor must these toils be such as to produce wildness, and they will not do so if, contrary to the Spartan practice, other subjects are learned as well (things that, like music, will prepare the young for other moral virtues, and, like letters, for the virtue of philosophy), and if these things are taught first, while growth is still going on.

It is not necessary to conclude[19] that Aristotle means these other subjects of learning to begin only at puberty. For the Greek is sufficiently ambiguous to allow the possibility that he means them to be *continued* into the first three years after puberty.[20] Moreover, when he says that physical and mental toil are incompatible, his emphasis must be on toil, for assuredly mental toil can go along with, and even be helped by, light physical exercise, as light mental exercise can go along with heavy physical toil (hence there is no reason, on this account, for mental education not to begin before puberty, or not to be continued, in some lighter fashion, after seventeen).

18. Aristotle would be in a good position to know this evidence as he himself drew up a list of all the Olympic victors, as Newman (3:526) recalls.

19. Contra Newman (3:526).

20. As for the time when Aristotle intended formal military training (or even formal philosophical training) to begin, whether before or after twenty-one, we cannot say on the basis of present evidence; Newman (3:526–27).

Chapter 5

~ MUSIC

~ PRELIMINARY DISCUSSION

1339a11   Gymnastics and physical training are subjects of education that concern the body, and since Aristotle says nothing further about training the body, it is reasonable to suppose that, in now turning to music, he is turning to consider subjects of education for training the soul in habits—a supposition that is supported by the fact that this aspect of music is what he proceeds to stress.[21] At any rate he begins, as is his wont, by laying out the difficulties associated with music (calling this, in a piece of verbal witticism, a "prelude," 1339a13) before turning to resolve them and to state his own view on the subject. Some of these difficulties were, of course, raised before (in chapter 3), when education in music was discussed, in order to show that some education for noble and cultured leisure was necessary. But Aristotle did not in fact decide there that music was absolutely necessary for this purpose, only that this was the purpose for its inclusion in traditional education. Now, however, he is turning directly to that question of whether music is thus necessary and if so how it should be taught. Consequently, while he raises some of the same questions again, he is doing so for a different purpose.

Aristotle's reason for raising questions about music as a prelude to setting out his own views is, as he says, that it is not easy to say what is the power of music or why one should participate in it. These are in a sense the same question (for why one should participate in music must be a matter of what participating in music does, or what the power of music is) and, of course, they refer back to the discussion of chapter 3. However, they are not yet, or not as such, questions about why music should be included in the education of the young. They are rather preparatory to this question, for only when we know what music does and is for can we say whether and how the young should be educated in it. At all events, in what follows, Aristotle first sets out the several possible purposes or powers of music and then raises questions about why, given these purposes, the young should be educated in it.

1339a16   As regards the power or purpose of music, the questions are whether music is for play and rest, like drinking, sleeping, and dancing (perhaps the most common use to which music, now as well as then, is put); whether it is for training the character of the soul, as gymnastics trains the character of the body (a possibility that seems not, either now or then, to be traditionally acknowledged); or whether it is for cultured pursuits and prudence (the use that the ancients

21. The discussion of subjects for training reason is lacking.

especially put music to).[22] These were, as he says, the three purposes of education stated before (in chapter 3). For usefulness for virtue (or specifically courage) was one of the traditional categories of subjects for education, and the category of pleasure turned out to be ambiguous as between play and noble leisure. So even if music was not traditionally associated with the category of training in virtue (but only with the category of the pleasures of play and leisure), philosophical completeness at any rate requires that the possibility be considered now.

1339a26 These, then, are the possible purposes of music, and Aristotle now proceeds to raise questions, in the case of each of them, as to why the young should be educated in it. For certain problems arise on this point and also on the point as to why they should be educated to perform music and not just to listen to it. So if music is to be taught for play, it cannot be for play now because education is painful while play is not; and if music is for the cultured enjoyment of leisure, which of course constitutes the end of life, then the young are not yet ready for this since by definition they do not possess the maturity or completeness of development required for enjoying the end.

1339a31 An obvious response, of course, to these arguments is that education in music is not for what children do now but for what they will be doing later. So Aristotle next considers this possibility. Here problems arise about all the possible purposes of music. So if education in music is for play in maturity then, contrary, presumably, to current practice, there will be no need for the young to learn to play music themselves. For, first, they could enjoy the pleasure of play by listening to others perform; second, experts who have devoted their lives to performance will provide this pleasure better than amateurs (which is all that most of the citizen young will be); third, if the young are nevertheless to learn to play music, then they should, by parity of reasoning, learn also to cook delicacies (fine food belongs to play and relaxation as well as music), which is absurd (the young are to be taught the deeds of free citizens, not of menials and slaves).[23]

1339a41 The situation is no better if music is for improving character, for this too could perhaps be achieved if the young only listen to others and do not

22. Prudence (*phronēsis*) was not expressly mentioned before, but only cultured pursuits. Newman suggests, following other scholars, that *phronēsis* here means "intellectual culture" (3:529). This does, admittedly, tie in neatly with the idea of cultured pursuits, for certainly such pursuits must have involved, even among the ancients, the cultivation of reason. Perhaps, however, *phronēsis* might still be taken here in the narrower sense of prudence, for the ancients seem to have cultivated reason primarily with respect to human affairs, which is the sphere of prudence. In addition, Aristotle argues later in this chapter that music helps the development of virtue by helping the development of right judgment as well as of right habits, and right judgment in the matter of virtue is prudence. So perhaps he adds *phronēsis* here on his own account, and in its sense of prudence, as a sort of anticipation of his later discussion.

23. See 1.7, and Newman (3:531).

themselves perform. As evidence, Aristotle adduces the claims of the Spartans. An appeal to Spartan opinion is perhaps sufficient for a dialectical discussion but, since Spartan pretensions to knowledge and possession of virtue are specious, these claims have no weight in themselves (and indeed Aristotle quickly rejects them later, in chapter 6, 1340b22–25).

1339b4 Finally the same problem arises if music is for cultured leisure later, since, first, this purpose too can be served by listening only, and, second, general opinion, both about Zeus, the chiefest of the gods (though not general opinion about lesser gods, like Apollo, who do play music), and about the mechanical character of professional musicians, dissociates performance from cultured leisure. These arguments too are dialectical, not demonstrative, and Aristotle does not entirely accept them in what follows, but only with qualifications.

∿ THE PURPOSES OF MUSIC AND EDUCATION IN MUSIC

∿ FOR PLAY AND CULTURED PURSUITS

1339b10 Having completed his prelude, Aristotle next turns to the main movement of his piece, which is his determinative answer to the questions just raised and to the arguments just rehearsed. Now an answer to the question about whether the young should learn to perform obviously requires first an answer to the prior question whether music should be included in education and for what purpose. So Aristotle deals now with this question, leaving the former till later (in chapter 6). He argues that music should be included in education for all three purposes. First he argues that music, because of its pleasure, has power for play and for cultured pursuits and that it should be included in education for these reasons. Then he argues, and at length, that it has power for character and should be included in education for this reason also, and indeed for this reason above all.

That music has power for play and cultured leisure he argues thus: (1) play and cultured pursuits need to be pleasant (play because it gives rest from the pain of toil, cultured pursuits because they are the end and the end must be pleasant as well as noble); (2) music, both instrumental (music "by itself," 1339a20–21)[24] and with song, is among the pleasantest things (as all agree and as Musaeus, an acknowledged authority, says); (3) therefore music, being pleasant, has power for play and cultured pursuits (and has, for this reason, reasonably been included in social gatherings). Of course, this argument will, as far as it goes, prove that anything that is pleasant has the power for play and cultured pursuits, including harmful and vulgar pleasures. But this need not matter for Aristotle's present purpose, because, first, the argument does prove the conclusion about music and because, second,

24. That music "by itself," or literally music "bare" (*psilēn*), means instrumental music is the view of Kraut (1997: ad loc.), Newman (3:533), and Susemihl and Hicks (1894: 587), but not of Lord (1982: 86–87), who wants it to mean words without music rather than music without words.

harmful and vulgar pleasures, though included by this argument, could easily be excluded by other arguments that would not exclude music, or not harmless and noble music (as the arguments, for instance, that cultured leisure is noble and that the citizens of the best city are not to enjoy vulgar or harmful things).

1339b24   From this fact, then, that music is a source of pleasure, and of harmless pleasure (as Aristotle expressly says here, 1339b25), it must follow that music should be included in the education of the young for both of the purposes that it thus has the power to effect, namely not only for training them to enjoy the end, or noble leisure, when older, but also for contributing to their rest and play even now while they are being educated. In confirmation of this last point in particular, Aristotle appeals to the general fact that the end is seldom enjoyed (even, presumably, by the mature, for contemplation, which is the end, is something human beings, unlike the god, only fitfully achieve; *Ethics* 10.8.1178b25–27, 7.14.1154b20–31). Enjoying pleasure, then, by way of rest and play and without thinking of anything further (whether of the past occupations that play is a rest from or of the future ones it is a preparation for), is useful as a sort of consolation and substitute for not always enjoying the end, or, in the case of the young, for not yet being able to enjoy it.

1339b31   As further evidence of this likeness between play and the end, and therefore of the suitableness, for the reason just given, of having music in education, Aristotle notes that it has led human beings to confuse the two. For it is not only the case that the end and play are pleasant but also that neither is for the sake of something that comes later. The end is certainly not, for, precisely as end, there can be nothing else for the sake of which one could choose it, and play is not, for it is rather for the sake of past toil, that is, to recover from it (play does, of course, enable one to take up toil again later, but it does this precisely because of the way it is used to give relief from the toil gone by).[25] The end and play are thus, in fact, very different, but also, for the same reason, sufficiently similar to make many people seek for the end in play and indeed in any pleasure, not just the noble kind of cultured pursuits. Nevertheless, music is enjoyed by people for rest, and hence has a place in education also for this reason.

~ FOR CONTRIBUTING TO CHARACTER

1339b42   Music, then, because of the pleasure it gives, has power for play and cultured leisure. But giving pleasure, as already noted, is not something proper to music; many other things also give such pleasure. So to justify the inclusion of music in education on this ground is to do so on the ground of something that may be merely incidental to music (and not peculiar or essential), and of some-

---

25. But see also the discussion in Susemihl and Hicks (1894: 589).

thing, moreover, that need not have anything grand or honorable about it. For children and animals can appreciate and enjoy the common pleasures of music (though, clearly, they are not fit for cultured leisure). One might accordingly wonder if music needs to be singled out, in the way it traditionally has been, for special mention among the subjects of education. Not inappropriately, therefore, does Aristotle turn now to consider if music may not have some additional and proper power for the third of the possibilities listed before, namely virtue of character. For this would certainly raise it above other common pleasures (as those of feasting, say, mentioned along with music in the quotations from Homer in 5(8).3), and would more adequately justify its special treatment. So Aristotle proceeds next to prove that it does have such power.

1340a7   Music will be shown to have this power if, as he says, it is shown to have power to make us come to be of a certain sort in our character (for virtue is good character or habits, so whatever has power for character will have power for good character if used appropriately). His argument for this conclusion is rather complex, but he first establishes that music affects the passions, and then, from this, that music must also affect character (for good or ill). The argument that music affects passions is a simple appeal to facts, first to the tunes of Olympus and second to imitations generally. As regards the so-called tunes of Olympus, it is not necessary to know much about them to know that music can have an enthusiastic effect (for some music today has this effect). Also, it is manifest that enthusiasm is a passion (it is a temporary state of high excitement) but also a passion with respect to the soul's character (and not, say, just a passion of the body or the intellect), since it urges us on to action and action belongs to the same part of the soul as does character, namely the desiring or appetitive part.[26]

As regards imitations, some problem arises as to what is meant by "imitations . . . even in the absence of rhythms and tunes" (1340a12–14). Perhaps they are mere imitative sounds (as perhaps a single note, or the creak of a door, or the call of an animal), which, by themselves, can make us feel certain passions;[27] or perhaps by "imitations" is meant poetic dramas and the like and the reference is to the effect such imitations still have even in the absence of musical accompaniment (so that Aristotle is meaning by "music" here poetry in general and is not confining it to music proper);[28] or perhaps, while the reference is to such imitations without their musical accompaniment, what is intended is the internal musical effect (and not the meaning) of the spoken words, for ancient Greek had a pitch accent and so

26. *Ethics* 1.13.1102b13–1103a10; Newman (3:536–37), Susemihl and Hicks (1894: 622–24).

27. Newman suggests this (3:537).

28. The opinion of Kraut (1997: ad loc.), Lord (1982: 88–89), and perhaps also of Jowett (1885: 2:300).

any recitation would have a marked singsong quality to it;[29] or perhaps, finally, the Greek should be translated differently to mean that people are affected by imitations even when the rhythms and tunes that accompany the recitation of the words are taken "separately," that is, such that one gets these alone without the words.[30] Any of these options would seem possible and make the point intended, except, perhaps, the second, for Aristotle's argument in this passage concerns the effect on character of certain sounds, not of certain meanings, so that he must be using "music" in its more narrow sense.

1340a14   Having thus shown that music has an effect on passions, Aristotle next turns to show that it can also thereby have an effect on character. First he lays down two premises and then proceeds to draw certain conclusions from them.[31] The two premises are: (1) music is something pleasant; (2) virtue concerns taking pleasure aright and liking and disliking. From premise (1) and from the point just made about music exciting passions in us, it follows (though Aristotle leaves the point to be understood) that: (3) music makes us find pleasure in the passions that it excites. For if music is pleasant and at the same time excites the passions, then to find pleasure in the music is also to find pleasure in the passions thereby excited. Premise (2) is a thesis central to Aristotle's whole doctrine about the virtue of character (or moral virtue), namely that such virtue belongs to the appetitive part of the soul and concerns establishing there, by a process of habituation, a fixed disposition for choosing and taking pleasure in the noble mean, the mean determined by reason, in actions and passions, and for being pained by and avoiding the corresponding but base extremes.[32]

From premise (2), and from the fact that it is necessary to become virtuous (in order to be happy, that is, and happiness is the point of the present discussion, not to say of the whole of the *Ethics* and *Politics* simply), it follows that: (4) there is need of nothing so much as learning and getting habituated to judging aright (that is, to reaching by prudence a correct determination of the mean) and to taking pleasure in decent characters and noble deeds (that is, to enjoying and choosing the mean in passions and actions as so determined). To these Aristotle now adds: (5) there are likenesses to be found in rhythms and tunes that are very close to the real natures of virtues and vices, and: (6) getting used to taking pain and pleasure

29. The opinion I suggested, though not with any certainty, in the translation; see Snell (1979) on the general musical quality of ancient Greek. But even modern languages that lack a pitch accent can be given a singsong quality and excite certain pleasures and passions accordingly (one might think of the way many Welsh speak English).

30. The opinion of Susemihl and Hicks (1894: 591). In illustration of this interpretation one may note how the modern blues still excite sadness and sorrow even if the usual accompaniment of words is omitted.

31. I follow here the suggestions of Barker (1946: 343).

32. The essentials of the doctrine are given in *Ethics* 2.1–6.

in likenesses is close to being in the same state with respect to the realities. Premise (5) follows in a way from the fact, established earlier and repeated here, that music excites the passions. It is now illustrated with respect to anger and mildness, courage and moderation (mildness is the mean with respect to the passion of anger, courage is the mean with respect to the passions of fear and boldness, moderation is the mean with respect to sensual pleasures and pains).[33] But the point is a general one that follows from the very idea of virtue. For if virtue is a mean with respect to certain passions, and if music excites such passions, then music can excite them either according to the mean (virtue) or contrary to the mean (vice). But as to how tunes and rhythms can be said to contain likenesses, Aristotle explains more fully shortly. Premise (6) is illustrated, and suitably enough, with an example from likenesses in visible forms.

From (5) and (3) it follows that: (7) music makes us find pleasure in the likenesses of virtues (and vices), namely those that, through the passions it excites, music contains. From (6) and (7) it follows that: (8) getting used to, and taking pleasure in, certain kinds of music is getting used to, and taking pleasure in, certain kinds of virtues (and vices). From (2) and (8) it follows that: (9) getting used to, and taking pleasure in, certain kinds of music is, to this extent, to acquire the corresponding virtues (and vices). From (4) and (9) it follows that: (10) there is need of such getting used to, and taking pleasure in, certain kinds of music. Conclusions (9) and (10) are what Aristotle is aiming at, since they mean that music has power to affect character and hence that it can and should be used in education (or rather that the kinds that promote virtue should be used and the kinds that promote vice avoided). But he leaves expressly stating these conclusions until later (at 1340b10–13). He turns first instead to explaining and proving (5) more fully.[34]

1340a28 Premise (5) is, in a way, the key to Aristotle's argument, but it might certainly be questioned, both in its own right,[35] and with respect to its confining likenesses to musical sounds only. For perhaps some might want to say that, if there are likenesses in music, there are likenesses in painting and sculpture as well, and hence these should also be singled out along with music as having the same power to form character. Accordingly Aristotle proceeds to defend his claims about music, first by explaining that the objects of the senses other than hearing do not contain likenesses, and then by explaining that music does.

On the first point Aristotle simply states that there are no likenesses in perceptions of taste and touch (or presumably in those of smell either), but slight ones in

---

33. *Ethics* 2.7.

34. Susemihl and Hicks (1894: 591) are thus, in a way, right to regard everything from the "since" at 1340a14 up to the conclusion at 1340b10 as a single "portentous" period.

35. As it has been questioned both in antiquity and since; see Susemihl and Hicks (1894: 592–93).

perceptions of sight, though, as he explains, what he means by "slight" here is rather that objects seen contain no likenesses, strictly speaking, but only signs. They contain signs in the sense that the colors and shapes of bodies in the grip of passion are signs of character relative to the passion (anger, for instance, can be portrayed by clenched fists, pursed lips, reddened face, and so on, and hence mildness might be portrayed by showing someone not angry while others are, or vice versa).[36] To the extent, then, that this is true, the young should naturally contemplate only the works of the better painters and sculptors.

1340a38 As regards the second point, that music does contain likenesses, Aristotle simply appeals again to the fact that different musical modes put hearers into different passions or emotional states, and that different rhythms too have different effects. The fact here is presumably not matter for dispute, for even if Aristotle's modes are no longer familiar to us and are not the basis of our own music, it is still true that our different scales or keys and their major and minor modes work different emotional effects. The point is anyway manifest in the case of rhythm. Marches affect us in one way, waltzes in another, and heavy rock in another. The general point, then, seems clear enough, that different sorts of music affect our passions in different ways.

What is less clear is how these facts prove that music contains likenesses while painting and sculpture contain only signs. Perhaps the stress is to be put on the idea that through music we are "put into" different states (1340a41) so that the effect of music involves no mediation or learning while visible forms require us to perform some sort of inference (we have to learn, for instance, to associate these sounds and shapes with these passions). One might also note that music is a motion, something that Aristotle mentions in the case of rhythm, and that passions and actions too are motions.[37] Music is, of course, a motion in sounds while passions are motions in the soul, but one motion can properly be said to be "like" another motion (while a shape or color cannot be); and since it is manifest that the motions of some music excite motions in the soul and also excite to physical motion (as in the case of dances and marches), it is perhaps not unreasonable to say that the musical motions contain "likenesses" of the motions they excite. But as Aristotle is

36. Newman (3:540) suggests that architecture too, and not just bodies, should be conceded an ethical suggestiveness. But perhaps Aristotle is not so much denying this as not, at this point, concerned to take notice of it. He is certainly not ignorant of the ethical significance of town planning, 4(7).12, especially 1331a28–32.

37. This similarity was already noted in antiquity, as it has also been noted since; see Susemihl and Hicks (1894: 593–94). Peter of Auvergne, by contrast (1951: 8.2.1308, 8.3.1334), understands the similarity between passions and music to consist, not in the fact that both are motions, but rather in the fact that both involve proportions: music the proportions of sounds, and passions the proportions of bodily humors.

relying heavily here on actual experience and empirical research, it is to such experience (our own specifically) that doubts and difficulties must be referred.

1340b10 Having thus stated and explained his argument, Aristotle finally draws the conclusion, first, that music does have power for character, and, second, that therefore it should be used in education for this purpose. In further support of the second conclusion he adds two other points: (1) that the young need things to be sweetened for them so that, since music has this sweetness naturally, to use music to teach virtue will be to use something that does not need any sweetening for the young willingly to respond to and enjoy; (2) that there is a natural affinity between the soul and the rhythms and modes of music (a sign of which is that some have thought the soul is a mode or harmony), so that, for this reason too, musical teaching of virtue will find a ready and willing response among the young.

Chapter 6

∼ THE MUSIC THE YOUNG SHOULD BE TAUGHT

∼ AS REGARDS PERFORMANCE

1340b20 Having determined that and for what purpose music is to be included in education, Aristotle turns next to consider the other question of which music one should participate in and how, or which music should be learned and how. He begins with the question of how music should be learned, namely with the question, broached earlier, of whether the young should learn to perform for themselves or not. He first answers this question in the affirmative and then responds to objections.

For his answer he gives two reasons. The first is: (1) sharing in the actual doing or performance of music is necessary to becoming a serious judge; (2) becoming a serious judge is necessary to coming to be of a good character; (3) therefore sharing in the performance of music is necessary to coming to be of a good character. Premise (2) is obvious from the idea of virtue (virtue requires one to judge character as well as to act accordingly). Premise (1) can be supported, at least as regards the fact, by the example of the Spartans, who did not share in performance (as they boast, 5(8).5.1339a42–b4), and who failed manifestly to acquire good character. It can also be supported by noting that the kind of judging in question here is a judging of character as present in the several modes and rhythms, and experience attests that a good understanding of modes and rhythms requires not just listening to them but at least sufficient familiarity with playing and singing so as to be able, however minimally, to reproduce them for oneself. Music in this regard seems different from the artistic products mentioned earlier (houses, rudders, dinners, 3.11.1282a18–23), which the user can judge better than the maker.[38]

1340b25 The second reason is: (1) children need diversion; (2) such diversion can be provided for older children by education (in performance, that is) as the rattle provides it for small children; (3) therefore older children should be taught performance. Premise (2) here does not say that music alone or best meets the need for diversion, so while it does establish the conclusion, it does not, by itself, prove that music is more to be included in education for this purpose than other possible diversions. But that hardly matters in the context, for performance has just been shown to be necessary for forming character, so the fact that it also fills this other need does genuinely provide an additional reason for including it, though not, of course, for including other diversions that are not otherwise necessary or desirable.

1340b31 Aristotle next turns to answering the objection, raised earlier (5(8).5.1339b8–10), that learning to perform is vulgar, and does so by drawing distinctions and determining which kinds of performance are vulgar and which not. His first determination removes the problem of vulgarity as regards the older. For since the point of performance is to learn to judge and enjoy music properly, once this ability has been achieved while young performance is to stop and not to be carried on into adulthood. Aristotle's meaning here need not, perhaps, be that performance is to stop entirely,[39] but only that it is to stop as something to be done and taken seriously, for performance was allowed by Aristotle earlier for those playing or drinking (5(8).5.1339b8–10), and some illiberal tasks were also allowed by him to the free provided they were not done in the service of others (5(8).2.1337b17–21).

1340b40 But this response, while removing the charge of vulgarity as far as it concerns adults, does not remove it as regards the young who are still performing (and hence it does not fully remove it as regards adults either, if vulgarity from youth can be carried over into adulthood). Aristotle, therefore, proceeds to further determinations, and specifically about the questions of how far learning to perform is to go, which tunes and rhythms are to be used, and which instruments are to be learned. He deals first with the first question, second with the third (later on in this chapter), and third with the second (in chapter 7).

1341a5 As preface to his answers, Aristotle lays down that performance must not be learned in such a way as to be an impediment to later activities, nor

---

38. Newman (3:546–57) notes certain problems at this point, which, however, admit of ready answers. That a multitude can sometimes judge the works of music and poets better than experts (3.11.1281b7–10) is only true of some multitudes and some experts and does not exclude the idea that these multitudes have some familiarity with performance. Also, the sort of familiarity Aristotle requires is, as becomes clear, only an amateurish one and solely for the purpose of judging character well; it does not include expertise.

39. As Newman (3:548) supposes, though not Susemihl and Hicks (1894: 599).

must it be learned so as to render the bodies of the young unfit, now or in the future, for the exercise and study of virtue, whether in war or peace. These two points follow from previous determinations (that earlier education has to be adapted to later education and that the end of education is the life of virtue, at 4(7).15), and observance of them will clearly ensure that musical education achieves the end of education as well as ensure that vulgarity of body, and indeed of thought too, is avoided. So, with respect to the first question, how far performance is to go, the end will be achieved and vulgarity avoided if, first, performance is confined to works that neither are aimed at artistic competitions (and the skills required for victory) nor excite astonishment or are extraordinary (it is such skills, as is explained at the end of chapter, that make the performer vulgar in body and soul); and if, second, even these works that are performed are performed only to the point required for being able to delight in noble rhythms and tunes (those, that is, which have power for a leisure of cultured pursuits and for virtue, and which take one beyond those elements of music that even animals, slaves, and small children can spontaneously enjoy).

1341a17   As regards the third question, what instruments to perform on, it evidently now follows that instruments that require the sort of artistic skills just excluded should also themselves be excluded, for the point of learning performance is to be able to judge well with a view to character, not to become an expert. Hence Aristotle rejects the pipes and the cithara (a kind of lyre or harp),[40] but rejects the pipes also for two other reasons, that their function is for purification, not education in virtue (a point developed in the next chapter), and that they prevent speech (so that learning to sing noble songs cannot go on at the same time).

1341a26   In confirmation of his rejection of the pipes (which rejection might perhaps raise questions), Aristotle refers to the fact that they were rejected, along with several other instruments,[41] in the past too, and for the same reason, that they were found, from direct experience (not prejudice or ignorance), to contribute nothing to virtue (which is the point of learning to play music). The events Aristotle records here, as well as the story about Athena (the goddess of learning), that she threw away the pipes after inventing them, are not merely anecdotal but stress the idea that learning to play was pursued by the noble minded in the past, as it should be pursued now, for the sake of virtue and noble leisure, and hence that only those instruments should be used which contribute to this end.

1341b8   Since in this discussion of how far performance is to go and on what instruments Aristotle has rejected everything that involves artistic expertise,

40. On these instruments see the notes and illustrations in Susemihl and Hicks (1894: 601); also Newman (3:551–52).

41. Some illustrations and discussion of these other instruments can be found in Susemihl and Hicks (1894: 632–36), and see also West (1992).

he now explains more fully what he means by this and why it is to be rejected for education. By such expertise, then, he means expertise for winning competitions, and this is contrary to education for two reasons. The first is that it is not undertaken for virtue but for crude pleasure (the pleasure of the crowd before whom the contest takes place). Such performance is therefore proper to laborers, not the free, because it is a toiling (learning artistic skills is certainly a toil, and the more so the more difficult the skill), and a toiling for the benefit of others. The second, which picks up on the last point, is that the performer or contestant is made into a vulgar mechanic. For the audience, being crude, make demands for cruder sorts of music and so, to give them pleasure and win their favor, which the contestant must do if he is to be successful, he has to perform crude music with crude movements and so becomes crude himself in both character and body.[42]

Chapter 7

〜 AS REGARDS MODES AND RHYTHMS

1341b19 Aristotle comes finally to consider the remaining question, which modes and rhythms are to be taught, though the discussion of rhythms is evidently missing. He divides the question into three: whether all modes and rhythms are to be used or distinctions made; whether the same division must be laid down for those engaged in toil with a view to education; whether some other division needs to be laid down. All three questions are about music education, and so I take it that the first is about which modes and rhythms are to be used for education generally (that is, for all the things that music has the power to effect and not for education in virtue only); the second about which the young are to learn specifically for education in virtue and hence for performance (performance, therefore, being the reference of "toil"); the third about the same question but now whether some further distinction is needed.[43]

This means, therefore, that Aristotle is now taking the question of modes and rhythms broadly, so that it also covers which ones are to be used in education generally, including any for play and cultured pursuits, and not just which ones are to be used in performance and for education in virtue (the question that occupied him in the previous chapter). But this is perhaps not unreasonable, for the broader

42. This "rake's progress" of musical performers is something that could be noted in many ages, including our own.

43. The Greek text here and its division of questions have been taken in several different ways by commentators, as Lord (1984: 239, 270; 1982: 107–8) and Susemihl and Hicks (1894: 606), and emendations are not infrequently proposed. My own interpretation is governed by the aim of leaving the text just as it is. In fact, I more or less follow Jowett (1885: 2:302) who also rightly points out that the third question is properly a subdivision of the second. That this third question is nevertheless included is presumably because Aristotle is going to decide that an additional distinction is indeed necessary.

question certainly needs to be asked, and a discussion of modes and rhythms to be used for performance is an appropriate place to ask it. For a determination about which modes and rhythms to use for other purposes would help make clearer the determination of which ones to use specifically for performance.

1341b23 As preface to his discussion of the three questions just distinguished, Aristotle notes two points. The first is that modes and rhythms, or tunes and rhythms (for modes only exist in music as realized in some tune), are different and that this difference requires a consideration of the different effects of each on education and whether goodness in one is to be preferred to goodness in the other. In other words, tunes and rhythms are to be examined separately, not together, and then later compared. But from this, of course, it necessarily follows that the three questions just posed will have to be asked twice, once about modes and once again about rhythms. Hence, in what follows, Aristotle turns first to ask them about modes or tunes, and his asking them about rhythms would naturally have come next. The second point is that since much has already been correctly said by others on these matters, he himself is not going to go into details but only to state things in outline manner (a procedure he follows elsewhere, as at 4(7).5.1326b39–40).[44]

1341b32 The first question, then, concerns distinguishing modes for use in education generally. Here Aristotle lays down a threefold distinction of tunes and modes: those of character, action, and enthusiasm. This distinction, especially as regards those of character, is evidently something different from what he said earlier about the power of music for character, because there he attributed this power to all music generally, using as examples also the tunes of Olympus and the Phrygian mode, which tunes and mode would here have to be put into the enthusiastic class (5(8).5.1340a9–12, b4–5). Tunes and modes of action would also seem to have, in a more general sense, power for character, since character is also a principle of action and what moves to action must move in a way that, at least in the particular case, does or does not accord with the virtuous mean. Modes and tunes of character are perhaps, therefore, to be taken as those that, of themselves, have power for character or rather good character, namely those whose nature, like Dorian, is already that of the mean (as noted later in this chapter, at 1342b14–16). Those of action and enthusiasm, by contrast, will be those that have, of themselves, power specifically for action or enthusiasm and only power for good character or the mean according to the particular way they are used.[45]

Having laid down this distinction, Aristotle next recalls, according to his pre-

44. As to which others Aristotle may have in mind, see Kraut (1997: ad loc.), Newman (3:544, 559–60), and Susemihl and Hicks (1894: 607).

45. As to which specific modes and tunes may fall into which class, see Lord (1982: 114–15), Newman (3:560–61), Susemihl and Hicks (1894: 607). Jowett (1885: 2:303) likens, and perhaps not unjustly, those of character to our sacred music, those of action to our military music, and those of enthusiasm to our music of the dance.

vious determinations (5(8).5), that music is to be used for several purposes, and not one only. These purposes were before stated as those of education in virtue, of cultured pursuits, and of play or rest, and these are all repeated here, though with two peculiarities. First, cultured pursuits and rest are listed together and it is not clear from the Greek whether they are meant to form a single third group or whether rest is to be taken as a fourth.[46] Perhaps either interpretation will do, or perhaps the ambiguity is deliberate. For while cultured pursuits are different from play and rest, they are not very different with respect to music since it is the pleasure of music that effects both (whereas it is music's likenesses to character, and not just its pleasure, that effect virtue). At any rate the two purposes of cultured pursuits and play are not treated separately in what follows.

The other peculiarity is that another purpose of music is now noted, that of purification or *katharsis*. This purpose, however, as becomes apparent, is not one that properly falls outside those initially distinguished but belongs to the two of play and cultured pursuits (for its purpose is a certain kind of pleasure). That it is nevertheless separately noted and discussed now (though it and some of its modes and instruments were mentioned before, at 5(8).5.1340a10–12, b4–5; 6.1341a21–24) is presumably because the discussion has come now specifically to modes and for what purpose each sort is to be used, and hence any modes that stand out for any reason with respect to one or other of these purposes deserve to be separately discussed (as Dorian and certain others are so discussed later in the case of music for virtue).

At all events, having distinguished the kinds of modes, and recalled that music is to be used for several purposes, Aristotle now concludes that all three kinds of modes are to be used but not all in the same way or for the same purpose: those of character are for education, that is, in this context, for learning to perform as part of training in virtue; those of action and enthusiasm are not to be performed but only listened to, that is, they are primarily for the pleasure of rest and cultured leisure (but perhaps also for virtue insofar as music that is merely listened to can still have power for character). Hence his answer to the first question at the beginning of the chapter is that all modes are to be used, but along with a certain distinction. This distinction will also now help further to answer the charge, from the preceding chapter, that learning to perform music is vulgar, for only modes of character are to be performed, not others, and the former need not involve any vulgarity in performance (as specifically the Dorian) while the others will (as specifically frenzied tunes and tunes for the pipes).

1342a4 Aristotle turns next to defend his answer as thus stated. Not much problem, however, is likely to arise about whether to include modes of character

---

46. The question is discussed by Newman (3:561–62) and Susemihl and Hicks (1894: 608). Kraut (1997: ad loc.) thinks there may be some corruption in the manuscripts.

and of action in education generally. For one could hardly doubt that the young, who are to train as soldiers, should listen at least to music for military action, and, as for modes of character, the only doubts here concern whether such modes should be learned for performance, and these doubts have already been answered, or can be more properly dealt with in the discussion of the second of the three questions stated at the beginning of the chapter. That leaves only the modes of enthusiasm, and there may well be doubt about whether these should be listened to in education, or whether they involve any vulgarity. In addition modes for purification or *katharsis*, which evidently fall under the same head, have been mentioned but not explained and some explanation is needed.[47] So Aristotle now leaves the other modes aside and confines himself in what follows to those of enthusiasm.

Aristotle's intention is, then, to defend the use of enthusiastic modes and tunes. His argument may be formalized thus: (1) passions that affect some souls strongly and with some force, as the passions of pity, fear, and enthusiasm, affect everyone more or less; (2) those strongly affected by such passions are seen to calm down under the influence of enthusiastic tunes, as receiving a cure and purification[48] (the point is shown by an example taken from the particular case of how the strongly enthused are affected by those sacred tunes that put the soul into an excited frenzy); (3) therefore everyone will, to the extent they feel the same passions, experience the same purificatory effect from the same tunes; (4) this purificatory effect is or is accompanied by relief along with pleasure; (5) therefore everyone will experience similar relief along with pleasure from the same sort of tunes. But if these sorts of tunes, which are all enthusiastic, have this pleasurable effect, then enthusiastic tunes are manifestly fit to be used for purposes of play and rest and cultured pursuits and hence, as Aristotle has just said, have a place in education, at least for listening to. Premises (1) and (2) are asserted on the basis of observation, but the inference from them to the conclusion (3) and thence to (5) also rests on the implicit premise (6) that like causes have like effects on like subjects. Hence, if those strongly moved by one passion feel a pleasurable purification when affected by one kind of enthusiastic music, then those mildly affected by the same passion, or strongly or mildly affected by other passions, will feel the same pleasure, whether strongly or mildly, when affected by the same or other enthusiastic tunes.

To this argument Aristotle then adds what looks to be another: (1) purificatory

47. I follow the suggestions of Newman (3:563) and Susemihl and Hicks (1894: 609).

48. What Aristotle precisely means here by purification or *katharsis* has become a source of endless debate. The secondary literature is vast and it would be impossible to list it. So, apart from Newman (3:564–65) and Susemihl and Hicks (1894: 610–11), note also the discussion and references in Kraut (1997: ad loc.), Lord (1982: chap. 3), and my own in Simpson (1988).

tunes also provide harmless pleasure. For if we combine with this the premise stated earlier (5(8).5.1339b25–27), that (2) all harmless pleasures are suitable for the end and for rest, then it follows that (3) purificatory tunes are suitable for the end and for rest. So again, enthusiastic music in general (to which class purificatory tunes belong) must, to the extent all such music is similar, be suitable for the end, that is, for cultured leisure, and for rest, and thus have a place in education as something, at any rate, to be listened to. Hence, Aristotle pointedly adds, contestants whose job it is to perform in the theater (and who, of course, cannot be citizens, since such performing will certainly be vulgar), should be assigned to play such tunes so that the citizens can listen to them and get the benefit.[49]

1342a18 This, then, justifies the inclusion of enthusiastic music in education. But there remains the question of vulgarity, a question brought back to the fore by the mention of the theater and contestants (whose activities were criticized in the previous chapter as vulgar). Aristotle, therefore, turns lastly to this question and adds the qualification that there are two sorts of theater or rather two sorts of audience, the free and educated on the one hand and the crude and vulgar on the other. Obviously the citizens are to be free and educated, so spectacles and contests for them will be free and educated too. The vulgar audience, however, made up of those in the city who are not citizens (but who perform necessary work for the citizens, 4(7).8, 9), will need play and rest too, for they must relax in preparation for continued labor. Accordingly they will need pleasure, but as each finds pleasure in what is akin to his nature, the vulgar, who have twisted souls, will need vulgar and twisted or deviant music for this purpose. Hence such vulgar music, the strained and highly colored sort that doubtless requires the display of artistic brilliance criticized in the previous chapter, has its place, but only for a vulgar audience. For an educated audience, by contrast, no such music is fit or needed. Music for them, even in the case of enthusiastic tunes, will lack any vulgar additions. The evident conclusion is that not only will the citizen young not play this vulgar music (as was argued in the previous chapter), they will not even listen to it. Hence, in this way too, the charge of vulgarity can be answered.

1342a28 Aristotle comes now to consider the second question, whether the same division as just laid down is to be laid down also for those learning to perform. His answer is in effect both yes and no. The same division is to be laid down because it is the division that contains the class of modes proper for performance, namely the modes of character. It is not, however, the only division that needs to be laid down because, as he indicates shortly in answering the third question, there is need also of another division, which, to some extent, cuts across the first. But as regards the present and second question, Aristotle first repeats the

49. From this it is evident that Aristotle intended some sort of theater or drama to be included in education, but his discussion of the other parts of education and specifically of poetry is missing.

answer, already given, that the modes of character are to be used for education (in the sense that they are also to be performed). Then he specifies these as the Dorian in particular and any others that the relevant experts recommend (for, as he said at the beginning, he is now relying on the determinations of experts).

1342a32   The experts just mentioned are specified as those who share in the pursuit of philosophy and in music education, that is, those who share in both and not those who share in one only, and specifically not those who share in the first alone. For Aristotle now in effect gives an illustration of how to use the opinions of experts in judging which modes to include and which to exclude, and in this he specifically criticizes the views of someone who was an expert in philosophy but apparently not in music education, namely the Socrates of Plato's *Republic*.[50] Socrates accepted the Dorian but kept the Phrygian along with it, and in this he seems to have erred in two ways. First, he was inconsistent, for he rejects the pipes but the pipes are among instruments what the Phrygian are among modes (both generate frenzy). Hence, if the Phrygian modes are to be kept, so should the pipes, and if the pipes are to be rejected, so should the Phrygian modes. Second, precisely because Phrygian modes are frenzied, they are not modes of character but of enthusiasm (and so do not belong among modes to be played but among modes to be listened to). In proof of the character of Phrygian modes and the pipes, Aristotle appeals to manifest examples and the views of experts about the particular case of the dithyramb.

1342b12   By contrast, Dorian gets the approval of all experts (including Socrates, of course) as a mode of character, in particular because it is the most steady and the one that most has a courageous character. Dorian also has the further support that it is like virtue, or characters that are praised, in being a mean between extremes, for it is a mean in relation to the other modes. Hence the young should manifestly be educated more in Dorian tunes (that is, educated in performing these tunes with a view to virtue).

1342b17   But Aristotle says that Dorian is to be used "more," not that it is to be used only, and that it is "most" steady and courageous, not that it alone is so (1342b13, 17). Hence there must be other modes that have a certain steadiness or courage to them, or are close to the mean, and are to be used as well. Thus Aristotle turns next to say which these are, but in doing so he lays down two other criteria besides the mean, namely the possible and the proper. He is now, in fact, laying down another division of modes and tunes and so has moved to the third question he posed at the beginning and is answering it in the affirmative. What is meant by the mean has just been explained, so he now explains what he means by the possible and the proper and first by the possible.

50. Socrates does in fact confess an ignorance of music in the passage of the *Republic* in question (399a3–c6), though this may be ironic.

The possible, he says, is distinguished by ages so that what is possible at one age is not necessarily possible at another. The example he gives is that of those "exhausted by time" (1342b20–21) who cannot easily sing the strained modes but rather the relaxed ones. This is usually taken to be a reference to old men, but since "strained" and "relaxed" (1342b21–22) naturally indicate modes that are high-pitched and low-pitched,[51] the reference would be more appropriately to puberty and to those whose voice has broken and who, for that reason, have lost the ability to sing the higher registers (for there is no natural break in singing ability at any other stage of life, and old age does not automatically take away one's ability to sing the sort of things one was singing in one's prime).[52] Hence, contrary to the objections of Socrates, learning to perform and sing some relaxed modes also has its place in the education of the young in virtue, because of their continued need for musical performance after puberty.

But the possible must be taken along with the proper (as well as with the mean), and this too is distinguished by ages. Learning to perform music is, of course, for the young, and what is proper for the young is modes that educate in virtue but also at the same time promote orderliness (the reason is presumably that orderliness is especially necessary in childhood when one is naturally full of energy and of an energy that will express itself in any and every way, including vulgar and base ones, if it is not directed and disciplined).[53] So orderly music, because of the natural attractiveness or sweetness of music generally, will be a most useful way of achieving this result. Hence, as regards which modes and tunes to use for teaching the young to perform (with a view to their education in virtue), these must not only be possible but also proper and have the nature of a mean. The latter criterion will ensure that the modes in question are those of character, the other two will ensure that these modes are correctly adapted to the age of the young being taught.[54]

With these remarks, Aristotle's discussion of education and of the best regime simply ends. Whether the further discussion has got lost or was never written is perhaps impossible to say. But the things immediately missing are a treatment of rhythms, with a comparison between them and tunes, and of other subjects to be

51. As noted by Newman (3:544) and Susemihl and Hicks (1894: 626).

52. Several commentators want to reject this whole final paragraph as spurious, as Lord (1978a: 39–41; 1982: 147, 215–19), Newman (3:571–72), Susemihl and Hicks (1894: 616–18), but not Kraut (1997: ad loc.). The main reason given is that Aristotle has earlier rejected performance after youth (5(8).6.1340b35–39), so he would be contradicting himself if he were now to imply that singing will go on into old age. But if one takes the reference of "exhausted by time" to be to the age of puberty and not to old age, this objection is removed (quite apart, anyway, from the fact that Aristotle seems to allow the older to indulge in performance when drinking or playing, 5(8).5.1339b8–10).

53. Cf. the discussion of shameful speech, etc., at 4(7).17.1336a39–b35. "Orderliness" is *kosmos*.

54. Which modes Aristotle has in mind, besides the Lydian along with the Dorian, is difficult to say, though one may begin with the extended discussion by Susemihl and Hicks (1894: 624–31). Perhaps he leaves the matter vague precisely because he is expecting the reader to consult the relevant experts.

included in education and how and at what ages (as notably military exercises and philosophy). Several other things mentioned earlier as needing later discussion might also suitably have been dealt with in what was to follow here, as: the censorship of speech and spectacles (4(7).17.1336b24–26), child managers (4(7).16.1335b2–5), treatment of slaves (4(7).10.1330a31–33), messes (4(7).10.1330a3–5), use of property (4(7).5.1326b32–35), homosexuality (2.10.1272a24–26), relations between men and women, and any education proper to the virtues of women (1.13.1260b8–13). But perhaps enough exists in other writings (as the *Ethics* in particular) to give us a fair idea of what Aristotle would have said on these matters. What other matters he would also have discussed must be left to speculation.

BOOK 6

Division and Description of
the Other Regimes

Chapter 1

~ THE QUESTIONS POLITICAL SCIENCE MUST STUDY

1288b10 Aristotle has completed his study of the simply best regime of kingship and aristocracy, and he turns next in the last books of the *Politics* to collect and study all the remaining regimes that are not simply best. Now it has seemed to many scholars that there is a conflict or tension between these last books about these other regimes and the earlier books about the best regime. Such scholars also tend to describe the earlier books as "ideal," since they treat of a best regime that does not exist, and these last ones as "empirical," since they treat, and with much historical detail, of regimes that do exist.[1] Yet it is manifest from this present chapter that Aristotle himself saw no such conflict or tension and that he did not divide his treatment of regimes into an "ideal" and a "real" part. On the contrary, he saw a comprehensive treatment of all regimes as constituting one and the same science, and he saw the difference between the best regime and the others as a difference between the best simply and the best under certain conditions and not as a difference between the ideal and the real.[2] Indeed, it is by seeing things in this same way that one best answers the question of how a treatment of inferior regimes can be necessary or appropriate in a study whose intention is the best regime and making men good (3.18.1288a39–b2, *Ethics* 10.9). For what Aristotle now shows is that such an intention includes within it, not just the simply best, but also the best in the circumstances, and not just making men simply good, but also making them as good as they and the conditions allow. He does this by showing,

1. The chief proponent of the thesis of a conflict between the "ideal" and the "real" books was Jaeger (1923/1934: chap. 10), and it became a major plank in his argument that the *Politics* is neither a doctrinal nor a structural unity. Schütrumpf is the most recent to have followed him in this respect (1991: 1:39–67, 94–102). Newman, however, expresses the sense of contrast more cautiously (1:489–92).

2. These points are correctly stressed by Pellegrin (1987). Jaeger (1923/1934: 269), despite being fully aware of them, fails to take them seriously, as Lord notes (1984: 15). Newman (1:489) only allows them to constitute an attempt at "softening" a tension that still remains. See also Barker (1946: xliv), Johnson (1990: xx–xxi), Miller (1995: 186–90), Mulgan (1977: 102), Rowe (1977: 166–69).

from both the nature and the usefulness of political science, what questions it must study in order to be complete.

As regards the nature of the science, Aristotle presents an argument that, in its general form, may be stated as follows: (1) among arts and sciences that are complete with respect to some one class of things, it belongs to a single art or science to study what is suitable in the case of each class (as shown by gymnastics); (2) the class of regimes forms one class of things; (3) therefore it belongs to a single science, if this science is to be complete, to study what is suitable in the case of the class of regimes. Premise (2) here is manifest (for all regimes are regimes, that is, ways of arranging control in the city), and premise (1) seems to be also since it merely states what is meant by the idea of a complete science (or at least a complete practical science). In explanation of what is meant by the suitable and the complete Aristotle gives examples from other arts. So the art of gymnastics studies: (i) what training benefits what body; (ii) what training is the best or suits the best body; (iii) what training suits most bodies; (iv) what training suits the less demanding desires of particular people. Likewise medicine, shipbuilding, and clothing have as their job knowing how to provide the sort of health, or ships, or clothes that will be suitable in each of the same categories (what suits whom, what suits the best, what suits most, what suits a particular desire). Each of these arts deals with knowing how to make something suitable and with respect to the whole of that suitability, both what is suitable for the best and what is suitable for something less than the best.

1288b21 The same is going to be true, therefore, of any other art or science with respect to its object. To be complete, it will have to study what is suitable or fitting with respect to the whole class of that object. Specifically this is going to be true of the class of regimes and of the science that has the class of regimes for its object, namely the science of politics. This science too must study: (i) what regime is best simply, or suits the best city; (ii) what regime suits what city; (iii) what regime is best given a certain supposition, or suits the particular desire of particular cities; (iv) what regime suits most cities. Aristotle lists the same four kinds of the suitable here as he did in the case of gymnastics but in a different order (he puts the second before the first and the fourth before the third). The reason, perhaps, is that he now wishes to show how all four are versions of the best, for the first is the best simply and all the others are, in various ways, the form of the best that is attainable.[3] These variants are also comprehensive, for all possible cases are in principle included under the best simply and the best attainable (even the

---

3. Smith and Mayhew, in Boudouris (1995: 1:191–94), argue against the idea that there is an exact parallelism between Aristotle's two lists. But they are only able to do so by not reading Aristotle's remarks in the way I suggest; and see also Miller (1995: 184 n87).

simply worst might be the best attainable in some circumstances), and the best attainable is either the best that people can attain, case (ii), or the best that they want to attain, case (iii). The final case (iv), the best attainable by most cities generally, is presumably added to the other two because of its generality, for the general is characteristic of science and permits the giving of advice to many together even in the absence of individual diagnosis (cf. *Ethics* 10.9.1180b7–28).

1288b35 So much may be true of the nature of political science or of the range of its object, but as regards the use to be made of it a problem may seem to arise. For whether, in the case of gymnastics, a given individual wants to develop the fittest body or not would seem to be a mere matter of choice, and no blame could attach to a gymnastic trainer who prescribed a course of training for someone who only wanted to be averagely fit and no more. But the opposite would seem to be true of regimes, for regimes are a matter of justice and not to want the best regime is not to want justice. So a political scientist who accommodated this desire would seem to be accommodating injustice, which is surely something reprehensible and not to be done.[4]

Aristotle's response is in effect that, on the contrary, this is precisely what ought to be done since otherwise one will fail to achieve the useful or to achieve the good that can be achieved, and hence fail to make politics the practical science it is supposed to be (what is reprehensible is to fail to achieve the achievable good not to fail to achieve the unachievable good). So what is required for usefulness is to study, not just the best regime simply, case (i), but also regimes that are possible, cases (ii) and (iii), and that cities already have more in common with, case (iv). As it is, however, among those who speak about regimes some seek out only the highest or best regime, the regime that requires much equipment (4(7).4–12), while others do speak about a more common regime but remove those that are already in place in cities and praise the Spartan or some other regime like it.[5] In other words, even these latter do not start from what is already there. On the contrary, they want, like the former, to start from scratch and, after removing first the regimes already there, then set up some Spartan sort of regime in their place. But usefulness requires one instead to introduce the sort of arrangement that, starting from the regimes already in place (and not, that is, from some regime like the Spartan that is not already in place), people will easily be both persuaded and able to participate in.[6]

4. Rowe (1977: 163–65) notes the problem, as do Smith and Mayhew, in Boudouris (1995: 1:194–97). See also Newman (4:137–38).

5. Aristotle is presumably thinking in particular here of Plato's procedure in the *Republic* on the one hand, and of his procedure in the *Laws* on the other; cf. 2.6.1264b26–1265a10.

6. The way I rendered this sentence (1289a1–3) in the translation, while not perhaps misleading as to the sense, is less accurate than it need be as to the words. I wrote: "But what should be done is to introduce the sort of arrangement that, given what people already have, they will easily consent to or could

Aristotle mentions persuasion as well as ability here because, of course, the legislator is limited, like the gymnastic trainer, not only by people's ability, case (ii), but also by their desire, case (iii).[7] For it is evidently pointless for a legislator to introduce a regime that people could share in but do not want to share in, or cannot be persuaded to share in. Of course, among the regimes that people could easily share in (even if not one that they could easily be persuaded to share in) is the regime that all cities have more in common with, case (iv). For what is more common to all cities must be more within the capacity of all cities. Hence usefulness requires the legislator to be familiar with all these cases, and not just with the simply best regime of case (i).

---

easily participate in." It would more accurately be rendered, as here in the commentary: "But what should be done is to introduce the sort of arrangement that, starting from those in place, people will easily be both persuaded and able to participate in." There is, in fact, dispute about the Greek at this point and, instead of "starting from those [regimes] in place" (the *huparchousōn* of the manuscripts), some have suggested an emendation to "starting from existing circumstances" (*huparchontōn*). But the emendation is not necessary and anyway weakens Aristotle's point, which is that the legislator is not to imitate the reformers just mentioned, who want to abolish existing regimes and start from scratch, but is rather to begin with those existing regimes themselves. For that is also what the gymnastic trainer and doctor do—at least if they want to be useful. They treat the trainees and patients they actually have and do not thrust them aside in the hope, someday, of coming across the perfect trainee or the perfect patient. That is why, as Curren rightly points out (1993–94: 118–22), much of Aristotle's advice in these last three books is directed at persuasion as well as at reform (or at reform through persuasion), or why, in particular, he appeals to stability as well as to justice. For rulers of existing, but defective, regimes are more likely to be persuaded to embrace reform by advice about how to preserve their regime than by advice about how to make it more just, even if, as a matter of fact, more justice is what makes regimes more stable.

7. Cf. 4(7).2.1324b29–41. This point is missed by Mulgan (1977: 130–38), Rowe (1977), and Smith and Mayhew, in Boudouris (1995), but not by Curren (1993–94: 103–26) or Miller (1995: 188, 279, 284–85). Smith and Mayhew also contend that Aristotle is not to be understood as telling legislators to help cities that want a deviant regime. Rather he is to be understood as listing all the facts legislators must be familiar with so that, in the case of deviant regimes, they can use these facts to overthrow, and not to preserve, these regimes. Now it is true that Aristotle is primarily concerned in the *Politics* to give legislators the materials for their task (just as a medical handbook does for doctors, *Ethics* 10.9.1181b2–9, 5.9.1137a14–17), and is leaving to legislators themselves how to apply these materials in particular cases. Nevertheless, he clearly expects legislators sometimes to be engaged in the task of preserving deviant regimes, as is evident especially from 8(6). For a deviant regime may be the best a given city may agree to put up with (and destroying it may only make things worse). Few democratic or oligarchic cities, for instance, can be persuaded to establish polity by giving up some of their power to the rich or the poor (8(6).3.1318b1–5), but they could perhaps be persuaded to be more measured in their behavior. To say that the legislator must not do what he can for such cities is harsh advice, just as it would be harsh advice to say that a doctor must not, say, do what he can for a smoker at risk for lung cancer who will not give up smoking. Must the doctor not even advise fewer cigarettes or less inhalation or cigarettes with a lower tar content? Or, again, must those working to help people living on the street refuse to do anything for them (as providing food, or clothing, or toilet facilities) if these people themselves refuse to leave the street and if force would only make them worse? Aristotle's position is surely more humane.

The reason Aristotle gives for starting thus from what is in place and not, or not only, from scratch is: (1) it is no less a work to put a regime right than to establish one in the first place (indeed perhaps the former may be a greater work if it is vastly more common); but (2) the reason for studying the best regime is that it is a great work to begin at once with what is right; therefore (3) this is just as much reason for studying also how to put a regime right when it already exists. Or, in other words, all regimes should be studied, the best and the less than the best, since the study of the second is no less important than the study of the first. Hence, as Aristotle stated initially, the legislator must be able to come to the aid of any regime anywhere, if not to change it into a better one, then at least to improve it where it is and stop it deteriorating, or deteriorating as fast as it otherwise might.[8]

1289a7 But if it is necessary to do all this, then it is necessary also to study a further question (v), how many sorts of each kind of regime there are, as specifically sorts of democracy and oligarchy (a point on which people currently err). For one cannot come to the aid of regimes if one does not know what all the regimes are: how many, of what sort, and how each differs from the others.

1289a11 In addition, it is necessary to study (vi) the laws that suit each regime. Aristotle evidently regards the need for this question as obvious and uses it rather to confirm the need for studying question (v). However, in doing so he also shows how he is understanding laws here and why a study of them is part of this same prudence (the prudence involved in aiding regimes). He presents the following argument: (1) a regime is the way cities arrange their offices (as in particular the controlling office), and the end of the community (cf. 3.6.1278b8–15); (2) laws are what the rulers or officeholders rule by and defend against transgressors (and against those in particular who wish to arrange the offices differently); (3) therefore laws are what the regime rules by and defends against transgressors. Hence (4) where the regime differs, the rules that the regime rules by must also differ and the same laws cannot be of benefit to all regimes. Thus (5) the differences among regimes must be studied for this reason too.

By laws, therefore, Aristotle is understanding mainly constitutional laws, or laws that determine the regime.[9] The regime itself is those who rule and the end

8. Some scholars believe that Aristotle's proposals for reforming regimes in the books that follow all involve changing the existing regime into another one, as say into a measured form from an extreme one, so Mulgan (1977: 134) and Rowe (1977: 172). But in fact a regime that is made less extreme, or stabilized where it is, is reformed but is still the same regime, for it will still have the same ruling body (which is what defines regimes) save that this ruling body will be less self-destructive in the way it exercises control.

9. An important phrase in Aristotle's text, which I translate as "but among the things that show what the regime is, laws hold a distinct place," can also be translated as "but the laws are distinct from those things that show the regime" (1289a18–19); see Jowett (1885: 2:150). The second translation makes less sense in the context of this passage and of this argument, as Lord rightly notes (1984: 256 n3), and

they propose to themselves (as, for instance, the poor and freedom in democracy, and the rich and wealth in oligarchy). The laws will accordingly be the rules that determine what offices there are to be, who is to be eligible for them, and how chosen (the matters discussed in 6(4).14–16). These laws must manifestly be relative to the regimes for they must ensure that in a democracy the poor rule, that in an oligarchy the rich rule, and so on with the others. Hence, setting up regimes, and coming to their aid as and when required, must involve above all laying down laws to support and preserve the regime in question.

Chapter 2

~ THE QUESTIONS REMAINING TO BE STUDIED
AND THEIR ORDER

1289a26   The questions just listed must manifestly revolve, in the concrete, about specific regimes, so Aristotle recalls now what those regimes are and how they relate to the questions to be discussed. The regimes are the three of kingship, aristocracy, and polity with their respective deviations of tyranny, oligarchy, and democracy. Of these six regimes, the first two have already been fully discussed in books 4(7) and 5(8) since they are both the best regime (and how they differ and when a kingship is to be adopted were also stated earlier, especially in 3.17).[10] Hence these regimes, or question (i) from the preceding chapter, need no further discussion. So only the other four regimes (and the other five questions) are left. In all the remaining books, therefore, we must suppose that Aristotle is no longer dealing with kingship and aristocracy in their true forms. The kingships and aristocracies that he does mention must all be construed as certain lesser kinds.

1289a38   As regards the other regimes and the other questions, Aristotle first orders the regimes and then the questions. These other questions, of course, all revolve in some way about the rank of regimes, since they all concern various

---

would also seem to refer to kinds of law that Aristotle does not much discuss in the *Politics*, whereas he does much discuss constitutional laws. These constitutional laws, or laws determining who should rule, would still be laws about education to virtue (the theme of *Ethics* 10.9). For the best regime in particular is that regime where rule is confined to those who have been properly educated in virtue, that is, who have successfully completed the education laid down by the regime. But the same need to confine rule to those educated to virtue, or the same need to educate rulers to virtue (at least relative to the regime), holds for the other regimes too, if they are to survive (7(5).9.1310a12–36).

10. Newman (2:xxv) raises the possibility that the reference here is to book 3. But there is no study as such of the best regime in book 3, only a defense of the division of regimes into six. The only part of the *Politics* that can reasonably be called a *study* (*theōrēsai*, 1289a31) of the best regime is books 4(7) and 5(8), and Aristotle says as much himself, 3.18.1288b2–4. Incidentally, Peter of Auvergne, who did not change the order of the books, thought (1951: 4.2.548) that the reference might be to the discussion of Plato's *Republic* and *Laws* in book 2, or to a separate treatise of Aristotle.

ways in which regimes are best. Consequently it is necessary to have a grasp of the relative goodness of regimes to serve as a guide while answering these questions. So Aristotle first states the order of goodness and then clarifies his view against a possible alternative view. The order is easily stated and easily proved: the deviation or corruption of the best is worst,[11] and tyranny is this as being the corruption of kingship, and oligarchy is next worst as being the corruption of aristocracy. Democracy will therefore be the least bad or keep most to the measure. This ranking has been reached by reference to the best regime, but it also sets up at the same time a ranking with respect to polity. For polity is a correct or good regime, and to be furthest removed from the best is to be furthest removed from the good.

1289b5 The idea that democracy is the most measured of the bad regimes recalls a similar view in Plato. Aristotle does not mention anyone's name here, perhaps because the view is actually put into the mouth of someone who has no name, the Eleatic Stranger.[12] At any rate this stranger's view is that there is a good and bad form of each of the three regimes in question depending on whether they rule with law or without law. The stranger's simply best regime, in fact, is the rule, without law, of those who have the true science of ruling, but other regimes can imitate this simply best one by ruling with law. When they do, democracy is worst, and when they do not, it is best. The stranger, therefore, is looking to the presence or absence of rule by law in regimes and is prepared to consider good any regime under law. But to look for this is not, as Aristotle says, to look for the same thing as Aristotle himself is looking for, which is evidently the end of the regime, whether this is the common advantage or the advantage of the rulers (3.6–7). Hence Aristotle is not prepared to consider good any regime that does not have the common good as its end, even if it is ruled by law. Instead he will only consider such a regime less bad. The stranger and Aristotle agree, therefore, that some other regime is simply best (both in fact agree that the simply best regime is a kind of kingship and aristocracy),[13] but they do not agree about which regimes are good, and they do not agree because the stranger looks to law and Aristotle evidently to the end. The difference here is not a merely verbal one,[14] for in fact Aristotle is quite happy to *say* on occasion that, for instance, one kind of democracy is better or best (for example, at 8(6).4.1318b6); it is rather a substantive one about how to assess goodness or correctness in regimes. Hence whatever words one happens to use, Aristotle's way of assessing goodness means that democracies and oligarchies

11. The corruption in question must be understood as a corruption in the principle of the regime. A mere corruption in certain accidents or externals would not make the best regime become the worst.

12. Plato *Statesman* 302e4–303a5. It is also conceivable, of course, that Aristotle is not thinking of Plato in the *Statesman* but of someone else altogether.

13. Though recall Aristotle's criticism of the stranger's argument in 3.15.

14. Contra Newman (4:147) and Jowett (1885: 2:152).

are never good regimes, even if the presence or absence of law makes some of them to be less extreme. For a less extreme deviant regime is still a deviant regime.

1289b11 This matter of the ordering of regimes is discussed again at suitable points later, so leaving it aside for the present, Aristotle orders the questions. The first, how many differences of regimes there are, was concluded fifth in the preceding chapter but it comes first in order of treatment, for without an answer to it none of the other questions can be properly treated. It is dealt with in chapters 3–10. When he says, however, "if indeed there are several kinds of oligarchy and democracy" (1289b13–14), he cannot mean that only these regimes have kinds.[15] He must, instead, be using them as the paradigm example, as he did also in the preceding chapter. For there he said that the reason for the need to study differences in regimes generally was that there are differences in kinds of democracies and oligarchies (1.1289a7–11, 20–25). So in a similar way, he may be taken here as saying that if these have kinds then it is likely that the others do as well. And, as it turns out, they do indeed have kinds (though since these other regimes are mixtures of oligarchy and democracy, there is a sense in which their kinds rest on the differences in the kinds of oligarchy and democracy).

The second question is which regime is most common and most choiceworthy after the simply best. This was listed fourth in the preceding chapter and the fluidity of the way Aristotle now phrases it (the regime that is most common or one that is aristocratic and nobly constituted but still suitable to most cities, 1289b14–17) reflects the fluidity in the answer he eventually gives, in chapter 11.

The third question is which of the other regimes is preferable for whom, or for which cities. This will embrace the second and third questions from the preceding chapter since which regime is preferable for which city will be the best regime each city is able, or wants, to attain. Sometimes, of course, and perhaps often, the regime a given city wants to attain will be some deviant regime, as oligarchy or democracy. A deviant regime may also be the only regime it can attain (if, say, it is so far from what is common that even the common regime is too hard for it, just as a common gymnastic program may be too hard for the very sickly or weak). But sometimes too the best regime that a given city can and wants to attain will be the regime that is most common and most choiceworthy after the best, namely the regime discussed under the second question. Hence this common regime gets discussed again along with the deviant regimes under this third question, in chapters 12–13.

The fourth question is how to set up these regimes, and this will correspond to the sixth question from the preceding chapter, about laws, since one sets up a regime according to the laws one lays down about the distribution and appoint-

15. Contra Newman (4:148, 191).

ment of its several offices. That Aristotle again only mentions democracy and oligarchy here need not be taken to mean that he only intends to speak about setting up the kinds of these two regimes.[16] One may suppose he is mentioning these rather as examples. Or one may suppose, alternatively, that he is mentioning them because, in a way, they include the other regimes, since polity is a sort of mixture of democracy and oligarchy (tyranny is also a sort of mixture of democracy and oligarchy, though it mixes them to produce something as bad or worse whereas polity mixes them to produce something better, 6(4).8.1293b33–34, 7(5).10.1311a2–22). Hence, to set up any of the remaining regimes (those that remain after the best regime of kingship and true aristocracy has been treated) is, in a way, to set up democracy and oligarchy, for it is either to set up one of these separately or to set up both of them together in some sort of combination. At all events this fourth question is dealt with in chapters 14–16.

The fifth question is how regimes are preserved and destroyed. This question has not been mentioned before and Aristotle in fact introduces it here as something additional. But it is clearly something additional to the question of how to set up regimes, for it will show what sort of things to avoid and what to pursue for this purpose. So it is perhaps best to regard it as a necessary supplement or continuation of the previous question. It is dealt with in book 7(5).

At any rate, as so explained, all these five questions neatly pick up on all the questions listed in chapter 1 that still remain, and neatly divide all the chapters that follow in the next two books.[17]

Chapter 3

∾ FIRST QUESTION: THE DIFFERENCES AMONG REGIMES

∾ THAT THERE ARE SEVERAL KINDS OF REGIME

1289b27 Aristotle turns first, as he said, to the first question, the differences among regimes. His discussion of this question is rather long and involved and has led to much confusion and difficulty of interpretation.[18] A way through can, however, be found if one notes that Aristotle first states, in this chapter, why in

---

16. Again contra Newman (4:149).

17. Many scholars deny that the connection between this chapter and the one preceding and those following is quite so neat, as Barker (1946: 159 nJJ), Jowett (1885: 2:152), Newman (1:492–94; 4:148–49), Robinson (1962: 72), Sinclair/Saunders (1981: 238). But this seems to be because they stress the verbal differences rather than the substantial similarities.

18. It is, for instance, a common scholarly view that chapters 3 and 4 especially contain much that is repetitious and discrepant, Barker (1946: 162 nKK), Newman (1:565–69; 4:150–52), Robinson (1962: 81), Sinclair/Saunders (1981: 243).

general regimes come in several kinds (for this will furnish the basis for showing how many such kinds there are), then repeats and defends, in the next chapter, his earlier doctrine (from 3.6–7) that there are six basic kinds of regime, and only after that comes to prove, in the rest of chapter 4 and in chapters 5–10, his main intention, that within these kinds there are several subkinds. But this detour, as it were, through a repetition and defense of his earlier doctrine is not mere repetition nor mere digression; rather it is required precisely by his intention to show that the kinds of regimes, oligarchy and democracy in particular, also divide into several subkinds. For, as becomes evident, there is a common view that all regimes are variations of oligarchy and democracy (as that aristocracy is a kind of oligarchy and polity a kind of democracy), and according to this view, while there will be kinds of oligarchy and democracy, these kinds will just be one or other of Aristotle's original six, not subkinds within these six. To establish his own claim, therefore, that oligarchy and democracy do have genuine subkinds that are not one or another of the original six, Aristotle must directly confront this view and show it to be wrong. So he must show again, but now in express opposition to and rejection of this common view, that his original sixfold division is correct.

Aristotle begins by stating the general reason for there being several kinds of regime, namely that there are several parts to any city. He first states these parts and then gives the reason that they cause differences of regime. His listing of parts here is merely stated, not analytically argued (as it is in the next chapter), because the argument he is about to present only requires the fact of such differences, not a comprehensive analysis of them. Nevertheless, this listing is not in any conflict with his analytic listing later (as will be shown later in the commentary on that place, at 4(6).4.1291a33). A city, then, is made up of households, which are the originating parts of cities (cf. 1.2), and the inhabitants of these households are going to be well-off, needy, or middling, and are going accordingly to have or not to have arms. The populace, or the bulk of the needy, themselves fall into several parts according to their several occupations, and so also do the well-off according to the amount and kind of their substance (Aristotle mentions wealth in horses in particular, perhaps because here there is manifest historical evidence of political differences springing from differences in wealth). In addition to these parts based, as it were, on material differences, there are also parts based on character differences (family descent and virtue). Aristotle refers also to any other part of the city mentioned earlier in the discussion of aristocracy,[19] though he would seem to have

---

19. This must be a reference back to 4(7).8–9, and especially 1328b2–33. The suggestion, made by Newman (2:xxv; 4:154–55), that the reference is in fact to 3.12.1383a14–22 is not convincing. The passage in book 3 cannot plausibly be called a discussion of aristocracy, since it is in fact a discussion of all regimes and of the principle of justice that should determine just distribution of shares in rule. The passage in 4(7).8–9, however, is manifestly part of a discussion of aristocracy, or of the best regime simply.

mentioned them all save for priests (those who judge and advise, of course, constitute the regime and must come from one or other of the parts mentioned, the poor, the well-off, the virtuous, and so on).

1290a5   Having stated the several different kinds of parts in cities, Aristotle now argues that there must be different kinds of regimes as a result. He states the following propositions: (1) the parts of the city are different in kind; (2) a regime is the way the offices are arranged; (3) the arrangement of offices is given or distributed by everyone to different parts according to the power of these parts, or to some equality of power among them. From (2) and (3) it follows that (4) regimes are distributed to the different parts according to the power of these parts or, in other words, that regimes differ as the parts that are powerful and have the offices differ. From (1) and (4) it follows that (5) regimes must differ in kind and, indeed, that there must be as many kinds of regimes as there are ways in which the different kinds of parts, or combinations of kinds of parts, can be powerful in the city. Premise (1) summarizes what Aristotle has just said at the beginning of the chapter; premise (2) repeats the definition of regime from before (3.6.1278b8–15); premise (3) is manifest from observation.

Aristotle has here traced the differences in regimes to differences, as it were, in material parts (namely which group of inhabitants in the city has the offices). But earlier he traced these differences to differences in the end the regime proposed to itself, wealth, freedom, virtue, or the like, or in what it supposed happiness to be (3.7, 4(7).8.1328a37–b2, 6(4).1.1289a15–18). There is no conflict or contradiction, however, because these different ends or conceptions of happiness will only make different regimes if they become the ruling principle in the city, and they only will become the ruling principle if some in the city with these ends or conceptions get the offices. But these some will have to belong to one or other part of the city; hence differences in regimes according to their end will follow differences in regimes according to the parts of the city that are in control. Or at least this will be true provided the material parts of the city differ also in their ends or their character. But this they manifestly do, as Aristotle has already shown when he excluded, in the case of the best regime, some parts of the city from sharing in rule (4(7).9.1328b33–1329a2), and as he shows more extensively in what follows when he comes to distinguish the several regimes from each other.[20]

Worth noting also is that Aristotle continues here, as he does throughout the *Politics*, to understand the parts of the city in terms of qualified groupings of individuals and not in terms of individuals simply (see 3.7–8). Aristotle's interest is not focused on numbers or quantities, but on qualities, and regimes are understood to

20. On the basic unity of Aristotle's views about the reasons for there being several different kinds of regimes, see in particular Johnson (1990: chap. 4, especially 52), but also Miller (1995: 160–61) and Newman (1:220–23, 565–69).

differ, and to be better or worse or just or unjust, according to what sort of persons in the city share in rule, not according to how many of them do. For since individuals differ in quality or character according to the part of the city that they belong to, and since these characters are not equal with respect to the true end of the city (some characters pursue that end, namely the virtuous, and others do not, namely the nonvirtuous rich and poor), the individuals are not equal either, and justice does not consist in giving each individual equal shares or equal rights, nor does it consist in majority rule. Rather it consists in giving greater rights and greater rule, or even total rule, to the best individuals, or the best grouping of individuals.

～ RESTATEMENT OF THE CORRECT VIEW AGAINST THE COMMON VIEW

1290a13 Now that the reason for differences among regimes has been explained, the next thing is to say how many regimes there actually are. But here is where the problem of the common view about this question arises, a view that, though having a certain plausibility, is nevertheless wrong. Aristotle therefore first states this view, contrasts his own view against it, and then proceeds to show why the common view is wrong and his own correct.

The common view is that there are only two kinds of regime, oligarchy and democracy, and that all others are deviations from these, with aristocracy as a sort of oligarchy and polity as a sort of democracy, because, apparently, aristocracy is like oligarchy in being rule by the few and polity is like democracy in being rule by the many. The view also gets support from similar ideas about winds and musical modes, where again two are set down as basic and the rest as deviations from them.

1290a22 Aristotle, however, earlier gave a different view and defended the correctness of it at length (3.6–17). So he briefly recalls that view now and then turns to refute the other view and to reconfirm his own. His statement of his own view is brief and has led to doubts about whether it really is the same as what he said before.[21] But these doubts can be allayed if, as I noted in the translation, the one or two nobly constituted regimes are taken to be kingship and aristocracy as the one (for these two together are the best regime) and polity as the second. For polity is a correct regime (so it is nobly constituted) but not the best regime (so it is not as nobly constituted as kingship and aristocracy). Hence there is in a sense only one nobly constituted regime (the simply best regime of kingship and aristocracy) and in a sense two (the simply best regime and polity). The other regimes are deviations from these, democracy from the well-blended mode of polity, and tyranny and oligarchy from the best regime of kingship and aristocracy respectively. Tyranny and oligarchy will be tighter and more despotic because they confine rule to too few (some of the excluded have as much or more of a just claim

---

21. See Barker (1946: 161 n3), Jowett (1885: 2:154), Lord (1984: 257 n14), Newman (4:157).

to rule), and democracy relaxed and softer because it extends rule to too many (some of the included do not have a just claim to rule).

Chapter 4

⌣ FALSITY OF THE COMMON VIEW

1290a30   Aristotle next turns to reject the common view. Now this view only works on the assumption that oligarchy is rule by the few (so that all regimes controlled by a few are kinds of oligarchy) and democracy rule by the many (so that all regimes controlled by many are kinds of democracy). Aristotle accordingly attacks the common view by attacking this assumption,[22] which he does by showing that it leads to false and absurd conclusions.

The idea that democracy is control by the multitude is, he first remarks, at least verbally wrong for in every regime the multitude is in a sense in control (namely the multitude of the ruling body). Noting this verbal error might seem trivial or pedantic, but it has the value of pointing out that "multitude" and "few" must be taken with respect to the city, and not with respect to the ruling body or the regime. It therefore sets up Aristotle's criticisms, which focus on problems arising from defining democracy and oligarchy by reference to the many and few in the city.

The first criticism is an appeal to an example of a city of 1,300, where, in the one case, the rich and many 1,000 rule and exclude from rule the poor and few 300, even though the 300 are free and otherwise equal, and where, in the other case, the situation is reversed and the poor who are few rule, excluding the many who are rich. No one would say that the first regime was a democracy nor that the second was an oligarchy. What should be said instead, and what most people would say instead, is that democracy is when the free are in control and oligarchy when the rich are in control (wealth and freedom are the bases of the claims that oligarchs and democrats make to rule, 3.8.1280a4–6). Accordingly one should, contrary to the common view, define democracy as rule by the free and oligarchy as rule by the rich, and regard the fact that the former are many and the latter few as incidental. In further confirmation Aristotle gives examples where rule is given to the few tall or the few beautiful. If oligarchy were rule by the few, these regimes too should be called oligarchies, which is absurd and would be denied by everyone, including oligarchs.[23]

22. I follow the analysis of Newman (4:158).

23. It is an interesting question what kinds of regimes these two are, and whether they fall under any of Aristotle's classifications, or are different kinds altogether. Perhaps they should be called attempts at aristocracy or at giving rule according to merit (tallness and fine proportions will tend to promote and enhance military virtue and skill, especially perhaps in horse riding). For nature tries to combine

1290b7 This first criticism has relied on universal opinion about democracy and oligarchy to refute the common view, and effectively too, for doubtless this universal opinion is also shared by those who embrace the common view. But while this universal opinion gives a correct account of oligarchy, it is misleading about democracy. Moreover, it is misleading in such a way as to allow democrats to claim that their regime is rightly called rule by the many or even rule by all, since all are free. It thus allows the possibility of calling democracy the one basic or true regime from which all the rest are deviations.[24] Aristotle's second criticism removes this possibility too.

He begins by noting that the criteria of wealth and freedom, as supposed by universal opinion, are still not enough to distinguish oligarchy and democracy. By this he must mean not that wealth is insufficient to define oligarchy but that freedom is insufficient to distinguish democracy from oligarchy. The reason is that the populace and oligarchy have many parts to them, or the poor and rich that form their respective ruling bodies may combine more than one feature at the same time, and so it is important to define by the essential feature, not by incidental ones. Aristotle shows this now in particular of the features of freedom and manyness which may be features of democracy but can also be features of oligarchy. So to say that democracy is rule by the free will lead to saying that wherever the free rule, even when they are few and those they rule are many and unfree, there is democracy. Now, while this may be true in some cases (democracies in the ancient world typically had fewer free than slaves), it will not be true of all. Specifically it will not be true of the cases Aristotle mentions of Apollonia and Thera, not because here only the free rule, but because here the free are the rich. They are the rich, of course, because they possess the property, but they possess the property for the same reason that they are free, namely their birth or their descent from the first colonists. So here the oligarchy is the free as well as the few and wealthy (it happens to combine all three features). And though it is an oligarchy because of its wealth, as are all oligarchies, the fact that it also comprises the free shows that freedom cannot be the definition of democracy.

The second example is an actual case of what was merely supposed in the first criticism just discussed, namely the rich ruling and also being the many (or an oligarchy that combines the features of manyness and wealth—and of course freedom). The supposition is repeated here with respect to an actual case, perhaps,

---

beauty of soul with beauty of body and people are inclined to believe the two go together (1.5.1254b27–36). In fact, if the tallest and most beautiful are presumed to have merit, they will probably also be distinguished by wealth and breeding, and other marks proper to the notables, so that their regime would be some kind of so-called aristocracy (6(4).7).

24. An opinion that gets expressed particularly in the idea that only the democracy is the city (3.1.1274b35–36, 3.1276a8–13). It also gets expressed, to some extent, in the widespread opinion today that justice requires everyone to be allowed to vote.

to forestall a possible response to the previous case of Apollonia and Thera. For someone might say that these were oligarchies and not democracies because they were rule by the few free and not by the many free. The case of Colophon is, however, a case of rule by the many free (those who rule are necessarily free), yet it is clearly not a democracy for it too is rule by the rich. Hence, as Apollonia and Thera show that democracy is not rightly defined as rule by the free, so Colophon shows that it is not rightly defined as rule by the many free—and indeed that oligarchy is not rightly defined as rule by the few.

Aristotle ends with the following remark: "But it is democracy when the free and needy who are the majority have control of rule, and it is oligarchy when the rich and better born who are few have control" (1290b17–20). This is usually taken as a general summary of how democracy and oligarchy should properly be defined, namely that democracy is to be defined as rule by the poor and free and many, and that oligarchy is to be defined as rule by the rich and well-born and few. But this conclusion is not only in conflict, as scholars have noted,[25] with the conclusion in book 3 (8.1279b39–1180a4) that manyness and fewness are only incidental; it is also in conflict with the teaching of this chapter itself. For this chapter also earlier asserted that manyness and fewness were incidental, and it ended with the case of Colophon, which is an oligarchy of *many* rich. Better, therefore, to take the conclusion, not as giving a general definition, but as responding to and explaining the cases just discussed. For since these cases are all of regimes with several features, and features that can be found in other and different regimes, it cannot be that these regimes are to be classified by all their features. Rather they must be classified by the feature that is peculiar to them and that cannot be found in different regimes. So Colophon is not a democracy because it is democracy when those in control are free and *needy* and many, but those in control in Colophon are free and *rich* and many. Likewise, Apollonia and Thera are not democracies because those in control there are rich and well-born and few, and it is oligarchy when those in control are *rich* and well-born and few. In other words, Colophon, Apollonia, and Thera are sorts of test cases, where the other features or criteria commonly used to distinguish regimes (few, many, free) turn out to give false results. So even if one describes these regimes using these other features or criteria, one will still have to include the criteria of wealth and poverty to classify them properly, and these criteria will prove to be the decisive and, indeed, the only necessary ones.

Taken in this way the final sentence accords with Aristotle's view that oligarchy and democracy are properly distinguished by poverty and wealth, not numbers or freedom. More particularly, it shows the falsity of the common view, or the view

25. As Barker (1946: 163 n1), Mulgan (1977: 64–65), Newman (4:158).

that these regimes are to be distinguished by their numbers. And that is what Aristotle was here intending.

✑ PROOF OF THE CORRECT VIEW AND REASON FOR THE COMMON VIEW

1290b21 Having thus shown the common view to be wrong with respect to how it distinguishes regimes, Aristotle next shows it to be wrong, and his own view, by contrast, correct, with respect to the number and kind of regimes. He first recalls what he has already stated (in chapter 3), that and why there are several kinds of regimes, and then says he is next going to show how many there are and why, and in particular that there are more regimes than the oligarchy and democracy of the common view. The principle he is going to use for this purpose is the one stated in chapter 3, that regimes differ because the parts of the city differ.

1290b25 To illustrate the force of this principle Aristotle takes an analogy from kinds of animals. He sets out the following program. To get the kinds of animals, (1) mark off all the necessary parts of animals (as parts to perceive with, to eat with, to move with). Next, (2) if these necessary parts are determinate in number but (3) they each have differences and come in several kinds (kinds of stomach, mouth, and the like), then (4) the number of ways of combining these several kinds of necessary parts will make several kinds of animals, for (5) no animal could have all the differences of each necessary part (as all the kinds of mouth or ears). Consequently (6) all the possible ways of combining these several kinds of necessary parts will produce kinds of animals, and as many kinds as there are combinations.

This account of species differentiation is brief and schematic but not misleading, provided that the possible combinations mentioned in proposition (6) are understood to be the physically and not the mathematically possible combinations. For otherwise the analogy would seem to imply that one could deductively work out from first principles, without ever looking at what exists, how many animals there are, and it would imply also that there must be as many kinds of animals as there are theoretical combinations.[26] But if the possibilities are physical, then seeing what are the combinations and the kinds of animals will be very much a matter of looking at what exists. In this way too the method proposed is less a way of finding the kinds of animals than a way of understanding and explaining the kinds one finds.[27] The application of the analogy to regimes is, however, complicated by the fact that, as was already stated in chapter 3, regimes differ, not so much because of the different combinations of different kinds of necessary parts, as

26. These are difficulties noted by Jowett (1885: 2:155–56) and Robinson (1962: 81).

27. There is thus no conflict between what Aristotle says here about animals and what he says in his biological works, as Newman (4:163–64) and Pellegrin (1982: 148–63) agree.

because of the different combinations of the other necessary parts with the necessary part of the offices. Still, the analogy holds in the sense that the differences arise from the necessary parts and from the combinations of these parts.

1290b37 At all events Aristotle now proceeds to apply the analogy by listing the necessary parts in the case of regimes. These parts are, of course, the parts of the city (for the regime is the distribution and arrangement of offices among these parts). First, he lists parts concerned with the provision of material necessities, the four of: those concerned with food; the mechanics or artisans (whether in necessities or luxuries); the merchants; and the laborers. Aristotle only mentions farmers with respect to food, but this must be shorthand for others such as fishermen and hunters (cf. 1.8). Moreover these parts need not all be necessary in the sense that they must all be present if the city is to be, but only in the sense that they must be present if the city is to be well (artisans engaged in making luxuries are only necessary for commodious living, and the same may be true of merchants if trading is only necessary for the same purpose and not also for basic subsistence).

1291a6 The fifth part, the warriors, goes beyond material things, whether necessities or luxuries, and is concerned with living freely. This part is also necessary, of course, because a city must be able to prevent itself from being enslaved by attackers, for those who are enslaved are not self-sufficient (they are reduced to dependence on others) and a city by definition is self-sufficient. At this point, however, Aristotle turns to criticism of the *Republic* (396b1–371e11), where Socrates is presented as giving a rival account of the parts necessary to the city. Socrates lists first certain artisans and farmers, and then adds other artisans, herders, and merchants. That this account is insufficient Aristotle has already shown by showing that soldiers are necessary. But he perhaps introduces and criticizes Socrates' account now, not just because the opinions of Socrates in the *Republic* are clever and deserve to be discussed, but also because they enable him to explain other parts that are necessary and that Socrates also omits. Socrates' error is twofold. First, he supposes that the city exists for what is necessary and not for what is noble (farmers and artisans provide necessities but warriors something noble, freedom),[28] and, second, he puts necessities on a par with other material goods that are not necessary, or not as necessary (one can live without shoes but not without food). So when he does introduce soldiers, he introduces them for the sake of gaining some other, and unnecessary, material good (extra land), and not for their true purpose of noble freedom.

1291a22 Aristotle next uses this criticism of Socrates to prove another necessary part of the city, the part that judges and deliberates. The reason is again

---

28. Thus, as Dobbs remarks (1994: 81), Aristotle in a way endorses Glaucon's criticism of Socrates' account of the parts of the city, *Republic* 372d4–5, where Glaucon complains that Socrates' city is a city of pigs.

similar, that this part is concerned with something necessary, in this case the something necessary of good rule, which, like the part of warriors, goes beyond the material necessities that the first four parts are concerned with. Aristotle first proves that this part is necessary and then answers an objection. The proof is: (1) these parts of warriors and judges and deliberators, which are concerned with the noble and with virtue, are to cities as the soul is to animals; (2) the soul is more a part of an animal than the body; (3) therefore these parts of warriors and judges and deliberators are more parts of the city than the parts concerned with material necessities. Premise (2) is manifest from the fact that a thing is more truly its form than its matter (the soul, or the principle of life, is the form of the body). Premise (1) is manifest from the fact that warriors and judges and deliberators rule the city and give it its form as the soul gives rule and form to the body (cf. 1.5.1254a34–b9).

The objection is that judges and deliberators need not be parts because they can sometimes be the same persons as some other part. The response is that this makes no difference. In proof and illustration Aristotle states the following propositions: (1) those who bear arms are often the same as those who farm; so clearly (2) if these latter (the warriors and farmers) must be set down as parts of the city, then the former (the judges and deliberators) should be as well; because (3) the armed part at any rate is a necessary part of the city. These propositions can be formed into the following conditional syllogism: (1) and (2) put together produce (4) if the armed part or the warriors must be set down as parts alongside the farmers, even though they may sometimes be the same persons as the farmers, then the judges and deliberators should also be set down as parts, even though they may sometimes be the same persons as some other part; proposition (3) then asserts the antecedent, that the warriors must be set down as parts; thence follows (6) the assertion of the consequent, that the judges and deliberators should also be set down as parts of the city. Premise (4) simply states a necessary parallel and premise (3) was proved just above.[29] That judges and deliberators are here regarded as constituting a single part in the city reflects the fact that they together form the controlling or authoritative part of the city (the part by which citizenship was earlier defined; see 3.1 and also 6(4).14).

29. This argument is only produced if one translates the text as I propose: "So clearly, if these latter must be set down as parts of the city, then the former should be as well, because the armed part at any rate is a necessary part of the city" (1291a31–33). The text is, however, standardly translated as: "So if both these and those must be set down as parts of the city, then it is clear that the armed part at any rate is a necessary part of the city." But on this translation there is an omission of the sixth part, as has been noted by all scholars, and a circular and lame argument is produced, as has been noted by Jowett (1885: 2:156). For now we have: "if both these (the armed part, the judges, and the deliberators) and those (the parts dealing with necessities) must be set down as parts of the city, then it is clear that the armed part at any rate is a part of the city," which is equivalent to "if the armed part is a part of the city, then the armed part is a part of the city."

1291a33 Aristotle lists finally a seventh, the well-off who provide the city with its needed public services (as, for instance, large estate owners), and an eighth part, the magistrates who provide the city with its necessary officials, or all those officials that a city needs over and above the controlling office of judgment and deliberation. That wealth is required for the city's public needs, as services, ships, temples, cavalry equipment, and so forth, is manifest. Officials are required because a city has many common functions to be managed for the common good (such as those noted earlier in 4(7).12). Aristotle expressly mentions this fact for it entails that, in addition to those in the city capable of providing public services, namely the wealthy, there is need also of people capable of exercising rule, whether continually or in part, and both in these offices and in that of judgment and deliberation. But the capacity for doing this is virtue, the virtue of ruling, which is prudence (3.4.1277b25–26). Hence, because of the sixth and eighth parts, there is need also for people in the city with the virtue of politicians.[30]

This list of eight parts of the city differs in certain respects from the list of parts given earlier in 6(4).3 and in the account of aristocracy in 4(7).8. The differences in this last case and the reasons for them were discussed earlier in the commentary on that place. But the differences in the list in chapter 3 present additional problems. Some scholars hold that the list here and the one there are simply incompatible, for here the list is according to functions whereas there it is according to social or economic class.[31] But, in fact, functions are mentioned also in chapter 3 (as farmer, merchants, artisans, and warriors) and social and economic class are mentioned here. For the wealthy are such a class and the first four parts mentioned here repeat, with the exception of laborers, the parts of the populace mentioned there, and they are evidently meant to indicate the populace again here. Further each list mentions the virtuous (and the virtuous are not really an economic or a social class). In fact the only main difference is that while there the parts are just listed, here they are, as Aristotle had intended, systematically accounted for. They are accounted for in terms of the city's functions, and it is these functions that also explain why cities have the classes that they do, for the classes follow the functions: the poor follow the functions of material necessities, the rich the functions of public service, the virtuous the functions of fighting (for warriors need military virtue) and ruling. The two lists, therefore, are in perfect accord.[32]

30. In agreement with Peter of Auvergne (1951: 4.3.568), I read the remarks beginning with *loipa de* (1291a38–40) as a continuation of the previous sentence and to be saying that there must be some able to judge and deliberate for the city, just as there must be some who can rule and perform public service in the offices. Most others translate these remarks as if they were listing an additional (and ninth) part of the city.

31. Barker (1946: 162 nKK), Newman (1:568, 4:151), Schütrumpf (1991: 1:48).

32. Cf. Johnson (1990: 57–61, 82–84).

Moreover, what Aristotle has just argued, about the virtuous, provides the necessary justification for his own account of the kinds of regimes. For if the city's need for rule requires it to have some with the virtue of politicians, then those with virtue should be the rulers and hence should form the regime. Consequently regimes based on virtue will not only be distinct kinds of regime, but they will be the correct kinds of regime. Regimes, by contrast, based on the poor and rich will be deviations because, or insofar as, they are not based on virtue. That Aristotle does not make this inference explicit here is perhaps because he has no need to, having just repeated it briefly in chapter 3, and defended it at large in book 3.[33]

1291b2   What Aristotle does do explicitly instead is explain why the common view of regimes arises and is so common despite being false. The reason is that many people assume two false, but apparently true, propositions: (1) that all the powers or parts of the city can be combined in the same persons, and (2) that everyone has virtue and is capable of office and of exercising rule. But proposition (2) is straightforwardly false (virtue requires much education and most people in the city do not have this education),[34] and so, as a result, is proposition (1) too, or if it is true it is only true in the sense that all the powers or parts can be combined in the same persons but not in the sense that all the powers or parts can be combined *well* in the same persons (farmers and artisans, for instance, are not fit to be rulers, 4(7).9.1328b39–1329a2). It is easy to see how most people would think proposition (2) was true (for vanity or shame or both would make denying it hard), and proposition (1) is in a sense true.

To these false but plausible propositions is now added the true proposition that (3) the poor and wealthy cannot be combined in the same persons. From (3) and (1) the conclusion is then drawn that (4) the poor and wealthy, or needy and well-off, are most of all the parts of the city. This conclusion, however, only follows on the (unexpressed) assumption that (5) the parts of the city are those powers or parts that cannot be combined in the same persons. This assumption is false to the extent that it supposes the parts of the city to be separate groups of persons and not separate powers or functions. Conversely the assumption is true to the extent that proposition (1) is false, namely to the extent that the separate functions cannot be combined *well* in the same persons and so should preferably be filled by different persons. The false sense of proposition (5) is however made plausible by proposition (3), for proposition (3) insinuates that the poor are parts of the city alongside the wealthy. Strictly speaking, however, the poor are not parts of the city qua poor but only qua filling certain functions (it is only thus that Aristotle has

33. Especially in 3.9, which closely parallels the argument in the passage here.

34. The error here is similar to the error exposed before, 4(7).1.1323a36–38, that only a modicum of virtue is necessary for the happy life.

listed them among the parts), in which being poor or needy is hard or impossible to avoid. By contrast the wealthy are parts of the city qua wealthy because the function they fill requires wealth.

To proposition (4) is now added proposition (6) that the wealthy are few and the poor many and that few and many are opposites, to give the conclusion (7) that the wealthy and poor are the opposite parts of a city (and so, in a way, the principal parts of the city, of which the other parts are variants). So regimes based on this division into opposites are the ones that people set up and, as a result, it seems that there are only two basic kinds of regimes, that of oligarchy and that of democracy, with all others ultimately reducible to these. Thus arises the common view about the kinds of regimes. But this view is false and based, as has been seen, on a series of errors and half-truths. Moreover, virtue and depravity make more of an opposition in cities (7(5).3.1303b15), so since these cannot be combined either, it should follow, even by the common view's account of regimes according to the principal division of parts of the city, that Aristotle's division of regimes into correct and deviant according to virtue and depravity was still the proper one.

~ THAT THERE ARE ALSO SEVERAL KINDS
OF DEMOCRACY AND OLIGARCHY

1291b14 Aristotle's first sentence here clearly marks the beginning of a new section. For he first states what he has done so far, namely show, in contrast to the common view, that there are more regimes than democracy and oligarchy and why there are more. Then he says what his intention requires him to do next, namely to show that democracy and oligarchy themselves divide into several kinds.[35]

The reasoning now is going to be straightforward enough: if regimes differ as those differ to whom rule is distributed, and if democracy is when rule is distributed to the poor or populace and oligarchy when it is distributed to the rich, then democracy and oligarchy are going to differ within themselves as the kinds of populace and wealthy differ to whom rule is distributed. Accordingly Aristotle first states the kinds of differences to be found in the populace and the wealthy, and then turns to list the kinds of democracies and oligarchies.

So the populace include: farmers, artisans, dealers in the market, seafaring folk (of several kinds and of varying numbers in different places), laborers and the unleisured with little substance, the free who are born of only one free parent, and any others there may be. Now one need not suppose that Aristotle means that democracies must differ according to each of these groupings, but only that they

---

35. Some scholars regard this opening sentence as a repetition from the beginning of the previous section at 1290b21 and as indicative of a misplaced doublet in the text; cf. Barker (1946: 164 n1) and Newman (4:162). But in fact it introduces the next stage of the discussion and there is no duplication.

may do so, namely when the groupings are large enough to be a distinct force (as in the case of fishermen in Byzantium and trireme sailors in Athens). Nor need one suppose that each group must produce a distinct kind, for perhaps some groups, because of significant similarities, will produce the same kind. All one need suppose is that some differences in democracies are going to be produced by these differences in the populace. But how many and which differences will only be discovered by looking at the facts (as in the case also of the kinds of animals). So the miscellaneous group of others is added at the end presumably because, depending on circumstances, any number of possible differences in the populace might become politically significant. Thus the miners, for instance, have been a powerful political force in some modern nations, though they were not in Aristotle's day (they were usually slaves and without citizen rights even in democracies).

1291b28 The notables include differentiations according to wealth, good birth, virtue, education, and other such marks of privilege. Since Aristotle is speaking here of oligarchy, these differences must be differences of the wealthy, though here, as elsewhere, he calls them notables. The wealthy, however, are notables, or the notables are wealthy, because wealth in particular makes people stand out and brings with it many privileges, as distinction of family (if the wealth is old enough), education (wealth provides leisure for learning), virtue (which here can hardly mean perfect virtue—for that would produce an aristocracy, not an oligarchy—but rather certain parts of virtue, as military virtue in particular, or certain approaches to and beginnings of virtue born of elegant and leisurely living), and other like things (as many and powerful friends). Manifestly the less wealthy differ from the more wealthy (the latter, for instance, and not the former, could create the oligarchy of knights or horsemen mentioned in chapter 3), so do the educated wealthy from the ill-educated wealthy, the well-born from the low-born wealthy (the nouveaux riches as it were), and the cultured from the crude or vulgar wealthy. But again Aristotle leaves the list of differences open-ended, nor does he presume to deduce the kinds of oligarchy immediately from them.

∾ KINDS OF DEMOCRACY

1291b30 Aristotle next comes to list the kinds of democracy and oligarchy, and first of democracy. However, he merely lists them first and leaves till later (chapter 6) relating them back to the kinds of populace and notables. The list must, therefore, in the first instance be taken from empirical observation.[36] This is certainly true of the first kind of democracy whose characteristics are evidently taken from actual political rhetoric. It is called, following this rhetoric, "the one

36. For a similar procedure in the case of animals see, for instance, *Historia Animalium* 1.1–6 and *De Partibus Animalium* 1.1–4.

that is said to be most in accord with equality" (1291b30–31), and whose law defines equality as when the needy are no more superior than the well-off and when neither of the two is in control.

About this case Aristotle says two things: first, that if freedom and equality do exist most of all in democracy, as some suppose, then such freedom and equality would most of all exist if everyone most of all has a like share in the regime; second, that, in point of fact, the populace is in the majority and what the majority think right is in control, so that the regime in question here is necessarily a democracy. It seems evident, therefore, that Aristotle is denying in his second statement that the first statement actually holds of democracy (the first statement is, anyway, only what "some suppose"), and hence that the democracy said to be "most in accord with equality" is not in accord with equality at all. This conclusion is confirmed by what Aristotle says later about this rhetoric when he points out that the claim to equality, typically made on behalf of democracy by democrats, will be realized, not when the view of the majority is in control, but when the balance between the independently assessed views of the rich on the one hand and those of the poor on the other is in control (8(6).3). Democrats, of course, assert that equality is when the majority rule, but this produces inequality, namely the dominance of the populace. In other words what is claimed for democracy by democrats is so much false rhetoric. The first kind of democracy is not how democracy is but how democrats say democracy is. In practice, therefore, this rhetorical democracy will be no different from one or other of the four democracies next listed and probably in most cases it will be the last and worst of them (for it is there that demagogues, to whom such rhetoric will be most dear, are especially to be found). Hence it is not surprising that this first democracy drops out of the later listing (in chapter 6).[37]

1291b39   The next three democracies are quickly listed and differ in that the first distributes rule on the basis of a property qualification, though a low one, while the other two do not but give everyone in the city this right, save that the second takes care to scrutinize the descent of those it allows as citizens and the third does not; but both are checked by the rule of law. These three democracies differ from each other by progressive extension of citizenship to more of the populace until, in the last of them, everyone in the city not obviously an alien or a slave has it. That such progressive extension of the franchise will produce populaces with very different complexions (and rather worse ones from the point of

---

37. Most commentators suppose that Aristotle takes seriously the equality attributed to the first democracy, and that he views it as some ideal and best democracy, or identifies it with the least extreme democracy next mentioned; see Chambers (1961: 20–21), Lintott (1992: 118–19), Mulgan (1977: 75) and in Keyt and Miller (1991: 317–19), Newman (4;xxxvi). Jowett (1885: 2:159) suggests that it is a general description of democracy. Peter of Auvergne (1951: 4.4.574, 578) does not take the rhetoric of equality seriously and says the first democracy coincides with the last kind.

view of good rule) seems evident. That Aristotle was using observation to get these kinds is supported by things he elsewhere says of democracy.[38]

1292a4   That the last democracy came from observation there can be little doubt.[39] This kind is described as being the same in other respects save that the multitude is in control and not the law. The sense must be that it is the same in other respects as either of the last two democracies and not as the last one only.[40] For earlier Aristotle indicated that the same democracies may, for the sake of numbers, first extend the franchise to those not of full citizen descent but then, when they have enough, revert to a stricter scrutiny (3.5.1278a26–34), so that either of the two previous democracies could thus be the last if law ceases to be in control.[41]

There is, however, a problem with the statement that the multitude is in control, not the law. For Aristotle explains that this happens when decrees, and not law, are in control, and that decrees come to be in control because of demagogues. But then he goes on to say that demagogues arise when the laws are not in control. Hence there seems to be a circle in his reasoning: laws not being in control causes the rise of demagogues, demagogues cause decrees to be in control, decrees being in control is the laws not being in control.[42] The circle can be broken by supposing, first, a distinction between law not being in control and the multitude or decrees being in control (or by supposing that the shift from the first to the second need not be immediate),[43] and, second, by supposing that the rise of demagogues means, not their existence merely, but their taking over from the best men the first place in the regime. For demagogues, or would-be demagogues, doubtless exist in other democracies though without the possibility of seizing first place. If such demagogues do seize first place in these other democracies, it is not by controlling the democracy but by abolishing it through force of arms and creating tyranny.[44]

The process then is somewhat as follows. First the populace, in any democracy,

38. Cf. the remarks at 2.12.1274a3–21 and 3.5.1278a15–34. The *Athenaion Politeia*, even if not by Aristotle, is a rich source of the sort of historical information he might have used; see Chambers (1961) and Rhodes (1981).

39. Athens is usually cited as the main source, but Aristotle himself was probably more impressed by happenings in Cos, Rhodes, Heraclea, Megara, and Cyme; see 7(5).5.

40. Contra Newman (4:177).

41. The fact that Athens, in both the fifth and fourth centuries, insisted on citizen descent from both parents, need not therefore be an indication that Aristotle's description of ultimate democracy could not be accurate if applied to Athens, contra Newman (4:xli), and see Strauss, in Lord and O'Connor (1991: 217–18). See also 8(6).4.1319b1–22.

42. Newman notes the problem (4:178).

43. A phenomenon that in fact Aristotle expressly discusses shortly, in 6(4).5.1292b11–21.

44. Such instances are noted later in 7(5).5.1305a7–28 where, since the populace is said to have been occupied in the fields and not at leisure to attend assemblies, the democracies dissolved by the advent of tyranny were doubtless not ultimate ones.

exercises control as a unit and not as individuals and hence has the character of a monarch or single ruler. Now such a populace will be subject to law when affairs are handled by offices regularly appointed (and subject, no doubt, to audit and review by the assembly). But this state of law may cease to be in control without the populace immediately coming to exercise control instead. For the populace may have obtained the leisure to handle affairs directly through the assembly and no longer be compelled to leave this to the offices. But they may not yet actually be using this power. Indeed they could refrain from ever using it and continue to rely on the offices. But they have the power and, having it, start looking how to exercise it. What gets them actually to exercise it and to overthrow law and the discipline of the offices is the flattery of demagogues. Under this influence the populace realizes its monarchical power in actual monarchical or tyrannical behavior, and despotizes over the best men (to whom before it entrusted affairs in the offices), and handles everything instead directly through particular decrees in the assembly. The demagogues egg the populace on to behave thus because they want to be great by controlling everything, and they control everything by controlling the populace which controls everything. But the populace only controls everything by making decisions about everything, so the demagogues have to bring everything before the populace to realize their ambition. At the same time they have to attack the offices (for the offices before did the deciding) and the populace gladly obliges.

Thus the law's not being in control is first a potential state and then, through the behavior of demagogues, gets realized in actual behavior. Consequently there is no need to suppose a circle in the description.[45]

1292a30 Aristotle ends with a final point that serves to clarify the difference between the rule of law and rule by decree. Law ought to rule over everything, he says, but it is of particulars that the offices and regime (the controlling office) ought to judge. In other words, the rule of law means a fairly severe and strict limiting of the power of discretion of offices and assembly to those particulars that universal law cannot decide because of its universality (see 3.11.1282b1–6). It is only such particulars, not also the law, that fall within the competence of offices and regime.[46] In the other democracies this is what happens: the offices and the assembly take decisions only on certain particulars, but all else is decided according to universal law. In ultimate democracy everything is subject to the assembly's decrees, and no decree can be universal in the relevant sense, not because it cannot be written in universal terms, but because a decree applies, as such, only to the

---

45. The description also recalls, in certain respects, the account given in 2.12.1274a5–15.

46. Aristotle would not, one thinks, be a friend to the doctrine of executive prerogative that one finds in Locke's *Second Treatise on Government*, chap. 14, and that has been carried over into the understanding of the United States Constitution—unless, of course, the one who had the prerogative possessed surpassing virtue.

particular case in hand and does not lay down any fixed principle of action to be observed indefinitely into the future. Universal law, however, does lay down such a fixed principle of action.[47]

When Aristotle approves the opinion (possibly from Plato's *Republic* 557c1–558c7) that ultimate democracy is not a regime, for where the laws do not rule there is no regime, he is perhaps recalling his statement that only where the rulers have the virtue of gods can they rule without law, because then they are themselves law (3.13.1284a3–14).[48] Everywhere else the rulers are not law and should rule subject to law (cf. 3.11.1281b1–6). For it is only the restraint of law that will keep the regime to be the regime it is, or even to be a regime at all. A democratic assembly, for instance, that decides whatever it likes could, and typically does, decide things that are destructive of its own continued existence and control (see 7(5).9.1309b18–1310a36 with commentary thereon). A completely unrestrained and lawless democracy, in other words, will not long remain a democracy. In addition, a regime is what has controlling rule in the city, and such rule is the exercise of deliberation and judgment about the advantageous and the just (3.6.1278b8–11, 4(7).8.1328b13–

---

47. See *Ethics* 5.10. Some of the discussion of how far Aristotle's description of ultimate democracy is, and is intended to be, true of Athens, as in Strauss, in Lord and O'Connor (1991: 212–33), does not perhaps pay enough attention to the difference between law and decree, nor to the difference between being extreme in principle and being extreme in practice. The other democracies, for instance, are not extreme in principle because they are never even going to choose rule by decree. Only the officeholders in these democracies have the necessary leisure to meet often, so that rule by decree here would effectively mean rule by the decree of the officeholders or, in other words, despotic rule by the wealthy few (who alone or predominantly occupy the offices), which is not democracy but extreme oligarchy. Hence, out of sheer self-interest, the assembly in these democracies will lay down and insist on abiding by laws that divide rule between assembly and offices and give the offices real, though strictly limited and conditioned, powers of decision (law thus rules in these democracies because the ruling body, the populace, *wants* law to rule). In an extreme democracy, by contrast, the assembly has the necessary leisure to meet often and thus also to decide everything by and for itself (taking all such power of decision away from the offices). Here the rule of law, or such division in ruling, will only be apparent, because it can in principle be ignored whenever the assembly wishes (and the assembly now has the leisure so to wish). Rule is thus effectively by the assembly's wish and decree, even if in fact some or most decrees go on being in conformity with law. For the point is that the conformity, if it exists, will be incidental, since law, given the assembly's leisure to control everything directly, forms no essential part of the principle of rule. That principle is, appearances notwithstanding, lawless in fact and can, at any point, issue in lawless deeds. For the assembly, having total power concentrated in its own hands, can ignore or change anything (including all the rules of procedure), and might easily do so, especially in times of high passion (see Plato *Apology* 32a4–c4). Note, however, that, as Aristotle has here explained (and as he recalls later, 7(5).5), it is demagogues who, by stirring up popular passions, are the instruments whereby the lawless principle becomes lawless deeds. In the absence of demagogues, a democracy lawless and extreme in principle could in its practice be very measured. That is why a legislator faced with setting up or reforming an ultimate democracy would seek ways to limit the influence of demagogues and to counter extreme behavior (8(6).4–5).

48. A suggestion of Peter of Auvergne's (1951: 4.4.583).

15, 6(4).4.1291a22–28, 34–40). But if deliberation and judgment are exercised without perfect prudence or without its substitute in the form of law, but by passion instead, then it will be as if no deliberation or judgment is being exercised at all (for passion is not deliberation or judgment).[49] In such a case there will be no true ruling nor, consequently, any true regime or any true city, for there will be no deliberation or judgment or even reasoned speech (which is the mark of the city, 1.2.1253a9–18). Hence an extreme democracy, which decides everything by decrees, or by its particular passions (even if these passions are sometimes good), and is not restrained in its decision making by universal law, will not even be a democracy in the true or authoritative sense—if, that is, democracy is one of the regimes. An assembly of beasts, after all, is not a regime (3.11.1281b15–20).

Chapter 5

~ KINDS OF OLIGARCHY

1292a39 The kinds of oligarchy are also four, of which the first differs from the others in not having a high property qualification and in allowing all to share in rule who have that qualification. That it must exclude the poor (even and especially when the poor are more numerous) is evident if it is to be an oligarchy. The other oligarchies do have a high property qualification and do not include everyone with that qualification. So the second oligarchy chooses whom to exclude and include (whether making the choice from all with the qualification or only from some), and the third has son succeeding to father. The fourth is the same as the third save that the rulers rule and not law. It exercises total control over everything, like the last democracy, and so is also analogous to tyranny. It carries the name of dynasty. The differences between these oligarchies lie not just in degrees of wealth, but also in other privileges associated with wealth, as family connection (evident in the third and fourth kinds), and perhaps also how long the family has been wealthy, and what ties it has with other families or with the founding and preservation of the city (the second kind).[50]

~ REASON FOR THESE KINDS OF DEMOCRACY AND OLIGARCHY

~ PRELIMINARY CLARIFICATION

1292b11 Having stated the kinds, Aristotle comes next to relate them back to the kinds of populace and notables, for, as he has argued at length, it is differ-

49. See Miller (1995: 82, 170).

50. Evidence for oligarchies differing in kind along these sort of lines is mentioned later in 7(5).6, 8, and recall also Apollonia, Thera, and Colophon from 6(4).4.1290b8–20. The twelve kinds of oligarchy listed by Newman (4:xxiv–xxvii) all seem to be instances of Aristotle's four.

ences in the kind of ruling body that make differences in kind of regime. However this fact can sometimes be obscured, and so, to remove any doubts about it, he begins with a preliminary clarification.

A situation can arise, he says, when the laws are popular or oligarchical but the habits and training of the regime are the reverse. Such situations are typical after a change in regimes when those now in control are content at first to use their power against opponents in small ways. So the laws associated with the previous regime still remain, but it is those changing the regime who dominate and are actually in control. Eventually, therefore, the old laws will be removed and new ones in harmony with the new regime will be introduced. The lag, however, between a change in regime and a change in laws should not be allowed to obscure the fact that the regime is the people in control and gets its character or kind from them. The laws clearly depend for their character and their force on the regime and not vice versa, and laws out of harmony with the regime will eventually suffer de iure, what they have already suffered de facto, namely abolition. Hence in judging regimes, and in determining which kind they are and why, one must look, as Aristotle has done throughout and continues to do in succeeding chapters, at the people in the ruling body rather than at the laws.[51]

By laws here must again be meant primarily constitutional laws, the sort that determine the offices, their appointment, their sphere of competence, their limitations, and so forth. A case in point might be where an oligarchical law, confining a certain office to certain property qualifications and endowing that office with certain important functions, remains in effect, even though the assembly has changed in character and strength sufficiently to throw the office open to anyone and to cut back its functions, or even to abolish it. Only later, however, does the assembly act and exercise its power in this regard.[52]

Chapter 6

~ RELATION TO THE KINDS OF POPULACE AND NOTABLES

1292b22   In stating the kinds of democracy and oligarchy, and in relating them back to the kinds of populace and notables, Aristotle does not, contrary to what one might initially expect,[53] designate a distinct kind of democracy and oligarchy for each of his listed divisions in the populace and the notables. But the

51. This point also confirms, of course, what Aristotle said earlier (6(4).1.1289a13–15), that in setting up a regime one must tailor the laws to the character of the ruling body for which one is legislating. Otherwise the laws one lays down will simply not be obeyed; cf. Johnson (1985).

52. Such seems to have happened with the office of the Areopagus at Athens, 2.12.1274a7–11, 7(5).4.1304a17–24; and cf. also Athēnaiōn Politeia 7–8, 23–25.

53. It is what Jowett (1885: 2:156), Newman (4:171), and Robinson (1962: 86) expect.

reason for this is not far to seek. Some of these divisions make no difference in regimes at all. For regimes differ according to the *character* of the ruling body, and not every difference in occupation need make a difference in the character of the populace nor every difference in wealth and privilege a difference in the character of the notables. Only where the differences in occupation, wealth, and privilege do vary the character of the ruling body will they also vary the regime. Thus, in what follows, Aristotle looks not to occupations and privileges but to certain distinctive groupings of occupations and privileges that do vary this character (which is perhaps why he listed all the occupations and privileges earlier, because, even if these operate as groupings and not individually, yet it is necessary to know them individually to know the groupings).

With respect to democracies, the kinds differ as shares in rule are extended to more and more of the poor. The first kind is the minimal extension necessary if there is to be a democracy. For a democracy is by definition rule of the poor, so some of the poor must be in control. But not all of them need be, and specifically not the completely poor. Instead shares can be limited to the poor who do possess some minimal degree of property, sufficient, perhaps, to make a living from. These will be above all the small farmers who own the land they farm (if they are hired hands they will be laborers rather than farmers). The decisive feature here is that these poor have no leisure and that all and only those who meet the property qualification are citizens.

The first fact, that they have no leisure, means that they cannot attend frequent assemblies so as to decide everything directly by themselves. Consequently they put law in charge instead and confine meetings of the assembly to a minimum. Most things, therefore, will have to be managed by the officials, and these officials will have to be the wealthy who do have leisure. But if the officials ran everything without check by the populace, the regime would become an oligarchy. So the populace imposes the necessary democratic check by laying down laws (laws defin-ing the offices, their powers, their limits, their duration, their appointment, and so forth),[54] and by having sufficient meetings of the assembly to ensure that the laws are kept and that anything directly affecting the regime is decided in the assembly.

The second fact, that all those who meet the property qualification are citizens, means, first, that the regime stays democratic and that property owners cannot start picking and choosing whom to allow into the regime (which would lead to oligarchy); and, second, that the regime does not become too democratic and let in a mass of poor who have no property. Such an additional mass would be more

54. The sorts of things discussed later in 6(4).14–16. We may note parallels in the United States Constitution, as for instance in the enumerated powers of article 1, section 8, which was similarly designed to put restraints on the activity of officials, though these restraints seem now to be but partially observed.

hostile to those with much property and less measured in its behavior. The balance in the meetings of the assembly would shift more against the notables, who would thus find themselves more jealously watched, less trusted, and more limited in the exercise of discretion.

1292b34 This shift will take place in the next two democracies, which differ from the first in no longer limiting shares in rule to property owners. So the second kind of democracy extends shares in rule to all who have a recognized family descent, and the third to all who are free (regardless of family descent). The second kind will therefore let in many artisans, dealers in the market, and laborers (or the urban crowd generally), and the third will let in all who are not manifestly slaves, including, therefore, those who have one parent an alien or a slave. Aristotle notes that here too law will be in control, because the populace do not have leisure to take an active part; but he does not say that assemblies will be confined to the necessary ones. Indeed, as he notes later (8(6).4.1319a26–32), since many in these kinds of populace are kept by their occupations about the town and the market-place, they will find it easier to attend more assemblies. Hence while the populace do not have leisure to take part in the offices or to decide everything through the assembly, they are certainly able to meet more often and to guard the notables and officeholders more closely.

The difference between the character of these two democracies will probably lie in the natural attachment of the populace to the city and to all the citizens of the city (including the notables). So everyone in the second kind at least comes from a native-born and free family and can be recognized as fellows of the one city, both by themselves and by the notables. But not everyone in the third kind need be either fully native-born or free. So this third kind will have less love for the whole city and will be less bearable to the notables (or even to the farmers). What keeps these kinds, especially the latter, from collapsing into ultimate democracy is not any inner lack of the requisite character, but lack of the leisure actually to manage affairs and to attack the notables. Farmers, for instance, share with the notables a love of the land and are kept on their farms away from the assembly also by this love, and not only by lack of leisure. Many artisans, by contrast, most laborers, and the like are kept back merely by lack of leisure, and, being landless, have less reason to feel at one with the notables.

1292b41 The fourth and last democracy is marked by two differences, increased size and public revenues. The size is going to increase mainly among those who inhabit the town (the land admits of little increase among those who live directly off it), and so among the populace enfranchised by the second and third democracies. Public revenues will give this increased populace the leisure to take over the management of affairs from the notables and the offices. For their work will not hold them back from frequent assemblies and from jury courts, but it will hold back farmers and the notables, both of whom have property to care for.

Notables may indeed have sufficient leisure for serving in the offices where the work can be made to fit a time and place convenient for them; but assemblies meet at set times in set places and are mainly spent in talking, not in actual management of anything. The urban poor, by contrast, have nothing to keep them away, provided they get enough to live on. What distinguishes this democracy from the previous one or two is simply the absence of restraint. This, however, amounts to a change in quality, for restraints can make people behave better than they are (cf. 4(7).15.1334a25–28, 8(6).4.1318b39–1319a1).

1293a10 Turning next to oligarchies, Aristotle notes that the first kind arises when shares in rule are confined to those with a property qualification that is not excessively great (though, clearly, it will have to be large enough to exclude the small farmers of the first democracy), and when everyone with the qualification takes part in rule. Here the circumstance of limited wealth and of shares open to all requires the oligarchs to rule subject to law. For they are too numerous to behave like a monarch and too lacking in leisure to manage everything themselves. Numbers will prevent the notables being a monarch, even though they do not prevent the populace being a monarch, because notables rule as individuals and not as a collectivity (their wealth and status would give them a sense of individual worth and make them scorn to act as one of a crowd). A council of the wealthy is like rule by many chiefs who consider each other as equals and so who can only share rule together subject to fixed and definite laws that ensure some equality.

1293a21 The second kind of oligarchy differs from the first both in greater wealth and in the privileges arising from greater wealth. This wealth makes the rulers think they deserve more power, and they secure this by limiting shares in rule, not to a general property qualification, but to those they themselves choose. Here the criteria of choice could in principle be anything indicative of privilege, from family descent, to virtue (perhaps especially martial virtue), to education (how they were brought up, by whom, and so forth), to friends; and the choice could be confined to certain of the wealthy only (as, say, members of certain clubs) or extend in principle to all of them.[55] Such an oligarchy decides more things according to its own wish (for now it thus decides its own membership), but subject to the law that requires oligarchs regularly to choose some from outside (the excluded are too strong to let the oligarchy reduce its numbers or become a few families only). The existing oligarchs cannot, therefore, do just whatever they wish, but must always be accommodating themselves to new members who will, as likely as not, have different wishes.

1293a26 The third oligarchy is marked by an increase in wealth and by a limiting of shares in rule to sons of existing oligarchs. In this case wealth and family (and primogeniture) are the criteria of rule. This oligarchy will differ

---

55. Several of Newman's twelve oligarchies will be instances of this type (4:xxiv–xxvii).

sharply from the previous one because no one from outside the oligarchical families will be allowed in the regime. But there is still law, the law about sons succeeding, which will be some sort of check on arbitrary action (for existing oligarchs will have to accommodate new sons as the fathers die). The fourth and last oligarchy is when the oligarchs are so powerful in the property they own, and in the multitude and closeness of their friendships, that they need not even abide by the law about succession, but can exclude everyone who stands in their way (or everyone, including any son, who is not inside or loyal to the circle of friendship). Here any check of law is wholly set aside.

One should note about all these democracies and oligarchies that what makes them the way they are is the character of the ruling body, and that what gives the ruling body its character is primarily external and social conditions. The measured behavior of the less extreme regimes is not virtue proper but the effect of circumstances (which, since it is a real effect, really modifies character). Virtue proper is the work of education, and only the simply best regime has and cares about the right education.[56]

Chapter 7

~ THAT THERE ARE ALSO SEVERAL KINDS OF
ARISTOCRACY, POLITY, AND TYRANNY

~ KINDS OF SO-CALLED ARISTOCRACY

1293a35   Having given the kinds of democracy and oligarchy, Aristotle now turns to give the kinds of other regimes. First he states that there are further regimes to consider, and specifically the regimes of so-called aristocracy and polity. Monarchy or tyranny is also dealt with, but dealt with last because it is least of all a regime. Of the regimes of aristocracy and polity, however, only aristocracy is recognized by current opinion. For this opinion posits four regimes: monarchy, oligarchy, democracy, and what they call aristocracy; the fifth, polity, is often missed out because of its rarity. Aristotle mentions Plato as omitting polity,[57] but some of those who made oligarchy and democracy the basic regimes, and who would classify aristocracy and monarchy as sorts of oligarchy, must also have failed to distinguish polity from democracy. As regards so-called aristocracy, this is not omitted in the way polity is (though such aristocracies too must be rare), presumably because of the famous case of the Spartans, who made express profession of

---

56. See Johnson (1990: 80–84).

57. Although Aristotle's reference to Plato is vague, it is nevertheless true that neither in the *Republic* nor the *Statesman* does Plato list polity.

virtue and whose regime was undeniably different from both oligarchies and democracies.

1293b1   These five regimes (provided monarchy is understood to embrace tyranny and kingship together) coincide, as far as names go, with Aristotle's basic six. But the introduction of aristocracy again is initially a surprise, since earlier Aristotle had said that it needed no further treatment and that only four regimes were left: polity, democracy, oligarchy, and tyranny (6(4).2.1289a35–38). But in fact, as he now explains, aristocracy is not being reintroduced nor does it need any further treatment.[58] For aristocracy properly speaking is the aristocracy discussed before as the simply best regime, where the citizens are also simply best and have the goodness of the good man (not the goodness relative to some lesser regime). But the aristocracies now in question are not aristocracies in this sense, nor indeed are they oligarchies or polities. For regimes that choose the offices on the basis of virtue as well as wealth are not aristocracies proper, for virtue is not the only criterion of rule, nor oligarchies or polities, for virtue is also a criterion of rule (though this virtue, by contrast with the virtue of true aristocracy, need not be perfect virtue but only partial virtue, or even a certain reputation for virtue). Instead, they are sorts of mixed regimes combining elements of true aristocracy, on the one hand, and of oligarchy and democracy, on the other.

1293b14   The kinds Aristotle gives of these so-called aristocracies are, first, a combination of wealth, virtue, and populace, as in Carthage; second, a combination of virtue and populace, as in Sparta; and, third, oligarchically inclined polities (which combine wealth and populace but incline more toward wealth). Now these kinds, unlike the kinds of democracy and oligarchy, are not so much variations within a single principle (populace or wealth) as combinations of one or more principles (populace, wealth, and virtue). They are, as Aristotle says, mixtures. Hence they still fall under his basic sixfold classification, not however because they are one or other kind or subkind, but because they straddle two or more kinds. For they acknowledge, in their distribution of rule, more than one of the principles that distinguish the kinds. So even if, as especially in the Spartan case, the virtue leaves much to be desired, these regimes do recognize virtue, or what they suppose to be virtue, as an independent title to rule and not merely as an appendage, say, to wealth (which is the only recognition that virtue or its reputation might get in an oligarchy).[59] That oligarchically inclined polities also get listed here under so-

---

58. Aristotle's remark that the regime that "it is noble to call aristocracy" is the one "we went through in our first discussions" (1293b1–3) must be a reference to 4(7) and 5(8), not to 3.7 or 3.13, for aristocracy is only set out in book 3 in general terms as one of the six regimes; it is not gone through in any detail. In addition, the immediately following sentence (1293b3–5) is strongly reminiscent of remarks at 4(7).9.1328b37–39.

59. This may explain the puzzle, noted by Newman (4:194), why regimes that combine virtue and wealth (as opposed, say, to virtue and populace) are not also listed as kinds of so-called aristocracy.

called aristocracy is, as is made clear in the next chapter, a concession to common opinion.[60] Strictly speaking they are not aristocracies, though they are mixed regimes.

The description of Carthage as a combination of wealth, virtue, and populace fits well the earlier discussion (2.11), but there may be some doubt about the description of Sparta as combining virtue and the populace since the earlier discussion makes it clear that Sparta is also marked by a very great fondness for wealth (2.9). But, in fact, the fondness for wealth, while it exists and affects the way things are run, is contrary to the intention of the regime (so especially 2.9.1271a29–37). Hence, with respect to its intention, Sparta is correctly described as a combination of virtue and populace, but with respect to how it actually is, it combines wealth too (so it can even be used as an example of the mixing of democracy and oligarchy, 6(4).9.1294b14–34).

Chapter 8

~ KINDS OF POLITY

1293b22   The two regimes left are polity and tyranny, but since polity is not a deviant regime, nor are so-called aristocracies (for both pay some attention to virtue, the latter expressly and the former in effect by mixing rich and poor in a virtuous way), the question why these kinds have been left for treatment among deviant regimes calls for explanation. Aristotle gives two reasons. First, these regimes have deviated from the most correct or simply best regime and, second, they are numbered with, and belong to, regimes that are deviations.

The point of this second reason is not immediately clear and the translation is disputed. The usual translation reads: "because they [polity and so-called aristocracy] are enumerated along with these deviations and these deviations are deviations from them" (1293b26–27). But there are two difficulties with this translation: one, it makes oligarchy a deviation from so-called aristocracy (whereas elsewhere oligarchy is said to be a deviation from aristocracy simply, at 3.7);[61] two, it does not

---

Such a combination would in fact not mix virtue and wealth but subordinate virtue to wealth (for virtue would never be allowed to count as a title independently of wealth, since no one would be allowed to rule who was not already wealthy). So these regimes would not be different from the second kind of oligarchy listed before (where new members are chosen from all those outside the regime and not from some only, 6(4).5.1292b2–4). By contrast a combination of virtue and populace would allow virtue to count as an independent title, for no one with virtue would be excluded from rule just because he did not, or did, have wealth.

60. There is therefore no inconsistency between this chapter and the next, contra Newman (4:195), since Aristotle is careful to distinguish between what he says when following what others say and what he says when stating his own view.

61. This difficulty is noted by Barker (1946: 174 n2) and Newman (4:195–96).

produce an acceptable reason for treating polity and the so-called aristocracies along with the deviations. For this translation makes Aristotle say that regimes should be treated along with their deviations, and this entails that the best regime of kingship and aristocracy should also be treated along with its deviations (namely tyranny and oligarchy), and this patently cannot be Aristotle's meaning. I offer, therefore, as an alternative translation: "because enumerated along with them [polity and so-called aristocracy] and belonging to them are these deviations." This translation avoids the first difficulty (for Aristotle is no longer made to say that oligarchy is a deviation from so-called aristocracy), and it can be read in such a way as to avoid the second. For it can be read as meaning that polity and so-called aristocracy and all the deviations are numbered and belong together because they are alike in falling under the other or second questions of political science (which questions all in some way involve each other, see the commentary on 6(4).1), and not under the first question of the simply best regime (which question can, and should, be taken separately). Read thus, this second reason now neatly complements the first, for the first explains why polity and so-called aristocracy do not belong to the treatment of the simply best regime (for they are not the simply best regime), and the second, why they do belong to the treatment of the deviant regimes (for they belong to the same set of questions as the deviant regimes).

As for tyranny, its being placed last is clear enough. Tyranny is least of all a regime (for, like the last democracy and the last oligarchy, or indeed more so, it departs furthest from the job of a regime, which is the common good of virtuous living, 3.6), so it has the least place of all in a treatment of regimes.

1293b31 These arguments for the arrangement of topics do not, except in the case of tyranny, specify a precise ordering: polity and so-called aristocracy are to be treated along with the deviations, but nothing is said about why they had to be treated after democracy and oligarchy and not before. A reason, however, is immediately suggested by what Aristotle says next, that polity is a mixture of oligarchy and democracy, for mixtures become manifest after the elements that they mix have become manifest (and so-called aristocracies also mix democracy and oligarchy, though differently).

Polity, then, is a regime that mixes oligarchy and democracy, in contradistinction to so-called aristocracy, which mixes these, or democracy only, and virtue. Aristotle does not, however, list its kinds; instead he immediately mentions how custom names two of them, those that lean toward democracy and those that lean toward oligarchy. He therefore presumably leaves the third possible kind, those that lean in neither direction, to be understood (all three seem to be mentioned together later, at 6(4).11.1295b36–39). At any rate custom is wrong to call only the first kind polities and the second kind, those that lean toward oligarchy, aristocracies (which were the third kind of aristocracies listed in the previous chapter). So

Aristotle first states why the custom arises and then shows that it should neverthe-less not be followed.

The custom of calling aristocracies those polities that lean more toward oligar-chy arises from a certain similarity between the well-off and the best. For first, education and good birth (which are marks of the best) go along with being well-off, and, second, the well-off have what people do wrong for. The force of the latter point may be either that the well-off are assumed to be just because, having abundant means, they are assumed to have no motive to be unjust, or that since they have what people think is best (and so what they do wrong for, namely wealth and the advantages of wealth), they are themselves thought of as best. At any rate, the well-off are called noble and good or gentlemen, and since aristocracies dis-tribute superiority to gentlemen, oligarchies, and hence also oligarchically leaning polities, are associated with aristocracies in being said also to be composed of gentlemen.

The custom, on the other hand, of calling polities, and not aristocracies, those mixtures that lean toward democracy arises from the fact that there seems to be an equivalence between aristocracy and a good state of law. For (1) a city not run by aristocrats but by the wicked cannot be under good laws, and (2) a city not under good laws cannot be an aristocracy. From (1) and the obvious, and unexpressed, premise (3) that democracies and democratically leaning polities are not run by aristocrats, but by the wicked (they are run by, or lean toward, the poor who are wicked or base compared with aristocrats), it follows that (4) such polities cannot be under good laws. From (2) and (4), it follows (5) that they cannot be, nor be called, aristocracies.

1294a3 Next Aristotle responds to these arguments on behalf of prevailing custom. First, he responds to the second argument, that democratically leaning polities are not under good laws and so are, for this reason, not aristocracies. He attacks this argument, not to show that such polities should be called aristocracies, but rather to show that the reason it alleges is not a good reason for saying that they are not aristocracies (and so not a good reason either for insinuating that polities leaning the other way are aristocracies). In other words, he is not rejecting the conclusion (5), but the reason for the conclusion, namely (2) and (4). He confines his attack to premises (1) and (2)—premise (3) is not as such wrong, for the poor are not better than aristocrats individually but only, if at all, collectively. First, he attacks both these premises directly; then he attacks an implication of premise (1).

First, then, he points out that "good state of law" (the condition of being under good laws) is a doubly ambiguous notion. For a good state of law is going to be absent, not only when the laws laid down are bad, but also when the laws laid down, though good, are not obeyed. Hence good state of law must mean, in one sense, simply that the laws laid down are obeyed (whether these laws are good or bad), and in another that the laws obeyed are also well laid down. Hence premise (2) is false, for a city not under good laws could still be an aristocracy, at least in the sense that it could have aristocratic laws, though not laws that were being obeyed (as is in fact true in part of Sparta, especially with respect to the laxity of its women and its love of money, 2.9). Premise (1) is false too, for a city not run by the aristocrats but by the wicked could be under a good state of law in the sense that it could be obedient to the laws that are laid down. But, further, even when good state of law means obedience to well-laid laws, there is still ambiguity. For well-laid laws can mean either the best laws people are capable of or the best laws simply. Consequently, premise (1) is false again, for cities run by the wicked could be said to be under good laws because the laws they are obedient to could be the best laws they are capable of.

But now it might seem that democratically leaning polities should be called aristocracies after all. At any rate there are senses in which they can be said to be under good laws, and it is an implication of premise (1) that a city under good laws must be an aristocracy. For if, as premise (1) says, a city not run by aristocrats cannot be under good laws, or if, in other words, no city not run by aristocrats can be under good laws, then, by conversion, no city under good laws can be a city not run by aristocrats, and, by obversion, every city under good laws must be a city run by aristocrats. So Aristotle attacks this implication by recalling that aristocracy is not properly defined by reference to good state of law. Rather its defining mark is virtue. Likewise the defining mark of oligarchy is wealth and of democracy freedom. Majority rule, by contrast, is not a defining mark of any regime, and specifically not of democracy, for it is found in all regimes. Consequently, even though polities leaning toward democracies can be said to be under good laws, they are not aristocracies, because aristocracies are not distinguished by this and what they are distinguished by, virtue, is not what democracies are distinguished by.

There is, however, a sense in which one might say that aristocracies could be defined by good state of law. For if good state of law is taken in its strongest sense, that is, in the sense of obedience to the best laws simply, it will coincide with the definition of aristocracy in terms of virtue. For the best laws simply must be the laws that do what laws are supposed to do, namely inculcate virtue in the citizens (*Ethics* 10.9); they are, in fact, the education of books 4(7) and 5(8). In this sense, indeed, premises (1) and (2) are going to be true, and hence in this sense they will also prove that democratically leaning polities are not aristocracies. But then they will also prove at the same time that oligarchically leaning polities are not aristocracies either, for such polities do not have the best laws simply and so are not under good laws.

1294a15 Next Aristotle responds to the reasons given for calling aristocracies those polities that lean more toward oligarchy, namely the alleged similarity between the well-off and the best. The opening sentence of his response, however, is a difficult one in the Greek (1294a15–16) and it may well be corrupt. Hence several translators give the sense they think is needed and not the sense of the Greek as it stands.[62] Translations that do try to follow the Greek include: "In most cities the form which is called polity exists," and "In most cities the form of the regime is called polity."[63] Both these translations, however, imply that most cities have a polity, which is contrary to what Aristotle said before (6(4).4.1291b11–13, 7.1293a39–42) and says again later (6(4).11.1296a22–b2), namely that most existing regimes are either oligarchies or democracies.

To avoid this problem, but to keep still to the Greek as it stands, I suggest the following: "In most cities the kind is the kind that is called polity," or: "The kind in most cities is the kind that is called polity."[64] I then understand this to mean that the kind *of mixture* in most cities (that is, in most cities that have a mixture or a mixed regime) is the kind that is (rightly) called polity, and not the kind that is (rightly) called aristocracy. In other words, in contrast to the two translations just given, Aristotle is no longer made to say that most cities have a mixed regime, but rather that most cities that have a mixed regime have a polity and not an aristocracy (which is not in conflict with anything he says about mixed regimes elsewhere). The next sentence now neatly follows on, for it provides the reason for this fact, namely that the mixture in most cities aims only at the well-off and the needy, at wealth and freedom. The mixture does not, that is to say, also aim at virtue because, as Aristotle immediately continues, among most people the well-off seem to be occupying the place of the gentlemen. The stress here must be on "seems" and "occupying the place of." For those who, in most cities, occupy the place of gentlemen are only apparent gentlemen and not really so, and hence most cities, if they were ever to have a mixed regime, would have no real gentlemen, and so no real virtue, to put into the mixture. The "gentlemen" they did put into the mixture would just be the well-off.

The facts stated earlier, therefore (that education and good birth go along with being well-off, and that the well-off have the wealth that others do wrong to acquire), are no guarantee, it is clear, that the well-off are in fact educated or well-born, or that they have used their wealth and their leisure actually to acquire virtue and to become gentlemen. Consequently, that a regime leans toward oligarchy, and is aiming at such pseudogentlemen in its mixture, does not mean that it is aiming at virtue, and so gives no ground for calling it an aristocracy. Indeed, there is a

---

62. As Barker (1946: 176), Lord (1984: 130), Sinclair/Saunders (1981: 260).

63. The first is Newman's (4:199), and the second Jowett's (1885: 2:164), though Jowett actually says "the form of the constitution is called constitutional" because "constitution" is the way he translates *politeia*.

64. I follow Newman in taking *kaleitai* ("is called") in an idiomatic sense, but I am not sure how accurately. At any rate this seems to me the only way to make good sense of the Greek in the context.

countervailing reason not to call it an aristocracy. For there is such a thing as real virtue, and such virtue forms an independent claim to rule alongside wealth and freedom (good birth is a combination of wealth and virtue and so not a separate factor; nor will it properly belong to the rich who are not virtuous at the same time or who are not really gentlemen). Hence mixed regimes that only aim at the well-off and needy, and not also at the virtuous (which would, for the aforesaid reason, be the case in most cities), should be called polities. It is only regimes that mix virtue as well, which is the defining mark of aristocracy, that should be called aristocracies—after the true and first kind, of course, the aristocracy of the simply best of books 4(7) and 5(8).

Chapter 9

∽ REASON FOR THESE KINDS OF ARISTOCRACY AND POLITY

1294a30 Having discussed the kinds of so-called aristocracies and polities, or mixed regimes generally, Aristotle turns next, as he did in the case of democracies and oligarchies, to give the reasons for them (he only mentions polity in his opening sentence but, as he indicates during the chapter, what he says about polities applies, with certain differences, to so-called aristocracies as well). That he is now going to give the reasons for these regimes may not initially appear to be the case. For he actually speaks of how these regimes come about and should be established, which seems to be a premature introduction of the question of how to set up regimes (the fourth of the questions for discussion in this book, dealt with in chapters 14–16). But mixed regimes seem to be especially dependent, as oligarchies and democracies are not, on legislative action for their existence. For they require a mixing of very different parts (poverty and wealth and virtue), which mixing could hardly happen spontaneously but must be a deliberate and conscious act. Oligarchies and democracies, by contrast, follow the spontaneously varying dominance in the city of their respective parts, and need legislative action rather for stable arrangement than for existence.[65] So to speak of the reasons for mixed regimes is really to speak of the sort of legislation that deliberately puts and keeps the middle (the mix of wealth and poverty and virtue) in a position of control. Accordingly Aristotle states the topic of this chapter as how so-called

65. One may note here that when Aristotle speaks later, in chapter 12, of which regime is preferable for whom, he says of democracies and oligarchies that, where their respective multitudes exceed or are superior in the city, there "it is natural" (*pephuken*) for these regimes to exist (1296b25, 32–33). Of mixed regimes, however, he says that, where the middle exceeds the extremes, there a lasting polity "can" (*endechetai*) exist (1296b39–40). I take this to be a sign, if only a passing one, of the point I am making here in the commentary.

polity comes about "alongside" (*para*, 1294a30) democracy and oligarchy and how it should be established. For I take this to mean that the topic is how so-called polity should be established so that it does indeed come about alongside, and does not, through poor legislation, collapse back into, democracy and oligarchy.

At any rate, if polity, and so-called aristocracy, are mixings, the reasons for their existence will consist in properly mixed legislation. So the legislator must have a grasp of all the elements that go into the mixing and also of the ways of mixing them. The thing to do, then, as Aristotle now says, is to take all the distinctive elements of the parts to be mixed, and of democracy and oligarchy in particular, set them out in separate lists, and pick and choose in turn from each list. Aristotle does not, however, set out such lists here. Perhaps he expects percipient legislators to do it for themselves from what was said earlier, especially in chapters 4–6, and from what is said later, in chapters 14–16; though he evidently thinks enough of the importance of this matter that, judging better, as it were, of his brevity here, he returns to the same point in his addendum in the last book and gives there such a list for democracy, and effectively for oligarchy too (8(6).2, 6.1320b18–20). At all events, what Aristotle contents himself with now is setting out methods for combining parts from the contrasting lists. He gives three such methods.

1294a35 The first method is to take contrasting elements of the legislation of each (the constitutional legislation, that is, or the legislation about the distribution of rule). The example is jury courts, where oligarchies, in order to ensure the attendance of the well-off and the nonattendance of the needy, impose a fine on the well-off but give no pay to the needy, and where democracies, in order to ensure the opposite, impose no fine on the well-off but do give pay to the needy. So if one takes the legislation of each and imposes fines on the well-off and gives pay to the needy so that both will attend, or if one imposes no fines and gives no pay so that those in the middle attend (the very needy not being able to, the very well-off not caring to), the result will be polity. The result will also be a polity leaning to oligarchy or democracy, or neither, according as the fines and payments are set higher or lower.

1294b1 The second method is to take the mean between the arrangements of each. The example is the assembly where democracies require no property qualification or a low one and where oligarchies require a high one. The mean qualification, then, between the high and the low, will produce a polity. Here again, of course, the polity will be oligarchic or democratic or neither depending on where the qualification is set. There may seem, however, to be a difference in effect between this method and the first, for the first would mix by including both needy and well-off whereas the second would mix by taking the middle and excluding the needy, or the very needy. But in fact the first method would do the same, namely if a low payment was not enough for the very needy to live on but was enough to give the less needy leisure to take a more active part in the regime, and if a low fine compelled the less well-off to come who could not afford to pay it but allowed the very well-off to stay away who could.

1294b6 The third method is to select from several different elements of the legislation of each. This method differs from the first in that the first balances out opposed elements of legislation whereas this one combines tangential elements, as it were, of legislation.[66] The example is taken from the appointment of offices where democracy uses lot and has no property qualification and where oligarchy uses election and has a property qualification. So to take no property qualification from democracy and election from oligarchy produces a polity or an aristocracy. Aristotle mentions aristocracy expressly here because what this combination produces is election from all and election from all is a feature of aristocracy—it is election from some that is a feature of oligarchy (6(4).15.1300b1–5). For election from all means that anyone with quality, however lacking in wealth, can be elected, whereas election from some, namely the well-off, necessarily excludes anyone with quality who is needy (the alternative combination, lot and a property qualification, would produce oligarchy, though the combination does not occur, 6(4).15.1300b2–3). One may note also that this example of a method of mixing, unlike the first two examples, does not admit of oligarchic or democratic leanings. It is distinctive, nevertheless, in leaving open a place to the claims of virtue. But different kinds of polity or so-called aristocracy will also be produced according to the way one does or does not combine the three methods.

These methods may perhaps be exhaustive, but whether they are or not, they are certainly sufficiently illustrative to serve the purpose, which is to explain how mixed regimes come to be, or can be brought into being.

1294b13 Having given this explanation, Aristotle next states ways of determining if the mixing of democracy and oligarchy is well done. He does not give a way of determining if the mixture of virtue is well done, perhaps because this will depend on the mixture of the other two: a regime will be more or less open to virtue the more or less well it tempers the extremes toward the middle, for virtue will get squeezed out if there is too much emphasis on freedom or wealth. At any rate Aristotle gives two signs, or defining principles, the first of which he states and then illustrates before coming to the second. So the first sign or principle that the mixing has been done well is when the same regime can be said to be both democracy and oligarchy, for if it can be, this must be because it displays equally the features of both. It will thus also be like the mean, for in the mean too both extremes appear (though as harmonized, of course, not as opposed).

1294b18 The illustration of this sign is taken from Sparta. For though

---

66. As Newman notes (4:201–2), and also Jowett (1885: 2:165).

Sparta is not a regime that aims to mix wealth and democracy and virtue (for rather it aims to mix democracy and virtue, 6(4).7.1293b16–18), it does in fact mix wealth and democracy (and even produces an inordinate love of wealth, 2.9.1270a14–15, 1271b15–17—though love of wealth, as opposed to wealth itself, is not peculiar to the wealthy). As features of democracy in Sparta Aristotle first mentions certain equalities of education, behavior, and sustenance. These are features indicative of the character of the ruling body. Next he mentions features to do with the distribution of offices, on the side both of democracy (that, of the two greatest offices, the populace elect the one, the senate, and take part in the other, the ephorate) and of oligarchy (that all offices are elected and that a few have control over the major penalties of death and exile). These are features indicative of the regime itself. Those on the side of oligarchy, interestingly enough, are ambiguous as between oligarchy and aristocracy[67] (offices chosen by election, for instance, is common to both). But this makes in favor of Aristotle's analysis, for it shows how Sparta can appear to be a noble mixture of democracy and oligarchy and yet be primarily, or in its intention, a mixture of democracy and virtue. Of course, that Sparta is a noble mixture takes nothing away from Aristotle's criticisms of Sparta elsewhere in the *Politics*, for he directed those criticisms at Sparta as a candidate for the best regime simply. Here he is talking of Sparta as a mixed regime and not as a candidate for the best simply.

1294b34   This then is the first sign or principle of a noble mixing, that the mixed elements should both appear and not appear in it (appear insofar as they can be traced, not appear insofar as the regime is neither of them but something in between). The second sign or principle is that the regime stands and is preserved through itself without need of being shored up from outside, not in the sense that the majority wishes it to exist (which would be true even of the evil regime of ultimate democracy), but in the sense that none of the parts of the city as a whole (and poor or rich in particular) would want a different regime. For if both poor and rich, and the virtuous too, are content with the regime and do not want it changed, then the regime must be giving all of them what they want, and hence it must have a noble mix of the elements favored respectively by each.

Chapter 10

~ KINDS OF TYRANNY

1295a1   The final regime and its kinds to consider is tyranny (though it is least of all a regime). It too has a part in the inquiry, since it is a part, if a degenerate

---

67. A point noted by way of query in Newman (4:206).

part, of the present subject matter, namely regimes.[68] Two kinds of tyranny were already mentioned earlier in the listing of kingships (3.14), so Aristotle first recalls these two here: barbarian kingship and Greek dictatorship (the *aisymnētēs*). These have features of both kingship and tyranny. They are kingly in being according to law (barbarian kings and Greek dictators arise in accordance with certain rules of appointment, as inheritance and election), and in being over willing subjects. But they are tyrannical in ruling like despots according to their own judgment. The total king also rules according to his own judgment but his judgment is law, and he rules over willing subjects because of his surpassing virtue; hence his rule too is according to law but is not despotic or tyrannical.

1295a17   However, what is most of all tyranny is the third and last kind. It is the direct counterpart of total kingship and has nothing in common with it, save its power. So it is unaccountable, that is, the tyrant has complete control like the total king; it is over subjects who are equal or better, that is, the tyrant, unlike the total king, is not surpassingly superior; it is for the tyrant's own advantage, unlike that of the total king, which is for the common advantage; it is coercive, unlike total kingship, which is over willing subjects. A slave indeed might willingly submit to a tyrant, but a free man would not, and the test of a regime must be what the free man, and not what the slave, would do, for a city is a community of the free, not of slaves. That barbarians and some Greeks willingly put up with their hereditary or elected despots is thus an indication that they are not free men and that their community is not really a political one.

1295a23   The reasons for these kinds of tyranny are implied in the descriptions given, and especially in the last remark about the third kind of tyranny, that it is "coercive monarchy, for no one who is free can willingly abide such rule" (1295a22–23). Thus, the difference between the first two tyrannies and the last is simply that the ruled willingly submit to the first two and indeed that they set up, or accept, a regular mode of appointment, whereas the ruled do not put up with the last. So the subjects of the first are slavish and of the last free and it is, evidently, this difference in the subjects that primarily makes for differences in kinds of tyranny.

68. Mansfield (1989: 99) wants to understand the remark that tyranny is "a part of regimes" (1295a3–4), not in the sense that it is part of the subject matter or part of the *class* of regimes, but in the sense that it is a part of each *individual* regime. His contention is that nature has a certain recalcitrance to what is good and best, and so each regime needs the force of the tyrant to coerce obedience. But while it is true that some people need to be coerced, there are others who do not (*Ethics* 10.9.1180a4–14); it is only nature corrupted, or nature uneducated, that is recalcitrant, not nature simply, and the force will not be that of the tyrant (who uses force also against the noble), but that of the king (who uses force only against the base). Besides, Mansfield's interpretation, while possible grammatically, is impossible contextually. For Aristotle says tyranny is "part" of regimes in explanation of why tyranny is to take "part" in the inquiry, and this must mean that tyranny is to take its part in the inquiry because it is part of the inquiry's subject matter, that is, because it is part, or member, of the class of regimes.

Chapter 11

∾ SECOND QUESTION: THE MOST COMMON AND MOST
CHOICEWORTHY REGIME AFTER THE BEST

∾ THAT THIS REGIME IS THE MIDDLE SORT OF REGIME

1295a25 Having listed all the kinds of regimes and the reasons for them,
Aristotle turns to his second question, about which regime is most common and
most choiceworthy after the best. So he first states this intention, that his question
now is the best regime and the best way of life if judgment is made by reference to
what most people and most cities can share in, and not if judgment is made by
reference to a virtue beyond the reach of private individuals, an education requiring a nature and equipment dependent on chance, and a regime one would pray
for—that is, if judgment is not made by reference to the virtue, education, and
regime of books 4(7) and 5(8).

Now this question, as so stated, is not just about a best regime after the simply
best, but also about a best regime that is at the same time the most common. Were
it just about a best regime after the simply best, the answer could be some so-called
aristocracy (some mixed regime that expressly aimed at virtue, as that of the Spartans perhaps, 2.6.1265b26–33). Such aristocracies, however, need not be within the
reach of most people and cities (as is indeed true of the Spartan). So, as if picking
up on this point, Aristotle immediately adds that so-called aristocracies cannot
(contrary to the opinion of some, 6(4).1.1288b39–1289a5) now be in question. Or
rather, they cannot now be in question as regards those features in which they fall
outside the reach of most cities. And as regards the features in which they come
close to most cities, they are not very different from polity (because, presumably,
in these features they will in some way be mixing the well-off and the needy and
not also virtue, 6(4).8.1294a19–25). So as regards these features too they are not
now in question, or at least they are not now *separately* in question, for as regards
these features they are at one with polity. Hence, for present purposes, they are to
be spoken of along with polity as if they were both one regime. True to his word,
therefore, Aristotle does so speak throughout the rest of this chapter, giving to
both the single name of "middle regime."

1295a34 The answer to the question about the best way of life and best
regime that is common to most people and cities is, in its essentials, given by
Aristotle in the following argument: (1) the happy life is unimpeded life in accordance with virtue; (2) virtue is a mean; (3) therefore the best or happy life for
everyone is the middle way of life, or the life of the mean that everyone can attain.
The conclusion (3) includes the qualification (not stated in the premises but
assumed by the context) that the best in question now is the best everyone can
attain, and this conclusion must also hold, as Aristotle immediately adds, of the

city and the regime. For since the city is human beings living together, and since the regime, being the way humans distribute rule, is the way they choose to organize their life in the city, the regime and city of those who live best must also be best.

Premises (1) and (2) are assumed from the *Ethics* (for example, 1.10.1101a14–21, 7.13.1153b9–21, 2.8.1108b11–13), where they apply, strictly speaking, to the best or happy life simply and to perfect virtue. They must, however, also apply to the best or happiest life attainable by most. For the mean in question is the mean of virtue, and this is the mean in actions and passions as determined by reason. So if there is a way in which all or most can reach, or at least somehow imitate, this mean in actions and passions (even if it is not the way of perfect virtue), then this must, for them, be the best life they can attain, and the corresponding regime the best regime they can attain. But while the present argument does establish this conclusion, it does not establish, nor is it meant to establish,[69] that this mean or this middle life is the life of the middle class or of those who have moderate property. That conclusion is a separate one that is separately argued in what follows.

1295b1 Evidently, to find such a mean of which all are capable, it is necessary to find something within reach of all cities where such a mean exists. Aristotle turns, therefore, to the parts to be found in every city, since only in such parts, and not in parts that may be found in some cities but not in all, could there exist a mean within the grasp of every city. The parts he now lists are three: the exceedingly well-off, the exceedingly needy, and the middle between them. This list is not the same as those he gave earlier (4(7).8, 6(4).4), but it follows from them. For those lists, in setting out the things that cities need, included both what cities need in order to exist and also what they need in order to exist well. Among the things a city needs in order to exist are the well-off and those involved in necessary occupations or the populace generally, and among the things a city needs in order to exist well are the virtuous or those who are fit to deliberate and judge. Now manifestly every city must have what is needed for it to exist, but not every city must have what is needed for it to exist well. For a thing can continue to exist even if it exists badly (and in fact most actual regimes, as oligarchies and democracies, do exist badly). But since Aristotle's concern here is with what is within the reach of every city, he cannot consider, from among the parts of the city, those that most cities do not have, namely perfect virtue in the rulers (for that is something only found in the simply best regime). So he only considers what every city does have, namely the several degrees of property, or the several parts of the populace and the well-off.

But Aristotle's concern is, further, with a mean that is within the reach of most cities, so if such a mean is to be found it will have to be found somewhere among these parts of the populace and well-off. But wealth obviously admits of a mean

---

69. Contra Mulgan (1977: 107).

and extremes, namely the mean of moderate wealth and the extremes of great wealth and little wealth. That there would indeed be some among those previously classed as populace and wealthy who would fall into such a mean was implied in the earlier discussions of oligarchy and democracy, for the less extreme kinds of these regimes were said there to be based on the moderately rich and the moderately poor (6(4).4.1291b39–41, 5.1292a39–b2), and these will form the basis for such a mean. At any rate Aristotle draws express attention to such a mean now. For all cities need wealth to survive, and so a mean in wealth is something that must be within the reach of all cities. The question then is whether this is the mean required. That it is so, Aristotle now argues, and first about the human beings and then about the regime based on them.

He lays down the proposition that (1) the mean and middle is agreed to be best, and then at once draws the conclusion that (2) therefore a mean or middle possession of the goods of fortune must be best. Now this conclusion does not, of course, follow from premise (1) alone. It needs, in fact, the further premise that (3) such a middling possession is, or best promotes, the mean and middle. But the mean or middle in question here, or the mean and middle that is agreed to be best, is the mean of virtue, and not any mean or middle, so premise (3) must be understood as asserting that to have a middling possession is also to observe, or to be best disposed to observe, the mean of virtue. Not surprisingly, therefore, Aristotle immediately proceeds to prove such a premise, and in several ways.

The first way or first proof is: (1) whatever has a middle possession of such things as beauty, strength, birth, and wealth most easily obeys reason, while whatever has too much or too little of them finds it hard to obey reason; (2) to obey reason is to observe the mean of virtue; (3) therefore whatever has a middle possession most easily, or best, observes the mean of virtue. Premise (2) is implicit here in the context. Premise (1) is an empirical observation and is obviously meant as a general truth. Aristotle does not say that those with a middle possession always obey reason, nor that those at the extremes never obey reason; doubtless there are exceptions. What he says is that having a middle possession makes it easier to obey reason while being at the extremes makes it harder (for this produces insolence and villainy and so acts of injustice). Aristotle is, after all, now talking of the best commonly attainable regime, not of the best regime simply, and the best commonly attainable regime need not be free of all possibility of abuse or corruption, but only freer than any other commonly attainable regime.

1295b12 The second proof is: (1) those in the middle are least affected by love of ruling when they have it or by desire to rule when they do not, both of which passions are harmful to cities; (2) what is least affected by such harmful passions keeps closer to the mean of virtue; (3) therefore those in the middle keep closer to the mean of virtue. Love and desire of rule and office are harmful, evidently, because these passions induce people to commit crimes and to stir up faction in order to keep or to get office. But such things are evidently contrary to the mean of virtue (virtue does not cause crime nor destroy the city), so to be less prone to them is necessarily to be closer to the mean of virtue. But that those in the middle are indeed, in comparison with the extremes, least affected by these passions is another empirical generalization. Certainly they are more likely to be satisfied with the share of rule that they actually have, for wealth generates pride and poverty generates need, and pride and need make people want more.

1295b13   The third proof is a bit more involved but may be summarized thus: (1) too much in the way of the goods of fortune (strength, wealth, friends) and too little wealth produce what is contrary to the city and good government, while a middle amount produces what promotes and preserves the city and good government; (2) what promotes and preserves the city and good government, as opposed to what destroys it, is the virtuous mean; (3) therefore a middle amount produces the virtuous mean, while too much and too little produce the reverse. Premise (2) is again evident or implicit in the context. Premise (1) is proved first about the extremes and then about the middle. About the extremes the proof is: (4) too little and too much good fortune produce slavery and mastery, envy and contempt; (5) these are furthest removed from good rule and from the friendship and community that a city is; (6) therefore too little and too much good fortune produce what is contrary to and destroys the city and good government. About the middle the proof is: (7) the city wishes to be made up of similars and equals (similarity and equality are bases of friendship and community; see *Ethics* 8.1–6); (8) those in the middle are most similar and equal; (9) therefore the city composed of the middle has what the city wishes; (10) a city that has what it wishes, or what it is naturally made up of, is best preserved and best governed; (11) therefore the city composed of the middle is best preserved and best governed.

The claim in proposition (4), that those with an excess of good fortune only know how to rule as masters and that those with an excessive lack of good fortune only know how to be ruled as slaves, is not about what they desire to do but about what they know how to do. For the poor, as Aristotle has made clear elsewhere (6(4).4.1292a15–30), can have a great desire to rule. What they do not have, however, is the knowledge of how to rule, for they have no virtue.[70] They know, indeed, how to be slaves, for their mean and abject position inures them to slavish habits. The excessively fortunate, by contrast, only know how to be masters, or how to lord it over the mean and abject. Neither is fit for rule in the city, for the city requires of its citizens the ability to rule and to be ruled politically, not the ability to rule and be ruled despotically. Indeed both the fortunate and needy, or the excessively rich and poor, would seem to *deserve* only to be slaves, for both are

70. Mulgan (1977: 108–9) fails to distinguish these two points properly.

marked by vice, though by vice at opposite extremes (the fact that the fortunate only know how to be masters does not show that they deserve to be masters).

The claim in proposition (8), that those in the middle are most similar and equal, is not contradicted by the fact that the rich may be similar and equal among themselves and the poor similar and equal among themselves. For those in the middle, by contrast, are not only similar and equal in this way, they are also similar and equal to the extremes (they have something in common with both the fortunate and the needy), while the extremes are not similar or equal at all in this way. But it is evidently this similarity and equality, a similarity and equality that those in the middle have to the whole city and not to themselves alone, that is relevant to Aristotle's argument.[71]

1295b28   The fourth proof is in effect another argument that those in the middle, as opposed to the extremes, have what preserves the city and so must be in the virtuous mean: (1) those in the middle are most preserved in cities, whereas the poor and wealthy are most destroyed; (2) that city is most preserved which is based on those who are most preserved; (3) therefore the city based on the middle is most preserved. Premise (2) is obvious and again implicit. Premise (1) is another empirical generalization whose truth as a generalization also seems evident. The quotation from Phocylides is apt and serves its purpose in this context, as Aristotle's quotations generally do, regardless of what the original context was.

It is worth noting, however, that these arguments about the superiority of the middle to the extremes are all about how the social position of those in the middle makes them behave in a moderate way.[72] Those in the middle are not shown to be in the mean because they have been educated in virtue and possess the inner habit of virtue (such education only exists properly in the simply best regime). Someone taken from the middle and suddenly thrust among the poor or the wealthy is likely to behave as badly as the poor and the wealthy. But the socially conditioned virtue of the middle is precisely what Aristotle is now in search of, for it is something both good and within the reach of every city: it is good because to behave virtuously is good (even if to behave virtuously from the true habit of virtue is better), and it is within every city's reach because the mean of wealth that produces the mean of behavior is within every city's reach.

1295b34   Having thus shown that those in the middle are best, Aristotle now shows that the regime based on them is best too. The first argument is a direct conclusion from the arguments just given, namely that the regime through the middle, or based on the middle, must be best. For, of course, those in the middle are themselves best, and since the ruling body is the regime, where those in the

71. Contra Mulgan (1977: 109).
72. So Mulgan rightly (1977: 109).

middle are this ruling body, or the dominant element in the ruling body, the regime they thus form must itself be best.

The second argument is: (1) a large middle, one that is stronger than both extremes together or than each one of them separately, prevents the emergence of the deviant regimes of oligarchy, democracy, and tyranny; (2) a city where the emergence of deviant regimes is prevented is capable of being well governed; (3) therefore a city with a large middle is capable of being well governed. Premise (1) is evident for the reason given, that a large middle can be used to tip the balance in turn against the emergence of an excess at either extreme by being added to the opposite extreme. Hence democracy and oligarchy, which are at the extremes, will be thus prevented, and thereby tyranny too, since tyranny is most apt to arise from these extremes and not from the middle (7(5).1.1302a2–8, 13–15; 8.1308a20–24, b30–31; 9.1309b18–1310a12). Premise (2) is true by definition, since to be badly governed is to be ruled by a deviant regime, and vice versa, so any city that can prevent deviant regimes must be capable of good government.

1296a7 The third argument is: (1) the regime of the middle is most free of faction while the other regimes, based on the extremes, are not, or are less so; (2) what is most free of faction is better than what is not; (3) therefore the regime of the middle is better than the others or is the best one among them (the best attainable for most cities). Premise (2) is obvious.[73] Premise (1) is implied by the earlier claim that those in the middle are most similar and equal, but is here expressly backed up by the stability to be found in large cities as opposed to small cities, and in democracies as opposed to oligarchies, both of which have comparatively large middles. It is also backed up by the instability to be found in democracies that forsake the middle.

1296a18 The fourth argument is an appeal to a sign. For if the best legislators, like Solon, Lycurgus, and others, come from the middle citizens, then the best regime is likely to come from them too.[74]

The middle regime is thus best, but a question has arisen among scholars as to whether this regime is the same as polity or not. A main objection is that polity is described as a mixture of the rich and poor, or of oligarchy and democracy, while

---

73. Or it is obvious if one's subject is the city and if the city is the community for pursuing the good life, as it is for Aristotle. If one's subject is rather some large modern state, not a city, and if one's aim is to prevent any one section becoming dominant and despotizing in that state (and the concern with pursuing the good life is to be left to other and much smaller communities), then perhaps faction is a good thing; cf. Madison in *Federalist* 10, and Rahe, who refers to Machiavelli as the origin of this modern idea (1992: 421–22, 588–90, 596–99, 735, 994 n107); also Simpson (1990, 1994).

74. For the evidence about Solon, see *Athēnaiōn Politeia* 5. Lycurgus was said to have been king by some, and if so he could well have been rich. By denying Lycurgus was king Aristotle does not so much prove Lycurgus was of the middle (this must have been evident from other facts), as remove an argument that he was not; so Newman (4:218–19) and against Jowett (1885: 2:168).

the middle regime is not so much a mix of the two as a mean between them and is described as based on the middle, not on a combination of rich and poor.[75] But polity was earlier compared to a mean or middle (6(4).9.1294b14–18), and indeed, if polity is supposed to be well mixed, it will turn out to be resting on the middle. For the ways of mixing it mentioned before (6(4).9) all tend to exclude the very poor from rule and to deprive the very rich of dominance, and so tend to put the regime into the hands of the middle. Further, the second of the arguments just given speaks of the middle as being stronger than both extremes or of being strong enough to outweigh each extreme when added to the other. This suggests that a middle regime could either keep in the middle or be more oligarchic (if the middle is added to the rich to outweigh the poor) or more democratic (if the middle is added to the poor to outweigh the rich), and these are varieties of polity.

But recall also what Aristotle said at the beginning of this chapter, that both polity and so-called aristocracy must be spoken of as one regime (1295a31–34). "Middle regime" and "regime based on the middle" are suitable names for what is common to polity and so-called aristocracy, and Aristotle seems to want to leave open the possibility that some middle regimes might be more like so-called aristocracies than like polities. In addition, a polity might, precisely by giving precedence to the middle and to the sociologically generated virtue of the middle, open the way to the regime's giving weight to virtue as such or by itself, which would therefore be aristocracy. Certainly Aristotle seems to have some such possibility in mind earlier (6(4).2.1289b14–17), and to advert to it again later (6(4).12.1297a7–8).

❧ WHY MOST REGIMES ARE NOT OF THE MIDDLE SORT

1296a22 The middle regime has thus been shown to be the best regime within the reach of all or most cities. But that it is the most reachable or attainable regime does not mean that most cities have reached or attained it. In fact most cities have not reached it but have adopted oligarchy and democracy instead. A question arises, therefore, as to why the best attainable has not often been attained. The answer, as Aristotle now explains, is evident from the nature of this best attainable regime, namely that it is based on the middle.

The first reason he gives in explanation is that the middle in most cities is small while one or other extreme is in excess. So this extreme uses its excess to arrogate rule to itself and to ignore the middle. But this middle could, nevertheless, have been used to moderate the city toward a middle regime. A middle regime was thus evidently attainable, even though it was never attained.

1296a27 The second reason is that the populace and well-off, as was noted before when it was shown how the first are full of envy and the second full of contempt, naturally fall to faction and fights against each other. Hence, in a spirit

---

75. Johnson most presses this objection (1990: 148–52); but see Miller's reply (1995: 262 n26).

of rivalry, the dominant party regards controlling the city as the reward of victory and sets up an extreme regime to favor itself, not caring for a middle regime that would be fair or equal to both sides. But here again, of course, a middle regime was clearly possible; only neither side wanted to realize it.

1296a32   The third reason is that cities that won leadership in Greece, notably Athens and Sparta, took leadership, in a similar spirit of rivalry, as an opportunity to impose regimes favorable to their own advantage, not to favor the advantage of the cities in question. Still, they too could have imposed middle regimes if they had chosen.

1296a36   The first two reasons were about why middle regimes have failed to arise from within cities, and the third about why they failed to get imposed from without. The fourth reason, while reinforcing the third, points also to how middle regimes could become the norm. This fourth reason is that only one leader in Greece has so far been persuaded to impose the middle regime on cities. The prevailing custom, which evidently persuades everyone else in cities, is not to share and have equality but either to dominate or to be dominated. Still, the possibility of imposing middle regimes exists, and if prevailing custom could be changed, first no doubt by the force of one or more leaders from without, but later by habituation from within, then middle regimes might become the norm rather than the exception.[76]

∾ THAT OTHER REGIMES ARE BETTER OR WORSE
  BY REFERENCE TO THE MIDDLE

1296b2   Having thus shown which regime is best for most cities, Aristotle now uses this conclusion to show which of the kinds of democracy and oligarchy classified earlier are better and which worse (for knowledge of the relative goodness of the several regimes is integral to the tasks of political science, as explained in 6(4).1). This was in a way indicated before (the kinds that are counterpart to tyranny must certainly be worst), but now it is given a deductive basis. The kinds nearest to the middle regime (as the first democracy and the first oligarchy) must be better because nearest the best, and those furthest away (as the last democracy and the last oligarchy) must be worse because furthest from the best. This measure of goodness is, however, only the measure for these kinds of deviant regimes. The measure for all the kinds of regimes generally is the best regime of kingship (6(4).2.1289a38–b5), according to which, of course, the middle regime is itself not simply best.

Still, the measure of goodness as taken from the middle does establish a fixed

---

76. The one man who was persuaded to impose middle regimes is, despite the proliferation of other candidates, almost certainly Philip of Macedon; so Weil (1960: 412–15) and Lord (1984: 6–8). The peace he devised for all Greece at the Congress of Corinth in 338 seems to fit very well the sort of imposition of middle regimes that Aristotle speaks of; see the details in Defourny (1932: 536–39).

hierarchy for the deviant regimes. The only qualification, immediately added, is that a worse regime may be better relatively to a supposition, the supposition that some city may want a worse regime, or may find a worse regime more advantageous than the best attainable. For then this regime, though worse absolutely, will be better for this city. Such would be the case for cities having a small middle and an excess at either extreme. For, as just noted, the dominant extreme will then want its own regime, not a middle regime that it has to share; and its own regime will be more to its own private advantage, though not to the common advantage of the city as a whole. Certainly Aristotle turns to such cases next in the following chapter, though he perhaps recalls the general point here to ensure that the relativity of the best to the actual circumstances, and the flexibility of the legislator's task (as explained in 6(4).1), are not forgotten.

Chapter 12

~ THIRD QUESTION: WHICH REGIME IS PREFERABLE FOR WHOM

~ DEMOCRACIES AND OLIGARCHIES

1296b13 Aristotle's third question is which regime is advantageous for which cities or which sorts of people. To answer it, he first lays down and explains a general principle and then applies it to the particular cases. The general principle is that the part of the city that wishes the regime to continue must be stronger than the part that does not. This principle is obvious enough and is implied by the fact, mentioned elsewhere, that the legislator's task is to see how to make regimes lasting (6(4).1.1288b28–30, 8(6).5.1319b33–37). For it is evidently pointless to set up a regime, however good in principle, that soon collapses, for no improvement is thereby gained, and the same task is left to be done all over again. But the way to make a regime lasting, or as lasting as it may be, is to ensure that the stronger part in the city wants it to last.

The principle, then, is clear, but what is less clear and needs clarification is the meaning of "stronger." This term suggests quantity but in fact quality is also a part of strength. The reason is that the city is itself made up of quality and quantity (a city is self-sufficient and to be self-sufficient it needs not just a multitude of people but a multitude of a certain sort). So quality is things like freedom, wealth, education, and good birth, and quantity is simply numbers. The weight of both these must be assessed together in determining which part of the city is stronger. So the low-born or needy may be greater in numbers than the high-born or wealthy but not so great as to make up for their inferiority in quality. These needy, for instance, may be so poor and so abject, and the rich so wealthy and so much in control of land, weapons, and military expertise, that, for all the difference in numbers, the rich can easily dominate (an example might be the cavalry oligarchies mentioned earlier, at 6(4).3.1289b35–40). In such a case the superior part of the city will be the few rich and not the many poor. It will be otherwise, of course, if the needy are too many to control, or if they are not so abject and poor.

1296b24 Having stated the principle, Aristotle now applies it, and first to democracies and oligarchies. Here he notes, simply and straightforwardly enough, that it will be "natural" (1296b26) for each kind of democracy or oligarchy to exist as each of the respective multitudes is predominant or stronger according to the above principle. Aristotle doubtless does not mean "natural" here in the way he used it earlier, when he said that only correct regimes were natural or according to nature (3.17.1287b37–41). He must mean it rather in the sense that these multitudes have the natural composition to make the respective democracies and oligarchies lasting. In fact, however, if such multitudes cannot also be got to accept a middle regime or polity, they will not be political multitudes, fit to form a city, but despotic ones, fit only for slavery (6(4).11.1295b21–25). This point gets some confirmation from Aristotle's next remark, that the legislator should always take up the middle sort into the regime and frame oligarchic and democratic laws so as also to include the middle. For the effect of this will be not only to make the regime more lasting, but also to move the democracy or oligarchy in question as close to the measured forms, and indeed as close to polity and the middle, as they can be made to go. Thus the capacity of each multitude for a correct regime will be exploited to the fullest possible extent.

MIXED REGIMES

THE GENERAL CASE

1296b38 Aristotle next applies the principle to polities and mixed regimes, and first in general about when such regimes are advantageous and how to realize them, and second about certain particulars. The principle, then, applies in a fairly obvious way. Polities will naturally be lasting, and so advantageous, where the middle is stronger, either than both extremes together or than each of them separately, for then it will either be the predominant group, or will at least always be able to tip the scales against the extremes.

An objection arises, however, about this latter case, that a middle only stronger than each extreme separately, and not than both together, could be overwhelmed by a combination of the rich and poor against it. Aristotle responds that such a combination could never in fact be realized. For the extremes, in order to combine, will have to form a regime together against the middle. But then this regime will either be dominated by one extreme or it will be shared in common. Dominance by one extreme, however, means, in the case of rich and poor, enslavement of the other (as noted in the previous chapter), which neither side would accept;

and a common regime, instead of opposing the regime of the middle, would in fact be such a regime. For rich and poor would never agree to rule by turns (the rich ruling first and then the poor and so on), since neither would trust the other to hand over power when the time came. They would, however, trust an arbitrator, but the arbitrator between rich and poor is the middle. Hence the only common regime they could agree to set up together is a regime mediated through the middle, that is, precisely a middle regime.

1297a6 But if a lasting polity or mixed regime can exist where the middle is stronger in the way described, it will only do so if the regime is made to rest on the middle. For this reason the regime must be well mixed, since, if it is not, it will really be resting on the populace or rich and so will really be a democracy or an oligarchy, and a democracy or oligarchy that, in the circumstances, will be less advantageous than a properly mixed regime. Aristotle, however, adverts particularly to the error of making the regime lean too much toward the well-off, evidently because, in the case of both polities and so-called aristocracies, it seems to many to be the better course.[77] Assigning more to the well-off and deceiving the populace can seem better (for the well-off have the reputation of being better, and if the populace are deceived about their own real inferiority in the regime, they will keep quieter and be more content), but in fact it results in real evils. Deceit when discovered (as it is always likely to be) manifestly makes resentment worse, and the graspings of the rich, Aristotle expressly adds, do more to destroy the regime than do those of the populace.

Chapter 13

~ PARTICULAR APPLICATIONS

1297a14/34 So much, then, concerns the general case. Aristotle turns next to note some particular applications of it, first about how to achieve a good mixture and second about how to determine those in the middle who are to be dominant in the regime. Aristotle speaks generally of regimes in this chapter but evidently has in mind mixed regimes (for his topic is mixing and the middle), and polities in particular.[78]

A good mixture is achieved when, as noted earlier (6(4).9.1294a32–35), elements from both sides are combined. Here the elements are the sophistries used to shift the mixture toward the well-off, and the opposing sophistries used to give control to the populace. They are called sophistries, no doubt, because they are devices of deceit, and devices that operate not unlike sophistical arguments. For in each case the inferior party is induced, by some apparent equality, into thinking it has real equality. Aristotle lists the oligarchic sophistries first and in detail. The

77. Aristotle may have Plato's *Laws* particularly in mind here, 2.6.1266a7–30, Newman (1:502 n2).
78. So Barker (1946: 186 n1), Lord (1984: 258 n44), Newman (4:226).

sophistries concern the several offices (or the three parts of the regime), and arms and physical training (for the armed part in any city is necessarily capable of imposing its control). In every case the trick consists in giving the poor the appearance of sharing in the regime but in practice depriving them of it, principally by discouraging them from taking part or from getting and practicing arms, while compelling the well-off to do so.

The contrary sophistries typical of democracies naturally do the opposite. So where in the previous case, for example, a fine was imposed on the well-off for not participating, here in this case pay is given to the needy for participating. Aristotle only gives the example of this sophism with respect to assembly and juries, but the same sophism could presumably apply to arms and training too (the populace could be paid to train). At any rate, to achieve the right mixture mentioned in the preceding chapter as necessary for mixed regimes, the thing to do is to mix the opposing sophistries.

1297b1 So much concerns the mixing of the regime. Aristotle turns next to those in the middle who are to be dominant in it. He lays down the following principle, that the regime should be composed only of those who possess or own arms. It is a general truth of all regimes, of course, that those who possess arms should be included in rule, for these have power over the regime's preservation and destruction. But Aristotle speaks here of having the regime consist *only* of those who possess arms, and evidently because this will ensure the predominance of the middle. For it will ensure the exclusion of the very poor, who cannot afford arms, but will not give control to the very rich, who can afford arms, because the middle can afford arms too. It is worth noting also that possessing arms requires being trained in arms (it is useless to have weapons and not know how to use them), and such training imposes discipline and moderate behavior (cf. 2.9.1270a1–6), the sort of discipline and moderate behavior also imposed by moderate wealth (polity was in fact earlier distinguished as the rule of the many who have such military virtue, at 3.7.1279a39–b4).

Defining the property qualification, however, to ensure this predominance of the middle, is not a matter of laying down some general amount. It requires looking at each particular case and choosing the highest figure that will still leave those who share in the regime more than those who do not. If it is set lower, it will likely include too many of the poor and so produce democracy, and if it is set higher it will likely exclude too many of the middle and so produce oligarchy. But by "more" (1297b5) Aristotle presumably means more both in quantity and quality (according to the principle of the preceding chapter).[79]

79. In the translation I wrote "more numerous" (the Greek is *pleious*), but perhaps "more" might be better by itself. For a merely numerical "more" could in fact be a democracy, if the rich and middle were rather few but the poor were exceptionally many.

1297b6   This way of defining the property qualification has two particular features: it excludes the poor and it is relative to particular cases. So Aristotle next proceeds to justify the first and to illustrate the second. As regards excluding the poor, he says that this need not be a threat to the regime for, first, the poor do not mind being excluded from rule provided they are not abused or robbed (which, if generally difficult to achieve, will at least be easier in middle regimes where the rulers behave moderately), and, second, the poor are not anyway keen to start a fight, since even in time of war they will not take up arms unless properly fed and cared for.[80]

1297b12   As regards the relativity of the property qualification, Aristotle notes ways in which the middle has varied or shifted in different cities and at different times. There is some dispute, however, about whether "regime" (*politeia*) in this paragraph has its generic sense or its specific sense, that of polity. But to suppose it has the generic sense is to suppose that Aristotle is no longer speaking of mixed regimes but of all regimes generally, and this does not fit well the present context.[81] It seems better, therefore, to suppose that he is speaking only of polities, or at least only of mixed regimes.

So in Malia the regime included also those who had passed beyond the regular age for active military service (doubtless to ensure that the middle was large enough), but the offices, in electing which the retired obviously shared, were confined to those still active (doubtless to ensure that the armed part thoroughly supported the regime). Again, the first polities, or middle regimes, were based on the cavalry, not the heavy armed foot soldiers. The reason was that the cavalry were then the armed and stronger part in cities, and hence the principle for determining the property qualification would necessarily shift the balance toward the cavalry (who would be more in strength if not in numbers), and so toward oligarchy.[82] By contrast, when cities increased in size and the hoplites or heavy armed troops, rather than the cavalry, became the armed and stronger part, the balance shifted back the other way and the principle necessarily included more people in the regime (for more people would now fall into the "more" as defined by the principle). Hence these polities appeared to be democracies (for more people shared rule than in the cavalry regimes). The previous polities, by contrast, were oligarchic and kingly (that is, they leaned in that direction), because the fewer numbers of people and the weakness of those in the middle shifted the balance toward the fewer and

80. I follow here the comments of Newman (4:231–32).

81. Barker, for instance, takes "regime" generically and so is forced to regard the present passage as a digression, (1946: 187 n1). Newman also takes "regime" generically (4:232, 234).

82. The cavalry regimes mentioned earlier, 6(4).3.1289b35–40, are called oligarchies by Aristotle, but presumably because they had shifted away from the middle altogether. Here he seems to have in mind cavalry regimes that did not do this but were polities leaning toward oligarchy, or perhaps were even aristocracies, if some special stress was laid on education and virtue in the rulers.

richer, and it is these, and certain outstanding men among them, who would, at that time, constitute the bulk of the "more" or "stronger" in the relevant sense.

1297b28 Aristotle concludes with a summary that essentially serves to indicate that his first three questions have now been dealt with. Consequently he is ready to turn next to the fourth.

Chapter 14

~ FOURTH QUESTION: HOW TO SET UP THESE REGIMES

~ BY MEANS OF THE DELIBERATIVE BODY

1297b35 The fourth question concerns the setting up of regimes (those now under discussion, namely oligarchy, democracy, and the regimes mixed from oligarchy and democracy). To set up a regime is to distribute rule to certain parts of the city (for a regime is a certain distribution of rule); hence to know how to set up a regime it is necessary to know what the rule to be distributed consists of and what the ways are of distributing it. Aristotle begins therefore by listing the parts or constituents of rule, that is, of the regime, for the regime will be better or worse set up, and will be a regime of this kind rather than of that, according to how the parts of rule are distributed.

The parts in question are, of course, the parts of the regime, not of the city. But regimes were earlier said to differ according to the parts of the city. There may seem to be some conflict, then, in the statement now that they differ according to the parts of the regime. But this appearance is deceptive, for regimes were said earlier to differ according to the parts of the city in the sense that the distribution of rule, which is the regime, was made to different parts of the city. What Aristotle is now saying is that the rule that gets distributed itself has parts, and if so, then the distribution of rule is just the distribution of these parts to the parts of the city. Hence, to say that regimes differ according to the way the parts of the regime differ is to say that regimes differ according to the way the parts of rule are differently distributed to the parts of the city.[83]

The parts of the regime are three: the deliberative, the offices, and the judiciary. These are briefly characterized as, first, the part that deliberates about common matters; second, the number, kind, and appointment of offices; and, third, the part that decides lawsuits. This distinction is not, however, a matter of separate spheres of influence for, as shortly becomes evident, the common matters over which the deliberative deliberates include some judicial matters, and the deliberative can itself be divided up among certain offices. Further the offices themselves are de-

---

83. It is important not to confuse or ignore the difference between parts of the city and parts of the regime, contra certain inferences of Mansfield (1989: 50).

fined by reference to deliberation and judgment (6(4).15.1299a25–27). The distinction turns rather on the phrase "common matters" (1298a1). This must mean, especially judging by the list Aristotle gives shortly, everything common to the whole city in the sense of all matters that directly affect the survival and functioning of the regime. For the deliberative part is the controlling part of the regime (as recalled at the end of the chapter, 1299a1–2) and is that by which the regime, and the city as determined by the regime, stands or falls. Hence any matter of any sort, including judicial matters, that is common in this sense (whether by its nature or by the particular circumstances) must belong to this deliberative or controlling part. The offices and the judiciary, by contrast, include matters that concern only parts of the city and that do not, or need not, affect the regime.

Aristotle's division of the parts of the regime is not, therefore, the same as the modern division into legislative, executive, and judicial.[84] The modern division is one of separate functions or powers in the sense of distinct areas of competence: as the making of laws, the carrying out of laws, the interpreting of laws. Aristotle's division cuts across this division and unites and separates in different ways, for it first divides the powers, not from each other, but each within itself (according as the object of the power is common or not), and then combines something from each power in each of the parts of the regime (for both the deliberative and the offices legislate, judge, and execute, and the judiciary judges and executes even if it does not legislate, 8(6).8.1321b40–1322a29). The thing Aristotle seems deliberately to avoid is a *unitary* executive or legislative or judiciary. For one should note that the modern separation of powers concentrates as well as separates: it concentrates all executive functions in one body, all legislative functions in another, and all judicial functions in a third.[85] Aristotle, by contrast, dissipates the powers, as we have seen.

But there is yet another way in which he dissipates the powers. For he separates them out, at least in the case of mixed regimes, among different parts of the city. So some parts of the deliberative and the judiciary he would give to the populace, and other parts, and the offices, he would give to the notables (3.11). Hence Aristotle's balance is between parts of the city, not, as in the modern case, between parts or powers of the regime. We may conjecture, therefore, that he would find fault with our modern separation of powers because our separation does nothing to prevent all powers from falling into the hands of the same part of the city (as the rich in particular). For it can matter little that the powers are separate if all those who separately exercise them come from the same part of the city. There is going to be injustice and despotism all the same, and the true end of the city, noble life, will be

84. As has often been pointed out; cf. Barker (1946: 193 nNN), Miller (1995: 166), Mulgan (1977: 57–60), Newman (4:236–37), Robinson (1962: 116), Sinclair/Saunders (1981: 276–77).

85. See in particular Rahe (1992: 605–14), and also Mansfield (1989: 47, 69–71, 293–94).

thwarted, unless the part that has all the power is surpassingly virtuous, like true aristocrats or the total king. Aristotle might even see the modern separation of powers as another (oligarchic) sophistry to deceive the populace. For under color of dividing power into different parts, it actually concentrates all of it into the same hands.[86]

1298a3 Having divided the parts of the regime, Aristotle turns next to his main question, which is how each part may be distributed to establish the different regimes. He begins in each case with a characterization of the powers or functions of the part in question (for these define what the part is). So here first, in the case of the deliberative, he begins by listing the matters concerning which it has control, of which there are four (if we judge by the repetition of the word *peri*, "concerning" or "over," at 12998a3–7): concerning war and peace, alliances and their dissolution; concerning laws; concerning penalties of death, exile, and confiscation; concerning the selection and auditing of offices. These are all manifestly serious matters of common concern.[87] The concern of the first is common defense; of the second common goals and the distribution of the common offices among the parts of the city; of the third common justice; of the fourth the filling and management of the common offices. Note that control concerning or over laws here cannot mean that the deliberative is superior to the laws (for that would be tyranny). Rather it must mean that the deliberative has control with respect to laying down those rules which will count as laws and which will control the regime (for, at least in more measured regimes, the ruling body wants the laws to rule and will ensure that they do). Control over the laws will only abolish the rule of law if no laws are in fact laid down and kept, or at any rate if no rules count as laws but only as decrees (see 6(4).4.1292a23–37 and the commentary thereon).

Next, as regards the distribution, there are logically only four possibilities: either (i) all matters for decision are given to all, or (ii) all are given to some only, or (iii) some matters are given to some and others to others, or (iv) some matters are given to all and others to some. Of these possibilities, (i) will be characteristic of democracy (even though "all" will in practice mean the majority), (ii) of

86. I think Aristotle would regard modern political parties as rival oligarchical clubs that fight each other for rule by playing the demagogue to the populace, especially during elections (7(5).6.1305b28–33). Hence, whoever wins the popular vote, it is always oligarchs who are in control. There is, of course, nothing in the modern separation of powers designed to prevent all power from coming into the hands of one and the same political party.

87. They can also all be found, incidentally, distributed to one or other of the three powers of the modern division of powers. Apparent omissions are the revenue or common funds and citizenship; see Newman (4:238). But Aristotle doubtless intends these to be included under the heading of laws, and he does in fact mention them in the context of law elsewhere (2.9.1271a26–37 and 1271b11–15, 3.5.1278a21–34).

oligarchy (where the rich decide everything), (iii) and (iv) of mixed regimes (polity or so-called aristocracy depending on the case).[88]

1298a9 As regards democracy and type (i), there are several ways or modes—as many in fact as there are kinds of democracy. The first is for most matters to be decided, not by all together, but by all in turns, namely through offices to which all may be appointed in turn. Only a few things are decided by all meeting together: passage of laws, matters to do with the regime, and the hearing of announcements from the rulers or magistrates. The things dealt with by magistrates would thus seem to be war and peace, alliances, penalties of death, exile, and confiscation, and selecting and auditing the offices. But perhaps the last two are better taken as included under the category of "matters to do with the regime," for the choosing of offices is manifestly such, and indeed any matter normally left to magistrates might fall into this category if it was serious or exceptional enough. Certainly the magistrates are to announce their decisions to the assembly, which suggests the assembly has some right to give or withhold approval, and especially on matters affecting the regime. This regime is evidently going to be a rather measured democracy, for only what is absolutely necessary for there to be a democracy at all is decided in open assembly, namely those matters, laws and the regime, which determine who has final control and how. Everything else is handed over to the magistrates. It will correspond to the first of democracy's four kinds.

One should note here, however, an ambiguity in the assertion that democracy is when all decide about everything. This can mean either that all do decide about everything and decide directly, or that all can decide about anything, whether directly or indirectly. The first alternative is only true of ultimate democracy, but the second is true of all the others (though not, significantly, of oligarchy or mixed regimes). For in these other democracies, since the populace by definition have the control, any matter ordinarily reserved to the magistrates can become a matter affecting the regime to be decided in open assembly, or any matter ordinarily reserved to the magistrates can become, if not a matter for decision by the assembly, a matter for regulation by the assembly, so that the assembly decides how and which magistrate is to decide (for the assembly passes the laws).[89]

---

88. Newman (4:239) takes (iii) along with (ii) as characteristic of oligarchy, which is possible if the "some" and "others" are the rich only; but (iii) must also be characteristic of mixed regimes, since Aristotle doubtless means by "some" and "others" different parts of the city, not different groups within the same part.

89. In this way one can answer the doubts of those, as Barker (1946: 190 n4) and Newman (4:241), who think these forms of democracy are not cases of all deciding all matters. One can also thus reject Mansfield's contention (1989: 307 n18) that all regimes are contained in each and that each is a mixed regime. For, on the contrary, each regime is distinguished by which part of the city has control, and if the populace have control, even if they do not behave in extreme ways, the regime is a democracy, not

1298a19   A second mode is for all together to decide more matters, as legislation, war and peace, and selecting and auditing of offices. Magistrates, then, must be deciding matters of alliance, and penalties of death, exile, and confiscation. These magistrates may also be chosen by election or lot. Nothing was said about the manner of appointment of offices in the previous mode, but the fact that now some of them are allowed to be chosen by lot (a characteristic of democracy), along with the greater competence of the popular assembly (it now has control over war and peace as well), clearly indicates that this is a democracy of a more thoroughgoing sort. On the other hand, it is less thoroughgoing than the next one listed. It doubtless corresponds to the second of the four kinds of democracy.

1298a24   A third mode is for all together to decide about the offices, audits, war, and alliances. Here the competence of the assembly has been extended to include alliances and only penalties of death, exile, and confiscation are reserved to magistrates. True, legislation is here omitted from the list of what the assembly decides, but it is doubtful if Aristotle means this now to be handed over to the magistrates when it was not so handed over in either of the first two forms.[90] The clue perhaps lies in his saying that the assembly here decides "about the offices" (1298a24–25), for this is broader than saying it decides about "the selection of offices." To decide about the offices doubtless means, therefore, deciding everything about the offices, not just their appointment but also the laws that govern the number and competence of offices. At all events, the more extreme character of this democracy is indicated by the fact that now only those offices are elected that have to be (because they require special knowledge in the officeholders), and all the rest are appointed by lot. In the previous democracy, even though lot was also used, there was no such restriction placed on the use of election. Still, the fact that this democracy does not decide everything, but is subject at least to laws reserving determinate things to determinate offices, means it is not ultimate democracy. It must correspond to the third of the four forms.

1298a28   The fourth and last mode manifestly corresponds to the last or ultimate democracy, and is said by Aristotle expressly so to do. For here no matters are reserved to the offices and everything is decided in open assembly. The offices are merely used to facilitate the process and their judgments are preliminary, needing to be laid before the assembly for final decision.

1298a33/40   As regards oligarchy and type (ii), where all matters are decided by some, and none by all, there are again several modes corresponding to the kinds of oligarchy. The first mode corresponds to the first oligarchy where the some who decide all matters are without excessive wealth and are many in number,

---

an oligarchy or a polity. A similar error is made by Mulgan (1977: 134). A regime is a democracy if the populace are in control. How they behave is a separate issue.

90. I follow the suggestion of Newman (4:245), but contra Barker (1946: 190).

where the laws are observed (and not suspended whenever the rulers please), and where all possessing the relevant amount of wealth share the regime. Such a regime, because of its measured quality, is a political one, that is, of the character of a polity because not far from basing itself on the middle. The second mode corresponds to the second oligarchy where things are otherwise the same save that not all those who have the relevant amount of wealth (which amount, however, is likely to be set higher) share in rule but only some chosen from among them.

1298b2 The last two modes and last two oligarchies are treated together as one. For they are alike in differing from the first two in confining rule to certain rich families and not to the wealthy in general or to anyone elected from the wealthy in general. They differ from each other, as was explained before (6(4).5.1292b4–7), in that the third is still subject to law and the fourth is not.

1298b5 As regards the mixed regimes and types (iii) and (iv), Aristotle speaks more briefly and generally, but his meaning is clear enough. So, as regards (iv), where all have control over war, peace, and taking audits, and certain rulers or magistrates control the rest (law, alliances, election, penalties of death, exile, and confiscation), and these magistrates are elected or chosen by lot, the result is aristocracy or polity. The fact that here the important matters of law and the choosing of offices are not decided by all makes these regimes not to be democracies; whereas the fact that all do decide about war and peace and audit the officials makes them not to be oligarchies. They are manifestly mixed regimes. Lot is a democratic feature and will make them polities by opening up office to many;[91] election is an oligarchic and aristocratic feature and will either confine office to the wealthy (in which case the regime will be an aristocracy in the sense in which oligarchic polities are aristocracies) or to those with a certain quality or virtue (in which case the regime will be genuinely aristocratic, after the pattern of Sparta or Carthage).

As regards (iii), some who are elected decide some matters and others who are chosen by lot decide others, and these others are either chosen directly by lot from all or from certain preelected candidates, or the elected and those chosen by lot act together in the same offices. The fact that these regimes have nothing decided by the assembly makes them not to be democracies, and the fact that office is open to all makes them not to be oligarchies. For office is open to all either because the lot is taken from all or because those preelected for the lot are taken from all. In the first case the regime will be a polity as being more democratic; in the second case it

91. It will not, however, make these mixed regimes indistinguishable from those democracies that also have some matters decided by offices chosen by lot. Barker (1946: 191 n1) and Newman (4:247) think it will and therefore want to remove the alternative "or chosen by lot" from the text. But this emendation is unnecessary for there are two significant differences that will remain: first, these mixed regimes reserve different and more important things to the offices, and, second, decisions made by these offices are not subject, even indirectly, to the assembly.

will be an oligarchic polity, if election is from the rich and if the rich, as well as the poor, are also among those preelected for the lot (for then the rich will predominate), or an aristocracy proper if election and preelection are from the more virtuous. The case where the elected and those chosen by lot act together will also be polity or aristocracy depending on how the election and lot operate.

1298b11/13   Such, then, is how the several ways of constructing the deliberative divide up among the several kinds of regime. But since Aristotle's intention is a practical one, especially here in discussing the fourth of his five questions from the end of chapter 2, he ends with some particular pieces of advice. These are confined to the question of establishing democracies and oligarchies, but they could be of use for mixed regimes too, since to establish a mixed regime is in effect to establish a democracy and an oligarchy at the same time.

His advice in both cases is designed to limit the excesses to which each regime is prone. So, in the case of democracy, he focuses on its ultimate form, for here the excesses are particularly extreme. He gives three recommendations. First, to imitate oligarchies by imposing a fine on the rich (in addition to the standard democratic practice of giving pay to the poor), so that the rich too will attend the assembly. This will make for more measure in the deliberating, since the rich will naturally tend to vote against democratic measures and, especially in extreme cases, may be able to form with those in the middle (who would not be sufficient on their own) a sufficient number to vote such measures down. The second and third recommendations (to ensure, whether by process of selection or by limitations on payment for attendance, that the populace do not outweigh the notables) work even more to the same effect, since both will expressly even out the numbers of rich and poor so that the poor cannot dominate as they wish, or as demagogues wish, but are forced to compromise.

It is to be noted that none of these recommendations alters the fundamentally democratic character of the regime. They could all be implemented and still leave the popular assembly in control of everything with nothing left to the decision of the offices. What they would do, and are designed to do, is to make the decrees of this absolute assembly more measured in character and less subject to the excesses of demagogues (for demagogues win preeminence by appealing to the poor against the rich and so will not be able, by their demagoguery, to win over the rich, or the middle either since those in the middle are opposed to extremes). An ultimate democracy, in other words, may be extreme in the control it has (for it has control and not the laws), but it does not have to be extreme in the way it exercises this control.[92]

92. Aristotle is therefore not guilty of the charge, leveled by some, as Mulgan (1977: 134) and Nichols (1992: 101–2), that his policy of preserving regimes by imposing measure on them is really a policy of changing them from one kind to another.

As regards the chances of getting any of these recommendations implemented in an ultimate democracy,[93] one may note that the first will have a certain natural attractiveness because it looks to be another way of getting money out of the rich. But either of the other two might also seem attractive, when, say, the populace has not yet become too proud in its strength or when, because of some setback, it is feeling particularly chastened and humbled and ready to impose some restraints on itself, or at any rate on the demagogues whom it will typically regard as responsible.

1298b26 Aristotle's recommendations for oligarchies are also three. The first is to co-opt some of the poor into the deliberative body or to conduct business in meetings of the assembly but only such business as has been approved for this purpose by a constitutional board. The effect of this is to keep the regime an oligarchy (for control over the regime remains in the hands of the rich and the poor are prevented from deciding anything that might alter that control), but to reconcile the poor to it by associating them in the process of deliberation and hence, at the same time, to limit oligarchic excesses, since the poor too must be got to agree. The second recommendation (to allow the populace to vote on the resolutions presented to them) will have the same effect of giving a voice to the poor but not of enabling them to change the regime. For they cannot vote on any resolutions not laid before them (that is, not only the business but also the resolutions relative to this business are limited beforehand), or cannot introduce any resolution contrary to those laid before them.

The third recommendation, or perhaps a continuation of the second, is to allow the populace to share in giving advice but not in deliberating about the final decision (which will rest with the rulers or magistrates). Aristotle's concluding remarks seem to be relative to this recommendation:[94] that what the multitude decides should only be binding if it is negative, but any positive proposal is to be referred back to the rulers or oligarchs. What Aristotle must mean by this is not simply that the oligarchs give the final approval to any proposal, for this is simply to give them the veto too (not to approve a proposal approved by the assembly is effectively to veto it).[95] He must mean that what comes before the assembly for approval is also controlled by the oligarchs. So if the assembly introduces any matter on its own account and passes some resolution about it, the whole matter

93. Newman (4:248) doubts they ever could be.

94. So Barker (1946: 193), but against Newman (4:252).

95. This is the opinion of Creed (1983), which, however, as he implicitly concedes, amounts to abolishing the control of the rich (the condition for oligarchy) by giving the assembly an equality with them. For if the rich only differ by approving proposals last and not also by controlling the agenda, then the assembly is their equal: both may put forward any proposal; both may veto any proposal (the assembly by rejecting proposals from the oligarchs, the oligarchs by not ratifying proposals from the assembly); and both need the support of the other to pass a proposal.

will be referred back to the oligarchs in the sense that the oligarchs will decide even whether to accept it for decision in the assembly. If so, they will then resubmit it in the way that they themselves wish and as their own recommendation. If not, the matter will simply die. In other words, only those affirmative decisions by the assembly will be accepted by the oligarchs which are on proposals that the oligarchs themselves form and introduce. The effect of this practice will be the same as before: the rich retain control of the regime, for they control the agenda, but the multitude can serve as a check on extreme proposals by the use of the veto.

The opposite practice of polities would, by contrast, shift control away from the oligarchs to the larger number, that is, to those in the middle who dominate the assembly in polities. For the middle would now determine the agenda, in particular by laying down what things the magistrates, or the notables, are to control and how. Proposals coming from the magistrates would be reserved to the middle in the same way, that is, the middle would decide whether and in what form the proposal was to be put forward. The magistrates would, however, be able to check extreme proposals from the assembly by the use of the veto.

Chapter 15

<~ BY MEANS OF THE OFFICES

<~ THE DIFFERENCES AMONG OFFICES

1299a3 Aristotle comes next to the offices, and first he lays down the questions to consider. They are: (i) the number of offices; (ii) their spheres of control or competence; (iii) their tenure, as regards both duration and repetition; (iv) their mode of appointment.[96] Regimes differ from each other in the ways they arrange offices in each of these respects, so since the context here is the practical one of setting up regimes it is necessary to know which arrangement fits and benefits which regime. Aristotle deals with the fourth question separately at the end, but the first three he deals with first and more or less together, since the answer to one will in a way determine, and depend on, the answer to another. So, for instance, if the number of offices is large, their spheres of competence will have to be small (so that they do not overlap and interfere with each other); conversely, if the number is small, their competence will have to be large (so that everything

96. Newman (4:254) lists other possible questions, as whether offices are to be salaried, or subject to review and by whom, or whether one man may hold more than one office at the same time, or whether and how offices should be combined into joint boards. But these are perhaps all reducible to questions of tenure, and besides Aristotle is presumably not intending to be comprehensive, but is content to lay out for potential legislators the sorts of questions to ask and the sorts of answers to give, leaving the rest to be filled in as occasion demands.

falls under the control of some office). Tenure will be a function of the number of offices too, but also of the number of citizens available and of the kind of regime.

1299a14　But even before these questions are broached, there is the prior question of what is meant by an office (just as there was the prior question in the preceding chapter of what was meant by the deliberative, or what were its powers). Aristotle proceeds by appeal to examples, and first to show how not to define offices. For while offices are manifestly cases of people taking care of something on behalf of the city, not all such cares are going to count as offices. So to define offices without specifying which cares are to count as offices and which are not will be to include too much in one's definition. To define them, for instance, in terms of mode of appointment (election or lot) will include priests, chorus masters, heralds, and ambassadors among the offices. But none of these are offices, at least not in the sense now in question. For by office is now meant one of the parts of the regime, that is, one of the parts of rule in the city, but priests, chorus masters, heralds, and ambassadors are not exercising rule (they are rather offering sacrifice, or managing music festivals, or announcing and conveying messages).

So Aristotle turns to consider next the kinds of care that go on in the city, and he lists three general ones. First, there are political cares, which concern the directing of all the citizens in some common action, as a general directing soldiers on campaign (generals are manifestly an office and soldiers are citizens), or concern the directing of a part of them in some common action, as managers of women and children directing women and children in virtuous habits and behavior (these managers are manifestly offices in aristocracies, where virtue is an express object of the regime, and women and children are derivatively citizens). Second, there are economic cares or cares to do with household management, as looking after the corn supply. Third, there are cares of an assisting or subordinate sort that, if possible, are handed over to slaves. Perhaps Aristotle has in mind here, among other things, certain cares of policing, as arresting offenders and guarding prisons, which are indeed necessary but which, because of their hatefulness, it is hard to get citizens to perform or to perform well (cf. 8(6).8.1321b40–1322a18).[97]

It is manifest that, of all these cares, the first above all are offices, the second less so, and the third least of all (especially if slaves can be used to perform them). But the difference between these is now not in terms of objects cared for (since all take care of common matters necessary to the life of the city), but in the kind of control that they involve or require. So the first, and generals most obviously, are distinguished for acts of deliberating, judging, and issuing commands, and especially for issuing commands as this is more characteristic of rule. In the other cases, these

97. In democratic Athens the policemen were Scythian slaves. Newman (4:257) also mentions public slaves serving as clerks and the like. Why policing and clerking activities should now be regarded very differently is interesting matter for speculation.

acts are less marked, or those in charge are rather following the deliberations, judgments, and commands of others than acting on their own account. So Aristotle concludes that those offices are above all offices that have assigned to them some common care of the city for deliberation, judgment, and the issuing of commands. Other common cares may indeed be *called* offices (as heralds and policemen), but that is not important, for it concerns the name only and disputes about names seldom if ever get resolved (they concern convention and convention varies widely). What is in question here is the thing and the thing has been sufficiently determined for the present practical purpose of establishing regimes. Anything more is matter for thought (thought, presumably, about how and why the conventions differ).

1299a31   Aristotle's practical purpose does, however, require him to discuss the questions he raised at the beginning, namely the kind, the number, and the duration of offices (though this last only gets treated implicitly), so he turns to these now. But he does not so much give answers as show how to find answers by listing the several factors that any legislator setting up a regime must take into consideration. For his aim here (so *Ethics* 10.9.1180b20–29) is the general one of training legislators by teaching them the science of legislation, so that they can meet any case that might arise; it is not the specific one of setting up this or that individual regime (though he does give more particular advice, especially about the kinds of democracy and oligarchy, in his addendum in book 8(6)).

Thus a first point to note is the difference between those offices that any city needs in order to exist and those it needs in order to exist well or to have a serious regime. For the latter offices can and will be dispensed with in deviant regimes (managers of women and children, for instance, do not exist in deviant regimes).

A second point is the size of the city that is to be legislated, for large cities can have many offices but small ones, through lack of numbers, must have few. In the case of large cities this question can be fairly easily settled: have one office for one task, and have tenure short and seldom repeated. For there are enough citizens to go around and works get done better when each is looked after separately. In the case of small cities, by contrast, several offices will have to be combined together and each office or official board will have to have several functions instead of one only. Such combination is in principle possible because, while small cities may need the same offices and laws as large ones, they will not need them as often. So a board that has many functions need not perform them all badly because these functions will arise serially or after long intervals and seldom all at once. One may also suppose in the case of small cities, though Aristotle does not say it, that tenure of office will have to be longer or more often repeated.

1299b10   However this answer about combining several functions in one office, while easy to state, is difficult to put into practice because of the need to distinguish which functions to combine with which. Aristotle therefore spends some time on the matter by listing the sorts of things to consider.

So a first point is to note what was mentioned just before, the difference between offices that cities must have and those that they need not have but would be better off having (that is, if they are to have a better regime). One could then either dispense with the latter, if the city did not care for a better regime, or, since the former offices must exist in any case, hand over to them some of the functions of the latter as well.

A second point is to note offices whose functions differ rather by place than by object. For it may be that while some of these offices must be different, others need not be but one and the same office could do the same task for several places. So perhaps good order in the marketplace could be managed by an office that also managed good order elsewhere (as, say, in the port).

A third point is to note the same thing about offices whose functions differ rather by the persons cared for. So the good order of women and children, normally divided into the separate offices of managers of women and managers of children, could perhaps be combined under one office.

1299b20   A fourth point is to note how offices differ according to regimes, whether the same offices exist in all regimes and differ only in who fills them (the educated in aristocracy, the rich in oligarchy, the free in democracy) or whether the offices are different in different regimes so that an office that is great or powerful in one is not in another (as the assembly must be great in a democracy, less great in a polity and aristocracy, and least, or even nonexistent, in an oligarchy). If the latter is true, then many functions can be combined in a certain office in one regime that will have to be combined in a different office or offices in another regime (many functions, for instance, could be combined in the assembly in a democracy but not in an oligarchy).

1299b30   This point about different regimes having different offices is obviously more general in scope than the question of combining offices in small cities, for it will apply to large cities too. So Aristotle notes some of these different offices (his remarks are presumably more suggestive than exhaustive), since it will be necessary, in setting up a regime, to include the offices proper to it but none that are opposed to it. Precouncillors, then, are an oligarchic body, for, as noted at the end of the previous chapter, they control the agenda and limit what is to be laid before the assembly. A council, by contrast, is popular because, though the assembly needs some office or body to deliberate on its behalf (so that it is not always meeting and can attend to its own affairs), it, and not the council, controls the agenda and can tell the council what to deliberate about on its behalf and how (for by definition the assembly is in control of the regime).

A council would, however, have an oligarchic character if its numbers were small. For then these few people would have to meet long and often to complete all the business, and only the rich could afford the time. A large council, by contrast, would be able to split itself into sections and divide the business, so that individual members would meet less often and the poorer could also find the time to take part. A precouncil combined with a council would be for checking the council (for the precouncil would presumably be set up to exercise some control over the agenda of the council). These two instances, a small council and a precouncil combined with a council, would thus be characteristic of polities or mixed regimes.

In an ultimate democracy the council, despite being democratic, will lose its powers, for here the assembly has the leisure to meet often and to deliberate and decide everything from the beginning itself. A strong council is thus proper to the more measured kinds of democracy.

1300a4 An office to manage or oversee women and children (and any other office similarly designed to regulate manners and conduct) is necessarily aristocratic as being concerned with the promotion of virtue. It cannot be democratic, for the women of the poor need to be out and about helping make ends meet and cannot be kept and regulated at home. It cannot be oligarchic either, not because the women of the rich have no leisure, but because wealth and the love of wealth characteristic of oligarchies inure the women to luxury and make them resistant to restraint and control. The same will hold of children in democracies and oligarchies.

∽ THE APPOINTMENT OF OFFICES

1300a9 Aristotle turns last to the way the offices are appointed and, in order to find all the possible varieties, resorts, as he must, to mathematical computation. First, he sets down all the divisions or terms involved in any appointment of anyone to office, of which there are three: (i) who does the appointing; (ii) from whom they do the appointing; (iii) how they do the appointing. Second, he sets down all the varieties or differences within these three terms, of which again there are three (though he states the first two members in each term first, adding the last members, the conjunctions of the first two, at the end). So: (i) all appoint, or some appoint, or all and some appoint (all appointing to some offices and some appointing to others); (ii) appointment is from all, or from some, or from all and some (from all in the case of some offices and from some in the case of others); (iii) appointment is by election, or by lot, or by election and lot (by election in the case of some offices, or some of the members of some offices, and by lot in the case of others). In the case of the some from whom appointment is made, term (ii), these will be marked off from the rest by such things as wealth, family, virtue, and the like (or the several features that distinguish the "some" of oligarchies and of aristocracies).

1300a22 Thus far everything is fairly clear, but what comes next seems puzzling. For one might expect Aristotle now to compute the modes by simply multiplying the three differences in the first term by the three in the second by the three in the third (which is the standard way to calculate combinations) and so get the twenty-seven possible modes. Instead what he does is take the three differences in one term and combine them with only two of the differences in each of the other two terms (omitting the third difference, or the conjunction, in these other two terms) to give a total of twelve modes (three by two by two). To get the remaining possibilities it is necessary, as Aristotle's note at the end is perhaps meant to indicate ("not reckoning the two pairings," 1300a31), somehow to compute the other two conjunctions.[98] Furthermore, although Aristotle says that he is counting twelve modes, he does not give us twelve modes for the term he seems to take as the starting point (the first term of who appoint), or even the modes we would expect. For we would expect the following twelve modes for the differences in the first term: (1) all appoint from all by election, (2) all appoint from all by lot, (3) all appoint from some by election, (4) all appoint from some by lot; (5) some appoint from all by election, (6) some appoint from all by lot, (7) some appoint from some by election, (8) some appoint from some by lot; (9) all and some appoint from all by election, (10) all and some appoint from all by lot, (11) all and some appoint from some by election, (12) all and some appoint from some by lot.[99] Aristotle, however, does not give us any of modes 9 to 12, and in fact adds other modes that are out of place here, because they include one of the conjunctions that were supposed to be omitted (the conjunction of election and lot).

These difficulties can be removed, however, by adopting a different interpretation[100] and supposing that Aristotle is taking the third term as his starting point, not the first term, and that the twelve modes are: (1) all appoint from all by election, (2) all appoint from all by lot, (3) all appoint from all by election and lot; (4) all appoint from some by election, (5) all appoint from some by lot, (6) all appoint from some by election and lot; (7) some appoint from all by election, (8) some appoint from all by lot, (9) some appoint from all by election and lot; (10) some appoint from some by election, (11) some appoint from some by lot, (12) some appoint from some by election and lot. The advantage of this interpretation is that Aristotle does give us all these twelve modes (provided we supply at 1300a24 the words "or all appoint from some by election or all appoint from some by lot," which have anyway to be supplied also for the first interpretation).

98. See the note in Sinclair/Saunders (1981: 287–88).

99. This way of interpreting the text is adopted by Barker (1946: 198–200), Jowett (1885: 2:177–78), Newman (4:266).

100. The interpretation of Lord (1984: 259 n58), Miller (1995: 178), Welldon (1883: 303–4).

But, further, computing the other modes is now straightforward. For these twelve modes have been computed according to a simple pattern, that of combining each of the three differences in a given term one after the other with combinations formed by differences in the other two terms. Thus: election, lot, election and lot (the three differences in the third term) are combined, first with the combination of all appointing from all, second with the combination of all appointing from some, third with the combination of some appointing from all, fourth with the combination of some appointing from some. All that is necessary, then, is to continue this pattern to the remaining combinations (those formed from the conjunctions in the other two terms). So, in the case of the conjunction of appointment from all and some, each of the three differences (election, lot, election and lot) will have two more ways of being combined: with all appointing from all and some (which will complete the modes when all appoint), and with some appointing from all and some (which will complete the modes when some appoint). Then, in the case of the conjunction of all and some appointing, each of the same three differences (election, lot, election and lot) will have an additional three ways of being combined: with all and some appointing from all, with all and some appointing from some, with all and some appointing from all and some (which will be all the modes when all and some appoint). Three differences combined in five ways give fifteen more modes, which, added to the original twelve, make, as required, twenty-seven modes. That computing all twenty-seven modes is thus relatively straightforward helps explain why Aristotle does not himself bother to compute them (though he may also have intended a diagram to be to hand from which all the modes could, as it were, be read off).

Only one difficulty remains. For while it is clear that there is a difference between all or some appointing by election (who gets elected depends very much on who does the electing), it is not clear what the difference is between all or some appointing by lot. For if an appointment is made by lot, how can it make any difference who is in charge of administering the lot? The result is going to be the same in either case.[101] The answer must be that while lot is, as such, indiscriminate, in the process of being administered it is not. For, first, some people are manifestly unfit for rule, as the insane, and such must be excluded from the lot, or if the lot falls on them, their selection must be annulled. There are other disabilities too, as say doubtful citizenship, debt, indictment or conviction for crime. There is even hostility to the regime (for no regime can want those to be in control who will try to overthrow it, 7(5).3.1303a16–20), which may be manifest or only suspected. Second, disputes may arise over whether a given lot was properly administered or whether a certain person did really win a given lot. Third, there is the possibility of

101. Newman raises this puzzle (4:266).

cheating or rigging the lot. Those who administer the lot will have control over all these things and hence will, through the way they decide them (and "some" and "all" will decide them differently), have no little control also over who is eligible for appointment and who gets appointed.

1300a31   With the modes thus computed, Aristotle comes next to explain which ones are proper to which regime (for that is what the legislator most needs to know in setting up regimes). The general pattern is clear enough, that, as one would expect, the pure modes—all appointing from all and some appointing from some—are characteristic of democracy and oligarchy respectively, whereas the mixed modes—formed from variations of all and some appointing from some and all—are characteristic of the mixed regimes, polities and aristocracies.

The popular or democratic modes are when all appoint from all, by election or lot or both, and in both the ways of doing this, when appointment is made from all the citizens together or when it is made from all one after another according to their divisions into tribes, clans, and so forth.[102] Democracy, of course, is when the populace are in control and everyone is individually equal, which will be if all appoint from all and the some who are rich have no special advantage either in appointing or being appointed.

The modes proper to polity are several: one is when all appoint from all but the appointment is not made by all together (as opposed to the democratic mode when the appointment is *by* all together but not made *from* all together); another is when they all appoint but from some and not from all, by election or lot or both; another is when they all appoint but from both all and some, by both election and lot. These are modes of polity because they are all ways of shifting the control of the populace toward the rich and the middle. So the first gets the populace to appoint, not as a populace, but as members of clans, tribes, and so on, where their class interest as the mass of the poor will be minimized and the influence of other ties, as those of family, friendship, and obligation, will be stronger, and so where they are more likely to appoint to office on the basis of these ties, that is to say, more likely to appoint from those who are notables. The second and third ways more obviously achieve the same result, for now appointment is expressly from some (and not, or not only, from all), that is, from the some who will again typically be the notables.

These modes of democracy and polity exhaust the nine modes of when all appoint: from all, or from some, or from all and some, and by election, or lot, or both (I take it that all the modes of all appointing from all and some are meant to be covered, the modes of election or lot or both, though only the last is expressly mentioned). Aristotle turns next to the modes of when some appoint. The modes

102. I follow the interpretation of Newman (4:267).

he first mentions are when some appoint from all by election and lot, and when some appoint from both all and some[103] by election and lot (though again I take it he intends, by a sort of shorthand, to be including here as well the modes of appointment by election *or* lot). These modes are also, and obviously, proper to polity, for they mix oligarchic and democratic features: they are oligarchic in that only some do the appointing (which is characteristic of oligarchy) and they are polities in that they mix this with appointment from all (which is characteristic of democracy). Aristotle's remark, however, that these modes are oligarchic must be taken in the sense that they make the polity more oligarchic or lean it in that direction. For they are not purely oligarchic modes (which are when some appoint from some), but, in comparison with the polities just mentioned (where all appoint from some or from all and some), they mix the "all" and "some" in the contrary way and have the some alone to do the appointing. These some, therefore, or the notables, have greater control since it is they who now entirely determine who gets appointed. What keeps them as polities, and away from being pure oligarchies, is that they still appoint from all.

Aristotle adds, however, about these two groups of modes (some appointing from all and some appointing from all and some—whether by election, or lot, or both), that to appoint *from* both (which he says is the practice of aristocratic polity), is more oligarchic than to appoint *by* both,[104] that is to say, the modes of the latter group, appointment by some from all and some (by whatever means), are more oligarchic (or make the polity more oligarchic) than the mode when some appoint from all by election and lot. For evidently if appointment is from both all and some (whether by election or lot or both), then some offices are not only appointed by some but also from some, and so over these offices the some will have a more complete control (whereas over those offices that have to be appointed from all they will have only partial control). Hence this mode will make the polity more oligarchic than the mode when all offices have to be appointed from all, even if some of these offices are chosen by election (which is oligarchic) and not by lot (which is democratic). Such a mode of appointing from both all and some will be characteristic, as Aristotle adds, of aristocratic polity, at least in the sense in which polities that lean more toward oligarchy are called aristocracies.

The remaining modes of when some appoint are when some appoint from

103. Note that to get this sense from the Greek one must read *amphoin* at 1300a39 as genitive and take it to mean *from* both, and not as dative and to mean *by* both, that is, by both lot and election. The latter interpretation anyway makes little sense in the context and forces emendations on the Greek.

104. Note, again, that to get this sense from the Greek one must read the words about aristocratic polity at 1300a41–b1 as parenthetical, and one must read *ē* at 1300b1 as "than" and not, following other translators, as "or." The sentence will then run as follows: "it is also more oligarchic when appointment is from both (the practice of aristocratic polity, some offices appointed from all and others from some) than when some offices are appointed by election and others by lot."

some alone, whether by election, lot, or both, and these are all oligarchic modes (even if, because oligarchs prefer election, appointment by lot is not actually found anywhere among them). These modes of oligarchic polity and oligarchy thus exhaust all the nine modes of when some appoint (from all, from some, from all and some, and by election, or lot, or both).

The last nine modes are when all and some appoint. But it is not clear if Aristotle goes on to mention these. What he says next is that it is aristocratic when some appoint from all and when all appoint from some by election (1300b4–5). There seem to be two ways to take this. First, Aristotle could mean that the mode of some appointing from all by election and the mode of all appointing from some by election, which have both just been included under the modes of polity, are characteristic of polities that are, or are becoming, more like aristocracies. For election, unlike lot, is not indiscriminate and allows candidates with some quality to make an impression and get elected. But if all are electing from all, or some electing from some, the chances are that bad qualities will catch attention (either, in the first case, those of demagogues, or, in the second, those of the very rich). If, by contrast, some are electing from all, and not just from the rich, then while they will not be influenced by the qualities of demagogues (for the some do not want ultimate democracy to arise), they are likely to be influenced by better qualities (say if one of the less rich or poor was very courageous or just or skilled in war). Or again, if all are electing from some, then while they will not be influenced by the quality of much wealth (the all do not want ultimate oligarchy to arise), they are likely to be influenced by better qualities (say if one of the wealthy was very moderate or just or benevolent).

But second, Aristotle could be talking instead about the remaining modes of when all and some appoint, and saying that the mode of when all and some appoint from all and some by election is aristocratic. This would be aristocratic for the reasons just mentioned, that election allows for appointment of men with quality. But it would in fact be more aristocratic (and so more appropriate to so-called aristocracy) than when all appoint from some or when some appoint from all. For now anyone with quality, whether rich or middle or poor, can be elected to some offices, and anyone with quality, whether rich or middle or poor, can do the electing to some offices. But because the electing is mixed, all and some from all and some, the chance of those with bad qualities getting elected is removed or minimized.

The other modes of all and some appointing would, in one way or another, dilute the aristocratic effect. For lot is indiscriminate and does not allow quality to count, and if all and some appoint from all, or from some, by election or lot or both, then there will be some offices that are appointed by all from all or which are appointed by some from some, and this will clearly shift things away from aristocracy back toward democracy or oligarchy. Maybe that is why Aristotle does not mention these other modes here, because they are not aristocratic. They are just variations, and seemingly not very significant variations, on the modes of polity already mentioned.

This second interpretation of the text is perhaps to be preferred, both because it gives modes that are more completely aristocratic, and because thus all the modes get a mention, including the last modes of when all and some do the appointing.

1300b5 So much, then, concerns the modes for appointing offices and which modes fit which regimes. But there remains the question, at least as regards modes that combine one or more conjunctions (all and some appointing, from all and some, by election and lot), of which offices these modes fit, as which offices should be appointed by all and which by some, which from all and which from some, and which by election and which by lot. These questions will arise for any regime (for in the case of all regimes there are modes that include conjunctions). The answer is to be found by considering the power or kind of office. So, for instance, it would be better to have a general appointed by election than by lot (even in democracies), and from all than from some (for quality can exist anywhere, though oligarchies would have to avoid appointing a general from anyone other than themselves, 7(5).6.1306a19–31). Conversely an office in charge of agreements in the market could more safely be appointed by lot and from anyone (even in an oligarchy). But much of this is perhaps straightforward so Aristotle leaves it aside. He does, however, return to it later (or so it would seem) when he also returns, in his addendum in the last book (8(6).8), to the question of the powers of the different offices.

Chapter 16

~ BY MEANS OF THE LAW COURTS

1300b13 With respect to the law courts, again it is necessary to compute their modes and to know what is meant by courts or what are their spheres of competence. The modes are, says Aristotle, to be found in three terms: from whom the courts are appointed, whether from all or some; about what things they judge, or what the kinds of court are; by what means they are appointed, whether by election or lot.

An initial puzzle here is that nothing is said about the other term, prominent in the preceding chapter, of who does the appointing. But in fact that term has already been fully dealt with there. For courts are a sort of office, so that what was decided there about the ways of all, or some, or both all and some appointing to office will simply carry over to what is said here about ways of appointing to the courts from all, or from some, or from both all and some. Aristotle did, anyway, proceed after this fashion in chapter 14, where he mentions choice by election and lot but leaves the determination of who those are who do the choosing to be understood from the regime he is then talking about (whether the all of democ-racies, or the some of oligarchies, or the all and some of mixed regimes). In chapter 15 he made this explicit since then he was not talking of the deliberative in general (as he was in chapter 14), but specifying one particular function of it, the selecting of offices, and showing how the handling of this function can vary according to the all, or some, or all and some of the several regimes. So in the case of courts too, it would now seem sufficient to specify only what is proper to them, namely what is meant by them or what their powers are (as he earlier specified the deliberative and the offices) and how one can, assuming for each regime its own ruling body, vary their distribution among the parts of the city.

1300b19   The courts are eight in number, having jurisdiction over: (i) au-dits; (ii) crimes involving common matters; (iii) matters affecting the regime; (iv) disputes between rulers or magistrates and private persons over fines; (v) private transactions of some magnitude; (vi) homicides (of which there are four kinds); (vii) foreigners (of which there are two kinds); (viii) small claims. These categories may not look exhaustive (though presumably they are meant to be), but one can perhaps include under one or other of them many things not expressly men-tioned.[105] So category (v), for instance, will include assault and injury, and crimi-nal cases generally, since Aristotle understands these as cases of involuntary trans-actions (*Ethics* 5.4). Also disputes over inheritance and heiresses will come here, except where they involve the regime and fall under (iii). Indeed any matter otherwise falling under some other category would fall under (iii) in particular circumstances. But one need not assume that each category must belong to a different court; the same court could perhaps have jurisdiction over several of them. These categories also proceed more or less in order of importance from the more common to the less common, and from the more serious to the less serious.

As regards the cases of homicide in particular, the four kinds (premeditated murder, involuntary murder, murder when the fact is admitted but the justice disputed, fugitives for murder) doubtless could be further specified (as premedi-tated murders could be further specified into first and second degree), and anyway Aristotle seems to say that the kinds he does mention need not specify different courts (for the same or different jurors, that is, the same or different courts, may hear them). The peculiarity is the last kind, fugitives for murder. But a city is a thing of special worth and so someone who has denied it by fleeing, and may have damaged it by killing, perhaps deserves to be treated in some exemplary way.

Of these courts, it is manifest that (i) to (v) are political in a way that (vi) and (vii) are not, for the former all directly involve the fate of the political community (the first four by their nature and the fifth by its magnitude), and if not managed

---

105. Newman (4:269) notes as missing cases of insolence and injury, of offenses against the gods, and of inheritance.

nobly will all, as Aristotle says, occasion factional conflict and change of regime. Of course, cases of murder and those involving aliens can also be such as to affect the regime, but insofar as they do so they will fall under category (iii). The same will be true of (viii) where the cases will not ordinarily affect the regime because so minor, but where, if abuses become common and a cause of alienation among the poor, the matter would fall under category (i) or (iii) or both.

1300b38 With respect to the setting up of these political courts (for, given what was just said, "all the cases just distinguished" must mean "all the political cases just distinguished"),[106] there are several modes. For there are again three terms: from whom the courts are chosen; about what matters they decide; how they are chosen. There are not, however, three differences in each mode. The second difference, about what matters the courts decide, can only be taken in one way, that is, wholly and never partially (always as "all" and never as "some"). For all the matters must have someone to decide them in every regime (one cannot just leave some cases unattended to). Hence the number of modes will vary only according to the differences in the first term, whether appointment is from all, or some, or all and some, and in the third term, whether appointment is by election, or lot, or election and lot. Hence there will only be nine modes: three when appointment is from all about all matters, three when appointment is from some about all matters, and three when appointment is from all and some about all matters. These are, therefore, the modes Aristotle goes on to list, save that he gives four modes for each instead of three. The reason is that appointment by the combination of election and lot can itself happen in two ways: either some courts are appointed by election and others by lot, or certain courts are appointed by election and lot at the same time (some of their members by election and others by lot).

So the modes of all deciding all matters are: (1) when appointment is by election; (2) when it is by lot; (3) when it is by election for some courts and by lot for others; (4) when for some courts it is by both election and lot. The modes for some deciding all matters are the same: (1) when appointment is by election; (2) when it is by lot; (3) when it is by election for some courts and by lot for others; (4) when for some courts it is by both election and lot. The modes for all and some deciding all matters (an obvious combination Aristotle did not mention at the beginning but introduces now) are similar, though he explains "all and some" as meaning when some courts are appointed from all, others from some, and yet others from both all and some. This combination too can be appointed in the same ways: by election, by lot, by both (and presumably again in both ways of both).

Technically, of course, one could have further options in the case of all and some deciding, as: some courts appointed from all and the rest from some; some courts appointed from all and the rest from all and some; some courts appointed

106. Contra Jowett (1885: 2:181) and Newman (4:272–73).

from some and the rest from all and some; all courts appointed from all and some. One could also have further options in the case of the second way of appointing by both election and lot, I mean the way when certain courts are appointed by election and lot at the same time (some of their members by election and others by lot). Such further options would be: some courts composed of members, some of whom are chosen by election and others by lot, with the other courts chosen by election; some courts composed in this way with the other courts chosen by lot; some courts composed in this way with some of the other courts chosen by election and others of them by lot; all courts composed in this way. If all these options are included, then the total number of available modes, for all ways of composing courts (whether from all, from some, or from both all and some) will considerably increase. Aristotle does not mention these further options but he may have meant them to be understood (they are easy enough to work out). It may, however, also be that many of these additional modes would not make very much difference to the character of regimes. The modes that are given, which are the basic ones, do make such a difference.[107]

1301a10 Aristotle concludes, as in the previous two chapters, by saying which of these modes are characteristic of which regimes. The pattern is straightforward and the same as before: the first set of modes, when all decide all things, is popular; the second set, when some decide all things, is oligarchic; the third set, when all and some decide all things, is characteristic of the mixed regimes, polities and aristocracies.

There remains, of course, the fact (adverted to in the commentary on the beginning of this chapter) that the appointment of these courts must not only be *from* all or some or both (which Aristotle has expressly talked about) but also *by* all or some or both (which, for the reasons stated earlier in the commentary, Aristotle does not expressly talk about). For all these twelve modes for courts could themselves be appointed in any of these three ways: by all, by some, or by all and some. But even so these twelve modes will remain popular or oligarchic or mixed as described, save that now there will be popular or oligarchic or mixed ways of appointing popular or oligarchic or mixed courts (and the same will hold, of course, for appointing popular or oligarchic or mixed deliberatives). This will greatly increase the options available to legislators in setting up regimes and, more significantly, greatly increase the options in setting up mixtures. The numbers of possible regimes may not thereby increase, but the numbers of ways of making these regimes will, and also, in particular, the numbers of ways of limiting excesses.

107. It is interesting to speculate about these additional modes also in the case of the offices, for some offices are composed of several members who could therefore be chosen from all and some and by election and lot in the several ways Aristotle mentions for courts. Perhaps, however, these variations, for both offices and courts, are getting too subtle and too nice to be of any consequence.

BOOK 7

Destruction and Preservation
of the Other Regimes

Chapter 1

~ FIFTH QUESTION:
DESTRUCTION AND PRESERVATION OF REGIMES

~ DESTRUCTION OF REGIMES IN GENERAL

~ THE STARTING POINT OF CHANGE

1301a19　Aristotle comes now to the last of his five questions, the one that, as he said (6(4).2.1289b22–26), is about the ways regimes are destroyed and preserved. So he first recalls and specifies the question. It concerns the number and kinds of things that originate change in regimes, the ways in which each regime is destroyed, and from what regimes into what regimes they alter most; how regimes are preserved, both in general and in particular, and what are the means whereby each regime can most especially be preserved. This question thus divides into two parts, about destruction and about preservation, and these parts again into two, the general and the particular. Change or destruction in general is dealt with in chapters 1 to 4, and in particular in chapters 5 to 7. Preservation, conversely, is dealt with in particular in chapter 8 and in general in chapter 9. Chapter 10 deals with the destruction of monarchies in general and in particular, and chapter 11 does the same for their preservation. Chapter 12 continues chapter 11 but finishes, in confirmation, as it were, of the discussion in all the preceding chapters, by exposing the faults in Socrates' rival account of change from Plato's *Republic*.

The main peculiarities here are that monarchies are treated separately and last and that they are also contrasted with regimes (7(5).10.1310a39–b2). But the same reason can perhaps be used to explain both peculiarities. For by monarchy Aristotle means tyranny and the several kinds of kingship other than the best. But tyranny is least of all a regime (and was indeed barely discussed in the preceding book), and the kingships in question are themselves either sorts of tyranny or more like an office than a regime (3.14, 6(4).10). Hence it is reasonable to contrast both tyrannies and kingships with regimes and to treat them last. For the kingship that is a regime, and indeed the simply best regime, is not at issue here, as neither is its companion, true aristocracy. These two regimes were dismissed in the preceding book as already sufficiently treated (6(4).2.1289a30–38), and anyway the faults within, or chances without, that could destroy them are assumed, by prayer and education, to be absent.[1]

1301a25 There can be no question, however, of regimes changing if there are not several kinds of regime but one only (for then there would be no other regime for a given regime to change into). So the first thing to consider is the different regimes, and specifically their genesis in human desires. For regimes are the distribution of rule in the city, and rule is distributed according to what the city, or some part of the city, wants or can be persuaded to want. So if a regime is to change into another, the desires of one or more parts of the city must win out against the desires of the remaining parts. That is why Aristotle speaks much in what follows of faction as well as of change; indeed he often treats the two as one. For people typically try to accomplish their desires by starting factions. Faction is thus integral to the study of change, because desire is integral to the sort of change in question.[2] Accordingly Aristotle turns his attention to the different desires that generate the different regimes.

Now these desires focus on justice, for each regime, as a distribution of rule in the city, is an expression of how people think that rule should be distributed, or of what they think justice is (cf. 1.2.1253a37–39). Hence, as people's conception of justice differs, so do the regimes differ that they want to set up and do set up. Aristotle has, of course, discussed this matter before (especially in 3.9–13), so here he contents himself with repeating the essential facts as they bear on the topic of change. What justice is in principle, then, is agreed to by all, namely that it is proportional equality, or the distribution of equal shares to equals and of unequal shares to unequals. What they disagree about is who is equal and who unequal, or what the criterion of worth or merit is. It is this disagreement that generates the different regimes (3.9, 12–13; cf. *Ethics* 5.3.1131a18–29). So democrats take freedom as the criterion and suppose that, because all are equal in freedom, all are equal simply and should have equal shares; oligarchs take wealth or substance as the criterion and suppose that, because some are unequal in wealth, they are unequal

---

1. Some modern thinkers have thought it possible to have political communities that would be free of change without the benefit of prayer and education. But that is because they abandoned the attempt to set up regimes or communities ordered to good life and counseled instead the setting up of nations or states ordered to life alone (leaving good life to individual opinion and choice). Moreover the states they had in mind were intended to be huge (unlike regimes that have to be small, 4(7).1326a25–b24), both for the sake of an emancipated economy (so as to provide in abundance the means of life; cf. 1.9.1257b40–1258a14), and for the sake, not of removing faction, but of rendering it powerless; see the references collected under *Stasis* in Rahe (1992: 1193).

2. Change and faction are thus one topic, not two, contra the ruminations of Mulgan (1977: 118–19); cf. Polansky, in Keyt and Miller (1991: 334), and Wheeler, in Barnes et al. (1977: 159–61).

simply and should have unequal shares. Thus democrats set up democracy or rule of the populace thinking this to be the equality demanded by justice, and oligarchs set up oligarchy or rule of the well-off thinking this to be the inequality demanded by justice.

1301a35 Democracy and oligarchy are mistaken or deviant regimes because, although freedom and wealth are indeed titles to rule, they are not the only or the chief title, which is rather virtue. So equality or inequality in freedom or wealth is not enough to settle equality or inequality in rule. Still, these regimes are just in a way, or have some justice to them, and it is this combination of justice and injustice that is the engine, as it seems, of change and revolution. For the element of justice generates in the partisans of each regime the conviction that they have justice on their side and so, whenever their share in rule does not accord with this understanding of justice, they resort to faction to change the existing regime and to put themselves in control. But, of course, since they are wrong about justice at the same time, the regime they want to set up instead, and do set up if successful, is itself unjust in another way. Conversely the regime they changed was itself in a way just. Accordingly their opponents have an equal sense of being wronged and of having justice on their side, and so they too, motivated by their understanding of justice, resort to faction in order to regain control. And so the cycle of faction and change goes on indefinitely.

But democrats and oligarchs are not the only ones who have some just claim to rule. The virtuous, or those superior in virtue, have a claim as well, and they indeed would be most justified in resorting to faction to gain control. For they are simply unequal and their claim is simply just. Why they nevertheless resort least to faction is not explained here by Aristotle, though he attributes it to lack of numbers later (7(4).4.1304b4–5). But an additional reason might be that they are virtuous, for the virtuous will always choose the best, and faction, because of the havoc it usually causes and the uncontrollable passions it usually stirs up, must seldom be best, even in deviant regimes. The virtuous then will prefer the measured path of unhurried reform, though they will doubtless be ready to act differently if an opportune moment presents itself.[3]

In addition to the virtuous, there are also the well-born, who seem or are reputed to be virtuous (because of inherited wealth and virtue in their ancestors). They believe that they should not share equality with others, whether the poor or

---

3. An example might be Demetrius of Phalerum, a member of Aristotle's school (and possibly a student of Aristotle himself), who introduced major reforms in Athens that moved the regime from democracy to polity; see the discussion and references in Williams (1987). Peter of Auvergne (1951: 5.1.714) says that the virtuous, given the right sort of conditions, would do wrong not to start faction to change the regime.

the merely rich, but should have a superiority, and so they too might resort to faction on these grounds (though lack of numbers must generally hamper them as it hampers the truly virtuous). Their claim to superiority would be just to the extent that they really were virtuous, but if they were not, their claim would reduce to one based on their wealth and the privileges of their wealth, and hence to the claim of certain sorts of oligarch.

This account of political change makes human beings and their opinions and actions the fundamental cause or starting point, and one might wonder if chance or nonhuman factors might not also in some cases be fundamental, or more fundamental.[4] Doubtless these features can play a role (as Aristotle expressly admits in the next three chapters), but clearly they will only do so if there are people in the city to take advantage of them. An oligarchy, for instance, will not change to democracy merely because many of the rich are killed in war (7(5).3.1303a3–10)— or even in an earthquake. The populace or their leaders must act to bring about change. But what will make them act is the desire to act, not merely the opportunity to act, and what will move the desire is the conviction that their action would be good and just.

∿ KINDS OF CHANGE AND WHICH REGIMES SUFFER THEM

1301b4 So much then concerns the beginnings and springs of factions, namely the different conceptions of justice, the respective desires for which move people to faction and change. What Aristotle considers next is what kinds of change people bring about and in which regimes. The kinds of change are two: from one regime to another and within the same regime. The first case, when a different regime takes the place of the existing one, is clear enough but the examples used suggest that Aristotle has in mind only changes from one whole class to another, as from democracy to oligarchy, and not changes within a class, as from one kind of democracy to another kind of democracy. If so, then such changes within a class will be included under the changes, by more or less, that he mentions shortly.

The second case is more complex and admits of several varieties. The first variety is when a regime remains the same but those who control it change. This will generally be confined, as Aristotle indicates, to oligarchies and monarchies, where there can be some outside the regime of the same quality as those in it and so who could, while changing the personnel, keep the regime the same (tyrants often have rivals who would be tyrant in their place and some oligarchs exclude many who are as rich and as well-born as themselves). In democracy and polity and aristocracy, by contrast, all the populace or middle or virtuous of the same quality are already included. Those excluded would belong to a different part of

---

4. Wheeler, in Barnes et al. (1977: 159–69).

the populace or a broader middle or would be virtuous but lacking wealth or family or suchlike, and, if included, would either change the regime in kind, or at least in degree, as in the second variety of change.

This second variety is when the regime changes by way of more or less, as when democracies or oligarchies become more or less democratic or oligarchic or, in the case of mixed regimes, when the mixture is relaxed and leans more toward democracy, or is tightened and leans more toward oligarchy.

The third variety is when a part of the regime is changed, as by the establishing or removing of a certain office. In the two examples Aristotle gives from Sparta, attempts were made to remove a certain office, either the monarchical one by Lysander or the democratic one by Pausanias, though in fact both attempts failed.[5] In the example from Epidamnus the attempt was to set up a certain office and it succeeded: a council that took over some functions from the rulers or magistrates was added. Still, despite this move toward democracy (a council is generally a democratic office, 6(4).15.1299b32–33), the fact that only the magistrates were obliged to vote[6] and that the single magistrate of some greatness remained (cf. 3.16.1287a6–8) kept the regime otherwise an oligarchy.

These three varieties of change within a regime seem to proceed from the least to the most disruptive. For in the first, the regime, as such, does not alter at all but only the identity of the rulers. In the second, change is only in degree and not in kind (unless such changes as from one kind of democracy or oligarchy to another are also meant to be included here). In the third, change is in kind but only with respect to a part of the regime. A change less than the first would hardly be a change at all, and a change more than the third would be a change of the whole regime. The three changes, therefore, seem to run the extent of all possible partial changes, to which any others could presumably be more or less reduced.

1301b26 Having thus stated in what ways changes in regimes occur (and having stated, at the beginning, the fundamental reason for such changes), Aristotle next states where, or in which regimes, they occur. His basic contention is that they occur in regimes where there is inequality, and because of the desire for equality that this inequality gives rise to. At any rate what he immediately says now is that wherever there is no proportion among those who are unequal, faction arises because of the inequality. I take it that he means by this that faction arises

5. Lysander is the Spartan admiral at the end of the Peloponnesian War, mentioned again later at 7(5).7.1306b31–33. He seems to have wanted, not to abolish the kingship as such, but rather to open it up to all those of quality and not have it confined to one or two families (something that Aristotle also seems to recommend, 2.9.1271a20–22). Pausanias the king, or rather regent, at the time of the Persian Wars, was mentioned earlier at 4(7).14.1333b29–35, and is mentioned again later at 7(5).7.1307a2–5; see Newman (4:287).

6. If this is what Aristotle's somewhat vague remarks are intended to mean, as Jowett (1885: 2:185–86) and Newman (4:288–89) suggest. Nothing else is known about these events at Epidamnus.

both where equals have what is unequal and where unequals have what is equal, for in both these cases there is no proportion among the unequal—the unequal are either unequal in fact but not in worth (they have unequal shares but do not deserve to) or are unequal in worth but not in fact (they deserve unequal shares but do not have them). Certainly the instance Aristotle gives, that a perpetual kingship is unequal if it exists among equals, embraces both cases, for it embraces the examples of Lysander and Pausanias together. Lysander sought to destroy such a kingship because he thought it an inequality among equals, and Pausanias sought to destroy a check on such a kingship, namely the ephorate, because he thought the ephorate an equality among unequals. Both started faction, therefore, because of an existing inequality (whether that of an unequal office among equals or of an equal office among unequals), and in order to get the equality they desired (the equality of an equal office among equals or of an unequal office among unequals).

So much, then, illustrates the general contention, that faction arises in situations of inequality from the desire for equality. The proof is based on what was said at the beginning, that different parts of the city have different understandings of justice, and also on the thesis, now to be expounded, that these understandings are different understandings of equality or, to be more precise, of proportional equality (as the instance of perpetual kingship has just shown). For equality, continues Aristotle, can either be numerical or according to merit. By numerical equality he means what is the same and equal in amount and size, as the difference between three and two and between two and one, which is the same in amount (namely one); by equality according to merit he means what is the same and equal in ratio, as the difference between four and two and between two and one, which is the same in ratio (namely a half). Now people in fact agree that justice is equality according to merit (or proportional equality); where they disagree is, as said at the beginning, that some think they are altogether equal according to merit if they are equal in one respect, while others think they are altogether unequal according to merit if they are unequal in one respect. But what this means, of course, is that the first are in effect understanding equality as numerical equality, for numerical equality will be the result if all are equal according to merit. Numerical equality can thus be regarded as a sort of special case of proportional equality, or equality according to merit, namely the case where all have equal merit or where all deserve numerically equal shares.

From this exposition, it is possible to set out the following argument (it is too obvious now, perhaps, for Aristotle to bother making explicit): (1) the desire for justice as people understand justice is (as shown at the beginning) what moves them to start faction and change of regimes; (2) the different understandings of justice (as just shown here) concretize themselves in different understandings of equality; (3) therefore the desire for equality moves people to start faction and change of regimes. Hence, further, (4) it must be in situations or regimes of inequality, where there is no proportion among the unequal (in the way explained), that this desire must be most excited and that people must be most moved to start faction and change.

1302a2 The next thing to explain, then, is which regimes are unequal. The qualities on the basis of which people claim equality according to merit are freedom, wealth, good birth, or virtue (3.12.1283a14–22). Of these qualities the first two are the most common, and regimes based on these qualities, democracy and oligarchy, are likewise the most common. Regimes based on the other qualities, as so-called aristocracies, can arise but they are comparatively rare, for the necessary virtue and good birth are also rare (good birth here including virtue and virtue meaning imperfect virtue, not the perfect virtue of the simply best regime). The inequalities, therefore, that will be most widespread and most felt will be inequalities with respect to freedom and wealth, or numerical inequality on the one hand (for the equality sought by democrats according to their principle of merit is in practice numerical equality) and inequality according to the merit of wealth on the other. Consequently regimes that accord in every respect with one or the other equality—whether the numerical equality based on freedom or the equality according to merit based on wealth—will be base, because these regimes will be unequal with respect to the other equality, and so most prone to faction and change. The fact is well illustrated by the results, for none of these unequal regimes is lasting. Certainly in comparison with regimes that have really lasted, as Sparta in particular but also Crete and Carthage, which are all mixed regimes, the unmixed regimes of democracy and oligarchy have been short-lived.

The fault here can be stated according to a universal rule, that an initial error, and one in the first principle, must end up eventually in something evil. For oligarchies and democracies both err from the beginning, and in the first principle, by taking justice or equality partially and not wholly (justice is the first principle in regimes, 1.2.1253a14–18, 30–39; 3.12.1282b14–18). The cure is obviously to combine the equalities that democracy and oligarchy each divide, for then both real and perceived inequality will be reduced to a minimum: the two sides that most exist in cities and that most resort to faction will have some of the equality that they think just instead of one of them having everything and the other nothing. Mixed regimes, therefore, will have least inequality and be least prone to faction and change (that is, they will be least prone to change from within, though of course any regime could be destroyed by some chance from without; cf. 2.11.1272b29–33, 12.1274a11–21).

Still, of the two unmixed regimes, democracy will be more stable and free of faction than oligarchy. The reason is twofold. First, there are two factional conflicts in oligarchy, the oligarchs against themselves and against the populace, whereas in democracy there is only one, the populace against the oligarchs.[7] Second, democracy is closer to the mixed or middle regime, which is the most stable of these regimes (it is not the most stable of all regimes, for that is the simply best regime), and what is more like something stable will itself be more stable. Democracy is closer to the middle regime because, presumably, its rule is not only more broadly based as being based on more people, but also because it will always include those in the middle (6(4).11.1296a13–16), whereas oligarchies will often exclude them by setting the property qualification too high.

Chapter 2

~ BEGINNINGS AND CAUSES OF CHANGE

~ THEIR KINDS AND NUMBER

1302a16 The starting point or origin of change has so far been stated at the most universal level, the level of saying that change, in its several kinds, springs from the desire for equality in situations of inequality. But fully to understand the phenomena of change, it is obviously necessary to descend to a more concrete and particular level. The general cause of change in fact resolves itself into three: the condition or state of mind of those who resort to faction or agitate for change; what they do it for; what pushes or incites them into it.

1302a22 The condition or state of mind, stated in its most general terms, is what was already said, namely the desire for equality: numerical equality if people suppose themselves equals in a situation of numerical inequality, and proportional equality (and numerical inequality) if they suppose themselves unequal and superior in a situation of numerical equality. These desires can be both just and unjust: just if people really are equal or superior in the way they think, and unjust if they are not. This remark serves as a reminder that Aristotle is not now interested in excusing, justifying, or condemning change (he decided before who may justly claim equality or inequality in rule when he decided the justice of the several regimes; see 3.9–13). He is interested rather in understanding its causes.

1302a31 The desire for equality (or inequality), however, is not a desire for

---

7. Newman (4:292) and Jowett (1885: 2:187) both think that there can, in democracy, be factions of the populace against the populace, as, say of the peasant farmers against the artisans or the urban crowd. Doubtless such factions are in principle possible (and Aristotle's words do not strictly rule them out), but they are undoubtedly rare by comparison with faction among oligarchs (Jowett gives certain modern examples which do not seem relevant, or are exceptional). Oligarchs have an individual as well as a class interest (their wealth and privilege give them a sense of individual worth), and so can be moved by both interests; the needy or populace have only a class interest.

equality in the abstract; it is a desire for an equality or inequality in certain goods, the goods that regimes have to distribute and which control of the regime enables one to get. These goods are two: honors or office and profit or wealth. However their opposites also need to be included, for people pursue equality (or inequality) by trying both to get more of these goods and to avoid the loss of them, and whether on their own account or on that of friends (for friends are in a way another self).

1302a34   But while the desire for equality in profit or honors is what moves people to act for change, there must, further, be something to excite the desire. For until the desire exists, or until, if existent but dormant or weak, it is stimulated into life and strength, there will be no action. So the third cause is the things that generate or activate the desire, namely the beginnings of change. Aristotle numbers these beginnings in two ways, either as seven or as more than seven. The first way would seem to be when those beginnings of change are numbered which incite factions or incite them directly, and the second way when those are numbered that may or may not incite factions or not directly.[8]

Of those numbered in the first way, profit and honor appear again, but this time as provocations and not as goals, when people are incited by seeing others getting more profit or honor, and whether justly or unjustly. For people can still be incited to a sense of injustice and inequality even if those getting more are getting it justly, for either they may not think this just or, even if they do, they may not think it just that they themselves are not getting more too.[9] The other causes among the seven are insolence, fear, superiority, contempt, disproportionate increase. Those additional to the seven are campaigning for votes,[10] disregard, small things, dissimilarity. These seven or eleven causes, though they are not the immediate efficient cause of change (which is rather the desire for equality), are nevertheless the mediate ones. They stand, moreover, at the focus of attention. For they are the inequalities and provocations that, by stimulating the fateful desire for equality, are the first steps or beginnings in the downfall of regimes. They are the things that the legislator must especially concern himself with if he is to set up a regime in a way in

8. Barker (1946: 207 n1), Mulgan (1977: 124), Newman (4:296).

9. Newman (4:295) wrongly supposes that seeing others gaining justly cannot incite in the observers a sense of injustice.

10. It is interesting that Aristotle regards vote getting as a cause of faction and change when we regard it nowadays as the very condition of free and democratic government. But that is perhaps because we have institutionalized faction as part of the political process (we aim to use the clash of a multitude of factions to prevent any one faction getting the upper hand), and because the emergence of political parties (or oligarchical clubs, as Aristotle would doubtless call them) has made us regard elections precisely as opportunities for change, namely for change from rule by one party to rule by another. See below p. 383 n41.

which it is likely to survive (there is nothing, of course, that he can do about the inequality inherent in the regime itself if it is a deviant one; he can only try to mitigate the evil consequences).

These causes do not seem exclusive, or not in the sense that any particular change must fall under only one of them and never under more. For one and the same change could, for instance, have both contempt and superiority or disproportionate increase as its causes (as is evident from the next chapter). But these causes do seem exclusive in the sense that they can all operate independently, so that a legislator who manages to remove one has not as such removed another, unless perhaps what he removes is some third thing that carries with it the removal of two or more causes (as removing demagogues in a democracy could remove both insolence from among the rulers and contempt from among the ruled).

Contrariwise the causes can be seen as exhaustive, at least by reduction, in the sense that any other cause will be an instance or kind of one of these, or only operate by operating through one of these. So natural disasters or disease or famine can be causes but only because, say, they bring about disproportionate increase; differences of opinion among the citizens, as also differences in religion and excessive contrasts of wealth and poverty, are kinds of dissimilarity; change of character among those in the city is an instance of disproportionate increase, for better and worse characters follow better and worse parts of the city so that, if the character of a city changes, one or other of its parts must have changed; continual rule by the same men, or too narrow an oligarchy, is an instance of honor; the ambition of those in office, as demagogues who are generals, or oligarchs courting the favor of the populace, are instances of superiority or perhaps also of honor. Teaching pernicious opinions, by contrast, is already faction and not a cause of faction, or only a cause in the sense that it can get more people to join the existing faction.[11]

The list of causes is doubtless taken from empirical investigation of actual changes and attempted changes of regimes (as indeed the many instances given in the following chapters suggest). But Aristotle seems to leave the list in a certain empirical diffuseness. One may accordingly be tempted to group the causes under more general heads, as under the psychological or the sociological or the hard to detect.[12] One could also group them under some of the famous ten categories as under passions, actions (including failures to act), and relations. Significantly, however, Aristotle does not endeavor to reduce his list to any more basic groupings. He ignores how they may or may not so contrast with each other and shows

11. All these cases are taken from Newman (4:276–78, 296) who wrongly supposes that they cannot be fitted anywhere into Aristotle's list. He also includes others that can be similarly explained. See also Polansky, in Keyt and Miller (1991: 332–33).

12. As do Mulgan (1977: 125) and Newman (4:275).

interest only in how they relate to faction and change. His focus of attention is thoroughly practical.[13]

Chapter 3

~ THE POWER OF THEIR OPERATION

1302b5   The causes last mentioned are obviously in need of explanation and illustration, so Aristotle now does that. He takes the causes in a different order, though it does not seem that anything of great significance hangs on the difference.[14]

Insolence and profit are causes when the rulers use their position to mistreat the ruled and to make a profit for themselves (whether from common funds or private). This creates a manifest, and offensive, inequality between ruler and ruled. It incites people to faction against each other and against the regime: against each other, perhaps, in the sense that those out of office compete to get into office (to stop the inequality or to get their share of it), or also in the sense that those in office compete with each other to get more; against the regime in the sense that some, whether in or out of office, think a regime that gives rulers such unequal power deserves to be replaced by a different one altogether. That Aristotle takes insolence and profit together here is presumably not intended to mean that neither can have an effect on its own, though taking excessive profits is perhaps a very common case of insolence. Among private persons, as opposed to magistrates, insolence and profit would hardly incite the aggrieved to change the regime. This would only happen if these private persons enjoyed the protection and favor of the rulers. But then, in that case, the insolence and the profit would be on the part of the rulers too.

1302b10   Honor is a cause when people either lose honor or see others gaining it. For then they will manifestly think they are suffering inequality. Aristotle's parenthetical remark, however, about the honoring and dishonoring being or not being according to merit (1302b12–14) seems ambiguous. It could mean that people will start factions even if the dishonors and honors are deserved,[15] for they may not themselves think that they deserve a deserved dishonor or that an honor which others deserve they do not deserve as well. But it could also mean that trying to change a regime when dishonors and honors are undeserved is justifiable. If so, then adding such a comment here about honors rather than earlier about profits has a certain appropriateness to it, for the virtuous, whose attempts at change

---

13. See Polansky, in Keyt and Miller (1991: 326 n9).

14. Barker (1946: 208 n1) gives an explanation in terms of logical connectedness, and Newman (4:296) notes that the order of the first four is the same as that followed in chapter 10.1311a11–1312a39 about monarchies.

15. This is the way Newman would take it (4:297).

Aristotle expressly allowed to be most just of all (7(5).1.1301a39–40), would seek the honor of rule, if they sought it, in order to rule well, not in order to turn a profit.

1302b15   Superiority is a cause since those who are superior no longer think that equality with others is equality for them, because their superiority entitles them to more. So they try to get rule to themselves alone—as sole ruler if single, or as dynasty if several. The counter against it used by many cities, as in Athens and Argos (both democracies), is ostracism, though Aristotle recalls (from 3.13.1284b17–20) that it would be better to prevent such superiority in advance. He is thinking of superiority in strength, wealth, friends, and so forth. Superiority in virtue is something to welcome, at least in the best regime (3.13.1284b22–34).

1302b21   Fear is a cause when people fear to pay the penalty for their misdeeds or to suffer wrong at the hands of others. What they fear to lose is their honors or profits, and thus to become unequal, as they think, by the loss. This is clear in the case of those about to suffer an undeserved loss, but it is no less clear in the case of those about to suffer a deserved loss. People who commit a wrong do not often think they deserve the threatened punishment. For they may not think that what they did was wrong, or, if they think it wrong for others, they do not think it wrong for themselves; or they may think the punishment too severe; or they may not think they should be punished by those threatening the punishment (as the rich with respect to the poor, or the poor with respect to the rich). The case from Rhodes, about an undeserved loss or threat of loss when the populace provoked the notables because of hostile lawsuits against them, recalls earlier comments about evils in democracies (3.10.1281a14–17, b18–20; 6(4).4.1292a10–30).[16]

1302b25   Contempt is a cause, not by bringing about an inequality, as in the previous cases, but by disposing people to attack an inequality that already exists. So an oligarchy can come to be despised for its smallness by those excluded from it when the excluded are more numerous,[17] and a badly governed democracy can, when its rule gets particularly disordered and anarchic, come to be despised by those who suppose themselves better fitted to rule (as at Thebes, Megara, Syracuse, and Rhodes).[18] The contempt in both cases incites attempts at change.

1302b33   Disproportionate increase is a cause because a city, like a body,

---

16. Events at Rhodes are mentioned again shortly at 1302b32–31 and also in 7(5).5.1304b27–31, and all three passages probably refer to the same events, which are generally dated to 390. However, the matter is not certain; see Newman (4:299).

17. "More numerous" must, contra Newman (4:300), presumably be taken in the sense also of "stronger," according to the proportion stated in 6(4).12.1296b17–24. For those excluded from rule in oligarchies are almost always more numerous with respect to mere quantity, but they need not thereby be stronger or more numerous with respect to quality, or think themselves stronger.

18. Events at Thebes are dated to the period after the battle of Oenophyta in 457; the date of events at Megara is uncertain; events at Syracuse are dated to before 485 when Gelon seized power. See Newman (4:300–301).

consists of parts and if these parts grow disproportionately, in quantity or quality or both, the whole will be destroyed or changed. So a human body would perish if its foot was four yards and the rest of it two feet, or it would start becoming a different kind of animal if its skin became scaly like a fish or if the flesh and muscle of its foot stiffened into a hoof.[19] Likewise a city could have one of its parts increase disproportionately, and if so it would no longer be adapted to the regime it had but would have shifted in weight toward another (6(4).12). The newly superior part, sensing its new superiority, would come to think the existing regime unequal, as no longer giving it what it deserved, and would be incited to effect change as a result.

Aristotle notes about this sort of increase that it can happen undetected and by chance (thus being hard or impossible for the existing rulers to detect beforehand). So increase of the populace in democracies and polities, which will shift these regimes to more thorough kinds of democracy, is likely to go undetected because democracies and polities will have their eyes on changes among the well-off, to whom they are more opposed and whom they more fear, than among the needy. Besides, the needy are generally large in numbers and to detect a large thing becoming larger is harder than to detect a smaller thing doing so. In oligarchies, by contrast, the needy will be more carefully watched, for the well-off fear threats from the needy, and so their growth will less escape detection.

Increase can also happen by chance, and suddenly. The examples Aristotle gives are of cases where one part increases because another part decreases. So the death of many notables in war led to a polity becoming a democracy in Tarentum, to an oligarchy becoming a democracy in Argos, to a democracy becoming more strengthened and more extreme at Athens.[20]

An increase in the numbers and wealth of the well-off in democracies (which would make them greater, by a combination of quantity and quality, than a more numerous mass of the needy) can similarly cause a change into oligarchy, and even, if the wealth and influence of some grow enormously, into dynasty. This kind of change is likely to be less frequent as democracies are going to be on special guard against the well-off, though it could also happen by accident if the needy suffered more in battle than the well-off did.

This cause of disproportionate increase presumably differs from superiority in that it is about parts or groups whereas superiority is about individuals. It differs from contempt, though it may go along with contempt (as can also superiority),

19. Newman (4:302) gives such instances and also mentions diseases like elephantiasis.

20. Events at Tarentum are dated to 473, those at Argos to 494, and those at Athens to the Peloponnesian War of 431–403, or to its first part, the Archidamian War of 431–421; see Newman (4:303–6). For some speculations on the significance of Aristotle's ordering of examples in this passage, and for the suggestion that the Spartan War is not the Peloponnesian War only but the whole of the last half of the fifth century, see Adshead (1986).

because it can incite to change without contempt, as contempt can incite to change without disproportionate increase or superiority. All three, however, can operate independently, which is presumably why they are given separate notice.

1303a13/20   Aristotle turns finally to the other causes besides the first seven. The first three of them can cause change without prior faction. So electioneering or vote-getting in Heraea and disregard in Oreus caused change in this way, as did small differences in Ambracia.²¹ The changes here were without faction because the regimes were changed by, or with the consent of, the existing rulers and without any prior agitation or attempt at change by some disaffected individuals or groups. So lot was willingly introduced in Heraea, not because some were agitating for such a change, but to cure the evil of electioneering. In Oreus someone hostile to the regime was given control willingly and without prior faction. In Ambracia the property qualification for office was already low and in the end, again without prior faction, everyone just agreed to disregard it. Nevertheless, despite the lack of faction, these are still cases where the causes work by acting on some desire for equality. Heracleodorus in Oreus, for instance, would not have used his power to change the regime unless he had thought the existing regime unequal and wanted to make it more equal. The Heraeans would not have changed the means of election unless they had thought it unequal that vote-getters should have the offices. The Ambracians would not have abolished the property qualification unless they had thought it unequal for some to be eligible and others not when the difference between their respective property was so small.

1303a25   The last cause, dissimilarity, works through faction, like the first seven, but differs in that the faction it causes is about the city, not the regime, and the regime only gets changed because the composition of the city gets changed. Aristotle first takes cases of differences in tribe (what today might be called racial differences). The principle here is that a sense of unity among such disparate groups in a city takes time to develop, so that before then the city is likely to tear itself apart. In illustration he gives two examples of factions and expulsions in cities formed by joint settlers (Sybaris and Thurii), and then six of factions, and sometimes expulsions, in cities that take in later settlers (Byzantium, Antissa, Zancle, Apollonia, Syracuse, Amphipolis).²²

This section ends with the following remark: "In the oligarchies it is the many who, on the grounds of being wronged, start factions because, as was said before, though equal, they do not share things equally; in the democracies it is the nota-

21. Not much is known about events at Heraea; those at Oreus are dated to 377. See Newman (4:306–8).

22. Not much is known about events at Byzantium, Antissa, and Apollonia. Sybaris was founded in 720 and Thurii founded near its ruins in 444. Events at Amphipolis are dated to 370, those at Zancle to 497, those at Syracuse to 467; see Newman (4:311–16).

bles who start factions because, though unequal, they do share things equally"
(1303b3–7). This remark has seemed to many commentators to be out of place,[23]
but in fact it makes sense where it stands. Aristotle has just been talking of dissimilarity with respect to the city, but his topic is faction and change with respect
to the regime, and the question arises as to how the two relate, and specifically as to
how the former works on or stimulates the desire for equality (the fundamental
cause of faction and change). Aristotle's answer is in effect that differences in tribe
cause factions over the regime because the different tribes make claims to the
regime in the way everyone does, namely according to one or other principle of
merit. The dissimilarity thus causes faction by causing the different groups to
agitate for equality according to their respective principles of merit.

So, for instance, one of the rival groups will tend to view itself as the notables,
who deserve greater shares, and the other as the free, who deserve equal shares. So
the original settlers will regard themselves as notables (for, being the first to settle
there, they are the well-born and own more of the land), and the later ones as the
free (for they too are settlers and so similars and equals, not slaves). The same will
happen in cases of joint settlement, for it is most unlikely that one or other group
will not think itself somehow superior to the other (either because greater in
numbers, or because contributing more to the foundation, or as undertaking
greater risks and labors, and so on). Thus the difference in tribe will be the basis of
a political difference, and the faction will be a faction about the regime and
whether it should be democracy or oligarchy. Aristotle indicates as much in the
description of his examples. So in Thurii the Sybarites thought themselves worthy
of more because they were the ancient owners of the land. Their faction then
would be as oligarchs against democrats. In Syracuse the newcomers were of low
status in comparison with the ancient inhabitants. Their faction then would be as
democrats against oligarchs.

1303b7   What is thus true of dissimilarity in tribe, or racial differences, will
be true of other dissimilarities, as differences in location. Here too those in one
part will tend to view themselves as superior to those in another (as perhaps those
on the island at Colophon thought themselves superior to those on the mainland
or vice versa), or those in one part will want to push a certain principle of merit
further than those in another (as those in the Peiraeus at Athens, being a different
sort of populace, want a more extreme democracy than those in the town of
Athens itself).

Differences in tribe and in place are only two kinds of dissimilarity, but there
are others, as many in fact as there are possible sorts of difference in cities (among
which we should perhaps now include religion). Aristotle mentions as the greatest
difference that between virtue and depravity followed by wealth and poverty. The

---

23. Barker (1946: 211 n1), Lord (1984: 260 n18), Newman (4:316), Sinclair/Saunders (1981: 305 n10).

first is greatest because it marks the difference between the correct and deviant regimes, whereas wealth and poverty only mark the difference between two deviant regimes (and there is a greater difference between correct and deviant regimes than between one deviant regime and another). Differences of tribe and of place (and other differences) will follow these because they are not in themselves political differences, though always tending to become political differences, as especially the political difference of wealth and poverty.

Chapter 4

～ OCCASIONS AND MEANS OF THEIR OPERATION

1303b17 Such then is how these several causes work. But there remains the question of the sort of events or circumstances that call them into operation or that, so to speak, set them off. Aristotle therefore adds a further chapter about these occasions of change.[24] These occasions must, of course, be potentially infinite (for particulars are potentially infinite), and will also vary from regime to regime. There can nevertheless be some more general ones that occur often or in several kinds of regime, and it is these that Aristotle notes here. He gives four in particular.

First, he notes, as drawing a conclusion from the above discussion, that while factions may arise from small things they are about great things. They are manifestly about great things because they concern who has control of the regime, but they can arise from small occasions because small differences can lead to differences about the regime, as his last examples in particular showed.

Second, he notes, as closely connected with the first, that small factions, or factions about small things, can develop into factions about the regime when they involve men who are influential in the city. He gives two cases of this. The first is small factions between those who exercise control in the city. The example is of two young men possessed of office who fell out over a love affair and dragged everyone else in the ruling body into the quarrel.[25] The cause here would presumably be honor in the sense that each faction would be annoyed that the other still enjoyed the honor of office despite no longer being worthy of it (because supporting the wrong side). Such quarrels among the leaders need to be watched and stopped at the beginning so that they do not go too far. For that they will otherwise go too far is proved from the fact that the quarrel or fault is in the principle. But

24. Newman (4:306, 318) rightly notes, from the Greek, that this chapter is about the occasions *from* which (*ex hōn*), and not the causes *because of* which (*di' ha*), change occurs.

25. This event is usually dated to the period of the oligarchy at Syracuse before it changed to democracy, which democracy was then, as recorded at 7(5).3.1302b31–32, destroyed when the tyrant Gelon seized power in 485; see Newman (4:301, 319–21).

the principle is half the whole,[26] so a fault in the principle, if left alone, will have the same effect as faults left alone everywhere else.

1303b31 The second case is small factions among the notables, even if they are not in office. Here too the rest of the city is liable to be dragged in (the reason being, presumably, that notables have prominence as individuals, whereas the poor only have prominence as a mass, and so disputes among individual notables are more likely to engage everyone's interest and attention than disputes among individual poor). Aristotle gives five examples, where faction develops about the regime because of insolence, profit, or honor. In Hestiaea a private dispute over wealth between two brothers, one well-off and the other more needy, leads to the well-off and the needy as a whole fighting over the regime. In Delphi it is a supposed act of insolence between two families. In Mytilene the private loss in gain and honor of one prominent man leads even to attack by a foreign power. In Phocis faction arises from a similar loss in gain and honor of a notable. In Epidamnus it is supposed insolence and gain on the part of one of the notables in office against a notable who was not.[27]

1304a17 Third, Aristotle notes that the growth in reputation or power of some part of a city can be an occasion for the operation of causes of faction, notably those of honor and superiority. The first example is of an official board, the council of the Areopagus in Athens, growing in this way and making the regime more strict (or perhaps making the polity more strict). The following five examples are all of parts of the city growing and achieving, or attempting, change toward oligarchy or democracy. So the populace in Athens, having become responsible for naval hegemony, strengthened the democracy; the notables in Argos, after winning repute in the battle of Mantinea, tried to get rid of democracy; the populace in Syracuse, after winning victory against the Athenians, changed the regime to democracy; the populace in Chalcis and in Ambracia, after helping get rid of tyrants, changed the regimes to democracy.[28] The general conclusion is that any individuals or offices or tribes or parts that become a cause of power incite faction, either by way of the cause of honor, when some resent the honor these others have acquired, or by way of the cause of superiority

---

26. There is a play on words in the Greek at this point (1303b28–31), since the word I translate as "principle" (archē) also means both "beginning" and "rule."

27. Not much is known about events in Hestiaea; more details about the events at Delphi are recorded by Plutarch; events in Mytilene are dated to 428; the Phocians' Sacred War broke out in 356 (Mnason is said to have been a friend of Aristotle's); nothing much is known about events at Epidamnus, not even if they are the same as those recorded at 7(5).1.1301b21–26. See Newman (4:322–27).

28. The battle of Salamis, which led to Athenian naval hegemony, took place in 480 (*Athēnaiōn Politeia* 23–25); the battle of Mantinea took place in 418; the victory of Syracuse over the Athenians took place in 413; nothing is known about events in Chalcis; those in Ambracia are dated to 580. See Newman (4:327–30).

(or perhaps also disproportionate increase), when these others think they now deserve more.

1304a38   Fourth, Aristotle notes that when those parts of the city that seem to be its opposites, the rich and the populace, are evenly balanced and there is no middle to shift the weight to one side or the other, changes occur. The cause that is set into operation here will be honor. For both sides will feel, because of their equal strength, that they have a good chance of victory, and so when they see the other side getting the honors of office and themselves none or too few they will attempt to change the regime toward themselves. Conversely, if one side is greatly superior, this cause will not operate to incite the opposite side to attack because this opposite side will see no chance of success. That is why the part of the city that is more truly opposite (the virtuous against the vicious) seldom forms factions to change the regime, because its numbers are few.

1304b5/7   So much, then, concerns the beginnings and causes of factions and changes in all regimes generally, or the third division of causes from chapter 2. The only thing left to mention before proceeding to particulars is how in fact people manage to change regimes. For all that Aristotle has discussed so far is what leads or causes them to do so, and not what means they use to realize their desire. He here states the means to be force or deceit or both. So force alone may be used all the way through. Or deceit may be used to get control of the regime first, and then force is used to keep control when the deceived discover the deceit (an example being the 400 at Athens).[29] Or deceit may be used all the way through.

One might, however, wonder how legislators will change regimes, or whether there is not such a thing as honest persuasion. But presumably a legislator is not so much going to be changing a regime as helping those already in control to set up the regime they want, or that he can persuade them to want. He will thus use his persuasion honestly, in order to convince them both what regime to want and how best to set it up. Such would be the case if he set up a democracy for the needy or an oligarchy for the well-off, but it would also be the case if, having been asked by both sides to set up an equal regime, he were to set up a polity or middle regime, for such is the only regime that is equal between well-off and needy.[30] But if the legislator uses persuasion to set up a different regime from the one wanted, then his persuasion will be deceit.

1304b17   The final sentence looks like a repetition of the one just given (at 1304b5–7),[31] but it differs in that this one concludes the whole discussion from chapter 1 while the earlier one concludes the discussion from chapter 3 only.

---

29. The oligarchy of the so-called 400 seized power at Athens in 411.

30. Solon might be a case in point, 2.12.1274a15–21, 3.11.1281b25–38, 6(4).11.1297a2–6. See also *Athēnaiōn Politeia* 5–12.

31. As is supposed by Barker (1946: 214 n1) and Newman (4:332).

Chapter 5

~ DESTRUCTION OF REGIMES IN PARTICULAR

~ DESTRUCTION OF DEMOCRACIES

1304b19 Having discussed the origins and causes of change in general, Aristotle must now study, in the light of them, by what sorts of ways or occasions these causes are brought into operation in each regime, or what sorts of things happen in each regime, so that faction and change actually occur.[32] He begins with the deviant regimes and ends with the mixed regimes.

In the case of democracies pretty well all the changes are occasioned and caused by the licentious behavior of demagogues, whether these changes are from democracy into oligarchy, or into tyranny, or into more extreme democracy. The causes operative are, as becomes apparent, insolence, profit, honor, fear, contempt, superiority, and campaigning for votes. Demagogues engage in insolent pursuit of profit and honor in one way when they bring false accusations against the rich individually, and in another when they attack them by egging on the multitude in the assembly. Common fear thus forces the rich to combine, and then (along doubtless with contempt and resentment that such wickedness is winning honor) incites them to attack the democracy. Some demagogues, however, through the honor they thus win for themselves among the populace, will be incited by a sense of superiority to bid for tyranny.

1304b24 As examples of demagogues provoking change in these ways into oligarchy, Aristotle gives two where the revolt came from notables still in the city, Cos and Rhodes, and three where the revolt came from notables who had gone first into exile, Heraclea, Megara, and Cyme.[33] Summarizing, he says that demagogues were in each case responsible by wronging the notables and forcing them to combine. The aim of these demagogues is honor among the populace and gain, and they achieve both by attacking and seizing the property of the rich. The examples fit Aristotle's general analysis: change happens when, in situations of inequality (the notables oppressed by the populace), the unequal want equality (equality by ratio in the case of the notables), in honors or wealth or both (the notables want to keep their wealth and to get control of the regime), and are incited to act for what they want by one or more of the seven or eleven causes.

1305a7 All the examples so far are of democracy becoming oligarchy. The

---

32. If Aristotle does not include in the following chapters all the particular cases of change that are mentioned, if in passing, elsewhere in the *Politics*, as Newman notes (4:344–45, 364), we should perhaps recall that his aim is rather to speak of the principal causes of change, not of all of them simply, and especially, one presumes, not those that may be reduced to, or understood from, others, or that are occasions rather than causes; cf. 6(4).2.1289b22–26, 7(5).1.1301a19–25.

33. Little is known of these events; see Newman (4:336–38).

next ones are of democracy becoming tyranny, something that, however, happened more in the past than now. The reason is that the cause that incites to tyranny was present in the past but is not present now. This cause is superiority, and the ancient demagogues had this because they were generals on active service. Military readiness and skill combined with great honor from the populace were enough to make them feel that they deserved to seize, and could successfully seize, sole rule. More recent demagogues are only clever at speaking, and while this may give them a sense of superiority in the assembly, it will give them none in that control of arms which is indispensable for tyranny.

1305a15 Aristotle adds two further reasons for the greater frequency of tyranny in the past, but these refer, not to the *cause* inciting to tyranny, but to *occasions* for its operation.[34] The first such reason is the possession by individuals of great office, for anyone with such an office is in a perfect position to seize control, and all that will be needed to make him do so is a sense of superiority. The second reason is the smallness of the cities and the dispersion of the populace through the countryside, for to dominate a small and dispersed population is generally easier than to dominate a large and concentrated one. The tyrants, however, who won control from this cause and on these occasions were demagogues, as is evident from the fact that the trust they won from the people (which was part of their sense of superiority) they won by attacking the rich. So Peisistratus, Theagenes, and Dionysius all won trust and became tyrants in this way.[35]

1305a28 A final way in which democracy changes, and again because of demagogues, is when a more measured democracy becomes an ultimate democracy. This happens when the offices are elected by the populace, but there is no property qualification and anyone can be a candidate. Those, therefore, without property will not be able to win elections as the notables do, by generous acts of largesse, but only by flattering the populace and giving them control over the laws, which is the mark of ultimate democracy.[36] The cause of change here is demagogic campaigning for votes, not, as in the example given earlier (7(5).3.1303a13–16), because people change the regime in order to stop election campaigns, but because those having resort to such campaigns promise and effect changes in the regime in order to win and keep the popular vote. If there was a property qualification (as would be the case in polity), such demagoguery would be less likely. Aristotle, however, suggests as cure that the election be done by the populace in tribes and not en masse (see 6(4).14.1298a11–19, 15.1300a24–26). Demagoguery will then be harder because demagogues win by appealing to the whole populace through their

34. Newman (4:344) wrongly regards it as a cause.

35. Peisistratus became tyrant of Athens in 560; Theagenes was tyrant of Megara in the seventh century; Dionysius I of Syracuse became tyrant there in 405. See Newman (4:339–42).

36. Aristotle may be thinking of the sort of thing Pericles did at Athens; see *Athēnaiōn Politeia* 27.

class interest as the poor. But if the populace are divided into tribes they will feel more their local and particular ties, especially to this or that notable family, than their general class interest.

Chapter 6

〜 DESTRUCTION OF OLIGARCHIES

1305a37　In the case of the other deviant regimes, oligarchies, change here is of two main types, from those outside the regime and from those inside the regime (for democracies, unlike oligarchies, are subject to faction in both ways, 7(5).1.1302a8–13). Of the first there are again two types, from the populace or from some of the well-off who are excluded. For there are several kinds of oligarchy, and while all exclude the poor, some also exclude a part of the rich (namely all those oligarchies after the first and most measured kind).

So the first type of change from without is when the oligarchy wrongs the multitude. Here the causes are manifestly insolence and profit on the part of the rulers. These will incite the multitude against the regime and anyone will be able to perform the office of leader for them, though a leader from within the oligarchy will be even more effective, presumably because he will already be well known to the populace as well as used to occupying positions of authority over them. A democracy will thus come to take the place of the oligarchy. The example is Lygdamis at Naxos, though he also went on to change the democracy into a tyranny, incited no doubt by the sense of superiority he conceived from successfully leading the populace.[37]

The second type of change from without is when the populace are not wronged but the excluded, whether the rich or the populace, agitate for change, incited no doubt by the fact that others have all the honors and themselves none. So in the examples Aristotle gives from narrow oligarchies (the types where rule is confined to certain families and sons succeed to fathers), the well-off who are excluded first get older sons included with fathers and then younger sons too, but the change continues to polity in Massilia, to democracy in Istrus, to broad oligarchy in Heraclea.[38] Whether the intention at the beginning was to push these changes so far is unclear, but if some are claiming and winning shares in the honors of rule, others are likely to be incited to want the same for themselves too. In Cnidus the populace were presumably thus incited, and doubtless further incited by contempt at seeing the notables torn and weakened by faction. At all events they effected change to democracy. In Erythrae, by contrast, the mere fact that so few had the

37. Lygdamis became tyrant in 540; see Newman (4:346).

38. Massilia (modern Marseilles) is mentioned again later (8(6).7.1321a29); not much is known of events in Istrus and Heraclea. See Newman (4:347–49).

honors and so many were excluded was enough, even without internal faction and misrule, to incite the populace.[39]

1305b22 Of change from within the ruling oligarchy, there are again several types. The first is when some of the oligarchs resort to demagoguery, whether before the oligarchs themselves or before the people. Examples of the first are the Thirty and 400 at Athens, where Charicles and Phrynichus and their respective friends flattered the other oligarchs, persuading them to take control even against the laws.[40] The change would thus be making the oligarchy more extreme and the cause would be the sense of superiority on the part of the oligarchs, that they deserved to rule as tyrants. In both cases, however, the insolence of their rule incited a later change from without, when the populace reintroduced democracy.

Examples of demagoguery before the populace are when elections and court decisions are in the hands of those outside the regime, whether the middle or the populace, as at Larissa, Abydus, and Heraclea.[41] Then rival oligarchs, wishing to get the honors of office they see others having, or perhaps also regarding themselves as superior to others, seek election through giving favors to the electors, thus introducing change toward democracy and perhaps also to tyranny. Similar demagoguery before the populace also happens when some of the oligarchs are trying to narrow the oligarchy, for then those who see themselves deprived of honor and others more possessed of it have to appeal to the populace as the only source of help for regaining their position. Change here would also be toward democracy or to tyranny.

1305b39 A second type of change from within is when some of the oligarchs live riotously and waste their substance. Profligate oligarchs will find themselves excluded from honors because no longer having the necessary property assessment, and this will incite them to faction and change. For those who live riotously are unlikely to be held back by the thought that their loss is their own fault and in some sense just. They effect change in two ways. In one way they try at once to introduce change, and change into tyranny, whether for themselves or another (tyrants and their favorites are able to enjoy power and riotous living at

39. Not much is known of these events at Cnidus and Erythrae; see Newman (4:349–50).

40. The so-called Thirty tyrants ruled in Athens after the Peloponnesian War in 404–403, and the oligarchy of the 400 ruled there in 411; see Newman (4:350–51).

41. Not much is known of events at Larissa and Heraclea, but those at Abydus are probably to be dated to 411, when the Spartan admiral Lysander was setting up regimes based on oligarchical clubs; see Newman (4:351–54). One may note that here we have the closest parallels in the *Politics* to what goes on in modern liberal democracies (as we call them). For our rival political parties are sorts of oligarchical clubs (these parties must be rich, and must court the rich, in order to be able to finance election campaigns), and they compete with each other for election by playing the demagogue to the crowd. Recall that one form of change is when the kind of regime stays the same but those who control it differ (7(5).1.1301b10–13), which is exactly what happens when a different party comes to power after a modern election.

the same time). An obvious case is Hipparinus helping Dionysius get the tyranny in Syracuse. In Amphipolis Cleotimus used a more circuitous route, first bringing in settlers and then aiming at tyranny by exciting them against the well-off. In Aegina the attempt was made with the aid of foreign mercenaries.[42]

In another way the dissolute oligarchs first start stealing common funds (to recover both wealth and position), and then either they themselves form factions against the other oligarchs, doubtless through fear of being caught and punished, or their insolent behavior, connived at by the regime, incites others to do so. The causes here, then, are fear and insolence, but the occasion for their operation is disunity among the oligarchs. Where the oligarchs are united, these causes of change from within do not operate. Likemindedness among the rulers keeps them from mistreating each other and so from causes of change. Evidence is provided by Pharsalus where a narrow oligarchy has survived because they treat each other well.[43] The case of Erythrae, just mentioned (1305b18–22), might be added also, for this narrow oligarchy was also well run and it fell from without, not from internal disunity.

1306a12   A third type of change from within is when an oligarchy arises within the oligarchy. This happens when, among the few well-off who rule, even fewer possess the greatest offices, and these latter eventually exclude the former altogether. The example is Elis and the cause doubtless superiority, those in the great offices conceiving themselves to be too superior to share rule in any way at all.[44]

1306a19   A fourth type of change from within is because of problems with securing defense, and in both war and peace. In war their natural distrust of the populace compels the oligarchs to hire mercenaries and the leader or leaders of these mercenaries introduce tyranny or dynasty. The cause here is doubtless again superiority, for control of an armed force sufficient to master the city (and of a force that will follow their leader anywhere provided they are paid) is certainly a great superiority. So it was with Timophanes in Corinth.[45] Conversely, to avoid the risks of hiring mercenaries, the oligarchs enlist the support of the populace. But then this makes the populace grow disproportionately with respect to the oligarchs, for the populace now become responsible for protecting the city. Consequently they conceive themselves as deserving of shares in the regime and use the occasion of war as an opportunity to force such a concession from the oligarchs.

In peace, when the oligarchs need to secure themselves against possible attack

42. Hipparinus was a leading citizen of Syracuse whose daughter Dionysius eventually married; Amphipolis was mentioned earlier at 7(5).3.1303b2–3; Chares was an Athenian mercenary commander stationed in Corinth not far from Aegina in 367. See Newman (4:355–56).

43. Nothing much is known of Pharsalus in Aristotle's time, but earlier it had been racked by faction and was dependent on Macedon from the 350s; see Newman (4:357–58).

44. Not much is known for certain about these events at Elis; see Newman (4:358).

45. Timophanes became tyrant in 350 during Corinth's war with Argos; see Newman (4:359–60).

(from within and from without the city), but distrust each other, they hire mercenaries along with a neutral leader, one who will not favor one group of oligarchs more than the other. But he, sensing his superiority, uses his military strength to master both sides and becomes tyrant. Examples are Simus in Larissa and Iphiades in Abydus.[46]

1306a31 A fifth type of change from within is when oligarchs maltreat each other, as over marriages and lawsuits. The cases mentioned earlier (in chapter 4) are instances in point, as are also three other cases, in Eretria over a marriage and in Heraclea and Thebes over punishments for adultery.[47] In the last two cases outrage was added to the punishment, so the guilty parties would be all the keener to stir up faction as a result. The causes are insolence and honor, the dishonored or insolently treated being thus incited to faction and change.

1306b3 A sixth and last type of change from within is when some among the oligarchs resent the despotic way the oligarchy is acting. The cause here would again be insolence and honor, the resentful oligarchs thinking the others do not deserve the share of honor they have. The change might be into a broader oligarchy or into a different regime, as polity or democracy. Of the two examples, Chios and Cnidus, the latter was mentioned also in the case of overthrow from outside the regime (1305b12–18).[48] The two incidents may be different or perhaps the same, for it is not unlikely that some in a despotic oligarchy, especially if they resented the behavior of their colleagues, would sympathize with an attempt at change, even change into democracy, from those excluded. One of them might well have become the leader the populace chose for themselves.

1306b6 The final type of change is accidental and concerns the property qualifications for office. It would be especially true of the first kind of oligarchy (where everyone with the property qualification shares in the regime), but it would include other regimes where office goes with property qualifications, as in the case of polity in particular. So an initial property qualification high enough to make the regime an oligarchy of the few well-off or a polity of the middle becomes too low when the city grows in prosperity, either suddenly or over time, and all come to share in the regime instead of a definite some. The result would be a kind of democracy (the needy may now be well enough off to meet the old qualification, but they are still needy in comparison with the well-off). The reverse would doubtless also be true, democracies and polities becoming oligarchies, or oligarchies becoming narrower, if qualifications stay the same but prosperity decreases (cases noted later, at 7(5).8.1308a35–b10).

46. Simus brought Thessaly into subjection to Philip of Macedon in 342; not much is known of Iphiades. See Newman (4:360–61).

47. Not much is known of these events at Eretria, Heraclea, and Thebes; see Newman (4:362–63).

48. Events at Chios and Cnidus are not further known.

1306b16 So much completes Aristotle's review of faction and change in democracies and oligarchies. But since most of the changes he has noted in both cases have been into regimes of a different kind altogether, from oligarchy to democracy or tyranny and from democracy to oligarchy or to tyranny, he recalls, as he did at the end of the previous chapter, that change can also be within these kinds, as from democracy or oligarchy to more or less extreme forms of each.

Chapter 7

∿ DESTRUCTION OF MIXED REGIMES

1306b22 In the case of mixed regimes Aristotle first discusses cases of faction in aristocracies separately, and then discusses change and faction in both polities and aristocracies together. The particular case, however, of change in polities associated with property qualifications is not repeated, since it has only just been mentioned in the discussion of oligarchies. But there are in fact fewer occasions of faction and change in polities than in aristocracies, which reflects the greater stability of polities among all regimes other than the simply best (7(5).1.1302a13–15).

Aristocracy is prone to faction for the same reason oligarchy is, that few share the honors of rule. For while oligarchy and aristocracy differ with respect to who the few are (the well-off in oligarchy, the virtuous in aristocracy), both nevertheless give rule to few. Indeed, in the case of those so-called aristocracies that are really polities leaning to oligarchies, these few are the well-off. Aristotle notes five ways in which aristocracies thus suffer faction for their fewness, which ways divide, as in the case of oligarchies, into those from groups or individuals outside the regime (the first and third ways) and into those from individuals and groups inside the regime (the remaining three).

So the first way is when a group are excluded from honor who think themselves equally virtuous and so equally worthy of honor. The cause is honor which those excluded see others getting but not themselves. The example is from the Partheniae at Sparta who conceived of themselves as equal in virtue because equal in good birth with those who shared rule (the so-called Peers or Similars). The second way is when someone great and second to none in virtue is deprived of honors. Here probably both honor and superiority are at work. The example is Lysander and again in Sparta. The third way is when someone of a manly sort is altogether excluded from honor, where again superiority will also be at work (manliness comes from spirit, which is a superior thing, 4(7).7.1328a7). The example is Cinadon and again in Sparta. The fourth way is when there is a wide disparity between the well-off and the needy among those who share in the regime. The cause is perhaps dissimilarity (which would be particularly noticeable among a few), but also honor, if loss of wealth brings with it loss of shares in the regime, as it did in Sparta from where the example is again taken. The fifth way is when someone already great is able to make himself greater. The cause would be superiority and one of the examples is again from Sparta; the other is from Carthage.[49] That among all the examples given here only one comes from Carthage reflects the relative absence of faction already noted before as a sign of the excellence of its regime; that no example at all comes from Crete reflects only Cretan good fortune (2.10.1272a39–b1, b15–22; 11.1272b30–33).

1307a5 So much is peculiar to aristocracies among mixed regimes. As regards both aristocracies and polities together, what most destroys them is that they deviate from justice in the regime by not getting a noble mixture. The justice here must be the justice relative to these regimes, which is indeed not partial (as it is in democracy and oligarchy) but is nevertheless not the justice of the simply best regime (for the justice of mixed regimes lies in mixing what deviant regimes divide, and not in perfect virtue). Aristocracy differs from polity by mixing virtue (if of an imperfect sort) as well as democracy and oligarchy (though some, like Sparta, only aim to mix virtue and democracy). But they also differ in that aristocracies lean more toward oligarchy and polities more toward democracy. Hence, even in the absence of the problem of getting a noble mixture, the latter are more stable than the former. For the majority, toward which polities lean, are generally stronger and also more content to divide rule with the well-off. So they do not engage in faction themselves and are too strong for any who would form factions against them. The well-off, by contrast, are not only fewer but less content to divide rule with the mass of the middle and the needy. So when they have a superiority, as they do in most aristocracies, they try and use it in insolent fashion to get more for themselves. But insolence and profit are causes of change. Still, even polities will presumably fall if they lean too much toward the multitude.

1307a20 Mixed regimes, precisely as mixtures, can change in either way, toward or against the direction in which they are already leaning. They will change in the first way when each side uses its superiority to get more, being incited no doubt precisely by such superiority as well as by seeing others, the well-off or the needy, still having honors that they think undeserved. Mixed regimes will change in the second way when the superior side, by their insolence and their gaining more in wealth and profits, incites the other side to effect change in the opposite direction. The injustice and inequality here are manifest. For mixed regimes are supposed to be just and equal, not only relatively to themselves, but also relatively

---

49. The Partheniae were illegitimate sons of Spartan fathers or mothers or disenfranchised citizens at the time of the First Messenian War (eighth century); the Peers were the Spartiates, or full Spartan citizens; Cinadon's conspiracy at Sparta was in 398; the wide disparity between the well-off and the needy belongs to the Second Messenian War (seventh century); Hanno may be the Carthaginian general who fought against Dionysius I of Syracuse in about 400. See Newman (4:367–71).

to what makes regimes correct and deviant, by mixing the well-off and needy so that each has its own according to the merit of each. For, in the absence of some with perfect virtue, justice requires that rule be divided such that the multitude or populace, who have virtue as a multitude, should rule where their collective virtue makes them superior (in assembly and law courts), but that the notables, who have virtue as individuals, should rule where individual virtue makes them superior (in the offices, 3.11). So if these regimes deviate in either way, and give too much to poor or rich, they fail both to be correct regimes and to be properly mixed.

Aristotle gives an apt example from Thurii which is a case of a mixed regime changing in one direction and then in the other and then back again in the first.[50] It was, to begin with, a regime leaning too much toward oligarchy, for it had the offices chosen on the basis of a high property qualification. So an attempt was made to correct the imbalance and to shift the regime in the direction of democracy by lowering the qualification and increasing the number of available places among the offices. But the notables, incited no doubt by seeing themselves deprived of accustomed honors, nullified the effect of this by using the existing oligarchical imbalance of the regime, albeit in transgression of the law, to buy up the land and so to prevent anyone else acquiring even the lower amount of property to qualify for office. The populace then in their turn, incited by the insolence and gains of the notables, countered by the direct use of force, defeating the oligarchic garrisons and forcing the notables to disgorge their gains. The result was thus presumably democracy, or a more democratic polity.

The problem in Thurii was the notables getting too much for themselves, and, in illustration of how this is a general problem for aristocracies, Aristotle mentions Sparta and Locri where there was similarly too much in the hands of the notables. In Sparta oligarchic gains (as recorded in 2.9) eventually weakened the city so much that it could not resist foreign invasion. In Locri the oligarchs, presumably in pursuit of gain and, because of the imbalance in the regime, acting unchecked, allowed a dangerous marriage alliance with a tyrant, which eventually led to tyranny over the city by the son born of the marriage. A regime that was better mixed, whether polity or aristocracy, would have kept the notables under more control and would not have been keener to have a wealthy connection than to avoid a dangerous one.[51]

1307a40 A second way in which mixed regimes change is little by little. This is in fact a cause of change common to all regimes, but Aristotle says it particularly escapes notice in the case of aristocracies. Perhaps the reason is that

50. Thurii was mentioned earlier at 7(5).3.1303a31–33, but whether the two events are the same or not is disputed; see Newman (4:372–73).

51. In the 350s Locri was under the tyranny of Dionysius II, son of Dionysius I by a Locrian woman; see Newman (4:374–76).

aristocracy is not only a mixed regime but a regime that is more narrowly based. For a small change in any mixture, even a polity, is likely to have a larger effect sooner than in an unmixed regime, but all the more so when the mixture in the regime embraces fewer people anyway. So once a small change is allowed, it quickly becomes a bigger one as those who profited by the change take full advantage of it.

The example he gives is again from Thurii[52] and the small thing is not, as in the example he gave earlier, when a low property qualification is dispensed with that brings with it a significant change in customs (7(5).3.1303a20–25), but when a first and small change is allowed that makes it harder to resist further and greater changes. The causes in Thurii were superiority and contempt on the part of young and successful generals, who began by using their military strength to abrogate a certain law limiting tenure of the generalship. This might have seemed a small thing since abrogation of the law did not guarantee repeated tenure but only allowed it, and since the expectation was that no other changes would be made. The generals, however, being in possession of the army and assured of keeping possession because of their popularity among the voters, could no longer be resisted by the other rulers and, contrary to what these rulers had assumed, introduced more changes until the regime became a dynasty of themselves and their collaborators.

1307b19 This completes the discussion of change in mixed regimes and also, at the same time, of change in all the particular regimes. A final remark is added that is common to all these particular regimes and which, therefore, might have been mentioned earlier, but it is perhaps reserved until now because it does not concern changes that come from within the city (whether inside or outside the regime). It concerns something external and accidental, when another regime is nearby or powerful that is opposed to the existing regime and can use its power or its nearness to overthrow that regime, as the Athenians and Spartans did to oligarchies and democracies respectively.[53] Knowledge of this cause will obviously not add to the understanding of faction, change, and their causes insofar as these causes belong to the inner structure of regimes. So it will reveal nothing about the stability of regimes or about how to set them up in as stable a way as possible. The cause nevertheless exists and needs noting, for a prudent legislator might have to counsel against establishing a certain kind of regime in circumstances where such an external cause of change was operative.

52. Of these events, and of how they do, or do not, tie in with those about Thurii just mentioned, not much is known for certain; see Newman (4:376–77).

53. The Athenians did this during their naval empires in the fifth and fourth centuries, and the Spartans during their empire after the Peloponnesian War; see Newman (4:378–79). An obvious modern parallel would be what was done over most of the globe during the decades following the Second World War by the United States and its allies on the one hand, and by the Soviet Union and its allies on the other.

Chapter 8

1307b26 Having dealt with what destroys regimes, both in general and in particular, Aristotle comes next to what preserves them, both in general and in particular. But, as is his wont, he reverses the order and, as becomes apparent, discusses first what preserves regimes in particular (chapter 8) and second what preserves them in general (chapter 9). He takes as principle of his discussion that to have the causes of destruction of regimes is thereby also to have the causes of preservation. The reason is straightforward, that opposites are produced by opposites and preservation and destruction of regimes are opposites. Consequently, since we already know how regimes are destroyed in particular, all it should be necessary to do to find out how to preserve them in particular is to go back over their particular ways of destruction one by one and look for the opposites. Aristotle does in fact do just that, but again in reverse order. However, the reverse order does not exactly mirror the original order because some of the particular destructions, listed in different places for different regimes, are opposed by the same or similar sorts of preservation. Hence, for ease and logic of exposition, all these ways of destruction are taken and discussed together, regardless of their original order.[54]

1307b30 The last destruction listed was the extrinsic one of overthrow by foreign and opposed regimes. But there is nothing a legislator can do about such extrinsic causes, or nothing over and above making the regime able to resist attack by strengthening it as much as possible from within. Hence Aristotle passes at once to the next destruction in reverse order, when mixed regimes, aristocracies in particular, are destroyed little by little. For this does come from within and is therefore something the legislator can be expected to counter. The first preservation Aristotle proposes, then, is the opposite of this destruction: do not ignore small changes but guard against them. In particular do not be swayed, as the joint counselors in Thurii were swayed, by the argument that a small thing can be ignored because it is small. For this argument is actually a fallacy, the fallacy of composition, that the whole must be small because the parts that make it up are small. But this is patently false, as is shown by the examples of a ruinous total expense and of the whole universe, both of which are big though they are made up of small things. The same happens in the case of laws (constitutional laws), and a small change here followed by another there can soon lead to the big thing of the

---

54. Newman (4:569–70) carefully records how Aristotle's recommendations for preserving regimes generally respond to the ways they are destroyed. He says nothing, however, about their ordering. Polansky, in Keyt and Miller (1991: 338–39), says the ordering is according to practicality, but if so it seems to be incidental. Note that Barker (1946: 224–29) numbers ten means of preservation instead of twelve, as I do. He takes together my numbers 8 and 9 and my numbers 11 and 12. This difference does not seem to be of much moment.

laws being disregarded generally and, hence, to the overthrow of the regime that rests on these laws. So the legislator should make sure, perhaps precisely by teaching this piece of logic, that no one with control in well-mixed regimes should allow even small changes to the laws but keep the regime the way it is.

1307b40 The second preservation is opposite to the next destruction, when mixed regimes deviate from justice by being badly mixed. The solution here is instead to balance both sides in the mixture, the well-off and the needy, and not to trust to sophistries that, while appearing to give a balance, actually give one side too much, especially the well-off (regimes that lean toward the few well-off are less stable than those that lean toward the multitude of the needy). These sophistries, both oligarchic and democratic, were listed before, as was also how to combine them to produce a mixture that is noble (6(4).9,13).

1308a3 The third preservation is opposite to the destruction that came first in the preceding chapter, when aristocracies suffer change because few share in the honors of office. Preservation here, however, cannot be by sharing out the honors more broadly, for that would not preserve these regimes but change them into polity or democracy. Rather it must be by not making the narrowness irksome to the excluded or a temptation to the included, which will be secured if, as Aristotle says, those in office treat the excluded and each other well. But since this way of destruction is common to oligarchies too (for aristocracies are like oligarchies in being rule by a few), the preservation opposite to it responds to several of the ways oligarchies change (from chapter 6), as notably when the oligarchy is too despotic—which is (ii)(f) in the summary to my translation—when an oligarchy arises within the oligarchy (ii)(c), when oligarchs play the demagogue (ii)(a), when an oligarchy excludes many notables (i)(b), or when it wrongs the multitude (i)(a).

So, with respect to those excluded from the regime: none of these should be wronged; anyone with the quality of a leader should be brought into it (as Cinadon in Sparta, for example, though to include more than these few would be dangerous and shift the regime toward democracy); the ambitious should not be wronged through dishonor (as the Partheniae, and perhaps also Lysander, in Sparta); nor should the many be wronged through being robbed or deprived of profit (as they usually are in oligarchies). With respect to those inside the regime: the rulers should treat each other in a popular or democratic way, for among equals equal shares are beneficial and just (and the members of a ruling body, even in aristocracies and oligarchies, are equal with each other). Hence, to ensure that all can take part equally, democratic practices, like having offices of short tenure (and perhaps also preventing property getting too unevenly distributed), should be adopted. This would in particular prevent dynasties, as well as the sort of bids at tyranny made by Pausanias and Hanno. Proof is furnished by the fact that in ultimate oligarchies and democracies bids at tyranny are made by those who are in office a long time.

1308a24   The fourth preservation, getting people to keep more of a hold on the regime by making them afraid for its survival, may be prompted by the consideration that regimes can be overthrown by an opposed regime that is nearby,[55] but it is hardly a defense against such overthrow (the only sure defense would be a more powerful army). It seems rather to be a continuation of what Aristotle has just been saying. For insolence and superiority are what mainly cause people in power to abuse those outside and inside the regime, and fear opposes insolence and the sense of being superior. Moreover, those who are afraid for their regime will be especially vigilant against abuses, and above all against abuses whose only effect would be to increase the number of enemies.

1308a31   The fifth preservation, preventing rivalries and factions among the notables, opposes a destruction of oligarchy, namely factions over marriages and lawsuits—(ii)(e) from chapter 6—which is not next in reverse order. The destruction is, however, closely connected with, or rather part of, the one under discussion and would to a large extent be countered by the same policy, for notables afraid of losing the regime will fall into factions and rivalries less. The additional policy proposed here, preventing such rivalries and factions by means of the laws, is to the same effect but specifically designed to make the prevention institutional and not dependent on the presence of an able politician. For able politicians are not guaranteed in any regime save the simply best, and to ensure something like good rule in their absence laws must be put in control instead.

1308a35   The sixth preservation, changing property qualifications to accord with changing prosperity, opposes the destruction of oligarchy which is next in reverse order—(iii) from chapter 6—when oligarchies, and polities, change toward democracy or dynasty because the property qualifications remain the same but overall wealth does not. The solution is the obvious but necessary one of having regular reviews of the state of the city's prosperity, combined with a law requiring property qualifications to rise or fall so that the same parts of the city retain control and neither too few nor too many are admitted to office.

1308b10   The seventh preservation, not to magnify anyone with honors beyond proportion, is opposite principally to the destruction of oligarchies when one person has control of mercenaries in war and peace—(ii)(d) from chapter 6—which is next in reverse order. For the two prior to it—faction over marriages and lawsuits (ii)(e), and when the oligarchy is too despotic (ii)(f)—were dealt with under the third, fourth, and fifth preservations above. But it is also opposite to destruction in oligarchies when an oligarchy arises within the oligarchy, (ii)(c), and indeed to any destruction in any regime that comes from someone possessed of great honors, as generals who are demagogues in democracies, and people like Lysander and Pausanias in aristocracies. The answer here is not to give anyone

55. As Barker suggests (1946: 226 n1).

such great honors quickly (as by sudden elevation to total command of armies and navies), or if this cannot be avoided, not to give and take away great honors quickly (contrary to what happened in the case of Lysander); also to prevent, by the laws, the rise of men superior in power, friends, or money (as, say, by laws limiting property acquisition and the indiscriminate bestowal of gifts), or failing that, to send them abroad (as on foreign missions or by ostracism).

1308b20 The eighth preservation, an office to watch against those whose private lives are contrary to the regime, is opposite to the same destruction, when someone is far superior in wealth and friends (and whether in oligarchies or democracies). It is also opposite to the next destruction in oligarchies (ii)(b), when some oligarchs squander their private property in riotous living. For all such persons are living in ways dangerous to the regime. An office specially deputed to watching out for them would help nip things in the bud before they went too far.

1308b24 But a part of the city might also become superior to the other parts in the way that an individual can (through some special success or prosperity), and its success can likewise take on a political significance. It would in particular do so through the agency of demagogues who play on the differences between the parts of the city to win control for themselves, and demagogues in oligarchies are the next cause of destruction in reverse order, (ii)(a) in chapter 6. Demagogues operate the same way in democracies so this ninth kind of preservation will apply to democracies too. It will, in addition, apply to destruction coming from the success or disproportionate increase of a part, several cases of which were mentioned in chapter 4 and chapter 3. No such cases were mentioned in the previous three chapters, perhaps because they are not peculiar to any one regime. These cases are appropriate here nevertheless, partly because the present context is about preventing destruction from superiority, and partly because demagogues play on the differences between parts.

The cure here could hardly be by expelling whole parts of the city (as one can expel superior individuals); it could only be by trying to prevent parts winning success by themselves. So, if the parts were associated jointly in public acts and in the offices, the success of one part, say in battle, would at the same time be the success of others; or if the parts were somehow mixed together,[56] the prosperity of one part would easily get spread to the others; or if the middle was increased, the extremes of rich and poor would become correspondingly small and the city less easily split into opposed and hostile parts. These proposals might seem to work rather by changing democracies and oligarchies into polities than by preserving them as democracies and oligarchies. But that need not be so, for populace and

---

56. Newman (4:394) mentions intermarriage among other things. One might add the combining of well-off and needy in tribes and clans so that local ties and interests would be stronger than those of class.

well-off can retain control of a regime, through retaining control of the deliberative, without having to use their control to attack and oppress others.

1308b31   The tenth preservation, arranging things so that profit cannot be made from office, is opposed mainly to destruction happening to oligarchies because they wrong the multitude, which is the first, (i)(a), from chapter 6, and the next in reverse order. For the destruction prior to it—(i)(b), when oligarchies exclude some of the well-off—was effectively covered earlier, especially in the third preservation. This preservation would also oppose the way demagogues use their control over democratic assemblies to steal and confiscate the possessions of the well-off. It would, however, be particularly beneficial in oligarchies, since the needy are less concerned about honors than about wealth (their poverty makes getting money a daily need). So if office is not a source of gain for the officeholder, the needy will be content to be without it and so content to put up with an oligarchy. Otherwise they will be irked and want a share in office too, though not so much because of the honor as because of the gain.

But while this means of preservation will be beneficial in particular to oligarchies, its main advantage is that it will make possible the combination of democracy and aristocracy (a combination which Sparta aimed at, though with many faults). If the needy have the right to office, they will have democracy, and if they gladly forgo office to be busy about their own affairs the notables will fill the offices and so they will have aristocracy. Thus both sides will get what they want and the inequalities that separately mar democracy and oligarchy will be removed. For the notables will not suffer in honor by being ruled by their inferiors, and the needy will not suffer in wealth by being robbed by their rulers. Indeed the needy will be able to rise up toward the ranks of the well-off if they are prepared to work hard. The effect will be to enlarge the middle and so to stabilize the regime as more of the needy become prosperous.

One particular condition for achieving this democratic aristocracy, or aristocratic democracy, is to ensure that there is no theft of common funds. The way to do this is to hand over and record the common funds in a way that the populace can readily monitor—for then no magistrate will be able to steal or any who do can easily be caught and prosecuted. Another condition is that rule not be undertaken for profit. The way to do this is to lay down laws that give special honors to those with a reputation for virtue (and of course the best way to get such a reputation is actually to be virtuous). For, by making virtue and not wealth the object of honor (a fault with the regime of the Carthaginians, 2.11.1273a37–b1), both notables and needy will be induced to care about virtue and so the first will be encouraged to rule well and the second to choose those who will rule well.

1309a14   The last two preservations, the eleventh and twelfth, oppose, as did the previous one, the first of the ways in which oligarchies are destroyed, namely because the oligarchs wrong the multitude. But they also oppose all the three ways in which democracies are destroyed discussed in chapter 5, namely demagogues, by their license, inciting the notables to revolt, demagogues seizing tyranny by winning popular support through their attacks on the well-off, and demagogues putting the populace in control of the laws. For these last two preservations both concern treating well, instead of badly, the excluded part of the city (the needy in oligarchies and the well-off in democracies). So, as regards the eleventh, the well-off should be spared in democracies and not impoverished, either directly by having their property or incomes stolen, or indirectly by being allowed, or even encouraged, to spend lavishly on useless public services (as opposed, say, to useful ones like equipping a trireme or decorating a temple).[57] Conversely, the needy should be specially cared for in oligarchies: they should have access to offices that have an income, the well-off who treat them insolently should be more severely punished, and inheritances should be spread about and not concentrated in a few hands. The effect will be to keep properties more on a level (so that few of the rich become either exceedingly rich or poor, both of which things stimulate to faction), to prevent acts of insolence becoming causes of faction, and to increase the numbers of the needy who will rise, by industry or marriage, into the ranks of the middle. Thus, by these means, the hostilities between the well-off and the needy naturally incident to oligarchies and democracies will be much reduced.

1309a27 The twelfth preservation continues the same policy, but this time with respect to equalizing rather the distribution of the honors of office than the distribution of wealth. So provided the ruling body in each regime keeps the controlling offices in its own hands (for otherwise the regime will be destroyed instead of preserved), it can afford to allow those outside the regime to be equal or even superior in the remaining and lesser offices.

One notes about this piece of advice, as indeed about all the advice Aristotle gives throughout this and the next book, that it is expressly designed to mitigate the faults and inequalities in each regime as much as possible while still preserving that regime as the regime it is. For regimes are defined and distinguished from each other by which part of the city, well-off or needy or virtuous (and the several sorts of each), has control; they are not defined by how well or badly those in control treat those who are excluded.[58] A regime, therefore, even of a deviant sort can stay the regime it is while still doing a great deal, by measured policies and behavior, to lessen the causes of its destruction.

---

57. Newman (4:399) suggests equipping a trireme as a useful expense. He also notes that the (useless) expense of equipping a chorus could be as much as, or even exceed, 3,000 drachmas, which is 3,000 times the daily wage.

58. A point that Mulgan (1977: 133–38) fails to weigh sufficiently and thence concludes, wrongly, that Aristotle's ways of preserving regimes, because they are ways of making these regimes less badly behaved, are really ways of changing them into regimes of a different kind; cf. Miller (1995: 306–7).

Chapter 9

1309a33 Aristotle comes next to preservations that are of a more general sort and are not taken by way of opposition to the particular destructions listed for each regime.[59] They are taken rather by way of opposition to the fundamental origin of change mentioned at the beginning (7(5).1), the desire for equality, whether just or unjust, in cases of inequality, whether real or supposed. Preserving a regime requires keeping rule in its existing distribution against the resentments of those who want a different and, as they think, more equal distribution. But to keep rule in its existing distribution is, as has in effect just been said at the end of the preceding chapter, to keep the controlling offices in the right hands, which means both in the hands of those who are fit to rule and in the hands of those who come from the ruling body, or from the part of the city proper to each regime.

So the first way of keeping rule in the right hands concerns fitness to rule. Those in the controlling offices should possess three things: friendliness to the regime, ability, and the virtue relative to the regime. Friendliness and ability are obviously necessary so that the rulers will want and be able to do what is required to preserve the regime. Virtue is necessary, as Aristotle explains shortly, so that they will actually do what they want and can do, and will not be swayed by lack of control over their passions. But the virtue in question is to be taken in a broad sense to mean the habit relative to the justice that defines each particular regime (whether this justice is complete or only partial). It is not virtue in the proper sense of the habit relative to the common good, the true end of human life, and which distinguishes the correct from the deviant regimes (cf. 3.6). Two questions arise, however, about these three qualities, one as to which is to be preferred, and another as to whether and how the third is really necessary.

As regards the first question, a particular person may have ability for one of the controlling offices, that of general for instance, but be lacking in justice and friendliness, while another may have the justice and friendliness but be lacking in ability. The solution about how to make the choice, says Aristotle, is to keep an eye on two things, which quality everyone has more a share of and which they have less a share of. So, in the case of generalship, everyone has less in the way of ability but more in the way of virtue (few people know much about how to lead an army, but most are reasonably patriotic), and one should look rather to the former than the latter. In the case of the treasury, by contrast, it is the reverse, and one should look rather to virtue than ability (few people are very trustworthy when it comes to large sums of public monies, but most know how to do necessary accounting).

---

59. As Barker (1946: 230 n1) expressly notes.

Aristotle speaks of looking both to what everyone has less a share of and to what they have more a share of, so his advice does not seem to be that one should choose a general who is conspicuously lacking in justice and friendliness or a treasurer who is conspicuously lacking in ability. Such a choice would clearly be foolish, since the first would likely destroy the regime by force and the second by bankruptcy. Rather Aristotle must be saying that one should look to the quality everyone has less a share of, so that if one finds someone with that quality to a sufficient (but above average) degree, one is likely to have found someone who also has the other qualities to a sufficient degree; whereas if one finds someone with a sufficiency of a quality that everyone has more a share of, then one is not likely to have found someone who has a sufficiency of the quality that everyone has less a share of. But if, contrary to expectation, one finds someone with a sufficiency of the quality that everyone has less a share of and an insufficiency or a lack of the other qualities, then one should not choose him either but rather someone who has all qualities, even if he has the rarer to a lesser degree.[60]

As regards the second question, whether virtue is necessary if friendliness and ability are present, the answer is straightforward. People who are able and have a proper love for themselves can, because of weakness of will, fail actually to do what will serve their own interests and what they know they should do and what they really want to do (their passions make them do the opposite). So if people can be weak-willed when serving their own interests, they can also be weak-willed when serving the common interest of the city. Hence, as virtue is needed in the first case, so must it be in the other as well.

1309b14 The second and also the remaining two ways of keeping rule in the right hands concern how to keep it in the hands of the relevant ruling body (the populace, the well-off, the virtuous). So, the second way is to make use of the laws, the constitutional laws, for setting up regimes that were explained at the end of the last book, namely the several ways in which the parts of the regime can be set up and what arrangement fits what regime.[61] For a democracy will obviously be preserved by laws that give control to the populace and overthrown by those that

60. Newman (4:404) suggests that it might be better to look for the most indispensable quality rather than the rarest, as wisdom, say, in a confessor rather than piety. But Aristotle is talking of cases where all qualities are equally indispensable and where one of them is harder to find than another and so needs more looking out for. Should there be nobody found who has all three qualities, even to a moderate degree, then the city will be in a parlous state, though such a situation is not likely to arise often.

61. Some take the reference to laws here to be a vague and general one, or to be to everything Aristotle says about preserving regimes, or to be to a separate catalog of laws; see Barker (1946: 231), Jowett (1885: 2:213), Newman (1:537 n2, 4:405). But a reference specifically to 6(4).14–16 would seem to make most sense in the context.

give control to the well-off. But even getting the right laws for the regime will not help if the regime does not fit the city where it is. So Aristotle recalls, in addition, his oft repeated principle that the regime be favored by the stronger multitude, or, in other words, that control in each city be in the hands of those who are dominant in that city, and that a democracy, say, not be imposed where the well-off are stronger or an oligarchy where the needy are. If this principle is not observed, the regime stands little chance of surviving long, however well set up it is in other respects.

1309b18   The third way of keeping rule in the right hands (relative to the regime, of course) concerns the principle not to neglect the mean or the middle. This advice applies above all to the deviant regimes of democracy and oligarchy. For here the tendency of democrats and of oligarchs alike is to think that the only virtue is to go to excess (the excess of everything to the needy or everything to the well-off), and to embrace all the apparently democratic things and all the apparently oligarchic things. But that virtue here, as elsewhere, lies in the mean and not the excess or the extremes, Aristotle shows by resorting, in his drily humorous fashion, to an analogy taken from something even democrats and oligarchs cannot fail to notice, their own noses. For a nose that departs from being straight can still have a certain beauty, but if it goes too far it will not only become ugly, it will even cease to be a nose. So it is with democracy and oligarchy. These too are deviations from what is best (as has been amply proved, 3.9–13), and hence while they too can, like noses, be in reasonable enough condition if they do not go too far, they will, if pushed to extremes, become intolerable and destroy themselves.

The solution, then, is to distinguish between those (apparently) democratic and oligarchic things that destroy democracies and oligarchies and those that preserve them, and to adopt the latter but reject the former. In explanation, Aristotle notes that neither democracy nor oligarchy can exist and last without both the well-off and the multitude, but that when a leveling of substance occurs, the regime in question must necessarily be different (1309b38–1310a1). The meaning of this I take to be that, to survive, each regime must preserve within itself something of its opposing part. For a regime made up wholly of the many poor, or wholly of the few rich, would cease to be a regime (just as a nose pushed to either extreme would cease to be a nose). For a city is a self-sufficient multitude, but many poor will not be self-sufficient (they will lack resources), and few rich will not be a multitude (they will be too small to perform all the tasks necessary to a city). Democrats, however, would, by pushing things to an extreme, level substances by destroying the well-off and making everyone poor. For democrats and demagogues in particular, are good at taking and spending others' wealth but not at making or preserving it, so that when they destroy the well-off they do not make the needy rich, except temporarily (2.7.1267a41–b5, 8(6).5.1320a29–b2), but rather destroy the only source of future revenues.[62] Likewise, oligarchs would level substances by destroying the needy and leaving behind only the well-off (for oligarchs want to take from the needy even the little that the needy have), so that the well-off would have no one to labor, or be craftsmen, or work the land from which their own wealth comes.[63] Hence, in both cases, the regime in question must necessarily be different, that is, it must necessarily no longer be a regime, because by destroying its opposite with democratic or oligarchic laws carried to excess (laws that combine all the democratic or all the oligarchic things), it has truncated itself and no longer has all the parts needed to survive.[64] Consequently it must be in the interests of both regimes to adopt laws that will protect their opposing parts instead of attacking and destroying them.[65] Such laws alone will be truly oligarchic and democratic, however much oligarchs and democrats may think otherwise.

1310a2 Thus it is an error on the part of demagogues in democracies always to fight against the well-off; they should instead always seem to be speaking on their behalf. Democrats cannot, of course, really speak on behalf of the well-off, for then they would have to give up democracy in favor of polity (only in polity would the well-off have the share in rule they deserve). They can, however, seem to do so, by defending them against attacks and prosecutions in assembly and law courts, and by thus preserving them for continued service to the democracy. Likewise oligarchs cannot really speak on behalf of the populace (for, again, only

62. It is a case of killing the goose that lays the golden egg. Socialists and Communists in our own day have not seldom been guilty of a like folly, when they attack economic entrepreneurs and encourage thieves and sycophants.

63. Socialists and Communists in our own day have been guilty of this folly too, since they so oppress and discourage the multitude that these are no longer willing, or able, to do the hard work necessary to keep the national economy flourishing.

64. Barker (1946: 232 n3) understands Aristotle to mean by leveling of substance the equalizing of properties, so that everyone will be in the middle and none at the extremes. But the implication of this understanding is that the regimes of democracy and oligarchy become different because they become polities, and this conflicts with the context. For polities are regimes and, indeed, better regimes, but the present context is about how democracies and oligarchies, when pushed to extremes, become worse regimes and in the end no regimes at all (1309b33–35).

65. Newman (4:276) thinks it inconsistent of Aristotle to recognize that an increase in the numbers of the wealthy can be fatal to democracies (7(5).3.1303a10–13) and not to admit, with many democrats, that it would therefore be wise for democracies to thin the numbers of the rich and impoverish them; and cf. also Mulgan (1977: 135, 137). But Aristotle answers that complaint here, for the fact that one extreme (too many wealthy) will destroy the democracy does not mean that the other extreme (killing or impoverishing the wealthy) will save it. Rather both extremes will destroy democracy and only the mean will save it. Tyranny alone, it would appear, can survive through extremism, by attacking and enslaving everybody. For tyrants are not so much one part of the city relying on another part, and needing the whole city to be in some sense prosperous to survive, as a hostile presence despoiling the whole city and surviving on the aid of foreigners (7(5).11.1313a34–1314a12).

in polity would the populace have the share in rule they deserve), but they can seem to be speaking on behalf of the populace, particularly by swearing oaths opposite to those they now do swear. At any rate, whether seeming or not, both democrats and oligarchs would thus preserve their regimes by preserving, as well as their deviant regimes permit, the necessary, if opposed, part of the city. For both these regimes are really sorts of mastery over slaves (3.6.1279a19–21), but then, like any master, they must take care of their slaves if they want to go on receiving the benefit of their slaves' service (3.6.1278b32–37).

1310a12   The fourth, and last, way of keeping rule in the right hands (relative to the regime) picks up from the previous three, and in particular from the first. For it is a way of ensuring that all those in the ruling body (and not just those who occupy some particular office) have the character appropriate to the regime. For it is no use laying down even the most beneficial laws, such as laws about not harming the well-off in a democracy or the multitude in an oligarchy, if people do not keep them. But people will not keep them if they have not been trained to keep them, and trained above all to resist threats or temptations to do otherwise (for as one individual can be weak-willed, so can all the individuals who constitute a city). There is special need, then, in every regime for an education to that regime so that people will actually do what the preservation of the regime requires.

1310a19   But there is an error here similar to the error about observing the mean. For just as extremism appeared to be, but was not, beneficial to regimes, since it destroys regimes, so doing whatever the ruling body wishes appears to be, but is not, education to the regime, since it too destroys regimes. Truly democratic and oligarchic education must, like truly democratic and oligarchic actions and policies, be that which enables democrats and oligarchs to go on ruling. So it is not oligarchic education to have the sons of the well-off live in luxury and to have the sons of the needy exercised in hard work. For this will make the first inferior and contemptible and the second superior and contemptuous, and superiority and contempt are causes of overthrow of regimes. Rather, then, must oligarchic education be to have the sons of the well-off live under more restraint and with more training and discipline than the sons of the needy.

Likewise it is not democratic education for the populace to live in the way they do in democracies that seem to be the most democratic, that is, deciding and doing everything they wish regardless of its effect on the survival of the regime. The facts, again, that such democracies provoke their own overthrow would prove there was an error here, but the error itself, that democracy is when everyone lives as they wish, arises from a false understanding of freedom. For since freedom is standardly used to define democracy, a false understanding of freedom must necessarily lead to a false understanding of democracy. Democracy, of course, is properly speaking rule by the needy, but democrats define it in terms of majority control and freedom. For democrats claim that rule by the majority is just on the basis of freedom.

They argue, in fact, more or less as follows: (1) justice is equality; (2) equality is that whatever seems right to the multitude is in control; (3) therefore justice is that whatever seems right to the multitude is in control. Aristotle has already explained (in 3.9–13) the errors in this reasoning: the first premise fails because justice is equality only for equals but inequality for unequals, and because freedom, which democrats assume is that which makes all equal, is not the real title to shares in rule but rather virtue is; the second premise fails because rule by the majority is not equality but superiority for the populace. But explaining these errors again is not Aristotle's concern here. His concern rather is what he says next, that freedom and equality, or all being equal in freedom, are understood by democrats as doing whatever one wants (to do as one does not want seems rather the mark of the slave than the free). For, because of this definition, premise (1) comes to mean that justice is doing whatever one wants, and hence the conclusion (3) comes to mean that doing whatever one wants is what it is for the multitude, or for what seems right to the multitude, to be in control. Consequently justice, and the democracy based on it, come to mean each and all of the multitude doing whatever they want, which is in fact how people do end up living in such democracies.[66]

That this is base is manifest, because it means that any decision counts as just provided the populace agree that it is what they want. But the populace could not only agree to want great injustice (as robbing the well-off, 3.10.1281a14–17), they could also agree to want things that destroy democracy, as in particular provoking oligarchs against them and exciting the ambitions of tyrants. They could also agree to want things beneficial to democracy but fail to do them through weakness of will. For those who do whatever they want must be chronically weak-willed, since they will do whatever they want when they want it, even if not what they wanted earlier and not what they will have wanted later—which is what is meant by weakness of will. In short, if justice and freedom are the multitude doing whatever they want, and if the multitude doing whatever they want includes the multitude doing what will destroy the rule of the multitude, then justice and freedom are doing what will destroy justice and freedom, which is absurd. Accordingly, justice

66. Mulgan, in Harris (1970: 105), complains that this is an inaccurate description of democracies because few, if any, democrats advocated the complete absence of coercive rules to prevent people doing whatever they wanted. But Aristotle is not denying that democracies, even ultimate democracies, have coercive rules, for, on the contrary, he is asserting here that the majority decide things and that these decisions are in control, that is, get imposed on everyone. What he is saying is that democracies decide any rules they like, including especially rules that, when coercively imposed on everyone, lead to their own overthrow. His advice is that democrats should exercise restraint instead and not decide any rules they like, but only those that will not destroy the regime.

and freedom in democracy cannot be understood as the multitude doing whatever they want. They must rather be understood as the multitude doing whatever will preserve the democracy, including especially the getting and imposing of an education to the regime, and the not doing of whatever they, or their passions, may want. Such subordination to the regime is not slavery, as democrats may complain, but safety, for it preserves to the multitude control over the regime. And control over the regime is, even by their own confession, the condition of their freedom, without which they would be slaves. They should accordingly define freedom, not as each doing whatever he wants, but as each doing whatever is necessary, and each being educated to do whatever is necessary, for the preservation of the regime.[67]

1310a36   So much, then, concerns the destruction and preservation of regimes. But one might wonder how practical Aristotle's many pieces of advice actually are, or whether and to what extent democrats and oligarchs in particular might come to be persuaded to adopt them. There is no reason in principle that they should not come to do so, for none of the advice requires them to abandon control, or to change their regime into another one. It mainly requires them to restrain, in a variety of ways, their passions for dominance and oppression. They will be reluctant, of course, to oppose their passions, as most of us are, but past examples about the fate of others who did not do so might be enough to shock some into accepting the advice. If not, then the legislator will be in the same position as any doctor before a recalcitrant patient. He can give the best advice he has, but if the patient refuses to listen, the doctor can only issue a last, friendly warning and leave him to his fate.

Chapter 10

~ DESTRUCTION OF MONARCHIES

~ HOW KINGSHIPS AND TYRANNIES ARE LIKE REGIMES

1310a39   Having dealt with destruction and preservation in regimes, Aristotle turns to destruction and preservation in monarchies, which are so far unlike regimes that tyrannies are hardly a regime and kingships (other than the simply best kingship) are rather an office than a regime. Nevertheless, they both have their part in regimes and form part of the study of regimes. For kingships can exist in

---

67. Strictly speaking freedom is virtue, or living and choosing to live the best human life (cf. 1.5–6), so that only citizens in the simply best regime will be simply free. But freedom in the case of other regimes will be relative to those regimes, for the ruling body definitive of each regime will be free in its own estimation when it has its own regime and is not subject to some other ruling body in some other regime.

any regime and tyrannies are an abiding threat or temptation in all or most regimes (as the previous chapters have shown). There has not been much to say about them so far with respect to the questions for study outlined at the beginning of the preceding book. Their kinds were indeed distinguished with respect to the first question, but neither was relevant to the second (the most common and choiceworthy regime after the best), and as regards the third and fourth (which regime is preferable for whom and how to set up regimes), the answer was more or less stated before in the case of kingships and the first two tyrannies (3.14), and is obvious in the case of the worst tyranny (for this tyranny is of advantage to no one anywhere, and is not so much set up as seized by force). All that remains, then, is the fifth question, which is dealt with now. That Aristotle's discussion is extended reflects the extent of the subject as well as how attractive and tempting monarchies, and in particular tyrannies, have proved. But his discussion is also frank, sometimes shockingly so,[68] and this frankness has done much, by the end, to destroy the temptation.[69]

The first question to ask, however, if monarchies are not to count as regimes proper, is whether the same things are going to be true of their destruction and preservation as were shown to be true of the destruction and preservation of regimes. For if not, the discussion is going to have to start again from the beginning with a whole new treatment of origins and causes of change. But in fact no such new treatment is necessary, because monarchies accord with, or are of the same character as, some of the regimes and have the same defining features. Consequently what holds of regimes generally can be taken to hold also of them (as indeed is amply illustrated in the ensuing investigation). The two sorts of monarchy, however, while both monarchies, accord with different, and not the same, regimes, for kingship accords with aristocracy, and tyranny accords with ultimate oligarchy and ultimate democracy. So Aristotle first explains why it is that they should accord with different regimes, and then why with these regimes.

1310b8   The two monarchies must accord with different regimes because their genesis, right from the start, is from opposites, and indeed, as emerges, with respect to both their beginning and end (genesis is understood from both); and clearly, things that differ in beginning and end cannot be the same, nor can they accord with the same things. So kingship arose to provide help from[70] the popu-

68. Barker (1946: 242–43), for instance, relegates some of the "scandals" Aristotle reports to a footnote.

69. As suggested by Newman (4:413) and Polansky, in Keyt and Miller (1991: 339–43).

70. The Greek, taken literally, says "from" (*apo*, 1310b9), but most commentators and translators want to change this to read "against" and to give the sense "to provide help for the decent *against* the populace." But this reading makes of the king a tyrant in reverse and conflicts with what is said later in this chapter (at 1310b40–1311a4): that the king acts as a guardian for both the decent and the populace,

lace for the decent, and a king comes from the decent, ruling because of virtue. A tyrant by contrast uses the populace against the notables, to prevent the populace being wronged, and comes from the populace. A king, then, has his beginning only where there are some who are decent and virtuous, comes himself from the decent, and has his end in the unity of the city. But a tyrant has his beginning where there need only be populace and notables (notables may only seem to be decent, without being so), does not come from the decent, or notables, but from the populace (in the sense that he is a partisan of the populace, not in the sense that he is needy), and has his end in the division of the city.

1310b14 In proof of these assertions, Aristotle appeals, since the assertions are themselves empirical, to empirical facts, and first (following reverse order again) with respect to tyranny. Most tyrants, then, came from the popular party because they came from demagogues who won the support of the populace by slandering the notables. This happened in four particular sorts of case (cf. 7(5).5.1305a8–28): one, when cities had already increased in size (and so when the populace were presumably becoming more numerous and getting stronger than the notables); two, when kings deviated from ancestral traditions and sought despotism; three, when the populace set up offices of long duration; four, when oligarchies put one man in control in the greatest offices. For anyone in these sorts of situation, and so possessed of this sort of power, could easily seize tyranny provided only he had the desire so to do. Thus Pheidon in Argos became tyrant from a kingship, Phalaris and the tyrants in Ionia from positions of honor (probably in oligarchies), Panaetius in Leontini, Cypselus in Corinth, Peisistratus in Athens, and Dionysius in Syracuse from being demagogues (when, that is, the populace were increasing, or when these men held offices of long duration from the populace, or both).[71]

1310b31 As regards kingships, these are arranged on the basis of aristocracy, and so come from the decent or the virtuous, and are for the unity of the city because kings became kings through virtue (their own or, where hereditary, their family's), or through acts of beneficence (which are outstanding deeds of virtue), or through these together with capacity to perform more, and on behalf of their whole city or nation. So Codrus saved the whole city of Athens from slavery, Cyrus liberated the whole nation of the Persians from slavery, the kings of the Spartans founded or won territory for their city, and those of the Macedonians and Molos-

---

while the tyrant has no common good in view. I take Aristotle's meaning to be, as I explain here in the commentary, that the difference between kingship and tyranny is that the first aims at reconciliation and unity and the second at division and mutual hatred.

71. Pheidon was tyrant of Argos in the mid-seventh century; Thrasybulus, one of the best known of Ionian tyrants, rose from general, as did Phalaris of Agrigentum; for Peisistratus and Dionysius I among the demagogues, see 7(5).5.1305a21–28; see also Newman (4:418).

sians for their nation.[72] All also evidently did so by uniting the populace with the decent in the accomplishment of these beneficent deeds.

1310b40 That kingship and tyranny differ in their genesis, and so must differ in the regimes they accord with, is thus evident. But that kingship accords with aristocracy has also become evident at the same time, for, as Aristotle noted, by being in accordance with virtue and the deeds of virtue, kingship is in accordance with aristocracy, for aristocracy is based on the merit of virtue. Kingship further accords with aristocracy because: it is correct, for it pursues the good of all the parts of the city, property owners and populace, by protecting the first from wrong or injustice and the second from insolence; its goal is the good life of virtue, for virtue is nobility and honor is the reward of virtue; it is gladly accepted by the citizens, for they provide its armed guard. By contrast, tyranny cannot accord with aristocracy, because it opposes aristocracy in all these ways: it does not look to anything common at all, except incidentally, when something common happens also to be to the tyrant's private advantage; it does not aim at the good life and nobility but at pleasure and the wealth that is the means to pleasure; it is not accepted by the citizens, for the tyrant has to have a foreign guard to protect himself from them.

Tyranny must instead accord with ultimate democracy and oligarchy, as is evident from the fact it has the evil features of both. Like ultimate oligarchy, it has its end, not in the good life, but in wealth, for only thus can the tyrant afford the luxury he wants and the mercenaries he needs for defense. Also like oligarchy, it distrusts and ill treats the multitude and the crowd, taking away their arms, expelling them from the city, and dispersing them about the countryside (thus rendering them harmless). Like ultimate democracy, on the other hand, it wages war on the notables, destroying them in secret and openly (as demagogues do), and exiling them as rivals in skill and impediments to rule, because they have the capacity and desire to seek the tyrant's overthrow—hence the advice of Periander (which ostracism in democracies imitates) to get rid of the superior men (see also 3.13.1284a28–33).

∼ THAT THEY ARE DESTROYED IN SIMILAR WAYS

∼ IN GENERAL

1311a22 From the fact, then, that monarchies are like regimes in the way stated, it follows that they must undergo change for like reasons. So Aristotle now confirms this, first restating the reasons and then giving examples. He states the beginnings of change as injustice (or insolence and gain by the monarch), as fear,

---

72. Codrus was a legendary king at Athens who saved it from a Dorian invasion; Cyrus liberated the Persians from the Medes in the sixth century; the first and sometimes also succeeding kings in the other cases led campaigns of acquisition. See Newman (4:419–20).

and as contempt; and he states the objects aimed at as wealth and honor. The basic desire for equality or inequality on the part of those who launch attacks against monarchies is not stated but is evidently assumed (as the examples show). Some of the beginnings of change, however, are omitted. The original eleven were: wealth and honor (as accumulated by others), insolence, fear, superiority, contempt, disproportionate increase, campaigning for votes, disregard, small things, and dissimilarity. Of these Aristotle only mentions wealth, insolence, fear, and contempt, though, judging by the examples, honor seems included under insolence (for the insolence takes away honor), and superiority under contempt (for the contemptuous think themselves superior to the contemned monarch). The remaining beginnings of change seem little relevant to monarchies, where all or most rule is in the hands of one man and there is no distribution of rule among several parts that could be disrupted by these other beginnings, though examples of kingships changing to tyrannies because of disproportionate increase (when many in the city become similar in virtue) do appear later.

1311a31/b6/b23   Aristotle next illustrates how these beginnings and causes operate in monarchies. First he deals with cases of insolence on the part of the monarch. But here a distinction is necessary, because attacks due to insolence are directed at the body (or person) of the ruler rather than against his rule. The reason is that insolence, despite the many forms it can take, causes anger, and those who are angry attack for revenge, not to become superior in their turn. So honor is aimed at here, not as something for attackers to get by getting rule, but as something to get back by avenging a dishonor inflicted on them or their friends by the ruler (cf. 7(5).2.1302a31–34).[73] Of course, if the attack is successful, the rule will change too, either by passing into the hands of another monarch or by becoming another regime, but such change is more a result of the attack than the aim of the attack.

Examples of insolence are:[74] first, insults of a verbal or physical sort, such as provoked the attacks on the Peisistratids, Periander, Philip, Amyntas the Small, and Evagoras of Cyprus; second, sexual abuse or outrage, such as provoked attacks on Archelaus and Cotys; third, physical beatings, such as provoked attacks on the Penthilids and on Penthilus himself, and again on Archelaus.[75] The Penthilids are mentioned here presumably because, though not monarchs, they had, as oligarchic dynasts, a sort of monarchical power (for monarchies include monarchical

73. A point apparently missed by Newman (4:424–25).

74. I follow the division suggested by Newman (4:425).

75. The attack on the Peisistratids occurred in 514; Periander was mentioned earlier, 7(5).4.1304a31–33; Philip, Alexander the Great's father, was slain in 336; nothing further is known of Amyntas the Small; Evagoras was slain in 374; Archelaus was king of Macedon from 413 to 399; Cotys was king of Thrace and was murdered in 359; the Penthilids were a leading family in Mytilene in the seventh century. See Newman (4:426–33).

offices and are not just regimes). All these examples are cases of successful assassi-nation, though not necessarily of change from monarchy into some other regime.

1311b36 Second, Aristotle deals with cases of fear. The example is the slay-ing of Xerxes by Artapanes who feared to be punished or slain himself by Xerxes.[76] This sort of attack is evidently against the rule of the monarch, rather than against him personally or against his body, because it is as having the power to punish or inflict harm, and hence as monarch, that the monarch is attacked, and not neces-sarily because of personal resentment. So Artapanes slew Xerxes for this reason and not because he resented Xerxes personally for insolence.

1311b40 Third, Aristotle deals with cases of contempt. Here too the attack is also against the monarch's rule rather than against his body or person, for it is because the monarch is contemned as not worthy of rule, not because he is re-sented as this person, that he is attacked. Such at any rate is clearly what happened in the cases of Sardanapalus (who was overthrown and killed) and Dionysius (who was overthrown and not killed), though Aristotle adds that he is not certain of the story about Sardanapalus.[77] Indeed, it may be worth noting at this point that questions can and have been raised generally about the historical accuracy of Aristotle's examples (by others as well as by Aristotle himself), and different accounts of some of the same events are to be found in other writers.[78] But we may suppose that Aristotle did as much as others in weighing the reliability and proba-bility of the sources he possessed (which were certainly greater than those we now possess), and if in any case he happened to adopt the wrong account, at least he adopted plausible accounts, or accounts that, as he says of Sardanapalus, could well be true of somebody. His examples, therefore, are always philosophically to the point (they do illustrate what they are supposed to illustrate), even if they are not always historically accurate.

The other examples of contempt Aristotle refers to are also evidently cases of superiority, namely attacks by friends and by powerful men like generals, such as the attacks on Astyages and Amadocus, and also the attack on Ariobarzanes by Mithridates (who was motivated by the desire for wealth as well by the desire for honor).[79] That such attacks also spring from a sense of superiority is shown by the fact that they are principally made by those who are bold in their nature and pos-sess military honor or command, and who thus are or will readily think they are,

76. Xerxes was king of Persia from 485 to 465 and Artapanes the chief bodyguard. See Newman (4:434–35).

77. Sardanapalus was king of Assyria in 668–626; Dionysius II was expelled from Syracuse in 357. See Newman (4:435–36).

78. See Newman's notes ad loca (4:426–44).

79. Astyages, king of Media, was overthrown by Cyrus in 559; Seuthes was a local ruler in Thrace in the early fourth century and Amadocus was a neighboring king; Ariobarzanes is probably the satrap of Pontus in the mid-fourth century. See Newman (4:436–37).

with respect to both quality of soul and power, more than a match for the despised monarch. For their bold nature already gives them the courage, the natural courage, to attempt daring things, and when they have the power too, their nature will quickly move them to boldness in action, to the actual doing of something daring.

1312a21   The attacks on monarchs mentioned so far have been motivated by desire for honor, or also wealth, in the sense of the desire to avenge dishonor or to acquire the honor, and wealth, of tyrannical power. But while desire for honor does operate in these ways, it also operates in another way, when the honor desired is not that of being tyrant, but that of having attempted or accomplished some extraordinary deed that brings glory and renown. Since the aim here is simply the deed, only those are moved to it who will be satisfied by the deed, or the attempt, regardless of their own safety or survival afterward (for if they cared for their own safety too, the deed would not be their sole motivation). Such self-denying love of honor and glory is hard to find in many people and instances of it, while they do exist as in the case of Dion (also mentioned at 1312a4–6), are necessarily rare. They are cases nevertheless directed at the monarchy rather than the person of the monarch, though they will typically involve, as they did in Dion's case, contempt for the monarch, for it is only glorious to attack a despicable or wicked monarch, not a good one.

∾ IN PARTICULAR

1312a39   So much concerns monarchies in general, but with respect to tyranny in particular there are certain ways in which it is mainly destroyed, and also certain main causes why it is destroyed. As regards the ways tyranny is mainly destroyed, these are either from within or from without. It is destroyed from without, as are other regimes, by an opposed and stronger regime (an opposed regime will want to destroy its opposite and, since everyone does what they want when they can, a stronger regime will act on that desire). The examples of ultimate democracies, which oppose by way of rivalry of similars, and of aristocracies and kingships, which oppose by way of contrasting aims (nobility against pleasure), are not, I take it, meant to be exhaustive of opposed regimes (for any regime could come to oppose a given tyranny for some reason or other). Rather regimes of this sort have a natural opposition to tyranny and will, if they are stronger, not need any further reason to destroy it.

1312b9   Tyranny is destroyed from within when (rather like oligarchy) those who share in it, especially the tyrant's family, start factions against each other, as in the case of the tyrannies of Gelon and Dionysius II in Syracuse.[80] Their internal disunity then makes it easy for others to intervene and overthrow them.

---

80. The tyranny founded by Gelon (Hiero, his immediate successor, was his brother) was overthrown in 466; Dion, who expelled Dionysius in 357, was himself killed four years later. See Newman (4:440).

1312b17 As regards the main causes of tyranny's destruction, these are principally hatred and contempt. Tyrants always inspire hatred (the very fact that they rule is unjust, and they typically add theft and cruelty to this injustice, all of which are causes of hatred), but they are not always attacked for this reason, if their power and prowess make them feared. When, however, a tyrant is despised as well, this restraint on attack will be removed, for contempt removes fear. So the successors of those who won tyranny seldom last long after the death of the first tyrant, for they dissipate themselves in luxury and are easy to assail (while the first tyrant, in order to win and establish his tyranny, had to be strong and able and watchful). Anger has the same effect as hatred, and even more so because of its greater impetuosity, and it is inspired especially by insolence. Hence, of the causes of overthrow of monarchies mentioned at the beginning, the two of insolence and contempt are especially powerful in the case of tyrannies.

1312b34 But there is no need to go further into these and other ways and causes of destruction of tyrannies for they have in a way already been dealt with in the discussion of ultimate democracy and oligarchy. These two regimes are sorts of tyranny (and tyranny is a combination of the evils of these two regimes), hence tyranny must be prone to destruction in similar ways and for similar causes. A reference back to the earlier discussion, therefore, should supply any missing details.

1312b38 By contrast with tyrannies, kingships are seldom destroyed from without. The fact is presumably obvious, but Aristotle does not suggest any reasons for it. Reasons can be readily conjectured, nevertheless. Kingships are, for instance, less likely to be attacked by regimes similar to them, for while bad fights with bad, good does not fight with good. They are also less likely to be attacked by bad regimes, for the bad do not envy those who enjoy what is noble but envy rather those who enjoy pleasure; nor will the bad attack out of fear, or at least not until they are threatened, and a king is unlikely to threaten a tyrant who is too strong for him. Moreover, if kingships are attacked, they are more likely to stand because more internally united and supported by willing subjects. Kingships are mainly destroyed from within, but only indeed because they start to decay into their opposite. For thus they lose the internal unity and the willing subjects natural to them—the first when those sharing in the kingship, the king's court and family, fight among themselves, and the second when the king himself turns more into a tyrant.

This destruction of kingships through decline to tyranny also explains why kingships do not come to be anymore, because there are few who stand out from others in virtue and the deeds of virtue, or are so superior as to deserve the control over the rather great matters proper to a king. Where many are equal or similar, justice requires that rule be shared equally among them all, not concentrated in a single pair of hands. But if one man does try to set up a single rule over others who are his equals or superiors, and by force or deceit, and so without their will, his rule is by definition a tyranny, not a kingship (rule over unwilling subjects is only just if the ruled are natural slaves who resist enslavement, 1.8.1256b23–26).

1313a10   As for kingships that are not now coming to be, but already exist and are passed on by family, they fall for the same reason, that the successor is not worthy of the kingly power but is contemptible and engages in insolent behavior like a tyrant. Such a king will be overthrown as soon as the subjects cease to accept his rule willingly, for then by definition (as just noted) he will have become a tyrant and ceased to be king. Such change from kingship to tyranny (because the subjects change from being willingly ruled to being unwillingly ruled) is not merely a matter of words or definitions, for the definition only changes because the reality has changed: a rule that was just and good has become one that is unjust and bad.

Several kingships still existed in Aristotle's day, as the Spartan and Macedonian, which could in principle be regarded as kingships and not as tyrannies, for they ruled over willing subjects and, in the case of Sparta, by inheritance from outstanding families, or also, in the case of Macedon, by their own great ability. But Aristotle has given reason to doubt the goodness of the hereditary Spartan kingship; and elected kingships (as in Carthage, 2.11.1272b37–1273a2) presuppose that there is someone outstanding enough to deserve election, so that, if none is outstanding, these sorts of kingships must fall into abeyance, at least for a time, or become tyrannies. That there are few or none who deserve to be kings anymore seems to be not so much because virtue has declined as because it has increased, so that whereas before few had much virtue and one man could surpass most others, now many have it and none is surpassing. Whether Philip and Alexander were, in Aristotle's eyes, exceptions to the rule, is a question too broad and difficult to enter on here.[81]

Chapter 11

〜 PRESERVATION OF MONARCHIES

〜 KINGSHIPS

1313a18   Aristotle's discussion of the preservation of monarchies reverses, in familiar fashion, the ordering in the preceding chapter and begins with kingships. The principle here, as also before (7(5).8.1307b27–30), is that monarchies are preserved by the opposites of what destroy them. So since kingships are destroyed above all when kings become more tyrannical and retain or seize greater control than is deserved, they must be preserved when kings become more measured and give up control. For thus they will be less despotic, more equal in their character,

---

81. But see Newman (1:278–79), who thinks Aristotle did not regard them as deserving of their great power, and also Stern (1968) and Vander Waerdt (1985).

and less envied by (their increasingly equal) subjects. The kingships of the Molossians and of the Spartans have been preserved in this way, and though kings thus become less in power, they are nevertheless longer lasting and so in a way greater, as Theopompus realized. His wife, by contrast, was interested in more control, not more duration. She had, it would appear, the greed typical of Spartan women (2.9).

Nothing else needs to be said about kingships. For if they do not become more measured in the way stated, they will end up as tyrannies, and so they will have to be preserved as tyrannies are preserved.

∼ TYRANNIES

1313a34   That Aristotle should advise how to preserve tyrannies, the worst of all regimes, and should do it at such length, may seem surprising and even Machiavellian. But it is no more surprising or shocking than that he should give advice for preserving ultimate oligarchies and democracies, which are as bad as tyrannies. For as a legislator may find himself called upon to advise a democracy, so he may find himself called upon to advise a tyrant, and he needs to know what to say in both cases. Of course, nothing can be done to make a tyranny decent, just as nothing can be done to make an ultimate democracy decent either. But something can perhaps be done to make a tyranny less bad.

Aristotle's advice is divided into two parts: a first about the tyrannical way of preserving tyrannies, and a second about the royal way of doing so. The first is the traditional way and the way apparently preferred by most tyrants, but the second is better than the first and is evidently preferred by Aristotle. The legislator cannot, however, keep silent about the first way. For his silence would escape no one's notice, least of all the tyrant's, and the way in question is so obvious and so well known that, if the legislator did keep silent, he would lose any reputation he had for wisdom and honesty, and so would lose also the only claim he had on a tyrant's or would-be tyrant's attention. But, if the legislator cannot, for this reason, keep silent about the first way, he can and should point out that there is another way. Moreover, in describing the first way, he can, by being comprehensive and explicit, fulfill the requirements both of science and of giving advice at the same time. For the first way is altogether depraved, and so the legislator has neither properly described it, nor properly advised the tyrant about it, unless he has shown it to be altogether depraved. Many tyrants perhaps slip too easily into it, and many are perhaps too easily attracted to tyranny, because they do not realize, until too late, how evil this way is. Exposing the evil, therefore, is not the least of the services a legislator can perform for a tyrant and the admirers of tyranny.[82]

The two ways of preserving tyranny are opposite to each other, and in fact opposite as well to the ways of destruction (in accordance with the principle

82. See also the discussion by Polansky, in Keyt and Miller (1991: 339–43).

general to monarchies and regimes). They are opposite to each other as evil opposes good, and they are opposite to destructions as ruthlessness opposes softness or as measure opposes excess. The first way, then, is the evil and ruthless way, and it consists of a multitude of devices, handed down from Greek or barbarian tyrannies and from democracies, for rendering the ruled as slavish de facto as they are de iure.

Some are designed to deprive the ruled of high thoughts and trust, or to make them low and ignorant of each other. They are opposite to the destruction of tyrannies that comes through contempt, for those who think little of themselves and have no one to trust will be too low and too unsure of others to have, or to be moved by, contempt for a tyrant, however base the tyrant is. These devices include not only the already mentioned one of killing or expelling superior men, or those who already have high thoughts, but also forbidding anything in the city that is likely to produce high thoughts and trust in others (as all associations and clubs where people can meet and get to know each other or improve themselves through a noble use of leisure), and imposing instead the contrary activities of attending the tyrant like slaves.

1313b11 Other devices are designed to deprive the ruled of the power or capacity to do anything, whether at all or undetected. These are opposite again to destruction through contempt (for those who have no power will not despise someone who has much), but also to destruction through hatred and anger (for lack of power renders hatred harmless and does much to dampen anger). So sending out spies everywhere will hinder people from trying anything or escaping detection if they do; destroying friendships and setting everyone in the city against each other will make combined action by many hard or impossible; depriving everyone of wealth and leisure, as by labor on public works and high taxes, will take away the means and the opportunity for action; waging war will have the same effect, and also make the ruled dependent on the tyrant for survival, since they will always need him to lead them; distrusting his friends will help protect the tyrant from those most able to attempt something against him.

1313b32 All these devices come from tyrannies and barbarian kingships. The next ones come from democracy and have similar effects. Women are dominant at home and slaves undisciplined, so that both can inform on the menfolk (and keep them weak and low-minded). Women and slaves are indeed specially suitable instruments of tyranny, as of democracy, for the freedom they then enjoy from the control, whether of husbands or of masters, while unnatural (for they are by nature subject to men, 1.5.1254b13–14, 12.1259b1–2), is nevertheless pleasant and enables them to do many things hitherto denied them. But just as tyrannies and democracies give precedence to women and slaves over men and masters, so they give precedence to flatterers (or demagogues) and to the base over the free and decent. The effect here is to render the latter powerless by not letting them get anywhere near the tyrant to do him harm. Only base flatterers, who are unlikely to attempt anything, but who are nevertheless useful tools for carrying out the tyrant's dirty work, are allowed to get close. So for like reason, when the tyrant does associate with people other than the base and the flatterers, they are foreigners, not citizens, since the former have no reason to attack while the latter do.

1314a12 Such are the devices for the preservation of tyranny, which, as Aristotle pointedly remarks, leave nothing out in respect of depravity. They can also be reduced to the three main heads of making the tyrant's subjects mean in thought, for no one like this will plot against him; distrustful of each other, so that no one can band against him (hence tyrants attack the decent and virtuous most of all as being most opposed to tyranny and most faithful to themselves and others); and incapable of doing anything, so that they will attempt nothing against him.

The depravity of these devices, their vicious nature and intention, are thus obvious, and Aristotle is sufficiently blunt and direct in saying so. His advice to tyrants on how to preserve themselves thus becomes at the same time condemnation and rebuke, or an invitation to consider, and more seriously than they might have done initially, the second and more decent way of preserving themselves.

1314a29 This other way is the opposite of the first, as it makes the tyrant more kingly rather than more tyrannical. But since this is advice about preserving, not destroying, tyranny, the fundamental condition for there being a tyranny at all has to be maintained, namely that the tyrant keeps his power, his control of arms and soldiers, so that he can continue ruling even when his subjects are not willing. Holding on to this, then, as the necessary presupposition of tyranny, the tyrant must, in everything else, act the part of king.

This way consists of several particular pieces of advice but they all respond to the ways tyrannies are destroyed (injustice, fear, hatred, contempt) and contrariwise to the first way, not by having hostile subjects who are incapable of attack, but by having friendly subjects who are unwilling to attack.[83] Kingships have subjects of this sort because, although they have an unequal distribution of what people attack for, honor and wealth, they do not have it unjustly, but through merit, and they use it for the common good of both the decent sort and the populace, not for their own advantage. So to imitate the king in the way required, the tyrant must seem to deserve his inequality, in both honors and wealth, and to be using it for the common good of both parts of the city.

1314a40 First, then, with respect to wealth, the tyrant should seem to deserve his inequality by caring for the city's finances as if he were a steward guarding common and not private funds. He will thus particularly secure to himself the friendliness of the multitude, for they are angered most when they think they are being wronged with respect to wealth. The tyrant can easily do this

---

83. I follow Newman (4:448).

by not spending money on offensive indulgences, and by giving account of income and expenses. But he will not thereby be any the less wealthy, as some tyrants obviously feared, for he controls the city and so has all its resources at his disposal. Indeed, by leaving these resources in the hands of the citizens, instead of concentrating them in a single hoard, his wealth and his control of the city are more secure as affording less temptation to potential rivals. When, however, he does need or want to get some of these resources directly into his own hands, as by imposition of taxes and public service, he should manifestly do so under color of the common good.

1314b18   Second, with respect to honor, the tyrant should seem to deserve his superiority by his character and behavior, which he will do if he appears dignified and inspires reverence like a king (in this way he will particularly secure to himself the friendliness of the decent and the notables, who most love honor). Dignity and reverence, however, are inspired by virtue and acts of virtue, so Aristotle speaks of ways tyrants can have, or appear to have, the virtues. He touches on features of courage, justice, moderation, liberality, magnificence, and piety. Courage or military virtue is particularly necessary because without it the tyrant will readily be despised, and the despised are not reverenced. Something of the virtue of justice is necessary too, or sufficient of it to be conspicuous for not treating subjects unjustly by acts of insolence, as in sexual matters. The tyrant's entourage should be similarly conspicuous, including his women (who have all too much license under tyranny). For not only is insolence a cause of overthrow of tyrannies, but the insolent and those surrounded by the insolent are scarcely venerable. Moderation in the pleasures of the body the tyrant should also have, or make a show of. Many tyrants go wrong by making a show of the opposite, and thereby inspire contempt by manifest unworthiness as well as expose themselves to attack. Also the tyrant should, as was said, be like a steward and adorn the city, thus displaying liberality and magnificence. Finally he should always be conspicuous for great seriousness in respect of religion, thus displaying piety and justice toward the gods. Such piety will certainly give him dignity and reverence (provided he is not silly about it), and will, moreover, make people trust him more and plot less against him.

1315a4   So much concerns how the tyrant can appear kingly with respect to his own honor, by seeming to deserve it. The next two pieces of advice concern how he can appear kingly with respect to the honor of others, by the way he gives honors and refrains from causing dishonors. So, with respect to giving honors, he should: honor the good in such a way that they do not think they would be more honored by free citizens living under their own regime (for then the good, who least think they deserve to be ruled by a tyrant, will be less desirous of change); distribute the honors himself and have others hand out punishments (for then he will be loved for the former without being resented for the latter); not make anyone great, or only along with others, or not someone bold, or not give someone power and then, if it should later prove necessary to take it away, take it away all at once but gradually (for thus none of the honored will want, or be able, to attack him).

1315a14   With respect to dishonoring anyone through acts of insolence,[84] the tyrant should altogether refrain from this, especially in regard to corporal punishment and sexual enjoyment of the young, and especially in respect of the notables, who love honor. Or if he does inflict such punishment and enjoy such intercourse, he should do the first seeming to be a father, not an insulter, and the second seeming to be a lover, not an abuser. Further, he should compensate these apparent losses of honor by giving greater honors. Such advice will remove most attempts on the tyrant's life arising from insolence (examples of which were given before), but as regards those who might attack him heedless of their own life (such as Dion against Dionysius), insolence against them or their loved ones is especially to be guarded against, as once their anger and spirit are aroused, they will stop at nothing.

1315a31   But just as the tyrant must seem deserving of his superior position by his kingly behavior, in the ways stated, with regard to wealth and honors, so he must seem deserving of it by the performance of the king's proper task, which is to preserve and defend all parts of the city. The needy and well-off, therefore, should come to suppose that it is through his rule that they are being thus preserved and defended. In addition, he should associate the stronger part of the city in his rule, for then he will always be able to retain control by relying on this stronger part, and will not be forced instead to attack and alienate the citizens by confiscating arms and freeing slaves.

1315a40   In summary form, then, the tyrant must appear: one, a household manager and trustee with respect to wealth; two, measured and virtuous in his character and behavior with respect to honors; three, a friend to both notables and populace with respect to his defense of the whole city. In this way both the tyrant and his rule will be much improved: his rule will be better and longer lasting, because over better and friendlier subjects, and he himself will be on the way to virtue and only half wicked instead of wholly so (half wicked and not good simply because his virtues are apparent or imperfect and because his rule, being over unwilling and equal or superior subjects, is still fundamentally unjust). This second way of preserving tyranny thus brings about a real improvement, but not such as to abolish tyranny and therefore not such as to abolish all the evil. Still the evil that remains is suffered most by the tyrant himself, since his very being in control is unjust; it is suffered least by the ruled, who are treated well, even if the tyrant's benevolence is mainly for the sake of appearance.

84. Which insolence (*hubris*) can also carry the connotation of rape.

Chapter 12

〜 DURABILITY OF TYRANNIES

1315b11 Aristotle has just said that the second way of preserving tyranny makes the tyranny more lasting, but while this may be a recommendation for the second way of preserving tyranny, it is not a recommendation for tyranny itself. For, as he now proceeds to show, tyranny is a short-lived regime even if those that were of a kingly sort lasted longest. This discussion of the durability of tyrannies seems, therefore, natural and appropriate enough in the context, despite the doubts of scholars.[85] There are certain internal problems, however, the first of which is that Aristotle mentions oligarchy along with tyranny, even though oligarchy belongs to the previous discussion of regimes and is not mentioned further here. But such a reference to oligarchy can be defended in a way, for oligarchy is like tyranny in being deviant and concentrating power in few hands, so that if it too is short-lived, then the short-lived character of tyranny receives further support and confirmation. But that oligarchy is short-lived was stated and explained before (7(5).1.1302a2–15) and does not need repeating.[86]

Still, however that may be, the longest lasting tyranny was that of Orthagoras and his sons at Sicyon. It endured a full hundred years because, as Aristotle notes, it followed mainly the second way of preserving tyranny: the tyrants were measured in their behavior, obeyed the laws, were hard to despise, and courted the favor of the populace. A story about Cleisthenes crowning someone who decided a victory in some contest against him is noted in illustration, and the apparently irrelevant reference to what the tyrant Peisistratus did in Athens (that he put up with being summoned to court) is perhaps added by way of confirmation. If the same people tell both stories, and if what they say of Peisistratus is true, then what they say of Cleisthenes is likely to be true as well. That Cleisthenes was Orthagoras' great-grandson, and not, as Aristotle says, his son, is not a problem, since "son" can be used in this loose way to indicate descendants generally.

1315b22/b34 The second tyranny is that of the Cypselids at Corinth, which lasted seventy-three years and six months and for similar reasons: Cypselus followed the second and kingly way, courting the populace and dispensing with a bodyguard, and though Periander pursued the first and tyrannical way he did at least follow the kingly sufficiently to acquire military virtue. The third tyr-

---

85. Such doubts are expressed by Newman (4:477), among others, but in fact they only raise questions about some of the particular details of the discussion and not about the general thesis and its relevance to the present context.

86. Newman (4:477) notes that some oligarchies lasted a long time, which, however, is compatible with oligarchy being in general short-lived. Certainly the longest lasting regimes mentioned in the *Politics* are all aristocracies (Sparta, Crete, Carthage).

anny is that of Peisistratus at Athens, which lasted thirty-five years but was not continuous, and also, among the others, there is that of Gelon and Hiero in Syracuse, which lasted eighteen years. Both these tyrannies were evidently less kingly than the others, if Peisistratus was twice exiled (his sons were also insolent, 7(5).10.1311a32–39), and if the tyranny of Gelon and Hiero fell through internal faction (7(5).10.1312b9–16).

The main problem with this list is that, while the first two tyrannies are the longest recorded, there were other tyrannies longer than the last two. The tyranny established by the older Dionysius at Syracuse lasted, if with interruptions, for fifty years or more. Some other tyrannies also lasted longer than that of the Peisistratids or than that of Gelon and Hiero.[87] It is hardly likely that Aristotle was ignorant of these other tyrannies (in fact, he has referred to both older and younger Dionysius more than once), so there is some reason here to doubt the authenticity or completeness of the Greek text. But Aristotle may have been following different sources of information (now lost); or, in the case of Syracuse in particular, he may have kept silent to avoid needless controversy about philosopher rulers and Plato's association with the older and younger Dionysius; or he may not have intended to cover all tyrannies but only, after the longest, the more famous and representative ones (hence his ordering them into second and third is not according to duration only but according to duration and significance or fame). At all events, if the longest tyranny lasted only a hundred years while all the rest were much briefer, then the thesis that tyrannies last a short time is sufficiently confirmed.

∽ REFUTATION OF THE RIVAL VIEWS OF SOCRATES

1316a1 So much, then, concerns the destruction and preservation of regimes and monarchies. To complete his discussion Aristotle ends with a criticism of a rival account of destruction of regimes given by Socrates in Plato's *Republic* (545a2–580a8). Such a criticism is appropriate, since this rival account exists and was doubtless both well known and respected, so some explanation of why Aristotle has so far ignored it and why his own account is so different needs to be given. Complaints, nevertheless, have been raised that Aristotle misses the point of Socrates' remarks. For Plato's intention, it is alleged, was not to make Socrates give an empirical or historical account of change, but rather a logical or psychological account, not unlike some of Aristotle's own accounts elsewhere.[88] But there is no need to suppose that Aristotle is either ignoring or denying this intention. We can suppose instead that certain students of the *Republic* were ignoring or denying it

---

87. See Jowett (1885: 2:231) and Newman (4:477, 480).

88. *Ethics* 8.10 is referred to by Jowett (1885: 2:231). See also Barker (1946: 250 n3), Bornemann (1923–24: 154–55), Newman (1:519), Sinclair/Saunders (1981: 351–52).

and that Aristotle's remarks are directed at them, to point out that this empirical way of reading the *Republic*, whether it was the way Plato intended or not, leads to many errors.

The account put into the mouth of Socrates is basically a progress of change beginning from the simply best regime and passing first into an aristocracy of the Spartan type, then into oligarchy, then into democracy, and finally into tyranny. Aristotle takes each aspect of this progress in turn. First he takes the first part of it, the best regime, then the whole progress, then the last part of it, tyranny, and finally the middle parts, Spartan aristocracy and oligarchy and democracy.

As regards change of the best regime, there are three criticisms. The first is that the cause of change given (*Republic* 546c1–d2) is not proper to the best regime but could be true of any regime. For the point of the mathematics (leaving aside its details)[89] is that sometimes nature may produce people who cannot be educated and who therefore alter the regime. But while people may well come to exist who cannot be educated, such lack of educability is a cause of destruction that could affect any regime (for all regimes need to educate their citizens to the regime if they are to survive, 7(5).9.1310a12–19). The point of this first criticism, however, is not, perhaps, that every regime must have a cause of destruction proper to it (for, on Aristotle's own account, very few of the ways each particular regime is destroyed are peculiar to that regime and cannot also sometimes be found in others), but rather that Socrates speaks as if this cause of change was proper to the best regime, when manifestly it is not. Aristotle, himself, of course has given no cause of change at all for his best regime (which has not been in question in this or the previous book), but that is because the best regime is according to prayer and so all causes of change, from deficiencies whether in nature or education, have, ex hypothesi, been removed.

The second criticism is that Socrates speaks of a cycle of time according to which a moment of change is determined universally for everything, and not for this or that particular. The consequence is that if the moment of change happens to be now, then a regime that came to be yesterday and a regime that came to be many years ago must both start to change now. Such a coincidence is perhaps not impossible, but it must be rare and, anyway, the common change would be a result of the coincidence of the cause, not a result of the lapse of the time. So, for instance, an invading army could destroy at the same time two regimes that came to be at different times, but only because of the coincidence that both cities were the object of, or in the path of, the same invaders, not that a certain period of time had elapsed.

The third criticism is that the change of the best regime is assumed always to be into the neighboring regime and never into the opposite regime. But this is con-

89. On the details see the references in the previous note.

trary to the empirical facts, for regimes are often observed to change into their opposites as well.

1316a20 As regards the whole progress of change, this same criticism applies, for any change can in fact go in the opposite direction. So there can be change from democracy to oligarchy as well as from oligarchy to democracy, and in fact democracy changes more to oligarchy than to tyranny (change to tyranny is, in the absence of military demagogues, not common nowadays, 7(5).5).

1316a25 As regards the last part of the progress, tyranny, the problem is that no discussion at all is given of whether it will change and why, or why not, and into which regime. Tyranny, of course, ends the progress Socrates speaks of, but it is false to suppose that tyranny never undergoes change. Indeed, Socrates himself seems to speak of the progress as being cyclical so that tyranny should accordingly change into the simply best regime and start everything all over again (*Republic* 546a1–7). But the meaning of Aristotle's remark, that Socrates could not have found it easy to explain change in tyranny because the matter is indeterminate, is a bit unclear. It could mean that the change back to the best regime is inexplicable on Socrates' own principles, for Socrates' account is all about how regimes get progressively worse, and contains nothing about how the worst of them could suddenly return to the best. This interpretation is perhaps to be preferred, as it more obviously explains that Socrates should have found it hard to say whether, why, and how tyranny changes. But Aristotle could also mean that the change of tyranny is indeterminate since tyranny can change into any regime and not to some single determinate one.[90] On this second interpretation Aristotle's criticism will be a general one, since any regime is indeterminate in this respect and not tyranny only, for any regime can, in principle, change into any regime. The examples adduced will support either interpretation, the second interpretation obviously (for the examples show how indefinite are the ways tyranny can change), but the first interpretation too (for the examples show that change of tyranny can, contrary to Socrates' apparent assumption, be into something better, and not just into another tyranny, and hence that a progress of change that is always toward the worse, as Socrates' progress is, cannot explain such facts).[91]

90. As suggested by Newman (4:484).

91. As for the examples, Myron was Cleisthenes' brother; Antileon is not otherwise known; the regime that followed tyranny at Syracuse is called a democracy here (though earlier it was implied to be a polity or an aristocracy, 7(5).4.1304a27–29 and 10.1312b6–9), presumably because Aristotle is now using Socrates' categories, not his own (for Socrates is his target), and Socrates does not distinguish polity from democracy; Charilaus was mentioned earlier, in 2.10.1271b24–26; the tyranny at Carthage presumably preceded the establishment there of the regime praised in 2.11 (see especially 1272b30–33), just as the tyranny of Charilaus is thought to have preceded the final establishment in Sparta of Lycurgus' aristocracy; see Newman (4:485–86). In this way one can solve the problems often noted in this passage; see Jowett (1885: 2:232), Lord (1984: 264 n121), Newman (1:519 n1).

1316a34   As regards the middle parts of the progress, and especially oligarchy, which is supposed to change from Spartan aristocracy and then into democracy, there are five criticisms. The first criticism is that change from oligarchy can be directly to tyranny without an intermediate change through democracy, as the examples show.[92] The second criticism is that a false reason is stated for the change from Spartan aristocracy to oligarchy, that those in office become lovers of money and businessmen (*Republic* 550e4–551b7). This is false for three reasons: one, mere love of money will not bring about any change unless those with the money think that their superior wealth entitles them to superior shares in the regime (for the cause of change is always the desire for equality in situations of inequality, which, in the case of oligarchy, is when those superior in wealth want superiority according to equality of ratio, 7(5).1.1301b28–40); two, some oligarchies forbid those in the regime to engage in business (as in Thebes, 3.5.1278a25–26); three, in Carthage, which is an aristocracy (or a timocracy to use Socrates' word),[93] the rulers engage in business and yet the regime has not yet become an oligarchy.

1316b6   The third criticism is that oligarchy is no more two cities, one of the rich and one of the poor, than other regimes where there is an inequality of property or an inequality of virtue (Socrates had posited this doubleness of oligarchy as a cause of its change into democracy, at *Republic* 551d5–7). For other regimes will also be two, either in the same way (as democracies, which are likewise split between rich and poor), or according to virtue (as in regimes like Sparta, for instance, which mix virtue and the populace).

The fourth criticism is that the change from oligarchy to democracy can have other causes. So one, democracy can arise without any increase in the wealth of the well-off or the poverty of the needy if the needy increase in numbers, just as democracy can change to oligarchy if, by contrast, the well-off become stronger and the multitude relax their guard; two, Socrates only alleges one reason for change of oligarchy, that the rich become poor through profligate living (*Republic* 555c1–e1), when the previous chapters have shown that changes in regimes generally, and in oligarchies in particular, can have many other causes.

The fifth criticism is that this reason anyway makes several false assumptions, as: one, that everyone was rich to begin with; two, that squandering of wealth on the part of anyone is a cause of change, and not rather squandering on the part of those who are leaders; three, that change is then only into democracy and not also into other regimes; four, that such squandering is necessary for there to be change,

---

92. For these examples see Lord (1984: 264 n122) and Newman (4:486).

93. The manuscripts actually speak of democracy and not timocracy, but the change to timocracy, suggested by Newman (4:486), seems required because Carthage is elsewhere said to be an aristocracy (6(4).7.1293b14–16) and Socrates' word for Aristotle's so-called aristocracy is timocracy.

whereas mere resentment at being excluded or wronged or treated insolently can cause change even in the absence of any squandering.

1316b25 As regards change in oligarchy and democracy generally, there is one criticism, that Socrates speaks as if there was only one kind of each regime, so that there is not, or cannot be, change from a less to a more extreme oligarchy or democracy or vice versa.

With this comment Aristotle's criticisms of Socrates come to an end. This ending is rather abrupt and also seems to leave the criticisms unfinished, for while all the rest of the progress has been examined, the change from democracy to tyranny has not been. Some, therefore, suppose the chapter is incomplete and a section has dropped out and been lost.[94] But this supposition, while possible, is not necessary, for the ending, if abrupt, is not inappropriate. Aristotle has no need to examine what Socrates says about change from democracy to tyranny since Socrates' account agrees in large part with Aristotle's own, that demagogues attack the rich and, securing or possessing military power, become tyrants (*Republic* 562a1–566d3). Indeed, there are many things in the *Republic*, as in the *Laws*, whether about change or other things, that Aristotle would clearly agree with but which, not surprisingly, he does not bother to discuss. Admittedly, in the case of what Socrates says about democracy, Aristotle would object that democracies can change for other reasons, that they can change into other regimes besides tyranny, including other kinds of democracy, and that change to tyranny is less common now. But since he has made all these criticisms already in the context of criticizing other aspects of Socrates' theory of change, he does not need to repeat them here. Instead, having just mentioned that democracy, like oligarchy, has several kinds and so can change into other kinds of democracy, he can regard his discussion of democracy, and so of Socrates' whole progress, as complete. This chapter, therefore, may well end the way Aristotle intended.

94. As do Barker (1946: 253 n1), Lord (1984: 264 n126), Newman (4:489).

BOOK 8

Addendum on Setting Up the Other Regimes

Chapter 1

∿ REASON AND ORDER OF THE ADDENDUM

1316b31 All five questions set out for treatment at the beginning of book 6(4) have now been dealt with, and one would accordingly expect the project of the *Politics* to be complete. But Aristotle proceeds to add some further discussion on the fourth of those questions, the question of how to set up the several regimes. Some scholars have thus supposed that the present book is the answer to that question and should be placed before the previous book.[1] But they can only do so by ignoring, or rather rejecting as a later interpolation, the opening section of this chapter, which makes it very clear that this book is meant to follow the previous one, and not to precede it. Other scholars suppose instead that this book is really a continuation of the previous one and answers the question of the preservation of regimes as the previous one answered the question of the destruction of regimes. But they in turn can only do so by regarding the chapters on preservation in the previous book (8–9, 11) as somehow out of place.[2]

By far the better course, then, is to reject both these approaches and, taking Aristotle at his word, regard this book as the addendum it professes to be.[3] Nevertheless the scholars just mentioned are right in a way. For this addendum is both an answer to the fourth question from book 6(4), about how to set up regimes, and a continuation of the question from the preceding book, about how to preserve regimes or make them endure. It is, in fact, a sort of combining of the two questions (for these questions are in a way the same question, or parts of the same question). So much seems suggested already by the fact that Aristotle begins the chapter with a reference back to these questions, as if to signal that they are both the focus of his attention. The difference is that now these questions are to be taken together and the results from the previous discussions of them to be set out in one place, not several, and along with any necessary additions.[4]

---

1. As explained in the introduction, p. xviii.
2. As does Barker (1946: 203 n1, 229 nRR).
3. This is the way Peter of Auvergne seems to take it (1951: 5.1.710).
4. Jowett (1885: 2:234) speaks along these lines in his notice on the character of this book.

Two reasons are given for such an addendum. The first is a general one about all regimes and appeals to the fact that the several regimes come in more than one kind. This multiplicity of kinds was stated in answer to the first question from book 6(4), but that question arose precisely because the answer to it was necessary for answering the other questions of how to set up and preserve regimes (6(4).1.1289a5–11). Setting up and preserving regimes constitute the proper task of the legislator, and treating of this task with respect to regimes other than the simply best has been the intention of the whole discussion from book 6(4) onward. But this task is necessarily rendered more complex and delicate if the kinds of regimes themselves have kinds. Hence, to ensure that the legislator is properly prepared for his task—and so to realize the intention of the *Politics* stated way back at the end of the *Ethics* (10.9.1180b28–1181b23)—a treatment of anything that is left, and a summary setting forth in one place of what is proper and beneficial to each regime, clearly cannot be a bad idea.

1316b39 The second reason appeals back to another of the questions from book 6(4), the second one about which regime is most choiceworthy for most cities or which regime cities have most in common with. It concerns, therefore, the mixed regimes in particular, the regimes of so-called aristocracy and polity, which combine the modes of more than one regime. These regimes have a special interest for the legislator, for they are correct regimes and the legislator will necessarily prefer correct to deviant regimes and will want to introduce them, or something like them, if he can. But setting up these regimes is also a complex and delicate task since it requires mixing different elements, and if the mixing is not done well, these regimes will not long survive (6(4).12.1297a6–13, 7(5).7.1307a5–27, 8.1307b40–1308a3). There is need, then, to examine the several possible combinations of modes by which mixed regimes can be set up and by which they can overlap with one or other of the unmixed regimes—as aristocracies with oligarchy when, say, oligarchic modes for the deliberative and the choosing of offices are combined with an aristocratic mode for the jury courts—either in order to be able to avoid these combinations when setting up mixed regimes, or in order to be able, if circumstances should require, to make a prudent use of them. The elements for these combinations were, indeed, stated earlier when all the parts of the regime and their several arrangements were discussed (6(4).14–16), but not all the relevant details were there discussed, nor the combinations themselves at any length. So again, if the legislator is to be properly prepared for his task and the intention of the *Politics* is to be fulfilled, some addendum about these combinations, bringing together previous results and supplying anything omitted, would clearly not be a bad idea.

1317a10 So much concerns the reasons for the addendum. As regards the order, Aristotle first notes that part of what is involved in the task of setting up regimes, namely knowing which kind of which regime suits which sort of city, does not need further treatment. This was the object of the third question from the beginning of book 6(4), and so Aristotle has now touched on all the previous questions in the opening section of this chapter. But if this question does not need further treatment, and if the other two questions, about the kinds of regime and about which regime is most choiceworthy for most cities, do not need further treatment either, but point instead to the need for further treatment of the questions about setting up regimes and about preserving them, then the addendum and the order of it will concern only these last two questions.

In stating the order, Aristotle only speaks expressly of democracy and oligarchy, but he thereby necessarily gives to understand that the treatment of the combinations for mixed regimes will follow these, since that is all that is left. These combinations must, anyway, follow democracy and oligarchy because they are combinations of parts of democracy and oligarchy, and the parts of a combination must be understood before the combination itself is understood. But as for the order of democracy and oligarchy, Aristotle says he will first speak about democracy, since its contrasting or opposed regime, the one some "call" oligarchy, will become manifest at the same time.

Opposites can, of course, in general be understood from opposites, but this by itself does not determine the choice to treat democracy first followed by oligarchy, instead of the other way round. Perhaps there is no compelling reason for Aristotle's choice of order, and he could as well have started with oligarchy as with democracy. But perhaps he begins with democracy because of lingering disputes about how to describe its opposite. For "oligarchy" is an ambiguous word, and while it properly means rule by the rich or the well-off, it literally says rule of the few. This may be the point of Aristotle's remark that the regime opposite or contrasting to democracy is the one some "call" oligarchy, because he wishes to remind us of the ambiguity.[5] For insofar as "oligarchy" is used to mean rule of the well-off, then it is right to call it the one that is opposite to democracy (as one bad extreme is opposite to the other); but insofar as "oligarchy" says rule of the few, it is not right so to call it. For the rich need not always be few (as they were not in Colophon, 6(4).4.1290b14–17), and, more to the point, aristocracy is also typically rule of the few, though it is not rule of the well-off, and aristocracy is not opposite to democracy but rather to oligarchy (as a correct regime is opposite to its deviation). No such problem arises about democracy, however (for "democracy" says what it means, rule by the *dēmos* or the mass of the poor), so to begin with it is safer and also the way to make clear that its opposite is oligarchy in the sense of rule by the well-off, not in the sense of rule by the few.

5. As Newman (4:492) suggests, and cf. 6(4).3.1290a13–29.

1317a18 With respect to setting up and preserving democracies, then, the first thing to do is to learn all the features characteristic of democracy. The reason Aristotle gives is clear enough: (1) democracies are put together from these features, and the different democracies arise from the different ways of putting them together; but (2) to put something together one must know the things from which it is put together; therefore (3) to know how to put each democracy together one must know all these features.

Premise (1) here gives a different account of the several kinds of democracy from the one given earlier (6(4).4 and 6), but it does not conflict with that earlier account and, indeed, in a way follows from it (cf. the commentary at 6(4).14.1297b37–41). The earlier account traced the different democracies to different kinds of populace, as farmers, mechanics, and laborers, and showed how democracies are not just better or worse but different in kind when, say, farmers are taken along with mechanics, or farmers and mechanics along with laborers. But, of course, these multitudes only constitute a democracy when they have control of the city, and the means whereby they have control of the city are precisely the features here spoken of (as distribution of office, manner of appointment, and so forth), and hence, as more or fewer of these features are present, so does the multitude that exercises control by means of them differ.

So, as regards the conclusion (3), it is thus manifest that knowing all these features is necessary for putting a regime together, both with respect to setting one up in the first place and with respect to the companion task of preserving it in being once it exists. For not only do democracies consist in these features, but they are sometimes destroyed too if they combine them all indiscriminately. Hence it is also necessary to know these features with a view to preventing such destruction and with a view to correcting the defects from which destruction originates.

These features are to be found in "the claims and character of democracies and what are the objects they desire" (1317a39). It is not immediately clear what Aristotle means by these words, whether he intends to mark out three distinct classes of things or is just describing the same things in three different ways. Judging by the next chapter one should probably adopt the latter interpretation. For the next chapter does not follow a division into three; it speaks rather of the supposition of democracy, or what it aims at, and of the features of popular rule that follow from this supposition. So one should perhaps best understand Aristotle as speaking of this supposition and its corresponding features in the same three ways, namely that both the supposition and the features are the things that democracies claim for themselves as their rights, that they are characterized by, and that they make the objects of their desire. A regime is at any rate characterized, or is the regime it is, above all by its aim or supposition, namely freedom or wealth or virtue. But by aim here is not meant what object people use rule in order to get (for democrats too, like oligarchs, can and do use rule to get wealth for themselves), but rather what claim to rule they desire to make dominant, whether the claim of freedom or of wealth or of virtue. For each regime aims or desires to put and keep control in the hands of that part of the city (the needy, the well-off, the virtuous) by which it is characterized. But from this aim, as so understood, necessarily follow also the particular things it desires in order to realize this aim, and these particular things are also what it claims for itself as its rights, and what typically characterize it.

Chapter 2

~ FEATURES OF DEMOCRACY

1317a40   The aim of democracy, or the supposition that distinguishes it from other regimes, is freedom. At any rate people say that only in democracy is there freedom, and they say this because they say freedom is what democracy aims at. This inference of theirs is strictly speaking invalid, since something is not necessarily attained just because it is aimed at. Still, this professed aim, whether attained or not, does determine the particular character, claims, and desires of democracy. However, the freedom that is democracy's supposition itself needs explaining. It has two senses, though senses that complement and reinforce each other. The first sense is ruling and being ruled in turn, which itself derives from the democratic understanding of justice as numerical equality. For if all are numerically equal, then no one should rule more than anyone else and hence all should rule and be ruled by turns. Numerical equality is distinctive of democratic justice even though justice in the case of the regime, as everyone in a way perceives (3.12.1282b18–21), is equality according to some principle of merit. For such equality reduces, in the case of democrats, to numerical equality because democrats say that everyone is equal in being free (oligarchs, by contrast, say that all are not equal, because all are not equal in wealth, and so for them equality according to merit is numerical inequality, 7(5).1.1301b29–40).

But if justice for democrats is numerical equality, then the practice of ruling and being ruled by turns itself reduces to the multitude being in control. For if all are numerically equal, then each citizen individually must have an equal say, and the only way to achieve such equality in practice is by majority decision. But majority decision is again in practice decision by the needy, for the needy are the majority. Hence numerical equality means the needy having more control than the well-off, or the needy ruling and the well-off being ruled—not in the sense that none of the well-off ever has any say in the assembly or ever holds office, but in the sense that their view of justice, that the well-off should have control, never has any say.

Democracy is thus in one sense all ruling and being ruled by turns and in another sense some always ruling and others always being ruled. For all rule and get ruled by turns taken as individuals (since the individual well-off can share as much in voting in the assembly as the individual needy), but all do not rule and get ruled by turns taken as qualified individuals, that is, as individuals belonging to this or that part of the city, the part of the needy or the part of the well-off. Democrats, however, ignore these differentiations and suppose the city to be made up directly of individuals and not of parts (or not of individuals qualified by the parts they belong to). Hence they judge equality to be equality of individuals and not equality of parts, and hence also, as a result, their equality of individuals is not only compatible with, but actually produces, an inequality of parts. The city, however, is made up of parts, or of individuals who differ in kind and not of individuals merely (2.2.1261a22–30). The reason for this is clear enough. The city exists for self-sufficient life and only those individuals can be said to belong to the city who in some way contribute to this life, that is, who carry out one or other of its necessary works. But these works determine the city's parts (3.12.1283a14–22, 4(7).8.1328b2–23, 6(4).4.1290b38–1291b2). Hence, if no one belongs to the city save by doing some work necessary to the city, no one belongs to the city save by belonging to one or other of its parts.

That is why democracy, despite all its talk of equality, is really inequality, for with respect to what the city properly is democracy is inequality, namely the dominance of one part of the city (the populace or mass of farmers, mechanics, laborers, and the like) over the other parts (the well-off and the virtuous). That is also why Aristotle has insisted throughout on defining democracy as rule by the poor or needy, for regimes are distinguished by which part of the city has control (6(4).3.1290a7–13), and democracy is when that part of the city which is needy has control. Rule by some other part, even if that part happened in some case to be the majority, would necessarily not be the same sort of regime, and so would necessarily not be democracy, at least so long as democracy is the standard name, as it is, for rule by the particular part of the city that is needy.

1317b11 This, then, is one sense of freedom, where freedom means dominance by the needy (and hence where it means slavery for the rest of the city, for democracy is by definition a despotic regime, 3.6–7). But there is another sense of freedom and this sense is, in a way, what lies behind the first sense of freedom. This other sense of freedom is to live as one likes, which sense is reached by deduction from the opposite, for they say that living as one likes is the mark of freedom since to live as one does not like is characteristic of the slave. For, to put the argument more formally, if (1) those who live as they do not like are slaves, and if (2) the free are not slaves, then (3) the free do not live as they do not like, or, in other words, they live as they do like. This notion of freedom was mentioned, and criticized, before (7(5).9.1310a25–36 and commentary thereon), where it was shown that living as one likes, instead of relatively to the regime, is self-destructive because it is destructive of the regime that supposedly gives one freedom and so is destructive of freedom. For even if the free live as they like, it does not follow that all those who live as they like are free. Indeed, if they live as their passions like (which is what effectively happens in democracies), they are not free but enslaved to their passions, and they will become enslaved to others too, when their intemperance has destroyed their regime. Strictly speaking, only the virtuous are free, for they are masters of themselves; and only they are fit to do what they like, for they like to do what is good and noble. The rest would be better off if they were ruled by the virtuous, since if they lived as they liked, they would become worthless and miserable (cf. *Ethics* 1.4.1095b4–13).

But be that as it may, this sense of freedom is certainly individualistic, just as was the first sense of freedom, for it says that freedom is when the individual does as the individual likes. That is why the first sense of freedom comes from this other sense of freedom. For the individual would most do as he likes if he was not ruled by anyone at all (since to be ruled is to do as the ruler likes), but, failing that, if he was no more ruled than ruling and so if he ruled and was ruled by turns (since then at least he is as little subject as possible to rule by others). This practice of ruling and being ruled by turns, however, is of individuals, not of parts, and so it necessarily results, as just explained, in dominance of the city by the needy.[6]

1317b17   These two senses of freedom, then—the individual doing as he likes and the corresponding distribution of rule according to numerical equality so that the poor control the regime—constitute the aim and supposition of democracy, and hence what its claims and character and object of desire are in general. From this aim then follow the other features of democracy, or what its claims and character and objects of desire are in particular. Aristotle lists eleven such features and he does so according to the three parts of any regime, speaking first of the offices, then of the law courts, then of the assembly (the deliberative body in democracies), and then finally of all three.

The offices are that part of rule in the regime which is not assigned to the whole assembly but is undertaken by particular persons. Offices are accordingly most opposed to democratic freedom and equality since they are cases of relatively few individuals exercising rule and giving commands to relatively many (the issuing of commands belongs necessarily to office and is particularly characteristic of rule,

---

6. The notions of freedom and equality in modern political thought and practice are no less individualistic and no less numerical. That they do not result in control by the needy is because modern states are too big for all to share in rule and hence too big for rule by direct decision of the majority. Rule is instead by certain representatives, as they are called. But these representatives are chosen by election and not by lot, and from some, the wealthy, and not from all. For only those are elected who are wealthy enough to finance an election campaign, or who belong to a party wealthy enough to finance an election campaign. Modern states are thus sorts of elected oligarchy (as noted earlier, in the commentary on 7(5).6.1305b29–36 p. 383 n41). Numerical equality and individualistic freedom are nevertheless preserved because all may do the electing and because the rulers, at least in theory, leave everyone to pursue whatever they wish and confine themselves to securing the conditions and means for such pursuit.

6(4).15.1299a25–28). The aim of democracy will, therefore, be best attained here if all, or as many as possible, have their share in such office, and if further these offices have as little control as possible. Thus the features concerning the offices are: (i) choosing all the offices from everyone (so that no one is deprived of a chance to rule); (ii) everyone ruling each and each ruling everyone in turn (so that all have an equal share in ruling); (iii) having all the offices chosen by lot (for election, as opposed to lot, always favors some over others), or as many as do not need experience and skill (for even democrats are sensible that some matters are particularly important, as defense, and that not everyone is equally capable of carrying out these offices well); (iv) having no qualifications for any office or the smallest qualification possible (so that poverty excludes only a few from office, as in the case of some kinds of democracy, or no one, as in the case of others); (v) having no one occupy the same office twice or rarely or only in the case of a few offices (so that some do not rule often and others never or seldom, except again in the case of particularly important offices, as especially those relating to war); (vi) having all offices, or as many as possible, of short duration (so that the chance of being chosen comes round often, which feature, combined with the previous one, will ensure that pretty well everyone gets a turn at some office or other).

So much, then, concerns ensuring that all, or as many as possible, share in office. But to ensure that the offices have as little control as possible, the thing to do will be to give all the control to the other two parts of the regime, to the law courts and assembly, where, in contrast to the offices, many or all the populace can participate and rule together. So, with respect to the courts, the feature here is (vii) having everyone, or those chosen from everyone, decide all court cases (as in ultimate democracy), or most of them or those which are most important and have most control (as in other democracies), such as cases to do with the giving of accounts, or audits of officeholders, and with the regime and private contracts (or those private contracts which are of the sort, especially among the well-off, to affect the regime). With respect to the assembly, the feature here is (viii) having the assembly in control of everything or the most important things and no office in control of anything or as few things as possible. The different democracies will, of course, differ in how complete they are in giving control, or final decision, to the assembly and in taking it away from offices, as Aristotle notes in particular of the democratic office of the council. For while in the other democracies this office will indeed have not a little control (for the populace do not there have the leisure to meet often enough to decide everything directly), in ultimate democracy, where they do have the funds for leisure, it will have none.

Finally Aristotle mentions features to do with all three parts of the regime, namely first (ix) having pay provided for everyone, for the assembly, the law courts, and the offices if possible, or if not, for the offices, the law courts, the council, and those meetings of the assembly invested with most control or for those offices where common messes are a necessity. For otherwise some of the populace will be too poor to take their turn in these activities of the regime. The second feature is (x) that the marks of popular rule (or of the kinds of persons active in the several parts of the regime and thereby controlling the city) are no family, poverty, and vulgarity.

About this last feature (x) some doubts have been raised by commentators, because it does not seem to be deduced, as the others are, from the aim or supposition of the regime, but rather by way of contrast with oligarchy (whereas Aristotle has just indicated that the features of oligarchy are going to be understood from those of democracy and not vice versa, 8(6).1.1317a17–18), and also because oligarchy is said to be distinguished by education whereas education seems characteristic rather of aristocracy.[7]

But in response one should note, first, that Aristotle did say about the aim of democracy that it amounts to control by the needy over the well-off, and so it must follow that a democracy will be dominated by those who lack the qualities of the well-off. Hence these qualities will, by reason itself of the supposition of democracy, be deducible by contrast with those of oligarchy. Second, the opposing qualities of oligarchy, from which those of democracy are here derived, are qualities common to oligarchy and aristocracy alike. For education, which, as already noted, is the mark of aristocracy, requires leisure, and leisure requires wealth, and hence education tends to be associated with those who are well-off (6(4).8.1293b37–42); at any rate, the well-off have the leisure for education and most of them will pick up some smattering of it, even if they do not bother to get an education that is proper and complete. Hence the term "oligarchy" here is perhaps to be taken in that loose and popular sense where it is not sharply distinguished from aristocracy, and so where to use it as a way to the contrasting qualities of democracy both makes sense and does not offend the policy of understanding oligarchy from democracy. For, as regards the persons in control in democracy, these are, in point of quality, as much opposite to aristocrats as to oligarchs (since, lacking wealth, they also lack the privileges dependent on wealth, which privileges include the education of aristocrats); and, as regards the policy of understanding oligarchy from democracy, that policy (as just argued in the commentary on 8(6).1.1317a17–18) relates to understanding oligarchy in the strict and not the loose sense, namely rule by the well-off alone, and oligarchy in this sense is to be sharply distinguished from aristocracy and is the true opposite of democracy.

The final feature of democracy, (xi) having no office perpetual but if one might be left over from an ancient revolution, stripping it of its power and having it chosen by lot and not by election,[8] seems added by way of supplement. It was, of course, implicitly included in the earlier remarks about the offices, for a perpetual

7. These doubts are raised by Newman (4:497, 502), and see also Jowett (1885: 2:236).

8. A reference in particular, no doubt, to what happened to the archonship at Athens, *Athēnaiōn Politeia* 21–25, but also to ancient kingships generally, 3.14.1285b13–19.

office is not compatible with everyone ruling and being ruled by turns. But it is perhaps noted here at the end because stripping such an office of its power is, while a distinctive feature of democracies, a feature of democracies as successors to other regimes and not of democracies as such, and the concern now is features of democracies as such.[9]

∾ HOW TO SET UP THE KINDS OF DEMOCRACY

∾ THE FIRST OR RHETORICAL DEMOCRACY

1318a3   Having thus stated the features of democracy, Aristotle comes next to explain how to set up each kind of democracy. He begins with the first one he listed before (in 6(4).4.1291b30–39), which has the very aim or supposition of democracy as its boast, namely numerical equality. For this reason, therefore, it is the democracy that seems most of all to be democracy. But ultimate or extreme democracy is also described as the democracy that seems most of all to be democracy.[10] The inference can only be, then, that the first and last democracies are the same (something I already argued in my commentary on the passage in 6(4).4, on Kinds of Democracy, p. 306). That they must indeed be the same is evident if the first democracy insists so much on the principle of numerical equality. For this principle necessarily results in the needy having complete control over everything, including the laws. As Aristotle explained at the beginning of the previous chapter, numerical equality (because it gives equality to individuals and not to parts) necessarily produces superiority for the needy.

Nevertheless this ultimate democracy professes, in its rhetoric, to be the only equal regime or the only regime where everyone would believe there was equality and freedom. It does this because it professes to give to the needy no greater share in ruling than to the well-off. The problem with this rhetoric, and what gives it the lie, is that it always interprets equality as numerical equality. This equality gives the appearance of equality, for the well-off as individuals do indeed have equal shares in rule with the needy as individuals. But in fact, of course, it produces inequality because, on the one hand, it deprives the well-off as well-off of all share in rule while, on the other hand, it gives total control to the needy as needy. Democratic equality does not, in other words, give the part of the city that is constituted by the well-off any say, as such a part, in the way the city is run. All the say belongs instead to the part of the city that is constituted by the needy. But to ignore the differences

9. Newman (4:498) notes some features of democracy mentioned elsewhere by Aristotle and omitted here, as uniformity of nurture, education, and dress; license of wives, children, and slaves; boards of magistrates and ostracism. All these features can, nevertheless, be deduced from, or reduced to, features that Aristotle does mention.

10. As at 6(4).14:1298b13–15, 7(5).9.1310a25–28, which Newman (4:504) notes as a puzzle because he thinks that the democracy listed here and ultimate democracy are different.

of parts in the city like this and not to care about equality between them is, as noted before (in the commentary on 8(6).2.1317b3–10 p. 427), to ignore what the city properly is and so also to ignore what equality in the city properly is. In short, in ultimate democracy the greatest inequality masquerades under the rhetoric of the greatest equality, and a tyranny of the populace is imposed on the city in the name of freedom.

Chapter 3: 1318a11[11]   But if democracy's rhetoric of equality and freedom thus serves as a cloak for inequality and tyranny, one can still ask the question of what regime would be produced if this rhetoric were taken seriously, or what the first kind of democracy would look like if it really were set up so as to be equal between the needy and the well-off in the way it claims to be. So Aristotle turns to this question.

Democrats say that equality between needy and well-off is to be found by considering numbers or quantity only, but the well-off too claim rule on the basis of quantity, namely quantity of property. Aristotle therefore considers a regime that combines the two quantities, of property and of individuals. For purposes of illustration, he supposes that the property qualifications of 500 well-off are divided through 1,000 less well-off, so that the total property qualifications of the 1,000 add up to the total qualifications of the 500, and the 1,000 have equal shares with the 500. Here quantity of property is balanced out with quantity of numbers, for the lesser properties of a greater number equal the greater properties of a lesser number. Presumably one could continue this process and, by dividing the property qualifications of the 500 through larger numbers of the less well-off, include more people in the regime, and give them, on each occasion, no greater power than the original 500. Thus 2,000 with lower property qualifications individually than the 500, or even than the 1,000, but having all together a total that equals that of the 500, could have equal shares with the 500. At all events, this will be the way to equalize the two quantities of wealth and numbers, since it allows both quantities to count without giving a preponderance to either. For though wealth is the measure, which is oligarchic, this wealth is allowed to be divided through greater numbers, which is democratic. Thus contrary, on the one hand, to standard oligarchic practice, a greater number of the needy will be allowed an equal say with the well-off if the greater number have equal wealth; and contrary, on the other hand, to standard democratic practice, a lesser number of the well-off will be allowed an equal say with the mass of the needy if the lesser number have equal wealth.

Aristotle proposes two ways of thus equalizing wealth with numbers: either what he has just said, that each group as a whole shares in assembly and law courts

---

11. Note that the chapter division here obscures rather than articulates the process of Aristotle's argument, for he has already, before this point, passed from listing the features of democracy to discussing the different kinds of democracy.

but the votes of the 500 count double those of the 1,000 (or quadruple those of the 2,000), or what he adds now, that equal numbers from each group are chosen, say 100 from the 500 and 100 from the 1,000 (or 100 from the 2,000), and it is these 200 who share in assembly and law courts but the votes of each count the same. The question is, then, whether a regime ordered in either of these ways would be more just according to the equality proclaimed by democratic justice, or whether a regime ordered according to quantity would be.

By quantity Aristotle means, first, the standard democratic position that shares should go entirely to quantity of numbers, and that whatever the greater number think should be considered just. But he also means, interestingly enough, the opposing oligarchic position that shares should go entirely to quantity of wealth, and that what the greater wealth thinks should be considered just. This interesting twist looks to be another way in which Aristotle undermines democratic (and oligarchic) rhetoric. For both views say that shares should be distributed according to quantity, though a different quantity, so if justice is to be found by distributing shares according to quantity, why not by a combination of both quantities rather than by one of them to the exclusion of the other? And if democrats and oligarchs say in response, as they will want to, that their chosen quantity is the only just quantity when it comes to shares in rule, they will have to give an account of why it is so, which is something they otherwise forget or ignore and leads, ultimately, to what both want to avoid, namely the supremacy of the claims of virtue (3.9).

1318a21   The truth is, of course, that neither the democratic nor the oligarchic view secures either justice or equality. The oligarchic view will justify tyranny, since if one man's property exceeds all the rest he alone should rule and whatever he decides will be just. Conversely the democratic view will justify robbing the wealthy since if the majority decides so to do, and if whatever the majority decides is just, then it will be just to rob the minority and the wealthy. But no regime can be just, and no regime can be equal either between well-off and needy, which justifies the injustice of attacks on needy and well-off, as oligarchy does by justifying tyranny, or the injustice of attacks on the well-off alone, as democracy does by justifying robbery of the well-off.

1318a27   Having thus refuted the democratic (and oligarchic) way of finding justice and equality between well-off and needy, Aristotle next turns to prove his alternative way. The starting point here is simple enough, that if one is going to find an equality between two opposing sides which both these sides can agree is equal, one must take the views of each together and not, as democrats do, the view of one alone and then boast that that is equality. In this case, indeed, combining the views of each is easier to do than the disputes between democrats and oligarchs would make it appear. For, as has already in a way been indicated, both agree that the greater part of the citizens should be in control. The difference is that democrats say that this part is the greater number and the oligarchs say that it is the greater wealth.

The answer, then, is to let the agreed proposition stand, that the greater part of the citizens should be in control, but to define the respect in which it is to stand and not let it be taken in any way at all. For since each side takes "greater part" in a different way, an equality to which both sides could agree may be found if both these understandings are somehow combined, that is, if both the "greater parts" share rule together. They can do this if the views of both parts are taken separately, and if, in particular, the view of the rich is not made to disappear in a single majority vote with the poor.[12] So the two sides will find equality if that view is in control to which both sides separately agree, or to which the separate majorities of both sides separately agree.

If, however, their separate views are opposed, then equality can still be found if the majorities on either side are proportioned with each other according to one of the ways Aristotle suggested at the beginning. For if the two sides of wealth and numbers are equalized by giving equal shares to greater numbers when the greater numbers have equal wealth, then, in the case of opposed views, a common view can be found by proportioning accordingly the respective majorities and minorities on either side. Thus, taking the first of Aristotle's original alternatives, suppose that there are ten rich and twenty poor all sharing rule together, and that the twenty poor have equal power with the ten rich so that the vote of one of the rich is worth twice the vote of one of the poor. Suppose further that six of the rich have voted one way and fifteen of the poor the other (so that the majorities of rich and poor are opposed). Then, necessarily, four of the rich agree with the majority of the poor and five of the poor with the majority of the rich. So add the votes according to their respective weighting. The four rich are worth eight votes when added to the fifteen poor bringing that side's total to twenty-three. Conversely the six rich are worth twelve votes when added to the five poor bringing that side's total to seventeen. Thus the side with the twenty-three votes wins (and this victory is not the victory of either rich or poor, but of a combination of both rich and poor). But suppose that, even after this adding up of votes, there is a tie. Then the answer is to do what is already done when there are tied votes in existing democratic assemblies and law courts: have recourse to lot, or a casting vote, or something similar.[13]

Such at any rate is how to achieve equality between rich and poor and so to real-

12. Note that Aristotle here ignores the other part of the city, the virtuous, though not, doubtless, because he no longer thinks they are a part, but rather because he is here confining himself to democracies and oligarchies and how to combine them to produce equality, and neither oligarchies nor democracies pay attention to virtue. Aristocracies, of course, do, and though such regimes are possible, they are rare and not relevant at present; cf. 6(4).11.1295a31–34.

13. In the case of Aristotle's alternative way of combining rich and poor, when 100 are taken from 500 rich and 100 from 1,000 poor, no weighting of votes will be needed, but a simple majority (which will always have to be a combination of votes from both rich and poor) will decide the issue.

ize in truth, and not in appearance, the claim of equality made by democratic rhetoric. The resulting regime, of course, will not be a democracy, for the mass of the poor will not be in control. It will in fact be a polity, or some sort of middle regime, that mixes rich and poor and shares control between both. Thus the first or rhetorical democracy becomes on the one hand, if the rhetoric is taken seriously, a polity, and on the other hand, if the rhetoric is used instead as a cloak for dominance by the poor, ultimate democracy. In neither case is it really another and fifth kind of democracy, unless polity be called, as it is by some, a sort of democracy.

1318b1   But it is one thing to find out the truth about equality and justice and another to achieve it, and if the first is very difficult it is still easier than the second. The reason is what Aristotle indicated before (6(4).11.1296a22–b2), that almost invariably one or other side, rich or poor, is in a position of superiority and has the power to gain more for itself, and when it is, it wants total control and is not prepared to share with opponents. It only wants equality and justice when it is inferior and so when, of course, it no longer has power to do anything.

Chapter 4

~ THE OTHER DEMOCRACIES
1318b16   Since the first or rhetorical democracy is deceptive and reduces in practice to the last or ultimate democracy, there are only four democracies properly speaking. So Aristotle turns his consideration to these. About the first of them he begins by showing that it is the best (for the aim of political science, as explained before in 6(4).1, is to set up the best regime possible or desired, and so the relative goodness of the several regimes needs to be stated), and then he shows how to set it up. As regards its being the best, he argues this in two ways, from the character of the populace who have control, and from how many of the democratic features it combines. For democracies, as he said (8(6).1.1317a22–33), are distinguished from each other, and are also better or worse, in these two ways: that their populace is better or worse and that they combine fewer or more democratic features.

The populace in the first democracy is an agrarian one, composed of farmers or herdsmen, and that such have the best character is shown by the fact that, first, they possess too little property to have the leisure to attend many assemblies, and, second, that the need to secure a living from this property keeps them busy and not desirous of the property of others (those who have their own farm and flocks to look after notoriously work long hours and have much respect for the rights of property). Both facts together will make an agrarian populace the best populace. For this populace will be better than the populace of ultimate democracy since it lacks leisure and so will have to control the regime through laws and offices and not directly by its own decrees; and it will be better than the populaces of the other democracies since it will not have any desire to rob the well-off, whereas these other populaces, because they lack property, have little respect for the rights of property and would rule without law if they could (6(4).4.1292a1–7, 6.1292b34–1293a10).

In support of these facts about an agrarian populace, or that such a populace will prefer honest work to the direct exercise of rule, is that the many in general, whether agrarian or not, love profit rather than honor (for their physical needs are manifestly more pressing). Hence, provided office is not a way to make money, they will prefer to be left to their work, which brings them profit, than to be bothered with rule, which will take them from their work and only bring them honor. Evidence for this claim about the reluctance of the populace to rule is that, first, the many have put up with being altogether deprived of rule, under tyrannies in the past and under oligarchies now, provided only they are allowed to work and are not robbed of the profits (for thus they improve their condition), and that, second, when the populace do want some share of the honors of rule, or have some ambition (*philotimia*, 1318b22, which literally means love of honor), they are satisfied with relatively little, as merely with electing and auditing the offices (the case in a polity or mixed regime, 3.11.1281b31–38).[14] The point is proved by Mantinea, even though the populace did not in fact elect the offices in Mantinea but were content to have control by turns over deliberation (Mantinea was thus a democracy, for those who control the deliberative body control the regime). For if the populace in a democracy can be content thus to be deprived of everything save that minimum share in rule necessary to make the regime a democracy (control by the populace over the deliberative), then they can be content to have a minimum share elsewhere too, and so in particular could be content to control elections and audits but not deliberation (as in a polity).

1318b27   An agrarian populace is also best because it combines fewer democratic features (for, as said earlier at 8(6).1.1317a29–33, democracies become worse and more extreme the more of these features they have). So, besides having general control over the regime through a popular assembly (the minimum for democracy), the first democracy only has in addition the features that the many elect and audit the offices and sit on juries.[15] It does not have the lot, nor are offices open to all, nor does the assembly control everything through its own decisions, nor is pay provided, nor are low and vulgar persons in the offices, nor need these offices be

14. Newman (4:511) quotes the following report about Bulgarian peasants: "A very little voting would be enough for the Bulgarian peasant, who grudges a walk to the polling-place as so much time taken from the more serious business of field-labor. In some districts it is difficult to find candidates for the Sobranje, and the village patriarch who lets himself be elected makes a virtue of his self-denial."

15. Newman (4:511–12) suggests that this description of an agrarian democracy fits Solon's regime. But Solon's regime did not give the populace control over the deliberative but only a share in it, so it was a polity rather than a democracy; see 3.11, especially 1281b32–38.

many nor held only once and for short periods. Instead it has a property qualification for office, and a higher qualification for the greater offices, or else it requires definite ability for office.

That such a combination of features is best is proved from the fact that such a regime must necessarily be nobly governed (insofar, indeed, as a deviant regime can be noble). For the offices will be in the hands of the best (the best, at least, that there are in the city) and the populace will consent and not envy the decent or the best. These best, or the decent and notables, will also have enough, both because they will not be subject to men worse than themselves in the offices, and because they will be forced to be just by having to give an account of their rule to others, that is, the populace. For only the simply best men, who have perfect virtue, will rule justly by their own unfettered choice. All the rest, in whom virtue has not fully mastered the base element in them, will only rule justly if that base element is restrained by something outside them, namely by the law that subjects them to the oversight of others. So in such a democracy the decent rule, and rule well, and the populace is not oppressed, which is necessarily something noble (and close, indeed, to polity and the middle regime). It has thus been proved in both ways (by the particular quality of the populace and by the particular combination of democratic features) that an agrarian democracy is best, but primarily by the first, that the populace is of a certain character. For it is because the populace is restrained in its character that the democracy is also restrained in the democratic features it combines.

1319a6 Aristotle now turns to the next topic, the setting up of such a democracy. Here, clearly, the essential thing to do is to ensure that the populace is and stays agrarian (for from this all else follows). Aristotle notes several proposals, and in particular laws prohibiting the acquisition of too much land and of land too near the site of the city. For the effect of such laws will be to prevent the emergence of a body of the well-off whose amount and quality of land would make them strong enough to wrest control from the populace and thus to institute an oligarchy. A third law is to forbid the sale of the minimal or original allotment of land, or to forbid the securing of loans against it. The effect of this will be to keep the numbers of small farmers large and so the strongest element in the city (and, if a regime is to survive, those in control must be the strongest part). It will also prevent these farmers from selling their land and migrating to the town where they would lose their agrarian character and swell the numbers of worse kinds of populace.

All these laws concern ways of keeping people on the land and of preventing the decline of an agrarian populace. But in present conditions this decline has already occurred, and so there is also need of laws to reverse it if an agrarian democracy is to be set up. One such law is that of the Aphytaeans who manage to have everyone farming despite having little land because they give shares in the assembly to those who have a certain part of the property qualification and not just to those who have the whole of it. Hence any of the populace who have sold or mortgaged some of their land will nevertheless be discouraged from selling or mortgaging all of it, and any who have no land will be encouraged to use their profits from other labor to purchase the necessary minimum amount of it.

Such laws, from ancient and modern times, are doubtless intended by Aristotle to be illustrative, not exhaustive, and sufficient to give the legislator a good idea of where to look and of which laws to choose for his purpose from any catalogs of laws he may have to hand (cf. *Ethics* 10.9.1181a15–b12).

1319a19 An agrarian democracy can be set up, then, under these sort of circumstances. But it can also be set up under other ones, as for instance if herdsmen are included in rule along with the farmers. For herdsmen are next best after farmers, being similar to them in habits and way of life and also well fitted for war. Herdsmen are presumably not as good as farmers, for, although they spend much time busy in the countryside, their work is less labor intensive and they have more idle hours (flocks generally need less looking after; cf. 1.8.1256a30–35). Still they are enough like farmers in their habits, and are similarly fit enough for serving as soldiers, that they could be included in an agrarian democracy, and so could help to make it stronger, without any real detriment.

The matter is different with the other sorts of populace, the mechanics and traders and laborers, who make up the other democracies. Not only does their way of life involve no virtue, so that they do not even have any goodness as a mass (whereas the life of farming and herding involves at least some military virtue), but they are also concentrated in the town and can easily attend more frequent assemblies and could, if possessed of leisure through the disbursement of common funds, wrest control away from the laws and the offices. An agrarian democracy could not be set up under these circumstances, but only some inferior democracy. An agrarian democracy requires the better sort of populace of farmers and herders, and consequently if, in addition to having such a populace, the city is situated such that its land is some distance away (as when, for instance, it is near the sea and its fields are in the interior, or when it is on a narrow headland or promontory),[16] setting up a decent democracy or a polity, such that the populace have control but exercise it infrequently or share it with the well-off, will be particularly easy. For such a populace will find it impossible to spend time in the city attending assemblies. But if there is nevertheless a crowd of people who do spend their time in the city and the public square (some of whom at any rate would meet the property qualification), control can still be kept in the hands of the agrarian populace, and so a decent democracy or polity can still be set up, if there is a law forbidding meetings of the assembly when the multitude from the countryside are not also

16. Newman (4:520) notes these as features of parts of the Greek world, and of colonies in particular.

present. For then assemblies will necessarily be infrequent and, when they do take place, the farmers and herdsmen will predominate, or be strong enough to prevent excesses.

1319a38 So much, then, concerns the first or agrarian democracy. As regards the others, that they are worse has just been shown in the preceding comparison of the kinds of populace, so what remains is to discuss how to set them up. Again, as before, the essential thing is to get the right sort of populace, which can be done if, at each stage, one brings the next worse element into the regime, adding first to the farmers and herdsmen all those artisans and traders in the market and laborers whose citizen descent passes scrutiny, which is the next democracy, and then adding to these all the rest who can claim to be free or citizens whether descended from citizens or not, which is the third democracy (6(4).4.1292a1–6, 6.1292b34–41). The second democracy would presumably be better than the third because its populace would feel, through established family descent, more affection and loyalty to the city and its existing traditions and so also to the laws, whereas the third, because of the multitude of those who have no such descent, would feel less affection and loyalty and so would be readier for change and for introducing a more lawless and disruptive sort of rule.

1319b1 The last and fourth democracy is the same as these two save that now the populace has enough leisure for frequent assemblies and for controlling everything directly without law by its own decrees. However, because it allows everyone into the regime, including the simply worst elements, it cannot be set up in some cities (those, doubtless, where the wealthier and better elements are too strong to let it come about), and in others where it can be set up it does not survive long if it is too extreme in its composition, that is, if it extends the franchise too widely. Such extremism is what demagogues aim at, supposing that the regime will be stronger if the populace is as great in numbers as possible and includes bastards as well as those with one parent a slave or an alien. But a larger populace is not necessarily a stronger populace (cf. 4(7).4.1326a8–25), especially since all it tends to do, as was noted before (7(5).5) and is again noted here, is to provoke faction and revolution. The path to follow instead is to extend the franchise only as far as is necessary to make the populace outweigh the notables and the middle (according, of course, to the proportion of both numbers and quality, 6(4).12.1296b15–31). For then the populace will have the necessary control of the regime (they will be dominant in the assembly), but will not, by their numbers and disorder, provoke a revolution. For the notables will more easily tolerate rule by a populace that is evil and base up to a point than by one that is excessively and offensively so.

1319b19 There are nevertheless ways of strengthening such a regime without increasing, like demagogues, the numbers of the overly base included in it. For, first (in imitation of Cleisthenes at Athens, 3.2.1257b34–39, and *Athēnaiōn Politeia* 21), the whole citizen body can be mixed up with each other and old groupings and family connections can be dissolved, the effect of which would presumably be to hide, to some extent, the base origin of those among the populace who need to be added to the regime and given shares in rule (for their origin will not appear in official records), and also perhaps to hasten their acceptance by the existing citizens, since these existing citizens will be having to accept so many other new things at the same time. Second, very large numbers can be got to support the regime, even without the extension to them of the franchise, if they are allowed more license and are not hindered from living as they wish. So one can, in imitation of tyranny, get slaves, women, and children to support the democracy in this sort of way. Indeed the many in general will support such a regime (including those of the needy excluded from shares in rule, and doubtless not a few of the well-off too), since the many prefer to live lives of disorder than of moderation and control.[17]

Chapter 5

~ HOW TO MAKE THE KINDS OF DEMOCRACY ENDURE

1319b33   There is no point, however, in setting up a regime if it is not going to last, for a regime is supposed to enable the city to function and live the best life it can, which it will not be able to do if its regimes keep on collapsing after a few days. Certainly there would be no need of study or legislative science in such a case, for any regime at all, set up in any way at all, could survive for one or two or three days.[18] There is need, therefore, for the legislator not only to get the right sort of ruling body for his regime (the topic just discussed) but also to order the democracy in such a way that it can preserve itself.

The first advice Aristotle gives here is to take all that was said in the previous book about the ways regimes are destroyed and preserved and to guard against the first and to embrace the second, and in particular not to suppose that measures are only democratic or oligarchic (or indeed suitable to any regime) which make the regime more extreme in type instead of those which make it endure.

This piece of advice is suitably general and comprehensive, for it applies in principle to all regimes and covers all possible measures. So it is, by itself, already

17. Of course, one faces here the problem that a lawless or licentious populace, that lives as it likes, is a cause of overthrow; see 7(5).9.1310a25–36. But this is mainly because their possession of rule is offensive to the notables and excites evil demagogues (7(5).5), and Aristotle has here cleverly contrived to have most of them excluded from actual shares in rule, so that they are not in the assembly to cause disgust to the notables and to become easy prey to the flattery of demagogues. One may also note, incidentally, that this device of allowing people to live as they like, while nevertheless denying them an active share in government, is much used by the political parties that divide rule among themselves in modern nation-states to hold on to their monopoly of power.

18. Mansfield (1989: 309 n34) interestingly suggests that there may be an oblique reference here to Platonic dialogues, where regimes are set up and endure in a speech that lasts a day or so.

sufficient. But Aristotle does not, in the particular advice he proceeds to give in the following sections (here about democracies and later about oligarchies), go over in detail everything that his general advice thus in principle covers. Instead he confines himself to certain points only. These points, therefore, must be taken as illustrative and suggestive, designed to get the serious legislator thinking along the right lines, and not taken as saying everything that could be said. The particular pieces of advice Aristotle gives about democracy here are all, nevertheless, instances of what he has just said, namely how to guard against what destroys democracies and how to introduce into the laws what will preserve them. They also apply in the first instance to the last kind of democracy, but most could also be put to good use in the other democracies as well.

1320a4 The first particular piece of advice is counter to the demagogues' habit of attacking the rich through the law courts. This habit was earlier said to be the main cause of destruction of democracies (7(5).5), and springs from the false supposition, just criticized, about what does and does not count as a democratic measure or policy. The advice, then, is that true democrats, those who care about the regime and want it to survive, should oppose the demagogues and introduce laws, not indeed to stop all prosecutions of the notables (which would indeed not be just if the notables do wrong, nor acceptable to the populace), but to make sure that these prosecutions are serious and are decided in court fairly.

So, first, any fines imposed in cases involving common matters (only such cases would produce revenue for the demagogues to distribute, as private cases would issue in restitution only to the aggrieved party) should be declared sacred, not public, and so for religious uses, not for handing out as doles to the populace. This will ensure that genuine wrongdoers will be no less afraid, since they will still face the same penalties, while also ensuring that the populace reach more unbiased verdicts, since they will have nothing personally to gain from conviction. The clever thing about this law is that it calls the demagogues' bluff, as it were, and beats them at their own game. For demagogues profess in their prosecutions to be serving the public good and punishing wrongdoers, though secretly they really want money to distribute. This law, however, allows prosecutions to serve the professed purpose of prosecutions, so that demagogues could hardly speak out against it without revealing their secret intentions, and yet makes it impossible for those secret intentions to be realized.

Second, the demagogues can be curbed from introducing lots of prosecutions, and the prosecutions that are introduced can be kept to those that are really serious, by imposing heavy penalties on prosecutions that are frivolous or random. For such prosecutions are invariably brought against the notables (since it is the notables who have the money the prosecutors want), and so make these notables ill disposed to the regime and eager to destroy it. But regimes are preserved and last longer if no one is ill disposed or at least does not regard those in control as enemies. This law, too, similarly traps the demagogues in their own rhetoric, for no one could seriously claim that random prosecutions, and prosecutions that always fall on the rich, serve the cause of justice and not of greed.

1320a17   But it is not just the demagogues who, to win the favor of the crowd, want to attack the notables in this way; for where there are no other sources of revenue the populace too want to attack the notables, so that there will be money to pay them for attending meetings of assembly and law courts. The only way to counter this is to reduce the number of meetings so that either the populace can attend without being paid, or so that the amount of taxes imposed on the rich for this purpose is not excessive. Thus assemblies should be reduced to those that are really necessary and the jury courts should be given competence over more cases (so that fewer courts meeting less frequently can complete more business). The result is that the rich will not become hostile to the regime through fear of having to pay heavy taxes to finance all the meetings, and that the decisions reached at the meetings that do take place will be better, for the well-off will be willing to take time off to attend and so will always be present in sufficient numbers to oppose extreme proposals.

1320a29   Where there are revenues, of course, this problem does not arise, but other ones do. To imitate the demagogues and distribute this revenue in doles to the multitude only excites in them greed for more and, in addition, does nothing to improve their character. They remain excessively needy (for the doles are not big enough to last long), and so a continuing provocation to the notables. The thing to do instead is to accumulate the revenues and to help the needy to improve their lot by giving out these revenues in lump sums, whether to all the needy or to sections of them in turn, so that the needy can become property owners or productive traders or farmers. They will thus be less offensive to the notables as well as less eager to confiscate their wealth. Such a policy would, of course, be useful in any democracy, including an agrarian one, since the agrarian populace could thereby be strengthened. But it would be particularly useful in an ultimate democracy, for though the assembly would remain directly in control of everything, its behavior and decrees would be less extreme and hostility between well-off and needy much reduced. But since, under this proposal, the revenues will not be available to pay for attendance at assembly and law courts, pay could still be provided for this purpose (as is required in ultimate democracy) if, first, the rich are taxed but only to provide pay for the few really necessary meetings, and if, second, they are not additionally burdened with pointless public services (as putting on public entertainments, perhaps, that are fleeting and do nothing but feed the passion for excitement).

The possibility of pursuing such a policy and the success that can be had with it is proved by the example of Carthage. For Carthage has managed to make the needy friendly to the well-off by giving them opportunities to acquire their own wealth. So if Carthage can make the needy friendly to the well-off in this way, even though the needy there have more reason for resentment because the well-off have more control (2.11), then so much the more must democracies be able to do the same, because the needy are in control and have no reason for similar resentment.

1320b7   The main problem in democracies is, of course, the hostility between populace and notables, and another way in which this hostility can be reduced and the notables protected is if the notables themselves take the initiative. So they can reduce the numbers of the idle poor or needy, those who demand pay and have time to meddle, by giving them a start to make their own living in useful labor. They can also make friends of the multitude by allowing them, like the Tarentines, the use of their own properties (which is a version of Aristotle's standing recommendation to make properties private but their use common, 2.5.1263a22–40, 4(7).10.1329b41–1330a2).

1320b11   The last piece of advice also comes from the Tarentines and concerns a way of including the populace in the offices while not worsening the quality of government. It is to have the offices double, one elected (where the notables will likely dominate) and one chosen by lot (where the populace will), and to make both offices together share rule. The same effect can, however, be achieved, and more simply, if one and the same office is filled by several persons at once, some of whom are elected and others chosen by lot. This piece of advice would be useful in ultimate democracy but would perhaps also help to prevent another kind of democracy from becoming an ultimate one, because it could be used to satisfy the populace's demand for more control without at the same time requiring all power to be taken away from the offices.

Chapter 6

～ THE SETTING UP OF OLIGARCHIES

～ HOW TO SET UP THE KINDS OF OLIGARCHY

1320b18   Having thus dealt with democracies, Aristotle turns, as he promised in the opening chapter, to oligarchies. Here the same procedure as with democracies is to be followed. First, the features of oligarchy should be listed, which will of course be the opposites of those given for democracy (in 8(6).2), and then each oligarchy can be understood and brought together, as the democracies were, by taking more or fewer of these features and by using the contrasting or corresponding democracy as analog. So, if the first democracy has such and such democratic features but not others, then the first oligarchy will have the opposites of the same features but not the opposites of the others, and so on.[19] Aristotle does not bother, therefore, to list these oligarchic features, because finding opposites is straightforward enough (for instance, as democratic justice is equality, so oligarchic justice is inequality; as democracies choose all offices from all, so oligarchies choose all offices from some; as democracies have rule by turns, so oligarchies have rule always by the same people; and so on in the same way with each of the eleven democratic features listed in 8(6).2). Instead he takes these features as understood and proceeds directly to explain how each oligarchy is to be set up.

In the case of democracies, Aristotle had first argued which one was best and which were progressively worse. But he need not do this in the case of oligarchies, for their ordering too will be evident from the corresponding democracies, with the oligarchy corresponding to the better democracy itself being better and so on. Nevertheless he does point out in the case of the first oligarchy, partly no doubt by way of identification, that it is close to polity, but from this its superiority to other oligarchies also follows, for what is closer to a better regime must itself be better (cf. 6(4).11.1296b2–9).

At all events, the essential thing in setting up oligarchies, as in setting up democracies, is to get the right sort of ruling body. In the case of the first oligarchy, the ruling body is a fairly large one and includes those who are not excessively rich. So, first, there must, in opposition to democracy, be a high property qualification but this property qualification cannot, in the case of the necessary offices (the deliberative in particular, which is determinative of the regime), be set so high as to exclude those without excessive wealth. The qualification can, and should, however, be set higher for the offices that are more in control, which must mean offices that give their holders greater individual control over major matters, though not so much as to control the regime (for that would make the regime an extreme oligarchy). In this way the regime will be an oligarchy, giving greater privileges to wealth as such, and not just a polity leaning toward oligarchy. Second, anyone who reaches the property qualification must have the right to take part (otherwise the oligarchy will be of some other and more extreme kind). Third, with respect to where to set the property qualification, this must be low enough to include as many of the populace as is necessary to ensure that those who share in the regime are stronger (in quality and numbers) than those who do not (otherwise the

19. The interpretation I give here of Aristotle's remarks is that of Newman (4:538). It makes Aristotle's procedure for oligarchies follow his procedure for democracies as closely as possible, and shows how each oligarchy is brought together or constructed on the analog of its contrasting democracy. For as the most measured democracy has fewer of the democratic features, so the most measured oligarchy has fewer of the oligarchic features, and so on, contra Barker (1946: 270 n1). Thus also the democracies become the guide and key to their opposites and so to the understanding of oligarchy as rule of the well-off, 8(6).1.1317a17.

regime will be easy to overthrow), yet high enough to exclude all but the better part of the populace (otherwise the regime will be too democratic).

1320b29   The next oligarchies can all be constructed by progressively tightening the qualifications for office (not just by requiring greater wealth, but also by requiring election, or election by certain people, or descent within certain families, 6(4).5.1292a39–b10, 6.1293a12–34). In this way the sort of ruling body necessary to constitute each kind of oligarchy can at each stage be properly separated out for exclusive shares in the regime.

Of course, the effect of this process is so to reduce the numbers of those in the regime, and so to increase the qualifications for rule, that the last oligarchy in particular, which, like the last democracy, is most extreme in its character and combines most of the oligarchic features, will include very few and exclude very many (even very many from among the well-off). It will accordingly have many enemies and few friends and be most in need of careful guarding if it is to survive (just as is true of other things, as bodies and ships, that are in a bad condition). The same will be true, to lesser degrees, of the other oligarchies after the first. Consequently, once the relevant ruling body for setting up each oligarchy has been secured, the need to introduce additional measures to make the regime last is going to be particularly urgent. For while democracies, including disorderly ones, can sometimes survive by the sheer size of their numbers and without much in the way of additional measures to restrain excesses, oligarchies by contrast do not have this advantage but must seek their salvation in how well they are arranged.

Chapter 7

~   HOW TO MAKE THE KINDS OF OLIGARCHY ENDURE

1321a5   Aristotle has explained before (7(5).6) that oligarchies are mainly overthrown either from without the regime, by those excluded from rule, or from within, by strife among the oligarchs themselves. In this chapter, however, he concentrates on setting up oligarchies to escape the first kind of overthrow only. Perhaps this is because it is no use putting efforts into making an oligarchy unanimous and safe from within the regime if it has not first been made strong enough to survive threats from without (for if it cannot do that, it will not survive long however well it is arranged internally, as is shown by the case of Erythrae, 7(5).6.1305b18–22). The chief concern of the legislator, therefore, would seem to be to ensure that the oligarchy he sets up is strong externally and is supported and preserved by the stronger part of the city—according to the principle set down in 6(4).12 (though some of Aristotle's advice could also be of help internally).

Such strength is itself primarily a military matter (for it is primarily a matter of defense), so an oligarchy, to survive, must have the necessary superiority in military strength over all the excluded. Consequently Aristotle begins by listing the parts of the multitude and the parts of military force, for these make it clear how an oligarchy can be rendered strong in the necessary way. The kinds of force in which oligarchs are naturally stronger will be those where expensive equipment is required and so where the multitude, because too poor to equip themselves in the same way, cannot make their greater numbers count. Thus oligarchs will be superior in cavalry and in heavy armed infantry. Moreover the wealthiest oligarchs will have exclusive possession of the cavalry, since the less wealthy will not be able to afford to keep and train horses. The first inference, then, is that the worse and more narrow oligarchies, which have very tight qualifications for office, are only going to be strong and durable, and so only safe to set up, where defense depends on the cavalry.[20] But where defense depends on heavy armed troops, such a narrow cavalry oligarchy would easily be overthrown, and some less narrow oligarchy would be called for, with the first and least extreme oligarchy being the strongest, for it would be nearest to polity, which is above all the regime of the hoplites (6(4).13.1297b1–2).

1321a13 No oligarchy, however, because of its smaller numbers, is going to be stronger than a large populace in those kinds of military force where the populace can fight on equal terms, that is, where little or no expensive equipment is required. Such forces are light armed troops and the navy (for even if the rich must provide the warships, they cannot provide the crews). Where defense depends above all on the navy (as at Athens), setting up an oligarchy is going to be fairly pointless since the populace are always going to be too strong for it. However something can be done to enable an oligarchy to survive when faction comes from a populace of light armed troops (who can get the better of cavalry and heavy infantry when fighting in narrow and rough spaces, as in hill country and the town, instead of in open spaces). The answer is for the oligarchs to imitate expert generals and complement their cavalry and heavy infantry with a force of light armed troops. These troops, however, cannot be taken from the populace for the populace are, ex hypothesi, hostile. Instead advantage must be taken of the younger generation of oligarchs who, when boys, can usefully be trained in light armed fighting and who can act in this capacity as they mature before passing on into the heavy infantry or cavalry.[21] In this way an oligarchy could be stronger than a much larger populace, for the oligarchs would have a full complement of forces, able to protect

20. Newman (4:540–41) suggests that Aristotle has Lysander in mind here, when the latter made this mistake in setting up a narrow oligarchy in Athens, a place not suitable for cavalry. He also suggests that Aristotle is remembering, in contrast, the narrow oligarchies set up by Philip of Macedon in Thessaly, a place very well suited to cavalry.

21. Newman (4:543–44) notes that this was the practice in Boeotia, though he also adds that Aristotle's suggestion would run counter to the prejudices of most oligarchs.

each other and to attack in turn as the opportunity arose, whereas the populace would always be one-sided and vulnerable in conditions not favoring them.

1321a26   So much concerns making the oligarchy strong by enabling it to defeat the populace if they become hostile. The final pieces of advice concern making it strong by lessening or even removing the chances that the multitude (or the excluded in general, among whom may be some of the well-off) will become hostile. The first concerns ways of continually drawing some of the excluded into the regime. So, as regards the first kind of oligarchy (from 6(4).5), its distinctive feature, that all those who have acquired the property qualification are to be admitted to shares in the ruling body, should be carefully observed. As regards the other oligarchies, where entry into the regime is by the choice of the existing oligarchs, those should be admitted who have abstained from vulgar occupations for a definite period or who are adjudged to be most worthy of rule. And, in the last case, the judgment should be made to work the other way too, and even those within the ruling body (those, presumably, who are entitled to vote and stand for office) should not in fact be elected to any office, if they are adjudged unworthy (this would reconcile the excluded even more to the regime, and make the regime itself less extreme, if office depends, and is seen to depend, on some sort of merit as well as on wealth). This policy could, indeed, be pursued up to a point by ultimate oligarchy too, where only sons of oligarchs succeed to rule. For the oligarchs could make a judgment about which one of the sons was most worthy to succeed, or allow two or more sons of the same father to succeed if all were worthy enough, or not choose any son who proved unworthy.

1321a31   The second and last piece of advice about lessening or removing hostility to the regime concerns ways of making the offices unattractive to those who are needy or not excessively rich. So the offices with most control, and which must be kept in the hands of the ruling oligarchs if the regime is to survive, should be burdened with heavy financial responsibilities or public services. For then the populace (and the less well off), who would be ruined by having to undertake such public services, will both be willing not to have a share in these offices and will be forgiving, or look with indulgence and not hostility, on the rulers who do share in these offices because of what they have to pay for the privilege. Also, oligarchs entering upon office should undertake some notable public project, as offering a magnificent sacrifice or setting up grand buildings and statues. For the populace will be glad to see the regime continue when they see how well adorned the city is. The notables too will be content (and oligarchies are also threatened, of course, by disgruntled oligarchs) to see permanent memorials of themselves everywhere.

These pieces of advice are evidently sound, and oligarchs sensible enough to do what is necessary to see their regime survive could readily be persuaded to adopt them. That many oligarchs do the opposite, and refuse to spend their wealth for the privilege of office, is because they are as much in love with making money as with honor, and so are more ready to have their regime short-lived than to give up the chance of gain. They are, therefore, more like the populace, whose distinctive feature, because of their poverty, is to prefer making money to having the honors of office. So it is well, concludes Aristotle in a last and pointed remark, to call such regimes small democracies rather than oligarchies. For as regards what motivates the oligarchs who rule in them, if not as regards their basis for rule, they are no different from the populace.

Chapter 8

∼ THE ELEMENTS OF RULE AVAILABLE FOR COMBINING

1321b4   The remaining topic from the program set out in the first chapter is the combinations of regimes, but it is not immediately clear that this is what comes next. For Aristotle now turns to distinguish the offices, their number, their kinds, and their power or spheres of control, which is not, as such, to examine the combinations of regimes.[22] But Aristotle immediately gives two reasons for what he does. The first reason is that cities need the necessary offices in order to exist and the offices to do with good arrangement in order to exist well or be managed nobly. The second reason is that small cities must have fewer offices and large ones more. Hence, he concludes, what offices are suitable for being combined and what for keeping separate must not be overlooked.

This sort of combination of offices is not the same as the combinations of regimes, for the latter are not combinations of offices but combinations of modes of setting up offices (if "office" is taken broadly to mean all three parts of the regime), such as the combining of an oligarchic mode of the deliberative with an aristocratic mode of the judiciary (8(6).1.1316b39–1317a10). But understanding the combinations of offices in this sense would seem a necessary preliminary to understanding the combinations of modes of setting them up. For any offices that are or must be combined into one must necessarily also have one and the same mode of being set up (whether this mode be itself mixed or pure), and only offices that are or must be kept distinct can be given the different modes of appointment needed for combined regimes. Consequently what sort of combined regime can suitably be set up in what sort of city (and getting the right sort of city, or the right sort of multitude, is the key to setting up any regime) will depend in large part on the size of the city. For large cities will admit of more complex combinations than small cities (a small city, for instance, might only be able to have one mode of appoint-

22. As is noted by Newman (4:547) and Sinclair/Saunders (1981: 379–80).

ment for all the parts of the judiciary while a large city could have different modes for different parts).

Further, combined regimes, being mixed regimes, are correct regimes (in contrast to democracies and oligarchies which are all deviations). Therefore, besides offices devoted to necessary things, they will also have to have some offices devoted to noble things (for noble life is the end of the city, which a correct regime must aim at in order to be correct, 3.6). So how and whether noble offices are to be combined with necessary offices will also determine how and whether a given combined regime can suitably be set up in a given city. The sort of discussion, therefore, that Aristotle now gives, about the offices and their powers (for offices admit of being combined or separated by how their powers admit of being combined or separated; cf. 6(4).15.1300b5–12), is not inappropriate as a beginning of a discussion of combined regimes.[23]

That Aristotle's interest is indeed now focused on the combined, and so correct, regimes can be further confirmed by the offices he lists. For he divides these fundamentally into the necessary and the noble and, of course, only correct regimes need the noble offices (the deviant regimes are even incapable of them, 1323a3–6 and cf. 6(4).15.1300a4–8). Furthermore, he distinguishes between necessary offices that are of lesser rank and necessary offices that are of greater rank, and these latter are of greater rank because they need more in the way of virtue (1322a30–33), which fact is specially noted, no doubt, because, in a correct regime, such offices should preferably be given a more aristocratic mode of appointment. In addition, he also distinguishes between necessary offices that are political and necessary offices to do with the gods (1322b17–19). But offices to do with the gods are only strictly speaking necessary in correct regimes, for these regimes, in caring about virtue, must care about the gods who are the guardians of virtue. Deviant regimes may indeed typically devote care to the gods, but more, it would appear, from selfishness or superstition than from genuine piety, for there is nothing in their aim that requires genuine, as opposed to apparent, piety (cf. 7(5).11.1314b38–1315a3).[24]

1321b12/b18/b27/b30 Aristotle begins his list with the necessary offices of lesser rank, before he comes to necessary offices of higher rank (at 1322a30), and then lastly to offices to do with leisure (at 1322b37). Although Aristotle's listing of all these offices is not perhaps exhaustive in detail, it would seem to be exhaustive in its general form. For it covers all the parts of the regime: the offices and the judiciary and the deliberative, and all the parts of the city: those to do with food and the arts and the market, those to do with a supply of wealth, those to do with

23. I have elaborated here on a suggestion of Lord's (1984: 265 n2).

24. It is worth recalling here that when speaking of the parts of the city in the context of the best regime Aristotle included the priests, but did not include them when talking about the parts of the city in the context of the deviant regimes; see 4(7).8.1328b11–13 and 6(4).4.1290b38–1291a36.

defense, those to do with judgment and deliberation, those to do with the gods. Any offices not expressly mentioned could accordingly be made to fall under one or more of these heads.[25]

The first necessary offices to be listed are the following three: offices to care for the market and the getting of material self-sufficiency; offices to care for the town property, both public and private; and offices to do the same for the property about the country. Aristotle groups these together as a threesome, by which he perhaps means to indicate that they could suitably be combined into one if necessary. For they all care for similar things, material goods, in a similar way (cf. 6(4).15.1299b14–18). A next, and related, office is that which collects and distributes the public revenues, for no office can perform its task, least of all these first three, without the necessary finances.

1321b34 Aristotle comes next and not unnaturally to offices relating to the administration of justice, for many disputes about what is just are likely to arise from the concerns of the previous offices. So there is need for offices to keep a record of such matters as contracts and court decisions, and to register the initiation of law suits. About this office he expressly notes that it can be subdivided among many offices (as would fit large cities), though it is one office and can be kept as one (as would fit small cities).

1321b40/1322a19 Next and manifestly required in matters of justice are offices to enforce and carry out the penalties imposed by courts.[26] But as Aristotle rightly notes, this office is difficult to set up, for exacting penalties is hateful work and without considerable remuneration no one will do it, or do it properly. Nevertheless it very much needs to be set up, for people cannot live together if there is no orderly way to settle complaints and disputes (they will instead settle things by fighting, and those who fight are not in community with each other), and therefore also if there is no office to carry out judicial decisions. The answer is to divide up this office and not have it as a single one (even though it is a single care). Aristotle suggests a number of ways of doing this, including ways suitable to small cities that lack sufficient manpower to multiply offices, such as dividing the functions between outgoing and incoming members of the same office or between other offices already existent for other purposes. Without such dividing this necessary care will never be done properly, and those on whom it is imposed will be the objects of excessive odium and hostility.

25. As, for instance, those noted by Newman (4:547–48), namely offices to make periodic valuations of property, to collect taxes, and to manage poor relief (reducible to the office that receives and disburses common funds), offices to look after public health (reducible to offices concerned with care of the town and country), offices to check spendthrift habits or riotous living (reducible to offices concerned with ordered adornment), offices to keep public records, citizen rolls, and the like (reducible to the office that records contracts and lawsuits).

26. On this whole section see the interesting disquisition of Mansfield (1989: 68–71).

For similar reasons the office that does the guarding of prisoners should be different from the office that carries out the sentence (as the collecting of debts or the execution of the condemned). For none of the decent sort want to do the guarding (there is nothing noble to it), and while some of the depraved might happily do it (for financial rewards, perhaps, or even love of cruelty), they are not fit for the job, since they are more in need of being guarded than capable of guarding others. A better solution is to divide this office too and always have different people doing it, whether taken from the young, who are being trained by garrison duty anyway, or from the offices.

1322a29 So much concerns the most necessary offices. Next come offices that are equally necessary but are of higher rank as requiring special qualities in the officers, namely experience and trust. Such are, first, all those that have to do with defense and war, for exercising command in these matters manifestly requires military experience and virtue (as even democrats acknowledge by having such offices elected rather than chosen by lot; see 8(6).2.1317b20–21). This care, too, though single in kind, can be divided through more or fewer offices as necessary.

1322b7 Another office likewise requiring virtue is the office that watches the other offices by doing the accounts and receiving the audits or by scrutinizing the use of common funds and official conduct generally. In combined or mixed regimes, as also in democracies, the assembly of the multitude would generally have the final say in this matter (and would have the final say in other matters too), but Aristotle seems rather to be thinking of a definite office, not the indefinite one of the assembly, and to have in mind experts who understand the complexities of accounting and who can go through the records on the assembly's behalf and advise it as to what they contain. Putting these officers in charge of this task alone, and of no other, would be beneficial since it would help remove conflicts of interest.

1322b12 Another necessary office of higher rank (and similarly in need of experience and virtue) is that which has the most control over everything, namely the deliberative body, which again may be a definite office (as in most regimes save democracies and polities leaning toward democracy), or the indefinite one of the assembly itself. In the former case, while some things may be referred to the multitude, the office itself has the final say; in the latter case, the multitude has the final say and the definite office only convenes it and prepares the business.[27]

27. There is an ambiguity in the Greek at this point. The remark that I translate as "for there must be something to convene the body that controls the regime" (1322b15) could also be translated more along the lines "for the convening body must be the part that controls the regime," as by Sinclair/Saunders (1981: 384). The latter translation, however, makes less sense in the context, for Aristotle here expressly speaks of the council (the convening body in democracies) as serving those who are in control, namely the multitude, and not as being itself in control, and also speaks of the precouncil (the deliberating body in oligarchies), which is in control, but because it controls deliberation and not just because it convenes the assembly; cf. 6(4).15.1299b31–38.

1322b17   The final necessary office, but the nonpolitical one, is that to do with the gods, which again, while a single care, can be divided among many offices or, as in small cities, confined to one alone.

1322b29   All these are the necessary offices, those to do, as it were, with occupation and with living. But before passing on to those that are to do with leisure and living well, Aristotle pauses to summarize them. He does so by dividing them, in effect, through the three parts of the regime: first those that are simply offices (those to do with matters spiritual, war, revenues and expenses, the market, the town, harbors and country), then the judiciary (the jury courts, registering of contracts, exacting penalties, guarding prisoners, accounts and examinations, auditing of officials), and finally the deliberative.[28]

1322b37   As regards the offices to do with leisure, these are all in some way concerned with educating the citizens in virtue. So there are offices to exercise care over women and children (for a regime cannot be in a condition of well-ordered adornment if its women and children are not properly educated; cf. 1.13.1260b15–20 and 2.9.1269b12–1270a15); guardians of the law (to help prevent innovations detrimental to virtue); presidents of the gymnasium and musical contests (to help ensure that these are, as they should be, instruments of education in virtue and not the opposite).

That these offices are indeed proper to leisured and correct regimes, not deviant ones, is shown by the fact that managers of women and children cannot exist in democracies (where the needy must, like barbarians, 1.2.1252b5–9, use their wives and children as slaves and cannot afford to have them stay at home to be properly educated), and that law guardians are aristocratic and do not exist in oligarchies and democracies. Presidents of the gymnasium and of musical contests could exist in deviant regimes but they would doubtless not have the same concern with virtue.

1323a9   With these remarks Aristotle's discussion ends before he has even started to say anything directly about the combinations of regimes. The form of the concluding sentence also seems to indicate that the chapter is incomplete, since it contains in the Greek an "on the one hand" (*men*) that has no answering "on the other hand" (*de*). We may not unreasonably suppose, therefore, that further chapters were to follow in which, using what he has just said, Aristotle proceeded to complete his study of the combined regimes, pointing out in which cities they can be set up and with what precautions to ensure continued preservation. But if Aristotle has not provided us with this discussion, he would seem to have provided us, both here and earlier in the two previous books, with most of the necessary

28. Barker (1946: 277 n3) and Newman (4:566) obscure this division according to the three parts of the regime by unnecessarily splitting the first division (those which are simply offices) into two distinct subdivisions, offices to do with the gods, war, and finance on the one hand, and offices to do with local affairs on the other.

materials to complete the discussion for ourselves. Indeed, it is not impossible that the missing "on the other hand" is to be supplied, not by chapters that are now lost or that Aristotle never had time to write, but by the reader's own further reflection on all he has read and, should he be a legislator, by his actually setting up a lasting regime somewhere (in his own household at least, if not in a city). For that, after all, is what *Ethics* 10.9 was about.

Adshead, K. 1986. "Aristotle, *Politics* v.2.7 (1302b34–1303a11)." *Historia* 35: 372–77.

Ambler, Wayne H. 1984. "Aristotle on Acquisition." *Canadian Journal of Political Science* 17: 487–502.

——. 1985. "Aristotle's Understanding of the Naturalness of the City." *Review of Politics* 47: 163–85.

——. 1987. "Aristotle on Nature and Politics: The Case of Slavery." *Political Theory* 15: 390–410.

Annas, Julia. 1996. "Aristotle on Human Nature and Political Virtue." *Review of Metaphysics* 49: 731–53.

Aubenque, Pierre, ed. 1993. *Aristote Politique: Etudes sur la Politique d'Aristote*. Paris: Presses Universitaires de France.

Barker, Sir Ernest. 1946. *The Politics of Aristotle*. Oxford: Oxford University Press.

——. 1947. *Greek Political Theory*. London: Methuen.

——. 1959. *The Political Thought of Plato and Aristotle*. New York: Dover.

Barnes, Jonathan, Malcolm Schofield, and Richard Sorabji, eds. 1977. *Articles on Aristotle*. Vol. 2. New York: St. Martin's Press.

Benardete, Seth. 1989. *Socrates' Second Sailing*. Chicago: University of Chicago Press.

Bien, Günther. 1968–69. "Das Theorie-Praxis-Problem und die politische Philosophie bei Platon und Aristoteles." *Philosophisches Jahrbuch* 76: 264–314.

——. 1985. *Die Grundlegung der politischen Philosophie bei Aristoteles*. Freiburg and Munich: Alber.

Bloom, Allan. 1988. *The Closing of the American Mind*. New York: Simon and Shuster.

Bodéus, Richard. 1982. *Le Philosophe et la Cité*. Paris: Les Belles Lettres. English translation: *The Political Dimensions of Aristotle's* Ethics. Trans. Jan E. Garrett. Albany: State University of New York Press, 1993.

Booth, William J. 1981. "Politics and the Household: A Commentary on Aristotle's *Politics* Book One." *History of Political Thought* 2: 203–26.

Bornemann, E. 1923–24. "Aristoteles' Urteil über Platons politische Theorie." *Philologus* 33: 70–158, 234–57.

Boudouris, Konstantine I. 1995. *Aristotle's Political Philosophy: Proceedings of the 6th International Conference on Greek Philosophy*. 2 vols. Athens: Kardaminski.

Bradford, Alfred S. 1986. "Gynaikokratoumenoi: Did Spartan Women Rule Spartan Men?" *Ancient World* 14: 13–18.

Bradshaw, Leah. 1991. "Political Rule, Prudence and the 'Woman Question' in Aristotle." *Canadian Journal of Political Science* 24: 557–73.

Braun, Egon. 1956. "Das Lob Spartas in der Nikomachischen Ethik." *Jahresheft des Österreichischen Archäologischen Institutes in Wien* 43: 132–38.

Bywater, Ingram. 1894. *Aristotelis Ethica Nicomachea*. Oxford: Clarendon Press.

Chambers, Mortimer. 1961. "Aristotle's Forms of Democracy." *American Philological Association Transactions* 92: 20–36.

Chan, Joseph. 1992. "Does Aristotle's Political Theory Rest on a Blunder?" *History of Political Thought* 13: 189–202.

Creed, J. L. 1983. "Aristotle and the Veto: A Puzzle in *Politics* 4.14." *Liverpool Classical Monthly* 8: 122–23.

Curren, Randall R. 1993–94. "Justice, Instruction, and the Good: The Case for Public Education in Aristotle and Plato's *Laws*." *Studies in Philosophy and Education* 11: 293–311 (part one), 12: 103–26 (part two), 13: 1–31 (part three).

David, Ephraim. 1982–83. "Aristotle and Sparta." *Ancient Society* 13–14: 67–103.

Davis, Michael. 1989. "Cannibalism and Nature." *Metis* 4: 31–50.

——. 1991–92. "Politics and Poetry: Aristotle's *Politics*, Books VII and VIII." *Interpretation* 19: 157–68.

——. 1996. *The Politics of Philosophy: A Commentary on Aristotle's Politics*. Lanham, Md.: Rowman and Littlefield.

Defourny, Maurice. 1932. *Etudes sur La Politique*. Paris: Beauchesne et fils.

Dobbs, Darrell. 1985. "Aristotle's Anticommunism." *American Journal of Political Science* 29: 29–46.

——. 1994. "Natural Right and the Problem of Aristotle's Defense of Natural Slavery." *Journal of Politics* 56: 69–94.

Dreizehnter, Alois. 1970. *Aristoteles' Politica*. Munich: Wilhelm Fink.

Düring, Ingemar, ed. 1960. *Plato and Aristotle in Mid-fourth Century*. Göteborg.

Finley, Moses I., ed. 1987. *Classical Slavery*. London: Frank Cass.

Fortenbaugh, William W. 1976. "Aristotle on Prior and Posterior, Correct and Mistaken Constitutions." *Transactions of the American Philological Association* 106: 125–37.

Gauthier, David. 1986. *Morals by Agreement*. Oxford: Clarendon Press.

Gauthier, René A., and Jean Y. Jolif. 1958–59. *Aristote. L'Ethique à Nicomaque*. 2 vols. Louvain: Publications Universitaires.

Gigon, Olof, and Michael W. Fischer, eds. 1988. *Antike Rechts- und Sozialphilosophie*. New York: Peter Lang.

Grene, Marjorie. 1963. *A Portrait of Aristotle*. Chicago: University of Chicago Press.

Guthrie, William K. C. 1981. *Aristotle: An Encounter*. Vol. 6 of *A History of Greek Philosophy*. Cambridge: Cambridge University Press.

Harris, B. F. 1970. *Auckland Classical Essays Presented to E. M. Blaiklock*. Oxford: Oxford University Press.

Immisch, Otto. 1935. "Der Epilog der Nikomachischen Ethik." *Rheinisches Museum* 84: 54–61.

Irwin, Terence H. 1988. *Aristotle's First Principles*. Oxford: Clarendon Press.

Jaeger, Werner W. 1923. *Aristoteles. Grundlegung einer Geschichte seiner Entwicklung*. Berlin: Weidmann. English translation: *Aristotle: Fundamentals of the History of His Development*. Trans. Richard R. Robinson. Oxford: Clarendon Press, 1934.

Jaffa, Harry V. 1952. *Thomism and Aristotelianism*. Chicago: University of Chicago Press.

Johnson, Curtis N. 1984. "Who Is Aristotle's Citizen?" *Phronesis* 29: 73–90.

——. 1985. "The Hobbesian Conception of Sovereignty and Aristotle's *Politics*." *Journal of the History of Ideas* 46: 327–47.

——. 1990. *Aristotle's Theory of the State*. New York: St. Martin's Press.

Jowett, Benjamin. 1885. *The Politics of Aristotle*. 2 vols. Oxford: Clarendon Press.

Kamp, Andreas. 1985. *Die politische Philosophie des Aristoteles und ihre metaphysischen Grundlagen*. Freiburg and Munich: Alber.

Keaney, John J. 1981. "Aristotle, *Politics* 2.12.1274a22–b28." *American Journal of Ancient History* 6: 97–100.

Keyt, David, and Fred D. Miller Jr., eds. 1991. *A Companion to Aristotle's Politics*. Oxford: Blackwell.

Koraes, Adamantios. 1821. *Aristotelous Politikōn Ta Sōzomena*. Paris: Didot.

Kraut, Richard. 1997. *Aristotle. Politics. Books VII and VIII*. Translation and commentary. Oxford: Clarendon Press.

Lachterman, David. 1990. "Did Aristotle Develop? Reflections on Jaeger's Thesis." *Revue de Philosophie Ancienne* 8: 3–40.

Lear, Jonathan. 1988. *Aristotle: The Desire to Understand*. Cambridge: Cambridge University Press.

Levy, Harold L. 1990. "Does Aristotle Exclude Women from Politics?" *Review of Politics* 52: 397–416.

Lindsay, Thomas K. 1992. "Aristotle's Defense of Democracy through 'Political Mixing.'" *Journal of Politics* 54: 101–19.

——. 1994. "Was Aristotle Racist, Sexist, and Anti-Democratic? A Review Essay." *Review of Politics* 56: 127–51.

Lintott, Andrew. 1992. "Aristotle and Democracy." *Classical Quarterly* 42: 114–28.

Lord, Carnes. 1978a. "On Damon and Music Education." *Hermes* 106: 32–43.

——. 1978b. "Politics and Philosophy in Aristotle's *Politics*." *Hermes* 106: 336–57.

——. 1981. "The Character and Composition of Aristotle's *Politics*." *Political Theory* 9: 459–78.

——. 1982. *Education and Culture in the Political Thought of Aristotle*. Ithaca: Cornell University Press.

——. 1984. *Aristotle. The Politics*. Chicago: University of Chicago Press.

Lord, Carnes, and David K. O'Connor, eds. 1991. *Essays on the Foundations of Aristotelian Political Science*. Los Angeles: University of California Press.

MacDowell, Douglas M. 1978. *The Law in Classical Athens*. Ithaca: Cornell University Press.

McGrade, Arthur S. 1996. "Aristotle's Place in the History of Natural Rights." *Review of Metaphysics* 49: 803–29.

Mansfield, Harvey C. 1980–81. "Marx on Aristotle, Freedom, Money and Politics." *Review of Metaphysics* 44: 351–67.

——. 1989. *Taming the Prince*. New York: Free Press.

Martin Ferrero, Francisco. 1984. *El Libro II de la Politica de Aristoteles: La Autenticidad del Capítulo 12*. Salamanca: Ediciones Universidad de Salamanca.

Mayhew, Robert. 1993a. "Aristotle on Property." *Review of Metaphysics* 46: 803–31.

——. 1993b. "Aristotle on the Extent of the Communism in Plato's *Republic*." *Ancient Philosophy* 13: 313–21.

——. 1995. "Aristotle on the Self-Sufficiency of the City." *History of Political Thought* 16: 488–502.

——. 1996. "Aristotle's Criticism of Plato's Communism of Women and Children." *Apeiron* 29: 231–48.

Meikle, Scott. 1994. "Aristotle on Money." *Phronesis* 39: 26–44.

——. 1995. *Aristotle's Economic Thought*. Oxford: Clarendon Press.

Milani, Piero A. 1972. *La Schiavitù nel Pensiero Politico. Dai Greci al Basso Media Evo*. Milan: A. Giuffre.

Miller, Fred D., Jr. 1989. "Aristotle's Political Naturalism." *Apeiron* 22: 195–218.

———. 1995. *Nature, Justice and Rights in Aristotle's* Politics. Oxford: Clarendon Press.

———. 1996. "Aristotle and the Origins of Natural Rights." *Review of Metaphysics* 49: 873–907.

Moffat, Ann. 1984. *Maistor: Classical, Byzantine and Renaissance Studies for Robert Browning*. Canberra: Australian Association for Byzantine Studies.

Mulgan, Richard. 1974a. "A Note on Aristotle's Absolute King." *Phronesis* 19: 66–69.

———. 1974b. "Aristotle's Doctrine That Man Is a Political Animal." *Hermes* 102: 438–45.

———. 1977. *Aristotle's Political Theory*. Oxford: Clarendon Press.

Natali, Carlo. 1979–80. "La struttura unitaria del libro I della *Politica* di Aristotele." *Polis* 3: 2–18.

———. 1989. *La Sagezza di Aristotele*. Bibliopolis. Naples.

———. 1996. "Aristotele o Marx? A Proposito di 'Aristotle on Money' di S. Meikle." *Phronesis* 41: 189–96.

Newman, William L. 1887–1902. *The Politics of Aristotle*. 4 vols. Oxford: Clarendon Press.

Nichols, Mary P. 1983. "The Good Life, Slavery and Acquisition: Aristotle's Introduction to Politics." *Interpretation* 11: 171–83.

———. 1992. *Citizens and Statesmen: A Study of Aristotle's Politics*. Lanham, Md.: Rowman and Littlefield.

Ostwald, Martin. 1962. *Aristotle. Nicomachean Ethics*. Indianapolis: Bobbs-Merrill, Library of Liberal Arts.

Patzig, Günther. 1990. *Aristoteles' Politik, Akten des IX Symposium Aristotelicum*. Göttingen: Vandenhoeck and Ruprecht.

Pellegrin, Pierre. 1982. "La Théorie Aristotélicienne de l'Esclavage." *Revue Philosophique de la France et de l'Etranger* 172: 345–57.

———. 1982. *La Classification des Animaux chez Aristote*. Paris: Les Belles Lettres.

———. 1987. "La Politique d'Aristote: Unité et Fractures." *Revue Philosophique de la France et de l'Etranger* 177: 129–59.

Peter of Auvergne. 1951. See under Thomas Aquinas, St.

Quinn, Timothy S. 1986. "Parts and Wholes in Aristotle's *Politics*, Book iii." *Southern Journal of Philosophy* 24: 577–88.

Rahe, Paul A. 1992. *Republics Ancient and Modern*. Chapel Hill: University of North Carolina Press.

Rawls, John. 1971. *A Theory of Justice*. Cambridge, Mass.: Harvard University Press.

Rhodes, P. J. 1981. *A Commentary on the Aristotelian* Athenaion Politeia. Oxford: Clarendon Press.

Robinson, Richard R. 1962. *Aristotle's Politics III and IV*. Oxford: Clarendon Press.

Romer, F. E. 1982. "The *Aisymnēteia*: A Problem in Aristotle's Historical Method." *American Journal of Philology* 103: 25–46.

Rowe, Christopher J. 1977. "Aims and Methods in Aristotle's *Politics*." *Classical Quarterly* 27: 159–72.

Saint-Hilaire, J. Barthélemy. 1848. *La Politique d'Aristote*. 2d ed. Paris.

Saunders, Trevor J. 1976. "A Note on Aristotle, *Politics* 1.1." *Classical Quarterly* 26: 316–17.

———. 1986. Review of Lord's translation of the *Politics*. *Classical Review* 36: 216–19.

———. 1995. *Aristotle. Politics. Books I and II*. Oxford: Clarendon Press.

Saxonhouse, Arlene W. 1982. "Family, Polity and Unity: Aristotle on Socrates' Community of Wives." *Polity* 15: 202–19.

——. 1983. "Further Reflections on Aristotle on the Peoples of Europe and Asia." *Polis* 5: 34–39.

Scaino da Salo, Antonio. 1577. *In Octo Aristotelis Libros qui Extant de Republica Quaestiones*. Rome.

Schneider, Bernd. 1973. Review of Dreizehnter's *Aristoteles' Politica*. *Gnomon* 45: 336–45.

Schofield, Malcolm. 1996. "Sharing in the Constitution." *Review of Metaphysics* 49: 831–58.

Schütrumpf, Eckart. 1991. *Aristoteles. Politik*. 2 vols. Berlin: Akademie Verlag.

Silver, Thomas B., and Peter W. Schramm, eds. 1984. *Natural Right and Political Right: Essays in Honor of Harry V. Jaffa*. Durham: Carolina Academic Press.

Simpson, Peter L. P. 1988. "Aristotle on Poetry and Imitation." *Hermes* 116: 279–91.

——. 1990. "Making the Citizens Good: Aristotle's City and Its Contemporary Relevance." *Philosophical Forum* 22: 149–66.

——. 1991. "Aristotle's Criticisms of Socrates' Communism of Wives and Children." *Apeiron* 24: 99–113.

——. 1992. "Contemporary Virtue Ethics and Aristotle." *Review of Metaphysics* 45: 503–24.

——. 1993. Review of Schütrumpf's *Aristoteles. Politik. American Journal of Philology* 114: 320–23.

——. 1994. "Liberalism, State and Community." *Critical Review* 8: 159–73.

——. 1996. Review of Miller's *Nature, Justice and Rights in Aristotle's* Politics. *Journal of the History of Philosophy* 34: 111–12.

——. 1997. *The Politics of Aristotle*. Chapel Hill: University of North Carolina Press.

Sinclair, Thomas A. 1981. *Aristotle. The Politics*. Rev. ed. by Trevor J. Saunders. Harmondsworth, England: Penguin.

Smith, Nicholas D. 1983. "Plato and Aristotle on the Nature of Women." *Journal of the History of Philosophy* 21: 467–78.

Snell, Bruno. 1979. "Das Musikalische in der Sprache." *Zeitschrift für Papyrologie und Epigraphik* 36: 1–14.

Solmsen, Friedrich. 1964. "Leisure and Play in Aristotle's Ideal State." *Rheinisches Museum* 107: 193–220.

Spyridakis, Stylianos V. 1979. "Aristotle on Cretan *Polyteknia*." *Historia* 28: 380–84.

Stern, Samuel M. 1968. *Aristotle on the World State*. Columbia: University of South Carolina Press.

Strauss, Leo, and Joseph Cropsey, eds. 1972. *History of Political Philosophy*. Chicago: Rand McNally.

Susemihl, Franz. 1886. *De Politicis Aristoteleis Quaestiones Criticae. Jahrbücher für classische Philologie* neue Folge der Supplemente 15 hft.1.

Susemihl, Franz, and Robert D. Hicks, eds. 1894. *The Politics of Aristotle*. London: Macmillan.

Swanson, Judith A. 1992. *The Public and the Private in Aristotle's Political Philosophy*. Ithaca: Cornell University Press.

Tessitore, Aristide. 1996. *Reading Aristotle's Ethics*. Albany: State University of New York Press.

Thomas Aquinas, St. 1951. *In Octo Libros Politicorum Aristotelis Expositio*. Ed. Raymond M.

Spiazzi, O.P. Rome: Marietti. [Peter of Auvergne completed this commentary at the point where St. Thomas left off, at 3.6.398 (the end of *Politics* 3.8).]

———. 1964. *In Decem Libros Ethicorum Aristotelis ad Nicomachum Expositio*. Ed. Raymond M. Spiazzi, O.P. Turin: Marietti.

Vahlen, Johannes. 1911. *Gesammelte philologische Schriften*. 2 vols. Berlin.

Vander Waerdt, Paul A. 1985. "Kingship and Philosophy in Aristotle's Best Regime." *Phronesis* 30: 249–73.

———. 1991. "The Plan and Intention of Aristotle's Ethical and Political Writings." *Illinois Classical Studies* 16: 231–53.

Weil, Raymond. 1960. *Aristote et l'Histoire*. Paris: Klincksieck.

Welldon, James E. C. 1883. *The Politics of Aristotle*. London: Macmillan.

West, Martin L. 1992. *Ancient Greek Music*. Oxford: Clarendon Press.

Williams, James M. 1987. "The Peripatetic School and Demetrius of Phalerum's Reforms in Athens." *Ancient World* 15: 87–98.

Winthrop, Delba. 1975. "Aristotle and Political Responsibility." *Political Theory* 3: 406–22.

Wolff, Francis. 1988. "Justice et Pouvoir (Aristote, *Politique* iii 9–13)." *Phronesis* 33: 273–96.

Yack, Bernard. 1991. "A Reinterpretation of Aristotle's Political Teleology." *History of Political Thought* 12: 15–33.

Zuckert, Catherine H. 1983. "Aristotle on the Limits and Satisfactions of Political Life." *Interpretation* 11: 185–206.

429, 432, 434–35, 438–39, 442; and oligarchy, 347–48, 351; and polity, 118, 191, 323, 338
Assistant/assistance, 29, 36, 46, 57, 62, 65, 68
Assyria, 407n
Astyages, 407
Athena, 275
Athēnaiōn Politeia, 137n, 145n, 307n, 311n, 332n, 378–79n, 381n, 430n, 439
Athens, xxiv, 121, 138, 227n, 252n, 305, 334, 349n, 364n, 389, 446; and change of regime, 311n, 374, 376, 378–79, 381n, 383, 404, 416–17, 430n; and Cleisthenes, 137, 139–40, 439–40; and ostracism, 179, 373; and Solon, 118, 142; and ultimate democracy, 307n
Athletes, xxv, 37, 246, 262
Audit, 118, 168–69, 178, 306, 308, 342–46, 359, 429, 436–37, 451
Authority: as translation of *kurios*, xxvi–vii. *See also* Control
Autophradates, 102

Babylon, 94, 138–39
Barbarian, 19–20, 27, 34, 42, 44, 52, 87, 112, 130n, 161, 179–82, 225–26, 234, 295, 326, 412, 452; two meanings of, 19n
Barker, Sir Ernest, xvin, xviiin, xxiiin, 11n, 29n–30n, 40n, 52n–53n, 59n, 66n, 69n–70n, 77n, 86n, 88n, 90n, 94n, 125n, 128n–29n, 139n, 145–46n, 163n, 168n–69n, 173n–74n, 196n, 200n, 202n, 204n, 216n, 219n–20n, 223n, 225n, 230n, 238n, 246n, 249n–50n, 270n, 284n, 292n, 295n, 298n, 302n, 304n, 317n, 321n, 337n, 339n, 341n, 343n–45n, 347n, 353n, 370n, 372n, 376n, 379n, 390n, 392n, 396n–97n, 399n, 403n, 417n, 421n–22n, 444n, 452n
Barnes, Jonathan, 254n
Beauty, 18, 36–37, 42, 167, 173–74, 198, 211, 228, 262, 296, 329, 398; as translation of *kalos*, xxvii. *See also* Noble/nobility
Belief: in god-man and prayer, 170n, 192
Benardete, Seth, 83n
Berti, Enrico, xxiiin

Bien, Günther, 112n
Birth, good, 305, 319, 321–22, 329, 335, 368, 386; continued in children from parents, 38n, 42–43, 191. *See also* Well-born
Bodéus, Richard, xviiin
Body: and soul, 31, 33–38, 42–43, 45, 67, 143, 197–99, 235–36, 244–48, 257, 275–76, 301; and gymnastics, 262–65. *See also* Soul
Bodyguard, 185–86, 416. *See also* Kingship/king; Tyranny/tyrannical
Boeotia, 446n
Boldness, 115, 271, 407–8, 414
Bornemann, E., 75n, 79n, 80n, 83n, 88n, 91n, 94n–97n, 417n
Bradford, Alfred S., 114n
Bradshaw, Leah, 67n
Braun, Egon, 115n
Bribes, 117, 122; modern public largesse, 123n
Brother, 77n, 79–82, 116
Bulgarian peasants: and voting, 436n
Business, 15, 93, 161, 214n, 420; and household management, 27–28; as meaning of *chrēmatistikē*, 27n, 50; nature and kinds of, 46–62
Byzantium, 305, 375

Cambiano, 38n
Campaigning for votes. *See* Election: campaigns
Cannibals, 48n, 263
Carthage, 121, 129, 161–62, 175n, 222–23, 394, 410, 416n, 419n, 420; analysis of regime of, 123–27; excellence of regime of, 112, 119, 124, 387, 442–43; as mixed regime, 125, 142, 316–17, 345, 368
Cavalry, 94, 336, 339, 446
Celts, 114n
Censorship, 249–50, 283
Chaeronea, 216n
Chalcis, 378
Chambers, Mortimer, 306n–7n
Chan, Joseph, 25n
Chance, 9, 22, 127; and change of regime, 129, 365, 368, 374; and equipment/external

Cooper, John, 150n

Corinth, 163, 384, 404, 416; Congress of, 216n, 334n

Cos, 307n, 380

Cosmoi: in Crete, 121–23

Cosmos, 9, 208, 211

Cotys, 406

Council, 99, 169, 314, 351–52, 366, 429–30, 451n

Courage/courageous, 56, 65–71, 120, 141, 145, 228–89, 241, 256–63 passim, 266, 271, 281, 357, 408, 414. *See also* Sparta; Virtue

Courts, jury/law, 105–9, 125, 129, 134–36, 146, 169, 313, 323, 338, 383, 388, 399, 434, 441–42; appointment of, 358–61, 423; features of in democracy, 429–30; kinds of, 359–60

Cowardice/cowardly, 66, 69, 228

Creed, J. L., 347n

Crete, 87, 89, 112, 127, 129, 223–24, 368, 387, 416n; analysis of regime of, 119–25

Crime, 26, 101–2, 119, 165, 207, 232–33, 329–30, 354, 359; and communism, 81, 83

Cultured pursuits, 163, 255–80 passim

Curren, Randall R., 252n, 287n

Cyclopes, 5

Cyme, 110, 307n, 380

Cyprus, 406

Cypselus, 404, 416

Cyrus, 404, 407n

Daedalus, 29, 35

Dancing, 265, 277n

Daughters, 100

David, Ephraim, 115n

Davis, Michael, xvn–xvin, 19n, 48n, 51n, 68n, 170n, 194n, 226n, 230n, 261n

Decent, the, 165, 169, 404, 412–13, 451

Decrees. *See* Law/legislation

Defense, 15, 102, 161–64, 214, 227–28

Definition. *See* Power; Work

Defourny, Maurice, 216n, 334n

Deliberate/deliberation, 34, 36–37, 67–68, 106; the part that deliberates, 66–67, 92,

148, 234, 300–301, 340–48, 361, 423, 436, 444, 451; and judgment, 135–36, 138, 142, 148, 168, 220, 222, 229, 239, 300–302, 309–10, 328, 341–42, 349–50

Delphi, 378

Demagogue: and democracy, 117, 129, 307–10, 346–47, 357, 380–82, 393–95, 398–99, 421, 439, 441–42; and modern politics, 342n; and oligarchy, 383, 391; and tyranny, 371, 404–5, 412, 419

Demetrius of Phalerum, 364n

Democracy/democratic, xxvi, 98–99, 109, 117, 119, 127, 138–39, 142, 144, 170, 175, 227, 292, 321, 332–33, 350; destruction and preservation of, 109, 252n, 335–36, 365–402 passim, 418–21, 425–43; kinds of, 117, 128–29, 288, 291, 293, 295, 304–14, 334–35, 343–47, 421, 431–35; modern democracy, 34n, 106n, 151n, 153, 222n, 252n, 383n; nature and features of, 60, 125, 146, 148, 152–69 passim, 177–80, 184–86, 221, 253, 287n, 289–90, 296–99, 308–10, 322–25, 328–29, 338, 345–46, 356–59, 363–64, 373, 398–401, 405, 408, 412–13, 424–32, 435–37; and offices and courts, 107n, 134–36, 342–44, 351, 355, 361, 451–52. *See also* Freedom; Many, the; Needy, the; Poor, the; Populace

Demont, Paul, 238n

De Partibus Animalium of Aristotle, 18n, 305n

Depew, David J., 209n, 210n, 238n, 239n, 242n

Desire: and soul, 101–3, 143; and change of regimes, 363–70

Despotic rule, 16n, 33–34, 43, 63–64, 98, 144, 154, 204–6, 240, 326

Dherbey, 228n

Dictatorship, 182, 326

Dion, 408, 415

Dionysius (I and/or II of Syracuse), 62, 128n, 186, 381, 384, 387n–88n, 404, 407–8, 415, 417

Discourses, external, 150n, 197

Disproportionate increase, as cause of change of regimes, 379, 384

Disregard: as cause of change of regimes, 370, 375

Dissimilarity, as cause of change of regimes, 370, 375–77, 386–87

Dithyramb, 281

Dobbs, Darrell, xvn, 25n, 36n–38n, 43n, 66n, 69n, 70n, 91n, 113n, 226n, 247n, 300n

Dole, 103

Dorian: invasion, 405n; mode, 278, 281–82

Dowries, 100, 103, 115–16

Draco, 130

Drama/dramatic (chorus), 139, 143, 249–50, 280n, 395n

Dreizehnter, Alois, 41n, 56n, 194n

Drinking/drunk, 95, 130, 265

Dynasty, 122–23, 310, 373–74, 384, 389, 391–92, 406

Economy/economic, 8, 56, 62, 349, 363n; modern, 84n, 363n, 399n. See also Household/management

Education/educate, 20, 89, 92, 124, 335; in best regime, 252–83; division and manner of, 143–46, 235–39, 243–44, 248–51, 262; as for virtue and noble leisure, 5–6, 10n, 14, 21n, 27, 38, 84n, 87, 193, 216, 229, 234, 255, 257–62, 363n, 452; and preservation of regimes, 70, 252–55, 400–402, 418; and wealth, 305, 314, 319

Egypt, 63, 223–24

Election, 98–99, 111, 117, 121, 324, 326, 344–46; campaigns, 118, 370, 375, 380–81, 383; in modern states, 99n, 118n, 123n, 342n, 370n. See also Lot; Office

Elis, 384

Empire, 114, 119–21, 123, 129, 161, 239–41, 256; and philosophy, 210

End/goal, 1, 30n, 55–56, 67–68; and city and regime, 21–22, 25, 37, 112n, 196, 203, 231, 288–90; and education, 243–44, 266–68, 280

Endurance, steadfast, 3–4, 114, 118, 241

Enthusiasm/enthusiastic, 269, 277–81

Environmentalists, 58n

Envy, 330, 333

Ephor/ephorate (in Sparta), xxi, 116–19, 121, 325, 367

Epidamnus, 187, 366, 378

Epimenides, 19

Equality/inequality, 160, 305–6, 363–69, 426, 433–35, 401, 428n, 431–32. See also Justice/just

Equipment, 40, 194, 201–2, 210–18, 222, 253, 286, 327

Eretria, 385

Erythrae, 382–84, 445

Ethics, the (of Aristotle), xxi–xxii, xxvi–vii, 1–16, 20, 22, 25–26, 27, 30n, 32n–34n, 36n–37n, 39n–40n, 43–44, 51n, 65–68, 71–72, 75, 85, 92, 94, 103n, 110–11, 115n, 120, 124, 132, 140–41, 143, 146, 149, 155n, 157, 161, 163n, 170–72, 178n, 182, 188, 193, 197, 199, 201, 206, 213n–14n, 217n–19n, 232–34, 238–39, 242n, 245, 250n–52n, 258n, 263, 268n–69n, 270n–71n, 283–84, 286n–87n, 289n, 309n, 320, 326n, 328, 330, 350, 359, 417n, 423, 428, 438, 453; Eudemian Ethics and Magna Moralia, 233

Etruscans, 161–62

Eubulus, 102

Euripides, 19

Europeans, 218

Evagoras, 406

Evolution, modern, 18

Exchange, 51–62, 161

Executive, modern, 341–42; and prerogative, 308n

Experience/observation, appeal to in argument of Politics, 2, 4, 15, 18, 24, 29, 32–34, 43, 47, 63, 79, 149, 161, 211–12, 216–18, 245–46, 248, 269, 272–73, 275, 279, 305–7, 329–31, 371–72, 404, 419

Experts/expertise, 214, 275–77, 281, 282n

Exposure (of children), 246–47

Faction, 127, 185, 216, 235, 244, 333; and destruction and preservation of regimes, 90, 101–2, 104, 119, 122, 124, 330, 332, 360, 363–67, 370, 372–73, 375–78, 383, 385–87, 392, 395, 408, 439; in modern thought and practice, 363n, 370n. See also Regime

Heracles, 178

Heraea, 375

Hermit, 23n–24n

Hero/heroic, 182, 230, 235

Hesiod, 19–20

Hestiaea, 378

Hiero, 408n, 417

Hipparinus, 384

Hippocrates, 211

Hippodamus, 104–12, 128, 224, 228

Historia Animalium (of Aristotle), 263n, 305n

Hobbes, Thomas, 26n, 151n, 153n, 162n, 173n

Holy/unholy, 81, 247

Homer, 5, 20, 23, 64, 260–61, 269

Homosexuality, 114n, 122, 283, 377. *See also* Sex/sexual

Honor, 118–19, 232, 405; and change of regimes, 101, 109–12, 126, 370–73, 377–83, 385–86, 388, 392–93, 395, 406, 408, 414–15

Household/management, 6–7, 10–11, 73–75, 90, 93, 113, 143, 149, 163, 182, 349, 415, 453; nature and parts of, 14–71

Human being: as naturally political, 21–27, 86, 149

Humor/wit (of Aristotle), 117, 228, 250, 265, 398

Hunting/hunters, 45, 47–48, 51, 60, 300

Husband, 28, 62–63, 115

Illiberal, 249, 274. *See also* Liberality/ generosity

Imitations, 269–70

Immisch, Otto, 11n

Increase, disproportionate: and change of regime, 370–71, 373–75, 393,

India, 235–36

Individual, 6, 168; and city, 134, 156, 195–210, 254–55; and equality, 156, 295, 426–28, 431–32

Injustice/unjust, 26, 89, 103, 118–19, 126, 181, 329, 341, 370, 372–73. *See also* Justice/ just

Insolence: and change of regime, 329,

370–72, 378, 380, 382–85, 387–88, 392, 395, 405–7, 409–10, 414–15, 421,

Instrument/tool, 18, 25, 29–31, 33, 45–46, 50, 58, 61, 189, 198, 219

Intellect, 26, 33, 36n, 188, 241, 243–44, 247

Intermarriage, 100, 163

Ionia, 216n, 404

Iphiades, 385

Irwin, Terence H., 11n, 86n, 135n

Isocrates, 8n

Istrus, 382

Italus, 224

Italy, 224

Jaeger, Werner W., xvin, xvii–xix, 233n, 284n

Jaffa, Harry V., xvn, xxiiin, 163n

Jason, 144, 150

Jeffersonians, 59n

Johnson, Curtis N., xvin, 136n, 140n, 284n, 294n, 302n, 311n, 315n

John the Baptist, 23n

Jowett, Benjamin, 14n, 30n, 94n, 59n–60n, 68n–69n, 70n, 77n, 97n, 200n, 202n, 226n–27n, 228n, 230n, 233n, 269n, 276n–77n, 290n, 292n, 295n, 299n, 301n, 306n, 311n, 321n, 324n, 332n, 353n, 360n, 366n, 369n, 397n, 417n, 419n, 422n, 430n

Judgment. *See* Deliberate/deliberation

Judicial power, modern, 341–42

Juror. *See* Courts

Justice/just, 23, 32, 137, 141, 183, 192, 229, 241–42, 263, 357, 450; and destruction and preservation of regimes, 287n, 363–64, 387–88, 396–97, 401–2, 413–15, 435; and household, 65–71; by nature, 27, 190; nature and kinds of, 25–27, 108, 139, 151, 156, 160, 163, 171–80, 212, 236, 295, 297n, 363; partial or deviant justice, 159–64, 254–55, 433–35. *See also* Equality/ inequality; Injustice/unjust

Kamp, Andreas, xxin

Keaney, John J., 128n, 130n

Keyt, David, 21n, 25n, 161n, 233n

Kingship/king, 239, 284, 289, 292, 295,

318, 339, 362–63; and destruction and preservation of, 367, 403–5, 409–11; and household, 5, 20, 45; nature and kinds of, 63–64, 154–58, 175, 177–93, 203, 234, 290, 326, 334, 362–63, 431n; in Sparta, Crete, and Carthage, 116–17, 119, 121–22, 126; total king, 170n, 182–83, 186–87, 190–92, 235–36, 290, 326, 342. *See also* God-man

Koraes, Adamantios, 35n

Kraut, Richard, xxvi, 202n–3n, 216n, 227n–28n, 233n, 238n, 247n, 251n, 267n, 269n, 277n, 277n–79n, 282n

Kullman, Wolfgang, 22n, 25n

Laborer, 61, 142, 144, 147, 215, 220, 257, 276, 300, 304, 312–13, 425, 438

Lachterman, David, xviiin

Larissa, 383, 385

Law/legislation, xxvii, 117, 123, 350; and decrees, 307–10, 342, 435–36, 439; nature and power of, 2–10, 14, 23, 25, 42, 87, 109–12, 162, 177–78, 184, 186, 188–89, 211, 214, 240, 288–89, 311–12, 390–92, 397–98, 437; and regimes, 72, 89, 165–66, 170–71, 179–92 passim, 204–5, 288, 291–92, 306–20 passim, 323, 342–46, 437–38, 452; and slavery, 39–44

Lawsuits, 373, 385, 392, 450

Leandri, Antoine, 157n, 168n

Lear, Jonathan, 44n

Legislative power (modern), 341–42

Legislator, 239, 332; education and virtue as work of, 4–13, 38, 70–71, 85, 91, 177, 193–94, 205–6, 216, 234, 243–44, 252; and setting up regimes, 72–131 passim, 133, 287n–88n, 309n, 335, 350, 355, 361, 370–71, 379, 389–91, 402n, 411, 413, 438, 440, 423, 453. *See also* Education/educate

Leisure, 60, 120, 156, 213, 238–39, 352; and education and virtue, 113, 183, 209, 220, 222, 241–43, 255–63, 321; and ruling, 99, 125–26, 175, 308–10, 312–14, 324, 352, 412, 429, 435, 438, 452–53

Leontini, 404

Lesbos, 227n

Leucas, 101

Levy, Harold L., 18n

Liberality/generosity, 2, 86, 95, 213, 414

Likemindedness, 78, 384

Lindsay, Thomas K., xvn, 167n, 226n

Lintott, Andrew, 306n

Lions, 178, 192, 263

Locke, John, 26n, 49n, 55n, 308n

Locri, 388

Lord, Carnes, xvin–xviiin, xxiin, 11n, 27n, 40n, 52n–53n, 59n, 70n, 124n–25n, 139n, 191n, 200n, 202n–4n, 209n, 216n–17n, 226n, 228n, 230n, 238n, 247n, 250n, 256n, 261n, 267n, 269n, 276n–77n, 279n, 282n, 284n, 288n, 295n, 321n, 334n, 337n, 353n, 376n, 419n–21n, 449n

Lot, 125, 324, 344–46, 352–61, 375, 429, 431. *See also* Election

Lycophron, 162

Lycurgus, 115, 120–21, 128, 332, 419n

Lygdamis, 382

Lyre, 233, 275

Lysander, 119, 366–67, 383n, 386, 391–93, 446n

MacDowell, Douglas M., 118n

Macedon, 384n, 404–6, 410

McGrade, Arthur S., 81n

Machiavelli, 332n, 411

Machines, 29–30, 113n

Madison, James, 332n

Magnanimity, 217, 262

Magnificence, 414, 447

Majority rule, 320, 325, 401

Male. *See* Female

Malia, 339

Mansfield, Harvey C., xvn, 41n, 49n, 55n, 170n, 194n, 326n, 340n–41n, 343n, 440n, 450n

Mantinea, 378, 436

Many, the, 1–2, 4, 44, 102–3, 205, 391, 436, 440. *See also* Democracy/democratic; Needy, the; Poor, the; Populace

Market/place, 304, 313, 315, 358, 450. *See also* Square

Marriage, 78, 244–48, 385, 388, 392

163n, 166n–71n, 173n, 175n, 179n–82n,
185n, 191n, 193n, 195–97n, 199n–200n,
202n–4n, 209n, 213n–14n, 216n–17n,
220n, 222n–23n, 225n, 227n–28n, 232n–
36n, 238n–39n, 242n–43n, 245n–46n,
248n, 250n, 254n, 256n–57n, 260n,
263n–64n, 266n–67n, 269n, 272n, 274n–
75n, 277n–79n, 282n, 284n, 289n–96n,
298n–99n, 302n, 304n, 306n–7n, 310n–
11n, 314n, 316n–17n, 321n, 324n–25n,
332n, 337n, 339n, 341n–45n, 347n–49n,
353n–55n, 359n–60n, 366n, 369n–85n,
387n–90n, 393n, 395n, 397n, 399n, 403n,
405n–8n, 410n, 413n, 416n–17n, 419n–
21n, 424n, 430n–31n, 436n, 438n, 444n,
446n, 450n, 452n

Nichols, Mary P., xvn–xvin, 67n–68n, 178n,
226n, 261n, 346n

Noble/nobility, xxiii, xxv, 2–4, 10, 12–13, 15,
18, 34, 56, 65, 78, 81, 85, 112n–13n, 123–24,
126, 149–56, 167, 180–81, 195, 200–201,
207, 211, 226–30, 257–63, 275, 291, 325,
387, 405, 437, 449; discernment of, 36–37,
44–45, 66, 69; as meaning of *kalos*, xxvii;
and utility and necessity, 198, 229, 232–
33, 238–39. *See also* Beauty

Nomads, 48, 60, 224

Noses, 398

Notables, the, 129, 297n, 305, 310–14, 341,
346, 348, 355–56, 373–76, 378, 380–82,
388, 394–95, 404–5, 414–15, 441–42, 437,
439

Occupation, 209, 241, 256, 258–59. *See also*
Leisure

Odysseus/Odyssey, 5n, 261n

Oeconomica, the (of Aristotle), 61n, 226n,
248n

Oenophyta, 373n

Office: appointment/distribution of, xxvi,
98–99, 124–27, 129, 148, 172, 174, 288, 292,
308–11, 324, 338–39, 342–46, 352–58, 361,
388, 391, 394, 428–31; nature and kinds
of, 92, 99, 118, 122, 134–35, 146, 162, 168,
340–42, 349–52, 393, 447–53

Oligarchy/oligarchic, 98–99, 119, 125–28,
133, 138–40, 142, 170, 175, 287n, 332–33,
338–39, 350, 359, 387; destruction and
preservation of, 109, 347–48, 365–66,
371, 373–76, 378–79, 380, 382–86, 391–95,
398–402, 418–21, 444–48; kinds of, xxvi,
123, 288, 291–93, 295, 304–15, 320–21,
334–36, 421; modern, 153, 342n, 370n,
383n, 440n; nature and features of, 60,
152, 155–56, 158–64, 177, 221n, 227, 253,
289–91, 296–99, 311, 318, 321–25, 328–29,
343, 356–58, 361, 363–64, 368–69, 391,
398–99, 405, 416, 424, 430, 436, 443–44,
447–48, 452; and offices and courts,
107n, 135, 146–48, 344–45, 356–57. *See
also* Notables, the; Wealthy, the; Well-
off, the

Olympic (games/victors), 15, 91, 264

Olympus, 269, 277

Onomacritus, 129

Opus, 187

Oracles, 229

Oreus, 375

Orthagoras, 416

Ostracism, 178–80, 373, 393, 405, 431n

Ostwald, Martin, 8n

Pagans, 37

Pain, 3, 23, 37, 77, 232, 241, 266. *See also*
Pleasure

Panaetius, 404

Parents, 42, 80, 83, 244

Partheniae, 386n–87n, 391

Passions, 2–4, 26, 44, 114, 116, 184, 188, 190,
279–80, 310, 329–30, 364, 396–97, 402,
428; and music, 269–73

Pausanias, 240, 366–67, 391–92

Pay(ment), 323, 338, 346, 429, 442

Peace. *See* War

Peers, the (in Sparta), 386n–87n

Peiraeus, the, 130, 138–39, 376

Peisistratus/Peisistratids, 381, 404, 406,
416–17

Pellegrin, Pierre, xviiin–xixn, 30n, 248n,
299n

Peloponnese, 138–39; Pelopnnesian War,
227n, 366n, 374n, 383n, 389n

Penthilus, 406
Periander (of Ambracia), 405–6
Periander (of Corinth), 179, 416
Pericles, 137, 381n
Perjury, 108, 129–30
Persia/Persians, 179, 404, 405n, 407n;
Persian Wars, 129, 216, 366n
Peter of Auvergne, xivn, 38n, 178n, 201n,
209n–10n, 227n, 242n, 247n, 263n, 272n,
289n, 302n, 306n, 309n, 364n, 422n
Phalaris, 404
Phaleas, 100–104, 112n, 122, 128, 130, 226
Pharsalus, 384
Pheidon (of Argos), 404
Pheidon (of Corinth), 96
Philip (of Macedon), 216, 334n, 385n, 406,
410, 446n
Philoctetes, 22
Philolaus, 129
Philosopher, 24, 91n, 204n, 224, 232n,
417
Philosophy/philosophic, 9, 45, 62, 87, 90,
101–2, 121–22, 137, 157, 172, 250, 263–64,
281, 283; as goal of life, 183, 203–10, 220,
223, 238–39, 241–43, 256, 261; meaning of
in *Politics*, 209n, 238n, 242n
Phocis, 378
Phocylides, 331
Phrygian mode, 277, 281–82
Phrynichus, 383
Physics, the (of Aristotle), xxi
Piety, 220, 414
Pipes (musical instrument), 145, 173–74,
275, 278, 281
Piracy, 48
Pittacus, 130
Pity, 279
Plato, 9n, 16n, 68n, 70n, 73–100 passim,
112n–13n, 122, 128, 130, 150n, 165n, 184,
187, 204n, 210, 213, 217, 221n–22n, 225,
228n, 246n, 248–49, 252n, 281–82, 286n,
289n–90n, 300, 309, 315, 337n, 362, 417–
21, 440n
Play, 258–59, 265–66, 268, 278
Pleasure, 1, 21, 37, 77, 85–87, 248, 266–67,
270–71, 279, 405; kinds of, 2–4, 23,

47–48, 56, 101–2, 161, 258–61, 268, 276,
280
Plutarch, 378n
Poet/poetry, 19–20, 68, 92–93, 167, 209n,
230n, 269, 274n, 280n
Polansky, Ronald, 363n, 371n–72n, 390n,
403n, 411n
Policemen, 349n–50
Political, xxii, xxv, 3–4, 21–27, 103–4,
137–38, 191, 204–10, 360; community,
3–5, 133, 140, 153, 174, 197, 203, 231, 235,
326, 359, 363n; parties, modern, 342n,
370n, 383n, 440n; rule, 33–34, 45, 63–64,
126, 144, 182–83; science/philosophy, xxi,
9, 57, 92–93, 104, 171–72, 284–89, 318, 334,
422
Politician, 7, 9, 58n, 133, 145, 205, 239,
302–3, 392
Politics, 7–11, 45, 62, 104–12, 170n, 171
Politics, the (of Aristotle), 13, 73; accuracy
of argument of, 9, 25, 43, 91, 93n, 142–43,
200–204, 236–37, 260, 298, 317–18, 322–
23, 331, 346, 376, 395, 399n, 401n, 407,
430, 440–41; order and coherence of,
xvi–xx, 2, 10–13, 28, 32, 59–60, 72–75,
77–81, 83, 86n, 88n, 127–28, 131–34, 136,
138, 140, 146, 149, 157–58, 161n, 164, 166,
168n–69n, 170–71, 180–81, 185n–87n,
191n–96n, 209, 213–14, 218, 220, 223–35,
232–33, 251, 255–56, 265, 276–78, 282n–
85n, 289, 291–95, 302, 304n, 323, 348–49,
362–63, 379, 390, 416–18, 421–22, 424,
428, 444, 448–49, 452–53; rhetorical
readings of, xv–xvi, 19–20, 43–44, 48n–
49n, 51n, 55n, 68n, 170n, 194n, 261n,
326n, 343n
Polity, xxv–xxvi, 112n, 127, 129, 175, 287n,
289, 365–66, 381, 419n; destruction and
preservation of, 365–66, 378–79, 382,
385–89, 391, 393–94; kinds of, 315–25;
nature and features of, 98–99, 125,
154–56, 164–71, 175–80, 185–86, 189–91,
192n–94n, 234, 290, 293, 295, 327–40,
387, 399–400, 423, 435–36, 444, 446; and
offices and courts, 107n, 343, 345–46,
348, 351–52, 355–58, 361, 451

Polynesia, 235n

Pontus, 407n

Poor, the, xxv, xxvi, 29, 100–101, 116, 142, 253, 296–97, 333, 346–47, 357, 360, 364, 373, 388; character of, 101–3, 152, 164–65, 302, 330–31, 336–39, 355, 382, 398–99; and parts of city, 89, 158–59, 303–4, 325, 393. *See also* Democracy/democratic; Many, the; Needy, the; Populace

Populace, 122–25, 140, 314, 316, 325, 337, 341, 403–4, 413; and change of regime, 128–29, 365–66, 368–69, 373–74, 378–79, 397–400, 381–84, 441; and character of, 116–18, 146, 333, 388, 435–39, 446–48; and democracy, 134, 136, 148, 306–10, 343, 346–47, 355, 364, 393–94, 427, 432; kinds or parts of, 293, 297, 304–5, 311–13, 328–29, 376, 425; as meaning of *dēmos*, xxvii. *See also* Democracy/democratic; Many, the; Needy, the; Poor, the

Poverty, 62, 95, 156, 159, 322, 329–31

Power: and definition and nature, 24, 28, 31, 212; separation of powers, 341–42

Practical: and theoretical, 204–10, 237–39, 242n

Pray/prayer, 3, 72, 94, 192, 194, 210, 220, 230, 234, 253, 327, 363, 418

Precouncil, 351–52, 451n

Pride, 89, 198, 330

Priests, 16n, 208, 220, 223, 229–30, 239, 294, 349

Prisons, 34n, 349

Profit: and change of regime, 370–72, 378, 380, 382, 387–88, 394, 405–6

Property/land, 29–31, 46–62, 83–86, 95, 100–103, 105–7, 115–16, 143, 219, 225, 283, 310–13, 328, 443

Property qualification, 306, 324, 338–39, 369, 375, 381, 383, 385, 388–89, 392, 429, 432, 437–38, 444–45, 447

Prudence, xxv, 26, 37, 112, 143–46, 148, 191, 216–17, 254–55, 265–66n, 270, 288, 310

Puberty, 250, 264, 282n

Punishment/penalty, 2, 4, 23, 34n, 123, 130, 232–33, 248, 325, 342–46, 385, 407, 414–15, 450–51

Purification (*katharsis*), 275, 278–80

Puritan/puritanical, 85, 249

Quinn, Timothy S., 133n–34n

Racial/racist, 217, 375–76

Rahe, Paul A., 59n, 111n, 114n–15n, 153n, 332n, 363n, 341n

Rake's progress (of musical performers), 276n

Rape, 415n

Rawls, John, 162n

Reason (faculty of), 2–4, 24, 35–37, 44, 143, 234, 237–39, 243–44, 329

Reciprocal/reciprocity, 75–76, 87

Regime, xxi, xxvii, xxviii–xxix, 8–9, 11, 70; best, 10n, 13, 27, 38, 71–132 passim, 158, 175n, 179–80, 193–284 passim, 289n, 316–18, 327–35, 418–19; change of, 92, 109, 123, 292, 309, 311, 335, 360, 362–402, 440–42; mixed/common, 33, 98, 125, 142, 186, 221n, 285–87, 291, 316–25, 327–40, 343, 345–46, 359, 366, 368–69, 386–91, 403, 423, 448–49; nature and kinds of, xxii–xxiii, xxv–xxvi, 10, 12–14, 25, 93, 125, 133–35, 141, 147–56, 158–64, 181, 190, 212, 219, 230–34, 252–55, 288–304, 311–12, 315, 317, 334–35, 340, 343n, 363, 396, 402, 425–27; and parts of, 126, 340–61, 351–52, 423, 428, 449, 452. *See also* Citizen/citizenship; City

Regimen, xxv, 5

Religion/religious, 230n, 246, 249, 371, 376, 414, 441. *See also* God/gods; Pray/prayer

Revenues, public, 313–14, 442, 450

Revolt/revolution, 100–101, 120, 122, 137, 236. *See also* Regime: change of

Rhetorical readings. See *Politics*, the

Rhodes, P. J., 307n

Rhodes (island of), 307n, 373, 380

Rich. *See* Wealthy, the; Well-off, the

Right, 23, 25–26, 145, 444; rights, xivn, 26n, 172n, 295, 305–6, 425–26, 435

Robinson, Richard R., 148n, 157n, 180n–81n, 187n, 292n, 299n, 311n, 341n

Robinson Crusoe, 22, 24n

Robots, 113n. *See also* Machines
Romans, the, 218
Romer, F. E., 182n
Ross, Sir David, 11n, 13n
Rowe, Christopher J., xviiin, 11n, 284n, 286n–88n
Rule/ruler, xxv–xxvi, 32, 89, 126, 135–36, 188, 207–8, 349, 448–53; advantage of, 151–56; kinds of, 14, 32–34, 44–45, 62–64, 144, 149–50, 174–80, 182, 190, 204–10, 240, 306; and ruled, 17, 32–71, 65–66, 88–91, 96–97, 142–46, 235–37, 426–27; by turns, 76, 150, 187, 191, 207
Ruling body, 10n, 148, 152n–53, 159, 219–20, 231, 253, 288n, 296, 311n, 315, 325, 331–32, 359, 377, 391, 395–97, 400, 402n, 440, 444–45, 447; as meaning of *politeuma*, xxv

Sacred: tunes, 277n, 279; War, 378n
Saint-Hilaire, J. Barthélemy, xvii–xviii
Saints, 230n
Sardanapalus, 407
Saunders, Trevor J., 21n, 32n, 36n, 40n, 47n, 51n–53n, 77n, 91n, 97n, 99n, 107n–8n, 127n–28n. *See also* Sinclair, Thomas A., and Trevor J. Saunders
Savages, 263
Saxonhouse, Arlene W., 67n–68n, 218n
Scaino da Salo, Antonio, xvii–xviii
Schofield, Malcolm, 16n, 36n, 40n, 69n, 135n
School, 3, 11, 15, 364n
Schütrumpf, Eckart, xvin, 17n, 29n–32n, 36n, 40n, 45n, 51n–53n, 56n, 59n, 69n–70n, 72n, 83n, 88n, 91n, 95n, 97n, 103n, 106n, 115n, 121n, 124n, 127n–28n, 130n, 132n–33n, 134n, 140n, 142n–44n, 146n, 150n–52n, 154n, 157n, 161n, 163n–64n, 166n–69n, 171n, 173n–75n, 180n–82n, 185n, 187n, 191n, 193n, 195n, 220n, 236n, 284n, 302n
Scylax, 235
Scythian slaves, 349n
Self-control. *See* Moderation/moderate
Self-sufficiency, 21–22, 24, 50, 52–55, 59n, 75–76, 85, 136, 203, 212–13, 300, 335–36, 398, 427
Senate/senators: in Sparta, 118–19, 122, 124, 223, 325
Separation of powers, 341–42
Serious, 5, 56, 64, 70, 141–45, 233, 258, 350
Service, public, 121, 302, 395, 414, 442, 447
Seuthes, 407n
Sex/sexual, 21, 26, 95, 81–82, 86, 121–22, 406, 414–15. *See also* Homosexuality
Shakespeare, 245n
Shame/shameful, 70, 242, 249, 303
Shoe, 22, 25, 51–52
Shulsky, Abram N., 226n
Sicily, 62, 121
Sicyon, 416
Simpson, Peter L. P., xivn, xviiin, 16n, 21n, 74n, 153n, 173n, 279n, 332n
Simus, 385
Sinclair, Thomas A., and Trevor J. Saunders, 52n–53n, 91n, 200n, 214n, 222n, 226n, 230n, 292n, 321n, 341n, 353n, 376n, 417n, 451n
Slave/slavery, 89, 93, 105–6, 123, 125, 140, 161, 163, 191, 211, 215, 240, 283, 305–6, 313, 349, 376, 402, 404; features of, 64–70, 231, 241–42, 249, 275, 326, 330–31, 412, 431n, 427, 440; and master, 17–19, 44–46, 50, 61–62, 70; natural, xv, 27–46, 181n–82n, 205, 219n, 222n, 226, 234, 240, 400, 410; and rule of, 16, 82, 105–6, 113, 120–21, 129, 143–44, 146–47, 150, 207, 237; slavish work, 144, 226, 237, 257, 266
Smith, Adam, 84n
Smith, Nicholas D., 36n, 45n, 67n, 285n–87n
Snell, Bruno, 270n
Social contract, 162
Socialists, modern, 103n, 222n, 399n
Society, xxiv
Socrates, 16n, 68, 73–93 passim, 104, 217, 224, 252n, 281–82, 300, 362, 417–21
Soldier, 92, 106, 116, 191, 208, 217, 264, 279, 349. *See also* Arms/armed
Solmsen, Friedrich, 209n, 238n
Solomon, 34n

Solon, 50, 101, 118, 127–29, 142, 332, 379n, 436n

Son, 7, 79–82, 100, 116, 244–45, 310, 314–15, 382, 388, 416

Sophist/sophistry, 7–9, 40, 73, 89, 200, 337–38, 342, 391

Sophocles, 68

Soul, xxvii, 31, 33–38, 45, 143, 202, 234–36, 244, 257, 279, 301; education of, 100, 262–66, 268–73; features and parts of, 33, 37–38, 42–43, 66–68, 72, 103n, 198–99, 237–39, 244, 259, 270, 280. *See also* Body

Soviet empire, 106n, 389n

Sparta, xxi, xxiv, 94, 98, 121–22, 124, 128, 131, 142–43, 181–82, 186–87, 213, 225, 228, 231–32, 286, 334, 383n, 389, 404, 410–11; analysis of, 112–25; education and practices of, 5, 85, 87–88, 104n, 110n, 127, 223, 239–43, 256, 262–64, 267, 273, 320; as mixed regime/aristocracy, 98, 125, 315–17, 324–35, 327, 345, 366, 368, 386–88, 391, 394, 416n, 418n–19n

Speech, 18, 23–24, 68–69, 72n, 104, 275, 310

Spies, 412

Spirit/spirited, 90, 113n, 182, 216–18, 225–26, 386, 415

Spyridakis, Stylianos V., 122n

Square, 229–30, 438. *See also* Market/place

Stalley, R. F., 77n, 81n, 86n

State, modern, xxii–xxiv, 15–16, 21n, 106n, 123n, 153n, 162, 252n, 332n, 363n, 383, 428, 440n

Stern, Samuel M., 410n

Stratford de Redcliffe, Lord, 144n

Strauss, Barry S., 307n, 309n

Superiority/superior, 235–36, 370–71, 373–75, 378–83, 384, 386–87, 389, 392–93, 400, 405, 407–8, 412

Susemihl, Franz, 35n; and Robert D. Hicks, xviin, xxvn, 40n, 52n, 69n, 88n, 95n–99n, 107n, 110n, 121n, 124n, 127n–28n, 130n, 132n–33n, 139n, 142n–43n, 146n, 148n, 157n, 166n–69n, 171n, 187n, 191n, 197n, 200n, 202n, 216n, 223n, 226n, 228n, 238n, 256n, 260n, 263n, 267n–72n, 274n–75n, 276n–79n, 282n

Swanson, Judith A., 36n, 67n

Sybaris, 375

Sycophants, 399n

Syracuse, 373, 375–76, 377n–78n, 381n, 384, 404, 407n–8n, 417, 419n

Tarentum, 374, 443

Taxes, 103, 120, 412, 414, 442, 450n

Technocrat/technology, 104–11, 212, 228

Tecmessa, 68n

Temple, 229–30, 395

Territory, 94–95, 213–15, 225–30

Tessitore, Aristide, xvn, 242n

Thales (of Miletus), 61–62

Theagenes, 381

Thebes, xxiv, 115–16, 129, 139n, 241, 373, 385, 420

Theodectes, 42

Theopompus, 411

Thera, 297–98, 310n

Theramenes, 145n

Thessaly, 446n

Thirty, the (at Athens), 383

Thomas Aquinas, St., xivn, xxin, 1n, 5n, 12n, 17n–18n, 19n, 21n, 23n, 25n, 33n–34n, 38n, 40n, 43n, 51n, 58n, 61n, 86n, 130n, 145n

Thought, 19, 24, 208, 216, 223, 246, 255–57, 275, 350, 412–13

Thrace, 406n

Thrasybulus, 179, 404n

Thurii, 375–76, 388–89, 390

Timocracy, 155n, 420

Timophanes, 384

Toil, 259, 264, 276

Tool. *See* Instrument/tool

Town planning, 228, 230n, 272n

Trade/traders, 48, 53–54, 58–59, 61, 214–15, 438

Tragedy. *See* Drama/dramatic

Tyranny/tyrannical, 24n, 45, 60, 62, 100, 117, 119, 124, 127, 133, 138–39, 142, 144, 151n–52n, 165, 186, 307, 310, 315–16, 365, 378, 388; nature and kinds of, xxvi, 82, 155–56, 158, 176–79, 181–82, 204–6, 289–90, 292, 317, 325–26, 332, 362, 402–5,

352, 412, 414, 431n, 440; and household
and marriage, 28, 62–71, 73–94 passim,
244–49; managers of, 349–52, 452; and
Sparta, 113–20, 320, 411; and virtue,
64–71, 145, 246, 249, 283. *See also*
Female
Work, 84, 126, 140–41, 288; and definition,
24, 28, 31; kinds of, 45, 61, 90, 145, 263,
427
Wrongdoer: three kinds of, 101

Xenophon, 16n
Xerxes, 407

Yack, Bernard, 22n
Young, the, 1–5, 142, 266–67, 451. *See also*
Education/educate

Zaleucus, 129
Zancle, 375
Zeus, 64, 179, 267
Zuckert, Catherine H., 24n